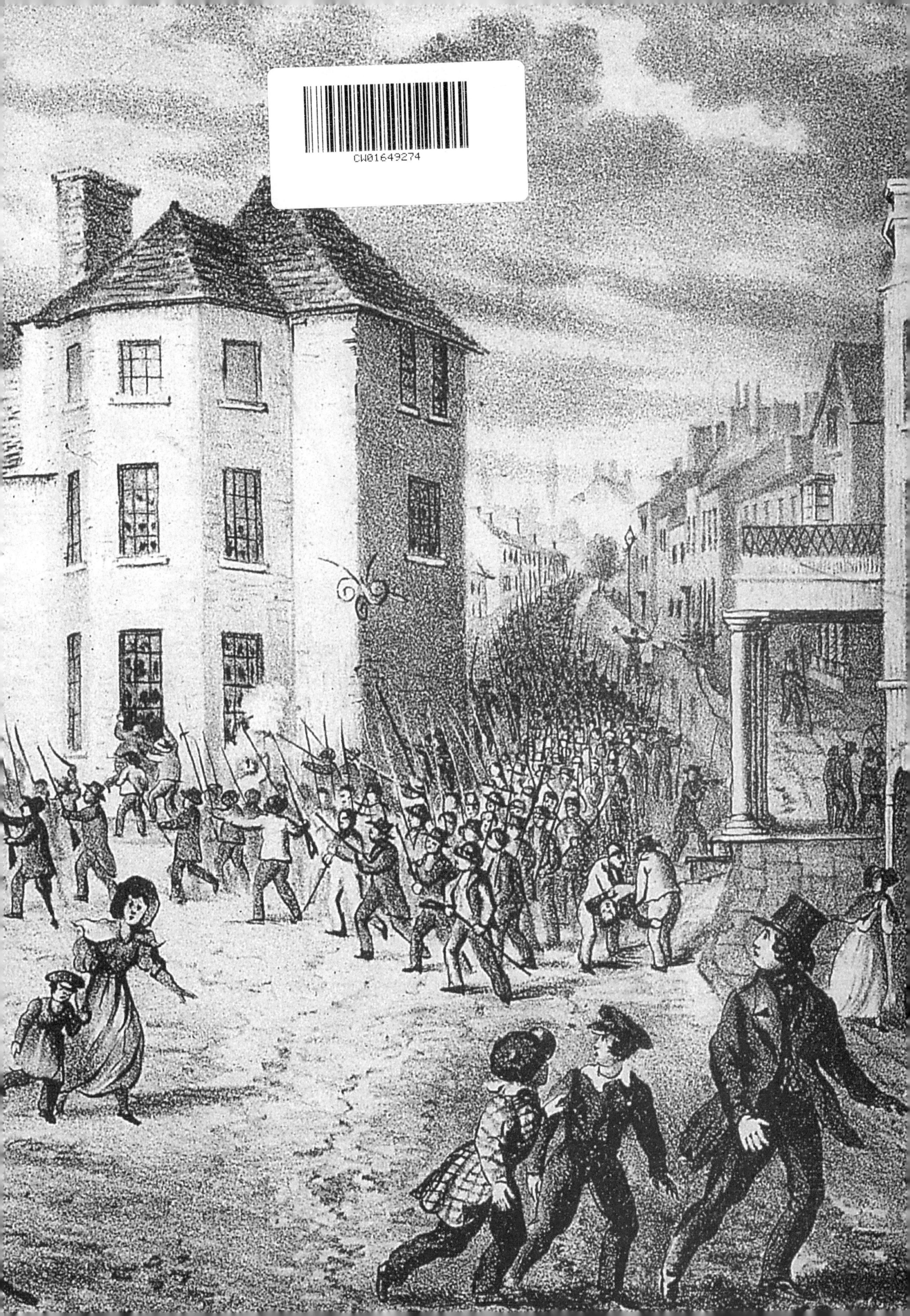

Artists in Wales
c.1740 - c.1851

Artists in Wales
c.1740 - c.1851

A handlist of artists
living and working in Wales from c.1740 up to c.1851

Paul Joyner

The National Library of Wales
1997

ISBN: 1 86225 003 0

Cover Illustrations

Front: Moses Griffith, *Self Portrait*, watercolour, signed & dated, 1811 (NLW MS 12706).
Back: Rev John Parker, *Porch at Llansaintffraid* [*sic*] *Glyn Ceiriog*, watercolour, 1838, PZ 7496.

Endpapers, Front: J. F. Mullock, *Chartist Riots*, lithograph, 1840, *NPT*.
Endpapers, Back: Charles Shone, *A design of a Bridge and Embankment across the River Conway* watercolour, 1808, PB 7434

Designed by Marian Delyth

Printed at the National Library of Wales

i
Ann
Siriol, Heledd a Llŷr

Contents

PREFACE

There are many people who have been responsible for seeing this work through press. However, the final form and, of course, the omissions and faults are all my own.

The most important influence on this text was my friend Dr Francis McCarthy who preceded me to Pembroke College, Cambridge, and undertook the first doctoral thesis on Welsh landscape. His encouragement to begin, continue and finish the research has been inspirational. At Cambridge the late Peter Bicknell shared his collection and knowledge of British Art.

My wife Ann has always been supportive to my search for artists and has visited many places with me - especially churchyards and churches. I thank her warmly for her patience.

About 75% of the text was originally produced for a doctoral thesis. My supervisor, Dr John Gage of the Dept of the History of Art, University of Cambridge, steered the research from the start in 1983 until 1989.

Two former Librarians of *NLW* have been instrumental in this work. Dr Geraint Gruffydd originally encouraged me to undertake the research and then Dr Brynley Roberts agreed for *NLW* to publish the text. Gwyn Jenkins has been generous to me in his post as Editor of *NLW* publications. The Editorial Assistant, Huw Ceiriog Jones encouraged and advised in all sorts of ways.

My colleagues have been unfailingly helpful. First Dr D.H. Owen and Mike Francis have supported this project. Colleagues such as William Troughton, Lyn L. Dafis, Iwan Jones, Mary Jewell, Louise Richards, Rita Johnson, Raymond Davies, Charles Parry, Cledwyn Fychan, Dr Huw Walters, Eiluned Rees, Donald Moore, Tudor Barnes, and the late Rhiannon Francis Roberts have provided valuable references. In fact, staff in all departments have checked many texts and manuscripts for me, and I thank them all. John Holmes has recently been especially helpful in checking references on his database of topographical prints. Gemma Entwistle helped with checking the illustrations for publication.

Colleagues and friends from all over Wales and the UK have provided important material. Dr Prys Morgan of Swansea University has given me much information.

Readers will see from the text, that three deserve special mention: Peter Lord, who has been a constant source of information and sometimes lively debate. I hope references to him have done him justice for his pioneering work. Thomas Lloyd has sent me all sorts of references and lent pictures. Every note has been helpful and often added to our knowledge of an artist. His energy and memory are phenomenal. Tony Parkinson has always been generous and encouraging. We have shared and discussed artists' information since we first made contact in 1984. May his next ten years be as happy as the last, now that he has entered full-time ministry with the Methodist Church.

I would like to thank all the institutions, libraries, museums and individuals mentioned in the text.

At the Library's Printing Press David Eldridge, Alan Thomas, and Michael Binks worked on the text with care, Marian Delyth designed the whole volume and the overall result, if the reader finds it pleasing, was accomplished with her enthusiasm and skill. The Paul Mellon Foundation generously provided a grant to produce the illustrations for this book. We should like to thank their Publications Committee and especially Dr Brian Allen for carefully considering our application.

Finally a word for those who typed the MSS. The original script was typed by Enid Jones; Annwen Isaac took over and finally Brigitte Morton completed the work with an efficiency and humour which has been a consolation.

Paul Joyner

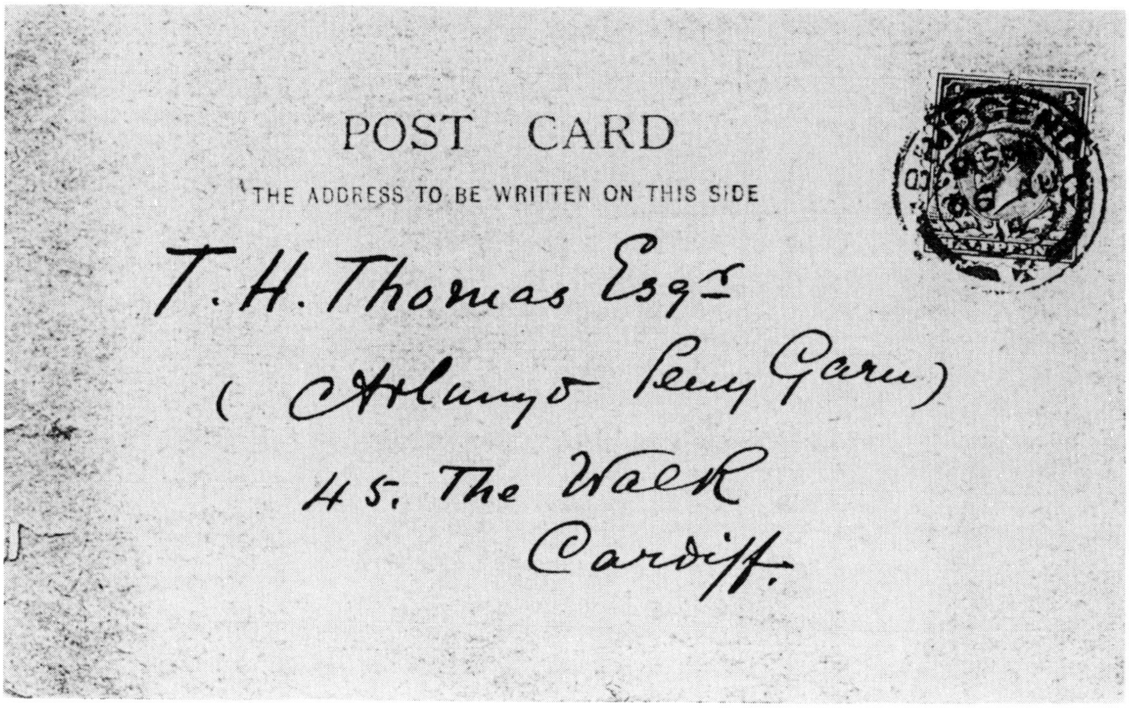

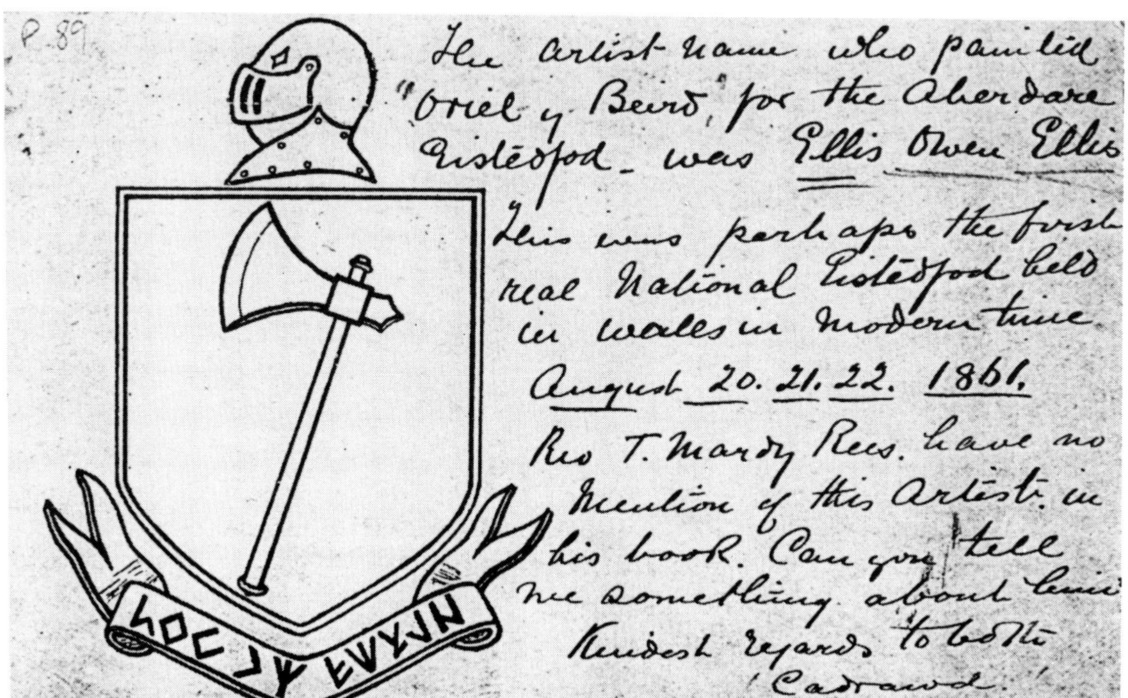

1a & 1b *Cadrawd,* Taken from a xerox copy of the postcard *NMW* files on Artists, Department of Art, from T.H. Thomas to Cadrawd concerning 'Ellis Bryn Coch.' Ellis Owen Ellis, 1914.

INTRODUCTION

'My general subject I have upon several occasions shewn to be worthy of all the Pains I, or a Better Hand Have taken, or Can take in treating it; and I know not any particular Branch of it that I have not Considered, and as fully as it Ought to be. If any Other shall think fit to undertake it hereafter, he supply the world with something Better; he may know more, or be Otherwise better qualified as a writer: But this is All I have been capable of Doing. I am Exhausted as to This Subject, whatever the Subject itself may be thought to be.'

(Jonathan Richardson's Preface to *Statues in Italy*, 1722)**(1)**

The compiler of this present publication empathizes much with Richardson. The subject before you is a 'hand-list' or 'dictionary' of artists and craftsmen who worked and lived in Wales from c1740 to c1851 and was the result of quite a long process.

This 'Dictionary' records all the artists, painters, architects, sculptors, photographers, drawing masters, and etchers who were living or working in Wales between c1740 and c1851. I have included amateur and professional artists. Amateurs were an important aspect of art patronage in Wales in this period and they also produced fine work themselves. One of the best examples was Charles Norris of Tenby who executed a large number of topographical views in that town, far surpassing anything else done at the same time in Pembrokeshire.

The dating of artists included in the hand-list gives birth and death dates where known, but where the only evidence is the artist's work the documented period of his *flourishing* is cited.

Craftsmen of various kinds are included, such as surveyors and monumental masons.**(2)** The original criterion has been whether they or their patrons considered their work fine or decorative, rather than utilitarian work. However, over the years I have noticed how often masons and painters, who had apparently no pretention to 'Art' produced work worthy of inclusion in this volume. For instance, we find surveyors who worked on tithe and estate maps also being known as 'Architects'.**(3)** Also, we note that many estate maps include pictographs, cartouches and landscape and genre studies.**(4)** Therefore I include here painter-decorators who worked both as artists and house painters, but I do not necessarily cite every example of a 'painter' which appears in Trade Directories as these were usually men without any other pretension except to cover walls with colour. For the same reasons I have included artists' colourmen and those who stocked artists' materials. As such, I do not recall any examples in Wales where a colourman did not also sell artists' brushes and equipment.

'Architects' as a term has caused me some problems. I decided to be inclusive rather than exclusive and so there are a number of craftsmen here who were builders but also drew plans for properties.

The majority of the artists included here were noted in a *Hand-list of Artists working in Wales, 1750 to 1850* which formed a substantial part of a doctoral dissertation written in 1988. Since that time new names have been discovered, in addition to a considerable amount of fresh material, which sometimes has transformed our understanding of an artist. One example is the recently discovered volume of original drawings by Edward Pugh for *Cambria Depicta*. We now, for the first time, can appreciate his art and some of the influences on his drawings. For instance Pugh included a watercolour copy of *Conway Castle* by Thomas Girtin and carefully prepared his original designs.

There have been a number of important projects, strangely many coming to fruition in 1993/94, which have significantly helped the present listing.

Inside the *NLW*, three projects have been of great benefit to the final format of this volume.

The Probate Project in the Department of Manuscripts and Records, supervised by Tudor Barnes, is invaluable. Tudor and his team have worked steadily through thousands of wills for the whole of Wales. He allowed me to consult original working copies of the project for the whole of the relevant period up to 1858. All references discovered are incorporated in the text. This is now available on computer, and the records are immensely rich.

What was clear from the Probate work was that many so-called 'masons' left wills and that they were spread throughout the country. In fact, the inference is that 'masons' and perhaps 'painters' were the artisans most numerous and therefore accessible to the population of Wales. As has already been discovered the 'mason' worked as a kind of 'rural' academician, sometimes encouraging talent for 'sculpture' or, as the case of Iolo Morganwg shows, retaining the status of craftsman and producing creative objects.

It was precisely because of the evidence presented in the Probate Project that the term 'artist' has been extended to encompass more than just those artists and craftsmen who can be conclusively shown to have produced aesthetically pleasing work. This extension has led to the inclusion of hitherto overlooked individuals, as well as some who merely cut and trimmed stone. It was worth taking that chance.

Another important project in the Department of Manuscripts and Records is the indexing of the Non-conformist Archives. This includes all the denominations of Wales, with the important Calvinistic Methodist material. Amongst the archives are about 275 original plans of chapels in Wales. Many of these are undated and unsigned. But one example which shows the possibility of this type of resource is the plan of *Castle Street Y Fenni, 1838*.**(5)**

In the Department of Pictures and Maps, the Topographical Prints Project showed a large collection of artists' work which could now be included. This has added depth and perhaps understanding to some of the more obscure artists.

Robert Davies's work on the tithe maps of Wales was completed in late 1993. For the first time it has been possible to list *all* surveyors working in that important scheme in the period c1835-c1841. All the people who appeared in *Davies Atlas* as surveyors (as opposed to valuers) have been recorded. As with the Probate Records this has meant an extension of the original term but we now have a more complete idea of how native craftsmen worked and combined activities. Besides these major sources of new information we should also mention the Great Sessions Records which record people (and occupation) up to c1830. Glyn Parry and Ann Davies kindly allowed me to examine some of their files. Once this project is complete it will no doubt add more names to the list.

Outside the Library, the *RCAM* Chapel Project will prove invaluable, as the intention is to record *all* chapels in Wales. Over the last few years some important relevant texts have been produced. These are given in the Bibliography. One particularly interesting example is Girouard's *Directory of British Architects 1834-1900*. This massive project gives us now a base-line for architects. *Girouard* records a number of previously unnoticed architects. The discovery of two Newport architects, Matthew Hubershon (1789-1852) and Robert Thomas (1820-1883), was a cause of elation for the me, a native of that town.

It will be clear that quite a few Welsh architects have escaped *Girouard*'s net and this only proves the importance of parallel and multifarious studies in a certain area of art-historical research.

Whilst the present volume was being checked at the page-proof stage, the Third Editon of Colvin's' *A Biographical Dictionary of British Architects 1600-1840* appeared. This prompted a renewed examination of the field and additional information has been included here.

The family history societies have become more active of recent years and the Dyfed branch have done much spade work in gathering information together. Their published texts have proved uniquely important.

Perhaps more important than any other development, the University of Wales began a research project, led by Peter Lord, on Welsh Visual Culture running from January 1995 for three years. I would expect that the results of the survey will put this volume into perspective.

In addition to all these major advances University of Wales, Aberystwyth has pioneered, since 1994 a course of Art in Wales. This presents under-graduates with Welsh Art in an academic context.

PURPOSE

The purpose of the list is to provide a source for the study of art in Wales in the period c.1740-c.1851.**(6)** It does not seek to include travellers who visited Wales to view the scenery, antiquities, or customs and thus avoids the muddled approach which confuses art about Wales with art produced in Wales.

The present work does not adopt a nationalistic stance that only examines art produced by Welshmen. This approach, taken by Rees, leaves the central questions unclear and unanswered.**(7)** It should be stated, however, that *Mardy Rees* has remained an essential text since the beginning of this century. His contribution to art in Wales was immense and crucial for later studies.

The dictionary is intended to show those who were working in Wales and receiving patronage from the Welsh population - both gentry, gentlemen and generality. One can therefore, have an overview of the sort of art which proved popular in Wales, in which areas and with which sections of society. Occasionally the list illuminates reactions to art and artists, for instance E.H. Brindley's comments on print prices.**(8)**

The dictionary also throws light on artists working elsewhere in Britain, firstly because a number of artists included were resident in Wales for only a few years, months or even weeks, and a discussion of their work in Wales often presents fresh material on their life and work in general.**(9)**

Secondly, the Welsh situation can be contrasted with that in the English provincial towns. There were many fewer artists, less stable art patronage, and a lack of public exhibitions. Certain points of comparison are evident such as the patronage of art by local Dispensaries, **(10)** craftsmen who function also as artists, migration of talent to London, and the establishment of local preference for one genre.

Thirdly, the study of art in Wales enables us to perceive what were the main influences from London, and more particularly how and when they operated. This can provide valuable information about the formation of Provincial Taste.

SOURCES

Primary sources such as pictures and other works of art have been researched for all artists. I have checked the collections of the National Library of Wales, National Museum of Wales, Welsh Folk Museum, Swansea Museum (The Royal Institution of South Wales), Newport Art Gallery and the Glynn Vivian Art Gallery. All other small galleries and museums in Wales have been checked for information, as well as the various properties owned by the National Trust.

A number of private collections have been examined both in Wales and elsewhere as these contain works by artists who may be overlooked by large institutions.

All record offices in Wales have been examined, including the archives of the Royal Institution of South Wales, Swansea (*RISW*), and the historical reference libraries at Newport, Cardiff, Swansea, Wrexham, Mold and Hawarden. Smaller libraries such as local search libraries at Carmarthen and Aberystwyth have given some additional information. The college libraries of the University of Wales, especially those at Swansea and Bangor, contain valuable MSS material which has helped to complete the list.

Outside Wales, the Grosvenor Museum at Chester, Chester City and Cheshire Record Office were major sources of information for artists in that city. A number of these had Welsh patrons and any study of Welsh art would not be complete without some comment on Chester artists.**(11)**

Many of the artists described in the dictionary were based in London, therefore various London repositories were researched, with special attention to the British Museum and the British Library, the National Art Library and the various Record offices in the Metropolis.

MSS sources have been gleaned from many collections. Undoubtedly the most important corpus is the *Cadrawd* MSS at Cardiff. The *NMW* Art Dept has notes on Welsh artists; the most important of these is the work of T.H. Thomas 'Arlunydd Penygarn' (1839-1915). He continued Cadrawd's pioneering work and it is particularly enjoyable to include, as an illustration, a postcard from Cadrawd to T.H. Thomas asking about Ellis Bryncoch (**Illustration 1**).

Besides the examination of primary visual or MSS material many secondary sources were consulted. These included all the available works on London exhibitions, and the Monmouth exhibition of 1840. Auction house catalogues and records (mainly Sotheby's and Christie's) were also searched.

All relevant dictionaries have been checked. The work of Mardy Rees, the first writer to attempt a list of Welsh artists and cite source material, was particularly important. Works such as the *Witt* list have also been used. There have been a number of exhibitions on Welsh art, the two most important up to 1975 were *Art in Wales*, 1964 (**Illustration 2**), and *Plans and Prospects*, 1975. Peter Lord's exhibitions in 1990, 1992, and 1993 have provided much information. Other references to particular exhibitions are given in the text.

Provincial newspapers have been extensively used to glean a large amount of new material, even upon relatively well researched artists such as James Harris (Senior). The newspapers have also provided evidence for many artists who had been forgotten. This is only the first step, and I hope that more attributions will be possible in the future, using ephemera.

It has been possible to attribute works solely on the basis of evidence in newspapers, for example, James Chapman's print, published in 1825.**(12)** In addition, the newspapers have revealed connections between artists such as the use of James Harris's shop as a venue for artists' exhibitions.

The local newspapers attest the variety of tasks of the craftsman or artist. One example is J. Parry, of Pwllheli, an architect who worked as a surveyor, rent collector and general estate manager. Without comparison with Parry, the career of Thomas Tudor would have appeared uncommon, but it is clear that the provincial architect had a large range of responsibilities and services. It, therefore, can be seen as quite natural that Tudor, who was at work on the Kentchurch Estate, should both collect rent and design an addition to Nash's facade in 1818.

Sometimes an advertisement can provide the reason for puzzling changes in an artist's career. Rigaud's move to Pembrokeshire had no apparent logic, until we discover that his wife opened a school in the region.**(13)**

Trade Directories have given numerous references to artists and are especially helpful to locate craftsmen and give the percentage of artists working in an area.

I have also consulted the Census Returns for a general overview of how artists were distributed in Wales and I have done some detailed work on the towns of Swansea and Aberystwyth extracting references to artists. The Census does sometimes confirm primary visual evidence. John 'Cambrian' Rowland, for example appears on the 1841 census as a resident of Aberystwyth, and in 1845 he published a portrait print inscribed, 'R.C. Rowland 1845 Aberystwyth'. There is a great deal of research which could be done on Census returns but I considered that the task would not be sufficiently fruitful to merit the time involved.

A large amount of information has been obtained from secondary sources such as biographies, catalogues, memoirs, and guide-books.

Some interesting objects still cannot be attributed (**Illustration 3**) and there remain many areas which could be checked and developed but the author presents this listing as the most complete he is able to provide at present.**(14)**

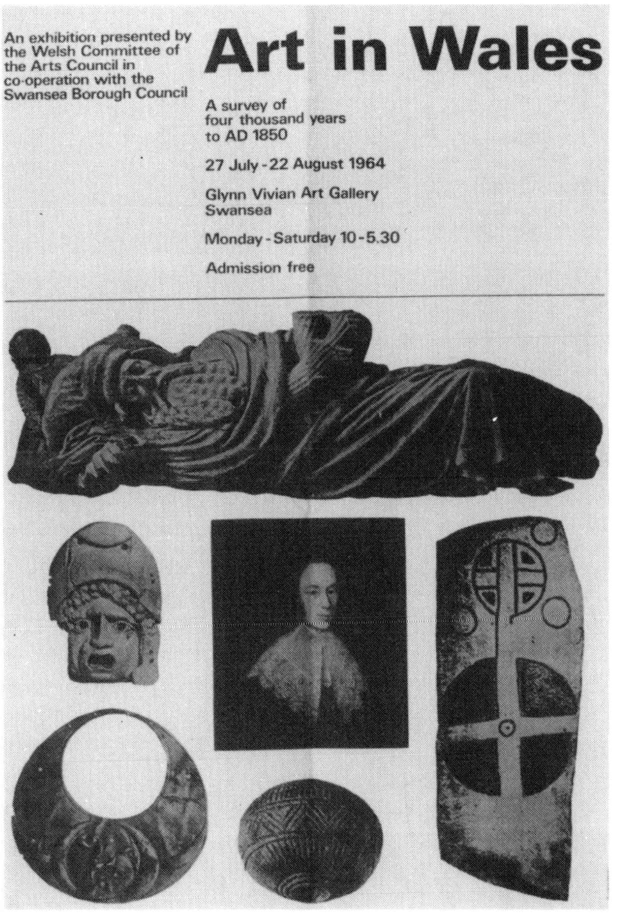

2 *Art in Wales* exhibition poster 1964.

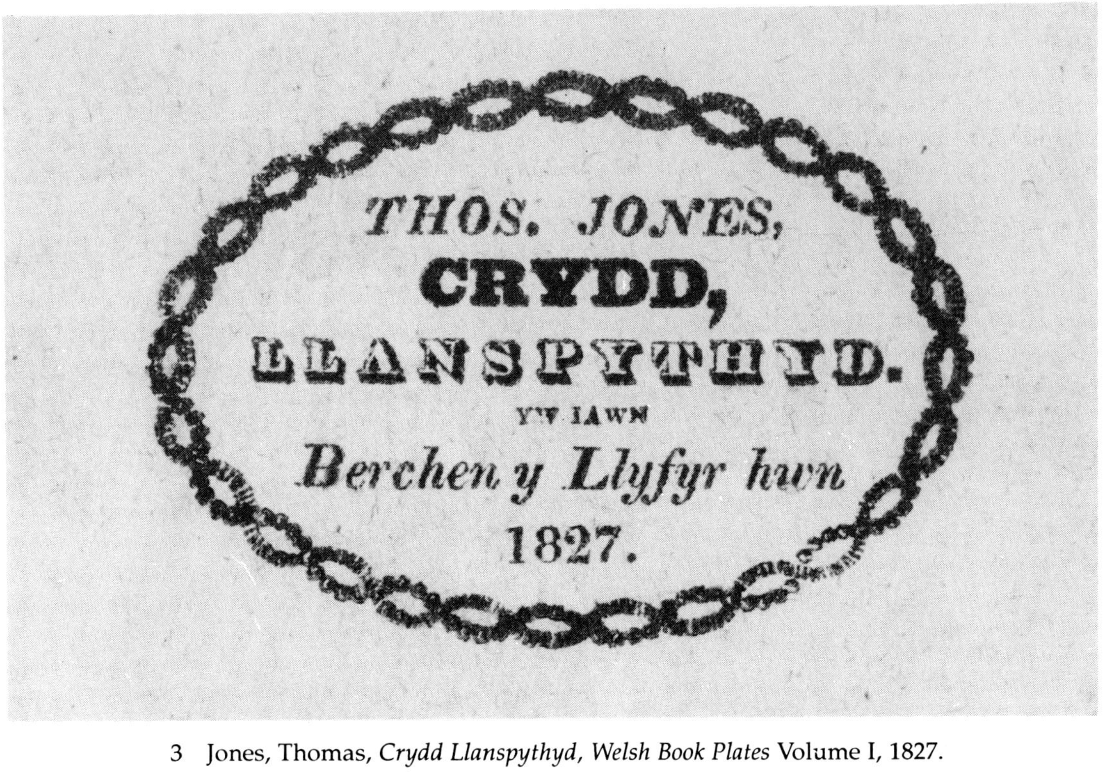

3 Jones, Thomas, *Crydd Llanspythyd, Welsh Book Plates* Volume I, 1827.

Notes

1. Richardson, Jonathan, *Statues in Italy*, (London, 1722), p.22.

2. For instance Slater and Lewis surveyors, *NLW* Map Volume Peniarth 4. The Brute family are a good example of this type of craftsman.

3. *Vide* John Evans, Hugh Hoare, Henry Kennedy for tithe maps.

4. William Morgan's portrait sketch on the *Perthin Llwyddin* [*Tŷ Bach*] map is a good example.

5. *NLW* MSS Dept, Non-Conformist Records, Monmouthshire (4623), dated 1838.

6. Artists' work is usually only discussed within these dates. However, where an important series of works appear later or earlier they are included, especially if they represent the major known output of the artists. This has occurred with Robert Taylor working c1747. A few references after 1851 have also been included with a final cut-off date at 1858.

7. *Mardy Rees* includes many who were of Welsh parentage, origin or had some Welsh connection. This does not, in my opinion, provide a coherent study of the subject, but a list of artists whose only connection is a vague 'Welshness'. This is why *Mardy Rees* devotes a large amount of space to Richard Wilson, the major 'Welsh' artist.

8. Brindley, E. H. (1829-1854) *vide* Dictionary.

9. Some good examples are Edouard Adolphe, L. Daguire and the Hubard Profile Gallery (all included in the Dictionary).

10. Compare the exhibitions at Monmouth Dispensary and Bristol Dispensary. For further discussion of early exhibitions, see *Joyner (1989)*, Vol. I, pp.47-50.

11. For instance, the Clowes family of Chester.

12. Chapman, James (*vide* Dictionary). There are two impressions known, one uncoloured at *RISW* and one coloured at the Glynn Vivian. Neither bears the artist's name.

13. Rigaud, Stephen F.D., (*vide* Dictionary) exhibited at the *BI* using an address in Jordenston, Pembrokeshire. The advertisement in the *Carmarthen Journal*, 15 January 1808, p.3, refers to an Academy organised by his wife.

14. **(Illustration 3)** shows a native printing of a trade card. There are many examples of this type of work which, one day, might be attributed to a local craftsman.

ARRANGEMENT

Name - The surname and Christian names of artists are given from the most reliable source. Where another name or spelling is available, this is added in brackets. Occasionally, pseudonyms were assumed especially where an artist had a Bardic connection. These are given with the actual name in the most common form. Where necessary, sources are indicated.

Dates of Artists - These are given in the top right corner, without detailing the month or day of birth or death (unless this is particularly significant). Where evidence is solely from extant work or contemporary references, the artist's flourishing is given.

Type of Artist - Wherever possible the sort of work undertaken is stated. More than one term means that I have seen or have information upon another aspect of their output.

Place of Residence/Working - This is given from available information, usually explicit in the text. Only obscure and little known place-names are given additional information concerning the county, or nearest town. For instance: Newport will be Newport, Monmouthshire unless otherwise stated. Where the artists address is known this will be included.

Descriptive Note - This includes some explanation of the artist's works. Where possible, subject matter of the artist, influences or similarities are noted. References are given in the notes. When it is not obvious, the main source of information is given. Where sources vary markedly this is mentioned in the notes. However I do not provide an index to all the common references and sources where the artist may be found.

Illustrations - Are almost all in alphabetical order according to artists. The size is given in centimetres, height first. Whenever, possible location of works is given. Readers will note that 'Private Collection' denotes that the present owners wish to remain anonymous.

References - The full bibliographic details of sources are given in the Bibliography. Abbreviations and short forms of titles and institutions will also be found there.

Square brackets - denotes uncertainty concerning the information shown. Internal evidence suggests that in all probability this is the case, but the author provides the brackets to alert the reader's caution.

COLOUR ILLUSTRATIONS

BLACK & WHITE ILLUSTRATIONS

Illustrations are owned by *NLW* unless otherwise stated

1a&b *Cadrawd,* Taken from a xerox copy of the postcard *NMW* files on Artists, Department of Art, from T.H. Thomas to Cadrawd concerning 'Ellis Bryn Coch.' Ellis Owen Ellis, 1914.

2 *Art in Wales* exhibition poster 1964.

3 Jones, Thomas, *Crydd Llanspythyd, Welsh Book Plates* Volume I, 1827.

4 Adolphe, Edgar, *Likeness, Cambrian* advertisement 5 July 1834 p.3.

5 Allen, Joseph, *Sir William Williams,* engraving, 1798, PA4254.

6 Attwood, John, *Milford Haven,* oil on canvas, 1776, *NMW.*

7 Baxter, Thomas, *Oystermouth,* engraving, 1818, P670 Top B8/3.

8 Bird, J.D., title page of *Eight Sketches in Glamorganshire,* lithograph, c1821 (*BV* 216).

9 Brigstocke, Thomas, *Self Portrait,* oil on canvas, c1830, PB5374.

10 Brute, Aaron, gravestone, c1768 (P. Joyner, 1984).

11 Brute, Thomas, *Williams family,* gravestone, 1759 (P. Joyner, 1984).

12 Chapman, James, *Wil Penmorfa,* oil on canvas, 1826, *WFM.*

13 Coulthart, William Ritson, *Design for Nanteos,* pen & ink, 1840 Nanteos Collection, 105.

14 Cox, David, *A Welsh Funeral,* engraving, 1843, PD5651.

15 Cox, David, *Royal Oak Hotel,* signboard, oil on board, 1847, Royal Oak Hotel, Betws y Coed.

16 Delamotte, George O., *Woman carrying a Jug,* watercolour, 1818, Drawing Volume 271, page 24, PB 4886.

17 Delamotte, George O., *Jane Harriot Talbot,* watercolour, 1821, *WPA.*

18 Dodd, John Josiah, *Cattle Watering near St Asaph,* watercolour, c1870, PE3883.

19 Dyer, Rev. John, *A Design for a landscape garden,* pen & ink, c1740, *WPA.*

20 Dyer, Rev. John, *Self Portrait,* oil on canvas, c1730, *WPA.*

21 Edwards, Joseph, *Female Mourner* (tombstone at Merthyr), illustrated in *Wales* II, 1895, p.194.

22 Edwards, Joseph, *Catalogue of an exhibition,* London Eisteddfod, 1855.

23 *Edwards, William,* engraving, c1779, P9793. [engraved by W. Skelton after a portrait by T.[homas?] Hill].

24 Ellis, Ellis Owen, *Morris Hughes,* watercolour, c1830, PB2425.

25 Ellis, Ellis Owen, *John Thomas Chwilog,* lithograph c1861, P9732.

26 Ellis, Ellis Owen, *Pwnch Cymreig,* wood engraving, April 17 1858, p.5.

27 Ellis, Ellis Owen, *Oriel y Beirdd,* [oil on canvas], c1847 (illustrated in *Cymru* Volume 52, 1917).

28 Ellis, Thomas, *High Street Haverfordwest* (original drawing 1822), published 1886, lithograph, PE 367, Top. B12/3 - B63.

29 Essery, William & T. B., advertisement in *Cambrian,* 13 September 1813, p.3.

30 Evans, E., *Philip Puleston, Welsh Book Plates,* c1800, Volume II p.110.

31 Evans, John, *Pistyll Rhaiadr,* engraving, 1794, PB3066, Top D6.

32 Evans, John, & Baugh, Robert, *Valle Crucis Abbey,* engraving, 1795, P6204.

33 Foulkes, Robert, *Inventory of Robert Foulkes, Caernarvon 'Plaisterer & Stucoman'* [*sic*], 1780 **B**/ 1780/69.

34 George, Thomas, *Self Portrait,* watercolour, c1824, *WPA.*

35 Griffith, Moses, *Cromlech at Plas Newydd,* watercolour, 1776, PA5608.

36 Gutch, John Wheeley, *Conwy,* photograph, 1857, Photograph Album 513, PE2514.

37 Harris, James, *Hafod Copper Works, River Tawe, Swansea,* oil on canvas, c1850, Glynn Vivian Art Gallery: Leisure Services Department: Swansea City Council.

38 Hornor, Thomas, *Picnicers at the Vale of Neath*, watercolour, c1812, PG4536.

39 Hubard, William James, advertisement, 1848 (Cardigan Printers file, Album 64).

40 Hughes, Hugh, *Conway Castle*, oil on canvas, 1846, PZ3938.

41 Hughes, Hugh, advertisement for the Cambro-British Picture Gallery, *Cambrian Quarterly Magazine*, Vol II, 1830, p.112.

42 Hughes, Hugh, A second advertisement for the Cambro-British Picture Gallery, *Cambrian Quarterly Magazine*, Vol II, 1830, p.255.

43 Hughes, Hugh, *Self Portrait with family*, oil on canvas, c1830, PB4599.

44 Ingleby, John, *Mount, Wrexham*, watercolour, 1793, PD9139.

45a&b Jernegan, William, *Copper works at Landore, near Swansea*, pen & ink, c1794, PE5213.

46 Johnes, Mariamne, *The Johnes Family* (After George Romney), watercolour on ivory, c1800, PG5516.

47 Jones, Rev Calvert Richard, *Margam Castle*, daguerreotype, 1841, PG726.

48 Jones, Rev. Calvert Richard, *Neath Abbey*, pencil, 1828, Drawing Volume 383, p.4, PE4038.

49a&b Jones, Hugh, The will of Hugh Jones, Beaumaris, signed April 1837, **B**/1838/3.

50 Jones, Roger, *Trade Card*, 1840s (Misc. Prints, A).

51 Jones, Theophilus, *Llanddewi'r Cwm Church*, watercolour, c1805, *A History of the County of Brecknock*, p.292.

52 Jones, Thomas, Pencerrig, *Hafod Sketchbook*, 1786 folio 9 Private collection, Friends of Hafod Archive.

53 Jones, William, *Dafydd Ddu Eryri*, oil on canvas, 1821, PA8239.

54 Lewis, John, *Pistyll Rhaiadr*, engraving, c1735-40, PZ5, PFC2M.

55 Lewis, John, *Disert* [sic], c1735-40, engraving, PB3044, PFC2M.

56 Linwood, Hannah, *The Library*, *Emral Hall sketchbook*, 1820, Drawing Volume 82, p.8, PA2755.

57 Llanover, Lady (Augusta Hall), *Self Portrait*, watercolour, 1837, PA3982.

58 Llewelyn, John Dillwyn, *Bonfire*, photograph, c1850, PB2376.

59 Marchi, Giuseppe, *Thomas Jones, Pencerrig* c1768, oil on canvas, *NMW*.

60 Morgan, Charles, *Tenby*, watercolour, 1851, *WPA*, Private Collection.

61 Morgan, William, *A Plan of Tŷ bach, Llanrhystid* [*sic*], pen & ink wash, 1827, Amphlett Lewis & Evans Deposit.

62 Morris, Lewis, *Self Portrait*, half-tone copy, c1900?, P8683. [Original, oil on canvas, 1740].

63 Mullock, James Flewitt, *Mr Hodges, Tredegar*, oil on canvas, c1843, *NPT*.

64 *Norris, Charles* by John Linnell, oil on canvas, 1837, *WPA*.

65 Owen, Richard, title page of *Survey of Ynys Maengwyn*, pen & ink with watercolour, 1776, Peniarth Volume 2.

66 Parry, John, *Ceubren yr Ellyll*, lithograph, c1813, PB8227 Top B9/6.

67 Parry, William, *R. Owen, Llwyn*, pastel on paper, c1770, PG2820.

68 Parry, William, *Richard Jones*, 1770, oil on canvas, *WPA* (St David's School, Ashford).

69 *Pennant, Thomas* by Joseph Highmore, oil on canvas, c1738, PG4534.

70 Pugh, Edward, *The Infant Hercules* in *Cambria Depicta*, aquatint, 1816, p.97.

71 Pugh, Edward, *Paris Mines* in *Cambria Depicta*, *book of drawings*, pen and ink, Drawing Volume, 407, p.12, PG672.

72 Pugin, Auguste, *Spilman Street, Carmarthen*, pen & ink, c1804, PE3753.

73 Rigaud, Stephen, *Carew Castle*, pencil, 1833, Private Collection.

74 Rigaud, Stephen, *Miss Evans of Neath*, c1823, Drawing Volume 115, p.2, PB7026.

75 Roberts, Thomas, trade bill, 1840s. (Misc Prints, A).

76 Rolfe, Alexander F., *Views at Crickhowell*, coloured lithograph, 1845, PB6379, BV2401.

77 Rolfe, Alexander F., *Sir Joseph Bailey*, oil on canvas, c1849, *WPA*, Private Collection.

78 Roos, William, *John Elias*, mezzotint, c1840, P7701.

79 Roos, William, [*William Morris Cilgerran*], oil on slate, 1849, PE1684.

80 Rothwell, Thomas, *Port & Bay of Swansea*, print on plaster, 1792, PG3432.

81 Rowland, John Cambrian, *Rev. John Hughes*, lithograph, 1845, P8492.

82 Rowland, John Cambrian, *John Salusbury Thelwall*, oil on canvas, 1849, *WPA* (Private Collection).

83 Sandby, Paul, *Bill to Sir Watkin Williams-Wynn*, Wynnstay MSS, 115/21/30, dated 21 June 1771.

84 Taylor, Robert, *Richard Gwynne*, oil on canvas, 1740, *NMW*.

85 Taylor, Robert, *Richard Gwynne*, mezzotint, 1747, P8677.

86 Taylor, Captain William, *After the Chartist Riots*, lithograph, 1839, PG5542.

87 Tudor, Thomas, *Dolbadarn Castle*, sketchbook, pencil, 1812, Drawing Volume 161, p.18, PZ130.

88 Watkeys, William, *Portrait of a gentleman*, oil on canvas, c1830, PG3415.

89 Welsh Primitive, *The Moon rising over Plynlimmon*, [*sic*] watercolour, 1846, PZ7329.

90 Williams, Edward, 'Iolo Morganwg', *Town Hall, Cowbridge*, pen & ink, 1782, MS 21416E (126), p.31.

91 Williams, Evan, *John Jones*, oil on canvas, c1840, PZ3611.

92 Williams, John, *William Williams Pantycelyn*, watercolour c1796?, PB8426 (Central Library, Cardiff has the original watercolour).

93 Williams, Penry, *Gwaelod-y-Garth*, watercolour, 1822, Drawing Volume 432, p.1, PG5346.

94a&b Williams, Penry, *Merthyr Riots*, oil on canvas, 1816, Cyfarthfa Castle Museum, Merthyr.

95 Williams, Penry, *Waterfall*, [*Ysgwyd Einion Fall*], oil on board, c1819, Cyfarthfa Castle Museum, Merthyr.

96 Williams, Taliesin, *Landscape, South Wales*, oil on board, c1830, PE4522.

97 Williams, William, *Miss Lovendon's Receipt*, 1830, Gogerddan Collection, Box 17.

98 Wilson, Richard, *Rev. John Wilson*, oil on board, c1728, PE 3545.

99 Wilson Richard, *Pembroke Town and Castle*, pencil, 1764-6, P6223.

100 Young, William Weston, *Neath Waterfall*, watercolour, c1791, Drawing Volume 15, p.4 PD5765.

101 Burt, Albin Robert, *Dic Aberdaron*, engraving, 1812, PZ8297.

I.

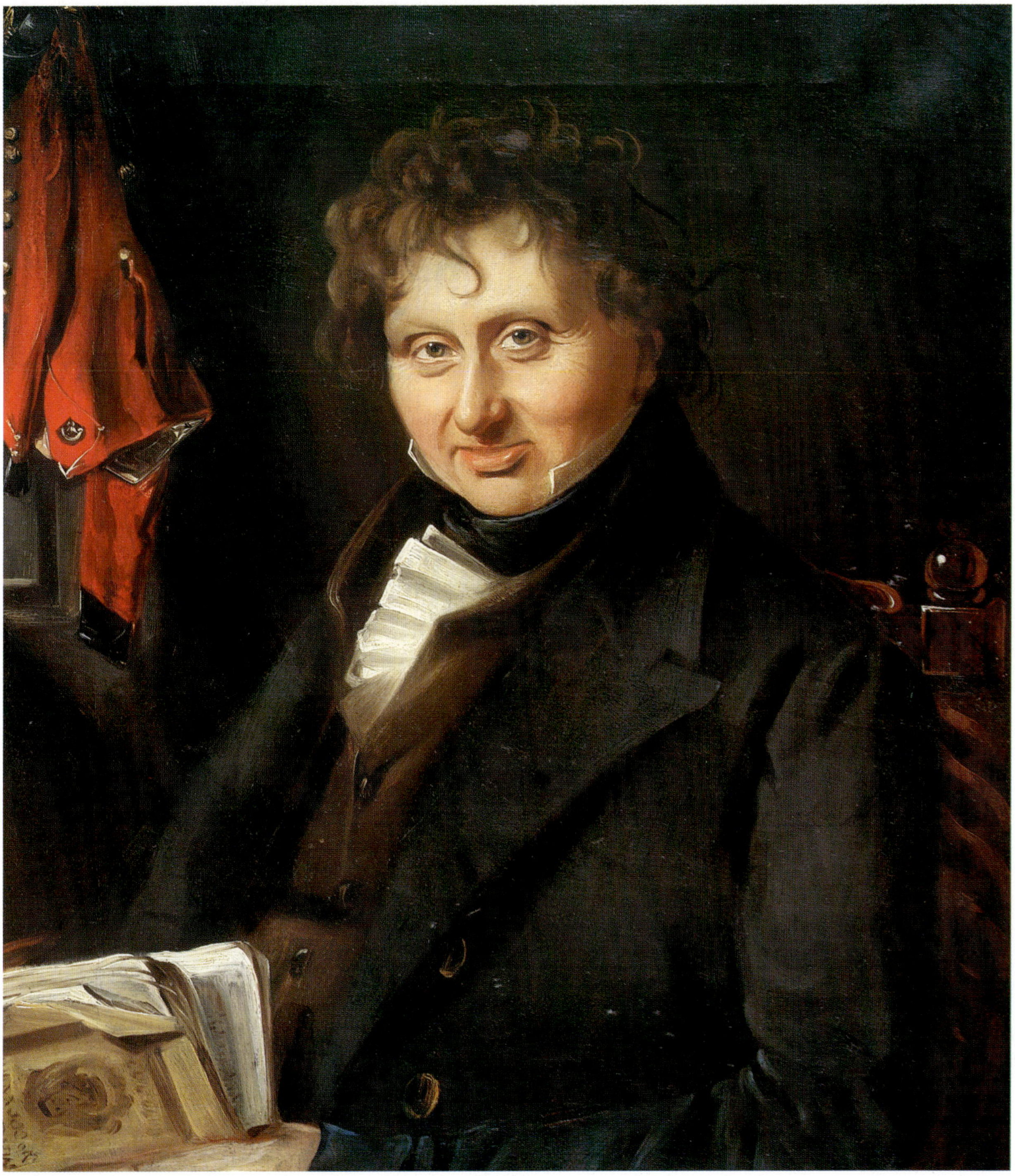

I. *Self Portrait* by William Jones, c. 1820, oil on canvas, PG 4585.

II.

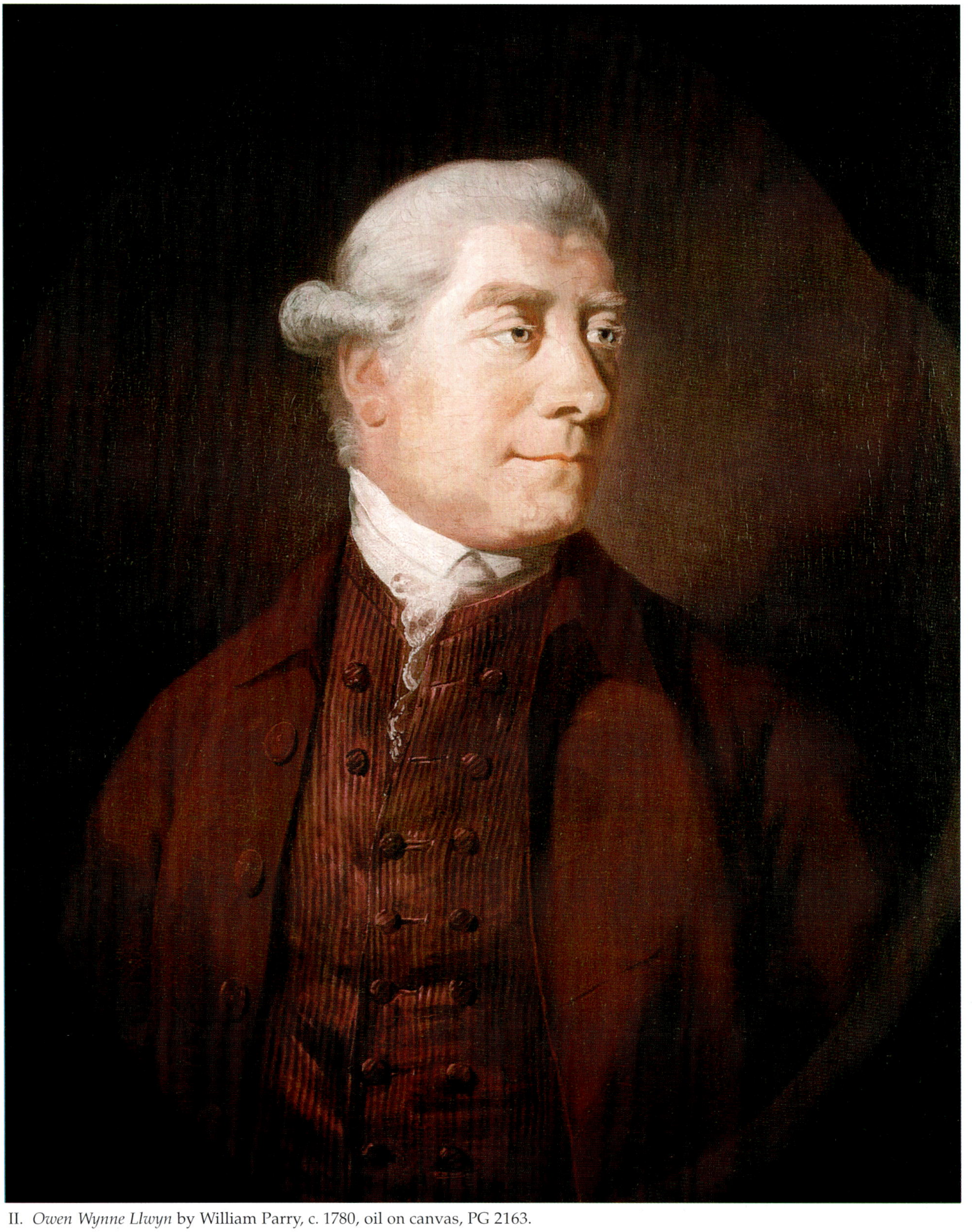

II. *Owen Wynne Llwyn* by William Parry, c. 1780, oil on canvas, PG 2163.

III.

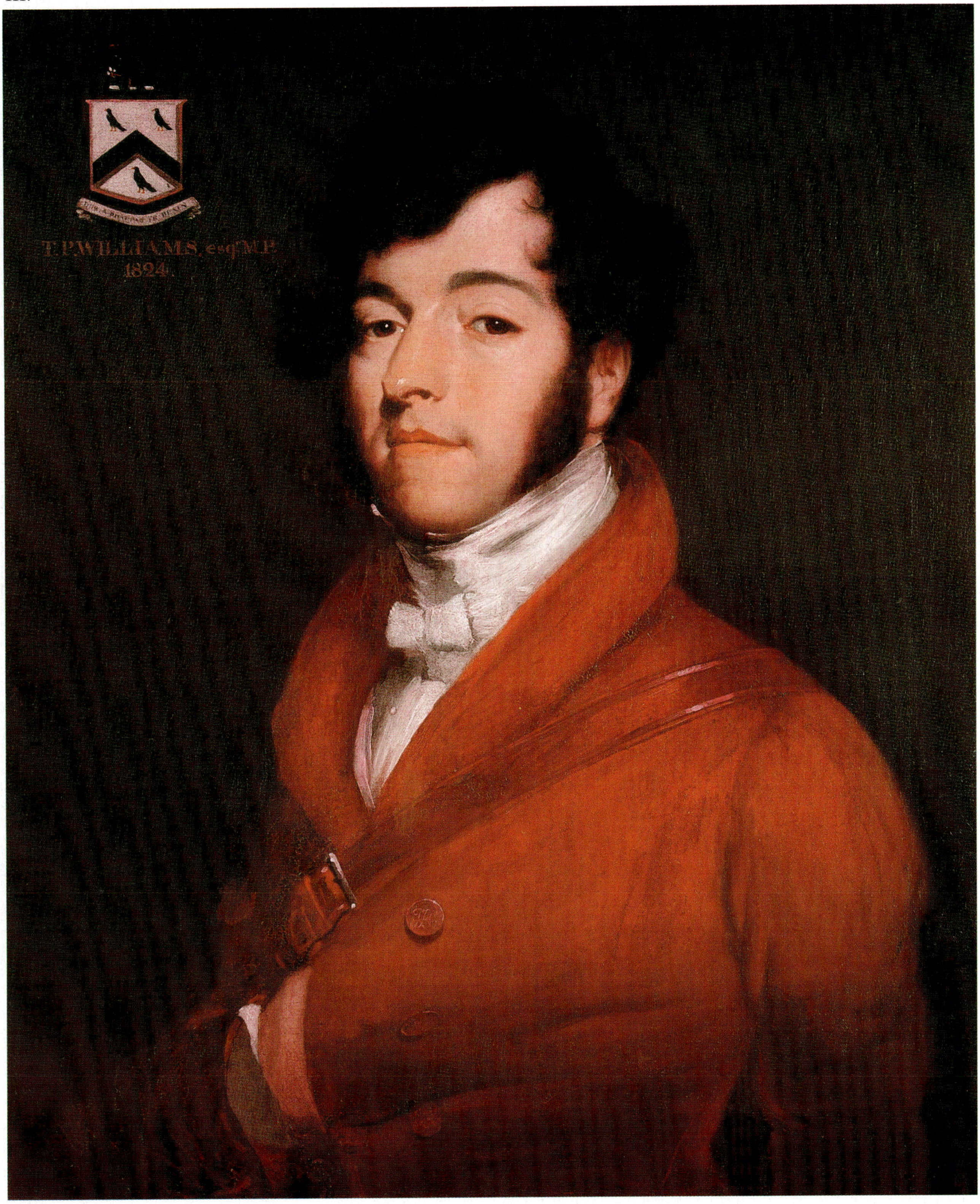

III. *Thomas Peeres Williams, Craig y Don Anglesey* by Hugh Jones, 1824, oil on canvas, PG8523.

IV. *Sarah Jones, Carmarthen* by John Deffett Francis, 1845, oil on canvas. Carmarthen Museum 1979. 549.

V. *Mrs Mary & Miss Sarah Williams, Carmarthen* by David Patrick, 1850, oil on board, Carmarthen Museum 1976. 1446.

VI. *Mr John Williams, Carmarthen* by David Patrick, 1850, oil on board, Carmarthen Museum 1976. 1445.

IV.

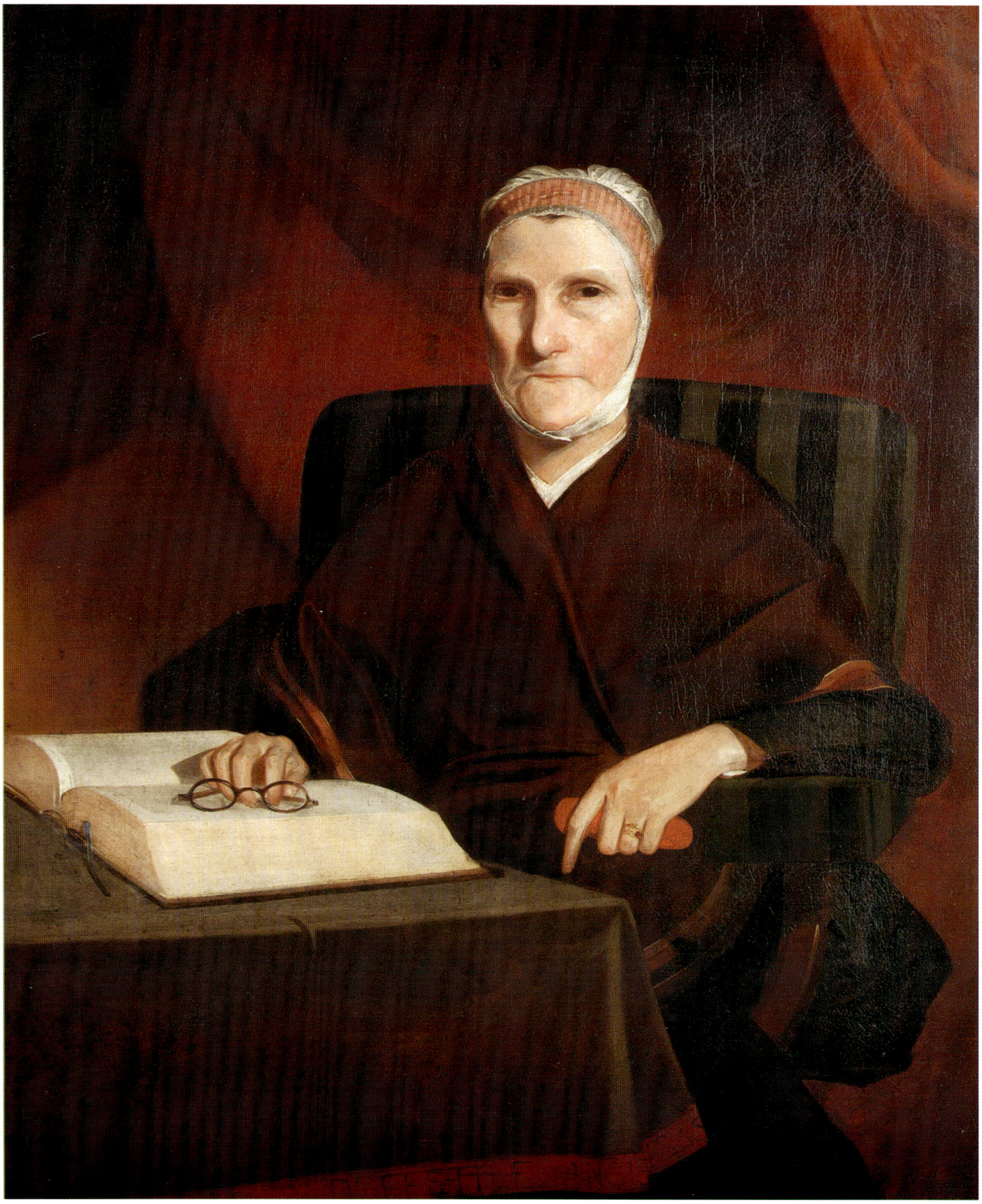

V.

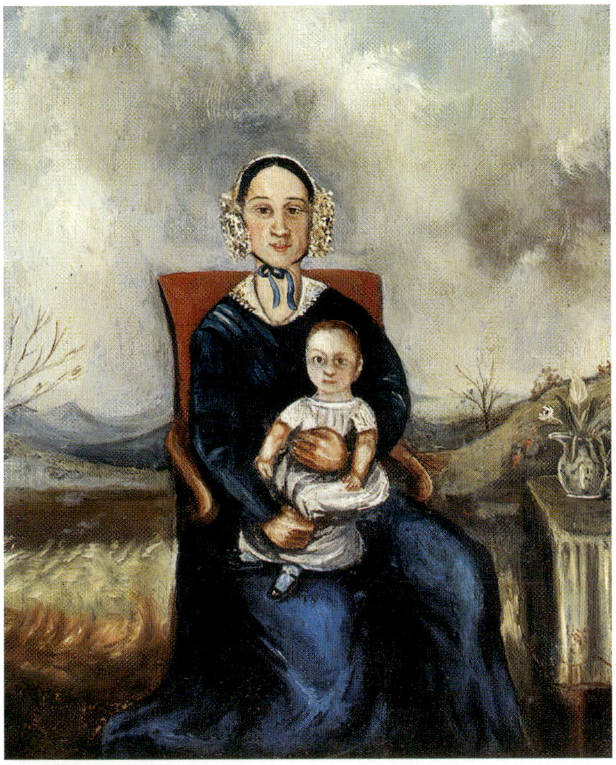

VI.

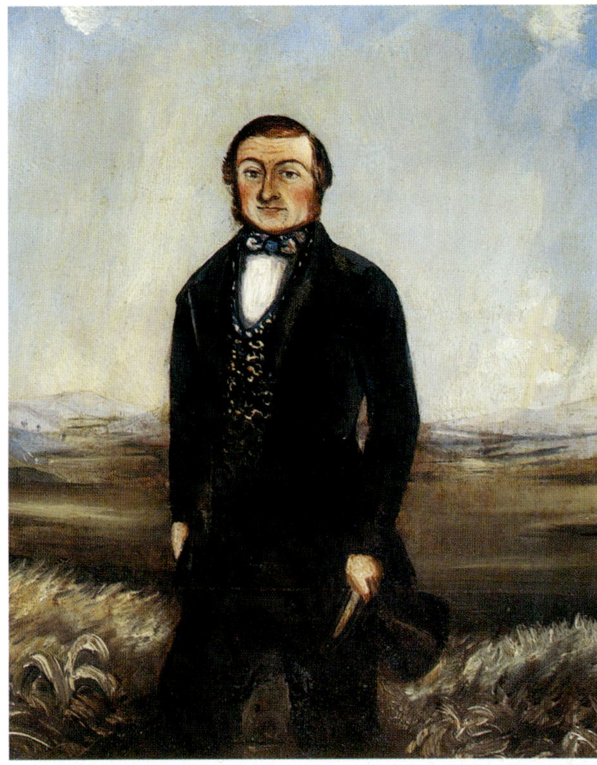

VII.

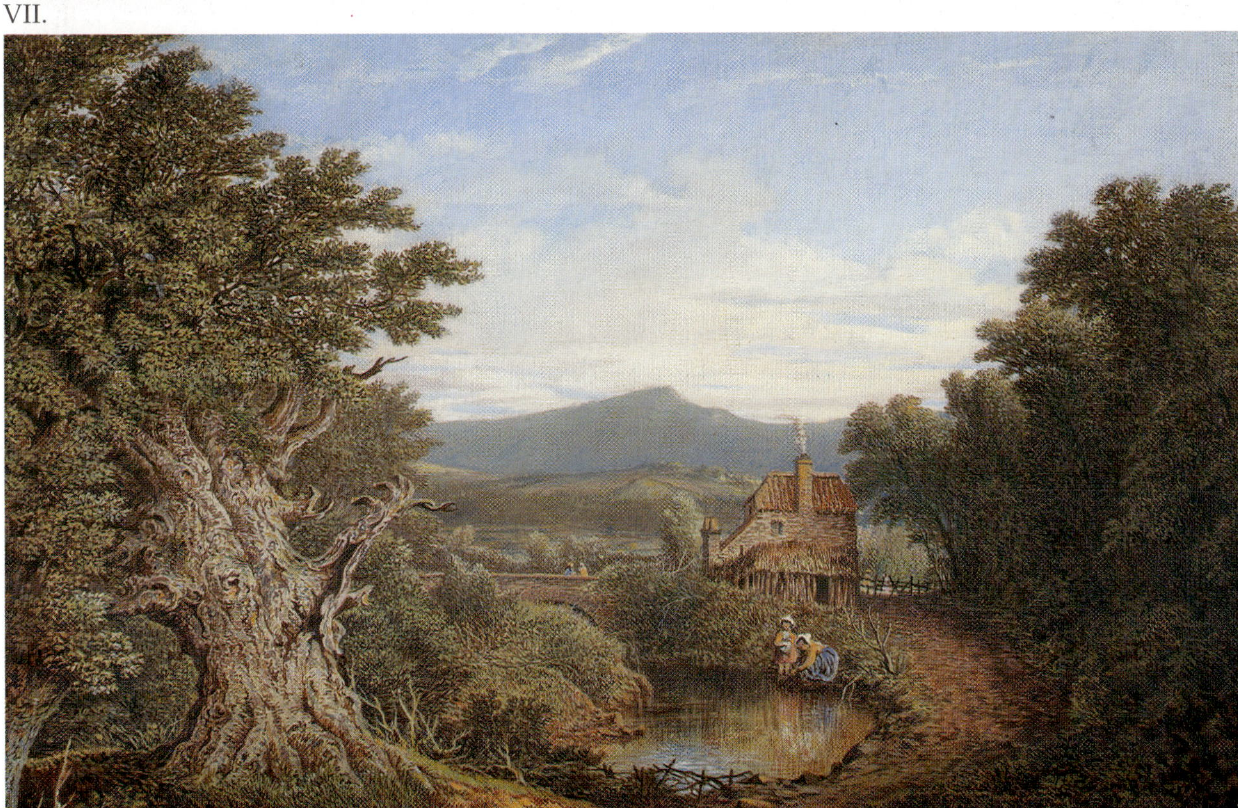

VII. *View taken from back of the old Turnpike house nr Porset [Caerphilly]* by Thomas Waters, oil on canvas, PG 5539.

VIII.

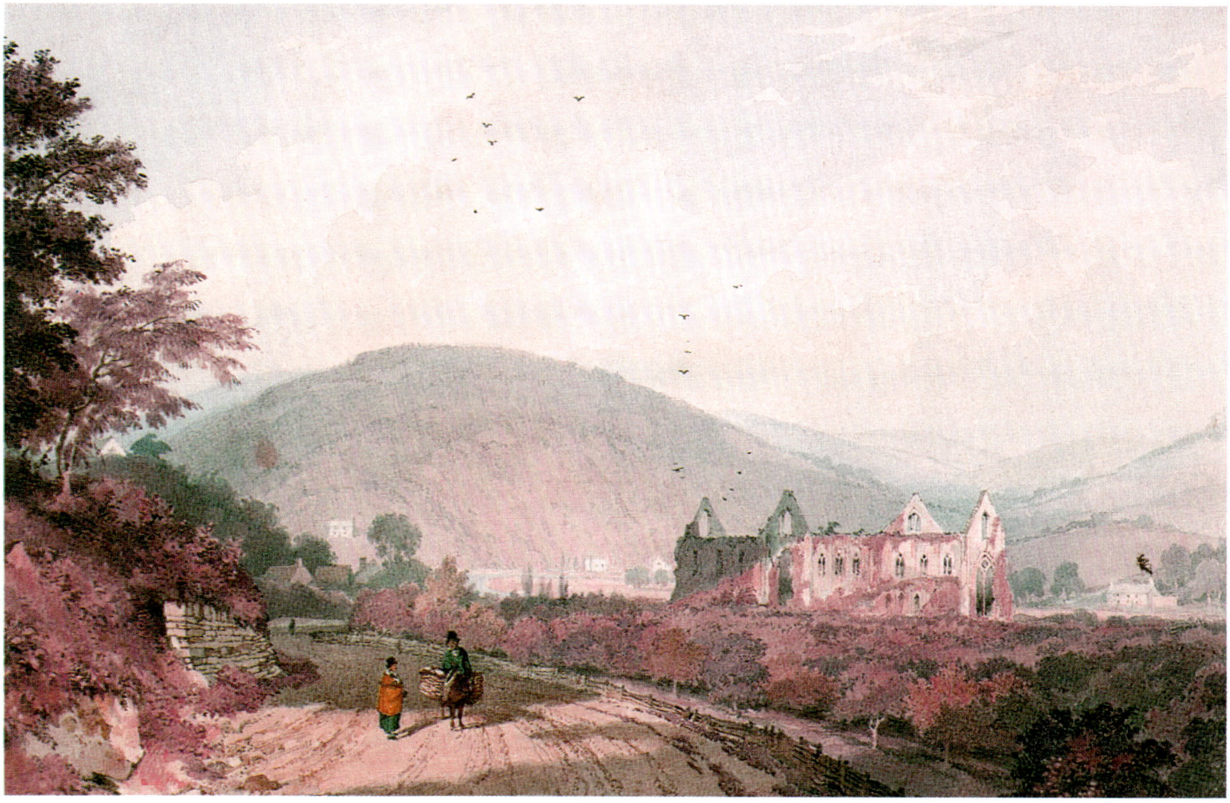

IX.

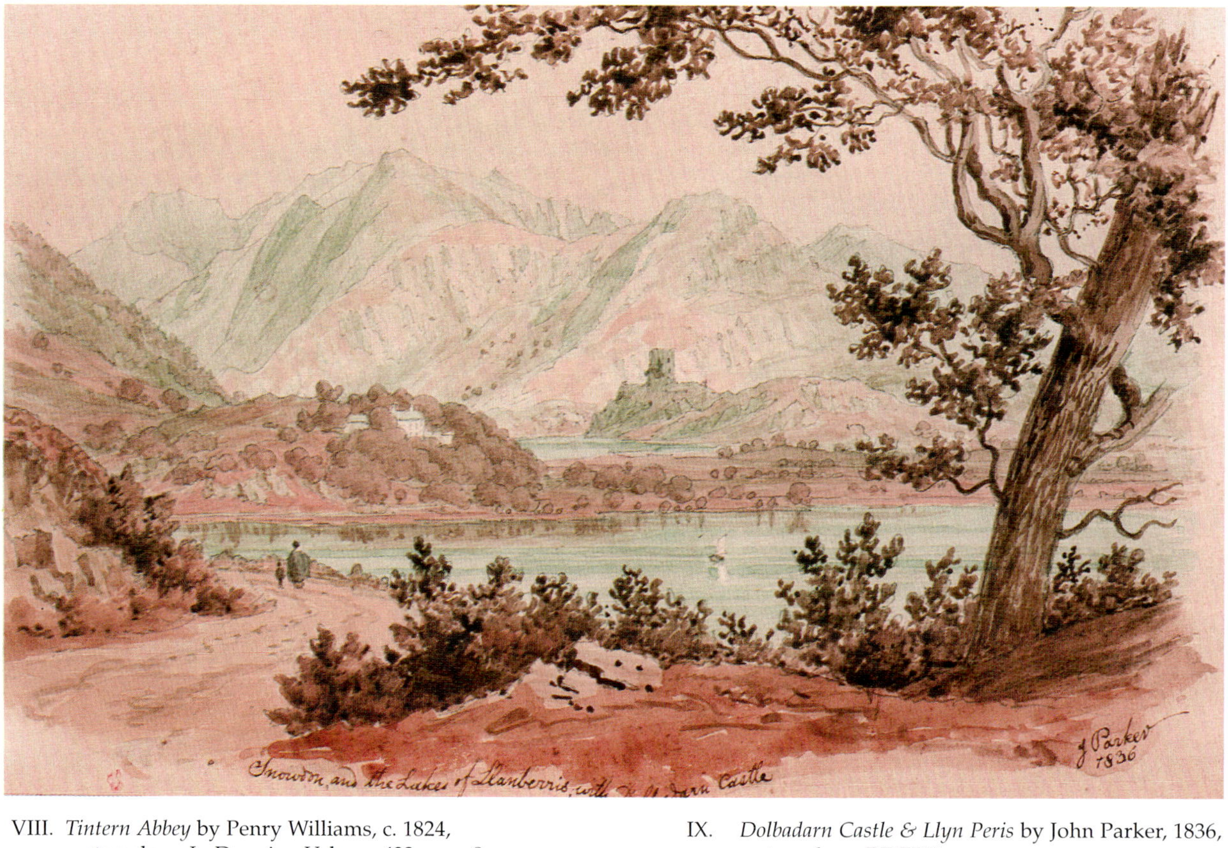

VIII. *Tintern Abbey* by Penry Williams, c. 1824, watercolour, In Drawing Volume 432 page 8, PG 5346.

IX. *Dolbadarn Castle & Llyn Peris* by John Parker, 1836, watercolour, PZ 7539.

X.

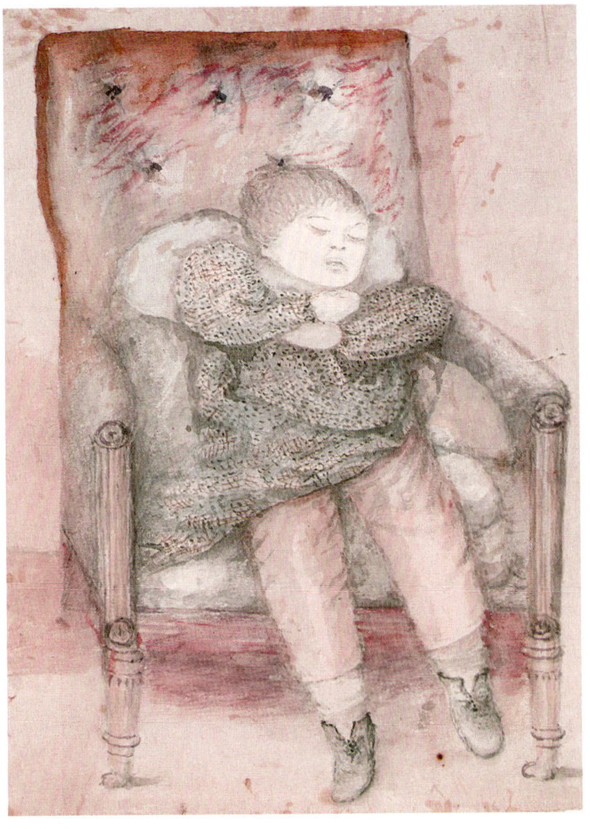

X. *Ivor Pughe* by William Owen Pughe, 1832, watercolour, Loosely inserted in Drawing Volume 58, PZ 364.

XI. *Ruins of Llangewydd Court Laleston* by Thomas Petherick, 1854, watercolour, PG 1292.

XII. *Two Peasant girls* by Thomas Pennant, c. 1780, watercolour, PD 425.

XI.

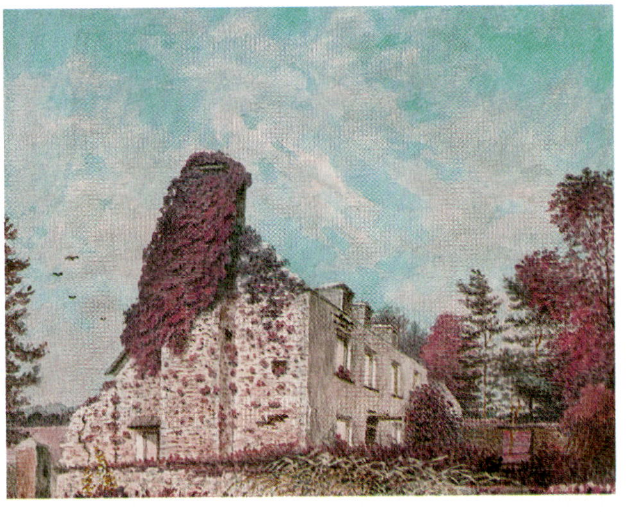

XII.

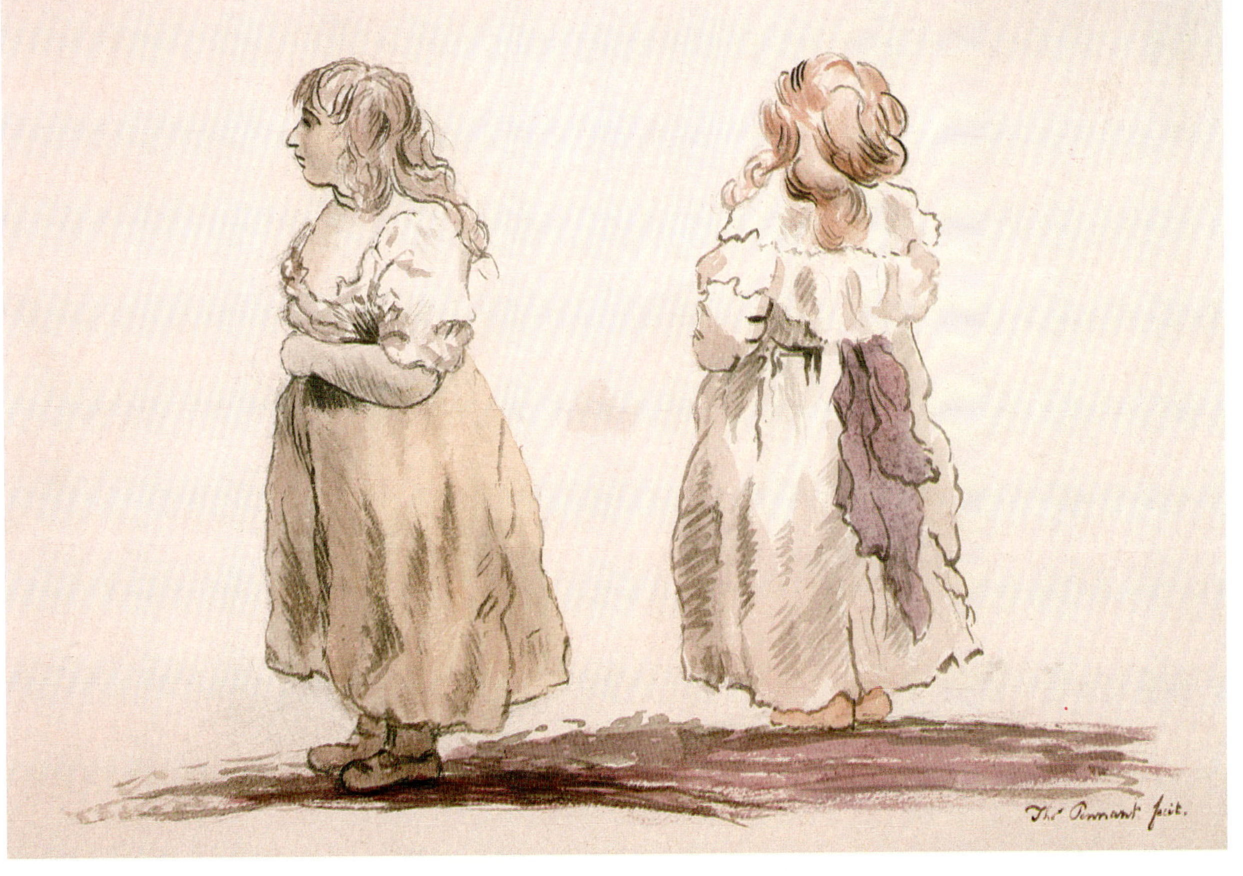

XIII. *Vicarage at St Brides Major* by John Prichard, 1847, watercolour, Church in Wales Records, Bounty Plans, Llandaff 111.

XIII.

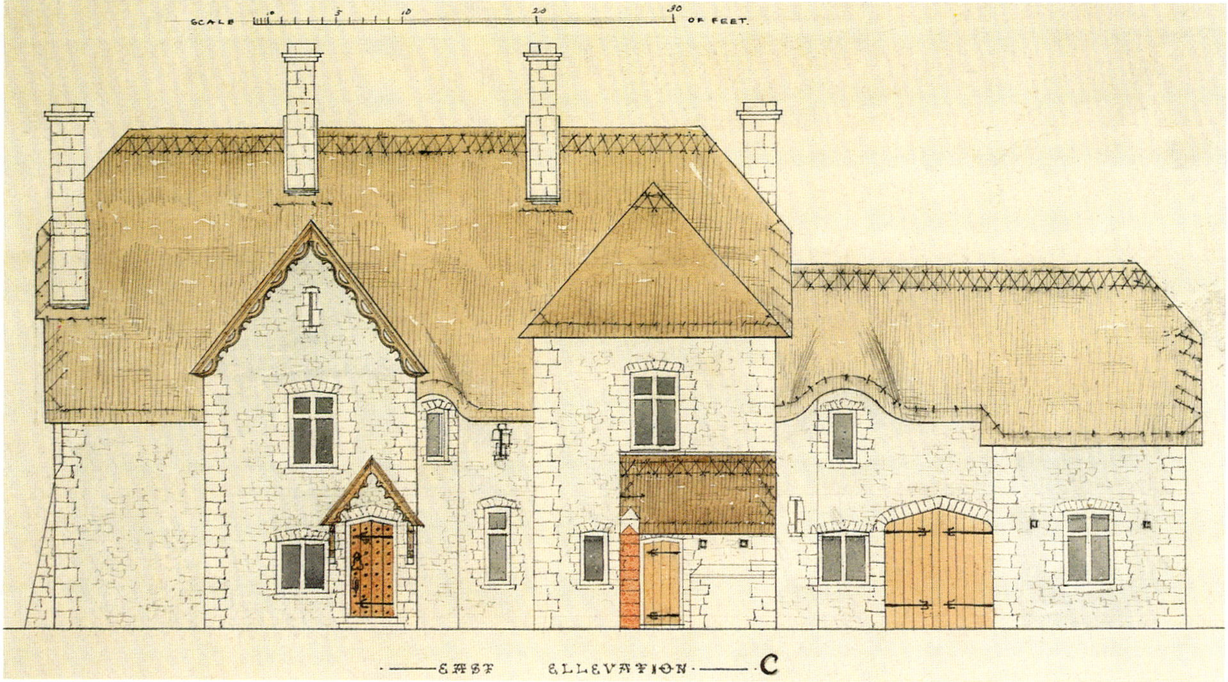

XIV.

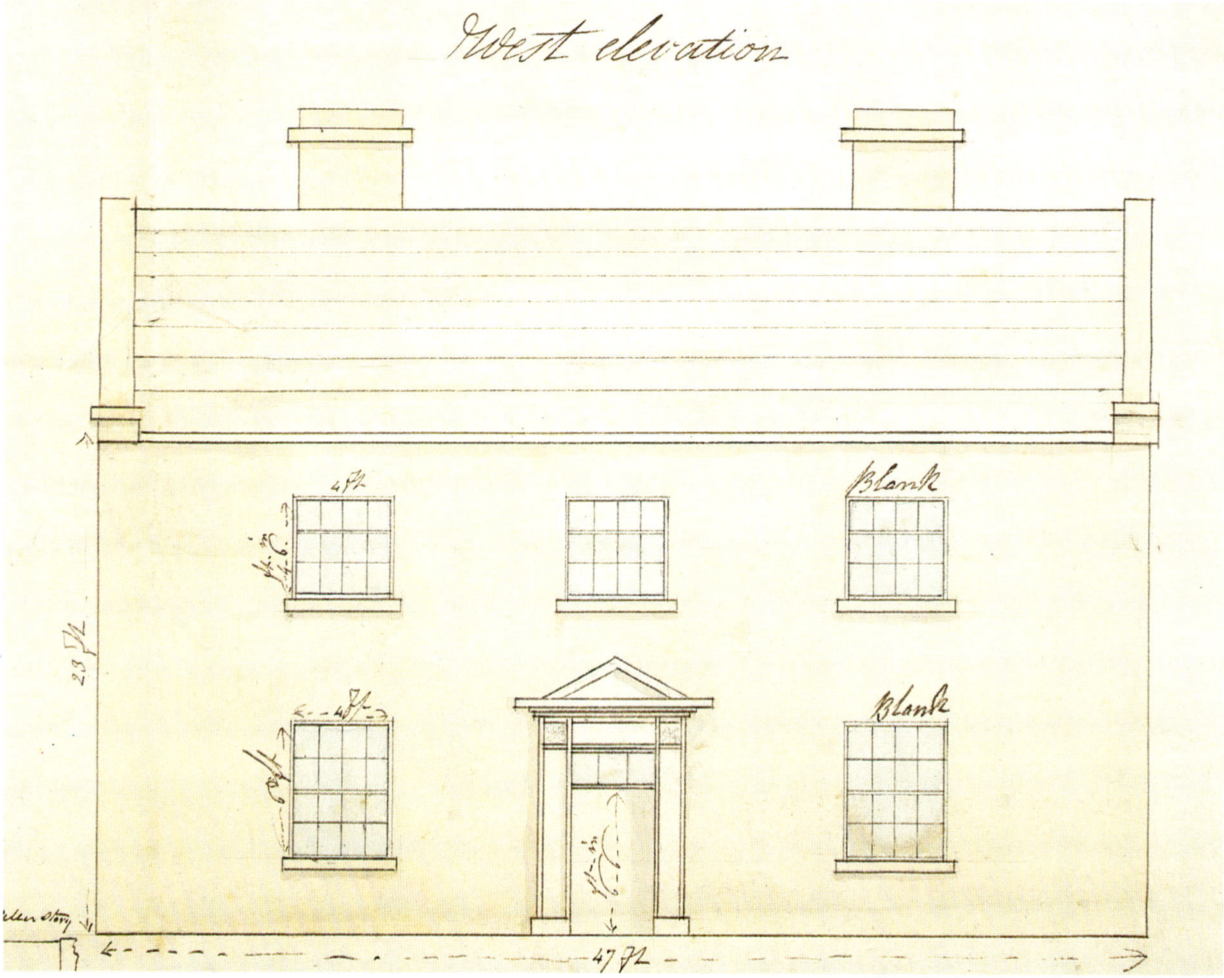

XIV. *Vicarage at Llanarmon* by James Pemberton, 1821, watercolour, Church in Wales Records, Bounty Plans, St Asaph 51.

A

ADAMS, George (- 1773)
Mason
Penally
Pembrokeshire

SD/1773/149 (I).

ADOLPHE, 'Monsieur' Edgar (fl1831 - fl1850)
Miniature and silhouette artist
Calligrapher and calligraphy teacher
Animal and portrait painter
Monmouth
Swansea
Neath
Carmarthen
Abergavenny
Newport
Chepstow

Adolphe was probably born in France, employed by Louis Philippe, King of France in the 1830s and apparently removed to Britain c1831.**(1)** We have no explanation for his leaving a secure and prestigious position to become a popular itinerant artist.**(2)**

McKechnie supplies much information but comments that before c1838, we know only what the wording of his trade labels 'and the appearance of known silhouettes tell us'.**(3)** She suggests that one silhouette was no later than 1833 but little else of this early period was available to her.

Most of his work in Wales covers this early period and there is firm evidence for his having visited Wales from 1831. The visits can be listed thus:

- 1831 - Monmouth, 14 days only [and possibly other parts of South Wales]**(4)**
- 1834 - Swansea, Neath, Carmarthen**(5)**
- 1835 - Monmouth, Abergavenny and possibly Swansea**(6)**
- 1837 - Newport, Chepstow, Swansea**(7)**
- 1850 - Monmouth**(8)**

The 1831 advertisement only mentions calligraphy, which suggests that his portrait work in this field commenced in the period c1833.

Adolphe's visits are of particular interest because he was a visiting artist using the newspaper media, with illustrations to encourage patronage. In 1831 he presented an elaborate image 'The Greatest Improvement of the Age is Adolphe's system of Writing'.**(9)**

When he began as a miniaturist he used a simple wood block of a well known Swansea character to illustrate his advertisements. He also utilised different typefaces to emphasise his skill.

His 1834 visit to Swansea documents the first occasion when a resident and visiting artist aided each other. Adolphe worked at the premises of James Harris and used Harris's window to exhibit silhouettes: 'numerous specimens of well known characters in the window'. The 1837 advertisement stated that Adolphe was at the Painting Rooms of Harris, which suggests that Harris used them for exhibition and painting.

The publicity for his visit of 1834 was quite exceptional in Wales. One does not find any such parallel campaign in this whole period. It is therefore significant that he claims to be a reputable miniaturist (and probably was not) and he used the local press to increase his opportunities. Like most popular portraitists, his pictures were 'warranted correct' but examples of his work show his generalising tendency which assured a correct, but facile portrait.

Adolphe had a good business practice. The gradual escalation of his genre appears symptomatic of commercial-mindedness. On his third visit to Swansea, he displayed his full talents which he expressed thus:

> 'A Striking likeness for 1s' [shilling]
> 'M Adolphe paints Portraits in oil, cabinet, or life size; Animals in oil or water; Miniatures in ivory ...'**(10)**

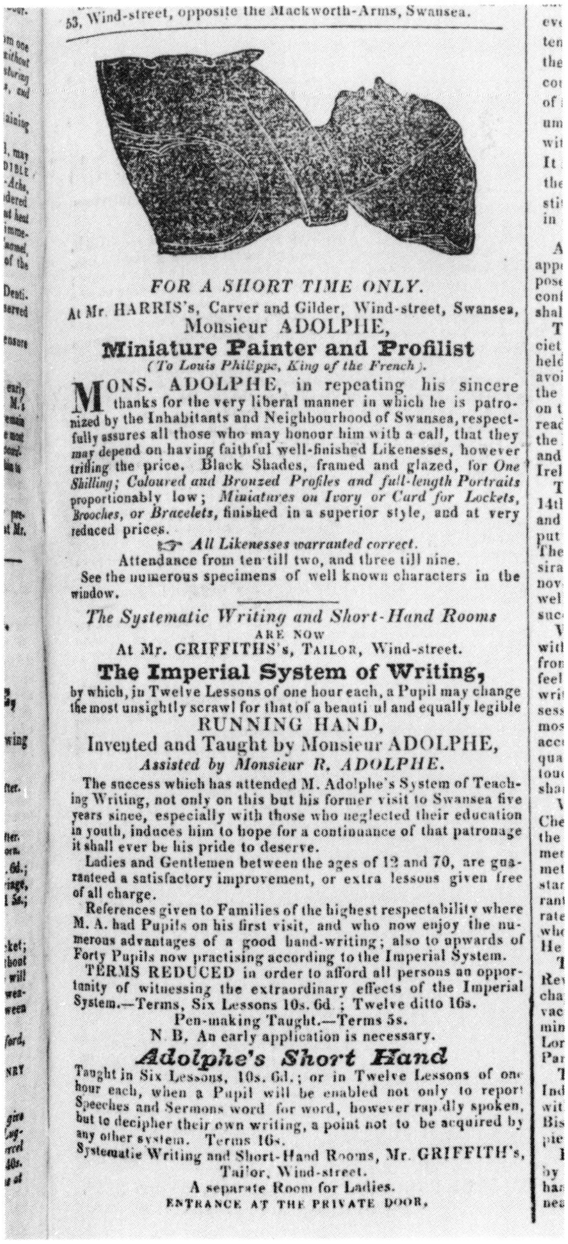

53, Wind-street, opposite the Mackworth-Arms, Swansea.

FOR A SHORT TIME ONLY.
At Mr. HARRIS's, Carver and Gilder, Wind-street, Swansea,
Monsieur ADOLPHE,
Miniature Painter and Profilist
(To Louis Philippe, King of the French).

MONS. ADOLPHE, in repeating his sincere thanks for the very liberal manner in which he is patronized by the Inhabitants and Neighbourhood of Swansea, respectfully assures all those who may honour him with a call, that they may depend on having faithful well-finished Likenesses, however trifling the price. Black Shades, framed and glazed, for *One Shilling; Coloured and Bronzed Profiles and full-length Portraits* proportionably low; *Miniatures on Ivory or Card for Lockets, Brooches*, or *Bracelets*, finished in a superior style, and at very reduced prices.

All Likenesses warranted correct.
Attendance from ten till two, and three till nine.
See the numerous specimens of well known characters in the window.

The Systematic Writing and Short-Hand Rooms
ARE NOW
At Mr. GRIFFITHS's, TAILOR, Wind-street.
The Imperial System of Writing,
by which, in Twelve Lessons of one hour each, a Pupil may change the most unsightly scrawl for that of a beauti ul and equally legible
RUNNING HAND,
Invented and Taught by Monsieur ADOLPHE,
Assisted by Monsieur R. ADOLPHE.

The success which has attended M. Adolphe's System of Teaching Writing, not only on this but his former visit to Swansea five years since, especially with those who neglected their education in youth, induces him to hope for a continuance of that patronage it shall ever be his pride to deserve.

Ladies and Gentlemen between the ages of 12 and 70, are guaranteed a satisfactory improvement, or extra lessons given free of all charge.

References given to Families of the highest respectability where M. A. had Pupils on his first visit, and who now enjoy the numerous advantages of a good hand-writing; also to upwards of Forty Pupils now practising according to the Imperial System.

TERMS REDUCED in order to afford all persons an opportunity of witnessing the extraordinary effects of the Imperial System.—Terms, Six Lessons 10s. 6d ; Twelve ditto 16s.

Pen-making Taught.—Terms 5s.
N. B. An early application is necessary.

Adolphe's Short Hand
Taught in Six Lessons, 10s. 6d.; or in Twelve Lessons of one hour each, when a Pupil will be enabled not only to report Speeches and Sermons word for word, however rapidly spoken, but to decipher their own writing, a point not to be acquired by any other system. Terms 16s.
Systematic Writing and Short-Hand Rooms, Mr. GRIFFITH's, Tailor, Wind-street.
A separate Room for Ladies.
ENTRANCE AT THE PRIVATE DOOR.

4 Adolphe, Edgar, *Likeness*, *Cambrian* advertisement 5 July 1843 p.3.

It appears that he alternated his visits to Wales, taking Monmouth and Monmouthshire as the main region for one year then Swansea and Mid Wales for the next. He tended to keep closely to the main coach roads and centres of population, venturing up to Carmarthen, but no further. This practice was typical of all the visiting artists described in this work

1. *McKechnie*, pp.364-365, 453-454.
2. His claim seems highly unlikely, Louis acceded in 1830 and Adolphe, when he advertised in 1831, does not refer to his connection to the King (*Monmouthshire Merlin*, 7 May 1831, p.3); rather he states that he is 'of the Systematic Writing Establishment, Rue Vivienne, Paris'. *McKechnie* suggests that Adolphe came to Britain c1832 but the *Merlin* evidence provides an earlier date.
3. *Op.cit.*, p.364.
4. *Monmouthshire Merlin*, 7 May 1831, p.3; *ibid.*, 14 May 1831, p.3, at 'Mr Protheroe's, Tailor, Agincourt Square, Monmouth'. He notes that he already had over two hundred pupils in Ross and Ledbury whom he taught at their own residences. At this date portraiture is not mentioned.
5. *Cambrian*, 5 July 1834, p.3 (wood-cut of silhouette), [written from Swansea].
   Ibid., 12 July 1834, p.2 (wood-cut of handwriting).
   Ibid., 19 July 1834, p.2: 'Last Week but one'.
   Ibid., 26 July 1834, p.3: 'Last Week you can have'.
   Ibid., 8 August 1834: 'in Carmarthen next week', information *TL*.
   Ibid., 16 August 1834, p.2: 'Positively the last week you can have...', [written from Neath].
   Ibid., 23 August 1834, p.2.
   Ibid., 30 August 1834, p.2. [In September it appears that he visited Carmarthen, a little later than originally planned.]
6. *Monmouthshire Merlin*, 3 January 1835, p.2: 'Monmouth for a short time only... Miniature Painter and Profilist. The accuracy of whose likenesses gained him such extensive patronage in Swansea.'
   Ibid., 10 January 1835, p.1.
   Ibid., 17 January 1835, p.1.
   Ibid., 24 January 1835, p.1.
   Ibid., 31 January 1835, p.1: 'his departure will not take place until Friday 6th February when his engagements at Abergavenny positively commence...' This advertisement was illustrated with a portrait profile.
7. *Monmouthshire Merlin*, 1 April 1837, p.2 [written from Newport]. Working at the Westgate Hotel and advertised as:
   'Professor of Portrait, Animal, Miniature and Profile Painting, Stenography, Arithmetic and Systematic Writing.
   M. Adolphe paints Portraits in oil, cabinet or life size, Animals in oil or water, Miniatures on ivory or card, of the smallest description, for rings, brooches, lockets, or bracelets, side or front sketches...'
   Ibid., 8 April 1837, p.1.
   Ibid., 15 April 1837, p.2.
   Ibid., 22 April 1837, p.1.
   Ibid., 29 April 1837, p.2.
   Ibid., 13 May 1837, p.2: 'For a Short Time only Chepstow and Newport.'
   Cambrian, 24 June 1837, p.3: 'Third visit of Monsieur Adolphe...in grateful remembrance of the extensive patronage which stimulated and rewarded his exertions on his two former visits...'
   Ibid., 15 July 1837 p3.
8. Reference given in *Kissack*, p.148, *Monmouthshire Merlin* 24/9/50. I have been unable to substantiate this reference, *Merlins* at *BL* (Colingdale) & *NLW* do not include this exact date and issues around this date have no reference to Adolphe.
9. See note **(4)**.
10. *Monmouthshire Merlin*, 1 April 1837, p.2, and *Cambrian*, 15 July 1837, p.3.

ALLEN, Lady Catherine (1821 - 1899)

Landscape artist — Cresselly, Kilgetty

She was an amateur artist,**(1)** who came to Wales after her marriage in 1843. Mostly her work is based on the Cresselly area, where she produced small watercolours. These are almost all in private hands.**(2)**

1. *TL*. *Steegman*, Vol. II, p.180, No.7 records a portrait of this artist, c1845.
2. *TL*. notes that the majority of the work dates from 1860 onwards.

ALLEN, Charles (fl 1858)

Photographic artist — Newport, Maindee

Slater's, 1858.

ALLEN, Joseph (1770 - 1839)

Portrait and genre painter — Wrexham

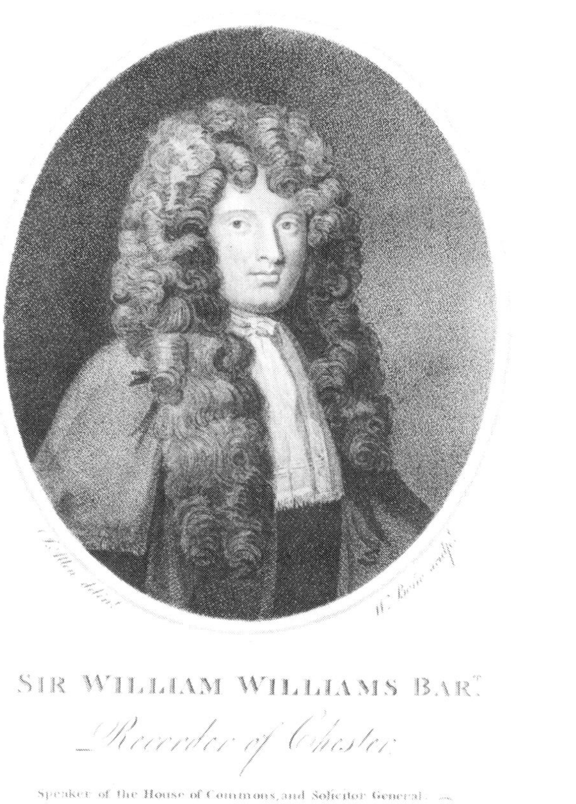

5 Allen, Joseph, *Sir William Williams*, engraving, 1798, PA4254.

He was born in Birmingham, went to London and became a student at the *RA*, 23 November 1787.**(1)**

Between 1798-9 he settled at Wrexham and probably built up many important business connections with Manchester, Preston and other Northern towns.**(2)** He seems to have returned to London where he remained intermittently, until 1822 after which he retired to Erdington near Birmingham. He exhibited at the *RA* 1792-1822, and from a Wrexham address in 1798.**(3)**

Philip Yorke of Erddig published prints after Allen which implies local interest in the artist.**(4)** By 1800 he had returned to London.**(5)**

1. *Hutchison*, p.149, 'Aged 19 [on] 12 January 1788, Painter'; he gained a Silver Medal in 1789.
2. *Bennett*, p.19.
3. *Graves, R.A.*, p.25: 1798, *Rev. Mr Strong*; 1799 (236) *Mrs Gray and Child*; (877) *Mr Dixon*.
4. *NLW*, PA4254, *Sir William Williams Bart*, J. Allen delint, W. Bond sculpt. 34.2 x 25.7 (image 14.4 x 12cm), 'from a Picture in the Town Hall of Chester, Published Aug 1 1798 by Philip Yorke Esqr. Wrexham'. Another is in BP109, *Sir John Trevor*, 1798, from the portrait at 'Brynkinalt' [*sic*]. See also PD 4718, C6/1 - C32, *Wrexham Church, North Wales*, c1810.
5. His address given in the *RA* exhibition 1800, was 5 Lower James Street, London. *Cadrawd*, Vol. I, p.1, mentions that he was 'for some time the chief scene painter at the Olympic Theatre'.

ANTHONY, Henry Mark (1817 - 1886)
Landscape painter — Cowbridge

He was born in Cowbridge.**(1)** Apprenticed in Harrison's Apothecary, who encouraged the young Mark,**(2)** after which he went to London to study art. As a boy he was a friend of Alderman Alexander and John Bird.

He also spent time at Paris and The Hague and exhibited from Paris at the *RA* in 1837. He never returned to Wales.**(3)**

1. *South Wales Daily News*, 10 November 1903. The article notes that his parents moved to Cowbridge.
2. *Mardy Rees* pp.5-6 notes this man was an amateur artist *infra* T. W. Davies.
3. Examples of his work are: *View of the Rhondda*, 1837 given as *Rhaidha, Glamorganshire* which was exhibited in the Arts Exhibition, Cardiff, 1884; *The Old School, Cowbridge*; [*Llanarfon*] *Church*.

ARNOLD, James F. (fl 1858)
Photographer — Cardiff
263 Upper Bute Street

Slater's, 1858.

ARONSON, J. (fl 1849 - fl 1851)
Medalist — Bangor

He produced medals for the following Eisteddfodau**(1)**:
1849 Aberffraw, medal signed 'A & M'.
1850 Rhuddlan, medal signed 'A & M'.
1851 Tremadoc, medal signed 'A & M'.

1. *WFM*, MS 3397/3 'Welsh Medals' [no pp.] Some medals are given in I.C. Peate, *Welsh Society and Eisteddfod Medals and Relics*, (Cardiff, 1938), p.28 ff.

ARTHUR, John (fl 1724)
Monumental Mason — (St. Michael's)
Cilycwm
Carmarthenshire

He painted the following in the parish church, all in English: Royal Arms, inscriptions, decalogues, *Moses & Aaron*, *Figure of Death*.**(1)**

All paintings were restored in 1986 by D. H. Jones & J. Davies, both local artists.**(2)**

1. *RCAM (TP)*, *The Transactions of Carmarthen Historical Society*, illustrates 'death' pre-1986 (1933, Vol. 24, pp.92-93).
2. The restoration aroused much local interest and dismay. For instance, *South Wales Evening Post*, 18 July 1986, pp.1 & 3. I am grateful to Mrs. M. White, Bryncoch for this reference. *Death* is illustrated, but unidentified, in colour, on a leaflet produced by the *RCAM*, 1994.

ATKINS, Alex (fl 1835)
Carver & guilder — St. Mary's Street
Carmarthen

Pigot's, 1835, p.753.

ATTWOOD, John (fl 1776 - fl 1816)
Drawing master — Swansea
Landscape painter — Burrows

A landscape by Attwood of Milford Haven was exhibited at Spinks in 1948. According to Spinks the work was signed and dated 1776.**(1)** This work appears to be the only surviving example of Attwood's *oeuvre*, and was engraved in the *European Magazine*.**(2)**

The *Swansea Guide*, 1802, p.43, mentions a John Attwood, Drawing Master, and again in 1816.**(3)** Attwood appears to have lived in Swansea and possibly remained there. From 1832 a solicitor, Thomas Attwood was in Swansea, he may have been a relative of the artist.**(4)**

1. Information from *Witt*. The painting is now at *NMW*.
2. *European Magazine*, Vol. 26, 1794, August, facing p.134: *Milford Haven*, 'Engraved by Thomas', published by T. Savell, Cornhill March 1, 1794. 10.1 x 16.9 cm (image size). This is a fairly accurate copy of the original.
3. *Swansea Guide*, 1816, p.19: 'John Attwood Drawing Master'.
4. *SD* 1832/329 notes a currier William Henry Attwood of Swansea, presumably the same family.

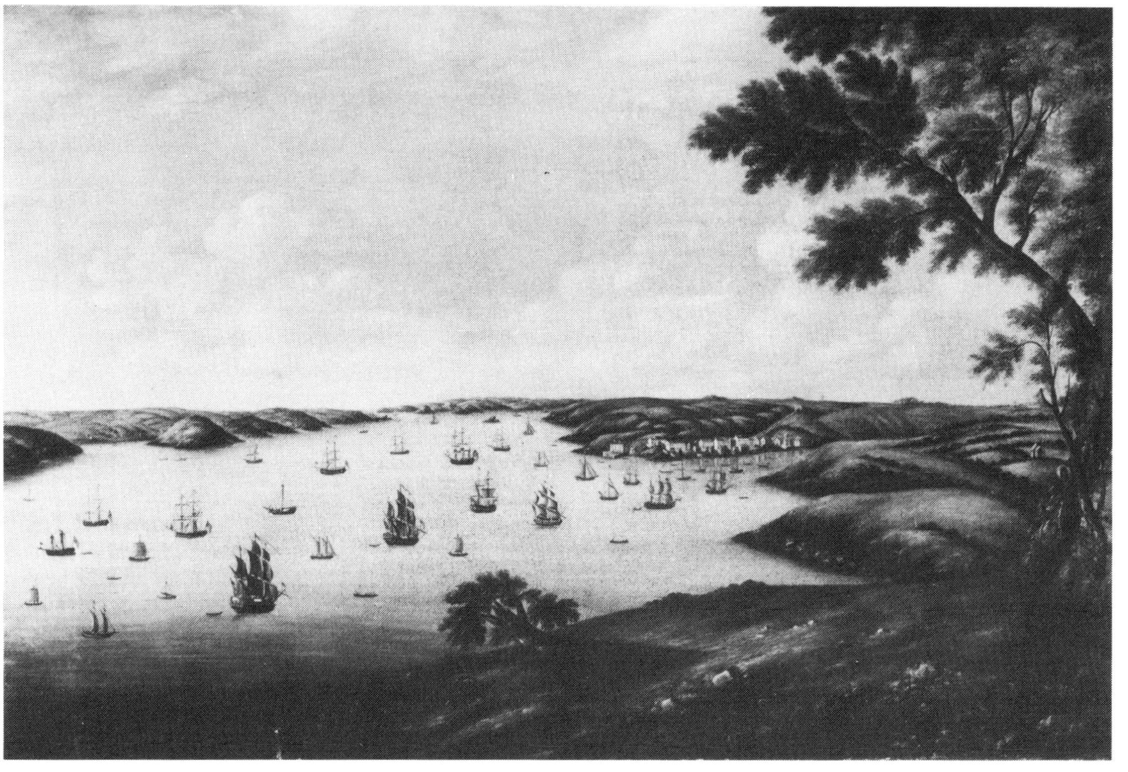

6 Attwood, John, *Milford Haven*, oil on canvas, 1776, *NMW*.

AUSTIN, Samuel (1796-1834)
Landscape and marine painter — Cefn-y-Cribin, Montgomeryshire

He worked mainly in watercolour both in London and Liverpool. He exhibited at the Liverpool Academy 1822-1832, *RA* 1820, *RSBA* 1824 and *RSPW* 1827-1834.

Although he lived most of his life in Liverpool, his death is recorded in Wales**(1)** and whilst no evidence has yet been collected to suggest his having painted in Wales there is a possibility that some work may have been done there between 1831/2-1834.**(2)** His will was proved at Chester, September 1834.**(3)**

1. *Bennett* (text), pp.29-30.
2. *VAM*, 1779-1900, *A Cottage in North Wales*, signed and dated 1831, 28.2 x 35.7 cm. At Christie's, 24 March 1987, lot 1, an album was sold of work by S.A. and others including views of Tintern and Raglan dated 1833-1861. This may represent work done whilst resident in Wales.
3. *Chester* (1980), p.6.

B

BAGGALEY, John (fl 1848)
Builder — Welshpool

He produced plans & built the Rectory at Manafon, 1848**(1)**

1. *NLW* St Asaph, Bounty Plans 1849. A neat plans. Not in *Eden*.

BAGGALEY, Richard (fl 1833)
Architect — Welshpool

He designed & built the Rectory at Llangyniew**(1)**

1. *NLW* St Asaph, Bounty Plans 89, 1833. He signed his estimate as 'Architect'. Not in *Eden* or *Girouard*.

BAKER, W. H. (fl 1848)
Drawing master — Caernarfon, Twt Hill

He was Principal of Caernarfon Grammar School and advertised private lessons in drawing, writing & French at his residence.**(1)**

1. *Caernarvon & Denbighshire Herald*, 29 July 1848, p.4.

BALL, Samuel (fl 1835 - fl 1843)
Surveyor — Kidwelly

Davies Atlas, *Eden* I p.28.
NLW, *Conwil Elvet* maps, 1841.

BAMFORD, Samuel (fl 1842)
Architect — Michaelston-super-Avon

He designed the rectory at Michaelstone-super-Ely, 1842**(1)**

1. *NLW* Llandaff Bounty Plans 83, 1842. Not in *Eden*.

BARBER, Edmund Scott (fl 1835 - fl 1848)
Surveyor
Newport
Commercial Street

Davies Atlas, Eden I p.28.

BARKER, Benjamin (Senior) (1720 - 1790)
Portrait painter
Enamel painter
Pontypool
Sporting, animal painter

He was a Foreman and enamel painter at the Japan works, Pontypool.**(1)**

He painted a Coat of Arms at Trevethin church in 1774. He worked as a portrait painter.**(2)** A portrait of *Mrs Edwards of Pontypool & her two daughters* on tin-plate was published in 1930.**(3)** He was a 'spendthrift who took to painting horses and who settled in Bath as a stable hand about 1783'.**(4)**

1. *DWB*, p.25. *Bell* I p.28.
2. *Leisure Hour*, Nov. 1899, pp.67-73: 'A British Painter's Travels in the Last Century', including a portrait of T.B. *NMW* has a self-portrait.
3. *Western Mail*, [7 March 1930], 'Famous Paintings in Wales XXIV', notes that this portrait was in the 'collection of Major Albert Williams, Llangibby Castle, Monmouthshire'.
4. (*NMW* files) Thomas Barker, *see Bath Chronicle*, 12 April 1862: F. Shum, 'Reminiscences of the late Thomas Barker'.

BARKER, Thomas (of Bath) (1769 - 1847)
Landscape & genre painter
Pontypool

He was born at Trosnant? near Pontypool. 'When quite young he displayed great skill in drawing'. He was entirely self taught.**(1)** His early work was presumably executed in Wales. The family moved to Bath c1783.**(2)**

1. *Mardy Rees*, p.8. Circumstantial evidence suggests he was taught by his father.
2. *Mallalieu* notes that Thomas Barker was then fourteen and his brother Benjamin (1776-1838) only seven. Eldest of four sons (*NMW* file). *vide* Barker, Benjamin.

BARKER, Thomas Jones (1815 - 1882)
Portraits, military scenes
Cardiff
History and sporting scenes

He was the son of Thomas Barker of Bath. 'His military pictures were in great demand 60 years ago. He used to exhibit his paintings in Cardiff in a shop near the Hayes. One of these, a painting of Nelson boarding a French Steamer, attracted great attention in the 1850s and was taken around the provinces on exhibition.'**(1)** This reference represents the unusual event of a single picture being exhibited, as were Daguire's works in 1830s.

He studied in the studio of Horace Vernet (1789-1863) at Paris in c1834.**(2)** Exhibited at *RA* 1845-1876, *BI* 1844-1867, *RSBA*, 1846-1874.

1. *South Wales Daily News*, 6 October 1910. (Reference given by *Mardy Rees* but incorrect. An extensive check of the newspapers around this date has so far proved unfruitful).
   One of his military pictures was sold at Sotheby's on 14 July 1993, lot 103: *Meeting of the Duke of Wellington...* This was published as a print in 1851.
2. *Mardy Rees*, p.11, quoting Bryan's *Dictionary of Painters*, Vol. 1, p.84. Mentions that Vernet was very popular in France & given a room for his military paintings in the French Exhibition 1855. This may explain Barker's popularity. *Millar*, Volume I, p.29, provides a little more information.

BARNETT, Mr (fl 1850)
Drawing master and house painter
Monmouth

Monmouthshire Merlin, 24 September 1850.**(1)**

1. Reference from *Kissack*, p.148 (not in the *Newport* edition but may be in the *Monmouth* edition).

BARRETT, Richard (fl 1836)
Surveyor
Pembroke

Barrett rebuilt the vicarage at Carew, 1836.**(1)** He also designed a vicarage at Saint Florence in 1838.**(2)**

1. Not in *Eden*. *NLW SD*, Bounty Plans 18, 1836.
2. *NLW SD*, Bounty Plans 168, 1838. He produced a surprisingly fine watercolours elevation of *St Ishmaels vicarage*, St Davids, Bounty Plan 169, 1836.
   Not in *Eden*.

BARROW, John (fl 1835 - fl 1843)
Surveyor
Bangor

Davies Atlas, Eden I p.30.

BARRY, Joseph T. (fl 1820)
Ship painter
Milford Haven
Pembrokeshire

An oil painting, signed and dated July 1820, *Milford of Pembroke*, is at Haverfordwest Museum. The naive style and colouring suggest a local artist.**(1)**

1. Circumstantial evidence suggests he lived at Milford.

BARRY, Thomas D. (fl 1835 - fl 1843)
Surveyor

Davies Atlas, Eden I p.30.

BARTLEY, Samuel (fl 1815**(1)** - fl 1843)
Surveyor**(2)**
Swansea
Pibwr, Carmarthen
Llandefaelog

Bartley was based in Swansea in 1815**(3)** and probably moved c1816. He took surveys in 1816-17 of *Blaenporth etc*. He also executed surveys in Carmarthen, Abergwili: 1825 and 1830.

1. *Cambrian*, 24 June 1815, p.1.
2. *Davies Atlas, Eden* I p.30.
3. *NLW*, MSS Estate maps.

BATCHELOR [& PROSSER] (fl 1830)
Architect & builder
Newport (Mon)
Canal parade**(1)**

(1) LL1836/118 notes the probate of Benjamin Batchelor, timber merchant of Newport.

Pigot's, 1830, p.522.

BATE, Thomas (fl 1835 - fl 1843)
Surveyor
Brecon

Davies Atlas, *Eden* I p.31.

BATTERSBY, Mrs (fl 1833 - fl 1839)
Amateur artist
Tenby

She exhibited water colours at Suffolk Street,**(1)** and exhibited at the *RA* as 'An Honorary Exhibitor' from Tenby the following:**(2)**

1833 (843) *The Maid of Athens*
1839 (803) *Leila*
(834) *Rose Maylie*

1. *RSBA*, 1833-1836, five watercolours, all figure and portrait studies of women.
2. Does not appear in *Pigot's*, Tenby 1830-1844, so may have been a summer resident at the resort.

BAUGH, Robert (1748 - 1832)
Engraver, draughtsman
Land surveyor
Llanymynech
Montgomeryshire

He was born in Llandysilio, Montgomeryshire and lived mostly at Llanymynech. Baugh engraved very fine prints for his friend John Evans (Llwynygroes).**(1)**

In 1795 he worked on the Evans *North Wales* volume, which displays a clean, fluid style. Several vignettes were included. The eagle is the most startling.**(2)**

In 1795 he engraved a map of North Wales which included a small view of Conwy Castle.**(3)** By 1803 he was surveying property in Montgomeryshire.**(4)** He engraved and published a map of Shropshire in 1808 which is characteristically well executed.**(5)** Later he worked for Thomas Telford during the improvement of the Holyhead Road.**(6)**

At Llanymynech he was much respected. 'He served for many years as parish clerk, played the bassoon in the band which accompanied the psalms in the parish church, and provided many engravings to adorn the village inns.'**(7)**

His obituary ends with the epithet 'The unassuming and merry-hearted Robert Baugh'.**(8)** He died in Shropshire.**(9)**

1. *BBA*, not in *Eden*, 1976, 1979). *Cambrian Quarterly Magazine*, Vol. V, p.312.
2. Evans, John, *North Wales* (1795, PG 1036), large folio sheets of maps. There is also a view of *Valle Crucis Abbey*, dedicated to Sir Watkin Williams Wynn, pub. by T. Evans, Llwynygroes, P 6204, D6-D11.
3. Folio map, dedicated to Sir Watkin.
4. *NLW*, Estate Map Volume (Dugdale Deposit), Map of the Manor of Brithdir [for John Humffreys], signed and dated 'Surveyed by R. Baugh in the year 1803'. Map 1, *Llwyn*, has a small decorative cartouche dated 1775. It is unlikely that the rest of this volume is in Baugh's hand.
5. *Robert Baugh's Map of Shropshire 1808* (*PA* 4004), Shropshire Archaeological Society, 1983, facsimile of the map with introduction by Barrie Trinder. The map bears the codicil 'Published August 1 1808 by Robert Baugh, Llanymynech *sic* Shropshire'.
6. *Ibid.*, p.2.
7. *Ibid.*, p.2, *Montgomeryshire Collections* VIII, 1875, 336-337:

   'Travellers have frequently expressed surprise at the excellence of the prints and maps at the village inns of Llanymynech, and still further when informed that they were all selected by the taste, and many etched and engraved by the ingenious talents of the parish clerk.'
8. *Cambrian Quarterly Magazine*, *op.cit.*, p.312. The obituary also notes 'a truly good man'.
9. His will records him as a 'land surveyor'. *NLW* SA 1833/131.

BAXTER, Thomas (1782 - 1821)
Enamel, porcelain and portrait painter
Engraver, draughtsman
Teacher of painting and drawing
Swansea

Trained at the *RA* from 1800.**(1)** He worked at Worcester as a drawing master and porcelain artist, then moved to London where he established an art school and painted china.

In 1816 he moved to Swansea.**(2)** Worked for the Cambrian Pottery and in 1818 published a set of engravings showing local scenes.**(3)** This venture was probably not greatly successful and he still possessed at least seven sets of the prints when he died.**(4)** An advertisement which he published shows his interest and prices:

> 'In a few days will be published, price 10s 6d six views in and near SWANSEA, by T. Baxter, Portrait Painter, and may be had at his house in Goat Street, or of T. Jenkins and Miss Oakey, Wind Street.
> Portraits drawn from One Guinea upwards.
> Miniatures painted from One Guinea upwards.'**(5)**

About 1819 he removed from Swansea. He returned to Worcester where he died.**(6)**

1. *Hutchison*, p.159, Baxter entered the *RA* schools on 23 October 1800 as a painter.
2. For details of Baxter's work, see *Nance* (pp.306-316). Matthew's *Swansea Guide* 1816 gives 'Thomas Baxter, Drawing Master, Goat Street'; *Long*, p.xxxiii, 'List of provincial artists in towns', lists only Baxter and T. George of Haverfordwest, working in Wales. He exhibited 1802-1811 as an enamel painter in the *RA* and in 1821 from Worcester. *Bell* p.86.
3. Examples of these prints are: P670, B8/3 - B60, *Caswell Bay*; PZ 3450, B8/6 - B139, *Mount Pleasant (Swansea)*; PZ 3451, B8/6 - B140, *The Willows and Mount Pleasant*. These were advertised in the *Cambrian*, 18 July 1818, p.2, just published 'Six Views in and near Swansea' and again on 1 August 1818, p.3 and subsequent

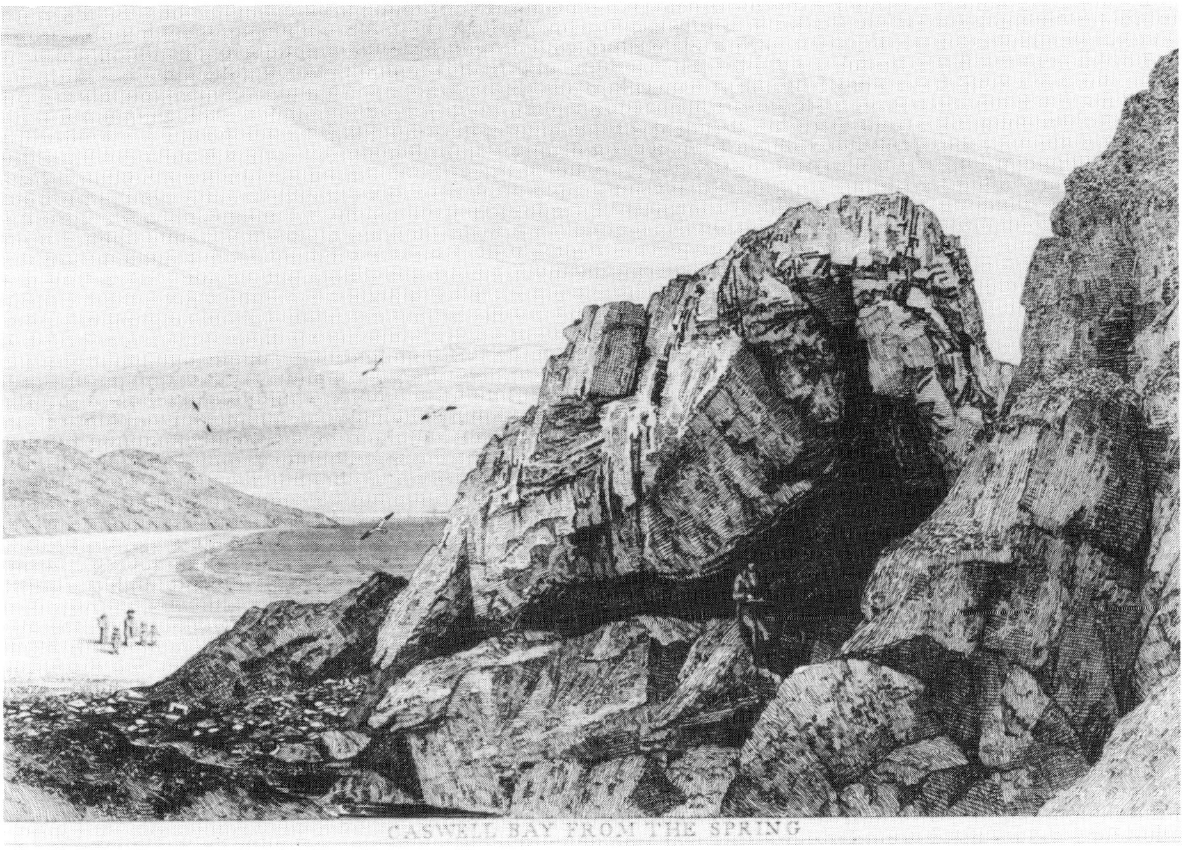

7 Baxter, Thomas, *Oystermouth*, engraving, 1818, P670 Top B8/3.

issues. Elis Jenkins wrote two articles in the *Gower* on Baxter, XIX (1968), 'Thomas Baxter's 1818 Drawings', pp.50-55, and XXIII (1972), 'The Return of the Natives - Postscript on Thomas Baxter', pp.34-39.

4. *Lugt*, 11499 (*BM* copy) 'Catalogue of Portraits and Engravings...' including the collection of the late Mr Thomas Baxter, auctioned by S.C. Southgate. 'Fifth Day's Sale' included lots (754) *Views taken near Swansea*, 3 copies; (759) *Views taken near Swansea*, 4 copies.
5. *Cambrian*, 30 May 1818, p.3.
   Cambrian, 6 June 1818, p.3
   Ibid.
6. In 1810 Thomas Baxter senior (fl 1782 - fl 1814) had a china painting studio and the *VAM* (782-1894) has a watercolour, *Painting Room of Mr Baxter No. 1 Goldsmith Street Gough Square*. This was exhibited at *RA* in 1811 as *China painting*. His son also worked in the studio. Father and son possibly worked together at Worcester.

BEARD, Joseph (- 1831)
Painter — Holyhead

B 1831/12: described as a plumber, glazier and painter.

BEDDOW, George (1813 - c1844)
China painter — Swansea
Heraldic artist

The only recorded example of his work is a painted coat of arms on a bowl.**(1)**

1. *Nance*, p.335.

BEDFORD, Thomas (1772 - c1817)
Architect — Carmarthenshire

He was the son of John Bedford of Acton Green, Middlesex (1741-1805). In 1797-8 he was employed by Sir John Soane as a clerk and he later established a practice in Carmarthenshire.**(1)**
Colvin p.117.

1. He designed Carmarthen Gaol, 1811, a *Villa 'Capel Isa'* near Llandeilo, 1811, Llangathen Church after 1811.

BEFFIN, Miss Sarah (1784 - 1850)
Miniature, portrait and landscape artist — Swansea

Itinerant artist**(1)** who visited Swansea Fair in 1815.**(2)** It is likely that Beffin often travelled with a fair or circus.**(3)**

1. *Foskett*, pp.165-166; *Bennett*, p.38ff. Both describe her unusual handicap, she had neither arms nor legs. She was apparently a very competent portrait artist. *Walker*, p.38, gives 'Sarah Biffin'. It also notes that she settled in Liverpool in 1842.
2. *Cambrian*, 1 July 1815, p.3.
3. Toole-Stott, R., *Circus and Allied Arts: A World Bibliography 1500-1962*, Derby: Harper & Sons Ltd, 1962, Vol. 2, p.138 (2590), *vide* index, Vol. 3, p.360. It

gives various references to Beffin. Many of these describe her work and history but none mention the appearance in Wales. I am grateful to my colleague Mr Charles Parry for bringing the text to my attention.

BENTLEY, George (early 19th century)
Clay modeller — Swansea

Worked at the Cambrian Pottery.**(1)**

1. *Nance*, p.38.

BERNARD, C.E. (fl 1855 - 1868)
Architect — Cardiff, 14 Trinity Street

Wakeford, 1855, p.70.
Girouard, p.76, gives fl 1868 at 5 Charles Street, Cardiff.

BEVINGTON, Hannah (1797? - fl c1810)
China painter — Swansea

Worked in the Cambrian pottery c1810, painted wild flowers.**(1)**

1. *Cadrawd*, p.9.

BIDDLE, Robert (fl 1858)
Photographer — Monmouth, St Monnow

Slater's, 1858.

BILLINGSLEY, L[e]vinia (fl 1776 - 1817)
China painter — Swansea, Nantgarw

She worked with her husband William Billingsley, *infra*, at Swansea and Nantgarw potteries.**(1)**

1. *Cadrawd*, p.9.

BILLINGSLEY, William (1758 - 1828)
Porcelain painter — Nantgarw
Designer of ceramics — Swansea

Born in Derby, his father had worked at the Chelsea porcelain factory.**(1)** He worked at Derby, then Worcester and moved to Nantgarw in 1813.**(2)** He worked in partnership with Samuel Walker who had moved with him from Worcester. He painted and designed porcelain and moved to the Cambrian Potteries in Swansea.**(3)** He remained in Swansea until 1816.**(4)**

He co-operated with William Weston Young (*infra*) who supported the production of translucent porcelain at Nantgarw.**(5)**

1. John, W.D., *William Billingsley* (Newport, 1968, pp.2-3. John, W.D., *Nantgarw Porcelain*, Newport, 1948), p.21. John, W.D., *Swansea Porcelain*, Newport, 1958. *Bell* pp.82-87 describes him as 'the genius who failed'. *Nance*, pp.291-293.
2. *William Billingsley, op.cit.*, p.37ff.
3. *Ibid.*, p.50ff.
4. *Ibid.*, p.94.
5. *Ibid.*, p.52.

BIRCHALL, Henry B. (fl 1840 - fl 1850)
Marine and landscape artist — Swansea, Bellvue Terrace

Appears to have painted many local cutters and shipping. There are several in Welsh private collections.**(1)**

1. *Hunt*, 1850, p.132; *Howells, 1987*, pp.110-116, illustrates Birchall's paintings, for instance *Pilot Cutter, Tom Rosser*, c1850, oil on board, 27 x 38 cm, signed. In private collection.

BIRD, Mr F. 'of Eton' (fl 1850)
Artist? — Caernarfon, Bangor, Beaumaris

Exhibited in 1850 the 'Grand Cosmographic Exhibition',**(1)** the subject of the show is unclear.

1. *Caernarvon and Denbighshire Herald*, 29 April 1850.
   Ibid., 30 April 1850.
   Ibid., 2 May 1850.

BIRD, John Davies (1784 - 1827)
Printer — Cardiff
Lithographer
Teacher of lithography

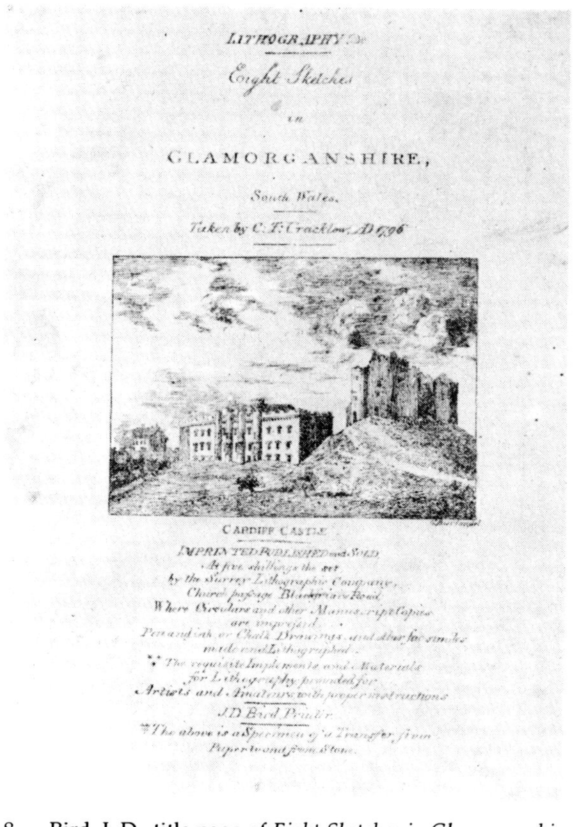

8 Bird, J. D., title page of *Eight Sketches in Glamorganshire*, lithograph, c1821 (*BV* 216).

The eldest son of John Bird (1761-1840). Diarist and estate manager for Lord Bute.**(1)** Bird published a book of prints *Eight Sketches in Glamorganshire South Wales***(2)** but nothing else is known about his career.

He may also have surveyed land.**(3)**

1. Thomas, H., *The Diaries of John Bird 1790-1803* (Cardiff 1987). The will of John Bird is noted as *LL* 1840/33; see Pedigree of Bird family, p.[iii].
2. *BV* 216 (4to); Cracklow, C.F., *Lithography etc Eight Sketches in Glamorganshire South Wales*, 'J.D. Bird, Printer', c1820. The original sketches appear to have been taken by C. Burton.
3. *NLW, Ystradfowg* map, 1778.

BLACKWALL, John (fl 1816 - fl 1840)
Architect — Llanbadarn Fawr, Aberystwyth**(1)**

SD/1840/255.

1. I am grateful to my colleague William Troughton for further information on this architect. Mary Blackwell, died c1836 (*SD* 1836/97), was recorded as patron of the Red Lion Inn, Aberystwyth, at about this date. *Aberystwyth Guide*, 1816, notes Blackwall as a builder in Great Darkgate Street. Not in *Girouard.*

BLATHWAYT, Edmond (fl 1835 - fl 1847)
Surveyor — Kidwelly

Davies Atlas, Eden I p.39 gives 'Edmund'.

BOND, Richard Sebastian(1) (1805 - 1886)
Landscape painter — Betws-y-Coed, Wern Cottage

Exhibited at the *BI* from a Betws-y-Coed address from 1846-1856. Exhibited each year except 1854-55. All views were in North Wales.**(2)** After 1856 he exhibited at *RA*.**(3)**

1. I am grateful to my colleague John Holmes for information on this artist.
2. For example, 1846 (152), *A Welsh Village*; 1849 (118), *A Welsh Pass in Winter*. Thirteen works were exhibited.
3. *RA*, 1856-1872, all from Betws-y-Coed (7 works). *Pavière* notes that he was born in Liverpool. *Witt*, p.23, gives (1808-1886) as Bond's dates.

BONNETT, John (fl 1844 - fl 1852)
Engraver & copper plate printer — Swansea, 39 Wind Street

Pigot's, 1844. *Hunt*, 1849, p.174.
Ibid., 1850, p.153.
Scammell & Co 1852, p.212.

BOURDON, Toussaint (fl 1812)
Landscape artist — Brecon, Monmouthshire

A watercolour by Bourdon is inscribed as follows:

> 'Toussaint Bourdon delin. June 5th 1812.
> To Sir Charles Morgan Bart. M.P. for the county of Monmouth etc. this S.W. View of the Castle of Brecon and adjacent Scenery in gratitude for Patronage etc. repeated favours, conferred upon a prisoner of War is inscribed by his obliged and obedient humble servant/Bourdon.'**(1)**

Bourdon was possibly an artist/craftsman in his native country (France ?) and he may have worked in some capacity for Morgan.

1. *NLW*, PZ 3910, 24.6 x 37.6 cm, watercolour. Print in *NLW* Tredegar Collection 843, engraved by E. Shirt, c30 x 45 cm., [it is a very accurate delineation of the original].

BOWEN, David
Mason — Swansea, Greenhill

SD/1824/254.

BOWEN, John (fl 1835 - fl 1843)
Surveyor — Glanthames, Llandeilo

Davies Atlas. Not in *Eden*.

BOWEN, Thomas (1788/9 - 1859)
Architect — Swansea, Green Dragon Lane

He designed the new Town Hall at Neath, 1820 & a similar building for Swansea in 1825.**(1)** There were financial problems in 1827 but he is recorded as an architect in the 1830s.**(2)** His obituary noted him as a 'master builder'.**(3)**

1. Not in *Girouard*. *Lloyd* Architects pp.65-68 illustrates his trade card & *Swansea Town Hall* design at *RISW*, *Colvin* p.146
2. *Pigot's*, 1830, p.862.
   Pigot's, 1831, [ref. *TL*].
3. *Cambrian* 15 April 1859.

BOWEN, W. (fl c1820)
Architect — Swansea

Designed the Old Town Hall, Neath, in 1820.**(1)**

1. *RCAM* records. Not in *Girouard*.

BOYDELL, Mrs (fl 1837)
Landscape painter — [Denbighshire]

Drew a view of Rossett mill, the style suggests this was done by an amateur artist taught by a drawing master.**(1)**

Possibly related to the Boydell family of Flintshire, Josiah Boydell (1752-1817).**(2)**

1. I wish to thank John Holmes for noting this artist. Photo Album 724, pencil drawing *c* 8 x 11 cm, inscribed 'from Nature the Rossett Mill, August 1837'.
2. *DWB* notes that Boydell was born at Manor House, Hawarden. *B.B.A.* gives Hanton, Shropshire, as his birthplace. His uncle John Boydell (1719-1804)

published the first large set of prints of North Wales c1750 (copy in *BM*).

BRIGSTOCKE, David (1771 - fl 1821)
House painter — Carmarthen
Stained glass dealer

The father of Thomas Brigstocke (1809-1881).**(1)** Besides his glazing and interior decoration business he occasionally sold pieces of stained glass. In 1821 he describes one work, the 'Nativity of Christ containing eight figures with the inscription "For unto you is born" measuring 6 feet 5 inches by 3 feet 7 inches with a richly ornamented double Border in a neat copper-sash'. The work of 'an Artist from London'.**(2)**

1. *AIW*, item 129, portrait of David Brigstocke by Thomas Brigstocke, dated 1841.
2. *Carmarthen Journal*, 27 July 1821, p.3. *Ibid.*, 17 August 1821, p.3.

BRIGSTOCKE, Job (Senior) (fl 1798)
Architect, builder — St Clears, Island House

Date-stone in Island House 'Job Brigstocke 1798'.**(1)**

1. *RCAM* (*TP*). Not in *Girouard*.

BRIGSTOCKE, Job (Junior) (fl 1841)
Glazier, carpenter & Painter — St Clears, Island House

RCAM (*TP*).

BRIGSTOCKE, Thomas (1809 - 81)
Portrait painter
Painter of still life — Carmarthen

His father *supra* was a tradesman at Carmarthen. Thomas attended Queen Elizabeth Grammar School and executed some work in Wales.**(1)** He worked there until 1825 when he was sent to work under Sass at the *RA*. He was in the *RA* Schools 1826.**(2)**

In 1833 he moved to Rome and met Penry Williams and John Gibson with whom he apparently spoke Welsh.

1. *AIW*, items 127-129; Thomas T.H., 'Versatile Welsh Painter', *Western Mail*, 16 April 1909, p.4, mainly discusses his origins and various anecdotes. *WW Price*, Vol. II, p.140, give additional references to this artist.
2. *Hutchison*, p.179, described as a painter. No prizes are recorded, yet Brigstocke claimed he gained a Silver Medal for *Study of Laocoon* and *Still Life Painting*, both were said to be at Dolaucothi.

BRINDLEY, E.H. (fl 1829 - 54)
Artist and engraver — Swansea

He produced a print of Swansea in 1829. The print was published by subscription via The Cambrian Office and the artist added:

> 'E.H.B. feels it his duty publicly and firmly to declare that should he not sell another print, the price will never lower one fraction; it is neither consistent with his interest nor his honour to lower the conditions as many expect.'**(1)**

He was presumably related to James Brindley.**(2)**

1. *Cambrian*, 22 August 1829, p.3; 29 August 1829, p.3. Prints cost 6s 6d and 16s 6d.
2. *Nance*, pp.539-540 (quotes Turner, W., *The Ceramics of Swansea & Nantgarw*, London, 1897), saying that J. Brindley was probably E.H. Brindley.

BRINDLEY, James (fl 1835 - fl 1852)
Engraver for china — Swansea

Mentioned by *Nance* as at Swansea 1835-45 and 1852.**(1)**

1. *Nance*, p.540.

BRODIE, Henry (fl 1835 - fl 1843)
Surveyor — Loughor

Davies Atlas, *Eden* supplement p.390 'estate surveyor'.

BROMLEY, Adelaide (c1839 - fl 1851)
Pottery painter — Llanelli, 10 Pottery Row

He was born in Tunstall and probably working at the South Wales Pottery in 1851.**(1)**

1. Census 1851, *DFHS*, Vol. I, folio 218, p.2. *Vide* Hughes, Gareth & Pugh, Robert, *Llanelly Pottery*, (Llanelli, 1990), p.84.

BROOK, Richard (fl 1835)
Portrait painter — Newport, Stow Hill

Pigot's, 1835, p.258.

BROOK, Richard (Junior) (fl 1835)
Portrait painter — Newport, Stow Hill

Pigot's, 1835, p.258.

In 1826 he visited Aberystwyth and later Carmarthen (for about two weeks) before returning to London.**(2)**

He was reported in Swansea in 1841,**(3)** then moved to Carmarthen.

He may well have returned in 1846 to take portraits, this time without the help of the Patent Delineator**(4)** and concentrated on Carmarthen and Cardigan.**(5)**

1. *Cambrian*, 8 September 1827, p.3. *ibid*, 15 September 1827, p.3.
2. *Carmarthen Journal*, 13 October 1826, p.3. *ibid*, 20 October 1826, p.3.
3. *Cambrian*, 7 August 1841; *Carmarthen Journal*, 6 October 1826; *Welshman*, 1 September 1848: 'Mr Brooke painter, student of Fuseli, thanks gentry for their patronage.'
4. For Patent Delineator, *vide McKechnie*, pp.431-432. James H. Millington (1799-1872) used the Delineator,

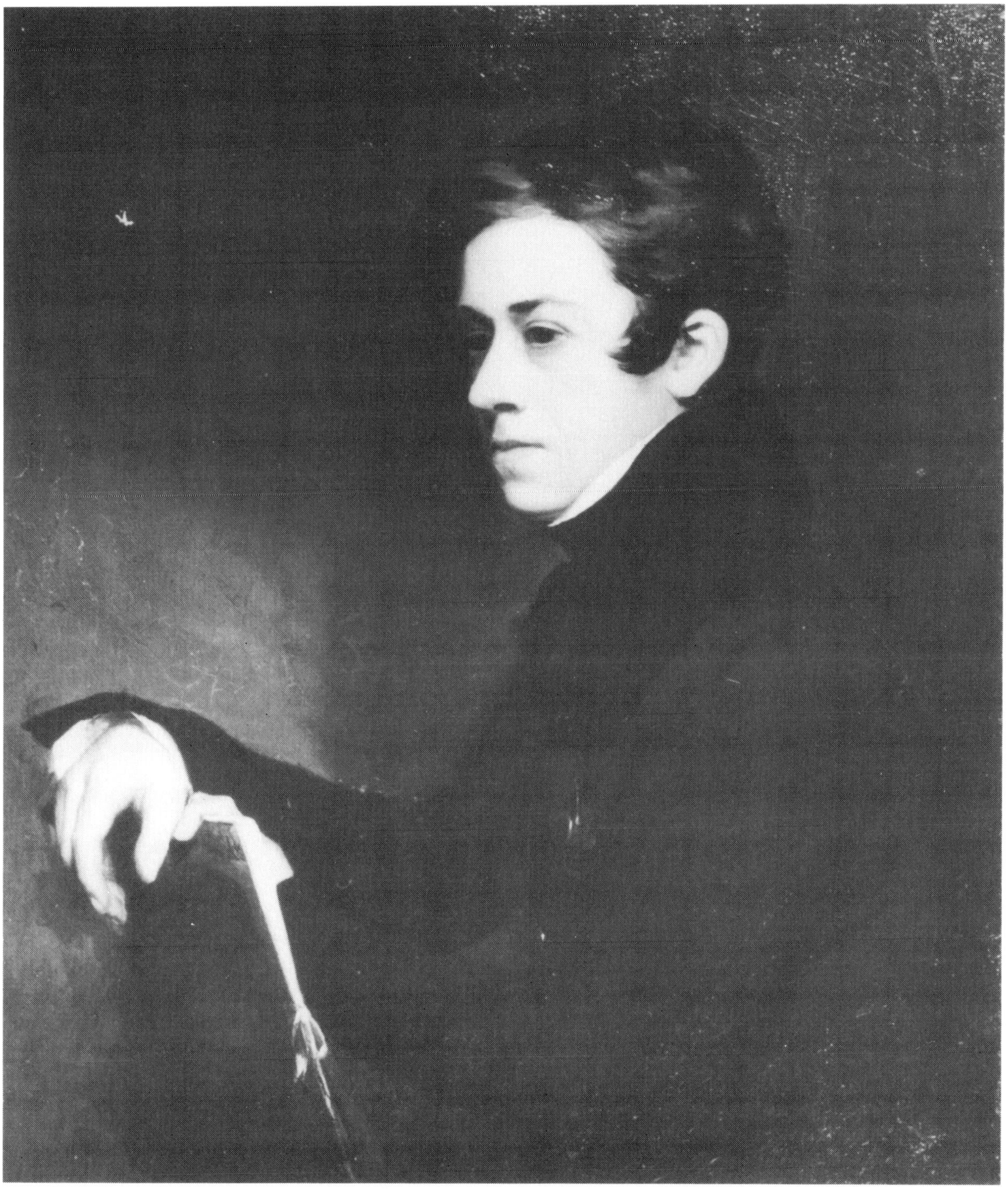

9 Brigstocke, Thomas, *Self Portrait*, oil on canvas, c1830, PB5374.

which is described as 'simple and unerring in its Principle'.

5. A poster in *NLW*, folder 117, advertises his visit to these places.

BROOKE, James (fl 1835 - fl 1847)
Surveyor Bridgend

Davies Atlas, Eden I p.46 notes that he was also an estate surveyor.

BROOKE, Mr (fl 1826 - fl 1846)
Portrait and miniature artist Swansea
Used the Patent Delineator Aberystwyth
Carmarthen
Cardigan

Soho artist who visited South Wales in 1826, 1827, 1841 and 1846. In 1827 he stayed at 'Mr Howell's Wind Street, Swansea'.**(1)**

BROOM, John (fl 1829 - fl 1839)
Carver & Gilder
St Mary Street
Carmarthen
Haverfordwest

Dale -Jones p.74

BROWNING, Miss (fl 1822 - 36)
Landscape Artist
Aberdovey

She produced small landscapes of Aberdovey.**(1)**
The Aberdovey Literary Institute has a picture signed by the artist.**(2)**

1. *NLW* has two sketches from the *Penhelig Album* in possession of W. Miles Wynn Cato. There are both c1820-30 PG5878 & PG5849 of *Penhelig House* 7x11.4cm. A further two watercolours from the album c12x8cm. showing yachts at Aberdovey are in a private Welsh Collection.
2. Pen & ink landscape of *Aberdovey* signed & dated 1836, approx 10x15cm. Seen by author, 1995 at the Reading Room of the Literary Institute, Aberdovey.

BRUTE, Aaron (fl 1754 - fl 1783)
Monumental mason — Llanbedr near Crickhowell
(Painted stones) — Breconshire

One of a family of masons who worked in the Breconshire and Monmouthshire area until c.1887.**(1)** There was a studio practice of collaboration, and a number of stones are signed. A. Brute.**(2)** Harthan and Wight note that 'his style is easily recognised. The crinkled, twisted borders festooned with garlands, the gilded cherub-heads and coloured sprays of flowers now represent one of the few examples of peasant rococo'.**(3)**

Painted grave stones were common in many parts of Britain and the Brute family are examples of artisans whose work has been well preserved.**(4)**.

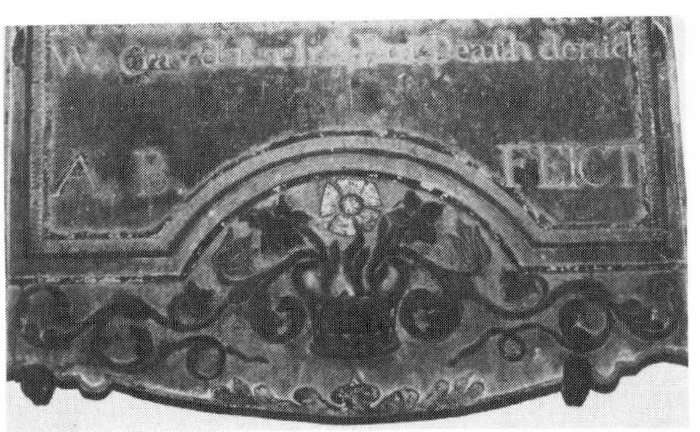

10 Brute, Aaron, gravestone, c1768 (P. Joyner, 1984).

1. Two members of the family were still living in 1887, John Brute and Thomas Brute. The family is discussed by John P. Harthan and M. Wight, 'Brute Fecit: a vernacular art of the Welsh Border', *Architectural Review*, Vol. 102, October 1947, pp.135-116.
2. Stones signed by A. Brute are found at St Martin's Cwmyoy, Monmouthshire, 1768; Llangatock Church, Monmouthshire 1777.
3. Harthan and Wight, *op.cit.*, p.136.
4. For discussion on stone painting, *vide* F. Burgess, 'Painted tombs', *Commemorative Art*, Vol. XXXIII, 1966, pp.238-242.

BRUTE, James (1773 - 1840)
Monumental mason — Llanbedr near Crickhowell
(Painted stones) — Breconshire

Worked in the family business, there are examples of his work at various sites in Breconshire.**(1)**

1. *Vide* Partrishaw Church, 1804, and T. Brute, *Country Life*, 5 April 1946, p.633, letter from Mrs E. Jones mainly relating to James Brute. Examples are also mentioned in Harthan and Wight, *Architectural Review*, Vol. 102, October 1947, pp.135-6.

BRUTE, Peter John (fl 1734 - fl 1768)
Monumental mason — Llanbedr near Crickhowell
(Painted stones) — Breconshire

Working with the Brute family business, he occasionally collaborated with Thomas Brute.**(1)**

1. At Llangattock Church there is a stone 'Pr and T Brute 1747'. *Vide* Harthan and Wight, *Architectural Review*, Vol. 102, October 1947, p.135.

BRUTE, Thomas (fl 1721 - *c* 1770)
Monumental mason — Llanbedr, near Crickhowell
(Painted stones) — Breconshire

Working with the family business, occasionally collaborated with Peter Brute.**(1)** A number of examples of his work survive.**(2)** Thomas Brute is the earliest known member of the family to work in painted stone and his style of ornamentation and calligraphy appears to have influenced later works by the Brutes.

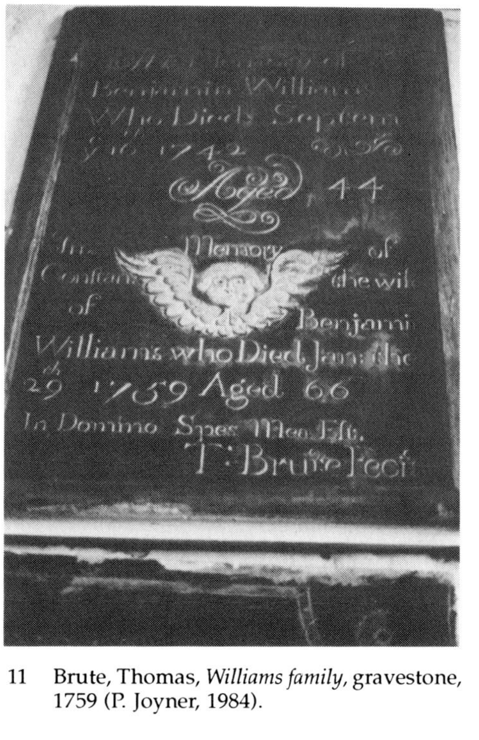

11 Brute, Thomas, *Williams family*, gravestone, 1759 (P. Joyner, 1984).

1. For instance the stone at Llangattock Church signed by P. & T. Brute. *BR* 1770/29 notes Thomas Brute but no occupation given, probate is not recorded for the other members of the family.
2. Partrishaw Church, stone dated 1757; Llantilio Pertholey near Abergavenny illustrated in Harthan and Wight, *Architectural Review*, Vol. 102, October 1947, Plate 1.

BURCHALL, William (fl 1846 - fl 1850)
Marine and landscape artist
Swansea
Gower Street

He is recorded in *Hunt*.**(1)** No extant works have been traced. He may have also acted as landlord of a Swansea Inn.**(2)** Possibly W. Burchall was J.W. Burchell.**(3)**

1. *Hunt*, 1848; 1849, p.153. *Vide Cambrian*, 7 May 1846, p.2.
2. *Rogers*, 1981, mentions that William Burchall may have been landlord of the Globe Inn near Padley's Yard between 1816-37. (Information from W.C. Rogers, correspondence with author.)
3. A scale drawing of a waggon is recorded in the Witt Library, c1815, which might suggest other interests.

BURNETT, Charles C. (fl 1858)
Photographer
Tenby
St George Street

Slater's, 1858.

BURTON, C. (fl 1822)
Landscape artist
Cardiff

Drew views for *Eight Sketches in Glamorganshire* published by J.D. Bird, Cardiff, *BV* 216, 1822.**(1)**

1. **(1)** There was a Charles Burton, Mariner of Newport, Mon. who may have been the same person (*LL* 1826/113).

BURTON, Richard. (fl 1825)
Surveyor
Monmouth

He repaired the rectory of Michel Troy in 1825.**(1)**

1. *NLW* Llandaf Bounty Plans 87, 1825. He provided a plan of *Llansoy rectory* - 1821, this was built by John Roberts of Llanishen, *NLW* Llandaff, Bounty Plans 68. Not in *Eden*.

BUTEL, Alexander (fl 1840)
Drawing master
Swansea

Butel is described as a French and drawing master. He was probably an immigrant and may be one and the same person as Edmund and Louis Butel.**(1)**

1. *Cambrian*, 1 August 1840, p.3; see other entries for E. & L. Butel.

BUTEL, Edmund (fl c1848 - fl 1852)
Drawing master
Swansea
43 Orange Street

Butel advertised as a French and drawing master in the *Cambrian*, 21 July 1848, p.2, stating 'he recommences duties...at 43 Orange Street.' He appears several times in *Hunt*.**(1)**

1. He is the only Butel mentioned in the following *Hunt*, 1848; 1849, p.169; 1850, p.148. *Scammell & Co* 1852 p.207 records Butel as 'BIRTELL'.

BUTEL, Louis (fl 1840 - fl 1846)
Drawing master
Swansea
6 Fisher Street
Neath
Mumbles

Advertised as a French, Italian and drawing master in the *Cambrian*.**(1)** He may have worked seasonally,**(2)** but was a resident in Swansea and one of the founder members of the *RISW*. **(3)**

Butel also attended Mumbles, Llanelli and Neath on separate days and probably taught both French and drawing.

1. *Cambrian*, 23 September 1843, p.2, refers to a change of address to 6 Fisher Street, Swansea (*vide* note 3).
2. *Cambrian*, 20 July 1844, p.2, mentions Butel resuming teaching. *Cambrian*, 18 Jan. 1845, p.2: 'Resumes his duties at his Residence, 10 Nelson Place'. (Butel also visited Neath & Mumbles on this ocassion).
   Cambrian, 2 August 1845, p.2, mentions teaching to resume.
3. *Pigot*, 1844, p.78, gives his address as Nelson Place. He appears in the annual reports of the *RISW* as 'BUTEL' Mons. L, Swansea' for the years 1841, 42, 46.

BUTLER, William (fl 1843 - 1870)
Marine and landscape artist
Drawing master
Swansea
7 Park Place

Evidence suggests that his career was based solely in Swansea.**(1)** Butler's early work **(2)** and later drawings**(3)** show an interest in buildings.

He is believed to have conducted drawing classes at the *RISW*.**(4)** An obituary appeared in the *Cambrian*, 5 April 1870, p.8: 'On the 31st ult. at 17, Brunwick Street in this town, Mr William Butler, artist aged 46. He was an honest man, and is deeply lamented by surviving relatives and friends.'

Butler was in contact with other artists in Swansea, for instance, Horlor stayed at Butler's address in 1846.**(5)**

1. *Hunt*, 1848.
   Ibid., 1849, p.153.
   Ibid., 1850, p.132, 'Rutland Street'.
2. *Rogers*, plate 55, *Ferry Boat at Ferryside with the Camera Obscura*. One example also suggests an interest in landscape. There appears to have been a set of prints of South Wales published by E. Pearce, Swansea, after *Butler* [n.d.]. Views include *Yscwd Gwladis, Vale of Neath; Yscwd Einon* [*sic*]; *Lower Cilhepste; Lower Glyngwyn*, P 4292-4297, A8/1 - A227 - A232 (c1860).

3. *NLW*, Drawing volumes 12, *Views in North Wales* 1853; 13 *South Wales*; 14 *Monmouthshire*, 1852. These contain evidence for his marine works, e.g. *South Wales, Windsor Castle at Pembroke Dock*, p.9. All were attributed to Butler in *South Wales Evening Post*, 27 November 1957, p.4, and are consistent with known work, subject matter and style.
4. I am grateful to staff at *RISW* for relating this oral tradition. No documentary evidence could be found to support the claim.
5. *Cambrian*, 17 July 1846, p.3: M. Horlor, animal painter.

C

C., S.

(fl 1827)

Profilist — Cowbridge

His style is very similar to Monsieur E. Adolphe. One extant silhouette is inscribed 'Price Jacob...taken by S.C. at Cowbridge in the year 1827.'**(1)**

1. *WFM*, 59-426/4.

CADWALLADER, A.

(fl c1830)

Costume artist — Llanover Monmouthshire

Painted watercolours from designs by Augusta Hall. Several examples in *NLW*, Drawing Volume 299 (4 to) are signed by this artist.**(1)**

1. *NLW*, Drawing Volume 299 (4to).

CALVERT, John

(fl 1778 - fl 1795)

Builder and possibly architect — Swansea

Built and possibly designed Slebech, Pembrokeshire, in an Adamesque style sometime before 1779.**(1)** On the evidence of this building, he understood both fine design and detailed ornament. He is recorded as working in at least one other South Wales house. The *Swansea Theatre* c1785 was also his work.

Colvin cites an advertisement in the *Hereford Journal*, 1784, in which Calvert offers 'patent slating'. He produced detail plans for a tunnel under the Severn river.**(2)**

1. Main source of reference is *Colvin* p.207. On 30 November 1983 Christie's lots 61-63 contained work attributed to Calvert. Lots 61-2 were designs for Slebech Hall, lot 63 'House intended for Mrs Williams at Cadoxton, Near Neath' (illustrated), *NLW*, PE 5129.
2. *Lloyd* gives an account of his life and work.

CARLISLE, Mr

(fl 1840)

Miniature painter — Caernarfon

Visited Caernarfon in 1840 with R. Carlisle a teacher of painting.

'Mr C. trusts his Style of Painting, and the striking fidelity of his likenesses, which he guarantees, will meet with the approval of the public.'**(1)**

1. *Caernarvon and Denbighshire Herald*, 6 June 1840, p.2. *Ibid.*, 13 June 1840, p.2.

CARLISLE, R.

(fl 1840)

Teacher of oil painting — Caernarfon
Teacher of drawing and painting 'in general'.

Visited Caernarfon in 1840 with 'Mr Carlisle', miniature painter.

'Mr R.C. will give lessons in his New System of Painting which will enable the Pupil, however deficient in the Art of Drawing, to produce the most expeditious and novel (though not in the least mechanical) process, Pictures in Oil, possessing all that depth and richness of colouring, and eminently characteristic of the Old School of Painting...

... course of six Progressive Lessons, for Two Guineas, including materials during the lessons; and that the most complete and satisfactory success will, in every instance, be guaranteed.'**(1)**

1. *Caernarvon and Denbighshire Herald*, 6 June 1840, p.2. *Ibid.*, 13 June 1840, p.2.

CARTER, J.M.

(fl 1842 - fl 1865)

Landscape and still life artist — Monmouth Parade

He possibly trained in London, then moved to Monmouth c1847.**(1)** He continued to exhibit at London in 1847.**(2)** Exhibited at Suffolk Street, *RSBA*, 1848, No. 13, *Interior of Tintern Abbey looking West*. From 1856 until 1865 he exhibited at the *BI* from a Monmouth address.**(3)**

1. Fenton, Richard, *A Historical Tour through Pembrokeshire*, 1811, includes a print after J. Carter, Vol. II, facing p.450, *Effigies of the Whites in Tenby Church*, dated 1809. This may be the same artist or a relative. In 1842 he exhibited at the *RA* from 'c/o Mr F. Grant, Sussex Villa, Regents Park'. Sir Francis Grant P.R.A. (1803-78) was an Associate of the *RA* from 1842 and an Academician from 1851. *Graves, B.I.*: He exhibited a landscape of Gibraltar in 1844, residence given as Gibraltar and 46 Pall Mall, London. Cox-Johnson, *Hand-list of painters, sculptors and architects associated with St Marylebone (1760-1960)* (London, 1963); p.18 also gives Carter at this address.
2. *Graves, R.A.* from Monmouth address, 1847:
   (686) *Fresh Spanish figs.*
   (687) *Muscatel grapes, apples etc.*
   (688) *Grapes, medlars, walnuts, etc.*
   (849) *Pomegranates and grapes.*
3. *Graves, B.I.*:
   1856 414 *Carew Castle.*
   1861 118 *Skenfrith Castle on the Monnow.*
   1865 208 *Corra Linn, a fall of the Clyde, and Corra Castle.*

CARTER, Robert

(fl 1845)

Surveyor — Pontypool

Rebuilt the vicarage at Trevethin, Monmouthshire, 1845.**(1)**

1. *NLW* Llandaff, Bounty Plan 121, 1845. A simple surveyor's plan was provided. Not in *Eden*.

CARTWRIGHT, J. (fl 1733)
Heraldic painter [and sign painter] Aberedw

Royal Arms signed and dated '1838/Thos Davies Churchwarden/J. Cartwright de Aberedow pinxit 1733' [on board c180 x 180cm] at St David's Church, Colva, Radnorshire.**(1)**

1. *RCAM* (*TP*); also, the author visited the church in 1986 and considers that there are other paintings in the church by Cartwright.

CARVER, William (fl 1827)
Architect and surveyor**(1)** Wenallt, near Carmarthen

'Begs leave to inform the nobility, Gentry and the Public in General, that he practices in the above Professions; and as he perfectly understands the practical part of Building as well as that of Architecture, feels convinced he would give satisfaction to those who will favour him with their commands.'**(2)**

1. Not in *Girouard, Eden, Colvin.*
2. *Carmarthen Journal*, 5 January 1827, p.3. *Ibid.*, 19 January 1827, p.1.

CHAPMAN, James (fl 1825 - fl 1826)
Marine and portrait artist Swansea
Surveyor Wind Street

Chapman probably moved from Bristol to Swansea c1825. His first recorded venture was the publication of 'A correct and Beautiful View of the Town and Harbour of Swansea, taken from the Pier Head.'**(1)** This large, well produced engraving may have encouraged local commissions.

In 1826 he painted a mature portrait of William Williams 'Wil Penmorfa' playing a red harp.**(2)** The strong colour sense, careful draughtsmanship and clear, precise composition suggest that Chapman was professionally trained.

A late 18th century map of Baglan may represent this man's work.**(3)**

1. Two examples, one coloured, the other uncoloured are at the *RISW* and *GVS*, 24.5 x 82.8 cm, aquatint with etching. The print was published in Bristol but bears no attribution. However, Chapman advertised the print in the *Cambrian*, 8 October 1825, p.3: 'size of the Print 2 feet 9 inches long by 10 inches wide. Price, Coloured 11s, Plain 15s, to be had of the Artist, Wind-Street, Swansea. An early application is requested in order to secure good impressions. N.B. the Artist's stay will be short.' Illustrated in *Howells, 1987*, p.9, unattributed.
2. *WFM*, oil on canvas, 350.7 x 97 cm (sight size) of Wil Pemorfa (1759-1828) signed and dated 'J. Chapman 1826'. A remarkably similar composition of a harpist, with comparable handling of paint and form is found at the church of Llanfair Talhaiarn, Denbighshire. Oil on canvas [*Dafydd with a Harp reciting Psalm 97*], c203 x 140 cm.
3. West Glamorgan Record Office, D/D Gn/E/128, *Map of Middle and Lower Hafdres in the Parish of Bagland and County of Glamorgan*, signed and dated 'Jas Chapman October 1791'. Also cited is Thomas, H.A., *Catalogue of Glamorganshire Estate Maps*, GAP Cardiff, 1992, p.69. Another Chapman is recorded as working in Swansea, but this may not be the same branch of the family. For instance, *vide Annual Exhibition of the Swansea Sketching Club*, 1895, advertisement on page 2: 'Henry A Chapman, Swansea', artists' colourman, dealer and frame-maker.

(*Illustration on p.16*)

CHAPMAN, W. J. [John Watkins] (fl 1830 - fl 1866)
Animal painter South Wales
[Engraver] [Carmarthen]**(1)**

He painted the *Cyfarthfa Hunt* in 1830 and *The Ostler at Nanteos* in 1836.**(2)** Another portrait is recorded, *James Philipps Lloyd*, in 1837.**(3)** By 1854 he was living in London and exhibited from there until 1866.**(4)**

1. *TL.* Carmarthen Journal, 11 March 1859, 'Mr Chapman, portrait and animal painter in Carmarthen for a period. Specimens on view in Carmarthen. Short visit as he has other engagements elsewhere'.
2. *Lord, 1993*, p.72.
3. *Steegman*, Vol. II, p.185, portrait at Penty Park, signed and dated W.J. Chapman, 1837.
4. *Graves, B.I.*, address given as 6 Great Russell Street, 1854, when he exhibited *Wild Fruit and Flowers*. He moved several times and his last address was at 7 St Philip's Terrace, Kensington.

CHITTENDEN, G. (fl 1855 - fl 1868)
Architect Cardiff
81 St Mary Street**(1)**

He was trained in London, but moved to Cardiff c1885.**(2)**

1. *Wakeford*, 1855, p.70.
2. *Girouard*, p.170, notes address in 1868 as Guildhall Chambers, St Mary Street, Cardiff. Also that he was a pupil of James Field, Adelaide Place, London.

CHRISTMAS, P. (fl 1840)
Surveyor Newbridge Monmouth

NLW, Llantrisant, dated 1840. Not in *Eden*.

CLAPTON, Mr (fl 1842)
Artist Carmarthen

Visited Carmarthen for five days in February 1842 and presented a 'Splendid Exhibition of Arts'.**(1)**

1. *Carmarthen Journal*, 11 February 1842, p.2.

CLARE, Mr (fl 1840)
Drawing master Swansea
Teaching of etching, stone seal engraver
Heraldic painter

Described as 'from London'.**(1)** Clare offered a course in

> 'Colouring and Chinese Penciling....he undertakes to perfect any Pupil, from the age of 10 to 50 in six lessons and engages that their productions shall be equal, if not superior, to those who have been taught under the old system twelve months.'

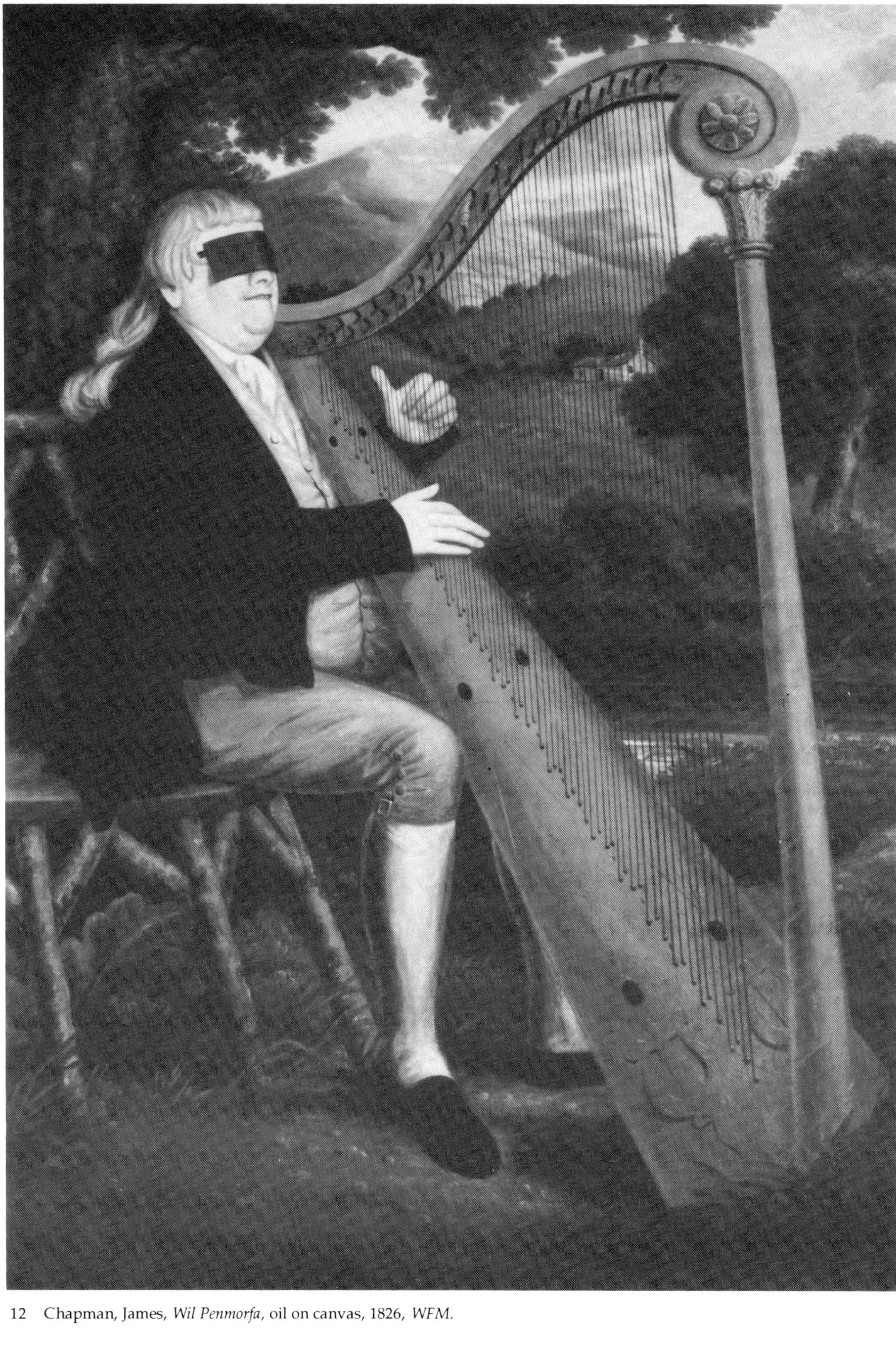

12 Chapman, James, *Wil Penmorfa,* oil on canvas, 1826, *WFM.*

'An extensive collection of Heraldry kept, from which Arms will be Traced and Painted in a superior style.'**(2)**

1. *POL*, 1840, no reference to Clare.
2. *Cambrian*, 26 December 1840, p.3.

CLARK, John (fl 1849)
'Potter' Newport
Potter St.

Hunt, 1849, p.131.

CLARK, William (fl 1858)
Photographer Pembroke Dock
Commercial Row

Slater's, 1858.

CLARKE, Thomas E. (fl 1850)
Landscape artist [Merthyr Tydfil]

He drew and engraved a landscape of Merthyr Tydfil.**(1)**

1. *NLW*, PZ 3466, Top. C8/1, C22, lithograph, 29.5x49.2 cm.

CLINTON, George (fl 1832 - fl 1850)
Surveyor and architect Aberystwyth
Cardiff
Hastings Villa

He worked at Aberystwyth for a while and rebuilt Eglwysfach Church, Cardiganshire in 1833. Also recorded as architect of Llanddeiniol Church and Llanilar rectory.**(1)**

Designed a Classical Church at Shrewsbury c1836-7 and was then given as living in Cardiff.**(2)** In 1840 he designed the Market House at Llandovery.**(3)**
He died at Cardiff.**(4)**

1. *Colvin* p.256, Not in *Eden*; *TL*; *Hunt*, 1849, p.17 (at Windsor Place). *NLW* St Davids, Bounty Plan 121, 1833. *Llandough rectory*. Llandaf Bounty Plan, 39, 1840.
2. *Slater's*, 1850, p.22.
   Not in *Girouard*.
3. *Civil Engineers & Architects Journal*, 1840, p.39.
4. *Robson's*, 1840, Glamorgan, p.9.
   Hunt, 1849, p.17.

CLOUGH, P. (fl 1785)
Copyist Denbigh

He copied the *Triumph of Turbulence & Mother Cambria Possessed* after Thomas Pennant.**(1)**

1. *NLW* PB8171, Illustrated in *Lord, WWP, p.79*.

CLULOW, Emma (c1830 - fl 1851)
Ware transferer Llanelli
19 Pottery Row

Clulow was born in Liverpool and presumably was a craftsperson/artist in the South Wales Pottery.**(1)**

1. Census 1851, *DFHS*, Vol. I, folio 219, p.5. *Vide* Hughes, Gareth & Pugh, Robert, *Llanelly Pottery*, Llanelli: Llanelli Borough Council, 1990, p.84, also gives the Census reference.

CLULOW, Mary (c1787 - fl 1851)
Pottery painter Llanelli
19 Pottery Row

Born in Stoke-on-Trent and may have moved to Liverpool, then Llanelli. Presumably working in the South Wales Pottery.**(1)**

1. Census 1851, *DFHS*, Vol. I, folio 219, p.5. *Vide* Hughes, Gareth & Pugh, Robert, *Llanelly Pottery* (Llanelli, 1990), p.84.

COLE, John (- 1787)
Architect Cowbridge

LL/1789/39.

COLLIER, Stephen (fl 1835 - fl 1843)
Surveyor Brides Minor
Glamorgan

Davies Atlas, Not in *Eden*.

COMER, Mr (fl 1829 - fl 1838)
Teacher of drawing Monmouth
Agincourt Square

Monmouthshire Merlin, 13 February 1829, p.3.
Ibid., 20 November 1838, quoted by *Kissack, Monmouth*, p.147.

COMLEY, James (fl 1858)
Photographer Haverfordwest
Dark Street

Slater's, 1858.

CONWAY, Charles (fl 1797 - 1860)
Flower & insect painter Pontnewydd

Born at Whitehall, uncle of Charles Conway (fl 1820-1884). 'The Botanical collection of the nephew and uncle formed the nucleus of the National collection.'**(1)**

1. *Mardy Rees*, p.19.

CONWAY, Charles (fl 1820-84)
Flower and insect painter Pontnewydd

Born at Whitehall, Pontnewydd.

'He made some good drawings and etchings and was greatly interested in the study of flowers and insects.'**(1)**

1. *Mardy Rees*, p.19. His uncle Charles Conway (*supra*) was also a artist of the same subject matter. *NMW* files, notes 'the late Mr Charles Conway, J.P. of Pontnewydd'. He exhibited at the Fine Art exhibition 1881 (Eisteddfod). An article in the file notes that 'he was

careless in the extreme of the original drawings' and his work is quite rare.

COOK, James (d.1812)
Glazier & painter — Kidwelly

SD/1812/33.

COOPER, John (fl 1783 - fl 1799)
Architect — Beaumaris, St Asaph

Commissioned for various large projects in North Wales, mainly employed upon alterations at residences.**(1)** In 1783-5 he altered Plas Newydd, 1796 Chirk Castle and 1798-9 Pennant in Denbighshire.**(2)**

1. *Colvin* p.269 main source of information.
2. He also is reported to have worked at Bodorgan, Anglesey (n.d.) Plans at *NLW* clearly show Cooper's influence from other contemporary buildings , specially evident in the plans of Pennant. These can be compared with the Assembly Rooms at Swansea & Aberystwyth, and the design by E. Williams for Cowbridge Town Hall. This suggests, possibly, a provincial standard for Georgian architecture in Wales. *Colvin* notes that his style was 'closely modelled on that of the Wyatts'.

COPE, James (1805/6 -fl 1842)
Engraver — Chapel Street, Caernarfon

Born in Caernarfonshire, & lived in Caernarfon, he produced a number of blocks for John Jones, Llanrwst. 'He produced political cartoons which are anti-Tory & anti-Church, suggesting that he was a radical Nonconformist... with the remarkable woodcuts of James Cope, printed pictures in the popular press finally blossomed in Wales'.**(1)**

1. *Lord, WWP* pp.93-4.

COULING, William (c 1783 - fl 1816)
Surveyor — Brecon, Carmarthen

Couling appears firstly as a surveyor, he proposed a plan of London Docks 1795.**(1)** He later surveyed estates in Cardiganshire, the Nanteos estate & Carmarthenshire.**(2)** By 1816 he applied, unsuccessfully, for the post of Principal Engineer, State of Virginia.**(3)** His plans are detailed & attractive.

1. Virginia Library, Richmond has a portfolio of plans including the set of drawings. I wish to thank Dr Anne Knowles for bringing his material to my attention. The collection includes collaborative ventures in England.
2. *NLW* has a number of important examples of his work, c1809-1815.
3. The project is discussed by Withers, Marianne 'William Couling: Mapmaker without Portfolio' *The Portolan,* Fall 1993, pp.6-7, all the drawings are at Virginia *vide Eden* I p.71.

COULON, Monsieur Pierre (fl 1839)
Drawing teacher — Bangor, Caernarfon, Beaumaris

'Professor of French at the Friars School, Bangor and at the Grammar School Beaumaris ... he attends private pupils in the above branches at Bangor, Menai Bridge and neighbourhood, Tuesdays, Wednesdays and Saturdays. Beaumaris and Neighbourhood Mondays and Fridays. Caernarvon and Neighbourhood Thursdays.'**(1)**

Coulon lived at Garth, Bangor and also taught music.

1. *Caernarvon and Denbighshire Herald,* 2 February 1839, p.1.

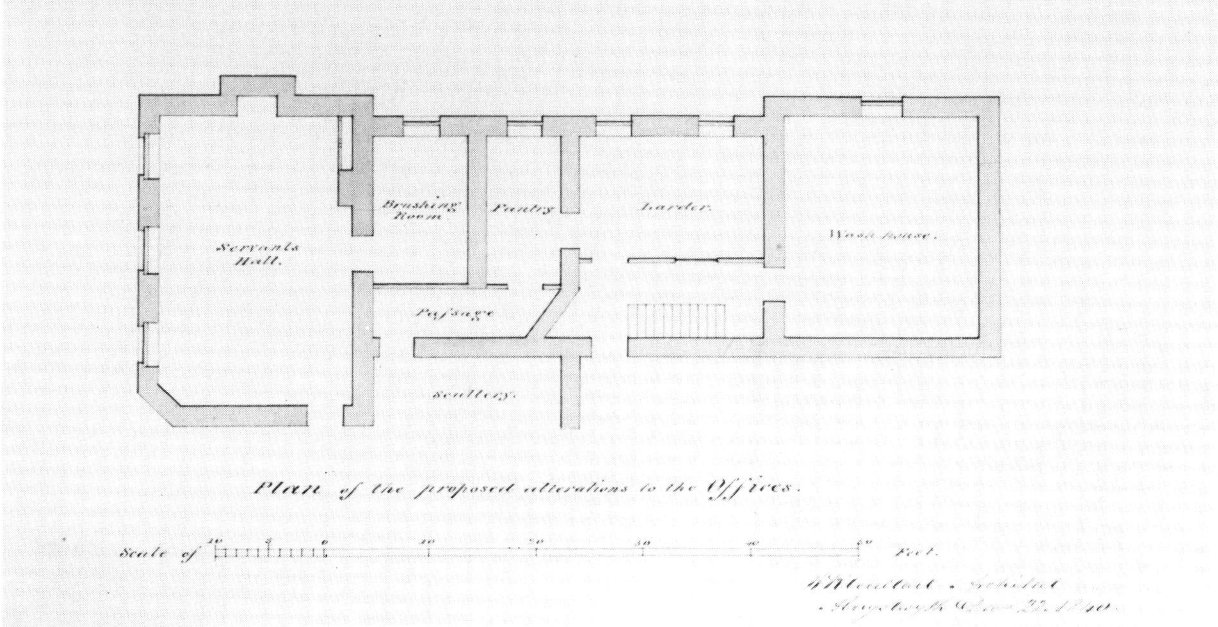

13 Coulthart, William Ritson, *Design for Nanteos,* pen & ink, 1840, Nanteos Collection, 105.

COULTHART, William Ritson

(fl 1820s - fl 1851)

Architect — Aberystwyth
Surveyor — 84 North Parade

Possibly born in Lancaster and certainly working there in the 1820s. He moved to Leamington Spa where he is recorded in 1833.**(1)** In 1836 he is recorded as surveying Yspyty Cynfyn Church. 'The work has recently been surveyed by a Mr Coulthart an intelligent architect from Leamington, lately come to Aberystwyth.'**(2)**

He was active in and around Aberystwyth. In 1839 he designed the Aberystwyth Workhouse.**(3)** Worked in Nanteos plans.**(4)** In 1841 he was commissioned to rebuild the Town Hall. This was completed in 1851.**(5)**

He worked on several other schemes, for instance, improvements at Hafod 1847-8;**(6)** Penparcau School 1841.**(7)** He clearly became a respected local architect and lived at Aberystwyth from 1840.**(8)**

Despite his importance locally he has not been recorded as working in Wales by any of the current standard texts.**(9)**

1. *Colvin*, p.273. Not in *Eden; TL & TP (RCAM)* kindly provided all the information in his entry. All citations, where possible were checked.
2. Information *TL* who gives source as ICBS 1756 (Incorporated Church Buildings Society, records held at the Society of Antiquaries, London).
3. *Cambrian*, 9 March 1839, p.1; *Carmarthen Journal*, 2 April 1841, p.4.
4. *NLW*, Nanteos Collection 20; 27; 105 are remodel designs for the facade.
5. *Carmarthen Journal*, 22 October 1841, p.3; *Welshman*, 7 April 1848, [p.3], mentioned the slow progress of the hall. The *Pembrokeshire Herald*, 13 June 1851, p.2, noted that the hall was 'nearly finished'.
6. *Welshman*, 2 July 1847, p.2.
7. *Carmarthen Journal*, 6 February 1846, p.3.
8. *Robson's*, 1840, p.11, 'South Wales' gives Coulthart's address as '84 North Parade'; *Pigot's*, 1844, p.8, the same address.
9. For instance, *Hilling;* the Penguin Pevsner of Dyfed, to be published, will no doubt prove the best source for his life and work. Not in *Girouard*.

COX, David

(1783 - 1859)

Landscape painter — Betws-y-Coed
Drawing master — Royal Oak Inn

Cox was an important and influential artist.**(1)** He was an excellent craftsman and an able teacher. Many of Cox's best works were of Wales and he first visited the Principality in 1805 and then regularly until 1844.

From this date he returned each year for several weeks at a time. He stayed at the Swan Inn for the first few years, then moved on to the Royal Oak where he stayed almost every summer from 1844 to 1856. In 1847 he painted a sign-board for the Inn. This remarkably impasto oil painting is extant and hangs in the Royal Oak Inn.**(2)** It is evident that this was not a 'one off' gesture by the artist because he asked his friend William Roberts to examine the sign in 1849.**(3)** In the same year he painted *A Welsh Funeral* which represented the sad event of the funeral of a young relative of the owner of the Royal Oak Inn.**(4)**

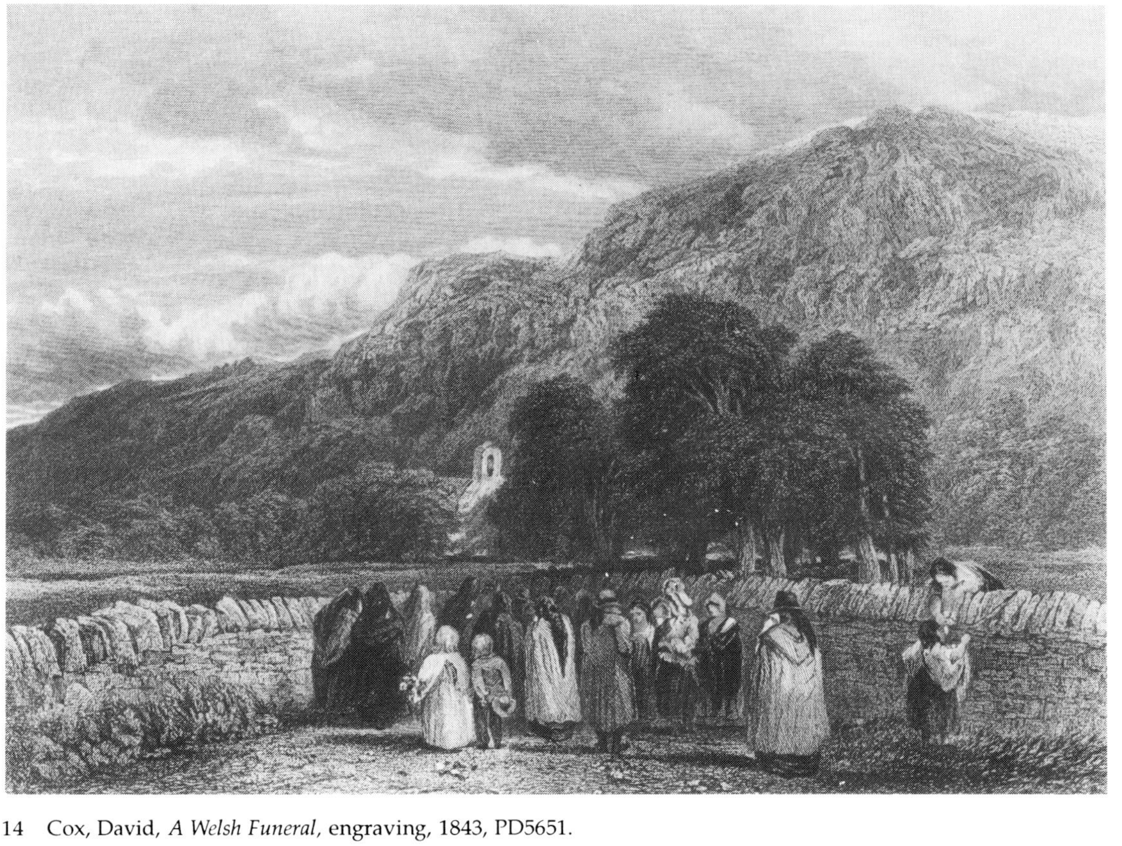

14 Cox, David, *A Welsh Funeral*, engraving, 1843, PD5651.

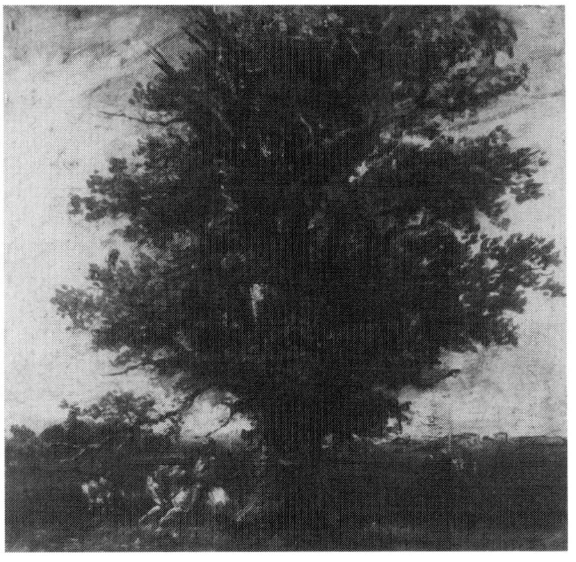

15 Cox, David, *Royal Oak Hotel*, signboard, oil on board, 1847, Royal Oak Hotel, Betws y Coed.

His affection for Betws was not curbed by several wet summers.**(5)** On his last visit to Betws in September 1856 he describes his love of the place and its people:

> 'I must tell you how glad I am to be at Betws y Coed, but I cannot paint out of doors; but I walk a small distance, and talk to some of the old travellers.'**(6)**

Cox probably encouraged many artists to visit, stay and eventually settle at Betws. Selby describes how Cox made the Royal Oak an academy and his letters are full of references to visiting artists.**(7)**

1. Wildman, Stephen, *David Cox*, Birmingham Museum & Art Gallery, 1983, is the best study of Cox to date. Wildman includes a valuable chronology. *Bell* pp.152-155 'The work of David Cox was so intimately connected with Wales and the Welsh landscape that it is easy to call him a Welsh artist.'
   Much of the additional information was gathered in course of preparing a lecture on Cox with J. Holmes (1993).
2. I wish to thank the owners of the Royal Oak for allowing me to examine the picture. The picture consists of three vertical panels, making an image of 57.1 x 60 cm. It is framed and the date 1847 is inscribed on a label.
3. Solly, Neal, *Memoirs of the life of David Cox* (London, 1973) (originally published 1873), p.169.
4. Cox, David, *A Welsh Funeral*. This was published as a steel engraving (see illustration).
5. *NLW*, 16093C (10), 29 July 1848, Cox writes to Grundy, in Liverpool: 'I have been here (Betws-y-Coed) nearly a fortnight and I believe it has rained every day more or less, some days the entire day...' In 1844 he noted that 'I cannot be home under a fortnight', Solly, p.162.
6. Solly, p.180.
7. For instance, *NLW* 16093C notes the following artists: Birch Gillott, Barber. Solly gives Creswick, Harry Johnston, William Roberts, Bennett, McKewan, Price.

CRACKLOW, C.T. (fl 1796)
Landscape painter — Cardiff

May have resided in Cardiff and is recorded as having taken the views in *BV* 216, *Eight Sketches in Glamorganshire*, 1822.**(1)**

1. *Vide* Bird, J.D. *supra*.

CRIDLE, James (1810 - fl 1841)
Coach painter — Swansea

Census 1841 (HO/107/1426/455, Swansea district 16, p.23).

CROWE, William (fl 1858 - fl 1878)
Photographer — Wrexham, Charles Street

Slater's, 1858.

CUMING, Robert (fl 1841)
Land surveyor — Denbigh

Son of T.G. Cuming?**(1)**

1. Not in *Eden*. Noted in *SA* 1841/32.

CUMMING, Thomas George (fl 1828 - fl 1841)
Land surveyor — Denbigh, High Street, Henllan Street

SA 1841/32.**(1)** He appears to have worked on title surveys & remained in Denbigh**(2)**

1. The probate record notes that Robert Turner (land surveyor), Denbigh, was the executor.
2. *Eden* I p.76 notes Thomas A. Cumming at High Street, 1828; Henllan Street, 1835. *Davies Atlas* notes T. G. CUMMINGS

D

DAGUIRE, P. and Co. (fl 1835)
Painter of panoramas — Cardigan

Daguire exhibited a 'dioramic' panorama of Paris and the Battle of Waterloo at Cardigan Town Hall during the summer of 1835. Posters were produced by a local printer and these provide the only extant information on this artist or company.**(1)** Music accompanied the revolving scenes and Daguire claimed that 'During its Exhibition in Paris it has been visited by Louis Phillippe and all the Royal Family, General Dubourg; and the greater part of the officers, and Thousands of those who bore a part in the Memorable Three Days....'

Such an important work was probably painted and marketed by L.J.M. Daguerre (1787-1839), the inventor of the Daguerreotype and painter of dioramas and panoramas from c1822.**(2)** He is known to have worked in London from 1823. Certainly works which he originally exhibited in Paris were circulated to the provinces such as Liverpool, Dublin and also to America.**(3)** His Welsh visit may well suggest a stop on a long itinerary from London to Dublin.

1. *NLW* Poster, Folder 56: 'For Ten Days Only'.
2. *Vide* Gernsheim, H. and A., *L.J.M. Daguerre - The History of the Diorama and the Daguerreotype* (London, 1956). Gernsheim discusses Daguerre's work & illustrates the Diorama in Regents Park. At this time his dioramas were fashionable and P. Daguire may have been a relative who undertook the itinerant exhibitions.
3. *Ibid.*, p.22.

D'ALLEGRE, Monsieur Louis (fl 1814)
Miniature artist — Swansea
Teacher of drawing, miniature painting

'Miniatures painted in a good style; and on reasonable terms.'**(1)** D'Allegre also taught French and Latin.

1. *Cambrian*, 23 July 1814, p.3.
   Ibid., 30 July 1814, p.1.

DANIEL, John (- 1845)
Mason — Ystradgynlais

BR/1845/62.

DANIELS, Joshua
(fl 1839 - fl. 1852)
Surveyor — Crickhowell

Designed & built rectory at Llangasty Talyllyn, 1852.**(1)**

1. *NLW* St Davids, Bounty Plan 106, 1852, very neat watercolour plan with a good detail of the facade. *NLW* Llandaff, Bounty Plan 58, 1839 Llangwm & Llandaff, Bounty Plans 117, 1839 Shirenewton vicarage. Not in *Eden*.

DAVIES, Dr [Thomas Woodwall]
(?fl 1820s - fl 1830s)
Portrait painter — Cowbridge

Physician who introduced Henry Mark Anthony (1817-1886), his apprentice, to painting c1832. Davies was 'a painter of talent, and several of his works are scattered throughout the Vale of Glamorgan'.**(1)**

Possibly he was T.W. Davies, surgeon, mentioned in contemporary directories.**(2)**

1. *Mardy Rees*, p.24.
2. 1822, *Pigot*, p.740: 'Salmon & Davies, Surgeon'. 1830, *Pigot*, p.833: 'Davies, Thomas Woodwall, Surgeon'. 1835, *Pigot*, p.754: 'Davies Thos, Woodwall' (under surgeons).
   Cadrawd, vol., p.[1]: 'Mr Harrison of Merthyr had a portrait by Dr Davies painted on parchment.'

DAVIES, Ann (fl 1834 - fl 1847)**(1)**
Ship and sign painter — Caernarfon
Artists' colourman — Crown Street
House painter

Widow of Thomas Davies, living at Crown Street until 1840 when she moved to Bangor Street. 'Paints, Oils, Varnishes and Brushes on Sale'.**(2)**

1. *B* 1848/88 is probate for Ann Davies. It mentions a Thomas Davies, Caernarvon, painter. So presumably T. Davies continued his family's business after 1847.
2. *Caernarvon and Denbighshire Herald*, 9 August 1834, p.2.
   Ibid., 14 November 1840, p.2.

DAVIES, David (fl 1740 - 1745)
Heraldic painter [& sign painter] — Denbighshire

Painted Royal Arms at Llanarmon-yn-Iâl, Denbighshire.**(1)**

1. TP (RCAM), oil on board, signed and dated 1740, c120 x 100 cm.

DAVIES, David (fl 1745)
Sign painter — Gwyddelwern, Merioneth

Painted the Lord's Prayer and a verse from the Acts of the Apostles (both in Welsh) at Gwyddelwern Church.**(1)**

1. *NLW*, MS 12646C, notes by Rev. Elias Owen, folio 31 (verso). Also includes sketch of the church and other inscriptions. Possibly the same artist as David Davies *supra*.

DAVIES, David (fl 1795**(1)** - fl 1813)
Surveyor and land agent — Llangattock, Crickhowell, Abergavenny

In 1803 he completed a survey of lands on the Gower for the Duke of Beaufort.**(2)**

His survey of Castle Madoc estate contains a fine naive rendering of Cil Hepste Falls, Breconshire. Such an addition was apparently solely for visual and topographical interest.**(3)**
He trained Thomas Morris ***supra.***

1. *NLW*, Estate map of *Llanelly*, dated 1795.
2. Thomas, H.A., *A Catalogue of Glamorgan estate maps* (Cardiff: 1992), pp.70-71. *Eden*, Supplement, p.403, notes a possible father and son. If so, the son was flourishing c1830 at the same address, Llangattock.
3. *NLW*, MSS Maps, Vol. 74 (PE 2924) 1813, commissioned by Hugh Price of Castle Madoc.

DAVIES, David (fl 1835 - fl 1843)
Surveyor — Tyn y Coed, Myddfai, Carmarthenshire, Llandovery, Brecon

Davies Atlas. *Eden* I p.79 notes him as an estate, coastal & tithe surveyor, at Llandovery & Brecon.

DAVIES, David (fl 1835 - fl 1843)
Surveyor
Froodvale
Conwil Gaio
[Cynwyl Gaeo]

Davies Atlas, Not in *Eden*.

DAVIES, David (fl 1840)
Builder and (architect)?
Llanelli
Wern

Robson's Directory, 1840, (Carmarthenshire, p.19).

DAVIES, Edward (- 1822)
Architect
Wrexham

SA 1822/113.**(1)**

1. Davies left most of his estate to his sister Margaret Parry.

DAVIES, Griffith (- 1824)
Mason
Cilcennin

SD/1824/34.

DAVIES, Hambury
Potter
Pillgwenlly
Newport

Hunt, 1849, p.131.

DAVIES, Henry (- 1831)
Mason
Swansea

SD/1831/306.

DAVIES, J. (fl 1792 - fl 1793)
Copyist and ?illustrator
North Wales?

He was probably a local artist, commissioned by Thomas Pennant to illustrate the Downing Library copy of the *History of Quadrupeds* 1793.**(1)** His drawings are probably accurate copies of the originals.

1. *NLW*, Grangerized copy, *History of the Quadrupeds*, Volume III, pp.52 & 54. Two watercolour drawings of *Weesels from Cochin's China*, both approximately 19.8 x 28.3 cm, are signed and dated 'J. Davies Pinxit 1792' and 'J. Davies Pinxit 1793' respectively.

DAVIES, John (1682 - 1755)
Gatesmith
Croes Foel
Wrexham**(1)**

Worked with his brothers on several important estates in North Wales.**(2)**

1. *SA* 1755/153 he is described as a'blacksmith'.
2. Edwards, I., *Davies Brothers Gatesmiths* (Cardiff, 1977). *Bell* pp.69-70. *See also* Robert Davies & Thomas Davies *infra*.

DAVIES, R. (fl 1763)
Surveyor
[Denbighshire]

Produced maps for John Wynne of Coed-coch, Denbighshire. These exhibit caricatured faces on the compass & also simple but original depictions of angels.**(1)**

1. *NLW* PE230 (Solander 495) map of Abergoley signed & dated by Davies. Also PE231 includes stylised depictions of trees. Not in *Eden*, but possibly I p.80 Robert Davies fl 1795-1800.

DAVIES, Rees (fl 1829 - 1850)
Architect
Llandysul

He is recorded, working on churches in Cardiganshire from 1829 onwards.**(1)** He drew simple but competent plans.**(2)**

1. *SD* 1850/255 he is described as a 'Carpenter/Builder'.
2. *TL* MSS notes Llandysul 1829-31, Capel Dewi church 1833-36, Llanfair Orllwyn 1842-44, Llanfihangel Rhos y Corn 1848. *Colvin* p.295.

DAVIES, Rees (- 1837)
Stone mason
Llandovery
Lower Street

SD/1837/116.

DAVIES, Richard (- 1827)
Mason
Amroth
Pleasant Valley

SD/1827/5.

DAVIES, Robert (1675 - 1748)
Gatesmith
Croes Foel
Wrexham

Worked with his brother John at his smithy. They made several famous gates in North Wales including Wrexham Church (1707), Chirk Castle, Eaton Hall, Chester and Leeswood Hall.

1. Edwards, I., *Davies Brothers Gatesmiths* (Cardiff, 1977). *Bell* pp.69-70.

DAVIES, Thomas (?fl1822 - fl 1838)
Surveyor
Llangattock Court?

NLW, Estate map *Llandrindod*, 1838.**(1)**

1. *Eden*, I p.80 with an Edward Davies.

DAVIES, Thomas (fl 1716 - 1755)**(1)**
Gatesmith
Wrexham

Brother of John & Robert Davies. He appears to have undertaken the work on the Erddig gates and some part of the Chirk Castle ironwork.**(2)**

1. *Bell*, pp.69-70.

2. Edwards, I., *Davies Brothers Gatesmiths* (Cardiff, 1977), p.25. *SA* 1729/298 notes as 'ironmonger' at Wrexham which is probably the same family.

DAVIES, Thomas (- 1857)
Painter & glazier Bangor

B 1857/59.

DAVIES, Thomas (fl 1840)
Builder Aberafan

Designed & built vicarage at Aberafan in 1840.**(1)**

1. *NLW* Llandaff, Bounty Plan 2, 1840. Not in *Eden*.

DAVIES, William (- 1853)
Mason Coed y Cymer Vaynor

BR/1853/73 (I).**(1)**

1. Inventory includes £30 worth of 'household furniture'.

DAVIES, William 'Mynorydd' (1826 - 1901)
Sculptor Merthyr

He may have worked for a short while in Merthyr and then left for London c1840.**(1)** He made busts of many Welsh preachers and statues, such as Thomas Charles of Bala, now in the Main Street, Bala.**(2)**

1. *DWB*. *Cadrawd*, p.24. *Lord, 1992*, pp.29-37.
2. *DWB*, p.160. Ffransis Payne Papers 847, pp.9-12, discuss William Davies, sculptor, of Merthyr (1800-1888). This Davies was born at Devynock and brought as a child to Merthyr c1806. He was apprenticed to his uncle, William Williams, a 'tyler & plasterer'. After an apprenticeship he moved from the provinces to London. Payne also notes that he returned to Merthyr between 1828 and 1842. It appears that he later removed to London and took three young men to study art: William Davies, Philip Davies and John Moses. This may be a confusion concerning William 'Mynorydd' Davies. Certainly no further reference is available on this earlier William Davies.

DAVIS, Edward (1813 - 1878)
Sculptor**(1)** [Carmarthen]

Davis was a native of Carmarthen and moved to London to train at the *RA* schools in 1833. Later he trained in the studio of E.H. Bailey (1788-1867).**(2)** He exhibited many times in the *RA* and the *BI*.

In 1851 Davis made a statue of Sir William Nott for Carmarthen.**(3)** This appears to be his only known early commission from Wales.**(4)**

1. *Lord, 1992*, p.37, (as E. Davies) notes that he exhibited at the Aberystwyth Eisteddfod in 1865. *Mardy Rees*, p.25, records that he flourished 1834 and exhibited at the *RA* and the *BI* 1861-63 from a London address. *Gunnis*, p.122, provides a good biography.
2. *Gunnis*, p.32, notes that Bailey was a native of Bristol. This exemplifies the connections between Bristol and South Wales.
3. This statue is still *in situ* at Carmarthen.
4. *Gunnis*, p.122, notes that he executed a bust of the Bishop of St David's in 1876 which was exhibited at the *RA* in that year.

DAVIS, Tyddesley R.T. (fl 1831 - fl 1857)
Animal painter Ruabon
Landscape painter

Exhibited from Ruabon in 1857.**(1)**

1. *Graves, B.I.* notes that he exhibited from Brighton in 1831, Oxford 1851-1852, then moved to Ruabon:
   1857 69 *Evening, twilight*, 30gs.
   438 *Moonlight*, 30 gs, 'The stag at eve had drank his fill, / Where danced the moon on Monan's rill.'- *Lady of the Lake*.

DAWSON, Richard Godwin (fl 1835 - fl 1843)
Surveyor Llanasa Flintshire

Davies Atlas, *Eden* I p.82.

DELAMOTTE, George Orleans
(fl 1809 - fl c1828)
Drawing master
Portrait painter Swansea

Delamotte was the brother of William Delamotte (1775-1863) who produced fine landscapes of North Wales.**(1)** He worked at Sandhurst, Reading and London as a drawing master. In 1809 he exhibited at the *RA* from a London address.**(2)**

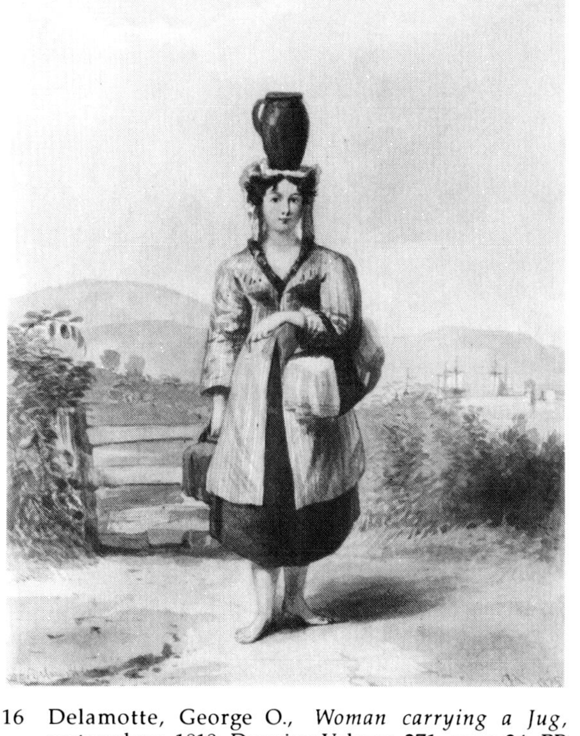

16 Delamotte, George O., *Woman carrying a Jug*, watercolour, 1818, Drawing Volume 271, page 24, PB 4886.

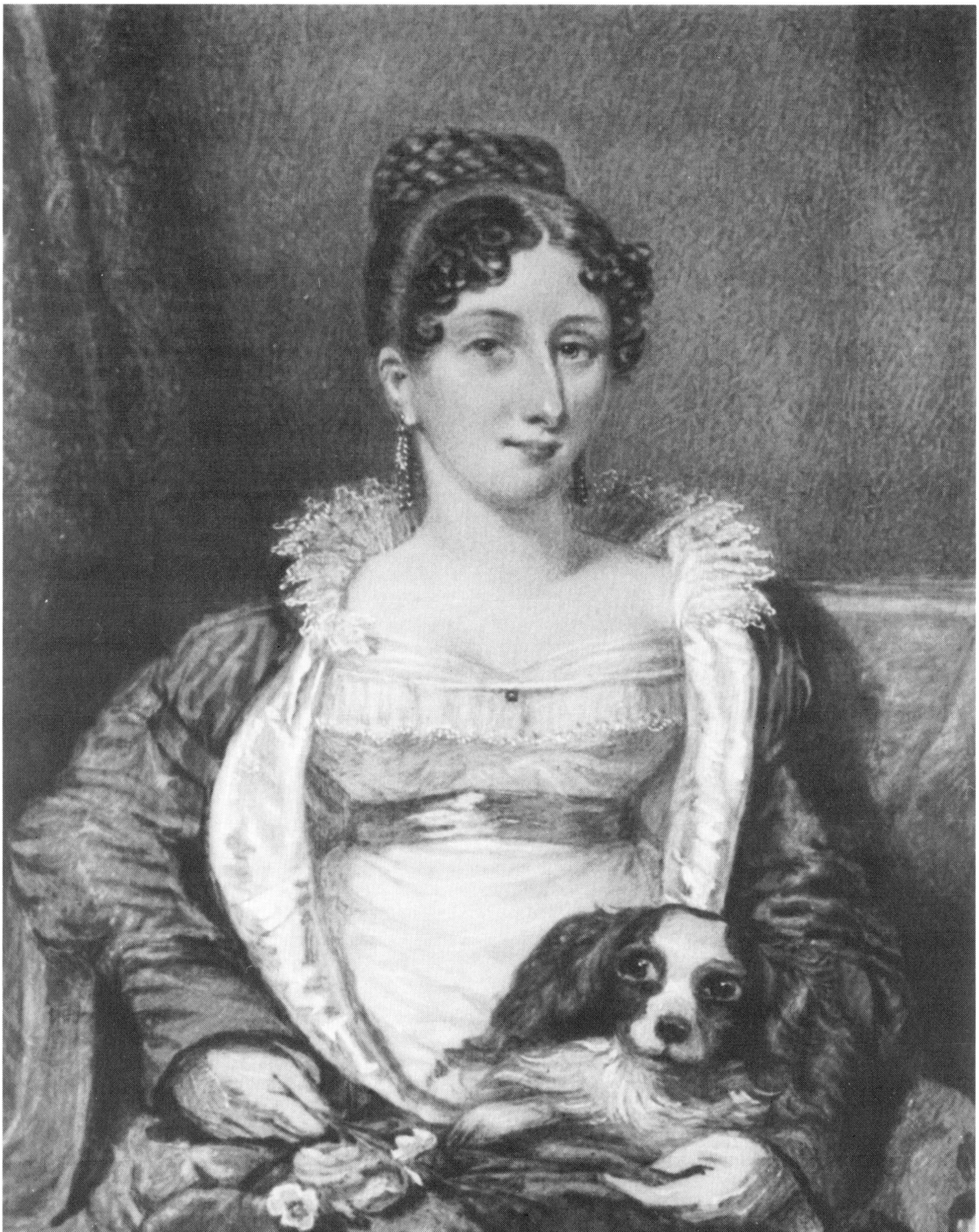

17 Delamotte, George O., *Jane Harriot Talbot*, watercolour, 1821, *WPA*.

By c1818 he was probably living in Bath. He visited South Wales gentry in 1818 (Aberpergwm) and Swansea in 1825.**(3)** In 1827 Lewis Weston Dillwyn records visiting Delamotte where the artist taught 'Mary' 'Miniature painting' and Delamotte took a likeness of John Dillwyn.**(4)**

About this period he published a set of prints of South Wales which are all landscapes in the Neath valley.**(5)** He is recorded at Sandhurst in 1828. Presumably his residence at Bath was seasonal.

1. *Mallalieu*, pp.104-5. William Delamotte's landscapes are illustrated in Joyner, Paul, *Dolbadarn Castle*

(exhibition catalogue) (Aberystwyth, 1990), Plates P65, P67, P68, dated 1832.

2. *Graves*, 'Great Marlow', *Carswell House, near Faringdon*.
3. *NLW*, Drawing Volume 271 (4to), [*Costume Drawings*], many portraits signed and dated by Delamotte. *NLW*, PB4174, 'Portraits A. John Rolls, Britton Ferry by Delamotte', pencil diary, c1825?
4. *NLW*, *Calender of Diary of Lewis Weston Dillwyn*, Vol. II, p.54, March 21-22 1827, at Bath. It appears the family knew Delamotte probably from previous visits to Glamorganshire. (I am grateful to Julian Cox for bringing this reference to my attention.) Whittaker, *The Boarding School and London Master's Directory* (London, 1828), p.77, cites Delamotte at 3 College Terrace, Royal Military College, Sandhurst.
5. *NLW*, *BV* 201 (4to), Delamotte, G.O., *Sketches of Scenery in South Wales*, printed at Moser and [imprint torn], No. 71, Cromer [imprint torn], brown paper wrappers, prints similar to soft ground etchings, 30 x 44 cm, all inscribed 'George Orleans Delamotte Print'. The following views are included: *Aberdylis Vale of Neath*; *Ysgwd Inon gam*; *Melincourt*; *Entrance to Porth yr Ogof Career*; *Ysgwd yr Rhyd*; *Kil Hepsti*. (Two examples are: PZ 3217, B2/1 - B24, *Kilhepsti, Vale of Neath*, c1820; PZ 3218, B2/4 - B77, *Ysgwd Inon gam* (Pyrddin River), c1820.)

DELAMOTTE, Philip (fl 1856)
Photographer — Swansea

A relation of Delamotte, *supra*.**(1)**

1. *Cox, 1990*.

DICKINSON, Joseph (fl 1835 - fl 1843)
Surveyor — Dowlais

Davies Atlas, Not in *Eden*.

DINGLY, Stephen (1821 - fl 1845)
Coach painter — Swansea
China painter — Clifton Terrace

Dingley is described on the 1841 Census: 'Aged 20 Coach Painter Not born in Glamorgan'.**(1)**

Nance reports that Dingly painted the Richardson Francis bowl with excellent armorial designs.**(2)** The bowl is now kept at the *GVS*.

1. Census Return (*PRO*), HO1O7/1426/p.1/[27].
2. *Nance*, p.164, and illustrations, LXVIIa.

DODD, John Josiah (c1821 - 94)
'Arlunydd Gwalia' — Bangor
Landscape painter — Caernarfon**(2)**
Drawing master**(1)**

He worked in London and Paris before settling in Bangor, North Wales.**(2)** No information is available concerning his home but he may have been born in Wales.

All drawings and paintings executed in his Welsh residence are dated later than 1850.**(3)** However, a large watercolour of Caernarfon Castle, c1825 attributed to Dodd,**(4)** may confirm an early residence in Wales before he moved to London.**(5)** There is evidence of his Bangor address in 1868.**(6)** He may have returned to the Continent, at least he worked in Spain in 1879**(7)**

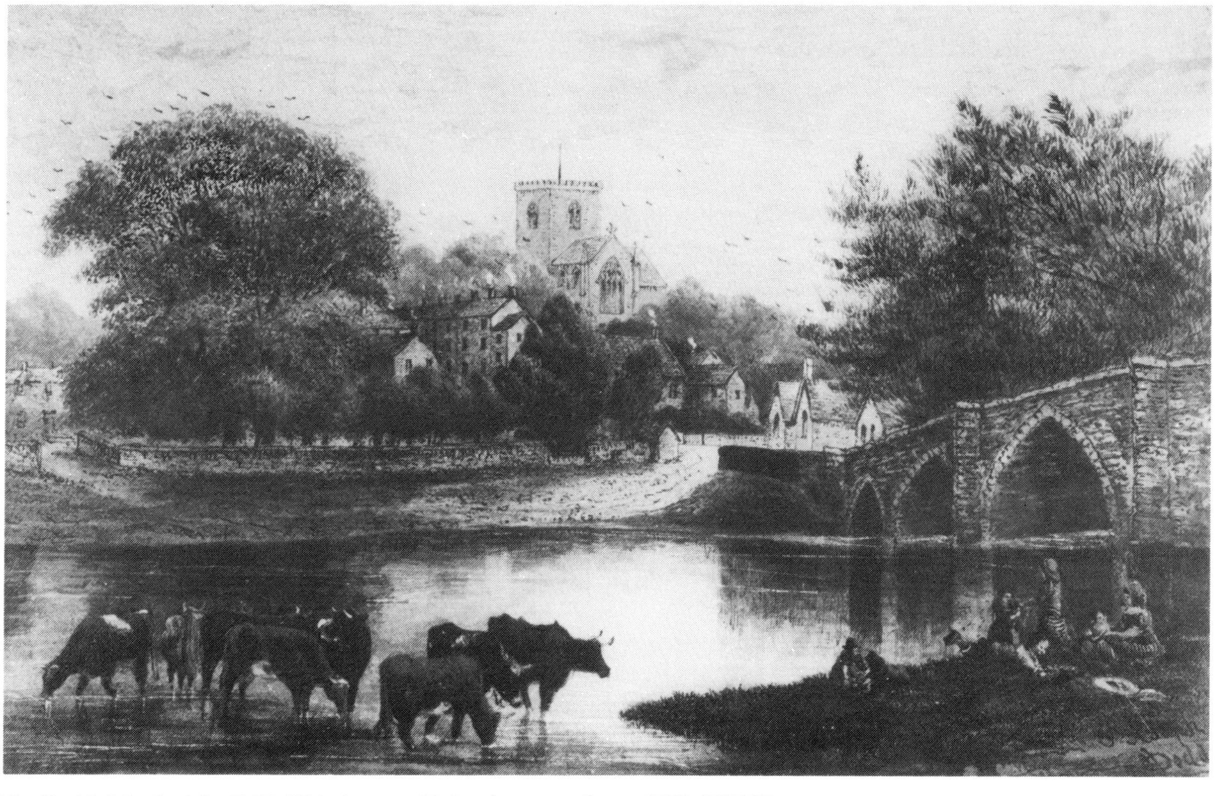

18 Dodd, John Josiah, *Cattle Watering near St Asaph*, watercolour, c1870, PE3883.

1. He is reported as drawing master to Lady Newborough (*NLW*, Dept of Pictures & Maps files).
2. Anglesey Inn, Caernarfon, *NLW*, Dept of Pictures & Maps files.
3. He exhibited at the *RA* in 1832-35 from a London address, 1838-39 from Paris. Lewis, Richard, 'Arlunydd Gwalia', *Y Casglwr*, 1988 (Rhif 34), p.17, gives a short biography.
4. *NLW*, PE 4304, 41.5 x 43.5 cm. The subject matter, style and composition are comparable with Dodd's work.
5. The *NLW* has a number of signed and dated watercolours produced in the 1860s and later, for example PE 3655, *Llanberis Lake*, 17.5 x 45.5 cm, 'J.J. Dodd, Bangor 187-'. The *NLW* also has a print, PB 5852, B3/22 - B415, *Snowdon from Nantlle Lakes*, 1854.PG2150-1 is a series of 4 oval watercolours of *North Wales* which are unusual, being small sketches of scenes, rather like views one would expect for book illustrations.
6. *Slater's*, 1868, p.13; Lewis, *op.cit.*, notes that the Census Return, 1871, gave Dodd as aged 50. In 1874 he exhibited as 'Arlunydd Gwalia' at the Bangor Eisteddfod, *vide Lord, 1992*, p.44. *Slater's*, 1880, gives 3 Mount Pleasant Terrace, Upper Bangor.
7. Abbott & Holder August 1994 list 292 nos 91 & 92 gives *Burgos Cathedral* dated 1879, watercolour, c16x10cm & *Interior of Burgos*.

DOWNMAN, John A.R.A. (1750 - 1824)

Portrait and miniature artist — Wrexham

Born at Ruabon, he was sent to Chester to study drawing, then to Liverpool, and in 1767 he moved to London. He trained at the *RA* schools and under Benjamin West.**(1)**

After a long and prosperous career in London, and provincial centres such as Cambridge, he returned to Chester, then to Wrexham 'where the artist had finally settled down'.**(2)** He probably resided there from c1817 until his death. He was buried in Wrexham church.**(3)** Acton Hall had several paintings by him.**(4)**

1. *Hutchison*, p.133: 'entered 17th March 1769'.
2. Williamson, G.C., *John Downman* (1907), p.xxxvi. Williamson is also the main source of biographical information on Downman.
3. Died 24 December 1824, *ibid* p.xxxviii notes a monument, Palmer, Alfred N. *History of the Parish Church at Wrexham* (Wrexham,[1888]) p.218 notes the stone in the church. *NLW* MS John R. Hughes, deposit 1561 has a file written c1924 on the artist with further information on his descendants.
4. *ibid* notes the portraits. Not included in *Steegman*.

DUBOURG, Mr (fl 1848)

Modeller — Swansea

Exhibited models of Jerusalem and lectured on the subject at Swansea.

Dubourg added the following to his advertisement:

> 'If I had stated on my first arrival it was the Work of a Welshman, you might have thought I wished to lay claim to your support as a countryman; but having gained your applauses as a stranger, I now state the maker is a Welshman. The Gentleman who lectures is a Welshman, and if there is any merit due for the Exhibition, it springs from the Principality of Wales.'**(1)**

1. *Cambrian*, 17 November 1848, p.2.

DUPONT, Monsieur A. (fl 1850)

Drawing master — Bangor, Caernarfon, Beaumaris

A 'Graduate of the University of Paris' taught at Bangor School and gave Rev. C.W. Totten, Friars School, Bangor and Rev. H. Price, Pen y Bryn, Bangor, as referees in his advertisement.**(1)** He also taught French.

1. *Caernarvon and Denbighshire Herald*, 2 February 1850, p.4.

DYE, Charles (fl 1858)

Photographer — Merthyr Tydfil, Glebeland Street

Slater's, 1858.

DYER, Rev. John (1699 - 1757)

Portrait, landscape and Religious painter — Mid and South Wales

Born at Abersanan, Llanfynydd, Carmarthenshire, he apparently worked locally before going to London to study under Jonathan Richardson.**(1)** Whilst he is probably best known for his poetry he was an artist.**(2)**

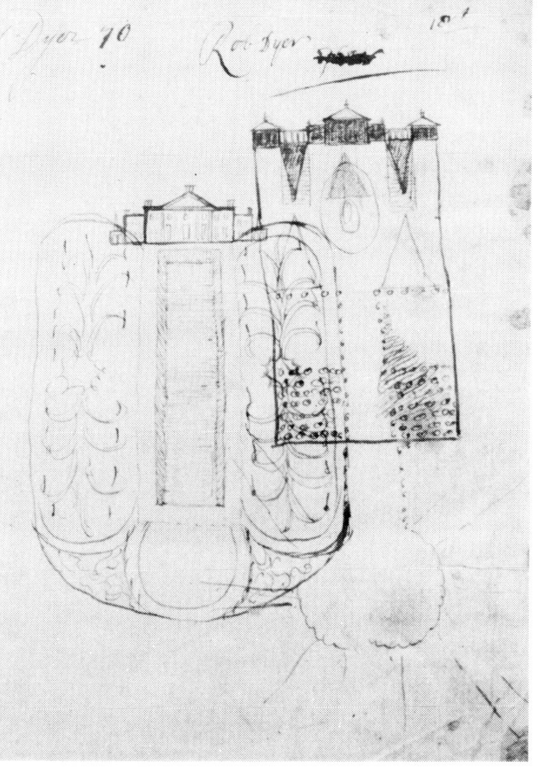

19 Dyer, Rev. John, *A Design for a landscape garden*, pen & ink, c1740, *WPA*.

A number of works survive which display his debt to Italian art. His landscapes suggest a freer response to nature, known paintings date from c1730-1750.**(3)**

A well preserved example, *The Last Supper*, is probably typical of his style.**(4)** There is also recorded a sketch by him of an antiquity.**(5)**

According to Williams, Dyer became an itinerant painter in Wales and the border countries in 1730.**(6)** Should this be true he was the earliest 18th century artist to attempt such a practice in Wales.

1. Humfrey, Belinda, *John Dyer* (Cardiff, 1980) (Writers of Wales Series) provides a biography with useful information on sources. Has self portrait as frontispiece (*WPA*). It is much in the style of his master, as is the portrait of his father also attributed by the present writer to Dyer. Dr Stephen Briggs, RCAM(W) informs me that there was a letter on Dyer in the *Times* 22 July 1939 p.437 by E. Parker. It is interesting to note that Rev. R.H. Newell in his *Letters on the Scenery of Wales* (London, 1821) p.52 mentions Dyer whilst discussing the region around Grongar Hill. 'Dyer was a Cambrian worthy, and a brother artist one of the very few that Wales can boast'. Newell provided a brief biography, presumably based on Dr Johnson's *Life of Dyer in The Lives of English Poets* (London, 1781), Volume IV, pp.335-339. All the Dyer manuscripts are now based at the *NLW*, MS 232294-23297. For a recent discussion on Dyer see Joyner, Paul 'Rev John Dyer', *Carmarthenshire Antiquary* (forthcoming article 1995/6).
2. Longstaffe, J.P., 'John Dyer as a Painter', *Montgomery Collections*, XI, 1878, pp.396-402. This is the earliest known discussion of Dyer's paintings.
3. Williams, Ralph M., *Poet, Painter and Parson: The Life of John Dyer* (New York, 1956), is the best source for illustrations of his work. These include a portrait of Dyer; a copy after Correggio c1725, portrait of *Bishop John Hough* 1740-1; *Vale of Neath* 1750. All are in private collections.
   AIW, p.79, item 130, cites *Caerphilly Castle* 1733 as the only extant drawing by Dyer.
   WPA has copies of exquisite Italian landscapes á la pen & ink drawings by N. Poussin (such as those in the *BM*). These include views of a *Roman Tomb*.
4. Now at Newtown Church, Montgomeryshire. Oil on canvas, approximately 100 x 450 cm, c1730. The painting, according to tradition, was given by Dyer to the original church. *Cambria Depicta*, p.225 tells us that the picture was repainted by a local sign painter and he has not left any trace of Dyer's painting: 'He has not left any traces of Dyer's paintings, with the exception of the ungrateful [*sic*] outline, which, if at all Dyer's, must have been one of his juvenile performances.' The author examined this picture in 1993 and suggests that the drapery is original work by Dyer but much else has been changed.
5. Recorded in *Carmarthenshire Antiquary*, Vol. XI (1), p.55, a drawing, now lost by Dyer of the Eiudon Stone. This is also noted in Camden, William, *Britannia* (London [Gough edition], 1789), Vol. II, p.510, 'Kaer Maen'.
6. Williams, *op.cit.*, p.77, describes a tour of North Wales in 1728, 'Probably he was doing more than just sketching, he may have been experimenting with living as an itinerant painter.' Williams records that Dyer settled in Hereford and from there travelled to Wales and the borders. Twiston-Davies, L. & Evans, A., *Welsh life in the 18th century* (London, 1939), p.77. 'Dyer painted his way' around South Wales. No source is given for this assertion.

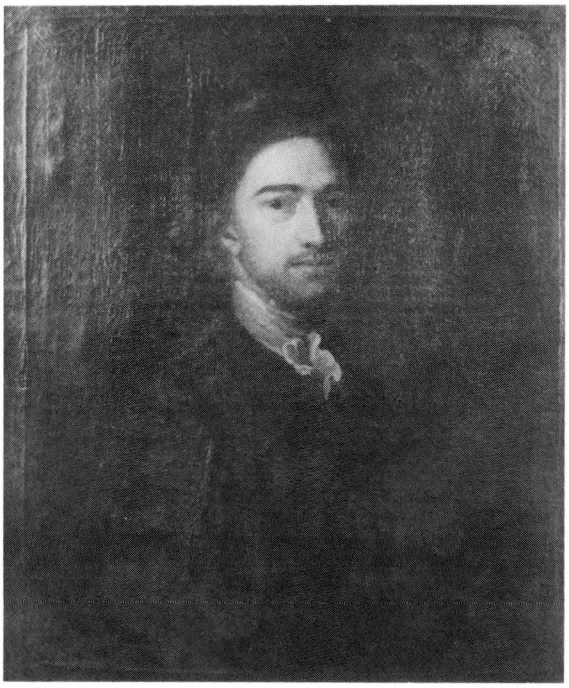

20 Dyer, Rev. John, *Self Portrait*, oil on canvas, c1730, *WPA*.

DYOS, Edward (1821 - fl 1866)
Surveyor? [Montgomeryshire?]

He produced a complicated map on vellum.**(1)** This included a landscape dated July 1821 showing gentlemen reading the title of the map & a hunt scene in the background. The title is Neo-Classical 'Corinthian' column, surrmounted with a decorative urn.

Over forty years later a surveyor of the same name is recorded practicing in the same region.**(2)**

1. 'Map of Llanllwchaiarn situated in the several Parishes of Llanllwchaiarn, Newtown & Bettws.' Book of References also signed by Dyos. *NLW* Harrison & Son Vol. 85, map 'Drawings Delinated by Edward Dyos'. 'Surveyed by F. Lloyd of Broseley, Shropshire' as vellum, *Cefn Mawr*, 1821.
2. *Eden* I p.93 1824-66, working at Garth Derwen, Montgomeryshire, Buttington in 1866.

E

EDMONDS, Paul (fl 1856)
Builder Skenfrith

He built & designed the vicarage at Skenfrith.**(1)**

1. *NLW* Llandaff Bounty Plans 118, 1856, no facade is given, only rudimentary drawings of the main structure - but detailed instructions for the building in his estimate. Not in *Eden*.

EDWARDS, Alexander Wilson

(fl 1806 - fl 1820)
Sculptor — Wrexham

Information kindly given to me by *PL*.

EDWARDS, John

(fl 1856)
Mason — Llanilar

SD/1856/153.

EDWARDS, John

(fl 1830 - fl 1846)
Surveyor — Cefn Bryn, Glamorganshire; Cardigan, St Mary's Street

Davies Atlas, Eden I p.96 probably same surveyor given as of St mary's Street, Cardigan..

EDWARDS, John

(fl 1835 - fl 1843)
Surveyor — Dolaugwyrddion, ?Dolau Gwyn, Merionethshire?

Davies Atlas. Not in *Eden.*

EDWARDS, Joseph

(1814 - 82)
Monumental mason — Merthyr Tydfil
Sculptor — Swansea

Edwards was born in Merthyr Tydfil and worked with his father as a stone-cutter. Joseph undertook the sculpting of ornamental pieces.**(1)** His mother was 'artistically inclined, could paint with taste'.**(2)**

He moved to Swansea where he worked for 'Mr Jones, a statuary mason'.**(3)** One example of his work in Wales is a head stone at Merthyr.**(4)**

By 1835 he was working in London, he never returned but appears to have kept close connections with Wales. It is interesting that Davies noted the effect the Mansel effigies at Margam had on Edwards's ambition.**(5)**

1. Davies, William, 'Joseph Edwards, Sculptor', *Wales* II, 1895, pp.134-137. This is the first in a series of articles on Edwards, pp.193-196, 273-278, 301-303, 355-360, 403-405, 468-472, 540-543. A recent study appeared in the *Merthyr Historian* (Vol. 4), 1989, pp.87, 103, by Holley, T. F. 'Joseph Edwards and Merthyr Tydfil'. *NLW* MSS, Ffransis Payne Papers 847, includes Edwards in biographical discussions of Merthyr artists.
2. Wilkins, Charles, 'Joseph Edwards the Sculptor', *The Red Dragon*, Vol. 1, 1882, p.100. Article issued as a pamphlet in March 1882, pp.[99]-107.
3. Davies, *op.cit.*, p.194.
4. Davies, *ibid.*, p.194, illustrated: *Female mourner leaning against a Classical Urn.* This is a standard but good image of the period. It shows ability but little imaginative design.
5. Davies, *ibid.*, p.194. These memorials are probably the finest in Glamorganshire.

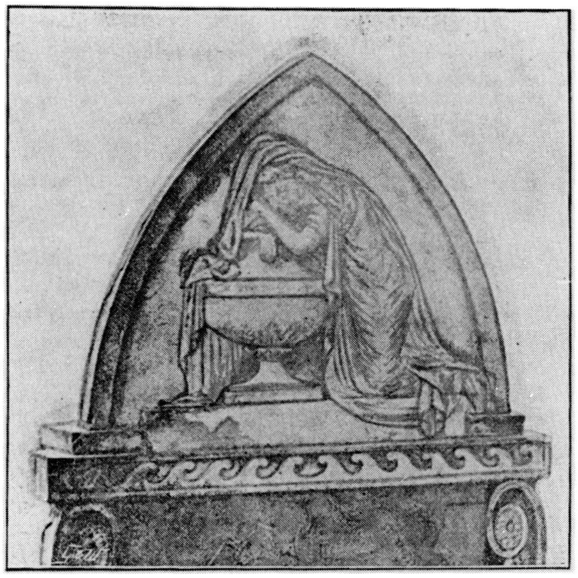

21 Edwards, Joseph, *Female Mourner* (tombstone at Merthyr), illustrated in *Wales* II, 1895, p.194.

EDWARDS, Robert

(fl 1844)
Architect — Bangor
Surveyor — High Street

Slater's, 1844, p.9.
Not in *Girouard, Eden.*

EDWARDS, Sydenham Teast [?Teak]

(1768 - 1819)
Botanical artist — Abergavenny, Usk

Edwards was born at Usk,**(1)** the son of Lloyd Pithell Edwards presumed a school master at the town.**(2)**

T. H. Thomas read a lecture on Edwards in 1910 & he noted that

'We first hear of Sydenham as having made copies of certain plates in the *Flora Londinensis* and these were brought to the attention of William Curtis... who was so pleased with their execution that he sent for Edwards to London.'**(3)**

He probably moved to London about 1788-90 and was producing first class work by 1793.**(4)** His subsequent career is well documented & it appears that he did not return to Wales. He is buried at Chelsea church which had a monument inscribed

'As a faithful Delineator of Nature few equal'd, none excel'd'.**(5)**

WORKS OF SCULPTURE
BY J. EDWARDS.

CONTRIBUTED TO

THE ROYAL LONDON EISTEDDVOD,

1855.

"Cas ni Charo y Wlad a'i Mago."

1. Bust of the late Ab Iolo.

On the scroll beneath the bust will be seen the following lines from his *Awdl ar Dderwyddon Ynys Prydain*:—

"Nid yw dyddiau dedwyddyd,
Och, i'n hwyl! ond bychan hyd;
Hawdd ammor y tymmor têg
A rêd i wewyr adeg."

"Nid bodd calon ond byw'n gyfion."

2. Lavinia.

"The modest virtues mingled in her eyes,
Still on the ground dejected, darting all
Their humid beams."

3. Religion Consoling Justice in her Grief.

"Thou, O God! workest all things after the counsel of Thine own will. The Day is Thine, the Night also is Thine!"
Eph. 1 11, & Ps. 74, 16.

4. Child Asleep.

"Oh 'tis a touching thing to make one weep –
A tender infant with its curtain'd eye,
Breathing as it would neither live nor die,
With that unchanging countenance of sleep!
As if its silent dream, serene and deep,
Had lined its slumber with a still blue sky,
So that the passive cheeks unconscious lie
With no more life than roses—just to keep
The blushes warm, and the mild odorous breath,
O blossom babe! So calm is thy repose,
So sweet a compromise of life and death,
'Tis pity these fair buds should e'er unclose
For memory to stain their inward leaf,
Tinging thy dreams with unacquainted grief."

5. The Spirit Ascending.

"The spirit shall return unto God who gave it, and sorrow and sighing shall flee away."—Eccl. 12, 7, & Js. 35, 10.

6. Bust of Samuel Bosanquet, Esq.
7. Bust of T. Snow Beck, Esq., M.D., F.R.S., &c.
8. The Last Dream.

"Her sun went down while it was yet day; but unto the upright there ariseth light in the darkness."
Jer. 15, 9, & Ps. 112, 4.

"Hark! they whisper, Angels say,
Sister spirit come away."

9. Bust of a Lady.
10. Bust of the Rev. John Guthrie, M.A.
11. Medallion of a Lady.
12. Medallion of J. Ewing Ritchie, Esq.
13. Medallion of J. B. A. Angell, Esq., and his Lady.
14. Bust of Sir Ivor Bertie Guest when 9 years of age.
15. Bust of Master Thomas Williams Angell Evans.
16. Sketch for a proposed Colossal Statue.

Intended to represent the *Future* High Poet-priest of Science, who, in the true light of the profoundest and most comprehensive Scientific Knowledge, when more perfected than at present, is to be to his fellow-beings, in all things excellent, an unequalled Guide, Father, and Educator; ever, as indicated in the Sketch, directing unwearied attention to the great modern precept, "Study Nature," inscribed on the tablet held in his hands.

On the pedestal will be observed the ancient Greek formula, "*Live Harmoniously with Nature,*" and the Roman apophthem, "*Nature never says one thing and Wisdom another,*" accompanied by the first aphorism from the *Novum Organum*:— "Man, the Minister and Interpreter of Nature, can understand and act—both with regard to Mind and Things—only in proportion as he observes the Order of Nature: more he can neither know nor do."

17. Sketch for a proposed large Relievo.

Intended to represent a Philosopher explaining to a Youth the full meaning of the celebrated Delphic precept "Know Thyself" inscribed over a niche containing a bust of Thales, the author of the precept. On the plinth supporting the figures are the following words of Marcus Aurelius:—

"The highest learning is to be Wise,
And the greatest wisdom is to be Good."

18. The Weary Reassured, being the Sketch of a—

"————Solemn Vision
Telling of things which no gross ear can hear."

"They that be wise shall shine as the brightness of the firmament; and they that turn many to righteousness, as the stars for ever and ever."—Dan. 12, 3.

19. Design commemorative of the Great Exhibition of 1851.
20. "Daughter of the Dawn—bright, rosy-fingered Aurora."

"———Look how the floor of heaven
Is thick inlaid with patines of bright gold!
There is not the smallest orb that thou behold'st,
But in its motion *like an angel sings*,
Still quiring to the young-eyed cherubim.

"Daughter of Faith, unfading Hope."

"Unfading Hope! when life's last embers burn,
When soul to soul, and dust to dust return!
Heaven to thy charge resigns the awful hour,
Oh! then, thy Kingdom comes! Immortal Power!"

"Calon wrth Galon."
"Yn Enw Duw a phob Daioni."

22 Edwards, Joseph, *Catalogue of an Exhibition*, London Eisteddfod, 1855.

1. Desmond, Ray, *Dictionary of British & Irish Botanists & Horticulturalists* (London, 1994), p.228 gives Monday 5 August 1768. It also provides a large amount of reference material on the artist's career.
2. *Mardy Rees* p.38 notes this possibility. Bradney, Joseph *A History of Monmouthshire* Volume III (London, 1923), pp.44-45 details the school masters at Usk but no mention of Edwards is given. *Mardy Rees* also suggests that Edwards was related to the Reece family of Usk *ibid* p.36 but this cannot be proved. Perhaps the family were based in Abergavenny.
3. Thomas, T. H., 'Sydenham Edwards of Usk', *Cardiff Naturalists' Society Transactions*, volume 43, 1910 p.15.
4. William Curtis (1746-1799) was a highly distinguished botanist & author. He began the illustrated *Flora Londinensis* in 1775 & founded the *Botanical Magazine* in 1787. From c1793 Edwards worked on both projects.
5. Hubbard, Clifford, 'A book at Random' in *Kennel Gazette* November, 1991 pp.33-37, monument destroyed in 1941. I am grateful to my friend & colleague Raymond Davies for reminding me of Edwards & providing much valuable information.

EDWARDS, William (1719 - 89)

Architect — Eglwysilan
Stone mason — Glamorganshire

A self-taught architect, particularly famous for his single span bridges.**(1)** His most famous bridge was Pontypridd in Glamorganshire.**(2)**

Edwards was engaged on a large number of commissions in South Wales which included smelting houses, forges and other industrial buildings. *Colvin* records that three of his four sons followed their father's trade, most notable was David Edwards who built Llandeilo bridge. Local tradition relates Edwards as the architect of Cenarth bridge.

There is a miniature portrait of Edwards in *NMW* by Thomas Hill dated 1779.**(3)**

1. *Colvin* pp.336-337 main source for this entry. *Cadrawd*, p.32, provides further details.
2. Wilson produced a painting and print of the bridge, *The Great Bridge over the Taafe*, J. Boydell, London, 1775, 54.3 x 40.6 cm (*NLW*, PG881).
3. *NLW* has a portrait print after Hill (Portraits (A) P9793), 13.8 x 10 cm which shows Edwards holding a plan of the Pontypridd Bridge.

EDWARDS, William Camden (1777 - 1855)

Portrait engraver — ?Monmouthshire

Born in Monmouthshire and may have worked there before moving to Bungay in Suffolk, c1803.**(1)** In Suffolk he engraved for various publications.**(2)**

1. *Mardy Rees*, p.248, main source for entry.
2. Edwards worked on publications of the Bible and *Pilgrim's Progress* and various portrait engravings.

ELLIS, Ellis Owen 'Ellis Bryn-Coch' (1813 - 61)

Landscape artist — Bryncoch (nr Pwllheli)
Portrait painter — Liverpool
Cartoonist — London
Illustrator

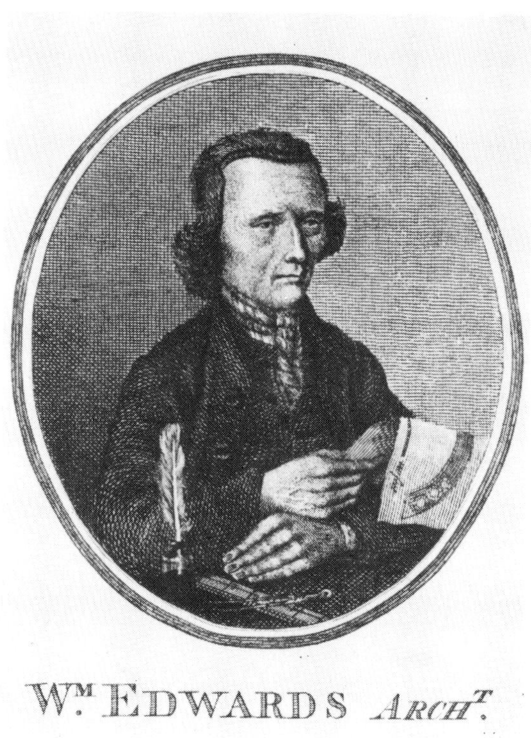

23 *Edwards, William*, engraving, c1779, P9793. [engraved by W. Skelton after a portrait by T.[homas?] Hill].

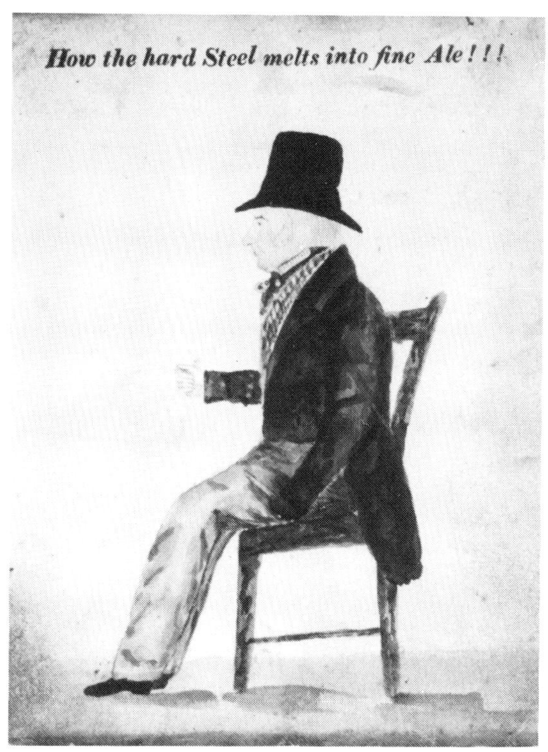

24 Ellis, Ellis Owen, *Morris Hughes*, watercolour, c1830, PB2425.

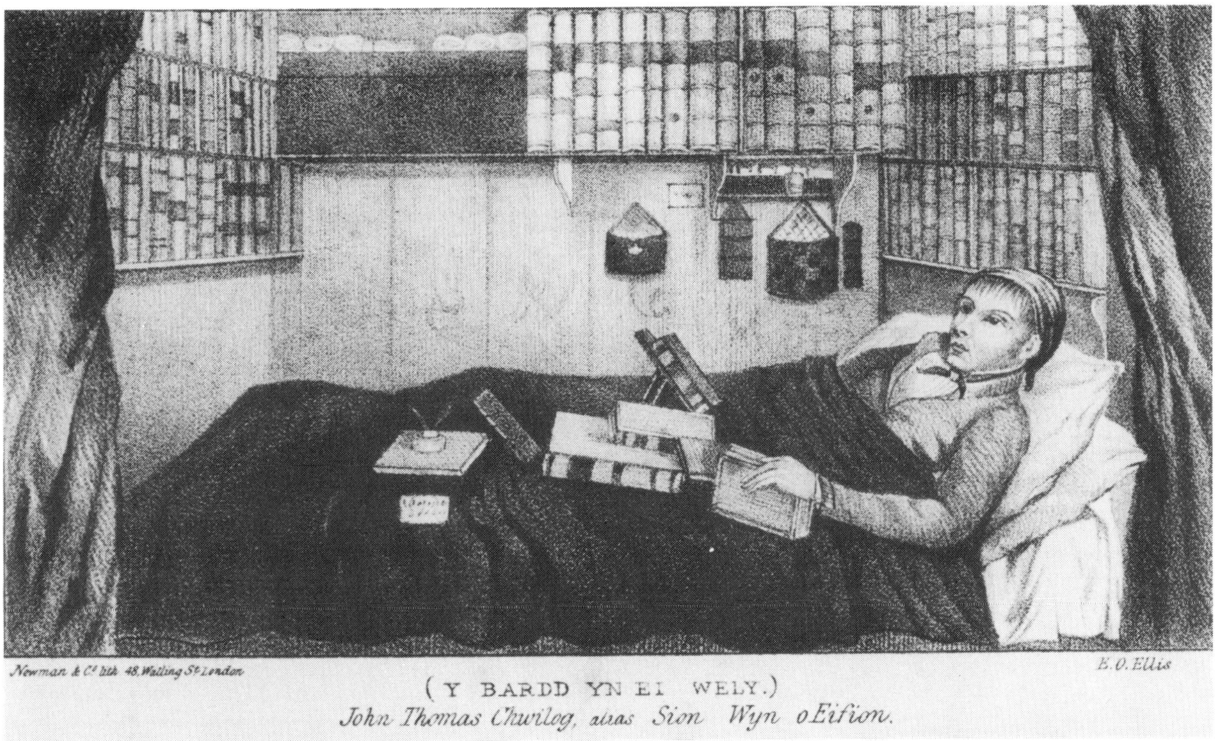

25 Ellis, Ellis Owen, *John Thomas Chwilog*, lithograph c1861, P9732.

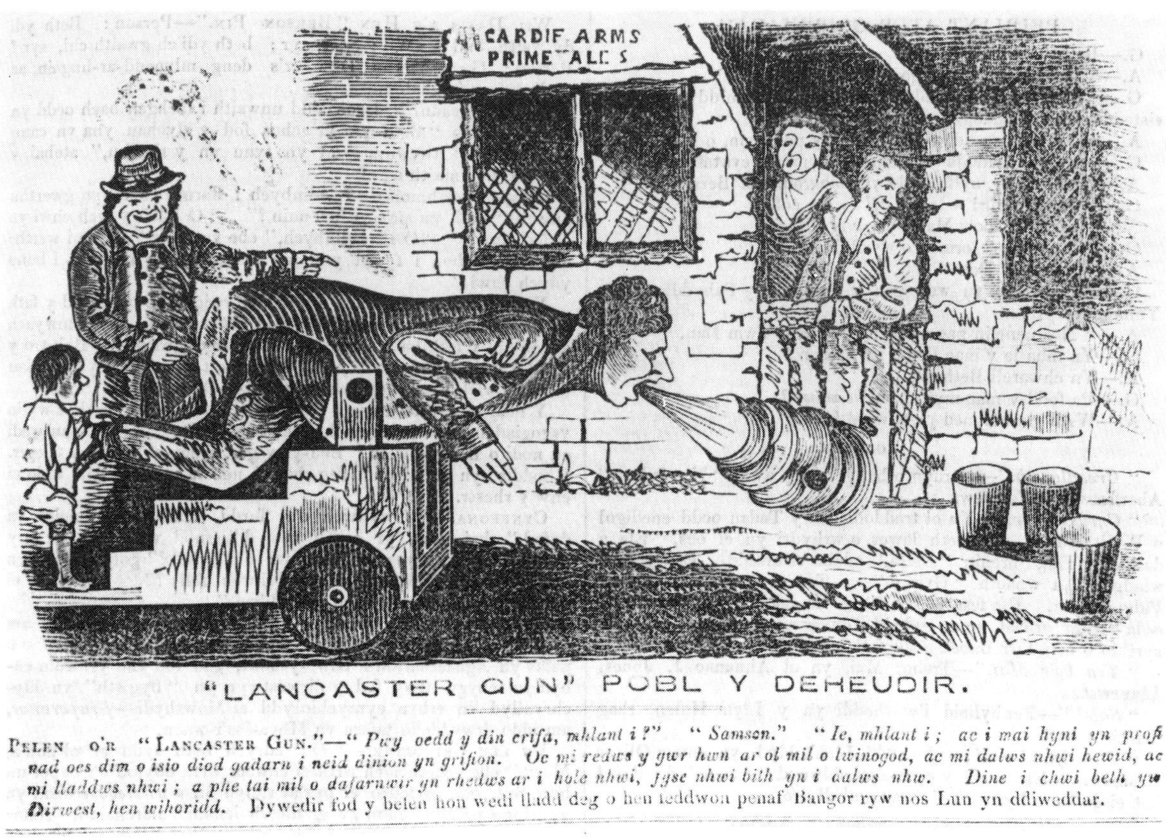

26 Ellis, Ellis Owen, *Pwnch Cymreig*, wood engraving, April 17 1858, p.5.

Born in Aber-erch, Caernarfonshire, and whilst an apprentice carpenter seems to have begun painting.**(1)** This may have been in connection with a sign writing or coach building business. It is reported that Sir Robert Williams Vaughan of Nannau saw Ellis's work and presented him with an introduction to Sir Martin Archer Shee (1769-1830).**(2)** In 1834, he met Shee and through him many important artists.

All the evidence available about Ellis suggests that his subject matter was wholly Welsh. There is little definite evidence concerning his whereabouts after 1834, but two references suggest that he spent some time in Liverpool.**(3)**

His biography is given in the *Pwnch Cymraeg*.**(4)**

Most important are his consistent innovations. In c1844 he drew seven illustrations of a Welsh ballad *Betty of Llansaintffraid. Drawn by Ellis Bryncoch, Pwllheli, Caernarvonshire*, and *Life and Times of Richard Robert Jones* (Dic Aberdaron). This was very much a Welsh *Odyssey*, including 'R.R. Jones shipwrecked' and 'Homer's Ghost appearing to Jones with the Geniuses of the Greek'. Of particular significance is the neo-classical Flaxmanesque style of outline drawing. In this way Ellis elevated Welsh subject matter to the value of the classics.

We also note that his historical works have the same tendency, titles such as *The Fall of Llywelyn the last Prince of Wales* and *Caradoc o flaen Claudius Caesar*.

In addition, he produced a series of exceptionally creative cartoons in *Y Pwnch Cymraeg*, between 1858-1860. These images do not derive from *Punch* illustrations but are a fresh treatment of Welsh matters in a style which varies from the near sublime to the grotesque. The 'cuts' are extremely bold and sure. They have the same earthy honesty of H. Hughes's satirical prints, combined with a coarser handling. His pastiche of the English *Punch* was a unique contribution in Wales at this period.

Ellis thought of himself as a serious artist. Perhaps this is particularly clear in his large group portrait *Oriel y Beirdd*. For instance, concerning the portrait of Gwallter Mechain he writes: 'I intend taking pains to execute the portrait in a style of masterly superiority.'**(5)**

Two other portraits that he painted were *Morris Hughes Llanrwst* and *Thomas Jones Chwilog*.**(6)**

Ellis was an artist who worked closely with literature, and many of his works were used to illustrate texts. Several of his pictures were portraits or studies of poets. A self portrait appeared in *Y Pwnch Cymraeg*.**(7)** This self portrait shows Ellis Bryncoch as a professional artist who had been trained in modern art theory. The pose is tense which suggests an artist ambitious for success.

The main collection of his work is at *NLW*. No extant portrait paintings are known and the *Oriel Y Beirdd* which was once kept at *RISW* may have been lost — possibly by war damage.**(8)**

1. The *DWB* gives a good succinct account of his life and work.
2. This statement appears to have only an oral tradition. I have examined the MSS of Shee at the *BL* and found no evidence to support this assertion. However, Vaughan did write a similar introductory letter at this period, for instance Vaughan to Sir Robert Peel, 21 December 1834, *BM*, Additional MSS 40407, f.36. Vaughan requests that a local young man be found a position.
3. *Y Pwnch Cymraeg*, 9 June 1860, Volume III, p.7, reports that Ellis was 23 while settled in Liverpool where he worked with Alexander Moses. *NLW*, 1889 E, Vol. II, letter 117, Ellis to Miss Davis, *NLW*, 1804, Vol. 1, letter 259, to Miss Davis, the latter giving 'No. 18 Phythain Street, Liverpool' is dated 1855. Certainly Ellis writes this letter stating that 'To you and my patron Mr Vaughan my greatest gratitude is particularly due'.
4. *Y Pwnch Cymraeg*, June 9, 1860, pp.6-7. This latter includes a self portrait wood engraving.
5. *NLW*, MS 1804, Vol. 1, letter 259, (1855). This portrait was offered to subscribers, *NLW*, 1889 E, Vol. 2, letter 117.
6. PB 2425, Ports A; *P* 9732, Ports A., both signed 'E.O. Ellis Portrait Painter'.

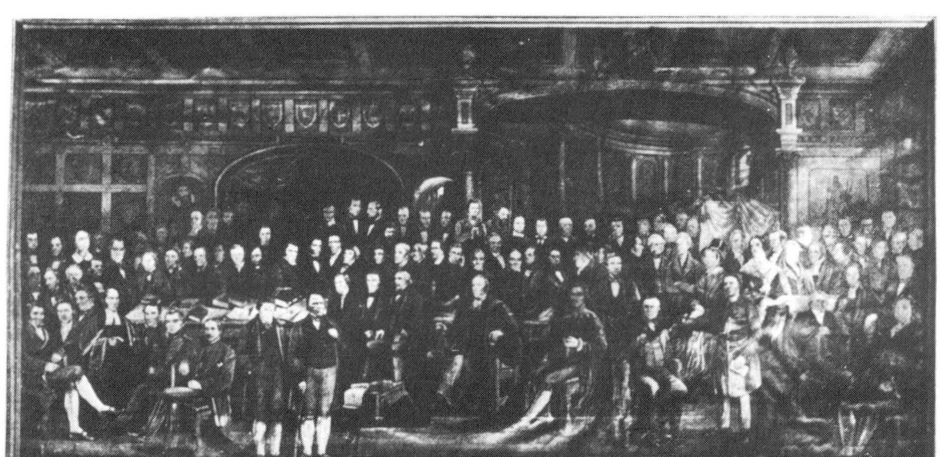

ORIEL Y BEIRDD

27 Ellis, Ellis Owen, *Oriel y Beirdd*, [oil on canvas], c1847, (illustrated in *Cymru* Volume 52, 1917).

7. *Y Pwnch Cymraeg*, 9 June 1860, p.6.
8. Oral tradition, recorded by the author at *RISW* in 1984-5. Miss Betty Nelmes informed me that she thought the painting had been kept in an outside store. This was destroyed in a bombing raid during the 1939-45 war.

ELLIS, Richard (fl 1835 - fl 1843)
Surveyor — Pwllheli

Davies Atlas, Eden I p.96..

ELLIS, Robert Lloyd (fl 1840 - fl 1850)
Architect — Caernarfon, Twt Hill
Surveyor — Bangor, Newborough Street

Slater's, 1844, p.16.
Slater's, 1850, p.20.
Davies Atlas.
Not in *Girouard, Eden* I p.96..

ELLIS, Thomas (fl 1822)
Drawing master? — Haverfordwest

Print published after Ellis by his son. This shows considerable skill in architectural drawing.**(1)**

1. *NLW*, Top B12/3 (B63) PE 367, coloured lithograph:

   'High Street, Haverfordwest in 1822, from a drawing by the late Thomas Ellis published for his son Mr Thomas Ellis of 4 Dew Street, Haverfordwest, June 1886.' [Lithographed in London, which may account for such a good image.]

ESSERY, Timothy Brumble (1792 - 1871)
House, sign and portrait painter — Swansea, Strand

The son of William Essery, who retired in 1813 leaving T.B. Essery to continue the business. T.B. extended the painting and glazing business of his father and included sign painting. In his advertisement he added 'N.B. PORTRAITS TAKEN at a moderate charge'.**(1)** He remained in Swansea.**(2)**

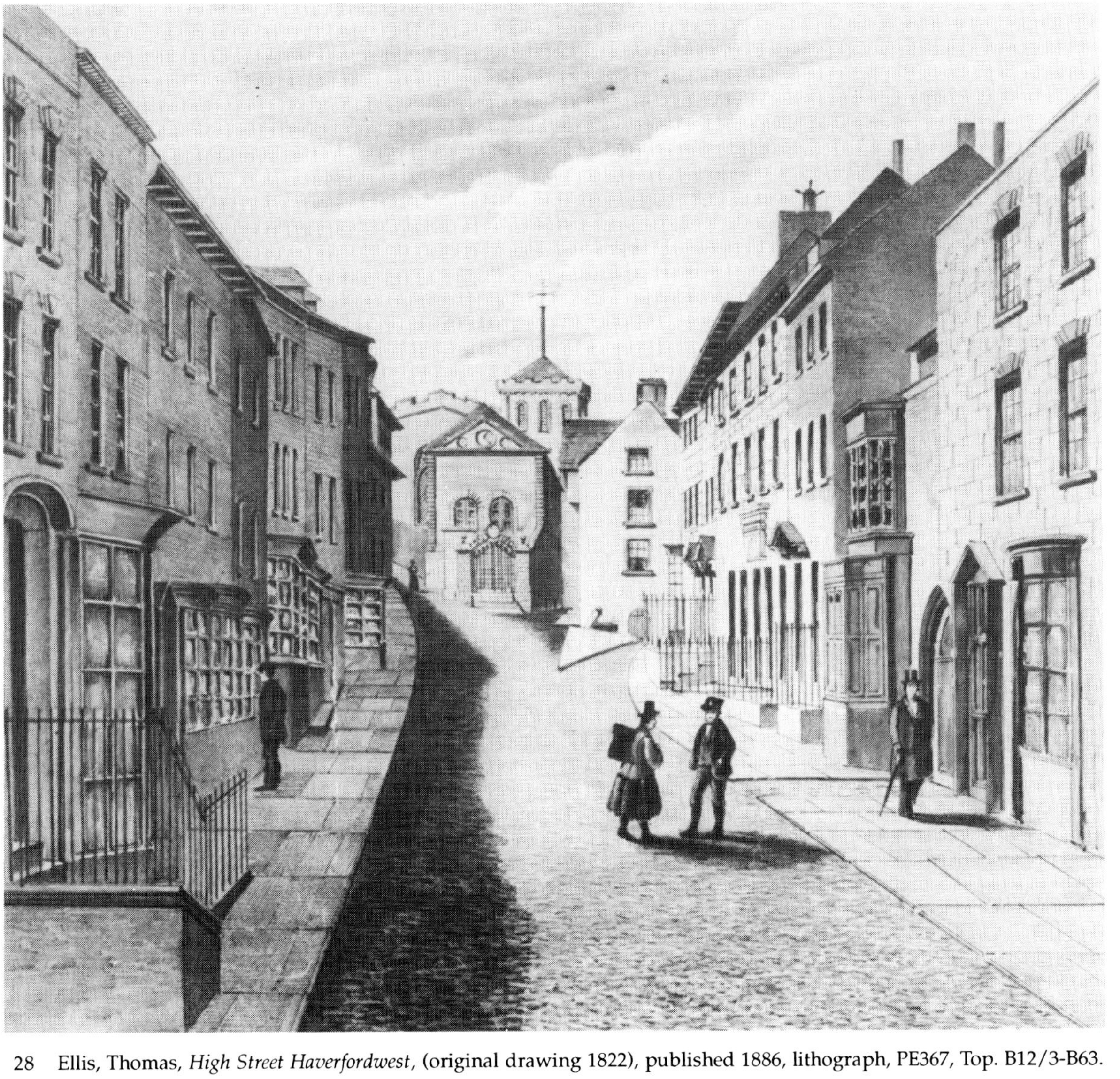

28 Ellis, Thomas, *High Street Haverfordwest*, (original drawing 1822), published 1886, lithograph, PE367, Top. B12/3-B63.

1. *Cambrian*, 13 September 1813, p.3.
2. Glamorgan Archive Service has a lease to T.B. Essery dated 12 January 1830, CL/BRA 190/148. Dates of the artist's life provided by the West Glamorgan Record Office. *SD* 1843/173 notes the will of Sarah Essery a Victualler at Swansea, possibly his mother.

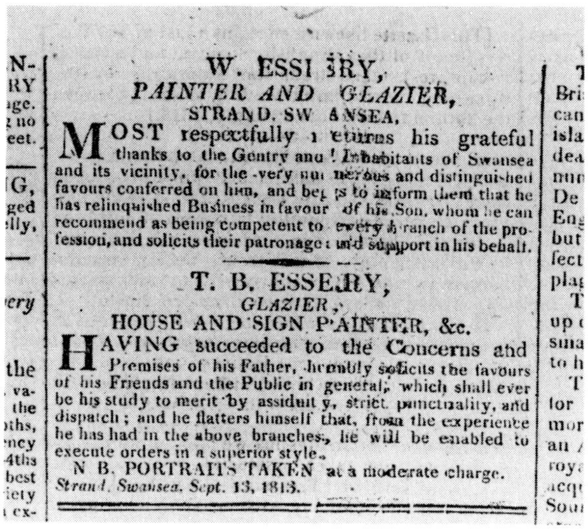

W. ESSERY,
PAINTER AND GLAZIER,
STRAND, SWANSEA.

MOST respectfully returns his grateful thanks to the Gentry and Inhabitants of Swansea and its vicinity, for the very numerous and distinguished favours conferred on him, and begs to inform them that he has relinquished Business in favour of his Son, whom he can recommend as being competent to every branch of the profession, and solicits their patronage and support in his behalf.

T. B. ESSERY,
GLAZIER,
HOUSE AND SIGN PAINTER, &c.

HAVING succeeded to the Concerns and Premises of his Father, humbly solicits the favours of his Friends and the Public in general, which shall ever be his study to merit by assiduity, strict punctuality, and dispatch; and he flatters himself that, from the experience he has had in the above branches, he will be enabled to execute orders in a superior style.

N. B. PORTRAITS TAKEN at a moderate charge.

Strand, Swansea, Sept. 13, 1813.

29 Essery , William & T. B. advertisement in *Cambrian*, 13 September 1813, p.3.

ESSERY, William (1766 - 1820)
House painter — Swansea
China painter?

He was the father of T.B. Essery, and appears to have retired in 1813.**(1)** *Nance* records Essery's name on a china bowl.**(2)** His obituary notice appeared in the *Cambrian*, 5 February 1820, p.3: 'House Painter, Master of Indefatigable Lodge of Free Masons'.**(3)**

1. *Cambrian*, 13 September 1813, p.3.
2. *Nance*, p.49: 'W. Essery' inscribed on a bowl dated 1806.
3. West Glamorgan Record Office, *St Mary's Burials*, p.296, records, 'William Essery of this town who died January 28th 1820'.

EVAN, John (1818)
Mason — Kidwelly

SD/1818/50.

EVANS (fl 1774)
Game painter — 'South Wales'

Exhibited at the Free Society of Artists in 1774, *A landscape, with dead game*.**(1)**

1. *Graves, F.S.*, p.89.

EVANS, Mrs (fl 1838)
Drawing mistress — Bridgend

'Professor of French and Italian...will receive a few young ladies to board and instruct at her residence in Bridgend...and instruct in English, French, Italian, Music, Drawing, Dancing, Geography, Writing and Arithmetic.'**(1)**

1. *Cambrian*, 7 July 1838, p.1.

EVANS, Daniel (1786 - 1852)
Architect — Cardigan
Bridge End
Fishguard**(1)**

Evans was the son & successor of David Evans. *Colvin* p.356 main source of information. He enlarged Llanrhian Church, 1835-6, rebuilt Cilgerran Church 1836-7, both in Georgian Gothick. Bethania Baptist Church at William Street, Cardigan, 1845-6 remains his most celebrated building, designed with an imposing Greek Doric porch.

At his death he was working as a landlord of the Castle Inn, Bridgend, Cardigan & an architect.

1. *TL* suggests that he also worked at Fishguard. Not in *Girouard. Hunt*, 1850, p.4.

EVANS, David (fl 1810 - 1840)
Architect — Cardigan
Muldan Street**(1)**
Fishguard

An architect and builder, born at Eglwyswrw. His first recorded work is Union Terrace, Carmarthen, 1810 & he also undertook buildings at St Dogmaels - 1830.**(2)**.

1. *SD*/1837/211. Not in *Girouard, Colvin* p.356.
2. *TL* MSS notes, quote the *Carmarthen Journal* 2 June 1810?, p.3 'the ingenious architect David Evans'.

EVANS, David (fl c1815 - 1851)
China painter — Swansea

'Rather famous locally as a flower painter, and also as a fruit painter.'**(1)**

1. *Nance*, pp.293-299, discusses Evans's work in some detail. *Bell* p.112 illustrates a *Pastille-Burner* by Evans at *GVS*.

EVANS, David (- 1856)
Mason — Llanfihangel-ar-Arth
Bwlch y clawdd?
Carmarthenshire

SD/1856/3.**(1)**

1. Described as a 'widower'.

EVANS, David (fl 1846 - fl 1858)**(1)**
Portrait painter — Newport
Photographer — Llandeilo

Evans had a practice in Commercial Street, Newport**(2)** and he visited Llandeilo in 1846.**(3)**

1. *Slater's*, 1858, gives us 'Photographic Artist & Portrait Painter', Commercial Road, possibly still working in Newport in 1871, *POL*, 1871, as David Brotherton Evans.
2. *Hunt*, 1849, p.115: 'Evans, David Portrait Painter 57 Commercial St'; *Slater's*, 1850, p.18.
3. Jenkins, D.C., *Diary of T. Jenkins*, (Bala, 1976), frontispiece illustrates a portrait of Thomas Jenkins by Evans signed and dated 'August 17th 1846'. This is the only known example of work by the artist. *PL* notes that there is a self portrait extant of a David Evans, this might be the same man.

EVANS, E. (fl c.1800?)
Engraver [Denbighshire]

A bookplate is included in Sir E.D. Jones Collection, p.110.**(1)**

1. *WBP*, Vol. II. (See illustration, *WBP*, p.110. Unknown to Fincham, H.W., *The Artists and Engravers of British American Book Plates*, (London, 1897).

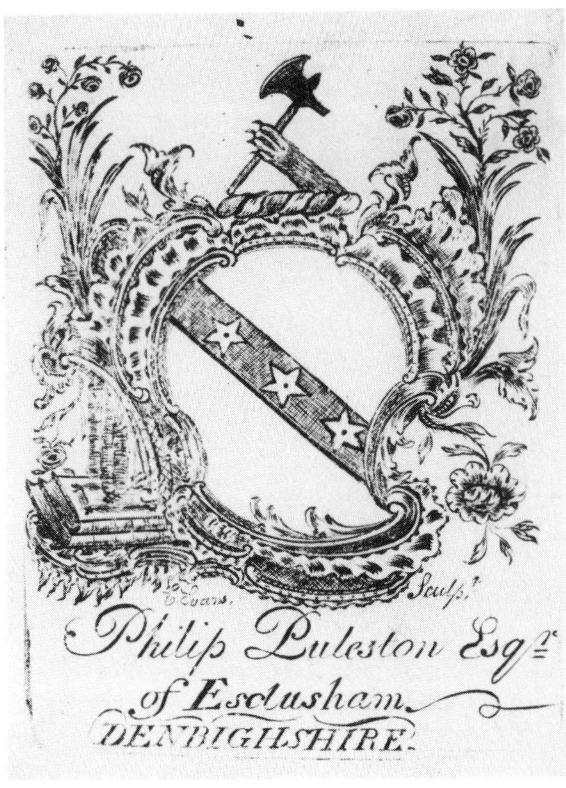

30 Evans, E., *Philip Puleston, Welsh Book Plates*, c1800, Volume II p.110.

EVANS, Evan (fl ? 1790s)
Earthen-ware painter Swansea

Worked at the Cambrian Pottery.**(1)** Reported by Turner as 'an inferior painter'.**(2)**

1. *Nance*, p.38ff.
2. *Ibid.*, p.295.

EVANS, Griffith
Stonecutter/[mason] Cilgerran

SD/1851/138 (I).**(1)**

1. The inventory included 'Household goods, furniture & working tools'.

EVANS, H[ugh] fl [1806 - fl 1830)
Land surveyor Holyhead

He produced a sketch of Holyhead Island including ship portraits of 18 wrecks, foundered 'within the last twelve months'.**(1)**

Evans was the Harbourmaster at Holyhead which accounts for his interest in the safety of shipping.**(2)**

1. *NLW* signed & dated November 1807. 58.5x86cm. watercolour, annotated plan, PB 7433 (BRN 12595). I would like to thank my colleague Dr Mark Rowlands for bringing this plan to my attention.
2. *Eden* I p.98, notes this status in 1830.

EVANS, John (1723 - 1795)
Cartographic draughtsman Llwyn-y-groes
Landscape artist Caernarfonshire

John Evans was 'a classical example of the gentleman amateur cartographer'.**(1)** In 1794 he published a print after his own drawing of Pistyll Rhaiadr, Denbighshire,**(2)** an excellent treatment of this waterfall.

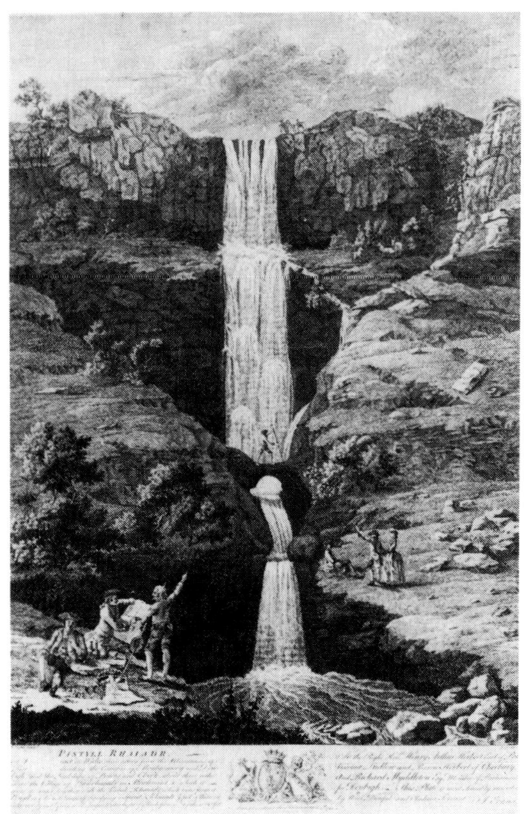

31 Evans, John, *Pistyll Rhaiadr*, engraving 1794, PB3066, Top D6.

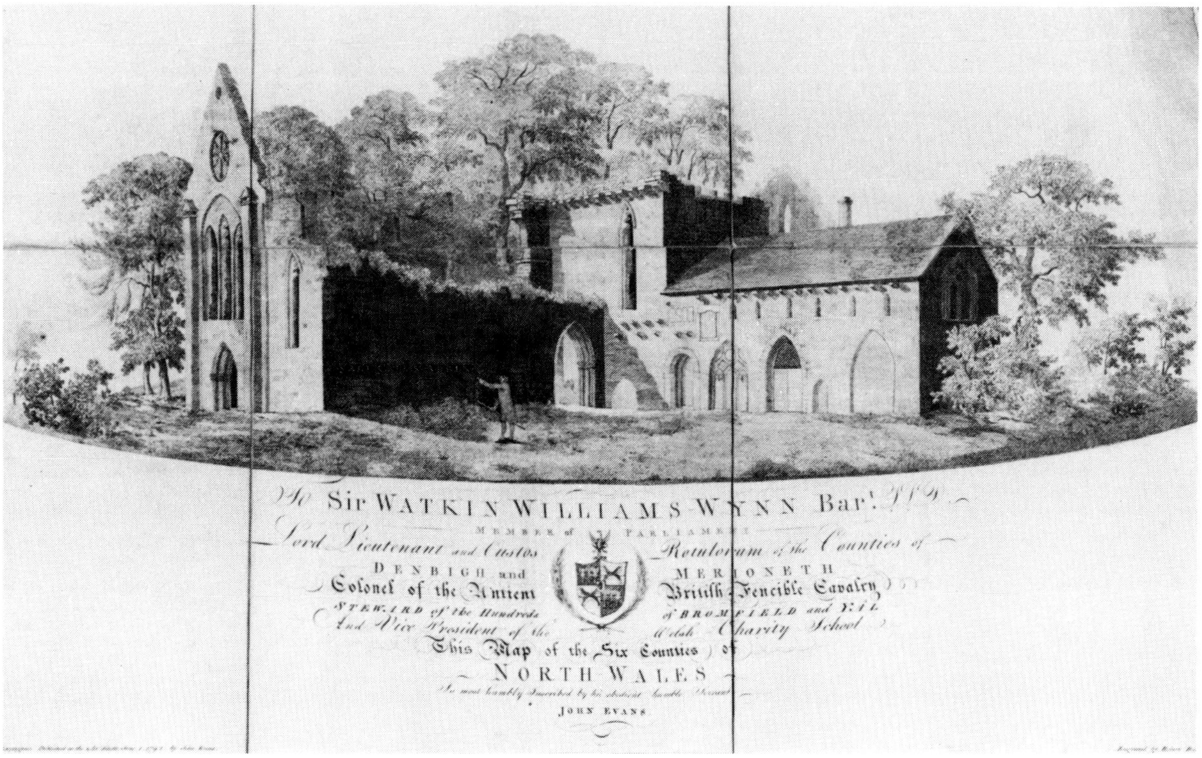

32 Evans, John, & Baugh, Robert, *Valle Crucis Abbey*, engraving, 1795, P6204.

He published a collection of maps of North Wales in 1795 which display a sophisticated use of topographical prints.**(3)**

1. *Roberts, I & M,* pp.18-23. The authors discuss several John Evanses and provide details for each.
2. *NLW,* PB 3066, D6 - D10, *Pistyll Rhaiadr,* J. Evans 'Pinxit' 'T. Green Sculp', 'Published according to Act of Parliament April 27th 1794', 55 x 37 cm.
3. *A Map of North Wales,* 1795 (large folio), contains a view of Valle Crucis Abbey, an elaborate but crude engraving of an eagle and a topographical print. *Roberts, I & M.,* p.22, discusses this work. *Vide* Robert Baugh, *supra* for details of his career and connection with Evans.

EVANS, John (fl 1806 - fl 1851)
Architect — Carmarthen
Surveyor — Cardigan

Evans was a sort of itinerant surveyor who worked for a while in one town then moved on.**(1)** He appears to have worked in Swansea, 1813 and may have moved from Carmarthen**(2)** up to Cardigan by 1830.**(3)**

1. *Eden Supplement* p.409 notes him working on inclosures, roads and estates.
2. *Pigot's,* 1822, p.738, 'Chapel Street'.
3. *Pigot's,* 1830, p.828, 'Mwldan'.

EVANS, John (fl 1810 - fl 1853)
Land surveyor — Rhuddlan**(1)**

He probably lived in Flintshire from c1810.**(2)**

1. *SA* 1853/206. Not in *Eden.*
2. *Roberts, I & M,* p.23, notes that he was working in 1810. It also notes that he was still living in 1851.

EVANS, John (fl 1824 - fl 1844)
Engraver and draughtsman — Penygraig
Aberystwyth
Rhuddlan
High Street

Evans lived at Penygraig which was described as a 'gentleman's house'.**(1)** He engraved a 'new map of Aberystwyth', signed and dated John Evans, Penygraig, and shows his own house. He probably moved to North Wales where he is described as an engraver.**(2)**

1. Prichard, T.J.LL., *New Aberystwyth Guide* (Aberystwyth, 1824). See Evans, John, *supra.*
2. *Pigot's,* 1844, p.54. It is possible that the North Walian Evans is a different artisan.

EVANS, Simeon (fl 1844)
Portrait painter — Newport
Stow Hill

Pigot's, 1844, p.14.

EVANS, Thomas (1790 - 1836)
[Sign] painter — Swansea

'of this town Painter who died December 27 1836'.**(1)** May have been a local sign and house painter.

1. West Glamorgan Record Office, *St Mary's Burials,* p.296.

EVANS, William Downing (fl c1800 - fl 1820?)
Portrait painter

He painted a portrait of Carnhuanawc.**(1)**

1. *PL* kindly gave me this reference, *NLW* 12353D, p.352.

EVINS Joseph Hancock (fl 1849 - fl 1854)
Architect — Merthyr
Surveyor — New Road**(1)**

Designed & built the rectory at Llanfoist, Monmouthshire.**(2)**

1. *Hunt*, 1849, p.60. Not in *Girouard*.
2. *NLW* Llandaf Bounty Plan 50, 1854 signed as 'architect'.

EVINS, Roger H. (fl 1843 - fl 1845)
Surveyor — Abergavenny

He re-designed the vicarage at Raglan & was possibly a brother to J. H. Evins or the same man**(1)**

1. *NLW* Llandaff Bounty Plans 105, 1843 plan signed R. H. Evins & Bounty Plans 76, 1845. *Llanvetherin Rectory*. Not in *Eden*.

F

FAIRCHILD, Adolphius (fl 1831)
Surveyor — Abergavenny

Designed & Built the rectory at Llanvapley, Monmouthshire - 1831**(1)**

1. *NLW* Llandaff, Bounty Plans 75, 1831.
Not in *Eden*.

FAIRCLOUGH, Henry J[ohn] (fl 1849)
Architect — St Asaph

Designed & Built the vicarage at Abergele, 1849.**(1)**

1. *NLW* St Asaph, Bounty Plans 1, 1849, very much surveyor's drawings for the vicarage.
Not in *Eden, Girouard*.

FENTON, [John] (fl 1800 - fl 1821)
Landscape draughtsman — [Fishguard] Pembrokeshire

He was the son-in-law of William Owen Pughe and executed two original drawings which were engraved by Hugh Hughes.**(1)**

Fenton was probably a relation of Richard Fenton (1746-1821) who lived at Fishguard, worked as a lawyer, and was a scholar and topographical author.**(2)** Richard Fenton produced an important text in 1811, *A Historical Tour through Pembrokeshire*.**(3)** Several drawings by J. Fenton were engraved for this work.**(4)** He executed simple antiquarian landscapes.**(5)**

1. *PL*.
2. *BBA.SD* 1821/56
3. Fenton, Richard, *A Historical Tour through Pembrokeshire* (2 vols) (London, 1811). The volumes were dedicated to Sir Richard Colt Hoare (1758-1838). *NLW*, XDA 1360, F34 (4to) is a collection of notes on Fenton by Edward Laws.
4. *Op.cit.*, Fenton, Vol. I, facing p.15, *The Hoopoe* [bird] 'Drawn from Nature by J. Fenton'; Vol. II, *Tomb of Elidore de Stackpole in Cheriton Church*, facing p.423, dated 1809. Fenton also did a view of *The Town of Tenby*.
5. *NLW*, PB 9345, *Cych*; PB 9346, *Dale*, dated 1806, are two good examples of this style.

FENTON, Roger (1819-1869)
Photographer — Llangibby

Fenton was trained as a solicitor and practised in law 1852-54. From 1854-62 he worked as a professional photographer before returning to the law.**(1)** It was in this period 1854-62 that he settled for a time in Wales.

1. I thank my colleague Lyn L. Dafis for this information. Browne, Turner, & Partnow, Elaine, *Photographic Artists & Innovators* (London, 1983), p.191. He was probably staying at Llangibby.

FIDLER, J. (Junior) (fl 1776 - fl 1803)
Landscape painter — Monmouth

Fidler exhibited at the *RA* from a London address in 1796 and 1797, then moved to Monmouth and exhibited the following works:

1798	(492) *Rhayader swy* [*sic*] *on the Wye*.
	(523) *The new wire on the Wye* [New Weir].
1802	(668) *View of Bangor, North Wales*.
1803	(512) *The old Welsh Bridge, Shrewsbury*.

He may have been the son of J. Fidler.**(1)**

1. Fidler exhibited at the *RA* 1784-1787, and was an architect living at Mr Yenn's, Charlotte Street, Bedford Square, London.

FOORD, William (fl 1771)
Surveyor — Caldicot

Eden, I, p.104.

FORSTER, Thomas (fl 1842 - fl 1849)
Portrait and miniature painter — Swansea, Cardiff

Artist from London**(1)** who lodged at 'Mr Harris's Wind Street'. He was living at Cardiff in 1844.**(2)**

1. *Cambrian*, 28 May 1842, p.3.
2. *Pigot's*, 1849, p.20: 'Crockherb Town'.

FOULKES, Robert

Plasterer & stuccoman — (- 1780) — Llanbeblig, Caernarfon

B 1780/69: His will includes an interesting and detailed inventory of goods, most notably plasterers' tools.

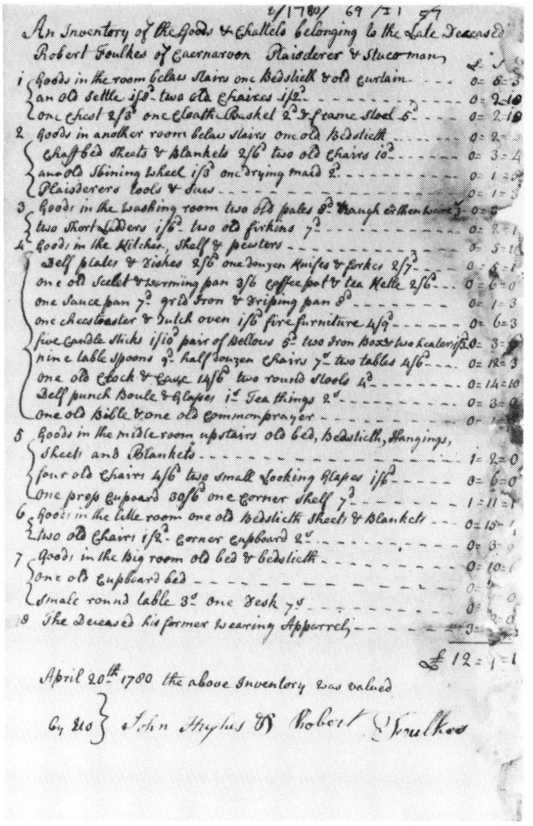

B/1780/ 69 /21 57

An Inventory of the Goods & Challels belonging to the Late Deceased Robert Foulkes of Caernarvon Plaisderer & Stucorman

		£ s d
1	Goods in the room below stairs one Bedstick & old curtain	0= 6=3
	an old settle 1/8 two old Chaires 1/2	0= 2=10
	one chest 2/3 one Cloath Basket 2d & frame stool 5	0= 2=10
2	Goods in another room below stairs one old Bedstick	0= 2=
	Chaff bed sheets & blankets 2/6 two old chairs 10d	0= 3=4
	an old Spining wheel 1/3 one drying maid 2d	0= 1=
	Plaisderers tools & ...	0= 1=
3	Goods in the washing room two old pales 8d rough earthenware	0=
	two short ladders 1/6 two old firkins 7d	0=
4	Goods in the Kitchen, shelf & pewters	0= 5=
	a delf plates & dishes 2/6 one dozen knifes & forkes 2/7	0=
	one old skelet & warming pan 3/6 coffee pot & tea kettle 2/6	0= 6=0
	one sauce pan 7d grid iron & driping pan 8d	0= 1=3
	one cheestoaster & dutch oven 1/6 fire furniture 4/9	0= 6=3
	five candle sticks 1/10 pair of Bellows 5d two iron Boxes two heaters 1/2	0= 3=
	nine table spoons 9d half dozen chairs 7/- two tables 4/6	0= 12=3
	one old Clock & case 14/6 two round stools 4d	0= 14=10
	delf punch Boule & glasses 1/- Tea things 2d	0= 3=
	One old Bible & one old common prayer	0=
5	Goods in the midle room upstairs old bed, bedstick, hangings, sheets and Blankets	1= 2=0
	four old Chairs 4/6 two small looking glasses 1/6	0= 6=0
	One press cupboard 30/6 one corner shelf 7d	1=11=
6	Goods in the litle room one old bedstick sheets & blankets	0= 15=
	two old Chairs 1/2 corner cupboard 2d	0= 3=
7	Goods in the big room old bed & bedstick	0= 10=
	one old cupboard bed	0=
	smale round table 3d one desk 7d	0=
8	The deceased his former wearing Apparrel	0=
		£ 12= 1=1

April 20th 1780 the above Inventory was valued by us } John Hughes & Robert Foulkes

33 Foulkes, Robert, *Inventory of Robert Foulkes, Caernarvon 'Plaisterer & Stucoman'* [sic], 1780 **B** /1780 / 69.

FRANCIS, John Deffett(1)

Portrait and coach painter — (1815 - 1901) — Swansea

He 'painted designs on the panels' of coaches built at his father's yard. Later Francis joined 'The Dolly Club', met country gentry and painted portraits in Carmarthenshire and Glamorganshire. After some time in London he removed to Wales c1890.**(2)** His collections of art were important additions to *BM* & *GVS*.**(3)**

1. *DWB* notes that 'He devoted himself to painting, particularly portraits at an early age'.
2. *Cambrian*, 22 February 1901, p.4. Carmarthen Museum has a fine portrait of *Sarah Jones* (Aberystwyth/ Carmarthen Artists Exhibition 1995 No.8).
3. He donated his library, prints & pictures to Swansea. As a collector, Francis was both influential & far sighted.

See Colour Illustration IV.

FURNIVAL, Edward

Surveyor — (fl 1835 - fl 1843) — Canal Cottage, Llanymynech, Salop**(1)**

This may be the same man as mentioned by Hugh Hughes in 1820.**(2)**

1. *Davies Atlas. NLW*, Estate map Llanymynech, dated 1837 (Powis Castle Collection, M51). *Eden* I p.108.
2. *PL.*

G

GABB, Robert

Architect, Surveyor — (fl 1824 - fl 1849) — Abergavenny, Merthyr, New Road

He surveyed several tithe maps in the Breconshire area.**(1)** He appears to have moved to Merthyr after some time at Abergavenny.**(2)**

1. *Davies Atlas. Eden*, II, p.109, records him as an estate surveyor or tithe, coal and tramway surveyor. *Hilling*, p.164, gives 'William Gabe'. Not in *Girouard.*
2. *Hunt*, 1849, p.60.

GABE, William

Architect — (c19th century) — Merthyr Tydfil

He built a number of chapels in Merthyr.**(1)**

1. *PP*, p.164. Not in *Girouard.*

GARNAUT, Mr

Portrait painter, Drawing master — (fl 1824) — Swansea, Wind Street

Garnaut worked from a studio in Wind Street, Swansea and advertised that he 'will paint portraits, for which he has never charged less than three guineas, for the reduced price of One Pound Ten Shillings.'**(1)**

There is a portrait of *Rev. Joseph Harris* at the Baptist College, Cardiff.**(2)**

1. *Cambrian*, 25 September 1824, p.2. At Mr Young's, Saddler, No 55 Wind Street, Swansea.
2. *Rees MS* (*NMW*, annotated copy) which also describes Garnaut as 'a refugee who supported himself by teaching language and drawing'.

GARVIN, Henry

Portrait and miniature artist — (fl 1848 - fl 1850) — Swansea, 48 Lower Oxford Street

Hunt, 1848; 1849, p.153; 1850, p.132.

GEORGE, David

Mason — (- 1844) — Llangattock

BR/1844/51.

GEORGE, Richard (- 1823)
Mason
Bayvil
Penygwndwn
Pembrokeshire

SD/1823/5.**(1)**

1. Also described as a 'farmer'.

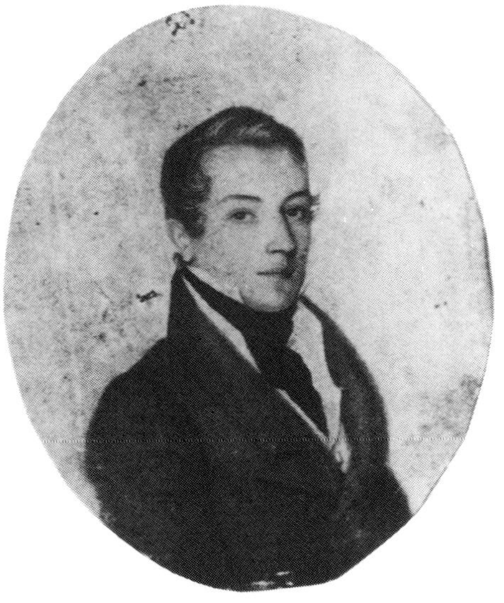

34 George, Thomas, *Self Portrait*, watercolour, c1824, *WPA*.

GEORGE, Thomas (1790 - c1840)
Miniature artist
Fishguard
Haverfordwest

Born at Fishguard and worked in the area until c1824. Some of his works, executed at this time, are still preserved in Pembrokeshire.**(1)** One work was inscribed 'Haverfordwest'**(2)** which suggests that he travelled in the district as commissions required.

He was working in London by 1826 and exhibited at the *RA* & *BI* for 1829-1838.**(3)** He died in Madeira.**(4)**

1. Vaughan, Herbert M., 'The Lost Works of a Welsh Painter', *Western Mail*, 21 September 1927, p.11. Vaughan mentions that 'whilst still in his teens' George painted miniatures, including three at Tregwynt, near Fishguard, for the Harris family. Also *Western Mail*, 22 September 1927: 'A Welsh Painter, The Works of Thomas George of Fishguard' (letter from Isaac J. Williams, Department of Art, *NMW*, Cardiff, p.8); 24 September: [Picture] *Portrait of a Gentleman* by T. George - *NMW*, b1790-1840. It was thought none of his paintings existed.
2. *NMW* has a miniature signed on the *verso* 'T. George fecit / H. West October 1824' watercolour, 30.5x25cm. *WPA* records 4 miniatures at Scolton Manor Museum, all c1824.
3. *Foskett*, Volume I, p.286.
4. *Ibid.*, p.286.

GISBOURNE, Edward Sacheverell (fl 1835 - fl 1848)
Surveyor
Bettws Newydd
Brecon

He worked on tithes and moved to Nottingham c1848**(1)**

1. *Davies Atlas. Eden* II p.113.

GOODE, George (fl 1835 - fl 1846)
Surveyor
Croft Cottage
Carmarthen

Davies Atlas. Eden, II, p.114.

GOODE, Harry Phelps (fl 1820 - fl 1873)
Lithographer and surveyor
Haverfordwest
High Street

He produced some competent and colourful surveys in Pembrokeshire**(1)** but had debt problems by 1842.**(2)** It is interesting to note that he surveyed a large number of tithe districts (about 80), and moved to St Martin's Place and then to St Mary's in the 1840s.**(3)** He remained in Haverfordwest until 1873.**(4)**

1. Haverfordwest Record Office, D/RTM/12/51, *Map of Porthyddy Llanrhian* [*sic*], July 1820; D/RTP/TRT/143, survey of the Trefguarne Estate (n.d.). *NLW*, Maps of Llanboidy, 1820; Haverfordwest, 1832; Slebech, 1829; Llanycefn, 1850.
2. Haverfordwest Record Office, D/CT/31.
3. *Davies Atlas. Eden*, II, p.114, notes he was in business with G. Goode, *supra*.
4. He appears in *Hunt*, 1850, p.48, as a lithographer. Other documents at Haverfordwest provide information on his career after 1850.
   There was also a James Goode (fl 1798 - fl 1820), many examples in *NLW* but no residence given.

GOODE, William (fl 1816 - fl 1843)
Surveyor
Llangadog

Davies Atlas. Eden, II, p.115. *NLW* has surveys dating from 1816-1832, all in the Llangadog area.

GRAY, E.A. (fl 1820s - fl 1840s)
Drawing master
Teacher of oil painting
Carmarthen
Pembroke Road

Gray was described as 'from London'**(1)** and also offered writing classes. He was a pupil of E.P. Carmical. Probably at Carmarthen from December 1828 - January 1829.**(2)**

1. *POL*, 1828, has no reference to Gray.
2. *Carmarthen Journal*, 1828, December 19, p.1.
   Ibid., 1829, January 9, p.1.
   Robson's, 1840, p.29, gives his address as 'Pembroke Road'.

GREGORY, Edward (1831 - 1851)
Artist
Swansea
Worcester Place

Born in Swansea, he is recorded as working there in 1851.**(1)**

1. Census 1851, HO/107/1426/455, Swansea District 8, p.37.

GREIVES, Jonathan (fl 1835 - fl 1844)
Drawing master
Tenby
The Green

Pigot's, 1835, p.796; 1844, p.83, notes address at The Green.
Robson's, 1840, p.29, gives his address as 'Pembroke Road'.

GRENVILLE, Lady Charlotte Neville (1734 - 1832)**(1)**
Landscape artist — Hawarden, Flintshire

An amateur artist who drew a landscape at Hawarden in 1832.**(2)**

1. *Steegman*, Volume I, p.135, notes her as Lady Williams-Wyn.
2. *NLW*, PB 6780, Top.B 7/1 B41, *Hawarden Rectory, Flintshire, 1832*, lithograph printed by W. Crow (Chester). This building is now the Record Office.

GRIFFITH, David (fl 1842)
Mason — Llan-non, Cardiganshire

SD/1842/135.

GRIFFITH, David (- 1857)
Mason — Pembroke, Primrose Cottage

SD/1857/17.

GRIFFITH, Hugh (fl? 1776)**(1)**
Surveyor — Brynodol, Caernarfonshire

1. *NLW*, Estate map Llanbeblig, pre-1776. *Eden* II p.119.

GRIFFITH, Moses (1747 - 1819)
Landscape and portrait artist — Whitford
Miniature painter — Flintshire
Engraver

He was described by Thomas Pennant as 'that treasure... He early took to the use of the pencil and during his long service with me, has distinguished himself as a good and faithful servant, and able artist.'**(1)** Griffith was one of several artists employed by Pennant but unique because he continued to work for the family until he died.**(2)** He was kept as a family servant and was hired to other antiquarians when required.**(3)** The patronage of Griffith reflected the foresight of Pennant and the quality of Griffith's art.**(4)**

Griffith was a fine miniature painter, producing copies and original designs.**(5)** These miniatures display the assured vision of a competent and experienced artist.**(6)**

His topographical work was precise and pleasing, somewhat in the style of S.H. Grimm (1733-1794). He was a natural colourist and his later colour sketches are freer and more expressive**(7)** than those works specifically commissioned by Pennant.

In 1809 Griffith defended himself against criticism of his accuracy in copying and drawing. Griffith's reply was to: 'promise to execute with all the fidelity and accuracy that care, honest intentions, and proportional compasses can effect'.**(8)** Griffith's work was popular with his contemporaries and evidence suggests that he had a fairly extensive private practice by 1796.**(9)**

He is buried at Whitford; the church has a memorial to him erected in 1990.**(10)**

1. Pennant, Thomas, *Literary Life* (London, 1793) p.10.
2. Moore, Donald, *Moses Griffith* (Cardiff, 1979), provides a useful synopsis of his life and work. Mr R.P. Evans has informed me that his research has covered Pennant and Griffith and should provide much more discussion on this artist.

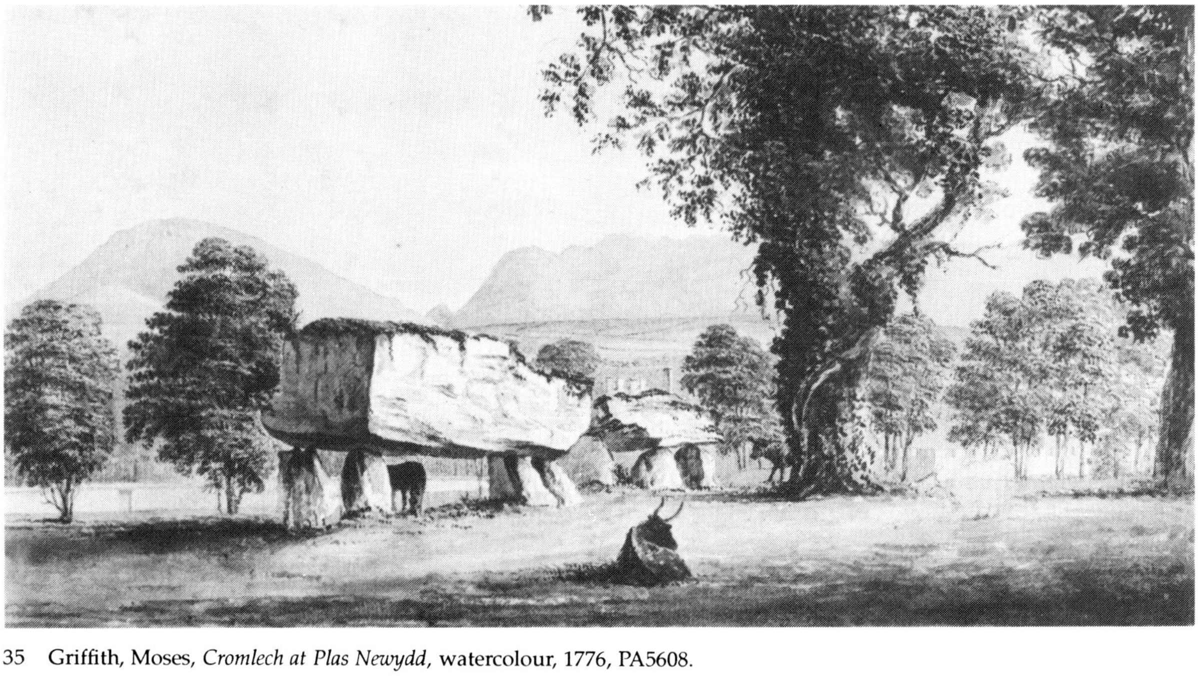

35 Griffith, Moses, *Cromlech at Plas Newydd*, watercolour, 1776, PA5608.

3. *Vide NLW,* MS 5500C, Letters of Thomas Pennant to Richard Bull, letter 6, dated 16 May 1780: 'I would chearfully [*sic*] permit Moses to copy for you; but I give you my word his time is... fully taken up.' Letter 24, dated 20 September 1782, describes charges by Moses to Bull.
4. *Ibid.*, letter 116, 24 June 1794: 'I do believe that Moses has out done any single artist in the Quadruped pair [*sic*] and Arctic Zoology.'
5. Pennant, Thomas, *Tour in Wales, NLW,* various editions, 8 volumes (London).
6. For instance, *NLW,* PA9333, *Rev. R. Williams,* oval miniature, 9.5 cm; *vide PA* 9330, oval miniature, 9.7 cm, of W. Edwards.
7. *NLW,* Drawing Volumes 38, for instance *Beddgelert,* watercolour, c1812, is a free treatment of the landscape. Many of Griffith's original drawings were published by Pennant; good examples of these would be: P3693, A3/1 - A136, *Caernarvon Castle,* c1780 and PZ 3237, A3/2 - A251, *Part of the Interior of Conwy Castle,* 1810.
8. *Gentleman's Magazine,* December 1809, Volume 79, pp.1112-1113, letter to Urban from Moses Griffith, dated 9 December 1809.
9. *NLW,* price-list of Moses Griffith's work (illustrated by Moore, *op.cit.*, p.15) mentions that he worked 'at his leisure hours' for the general public. *NLW,* MS 5500C letter 127, dated 12 May 1796, Pennant described that 'Moses has for a good while past been taken up with miniatures'.
10. 'Cofio Moses Griffith', *Y Glannau* 87, November 1990, p.1.

See front cover.

GRIFFITH, Moses Junior (fl 1782 - 1850s)
Landscape artist — Whitford

Son of Moses Griffith, *supra,* 'he inherited his father's talents.'**(1)**
He worked on Pennant's *Outlines of the Globe.* His style is superficially very similar to his father's, except that he tended to generalise & stylise landscape.**(2)**

1. *RCAM (TP).*
2. *NLW* MS 23412E *Outlines of the Globe: The View of Hindoostan,* 1798 folio 1, contains a watercolour signed & dated 'M. Griffith Junr' *Palace of the Rajah of Tassisudon* 8.5x14cm; MS 23413E folio 281b contains a watercolour *Aryut at Plough,* 1798, 26.7x34.7cm.

GRIFFITH, W[illiam] (fl c1740)
Surveyor — Llandysilio, Denbighshire

There is a fine *Plan of Llandysilio* by Griffith which includes a cartouche view of Llandysilio Hall & an inset lanscape in pen & ink of Valle Crucis, Dinas Brân & Llangollen.**(1)**

1. *NLW,* Harrison & Sons Collections 76. Pen & ink on parchment 61.5 x 70.5cm, signed W. Griffith.

GRIFFITH, William (fl 1844 - fl 1849)
Portrait painter — Caernarfon, Pool Street

Slater's, 1844, p.18; 1849, p.20.
Slater's, 1850, p.20.

GRIFFITHS, Mr (fl 1813)
Sign painter — Llansilin, Denbighshire

Painting of the *Lord's Prayer* at Llansilin Church.**(1)**

1. *By Gones,* 30 Jan. 1884, p.19, cost '£.3.3.0'.

GRIFFITHS, Evan (1824 - 99)
Architect — Aberdare?

From c1840-1870 he built chapels in the Aberdare District.**(1)**

1. *Hilling,* p.164. *Girouard,* p.381.

GRIFFITHS, Evan Jones (fl 1835 - fl 1843)
Surveyor — Llandeilo

Davies Atlas. Eden, II, p.119, notes that he worked in Breconshire, Carmarthenshire and Radnorshire.

GRIFFITHS, Lewis (fl 1835 - fl 1843)
Surveyor — Ynysgedwyn, Breconshire

Davies Atlas. Eden, II, p.119, records him as also an estate surveyor.

GRIFFITHS, Lewis Jones (fl 1835 - fl 1843)
Surveyor — Ynysgedwyn, Breconshire

Davies Atlas. Eden, II, p.119, son of L. Griffiths, *infra.*

GRIFFITHS, R. (fl 1851)
Genre painter — Caernarfon

He appears to have been a genre artist, probably living in Caernarfon.**(1)**

1. Print of *Welsh Fashions taken on a market-day in Wales 1851,* PB 8416, Welsh Costume, Ports B: 'Drawn by R. Griffiths Caernarvon', coloured lithograph, lively sense of design, well rounded forms, 26.8 x 37.5 cm. Illustrations in *Lord, Barn,* p.39. *PL* has informed the author that he considers R. Griffiths to be the same artist as the 'Welsh Primitive'. The present author does not agree, mainly on stylistic grounds. Griffith's forms appear to be considerably rounder and cruder than the 'Welsh Primitive'.

GRIFFITHS, Thomas (- 1850)
Stone cutter/mason — Llanelli, Erw Wastod

SD/1850/183.

GRIFFITHS, Thomas (- 1834)
Mason — Swansea

SD/1834/343.

GRIFFITHS, William (fl 1857)
Mason — Boughrood, New House, Radnorshire

BR/1857/5.

GRIFFITHS, William (fl. 1827 - 29)
Surveyor — Cardiff

Worked on Gelligaer vicarage 1827**(1)** & St Andrews Major 1828**(2)**

1. *NLW*, Llandaff Bounty Plan 24, 1827.
2. *NLW*, Llandaff Bounty Plan 107, 1828. Also *NLW* Llandaff Bounty Plan 115, 1829 *St Nicholas rectory*, Glamorganshire. Not in *Eden*.

GROVE, J. (fl. c1830)
Lithographer — Swansea

He lithographed a drawing by William Watkeys.**(1)**

1. *vide* Watkeys, William, information *TL*.

GROVES, Henry (- 1851)
Stone mason — Pembroke, Pembroke Dock

SD/1851/182.

GUMMOW, Benjamin (c1766 - 1844)
Architect — Wrexham? Ruabon

He was probably a pupil of S.P. Cockerell (1755-1827) and worked for that architect, on St Margaret's Church, Westminster, from 1799-1802. In 1803 he moved to North Wales whilst working on Eaton Hall in Cheshire.
He was given a number of commissions in Flintshire and Denbighshire and probably lived on the Wynnstay Estate. His works in Wales are as follows:

1804: some ornamental work on Halkin Mountain, Flintshire. From 1813-20 he provided Gothic additions to Nerquis Hall. He also worked on Halkin Castle (1824-7), Wynnstay (? 1825), Pool Park (1827-8) and Chirk Castle (1831).**(1)**

1. *Colvin* p.435-6 main source of information. He may have moved to Wrexham by 1850.
   Slater's, 1844, p.54; *Slater's*, 1850, p.81: 'Gummon & Park', Temple Place.

GUTCH, John Wheeley Gough (1809 - 1862)
Photographer — Swansea

Honorary Secretary to the Royal Institution of South Wales between 1835-1840. In 1854 he photographed several views in and around Swansea, including *The Mumbles Church of Glamorgan* and *Group of Colliers' Wives, Llansamlet*. By 1857 he was taking *Photographic Illustrations of North Wales*.**(1)**

1. *Cox, 1990*. *NLW*, Photo Album 513.

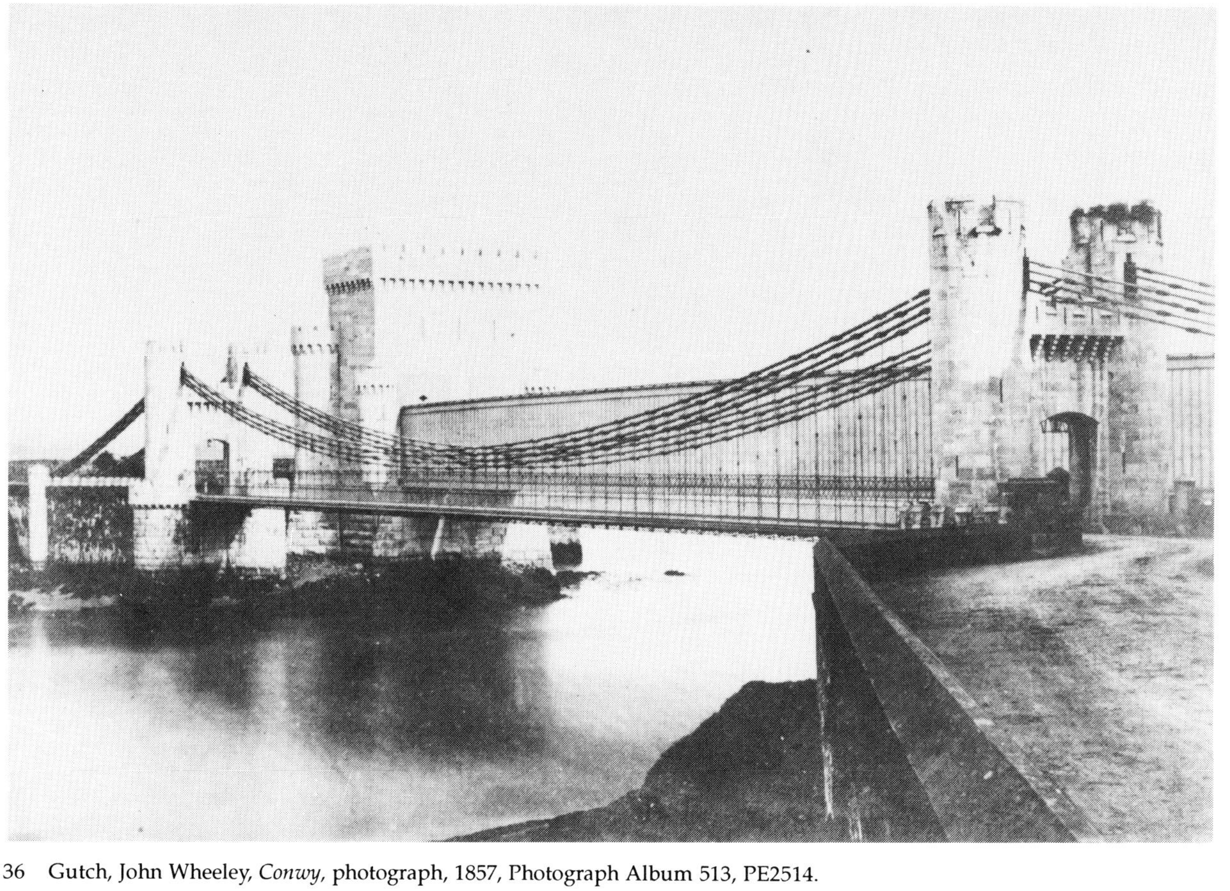

36 Gutch, John Wheeley, *Conwy*, photograph, 1857, Photograph Album 513, PE2514.

GWATKIN, Walter (fl 1817 - fl.1820)
Builder — Chepstow

Designed & built the vicarage at Llandogo, Monmouthshire 1820.**(1)**

1. *NLW* Llandaf Bounty Plan 37, 1820, also Llandaf Bounty Plan 29, Gwernesney, Monmouthshire, 1817. Not in *Eden.*

GWYTHER, George (fl 1844)
Builder — Pembroke

Designed & built rectory at Hubberston.**(1)**

1. *NLW* St Davids, Bounty Plan 62, 1844. Probably as a jobbing builder with a rudimentary gift for design. Also St Davids Bounty Plan 144, 1837. Not in *Eden.*

H

HABERSHON, Matthew (1789 - 1852)
Architect — Newport, Monmouthshire

Appears to have lived for some time in South Wales.**(1)**

1. *Girouard,* p.390. He also taught his son William H. (1818-1891).

HALL, John (fl 1821 - fl 1828)
Architect — Bangor
Surveyor

Hall worked on Bangor Cathedral (1824-28); he also designed the National School in Dean Street (1821-8) and provided some plans for terraced houses at Beaumaris (1824-5).**(1)**

It has been suggested that after 1828 he worked as an inn-keeper.

1. *Colvin,* p.448 main source of information, *see also* Clarke, M. L., 'A Bangor Architect of the Early Nineteenth Century', *Transactions of the Caernarvonshire Historical Society,* 1954, pp.49-50.

HAMMON, Henry J. (fl 1840 - fl 1868)
Architect — Welshpool
Surveyor — Church Cottage

After a practice in Wales, it seems that he moved to Finsbury Square & was recorded living there working as a District Surveyor of St Lukes in 1868**(1)**

1. *Robson's,* 1840, Volume II, p.27. Not in *Eden, Colvin, Girouard* p.402.

HANCOCK, John (1757 - 1847)
China painter — Swansea

Haslem records that 'shortly after the expiration of his apprenticeship he left Derby, and for a short time worked at Swansea'. This was probably c1790.**(1)** *Nance* was unable to trace this artist**(2)** but if he worked at Swansea it was before 1816.**(3)**

1. Haslem, John, *The Old Derby China Factory* (London, 1876), pp.125-126. This was reprinted in 1973 by E.P. Publishing, Wakefield. He adds that Hancock removed from Swansea to 'the Potteries, where he spent the remainder of his days'.
2. *Nance,* p.38 (note).
3. Haslem, John, *op.cit.,* p.127: 'From 1816 until within a few years of his death, Hancock was in the employ of Messrs. Wedgwood of Etruria.'

HAND, Thomas (fl 1835 - fl 1843)
Surveyor — Goodig Lodge, Pembrey

Davies Atlas, Not in *Eden* II p.124.

HAND, William (fl 1835 - fl 1843)
Surveyor — Goodig Lodge, Pembrey

Davies Atlas. Eden, II, p.124, states 'of Carmarthen' and also gives Hand as an estate surveyor.

HARGREAVES, Mr (fl 1850)
Miniature painter — Swansea

Visited Swansea in 1850.**(1)** Probably one of the Liverpool family of artists, either Francis Hargreaves (fl 1810-1854) or George Hargreaves (1797-1870).**(2)**

1. *Cambrian,* 2 August 1850, p.2.
2. *Foskett,* pp.309-310.

HARLEY, Miss (fl 1802)
China painter — Swansea

'She painted on the opaque china at the above place, in 1802 as appears by a jug on which is a Bullfinch in colours on the body, with oak leaves and acorns round the rim, the decorations are fairly well done, nothing more is known of her.'**(1)**

1. *Cadrawd,* Volume 1, p.57.

HARRIES, Alfred (fl 1852)
Surveyor — Dinas (Glamorganshire)

NLW, Estate maps Llanychlwydog, 1852. Not in *Eden.*

HARRIS, James (Senior) (1810 - 87)
Marine & landscape artist — Swansea
Teacher of drawing and painting — 4 Adelaide Place
Artists' colourman

Moved with his family to Swansea c1828.**(1)** In the 1830s he worked in the studio of George Chambers and he was presumably still there in 1839.**(2)** According to Watkins, George Chambers visited Swansea before the autumn of 1835 and 'returned with a pupil named Harris, who

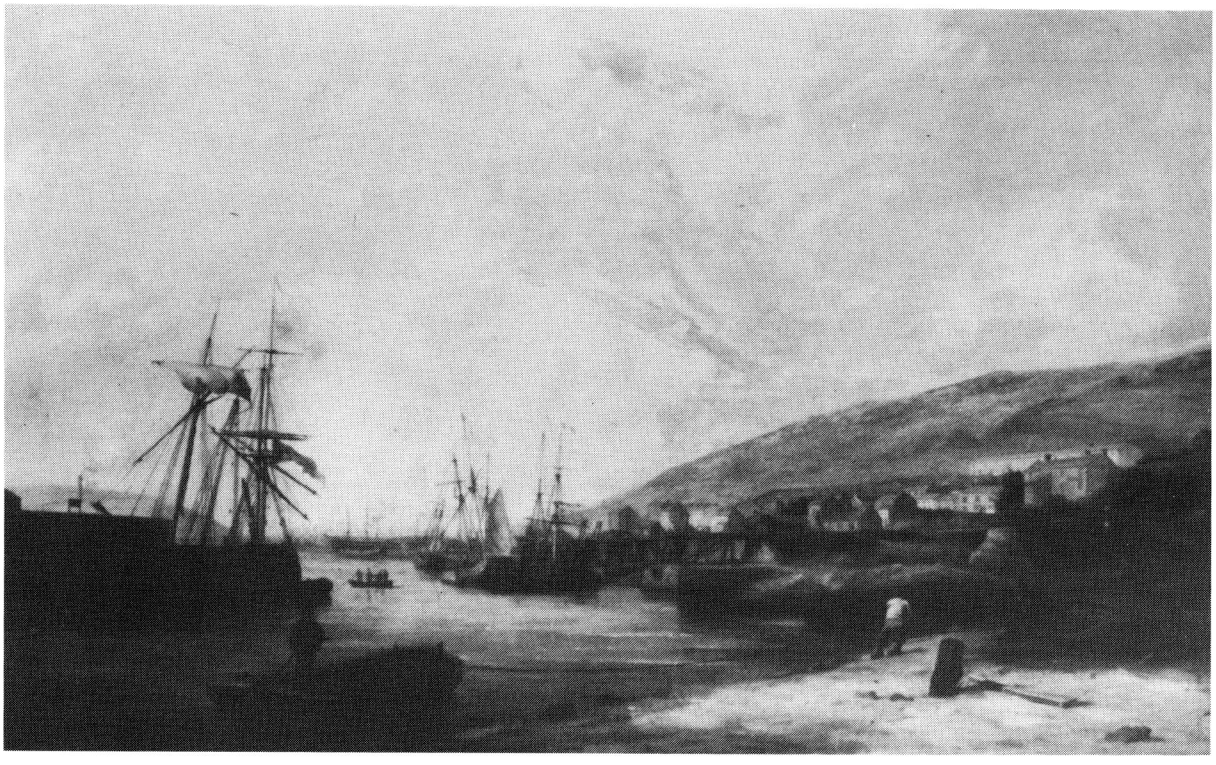

37 Harris, James, *Hafod Copper Works, River Tawe, Swansea,* oil on canvas, c1850, Glynn Vivian Art Gallery: Leisure Services Department: Swansea City Council.

copied a noble sea-view of Margate, done by his master'. Harris painted in a piecemeal manner, and Chamber's instructions to him were that he should 'Knock the colours more about'.**(3)**

He moved to Thistleboon c1844.**(4)** In 1846 he exhibited at the *RSBA* from an unspecified Swansea address. By 1847 he was at 4 Adelaide Place, and he moved to the Mumbles sometime before 1862.**(5)**

Harris advertised in 1842 that he was 'entering into' his late father's business in Swansea at the retirement of Sarah Harris. He stated: 'he has worked at every department of the Carving and Gilding Business, both in London and Swansea, for more than ten years; and has a most extensive stock of elegant Ornaments for looking glass and Picture Frames, from an Alter [*sic*] Piece to a Miniature...'**(6)**

Shortly afterwards he sold the family business to a London carver and gilder, William Palmer, and recommended his successor in an advertisement.**(7)** It appears he removed to Mumbles at this date.**(8)**

1. *The South Walian,* December 1902.
2. See *Cambrian,* 31 August 1839, p.2. His mother advertised for a youth to assist in her work continuing the framing business at Swansea.
3. Watkins, John, *Life and Career of George Chambers* (1841), p.86. *Howell,* pp.28ff, gives a clear account of his life and that of James Harris (Junior) (1847-1925). *Bell* p.180.
4. Swansea Record Office files (biographical).
5. *RSBA,* Volume 1:
   1846 *A View of Swansea Piers* (74);
   A distant View of Amsterdam (13).
   1847 *Rosselly* [*sic*] *Bay, Coast of South Wales* (2).
   He continued to exhibit in 1862, 1869, 1871-76 from an address on the Mumbles.
6. *Cambrian,* 8 January 1842, p.2.
7. *Ibid.,* 19 December 1845, p.2: 'he will relinguish business in the 25th inst. and Remove to No 4 Adelaide Place'. Palmer stated that he had 'succeeded to and purchased the business of Mr James Harris, including the Sale of Artists' Materials'.
8. *Hunt,* 1849, p.153 (Marine & Landscape Artist); 1850, p.132 (Marine & Landscape Artist).

HARRIS, John 'Old Harris' (1778 - 1836)

China painter — Swansea [Llandeilo]

'He was...a painter of merit.'**(1)** *Nance* records that he worked at the Cambrian Pottery in 1827.**(2)** May have worked in Llandeilo.**(3)**

1. Swansea Record Office files (biographical).
2. *Nance,* p.145 (note 2), gives the name as 'John Harries'.
3. (*PL*).

HARRIS, John (fl 1828 - 1836)

Marine artist — Swansea
Teacher of painting — 40 Wind Street

Possibly studied at *RA* in 1812.**(1)** He moved with his family from Exeter to Swansea c1828 and by 1833 had established a carving and gilding business. He also made picture frames and restored paintings.

He appears to have received patronage from a wide audience and in his advertisement he thanks 'the nobility,

Gentry and Inhabitants of South Wales'**(2)** for their support. He continues: 'He has a variety of OIL PAINTINGS constantly on sale, and that he is ready to wait upon any Gentleman at his residence to receive orders in the above Branches, and to give Lessons in Oil Painting.'**(3)**

Harris was the father of James Harris (1810-87), after his death Sarah Harris continued the business.**(4)**

1. *Hutchison*, p.166: '1026 John Harries' 20, P[ainter].
2. *Cambrian*, 13 July 1833, p.2; 27 July 1833, p.2; 3 August 1833, p.2. In two advertisements his name is given as 'J. Harries'. *Pigot's*, 1830, p.865: 'John Harries Carver & gilder'. Hugh Hughes mentions a John Harris at Llandeilo in 1821, this may be the same artist (*PL*).
3. *RISW, Swansea Bay in Stormy Weather*, signed and dated 'J. Harris 1834', oil on canvas, 70.3 x 89.5 cm, may be John Harris's work, *Howell*, p.39 (illustrated).
4. *Cambrian*, 31 August 1839, p.2. Sarah advertised the same business but without the sale of paintings or teaching.

HARRIS, Moses (c1787)
Caricature artist — Swansea

A print after Harris, dated 1787, is in the collection of the *RISW*.**(1)**

1. I am grateful to Michael Gibbs for this information. The print is called *Corporation Meeting 1787 discussing Harbour Improvements*, it includes a caricature of one famous Swansea celebrity. Illustrated in Williams, Glanmor, *Swansea Illustrated History* (Swansea, 1990), p.106.

HARRIS, Sarah (fl 1839 - fl 1842)
Frame maker — 40 Wind Street, Swansea

Wife of John Harris. She continued the family business after the death of her husband but reduced the range of services, from restoration and tending to frame-making and gilding only.**(1)** In 1839 she employed an apprentice and by 1842 the business was being managed by her son.**(2)**

1. *Cambrian*, 31 August 1839, p.2.
2. *Cambrian*, 8 January 1842, p.2.

HARRIS, William (fl 1858)
Photographer — Cardiff, 168 Bute Road

Slater's, 1858.

HARRISON, J.H. (c1840)
Marine artist — Swansea, 60 Carmarthen Road

Painted ship portrait, c1840.**(1)**

1. *Mary Lloyd, Portmadoc, Caernarvon* [*sic*], watercolour/bodycolour, signed and stamped at reverse, 20" x 29".

   'An example of a "ship portrait" or "pier-head painting" of the type often commissioned by a ship's captain or promoted to him by the artist. "Ship portraitists" were seldom trained artists, but people who used an intimate knowledge of ships, to produce works of authenticity and accurate detail, though unsophisticated in execution, and priced accordingly. They were produced in a variety of media, e.g. pencil, bodycolour and oils' (Philip Davies, *Spring Exhibition catalogue* (Cardiff, 1983), p.16).

HARRISON, John (fl 1850)
Artist — Cardiff, St Mary Street

Slater's, 1850, p.22.

HART, Mrs (fl 1814)
Teacher of drawing and ornamental works — Swansea

School mistress who also taught French.**(1)**

1. *Cambrian*, 16 July 1841, p.1.

HARVEY, John (fl 1835 - fl 1843)
Surveyor — Haverfordwest, 14 Gloucester Place

Davies Atlas. Eden II p.126.

HASLAM, John Ralph (fl 1839 - fl 1851)
Surveyor — Eiriannell Goch, Menai Bridge, Anglesey

Davies Atlas. Eden, II, p.127.

HASSALL, Charles (1754 - 1814)
Surveyor — Eastwood, Narberth

He surveyed estates, roads & canals**(1)**

1. *NLW* has surveys from 1772-1787, *Eden* II p.127.

HATHAWAY, W. (fl 1814)
Waxwork artist — Carmarthen

Exhibited 'large as life' waxworks of the Royal Family and Nelson's funeral, lying in State.**(1)**

1. *Cambrian*, 30 July 1814, p.1. He does not appear in *Pyke*. These figures were about life size.

HAVARD, J. (fl 1841)
Frame maker — Cardigan
Picture framer

McKechnie records that he framed a silhouette by G. Walker in 1841.**(1)**

1. *McKechnie*, p.346.

HAVERFIELD, Henry (fl 1818)
Portrait painter — Dolwilym, Llanglydwen, Carmarthenshire

May have been based in a West Country town.**(1)** He certainly worked in Bath and Dolwilym, Carmarthen, which he visited for four days.**(2)**

1. He claimed to work in London but does not appear in the *POL*, 1813, 1816, 1820, 1824.
2. Carmarthen Record Office has a manuscript *Diary* which refers to Haverfield, *vide Carmarthen Historian* XVIII, 1981, p.78. He drew a portrait of Emma 'extremely like her' and Mr Protheroe.

HAWKINS, Mrs Louisa [or Mrs W.] (fl 1839 - fl 1847)
Landscape and portrait artist — Monmouthshire

May have been based in Monmouthshire in 1838 or 1839.**(1)** She executed several pictures relating to the Llanover family.**(2)**

1. *RA* exhibition 1839 included *Lady Hall of Llanover* and *Abercarn landscape*.
2. *Steegman*, Volume 2, p.142, describes two portraits at Llanarth Court both dated 1838 of Lady Llanover (No 54) and Benjamin Hall (No 55).

HEMMING, William (fl 1838)
Surveyor? — Maentwrog

Provided a standard, competent design for the Trawsfynydd Rectory, 1838.**(1)**

1. Bangor Bounty Plan 85, signed & dated 1838. He described himself as a 'builder'. Not in *Eden*.

HENRY, Mr (fl 1848)
Exhibitor [of paintings] — Caernarfon, Denbigh, Bangor, Ruthin, Mold, Holywell

Based in Liverpool, Henry exhibited in various parts of North Wales, only staying one night at each town.**(1)** He accompanied the shows with fireworks. He exhibited 'Views of the World' and also a planetarium.

1. *Caernarvon and Denbighshire Herald*, 22 April 1848, p.4. *Ibid.*, 29 April 1848, p.1.

HERBERT, Lewis (- 1840)
Mason — Llannarth, Rhydyfydde

SD/1840/27.

HEWITT, Miss (fl 1800 - fl 1820)
China painter — Nantgarw

She was a daughter of a *thrower* at Nantgarw.**(1)**

1. *Cadrawd*, p.57.

HEYDON, Christopher (fl 1841 - fl 1867)
Surveyor — Chepstow

Davies Atlas. Eden, II, p.131.

HOARE, Hugh (fl 1792 - fl 1860)
Architect — Tenby**(1)**
Surveyor — Frog Street

He designed & built the vicarage at Rosemarket in 1855.**(2)** It seems he may have worked with his brother William *vida supra*.

1. *Hunt*, 1850, p.166. *Colvin* p.499.
2. *NLW* St Davids Bounty Plan 161, 1855, neat & fairly detailed facade.

HOARE, William (c1770 - 1830)
Architect — Lawrenny, Pembrokeshire

Hoare worked closely with his brother Hugh *vide infra*. His known buildings are *Lawrenny Hall*, 1800-04, *Cresselly*.**(1)**

1. *Colvin*, p.499.

HOOD, [Mr] (fl 1800)
China Painter — Swansea

Worked in the Cambrian pottery.**(1)**

1. *Cadrawd*, p.57.

HOOSON, William (fl 1836)
Surveyor — Cilcain, Flintshire

Designed & built the vicarage at Cilcain, [*sic*] 1836.**(1)**

1. St Asaph, Bounty Plan 29, 1836, a typical surveyor's plan, more concentration on detail with a rather plain, symmetrical facade. Not in *Eden*.

HORLOR, M. (fl 1846 - fl 1892)
Horse and dog painter — Swansea, 28 Adelaide place

This may be George W. Horlor who worked at Cheltenham at this period.**(1)** He stayed for some time at the same house as William Butler. His advertisements included the following statement:

> 'He will remain at Swansea for a short period, painting the PORTRAITS of Horses and Dogs for a gentleman of this town, which may be seen after next Monday, at the Cambrian office, where terms may be known, or at his residence.'**(2)**

1. An example of his work, *Figures and Cattle by a Mountain Lake*, 1862, is illustrated in Sotheby's Chester catalogue 18 April 1986, lot 3177.
   Millar (Volume I), p.123, noted Horlor exhibiting at the *RA* 1854-90, *BI* 1849-66, *RSBA*, 1854-66.

2. *Cambrian*, 10 July 1846, p.2.
Ibid., 17 July 1846, p.[3], address given as 7 York Place.

HORNOR, Thomas(1) (1785 - 1844)
Landscape artist South Wales
Map maker and surveyor

Although he was resident at Inner Temple, London, he spent some months in the Vale of Neath in 1814.**(2)** He appears to have worked for several patrons in South Wales,**(3)** and advertised his visit in advance:

'Wales and the Interjacent Counties to London
T. HORNOR
Pictorial Delineator of Estates etc.

Acquaints the Proprietors of Landed Property in Wales...being requested to delineate in his improved Style, some Properties in the Principality in the course of the ensuing Summer, he would be happy to increase the number of his engagements, with a view to reduce the expenses chargeable on separate journies to each property.'**(4)**

He executed large albums,**(5)** single watercolours**(6)** and panoramic maps.**(7)** All his work in Wales was of South Wales sites. Apart from views of Llandaff Cathedral**(8)** extant work is of the Neath Vale. It seems likely that most of his pictures were produced in his studio after returning to London.

1. *Mallalieu* gives 'Horner'.
2. Hyde, Ralph, 'Thomas Hornor: pictorial land surveyor', *Imago Mundi*, Volume 29, 1977, pp.23-34, gives a good account of Hornor's work. Hyde mentions that Hornor probably obtained Welsh patronage through a circle of Welsh friends at Clerkenwell, London. *See also* Hyde, Ralph, *Gilded Scenes and Shining Prospects* (New Haven, 1985), pp.140-145. *Eden*, Supplement, p.425, provides further references.
3. Jenkins, Elis, 'Thomas Hornor', *Glamorgan Historian*, Volume 7, 1971, pp.37-50. These included Sir John Llewelyn of Ynys y Gerwn, John Edwards of Rheola and Watson Taylor.
4. *Cambrian*, 2 April 1814, p.3, addressed to the gentry of North and South Wales.
Ibid., 30 April 1814, p.3 (longer advertisement).
5. Examples such as *NLW*, Drawing Volume 23, dated 1817, *The Vale of Neath;* Glamorgan Record Office, dated 1819, *Tours through the Vale of Glamorganshire.* Other copies are known to exist in private hands and the *BM*. All are handsomely bound and include a MSS text with a panorama of the Vale of Neath. The *BM* copy is dated 1817 and the *Bow Main* drawing illustrates a group using a Camera Lucida (*BM* 198.b.6*, Accession No. 1937-10-8-165). Another copy of this picture was sold at Sotheby's, 19 November 1992.Some copies are of a different format. For instance the *Vale of Neath* panorama represented in the volumes was also produced as a large single lanscape in 5 sections. A copy was sold at Spinks London, & illustrated: The *Western Mail* 5 October 1994 p.3.
6. For instance, *NLW*, PE 5122, *Town of Neath*, 1819, 24.7 x 43.8 cm. His advertisements mentioned that 'drawings and paintings of Properties from 5 to 3000 Acres are completed for the inspection of Landed Proprietors'.

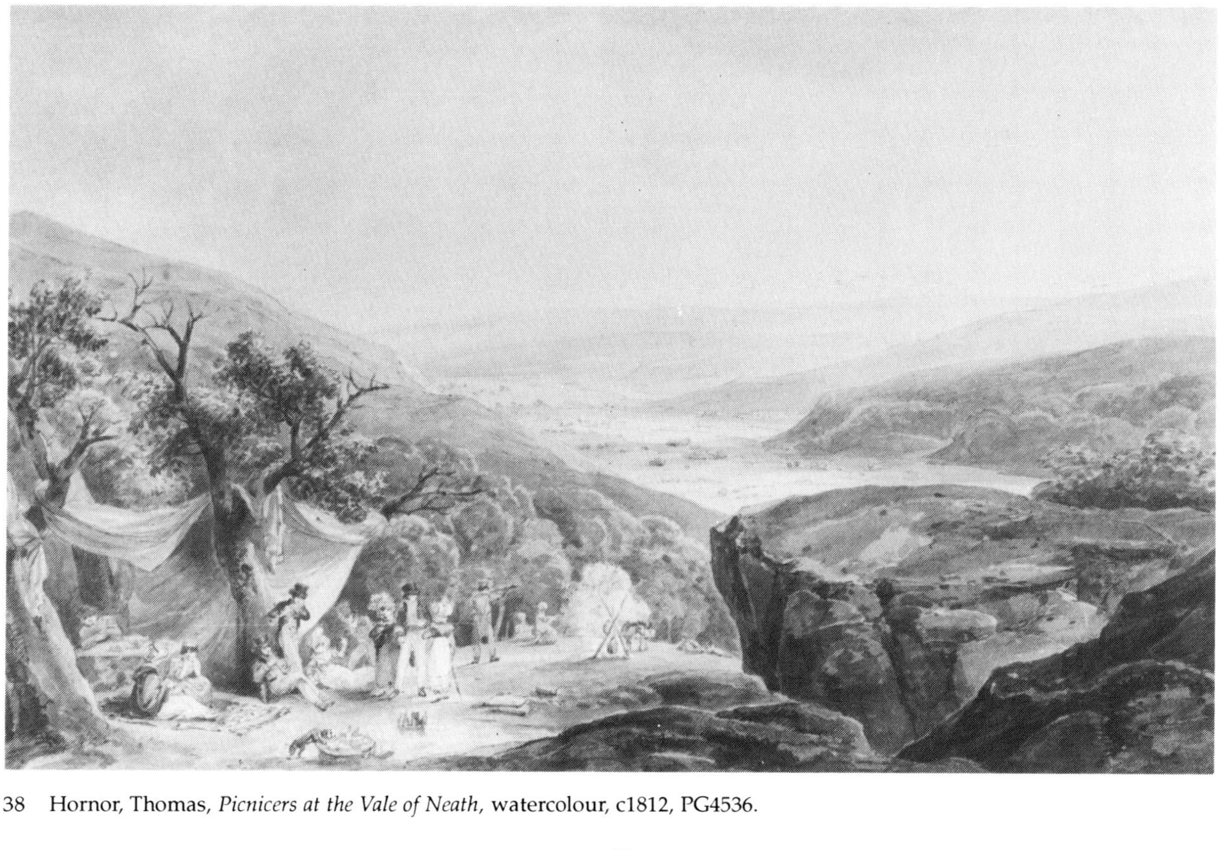

38 Hornor, Thomas, *Picnicers at the Vale of Neath*, watercolour, c1812, PG4536.

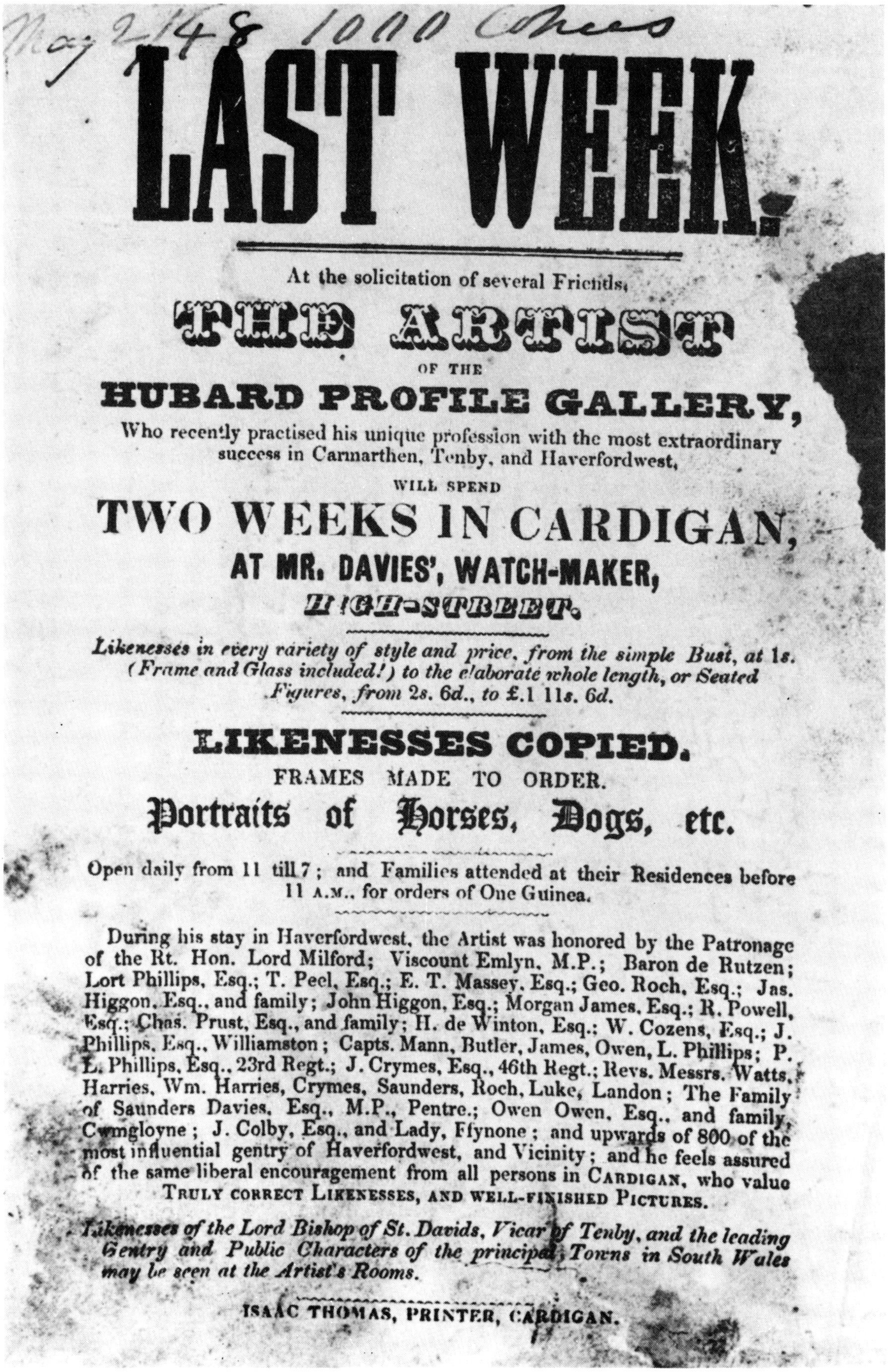

May 2/48 1000 copies

LAST WEEK.

At the solicitation of several Friends,

THE ARTIST

OF THE

HUBARD PROFILE GALLERY,

Who recently practised his unique profession with the most extraordinary success in Carmarthen, Tenby, and Haverfordwest,

WILL SPEND

TWO WEEKS IN CARDIGAN,

AT MR. DAVIES', WATCH-MAKER,

HIGH-STREET.

Likenesses in every variety of style and price, from the simple Bust, at 1s. (Frame and Glass included!) to the elaborate whole length, or Seated Figures, from 2s. 6d., to £.1 11s. 6d.

LIKENESSES COPIED.

FRAMES MADE TO ORDER.

Portraits of Horses, Dogs, etc.

Open daily from 11 till 7; and Families attended at their Residences before 11 A.M., for orders of One Guinea.

During his stay in Haverfordwest, the Artist was honored by the Patronage of the Rt. Hon. Lord Milford; Viscount Emlyn, M.P.; Baron de Rutzen; Lort Phillips, Esq.; T. Peel, Esq.; E. T. Massey, Esq.; Geo. Roch, Esq.; Jas. Higgon, Esq., and family; John Higgon, Esq.; Morgan James, Esq.; R. Powell, Esq.; Chas. Prust, Esq., and family; H. de Winton, Esq.; W. Cozens, Esq.; J. Phillips, Esq., Williamston; Capts. Mann, Butler, James, Owen, L. Phillips; P. L. Phillips, Esq., 23rd Regt.; J. Crymes, Esq., 46th Regt.; Revs. Messrs. Watts, Harries, Wm. Harries, Crymes, Saunders, Roch, Luke, Landon; The Family of Saunders Davies, Esq., M.P., Pentre.; Owen Owen, Esq., and family, Cwmgloyne; J. Colby, Esq., and Lady, Ffynone; and upwards of 800 of the most influential gentry of Haverfordwest, and Vicinity; and he feels assured of the same liberal encouragement from all persons in CARDIGAN, who value TRULY CORRECT LIKENESSES, AND WELL-FINISHED PICTURES.

Likenesses of the Lord Bishop of St. Davids, Vicar of Tenby, and the leading Gentry and Public Characters of the principal Towns in South Wales may be seen at the Artist's Rooms.

ISAAC THOMAS, PRINTER, CARDIGAN.

39 Hubard, William James, advertisement, 1848 (Cardigan Printers file, Album 64).

7. *NLW, PA* 2917 (RM C33), *Plan of Rheola*, 1815. Illustrated in Hyde, *op. cit.*, figure 2.
8. *NLW*, PB 7269, *Llandaff Cathedral*, c30 x 20 cm.

HOWELL, John (fl 1811 - fl 1817)
Surveyor Llanelli

NLW, Estate Map *Llanelly*, 1817, and *Llanwinio*, 1811, *Eden* II p.138.

HOWELL, William Jones (fl 1835 - fl 1843)
Surveyor Cardigan

Davies Atlas, Eden II p.426.

HUBARD, William James (and Company) (?1809 - 62)
Silhouette artists
Animal painters
Copyists
Aberystwyth
Cardigan
Haverfordwest
Tenby

This was a group of artists working under the direction of William Hubard. The company was referred to as the Hubard Gallery or the Hubard Profile Gallery.**(1)**

They worked in South and Mid Wales in 1835 and 1848. In 1835 the Hubard Gallery executed silhouettes at Aberystwyth.**(2)**

A poster was published on the 1848 tour of South Wales,**(3)** which clearly suggests that a single artist worked under the Hubard name on this occasion. A considerable number of portraits were taken, mainly of gentry families. The poster mentions that copies could be made of animal portraits which was, perhaps, an additional service for a rural community.**(4)**

Probably the Welsh tours were part of larger tours of Britain,**(5)** and it is significant that examples show Hubard in Wales in the winter and summer.

1. *McKechnie*, p.244 ff, discusses the Hubard Gallery and mentions that they visited the west coast of Wales (p.245).
2. *WFM* (F84.133/8-10) has three silhouettes all inscribed 'taken at Aberystwyth': *Ann Temple, Herbert Temple, Master Temple*. The last item is stamped 'Taken at the Hubard Gallery'.
3. *NLW*, Cardigan Printer's File Collection, Album 64. Dated in MSS 'May 2/48'. This evidence was first discussed by Ballinger, Sir John, 'Local history from a printer's file', *West Wales Historical Records*, Volume IX, 1920-23, pp.197-216, and Volume X, 1924, pp.155-176. I have been unable to trace any evidence concerning the Watchmaker Davies, of Cardigan, except to note he was W. Davies who also accommodated Mr Brooke in 1846.
   TL has kindly given me references to Hubard at Haverfordwest and Cardigan. *Pembrokeshire Herald*, 28 January 18[34], notes a portrait of *George Roch*. *Pembrokeshire Herald*, 28 April 18[34], notes Hubard at 2 High Street, Cardigan. The artists was named as 'G. Merryweather' and a lithograph of the Roch portrait was signed by that artist. *Pembrokeshire Herald*, 16 June 1834, lists 'families & horses painted'.
4. *McKechnie, op.cit.*, does not mention animal portraits as within the *oeuvre* of Hubard.
5. A fuller explanation of Hubard's practice may be found in McCormack, Helen, 'Duplicate books by Hubard', *Antiques*, February 1944, and McCormack, Helen, *W.J. Hubard and the Hubard Gallery* (exhibition catalogue), 1948, Valentine Gallery, Richmond, Virginia, USA.

HUGH, Peter (- 1793)
Mason Laugharne

SD/1793/56.

HUGHES, E.B. (fl 1841 - fl 1851)
Surveyor Narberth

The son of James Hughes *supra*.

There are examples of his estate maps in Pembrokeshire.**(1)** His best work was the wall map of Tenby which contains many cartouches of the town.**(2)** Hughes was employed as a surveyor for Tenby Corporation.

1. *NLW* Estate Maps *Cosheston* 1851, *Llandewi Velfrey* 1841, *Eden* II p.139.
2. In a private collection, c105x200cm, signed & dated 1849 in bistre wash.

HUGHES, G. (fl 1835)
Carver and painter Llechwedd

Presumably an amateur, he produced a miniature bureau in slate, embellished with a carved painted design.**(1)**

1. Sotheby's *English Naive Provincial Art*, 22 July 1986, lot 345 (illustrated), 23 cm long, signed and dated 1835.

HUGHES, Hugh 'Hughes the Limner' (1790 - 1863)
Landscape and topographical artist
Portrait artist
Caricaturist
Interior decorator
Diorama artist
Wood and copper plate engraver
Aberystwyth
Caernarfon
Carmarthen
Meddiant, Glan Conwy

The most important native artist working in Wales in this period.**(1)** Hugh had a polymathic ability in fine art. He began working as a wood engraver probably under Henry Hole. His first work was published in 1812, a fine copper-plate engraving.**(2)** This early print showed considerable ability and promise. Shortly afterwards he began to paint portraits, the majority of these are of ministers and their wives.

In 1819 he returned to Wales after some time in London. At Meddiant farm he engraved the prints for the *Beauties of Cambria*.**(3)** Later in his career he produced a number of prints of North Wales.**(4)**

He was involved in various literary, educational and artistic projects, a number of which were unsuccessful.**(5)** Hughes exhibited at the *BI***(6)** and the *RSBA* (Suffolk Street).**(7)**

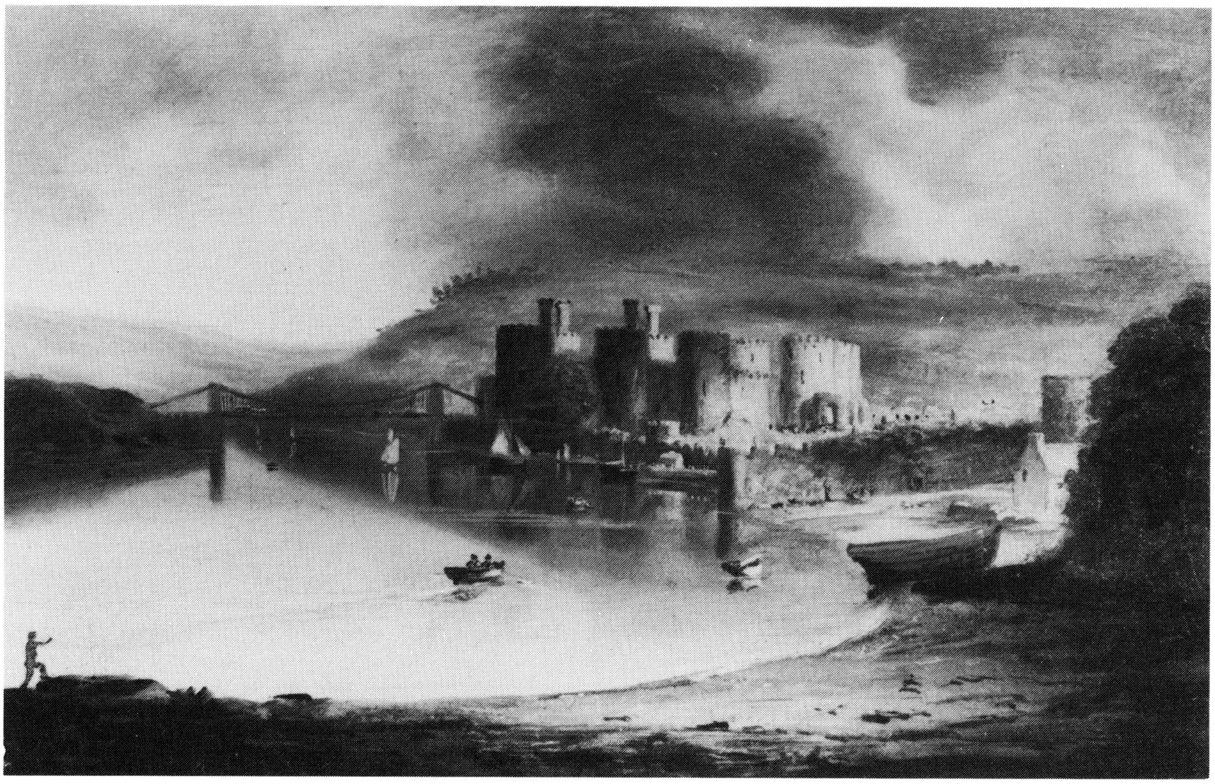

40 Hughes, Hugh, *Conway Castle*, oil on canvas, 1846, PZ3938.

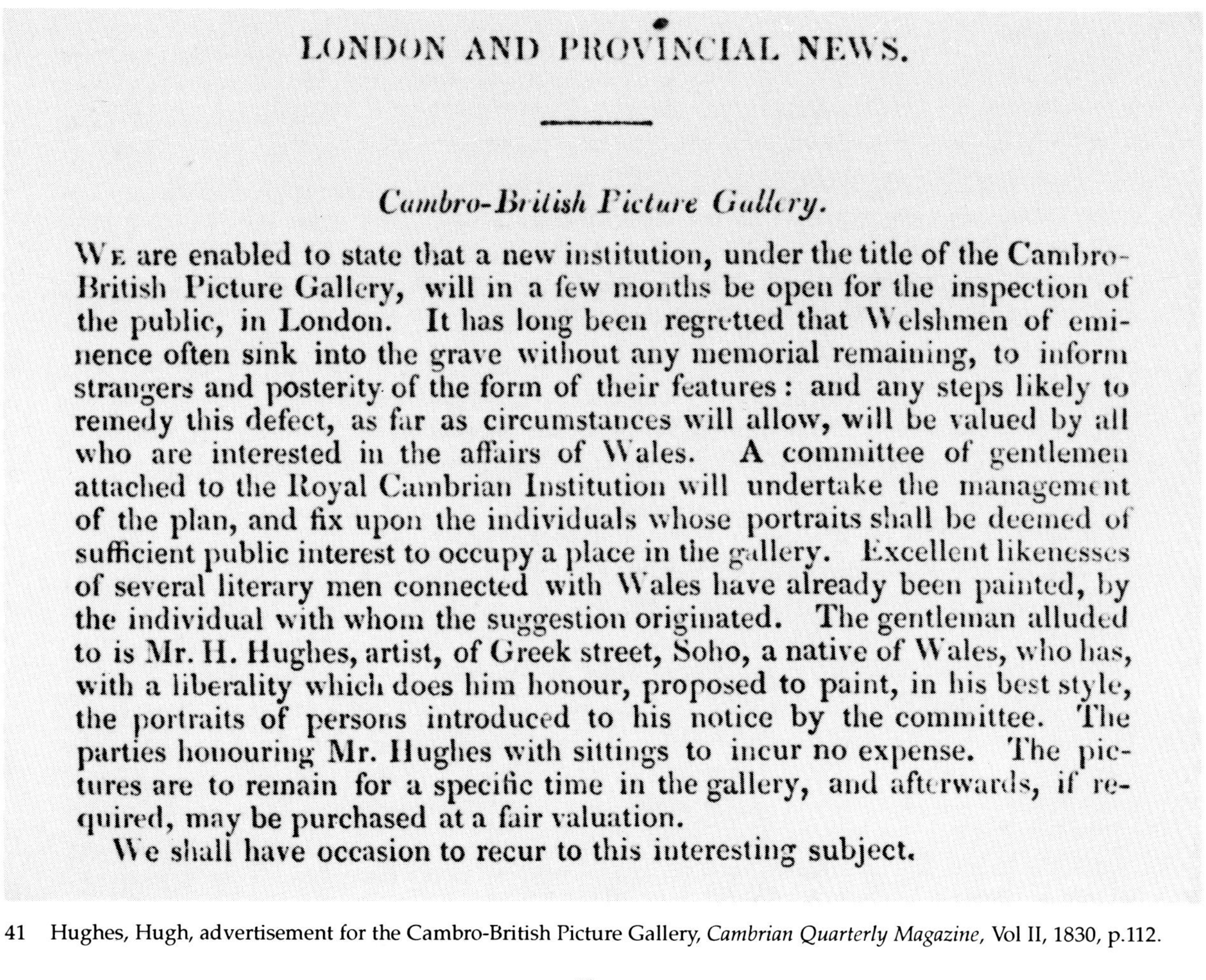

LONDON AND PROVINCIAL NEWS.

Cambro-British Picture Gallery.

WE are enabled to state that a new institution, under the title of the Cambro-British Picture Gallery, will in a few months be open for the inspection of the public, in London. It has long been regretted that Welshmen of eminence often sink into the grave without any memorial remaining, to inform strangers and posterity of the form of their features: and any steps likely to remedy this defect, as far as circumstances will allow, will be valued by all who are interested in the affairs of Wales. A committee of gentlemen attached to the Royal Cambrian Institution will undertake the management of the plan, and fix upon the individuals whose portraits shall be deemed of sufficient public interest to occupy a place in the gallery. Excellent likenesses of several literary men connected with Wales have already been painted, by the individual with whom the suggestion originated. The gentleman alluded to is Mr. H. Hughes, artist, of Greek street, Soho, a native of Wales, who has, with a liberality which does him honour, proposed to paint, in his best style, the portraits of persons introduced to his notice by the committee. The parties honouring Mr. Hughes with sittings to incur no expense. The pictures are to remain for a specific time in the gallery, and afterwards, if required, may be purchased at a fair valuation.

We shall have occasion to recur to this interesting subject.

41 Hughes, Hugh, advertisement for the Cambro-British Picture Gallery, *Cambrian Quarterly Magazine*, Vol II, 1830, p.112.

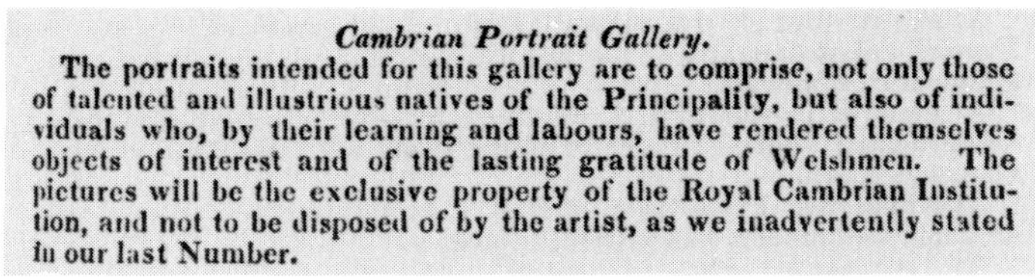

Cambrian Portrait Gallery.

The portraits intended for this gallery are to comprise, not only those of talented and illustrious natives of the Principality, but also of individuals who, by their learning and labours, have rendered themselves objects of interest and of the lasting gratitude of Welshmen. The pictures will be the exclusive property of the Royal Cambrian Institution, and not to be disposed of by the artist, as we inadvertently stated in our last Number.

42 Hughes, Hugh, A second advertisement for the Cambro-British Picture Gallery, *Cambrian Quarterly Magazine,* Vol II, 1830, p.255.

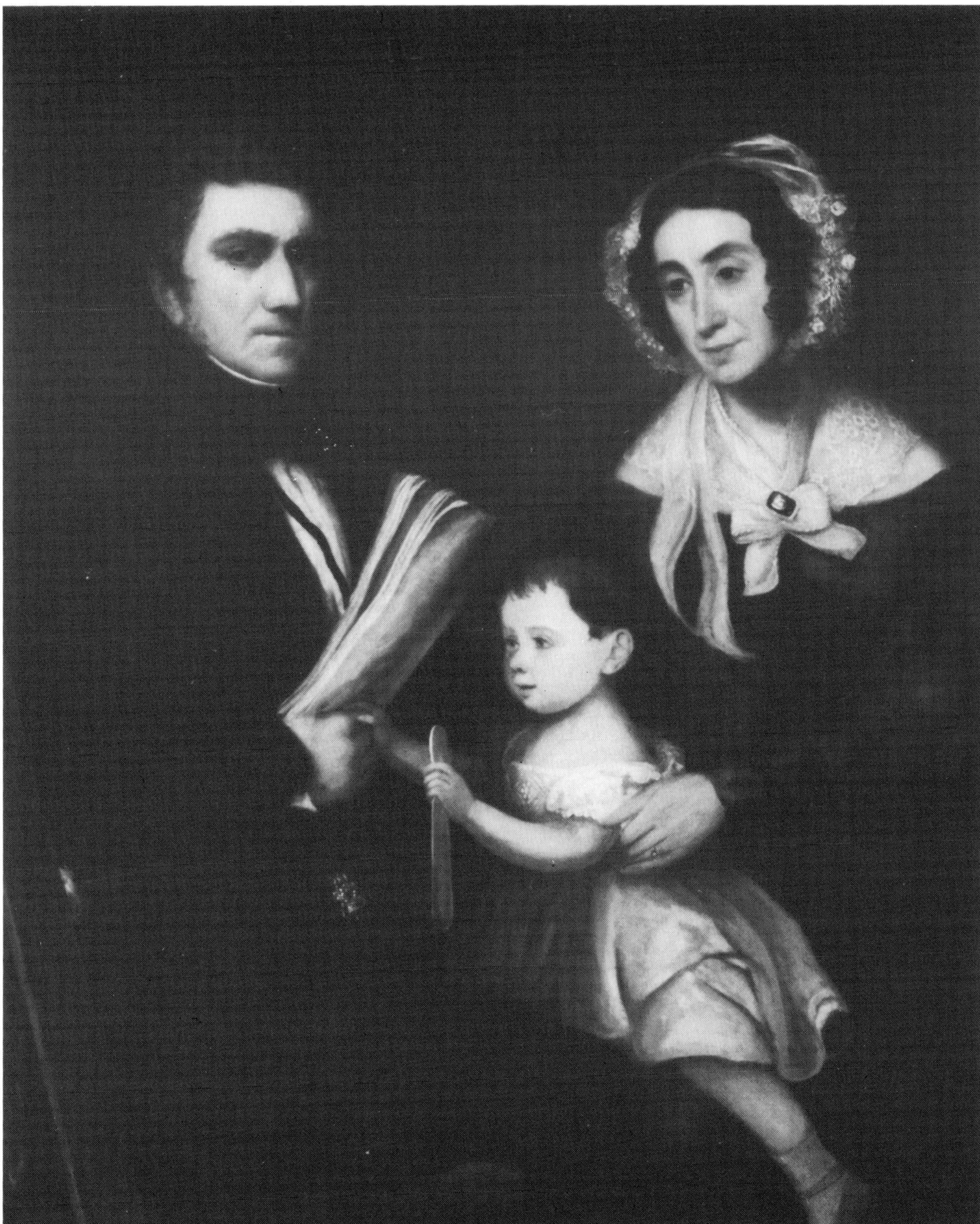

43 Hughes, Hugh, *Self Portrait with family,* oil on canvas, c1830, PB4599.

Between c1835-c1839 he was living in Caernarfon. There he began an interior decoration business, continued painting and executed a unique Diorama of Snowdon which he exhibited in the town in 1836.**(8)**

His caricatures are notably harsh and critical, somewhat in the style of Gilray.

1. For a discussion of his art and life, *vide Hugh Hughes, Arlunydd Gwlad, Artisan Painter* (Aberystwyth, 1990). Lord's biography *Hugh Hughes Arlunydd Gwlad 1790-1863* (Llandysul, 1995) is the standard text.
2. Morgan, William & Jones, John, *Tadau Methodistaidd* (Swansea, 1897), Volume 2, p.438, inscribed 'H. Hughes fecit Liverpool 1812', head and shoulders portrait of *Rev. John Elias*, oval, 9.7 x 8.5 cm.
3. Some good examples of these prints are *op.cit.*, Lord, 1990, p.17-18.
4. One example is *NLW*, P2855, P1 - B50, *Menai Bridge*, c1850.
5. Illustrations 42, 43 at the Cambrian Portrait Gallery.
6. 1827 (288) *The Falls of Helygog, Meirionethshire*, size 2.8x2.11 feet.
   1828 (346) *Pont y Glyn*, size 2.6x2.1 feet.
   1830 (283) *The Sentinel*, size 1.1x1.3 feet.
   1851 (519) *Flowers and Fruit*, [no size given].
7. 1827 (83) *The Sentinel.*
   (265) *The Minas Bridge, North Wales* [Menai Bridge?].
   1828 (301) *Falls of Helygog.*
   1850 (351) *Flowers.*
   (531) *Study of a Monk's Head.*
   1851 (110) *Lilies.*
8. All these aspects of his work are discussed in *Joyner, 1989*, Vol. I, pp.102-123, *Hugh Hughes 'The Limner'*.

HUGHES, James (1781 - 1832)

Architect — Narberth, Pembrokeshire

Worked in various parts of Pembrokeshire as a bridge builder and architect.**(1)** He enlarged Narberth Church in 1828-9 & was architect & builder of the Rectory 1829.**(2)**

He was described as'architect & bridge surveyor for the county of Pembroke'**(3)**

1. *RCAM* files. He may also have been a mason, builder and surveyor. Not in *Girouard, Colvin. TL* informs me that he is buried at Narberth & he was father of E. B. Hughes.
2. *TL* notes the *Narberth church* project in ICBS 767 & the Rectory in *NLW* MSS Dept, St Davids Bounty Plan 141. He also produced plans for *Narberth Market* in 1831-2 (*NLW* Slebech 3962, 4052). St Davids, Bounty Plan 86, 1831 *Llanddewi Velfrey vicarage* is a fine watercolour plan.
3. *Haverfordwest & Milford Haven Telegraph* 19 Nov 1862 notice of death of Miss Hughes, daughter of J. Hughes.

HUGHES, Lewis (fl c1810)

Portrait painter — Denbigh?

Twm o'r Nant, portrait *NMW*.**(1)**

1. Nothing further is known of this artist at present.

HUGHES, Meredith (fl 1774 - fl 1779)

Surveyor — Denbighshire

Executed several plans and maps for the Bagot Estate and introduced pictorial devices.**(1)**

1. *NLW*, Roller Map A205, *Cyffylliog*, Denbighshire map with hunting scene; MSS Map Volume, *Book of Refference* [*sic*], dated 1779, with haymakers.

HUGHES, Phillip (- 1800)

Japanner — Trevethin, Monmouthshire

LL/1800/12: given as Jepanner [*sic*].

HUGHES, Robert (1811 - 1892)

Portrait painter — Uwchlaw'r ffynnon
[Landscape painter] — Llanaelhaearn, Caernarfonshire

Born in Bodgared, Llanwrda, Caernarfonshire and as a child gained local fame as a woodcarver.**(1)** Moved to London in 1830 but by 1833 was farming at Uwchlawr-ffynnon. He was a preacher with a 'pictorial style'**(2)** and began painting in c1860.**(3)** Cadrawd notes that 'he was a self-taught portrait and landscape painter'.**(4)**

By c1870**(5)** he was painting fine, naive portraits. His self portrait is a good example of this style.**(6)** He was still painting portraits in 1888, and there is a series of small portraits extant.**(7)**

1. *DWB*, p.390. *Lord, Barn*, p.28, discusses this artist in some detail. Published in English *Lord, 1994* p.73 ff.
2. Hughes, Robert, *Hunan-Gofiant ynghyda Phregethau a Barddoniaeth* (Pwllheli, 1893).
3. He took a portrait of *Dafydd Pritchard.*
4. *Cadrawd*, p.64.
5. *NLW* has a portrait of *Rev. John Jones*, Tremadoc deposited, 1991 (PG 2451), 76 x 64 cm.
6. United Theological College, Aberystwyth (*WPA* 2159), has an oil on canvas, 73.7 x 61 cm. This is a recent acquisition by the college and shows Hughes at his naive best.
7. One of these portraits of Hugh Jones aned Jane Jones, Tŷ Uchaf, Clynnog, is illustrated in Roberts, Guto, 'Dechrau arlunio wedi'r hanner cant', *Y Casglwr*, Rhif 48, Nadolig 1991, p.1. *PL* discovered a whole series of these small portraits in c1989. Some are illustrated in Lord, Peter, 'Iconograffeg poblogaidd y pregethwyr', *Barn*, Gorffennaf/Awst, Rhifau 330/331, pp.37-52.

HUGHES, Samuel (fl 1849 - fl 1858)

Teacher of landscape painting — Bangor
Landscape painter — Bryndirwest

Hughes may have worked as a china painter**(1)** in addition to taking landscape painting.**(2)** There are several prints after Hughes.**(3)**

1. *Connoisseur*, January 1971, Volume 176, No 707, p.8, describes a piece of large Battersea ware with a painted landscape plaque signed 'S. Hughes', after Claude.
2. *Slater's*, 1849, p.13.
   Slater's, 1850, p.13.
   Slater's, 1858, p.15 (professor/teacher).

3. *NLW*, PZ 6457, A1 - A51, *Suspension & Tubular Bridge across the Menai*, c1850; P 2860, B1/5 - B95, *Plas Newydd, The Seat of the Marquis of Anglesey...*, c1850.

HUMPHREYS, John (fl 1801)
Architect Aberystwyth
Surveyor

A subscriber to William Morris, *Harbours*.**(1)**

1. Morris, William, *Plans of Harbours* (Shrewsbury, 1801), p.ix. Possibly the same man as worked with John Evans on the Montgomeryshire Enclosure survey, 1806-1815. Not in *Eden, Colvin*.

HUMPHREYS, Robert (fl 1832)
Portrait painter Abergele

Portrait of *Thomas Lloyd*, School Master of Hen Gapel, Mynydd Seion 19th century and died 2 August 1838 'at Abergele North Wales'.

Foskett, Volume I, p.344: Portrait '1832 Dublin'.

HUMPHREYS, William (fl 1806 - fl 1807)
Surveyor Berriew
Montgomeryshire

NLW, Estate Map & Enclosure Award maps. Not in *Eden*.

HUSTON, William C. (fl 1825 - fl 1850)
Portrait painter Swansea
Brecon
Haverfordwest
Carmarthen

Visited Swansea in June 1850; evidence suggests that he was an itinerant artist.**(1)** He worked at London, Bath, Gloucester, Brecon and Stowbridge. His advertisements in the *Cambrian* were typical of the provincial artists at this period, he writes:

> 'He will paint portraits in Oil, at Moderate Prices, and in every instance will warrant a Faithful likeness, in the most enduring colours that have been discovered in ancient or modern times.
>
> Mr H. will have pleasure in showing to the Gentry a few SPECIMENS OF PORTRAITS painted here of Persons well known, which he hopes will be a sufficient guarantee for the performances of what he professes.'**(2)**

Huston includes a list, mainly of ministers, in various towns and added 'With many other families of Distinction, who have patronised him for the last twenty five years.'

In 1851 he moved to Haverfordwest.**(3)**

1. He is unrecorded except for the *Cambrian* advertisements.
2. *Cambrian*, 14 June 1850, p.2.
   Ibid., 21 June 1850, p.2.
   Ibid., 28 June 1850, p.2.
3. *Pembrokeshire Herald*, 17 January 1851, p.3, notes him exhibiting at 'Mr Morgans Painter, High Street, & stating that likeness shall be warranted excellent or no money shall be received'. He wrote that he had 'made a sojourn to Haverfordwest.'

I

IBBETSON, Julius Caesar (1759 - 1817)
Landscape and Cardiff Castle
Portrait painter Hafod

He was employed by the Earl of Bute to paint a portrait group of Glamorganshire gentlemen in 1789.**(1)** He also executed a series of watercolours for Bute of Welsh views.**(2)** On his tour with Robert Fulke Grenville (1751-1824) in 1792 he met Thomas Johnes, Hafod, who asked Ibbetson to remain on the estate as a drawing master.**(3)** He also executed views in North Wales.**(4)**

1. Clay, R.M., *Julius Caesar Ibbetson* (London, 1948), Plate 24; p.132 provides a list of portraits in the painting; they include the Earl of Bute, Alderman Bloom Williams and William Morgan, Porter at the Castle; also illustrated in Thomas, H., *The Diaries of John Bird* (Cardiff, 1987), p.28.
2. *Ibid.*, pp.26-29, gives several South Walian views.
3. *Ibid.*, p.37. Thomas Stothard was employed at Hafod from 1803 - see Stothard (*infra*).
4. *NLW*, PZ 3209, A1/1 - A115, *Paris mine*, c1790.

INCE, Joseph Murray (1806 - 59)
Landscape artist Presteign
Lithographer Radnorshire

He was probably born in London but moved with his family whilst very young to Presteign. In 1823 he moved to Hereford, to work under David Cox and c1830 he returned to Presteign where he remained most of his life.**(1)** Between 1834-1840 he was in Cambridge and he apparently returned to Presteign c1840.**(2)**

His art is consistently rural with an interest in topography. Most of his extant watercolours are of Presteign or district and date from the 1850s.

In 1832 he published *Seven Views Illustrating the County of Radnor*.**(3)** Ince added a note:

> 'Should a sufficient number of Patrons be found, it is intended to publish a second series of Views, immediately after the appearance of the present Collection.'**(4)**

1. Oliver, R.C.B., 'Joseph Murray Ince', *National Library of Wales Journal*, Volume XVII, 4, 1972, pp.371-391. This short essay gives a biography of Ince. Oliver discusses the various moves of Ince and provides a family history. *NMW* files, MSS on Ince include notes about his paintings and art education.
2. Sotheby's *Eighteenth and Nineteenth Century British Drawings and Watercolours*, 20 November 1986, lot 9, a volume of Cambridge views by Ince dated between 1834-1840.
3. Published by Carpenter and Son, 14 Old Bond Street, [London]. Ince both drew and lithographed the plates.
4. No such publication was produced.

INGLEBY, John (1749 - 1808)

Landscape and topographical artist — Halkin
Book illustrator — Flintshire

Ingleby worked for Thomas Pennant, copying and executing drawings. In 1780 he was called 'an ingenious young man, one Ingleby'.**(1)** He was considered a lesser artist than Moses Griffith and was employed for minor tasks by Pennant and his contemporaries.**(2)**

Extant work by Ingleby dates from 1790s and on this evidence he appears to have been employed as a grangerizer**(3)** and an antiquarian research assistant.**(4)**

It seems likely that he executed other work, as yet undiscovered, because his obituary notice gave his profession as 'Limner'.**(5)**

1. *NLW*, MS 5500C, letter [6], dated 16 May 1780, Thomas Pennant to Richard Bull.
2. *Ibid.*, letter 7, dated 30 May 1780: 'Imgleby [*sic*] came to me yesterday and offered to copy any of my drawings at 5d [5 pence] a piece.'
   Ibid., letter 12 September 1780, Griffith charged 10s 6d [10 shillings and 6 pence] per drawing.
3. Good examples of his work are found at the *NLW*, for instance Pennant, Thomas, *History of the Parishes of Whiteford and Holywell* (1796), containing drawings dated 1794-5 by Ingleby. Often Griffith and Ingleby's work appears in the same volume, for instance the *Tours in Wales* collection at the *NLW*.
4. *NLW*, PD 9163, *Berrew* [*sic*], dated 1796: paper 24.5 x 30.5, is inscribed by Ingleby 'No Monuments worth Drawing'.
5. *NLW*, Bishop's Transcripts, Flintshire, Halkin, describes Ingleby, born in Halkin in 1749 and having died there on 26 August 1808.

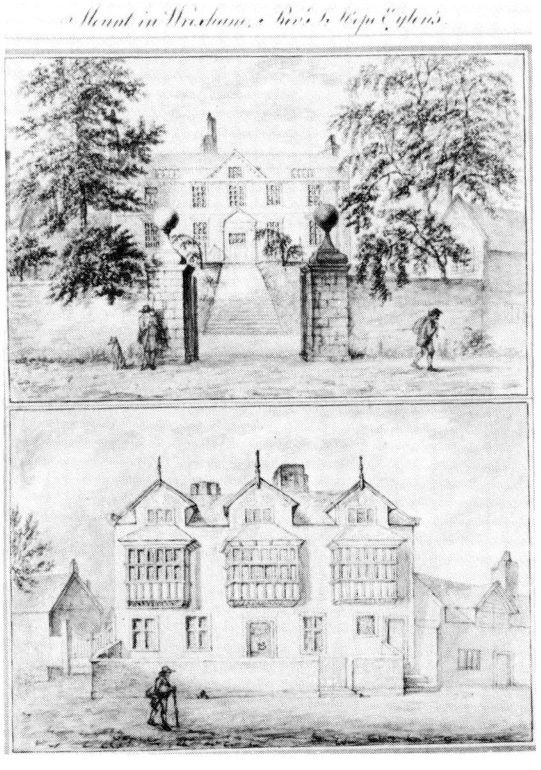

44 Ingleby, John, *Mount, Wrexham*, watercolour, 1793, PD9139.

J

J., J. (fl 1835)

Slate carver — Bethesda

Depiction of two figures (head and shoulder) with a cockerel and potted bush.**(1)**

1. G. Caffell, *Llechi Cerfiedig Dyffryn Ogwen* (1983), p.13.

JACKSON, Miss H. (fl 1803 - fl 1833)

Portrait and miniature painter — Aberystwyth
Teacher of painting and drawing — Carmarthen

Jackson stated that she was a London resident.**(1)** She worked in South Wales for a short time and exhibited her work at a local booksellers and a saddler.**(2)**

'Striking likeness warranted', she gave lessons in painting, which was very unusual for a woman.**(3)**

She was probably an itinerant artist for the Season and records that she had visited Liverpool, Shrewsbury, Aberystwyth and other towns where 'her likenesses have met with distinguished approbation'.

1. She does not appear in the *POL*, 1832-34.
2. *Carmarthen Journal*, 13 September 1833, p.4. She only presented one advertisement in which it is stated 'specimens may be seen at... Mr Dyer's Saddler (her lodgings), and the bookshop of Mrs White and Mr Evans'.
3. *Ibid.*, 13 September 1833, p.3: 'Gives lessons in Drawing [and painting] in all its branches — single lessons 2s 6d each, or £1.5s per dozen'.

JAMES, Benjamin (fl 1835 - fl 1850)

Architect — Llangattock
Newport
Stow Hill

Pigot's, 1835, p.755.
Slater's, 1850, p.18.

JAMES, Charles (1815 - 1852)

Surveyor**(1)** — Llanddewi Brefi

1. Rees, D. Ben, *Hanes Plwyf Llanddewi Brefi* (1984), p.76. Not in *Eden*.

JAMES, Horatio (1789 - 1850)

Landscape artist — Penralley
Rhayader

James was a commander in the Royal Navy who also worked as an amateur artist. He painted several watercolours of places around the world and continued to paint when he lived at Penralley.**(1)**

1. Williams, David H., 'Commander Horatio James R.N. of Penralley Rhayader', *The Transactions of the Radnorshire Society*, Vol. LXI, 1991, pp.9-18. The article

includes a portrait of James. The *NLW* Penralley Papers, 1992, item 551, gives a watercolour, *Castle in Wales*.

JAMES, John (- 1821)
Mason
Brongaist
Troed yr Aur
Cardiganshire

SD/1821/237.

JAMES, John (fl 1844)
Teacher of painting
Haverfordwest
Prendergast

Pigot's, 1844, p.36, 'professor of landscape'.

JAMES, Richard (- 1837)
[Architect]**(1)**
Llanbadarn Fawr
Aberystwyth

SD/1837/296: described as a 'master builder'.

1. Not in *Girouard*.

JANE, William (fl 1835 - fl 1843)
Surveyor
Chepstow

Davies Atlas. Eden, II, p.145.

JEAVONS, Mr (- 1867)
Landscape engraver
Welshpool

It appears that he retired to Welshpool and lived there for several years before his death in 1867.**(1)**

1. *Cadrawd*, p.77.

JEBB, William (fl 1835 - fl 1852)
Drawing master
Wrexham
Mount Street
Prospect Place

Worked as both a teacher of drawing and music.**(1)** His will catalogues oils paintings at the family residence at Prospect Place.**(2)**

1. *Pigot's*, 1835, p.730; 1844, p.67.
2. *SA*/1852/237/I, notes his wife Ann Jebb and daughter Margaret Eliza Jebb. Owned a small portion of land.

   'I give her

   all my oil paintings, namely the portraits of Ann Jebb, my said wife, myself & daughter aforesaid usually hung up in my sitting room on the ground floor, next to the street. Also I give her all my prints, drawings, materials for drawing, musical instruments...library of miscellaneous books.'

JEFFREYS, Thomas (1812 - 1870)
Carver and gilder
Carmarthen
King Street
Little Water Street**(1)**

Probably moved from Bristol to Carmarthen in 1846. Recorded frames by Jeffreys are at the Guildhall Carmarthen and Old Town Hall, Llanelli.**(2)**. In 1851 he was invited to exhibit at the Great Exhibition as a 'clever & deserving mechanic'.**(3)**

1. *Hunt*, 1849. p.68, gives address as Little Water Street.
2. Information Mrs Edna Dale Jones (1992). Possibly also still working in Carmarthen in 1859. See *Dale-Jones* for an account of his career. He also gilded the interior of Pantglas in 1854.
3. *Dale-Jones* p.76.

JENKINS (fl 1850)
Monumental mason
Bridgend

'Jenkins of Bridgend some 50 years later [c1850] usually gave his new memorials a couple of coats of paint...'**(1)**

1. Burgess, F., 'Painted tombs: some historical precedents', *Commemorative Art*, XXXIII, 1966, p.241.

JENKINS, David (fl 1765)
Surveyor
Lammas Street
Carmarthen

Eden Supplement p.429

JENKINS, Edward (- 1856)
Mason
Pen-bre
Portobello Inn
Carmarthenshire

SD/1856/185. Also described as a publican.**(1)**

1. Included an inventory:

'1 Chimney glass & ornaments	0-15-0
1 looking glass	2-0
Fine things	10-0
Old tools	2-0

JENKINS, George Thomas (fl 1856)
Surveyor
Haverfordwest

The son & successor of Joseph Jenkins.**(1)** He rebuilt the rectory at St Lawrence in 1836.**(2)**

1. Noted in *NLW* St Davids, Bounty Plan 171, 1856, but otherwise unrecorded, Not in *Eden*.
2. *ibid*.

JENKINS, John (- 1745)
Mason
Swansea
The Upper Lamb
Greenhill

SD/1845/211. Also described as a 'victualler'.

JENKINS, John (- 1787)
Mason — Kidwelly

SD/1787/32.

JENKINS, John (fl 1838)
Surveyor — Ruthin, Plas-y-ward

Eden, II, p.146.

JENKINS, John (- 1855)
Mason — Llangyfelach (Rhydypandy) Caernarfonshire

SD/1855/12 (I): Fairly detailed list of goods including '1 Clock'.

JERMAN, Hugh (1836 - 1895)
Landscape painter — Llanidloes
Teacher of drawing

Born in Llanidloes where his father Richard Jerman (1814-1866) was a master carpenter and joiner. He became a pupil teacher at the National School, Llanidloes and remained there until 1854.

By 1856 he was given a certificate of proficiency as a teacher of drawing.**(1)** He became one of the earliest art teachers in Wales and after a period in Lincolnshire moved to Connah's Quay in c1856.

1. Morris, E.R., 'A Montgomeryshire Artist - Hugh Jerman Llanidloes', *Montgomeryshire Collections*, Volume 72, 1984, pp.45-52. His extant work dates from 1885. *Montgomeryshire County Times*, 19 December 1970, p.8, illustrates a painting by Jerman, *Crownllwyn*. The article also some biographical details of the artist. I am grateful to my colleague Cledwyn Fychan for this reference.

JERNEGAN, William (1751 - 1836)
Architect — Swansea Burrows

Jernegan moved to Swansea in the 1780s and settled in the town. He became the 'Principal architect'.**(1)** He designed many buildings in South Wales; his more important works were *Marino* (1783), *Countess of Huntington's Chapel, Swansea* (1789) *Mumbles lighthouse* (1793), *Cardiff Goal* (1795-6), *Sketty Park* (c1820).**(2)** A recently identified drawing of the *Landore Copper Works* confirms his work there in 1794.**(3)**

He died in Swansea and was buried at St. Mary's Church.**(4)**

Despite being 'the leading architect in South Wales of his generation',**(5)** he was bankrupted in 1811 but later continued his practice & died leaving a well furnished residence in Adelaide Place, Swansea**(6)**

1. *Colvin*, pp.546-547. He appears in the *Swansea Guide*, 1802, p.43, as 'Jeringan, Mr William Architect'; *ibid.*, 1813, appendix (no pagination), and *Pigot's*, 1830, p.862. Not in *Girouard*. *Lloyd* pp.58-62 gives much new information & illustrates 3 structures by the architect.

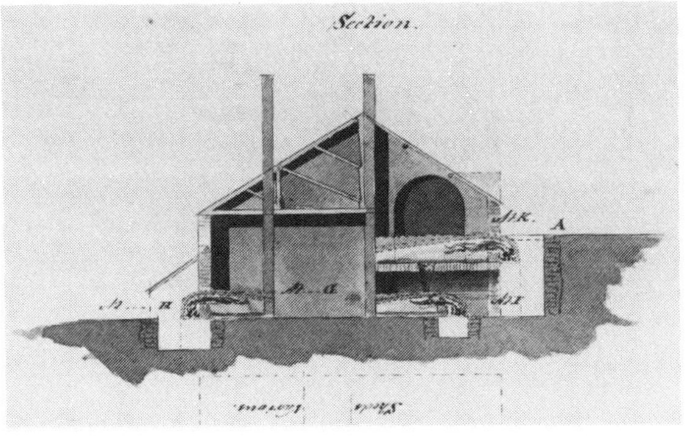

45a Jernegan, William, *Copper works at Landore, near Swansea*, pen & ink, c1794, PE5213.

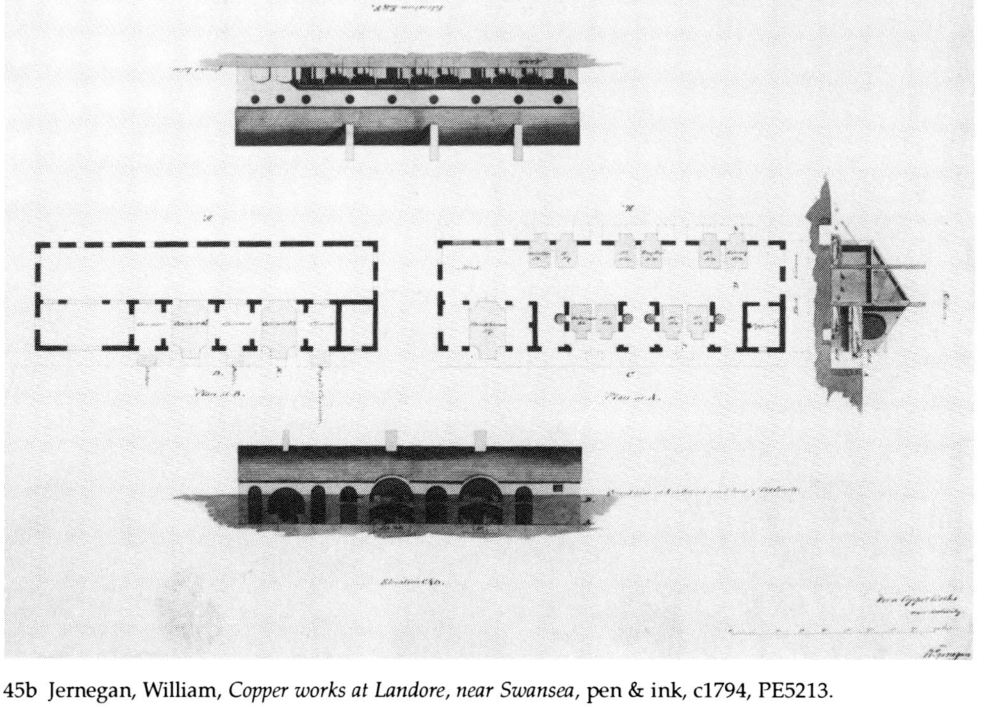

45b Jernegan, William, *Copper works at Landore, near Swansea*, pen & ink, c1794, PE5213.

2. Some are illustrated in *Rogers*, for instance *Marino*, Plate 126 of *PP*; *Gower* XXV, p.4, mentions that Stouthall near Penrice was probably by Jernegan, p.45, illustrates an unexecuted design for the Town Hall of Swansea 1825.
3. *NLW*, PE 5213, identified by the author and Stephen Hughes (RCAMW), November 1986. Christies, 16 December 1986, Lot 42 (illustrated).
4. West Glamorgan Record Office, *St Mary's Burials*, p.295, illustration 264: 'William Jernegan of this town Architect who died January, 11th 1836. Aged 86 years.'
5. *Lloyd* p.58.
6. *Lloyd* p.62, *Cambrian* 6th February 1836 p.2. The sale notice gives details of 'the whole of the valuable Oil Paintings, Prints & Engravings by Ancient Masters; together with the Library'.

JOHN, Alfred (fl 1850)
Portrait and miniature painter — Swansea, Goat Street

Hunt, 1850, p.132.

JOHN, Daniel Llewellin (fl 1844 - fl 1852)
Portrait and banner painter — Newport, Stow Hill

He was presumably a versatile craftsman, possibly employed by Institutions for their impressive banners.**(1)**

1. *Pigot's*, 1844, p.14. He was also given as a portrait painter in *Slater's*, 1850, p.18. *Hunt*, 1849, p.115, described him as a 'portrait and banner painter' & similar entry in *Scammell & Co* 1852, p.131.

JOHN, David (- 1777)
Mason — Llanybydder

SD/1777/171.

JOHN, David (- 1812)
Mason — Cardigan

SD/1812/14.

JOHN, Henry (fl 1758 - fl 1784)
Surveyor — [Pembrokeshire?]

NLW has a large collection of maps by John of Pembrokeshire and some in Carmarthenshire.**(1)** Several of his surveys were copied by Thomas Lewis *supra*.**(2)**

1. NLW Picton Castle Collection has a number of examples.
2. For instance Picton Castle MSS Map Volume, 1773, *Eden* II p.147.

JOHN, William (fl 1806 - fl 1851)
Coach painter — Haverfordwest, 36 Prendergast Hill

Born at Haverfordwest and lived close to James Devonald, coach builder (39 Prendergast Hill). This is one of the very few *documented* examples of craftspeople working and living in the same street.**(1)**

1. Census 1851, *DFHS*, IV Folio 212, p.9.

JOHNES, Mariamne (1784 - 1811)
Miniature landscape painter — Hafod

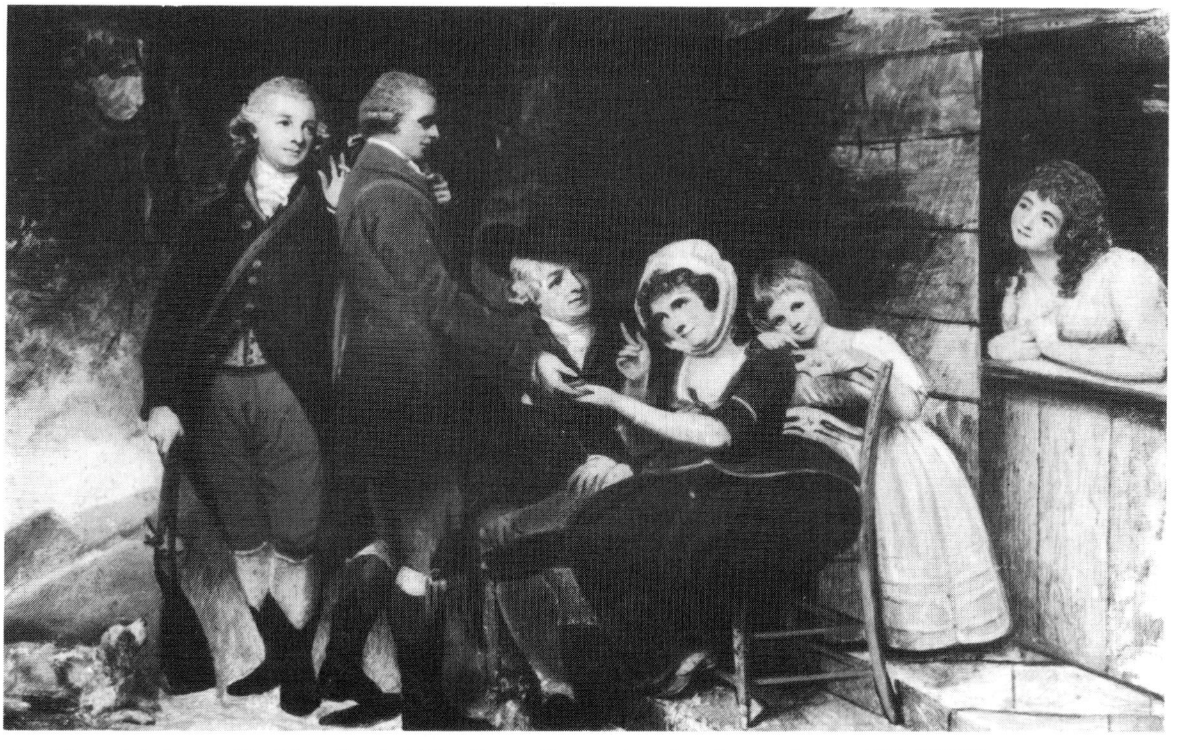

46 Johnes, Mariamne, *The Johnes Family* (After George Romney), watercolour on ivory, c1800, PG5516.

Mariamne was the only child of Thomas & Jane Johnes of Hafod. She was introduced to many important people of the time & would have known several artists. She was taught drawing by Thomas Stothard at Hafod**(1)** and Gasparé Trossarelli (possibly).**(2)**

It appears that she suffered much & was an invalid for the majority of her life. Thomas Johnes considered his daughter talented 'Viganoni leaves us on Tuesday. His improvement at Mariamne's playing & singing is wonderful, but I believe her talents for drawing are equally good.'**(3)**

Her monument by Sir Thomas Chantrey at Hafod Church [destroyed 1932] fittingly shows the emblems of music, literature & art.

In November 1994 a copy of the Hafod picture by George Romney (1734-1802) was bought by *NLW* which is almost certainly her work & clearly supports her father's opinion.**(4)**

1. See entry on Stothard & Trossarelli reference. It is also possible that she worked with Miss/Mrs Briane at London or Bristol. *Foster* p.499 notes a Mrs Elizabeth Ann Briane (1798-1807).
2. Moore-Colyer, Richard, *A Land of Pure Delight* Llandysul, (1992) p.93 notes Trossarelli at Hafod on 10 Nov 1792. This was either Giovani or Gaspari who emigrated to Britain from Italy c.1791. Both were miniature painters & could have taught Italian, music & painting. See *Foskett* I p.553. Ibbetson may also have taught her drawing.
3. Moore-Colyer p.178, Viganoni, Guiseppi was a Haymarket singer.
4. Christies 9 November 1994 lot 59, after George Romney illustrated in the *Western Mail* 11 Jan 1995 p.11. This was mentioned in Jane Johnes' will (1831, Crosswood II 938) 'Family group by Miss Johnes framed, a copy of the great picture at Hafod'. This was noted in the *Catalogue of Pictures & Books at Hafod* 1807, p.3. Inglis-Jones, Elizabeth, *Peacocks in Paradise* (Llandysul, 1990) illustration 23 shows Mariamne's dressing room at Hafod, which may be her work. *NLW* PG5516 watercolour on ivory, with wooden support 15.2 x 24cm, in a modern frame.

JOHNS, Naomi (fl 1851)
Pottery painter — Llanelli, 2 Vaux Hall

Born in Llanelli and working in the South Wales pottery in 1851.**(1)**

1. Census 1851, *DFHS*, Vol. I. Foster (1987) p.499 gives Mrs Elizabeth Ann Briane (1798-1807).

JOHNSON, E. & T. (fl 1835 - fl 1843)
Surveyors — Llan-rhos, Caernarfonshire

Davies Atlas, Not in *Eden*.

JOHNSON, John (fl 1811)
China painter — Carmarthen

He advertised thus:

> 'Ornaments of China and Earthen wares... J.J. flatters himself that on inspection his tea sets and table services are far superior to any ever offered the Public, and on terms equally low... orders received for table services, tea sets of any quality or pattern, in gold or colours, fancy lettered or cyphered jugs.'**(1)**

Johnson bought Staffordshire china and decorated it according to individual taste.**(2)**

1. *Carmarthen Journal*, 16 March 1811, p.3.
   Ibid., 4 May 1811, p.3.
   Ibid., 18 May 1811, p.1.
2. *Ibid.*, 4 May 1811, p.3, mentions that Johnson will paint 'Amorial bearings and other devices'.

JOHNSON, Kennedy (fl 1835 - fl 1843)
Surveyor — Bangor

Davies Atlas. Eden, II, p.148.

JONATHAN, Robert (fl 1849)
Portrait painter — Bangor
Teacher of painting

Slater's, 1849, p.13.

JONES (fl 1806)
Monumental mason — Llangynider, Breconshire

Painted on slate and executed grave stones with frames.**(1)**

1. Llangenni Church, Breconshire, grave stone signed and dated 4 April 1806, c152 x 76 cm.

JONES, Mr (fl 1832)
Marble cutter — Bangor

PL, Cambrian Quarterly Magazine, Vol. V, 1832, p.140.

JONES, Aneurin (fl 1853)
Surveyor — Gelligaer, Monmouthshire

Provided plans for the repair of the rectory at Mynydd Islwyn, Monmouthshire.**(1)**

1. *NLW* Llandaff Bounty Plans 90, 1853. These are particularly colourful. Not in *Eden*.

JONES, Benjamin (fl 1835 - fl 1843)
Surveyor — Talardd, Gwarallt, Llanllwni, Carmarthenshire

Davies Atlas. Eden II p.149. *NLW*, Estate map *Llanllawddog, Llanfihangel ar Arth*, 1840.

JONES, Rev. Calvert Richard (1804 - 77)
Marine and landscape artist Swansea
Photographer

An amateur artist of great skill and ingenuity. His paintings and drawings are sophisticated and worked in a contemporary style. Jones was rector of Loughor Church near Swansea from 1829.**(1)**

It is reported that Jones patronised James Harris (Senior) (1810-87)**(2)** to train under George Chambers. Calvert Jones' drawings clearly indicate his interest in shipping and landscape, and may suggest some formal art education.**(3)**

He was an important early photographer, probably receiving his knowledge from Fox Talbot.**(4)** Amongst the extant photographs by Jones are groups of shipping, and views in South Wales.**(5)**

1. A short biography and notes on Jones were published in an exhibition catalogue by Howell, R., *The Rev. Calvert Richard Jones of Swansea*, Glynn Vivian, March 1973. See also, Painting, David, *Swansea's Place in the History of Photography*, *RISW*, Swansea, 1982, pp.7-12. Three important recent studies concentrated on Jones's photographic work: Buckmann, Rollin, *The Photographic Work of Calvert Richard Jones* (London 1990); Kraus, Hans P. (Junior), 'The Reverend Calvert R. Jones', *Sun Pictures*, Vol. 5, (New York, 1990); Jones, Iwan M., 'Scientific Visions', *Transactions of the Honourable Society of Cymmrodorion* (1990), pp.112-172. Jones, Iwan Meical, 'Calvert Richard Jones, the earlier work', *History of Photography*, Autumn 1991, pp.174-

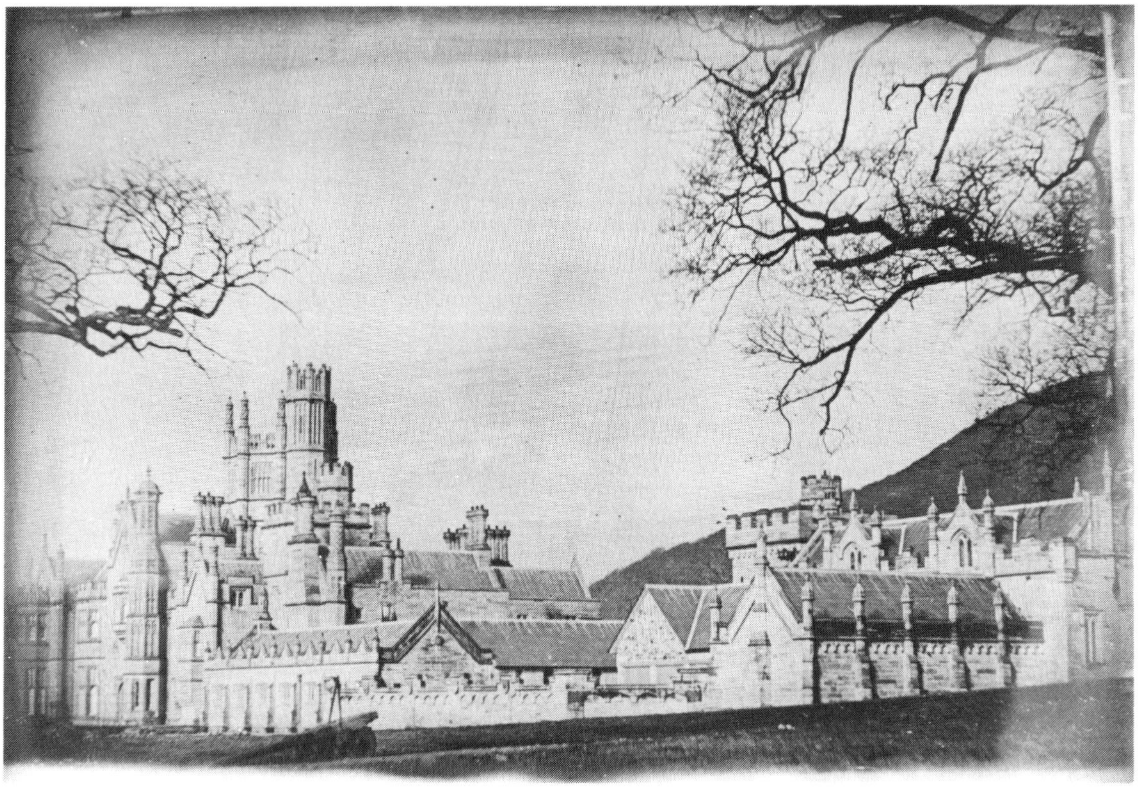

47 Jones, Rev Calvert Richard, *Margam Castle,* daguerrotype, 1841, PG726.

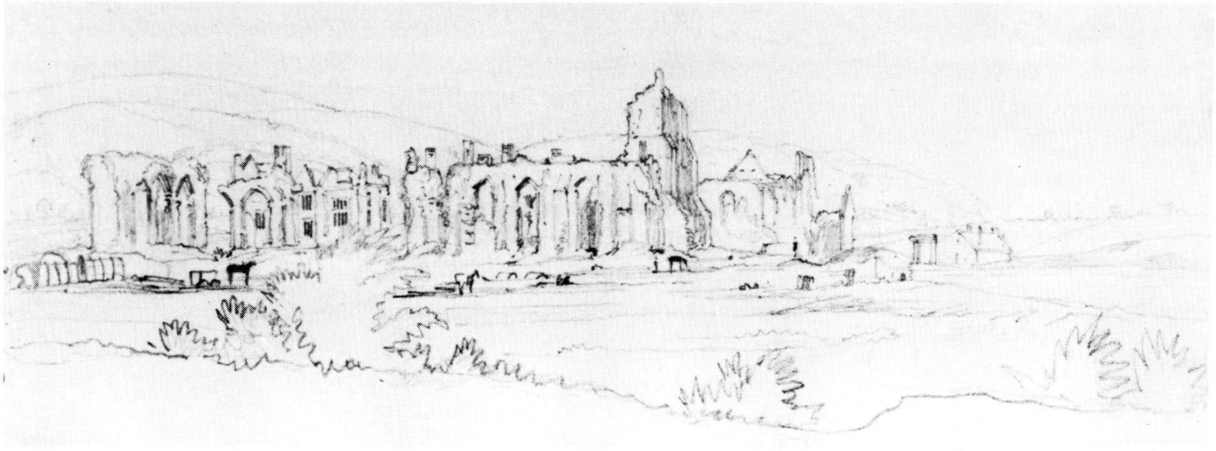

48 Jones, Rev Calvert Richard, *Neath Abbey*, pencil, 1828, Drawing Volume 383, p.4, PE4038.

179, Jones illustrates a self portrait, possibly c1820, *NLW*, PG 383, and the *Margam Castle* daguerreotype, 1841.
2. *Vide* James Harris, *supra*.
3. *NLW*, PE 4084, Drawing Volume 382 (4to) includes views of Rheola, Neath Abbey, Cyfarthfa Castle and shipping. Many are dated 1828.
4. Calvert Jones was an associate of Christopher Talbot, cousin to Fox Talbot.
5. The National Maritime Museum has photographs, dated c1845-50, of shipping. The earliest daguerreotype of Wales was purchased by the *NLW*. It is signed and dated 9 March 1841, PG 726.

JONES, Charles (fl 1844)
Engraver — Wrexham, Hope Street

Slater's, 1844, p.60, also a book binder.

JONES, Charles Woodfin (- 1856)
Painter — Ruthin

B 1856/78.

JONES, David (- 1818)
Mason — Llangyfelach, Glamorganshire

SD/1818/167.

JONES, Edward (- 1841)
Stone and marble mason — Llandygai, Caernarfon, Llwynon

B 1841/103: Hester Jones to have his books & premises.

JONES, Edward (fl 1835 - fl 1843)
Surveyor — Tanyberth, Llangar

Davies Atlas, *Eden* II p.431, possibly same person..

JONES, Edward (- 1835)
Architect**(1)** — Wrexham

There are no recorded buildings by Jones, but he died a relatively rich man.**(2)**

1. Not in *Girouard*.
2. *SA* 1835/219 (will dated 3 March 1835). He gave £100 per child and extra on reaching 24. Probably died late March 1835.

JONES, Elizabeth (fl 1827 - fl 1858)
Portrait painter — Beaumaris
Carver and gilder — 7 Castle Street

The Jones family were interior decorators and had an extensive practice in various crafts.**(1)** On her husband's will, 1827, he notes that his wife will continue the 'painting trade' with Hugh Jones, *infra*.**(2)** It is possible that the firm was still operating in 1858.**(3)**

1. *Pigot's*, 1828, p.1148 (also as painters and glaziers). *Pigot's*, 1835, p.688.
2. *B* 1838/3, Hugh Jones gives all his household goods to Elizabeth and mentions that her son James who was 'weak and sickly' will be looked after by his mother. And he requested that Elizabeth 'stays at home'.
   PL notes that there were seven children: William (1787-1873), *infra*; Eleanor, Elizabeth, Sarah, Hugh (c1800), Margaret and James.
3. *Slater's*, 1858, p.20, gives Richard Jones as a painter and glazier at this address.

JONES, George (- 1825)
Land surveyor — Oswestry

SA 1825/172: left £100. Not in *Eden*.

JONES, Griffith (fl 1829 - fl 1839)
Architect — Llanystymdwy

He presented a simple but well drawn plan for the Rectory at Cricieth.**(1)** His design for Llanystymdwy rectory is a more ambitious but still conventional & practical.**(2)**

1. *NLW*, Bangor, Bounty Plan 5, signed & dated 1829.
2. *NLW*, Bangor, Bounty Plan 101, signed & dated 1839. Not in *Colvin*, *Girouard*.

JONES, Rev. Henry Longueville (1806 - 1870)
Landscape painter — Beaumaris

He drew views of North Wales.**(1)** He also produced many illustrations for the *Arch.Cam.***(2)**

1. *NLW*, P17, A1 - A10.
2. *Cadrawd*, p.72.

JONES, Hugh (- 1827)
Painter — Beaumaris, 7 Castle Street

He was the father of Hugh Jones, *supra*.**(1)** His wife and son continued his painting business after 1827.

1. *B* 1838/3. Hugh Jones in his will writes to

   'my well beloved son Hugh Jones, whom I appoint to carry on the painting trade & in co-partnership with his mother & to have in care...& his other son James "weak & sickly".

   He also desired his daughter Elizabeth to 'stay at home'.

JONES, Hugh (fl 1835)
Coach painter — Bangor, Dean Street

Pigot's, 1835, p.685.

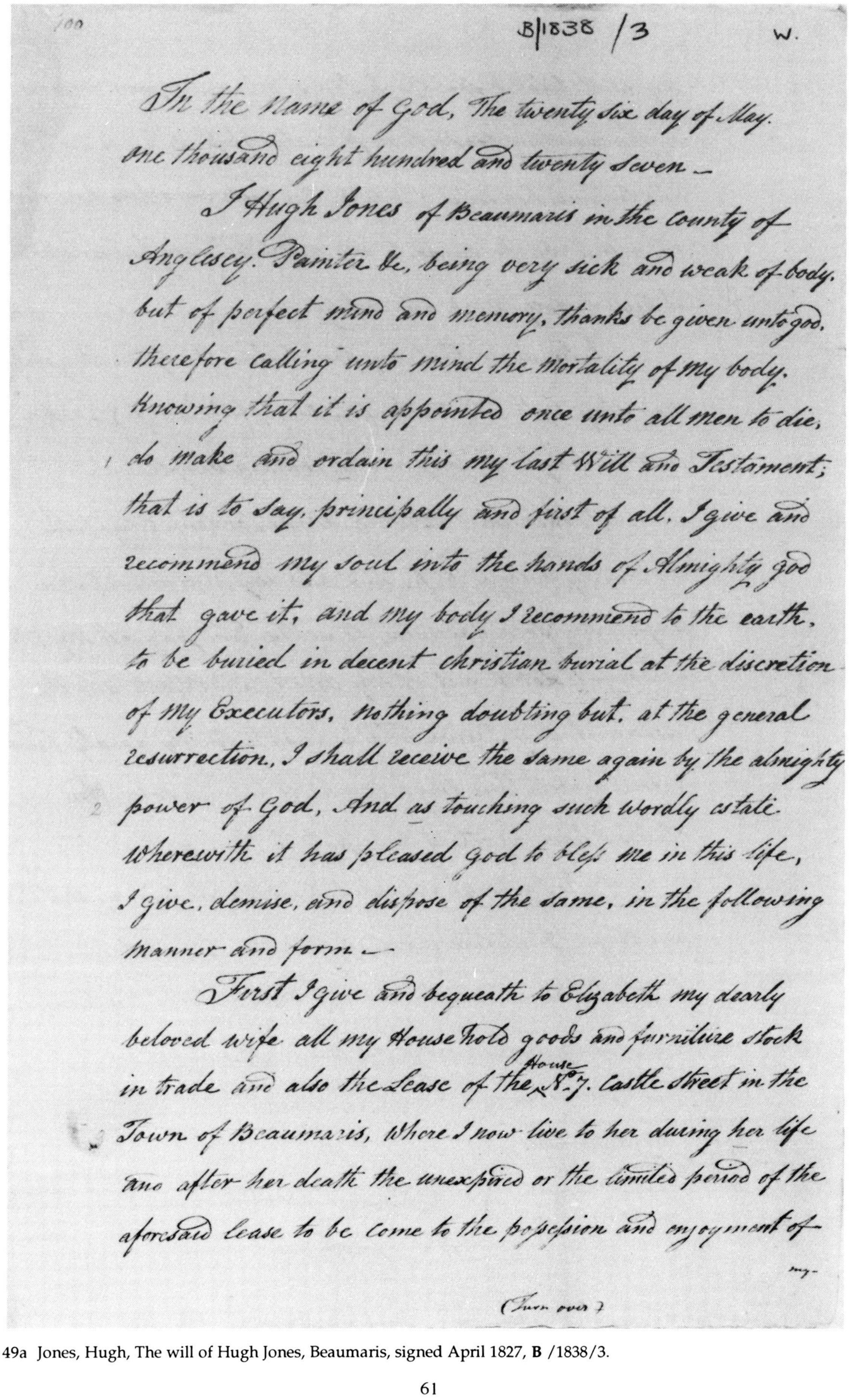

100 B/1838 /3 W.

In the name of God, The twenty six day of May.
one thousand eight hundred and twenty seven —

I Hugh Jones of Beaumaris in the County of Anglesey. Painter &c, being very sick and weak of body. but of perfect mind and memory, thanks be given unto god. therefore calling unto mind the mortality of my body. knowing that it is appointed once unto all men to die; do make and ordain this my last Will and Testament; that is to say, principally and first of all. I give and recommend my soul into the hands of Almighty god that gave it, and my body I recommend to the earth. to be buried in decent christian burial at the discretion of my Executors, nothing doubting but, at the general resurrection, I shall receive the same again by the almighty power of God, And as touching such wordly estate wherewith it has pleased god to bless me in this life, I give, demise, and dispose of the same, in the following manner and form —

First I give and bequeath to Elizabeth my dearly beloved wife all my Household goods and furniture stock in trade and also the Lease of the House No. 7. Castle street in the Town of Beaumaris, where I now live to her during her life and after her death the unexpired or the limited period of the aforesaid lease to be come to the possession and enjoyment of my

(Turn over)

49a Jones, Hugh, The will of Hugh Jones, Beaumaris, signed April 1827, **B** /1838/3.

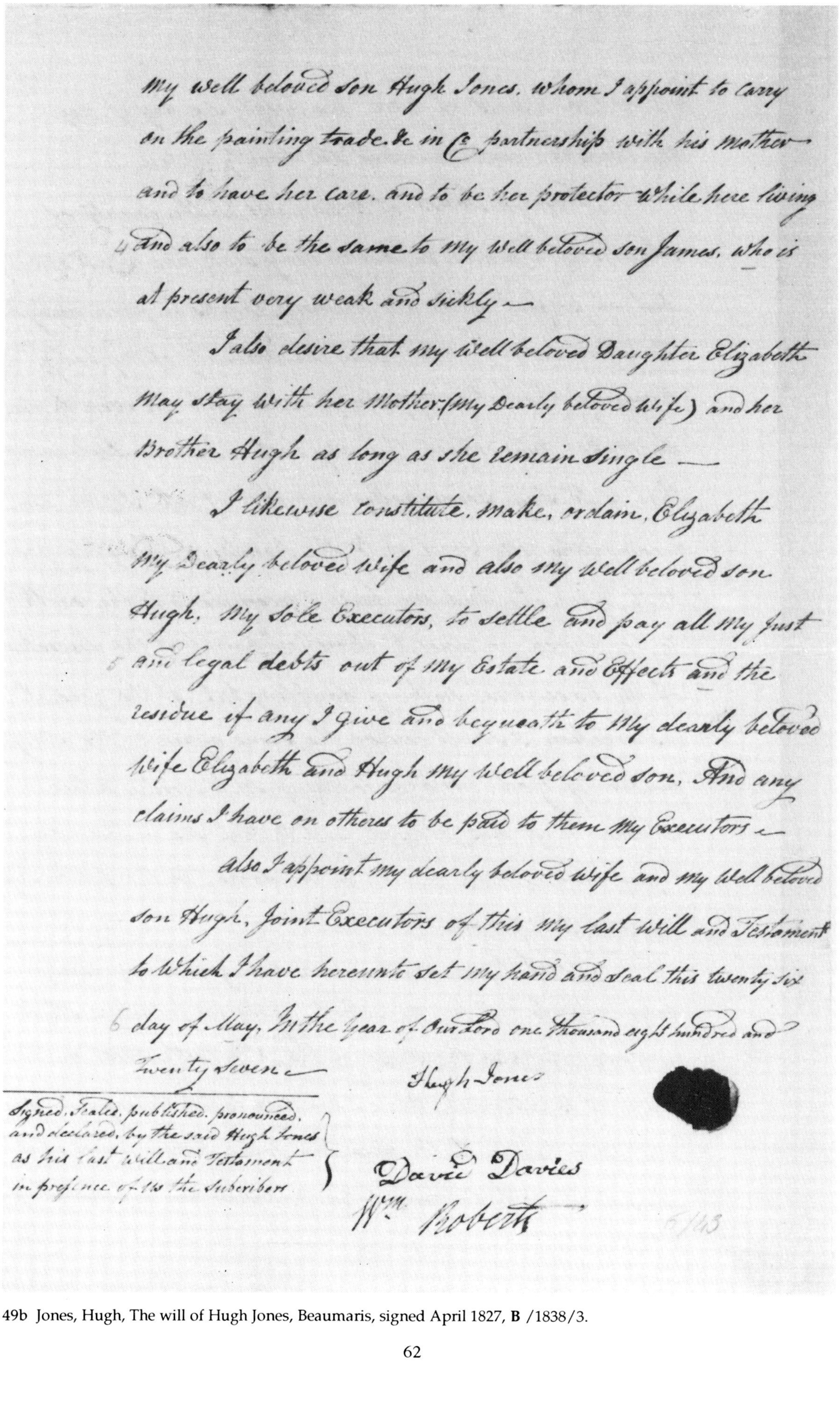
My well beloved son Hugh Jones. whom I appoint to carry
on the painting trade &c in Co partnership with his mother
and to have her care. and to be her protector while here living
4 And also to be the same to my well beloved son James. who is
at present very weak and sickly —
I also desire that my well beloved Daughter Elizabeth
May stay with her Mother (My Dearly beloved Wife) and her
Brother Hugh as long as she remain single —
I likewise constitute. make. ordain. Elizabeth
My Dearly beloved wife and also my well beloved son
Hugh. My sole Executors, to settle and pay all my just
5 and legal debts out of my Estate and Effects and the
residue if any I give and bequeath to my dearly beloved
Wife Elizabeth and Hugh my well beloved son, And any
claims I have on otheres to be paid to them my Executors —
also I appoint my dearly beloved wife and my well beloved
son Hugh, Joint Executors of this my last will and Testament
to which I have hereunto set my hand and seal this twenty six
6 day of May, In the year of Our Lord one thousand eight hundred and
Twenty seven —

Hugh Jones

Signed. Sealed. published. pronounced. and declared, by the said Hugh Jones as his last will and Testament in presence of us the subscribers

David Davies
Wm. Roberts

6/43

49b Jones, Hugh, The will of Hugh Jones, Beaumaris, signed April 1827, **B** /1838/3.

JONES, Hugh (- 1845)
Mason Denbigh

Chester Wills 1845/3.

JONES, Hugh (fl 1824 - fl 1849)
Landscape and portrait painter Beaumaris
Copyist 7 Castle Street
?Coach Painter Caernarfon

Edward Pugh recalled that he met Hugh Jones (father of H. Jones) in Beaumaris, and his son 'a fine youth lately studying the arts in London'.**(1)** By 1830 Jones was at work in Beaumaris and was commissioned by the Anglesey Hunt to paint portraits of the members. The Minute book records:

> 'that for the encouragement of native Talent, Mr H Jones of Beaumaris be recommended as the Artist to be employed and he be instructed to wait on the members for that purpose'.**(2)**

His work included original portraits and a number of copies.**(3)** It appears that he continued to work in Anglesey as a coach painter.**(4)**

He moved to Caernarfon in 1838 and took apartments at the house of Hugh Hughes in Segontium Terrace. Whilst there, he exhibited his 'portraits in oils'.**(5)**

He probably had a local practice of some success**(6)** and sometime between 1840-1848 he moved to London.**(7)**

In 1840 he published a print of *John Elias* which became one of the classic images of that preacher.**(8)** He also published sets of prints on Welsh costumes,**(9)** some important views of Beaumaris**(10)** an and excellent lithograph of the bridges across the Menai Straits.**(11)**

1. *Cambria Depicta*, p.91, *vide* Pugh. It is possible that Pugh met William Jones, *infra*, not Hugh Jones.
2. Anglesey Record Office (Llangefni) MD/I/1 p180.
3. 17 portraits were recorded by Lloyd, S.F., *The Anglesey Hunt Balls 1757-1957* (1956), p.21. *Steegman*, Volume 1, pp.1-2. *Steegman* wrongly attributes the paintings to 'T. Jones'. The majority are kept at Beaumaris Town Hall. The NLW has a portrait bearing the date 1824: Colour Plate III PB8523.
4. *Slater's*, 1835, p.685: 'Jones, Hugh (coach Painter) Dean Street, Beaumaris'.
5. *Caernarvon and Denbighshire Herald*, 9 June 1838, p.3. This was not Hugh Hughes the painter.
6. *Steegman, op.cit.*, Volume 1, p.20, gives a reference to the portrait of John G. Lewis signed (H. Jones on verso) and dated 1835 at Plas Gwyn, Pentraeth.
7. *Caernarvon and Denbighshire Herald*, 18 November 1848, p.4.
   Ibid., 2 December 1848, p.4.
   These record that Jones lived at Osnaburgh Street, Regents Park. He was still in London in 1849, *Slater's*, 1849, p.17: 'Hugh Jones Red H[ill], Portrait Painter.
   Robson's, 1840, Vol. II, p.11, gives his address at 'Castle Street, Beaumaris'.
   Slater's, 1844, p.14, 'Red Hill, artist'.
   Slater's, 1850, p.17, 'Red Hill'.
8. He painted the portrait and then advertised the print in *Caernarvon and Denbighshire Herald*, 11 July 1840, p.1. The print appeared on many chapel walls. For example a framed copy is in Llangefni R.O. (WSP/ 4). 'Painted by Hugh Jones Esq, Published by H. Humphreys, Caernarvon, engraved by W. O. Burgess Esq', 20.3 x 16.8 cm. *NLW* has several copies. *Lord, 1994* p.51 believes Jones's portrait was the original & W. Roos copied that version.
9. For instance those published by Day and Hayes c1850 and lithographed by T.H. Lynch, c23 x 28 cm.
10. These were published in 1845 and included three views of the town, approximately 16.8 x 35.4 cm. *NLW* has two of these views (P 2788, A1 - A12; PB 3298, A1 - A28).
11. *A West View of the Britannia Tubular and Menai Suspension Bridge*, published by T. Catherall, Chester and Bangor, 1850, 34.1 x 47.7.cm (*NLW*, PB 3508, C1 - C3).

See Colour Illustration III.

JONES, Hugh Lloyd (fl 1835 - fl 1843)
Surveyor Park
Llanarmon
Denbighshire

Davies Atlas. Eden, II, p.149.

JONES, James (fl 1828)
Builder Ewenny

Rebuilt the vicarage at Marcross, Glamorganshire.**(1)**

1. *NLW* Llandaff, Bounty Plan 80, 1828, a simple builder's plan of the house. Not in *Eden*.

JONES, John (1785 - 1815)
[Caricaturist] Llanrwst

John Jones was an important publisher and printer of Welsh ephemeral material. He may have produced some of his own illustrations but no firm evidence is available at present.**(1)**

1. Morgan, Gerald, *Y Dyn a Wnaeth Argraff* (Llanrwst, 1982). Morgan gives no specific reference to Jones as an artist but illustrates a number of interesting images.

JONES, John (- 1809)
Mason Brecon
St John Evangelist

BR/1809/6.

JONES, John (fl 1835 - fl 1843)
Surveyor Pembroke

He was an estate agent, registrar and Clerk to the Board of Guardians.**(1)**

Davies Atlas, Eden II p.149..

JONES, John (fl 1835)
'Engraver'
Dame Street
Carmarthen

Pigot's, 1835, p.753.
Robson's, 1840 (Carmarthenshire).

JONES, John (?fl 1844 - fl 1850)
Surveyor
Amlwch

Jones produced detailed plans & an attractive interior plan for Llanfachell Rectory in 1850.**(1)**

1. *NLW* Bangor, Bounty Plans 53, 1850. *Eden* II p.149 notes a J. Jones of Plas Isa, Corwen working in 1844, possibly the same person.

JONES, John (- 1857)
Mason
Llandyfriog
Pontgery
Cardiganshire

SD/1857/248 (I): Inventory includes '1 Clock & American Clock 2-10-0'.

JONES, John (1810 - 69)
'Talhaiarn'
Denbigh and Flintshire
Architect

Talhaiarn was taught his father's trade of joiner at Llanfair Talhaearn. He worked as an apprentice for Ward with the Bagot Estate 1825-30,**(1)** then moved to work under Thomas Penson (c1790 - fl 1857)**(2)** at Oswestry.

Although he moved to London, in 1851 he produced some work in Wales.**(3)**

1. *DWB* notes that he worked on bridges in Denbighshire and Montgomeryshire.
2. *Vide* entry under Thomas Penson (Senior), *infra*.
3. *NLW*, PB6406, *Llanfair Talhaiarn Church*, 21.8 x 27.2 cm, watercolour, inscribed 'Drawn by Talhaiarn 1841'.

JONES, John Emrys (mid-19th century)
Stone Mason**(1)**
Merthyr
Swan Street

This is probably the same man as John Jones described as a sculptor & stone mason at Swan Street, Merthyr.**(2)**

1. (*PL*)
2. Scammell & Co 1852 p.98.

JONES, John Waring (fl 1845)
Interior designer
Carver & gilder
Swansea
12 Castle Street
29 Wind Street

'Just returned from London', after seven years practice. He cleaned and varnished pictures and noted 'Rooms decorated in Gold & Ornamental Designs'.**(1)** He established a practice at Wind Street by 1849.**(2)**

1. *Cambrian*, 11 January 1845, p.2: advertised as a carver and gilder. *Dale-Jones* p.74 notes a J. Jones at Carmarthen in 1814, this could possibly be the same man.
2. *Hunt*, 1849, p.157, at Wind Street.
   Hunt, 1850, p.136.

JONES, Jonoval (1826 - ?)
Portrait painter
[Dolgellau]

Painted his father's portrait, *W.E. Jones, Cawrdaf*.**(1)**

1. Jones, William Ellis (Cawrdaf), 1795-1848, *infra*. There is a copy of this print in *NLW*, MSS 12, 353D, p.281.

JONES, Joseph (- 1844)
Land surveyor
Ystradgynlais
Ystrad Cottage

SD/1844/308. Not in *Eden*

JONES, Meredith (fl 1744 - fl 1764)
Surveyor
Brecon

NLW, has several Estate maps in Breconshire. Jones, Theophilus, *A History of the County of Brecknock*, includes a map of *Brecon* by M. Jones, dated 1744. *Eden* II p.431.

JONES, Phillip (- 1848)
Stone mason
Llanddewi Brefi
Penlan

SD/1848/339.

JONES, Rees (- 1759)
Mason
Llandingad
Llanymddyfri

SD/1759/63 (I).

JONES, Richard (1768 - 1815)
Surveyor
Pantirion
Pembrokeshire

NLW, Estate Maps in Cardiganshire, Glamorganshire, Pembrokeshire. Also possibly Pantygarn, *Eden*, II, p.150.

JONES, Richard (fl 1812 - fl 1815)
Builder
St Asaph

He produced very simple, plain buildings.**(1)**

1. *NLW* St Asaph, Bounty Plans 143, 1812 *Llandulas Rectory*, Bounty Plan 43, 1814 *Gwytherin*, Bounty Plan 56 St Asaph, 1815.

JONES, Robert (- 1828)
Architect**(1)**
Llanbeblig
Caernarfonshire

B 1828/88.

1. Not in *Girouard*.

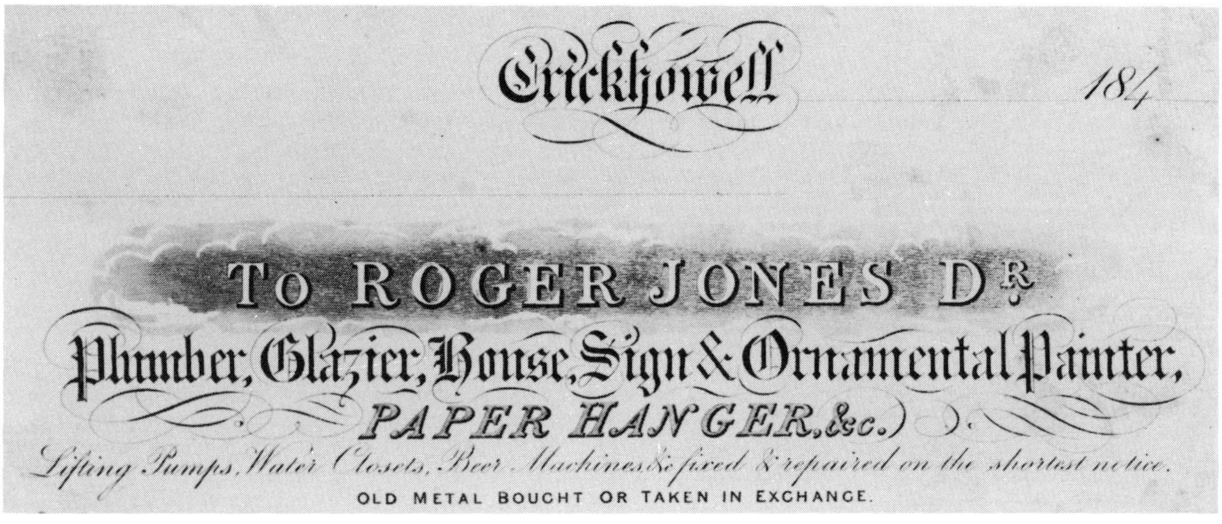

50 Jones, Roger, *Trade Card*, 1840s (Misc. Prints, A).

JONES, Roger (fl 1840s)
Plumber, glazier — Crickhowell
House, sign & ornamental painter
Paper hanger

His trade card indicates that this craftsman had an extensive and varied business.**(1)**

1. *NLW*, Misc. Prints (A).

JONES, Theophilus (1759 - 1812)
Landscape draughtsman — Brecon
Lion Street**(1)**

He appears to have produced drawings of Breconshire antiquities and landscapes.**(2)**

He was acquainted with Thomas Price 'Carnhuanawc' (*infra*), and presumably was taught drawing in the same intellectual circle.

1. *DWB* p.513.
2. *NLW*, XDA 1340 J78 (4to), *A History of the Country of Brecknock* (3 vols), Brecknock: T. Jones, 1805. This work contains sepia drawings attributed to Theophilus Jones, for example, Vol. II.1, facing p.292, has *Llanddewi'r Cwm Church*. In the same volume, facing p.320, there is a sepia drawing signed Jeston Humphrey, *Trebarriod* [*House*]. It may be that

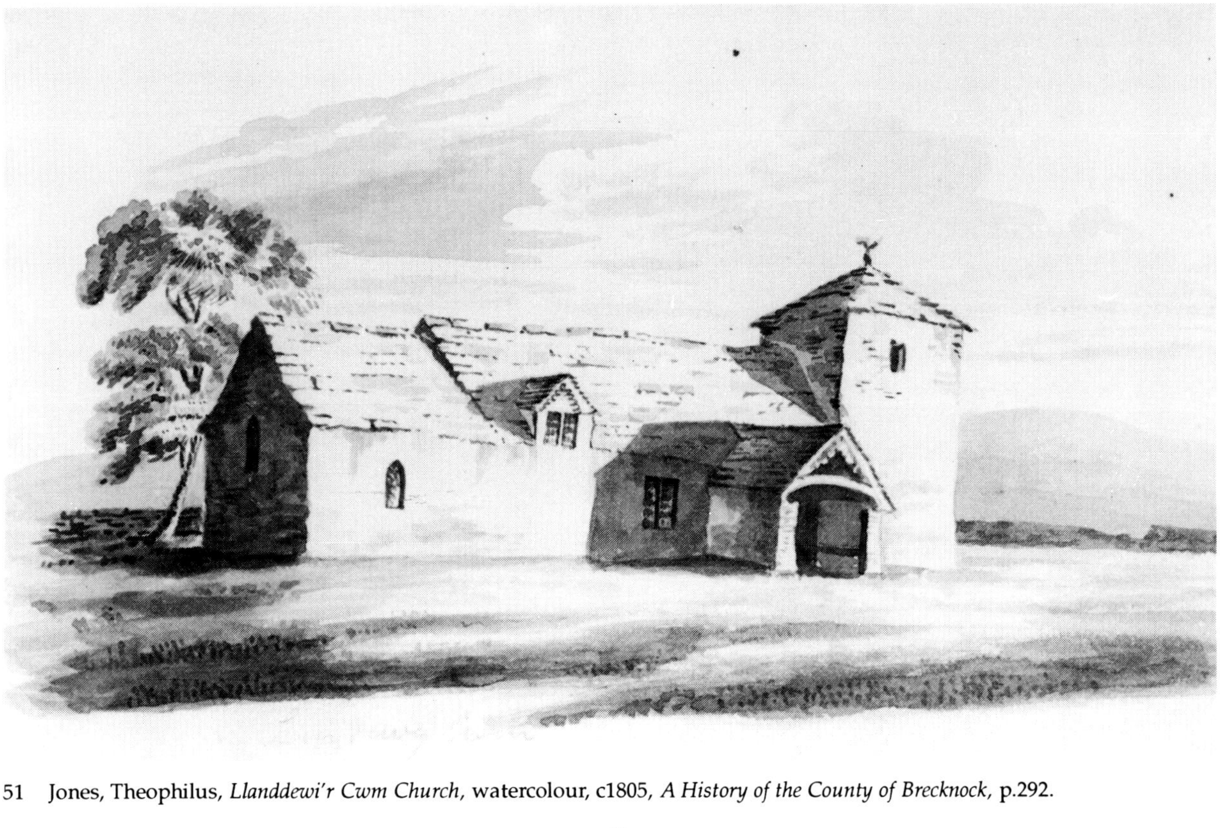

51 Jones, Theophilus, *Llanddewi'r Cwm Church*, watercolour, c1805, *A History of the County of Brecknock*, p.292.

Humphrey was the artist of the other pictures also. The style is very similar but the Humphrey drawing is slightly more embellished.

JONES, Thomas (fl 1791)
Sign board painter — Pennant Melangell, Montgomeryshire

Probably a signboard and grave-stone painter. He produced a large mural on the east wall of the nave at Pennant Melangell in 1791.**(1)** This remains the largest and best preserved wall painting extant in Welsh. It includes the Creed, the Lord's Prayer, Ten Commandments and has two angels which are reminiscent of grave-stone images.

1. *NLW*, MSS Dept, St Asaph Diocese, Pennant Melangell Parish, Vestry Book, 1791, 'Paid Mr Thomas Jones for doing Ten Commandments etc £3'. The mural is signed by Jones. It has been restored and rehung on the opposite wall of the nave. *Lord, 1993,* illustrates the painting, p.11.

JONES, Thomas (- 1815)
Architect/Surveyor — Oswestry

SA 1815/147. Not in *Eden.*

JONES, Thomas (c1794 - 1859)
Architect — Chester, Flintshire

He worked from a Chester office but was the County Surveyor of Flintshire.**(1)** In that capacity he designed many buildings in North Wales from 1830-43.**(2)**

He drew a view of the Deanery House at St Asaph.**(3)** Jones died in Barmouth.**(4)**

1. *Colvin* pp.563-564 main source of information. *Vide* Chester list *infra* for further reference to this architect. Not in *Girouard.*
2. In 1824 he designed Talacre Hall, Flintshire. He worked on churches, public buildings (*Bala Union House,* 1838). Also St Asaph, *Deanery* 1830 & *Cathedral; Llwynegrin,* near Mold, 1830; *County Hall,* Mold, 1833-4; *Holy Trinity, Rhyl, 1835-6; Wrexham Church,* 1835; *St George's Church,* Kinmel c1835, *Trevalyn Hall,* Denbighshire, 1836-8; *Ffestiniog, St David's church,* 1840; *Llangelynin church,* 1839-40; *Bryn Asaph,* c1840; *Harlech church* 1841; *Barmouth National School,* 1841; *Llanferres church,* Denbighshire, 1843; *Llangwstenyn church,* Denbighshire, 1843; *Llanarmon church,* Denbighshire, 1846.
3. *NLW*, PB 6781, B7/3 - B107, *View of the Deanery House, St Asaph,* lithograph c1845.
4. *Colvin* pp.563-564.

JONES, Thomas (1742 - 1803)
Landscape and historical painter, Engraver — Pencerrig

Jones practised landscape and historical painting in the studio of Richard Wilson from 1763. In 1769 he returned home and produced local views. He again visited Pencerrig in 1772, 1775 and 1776.

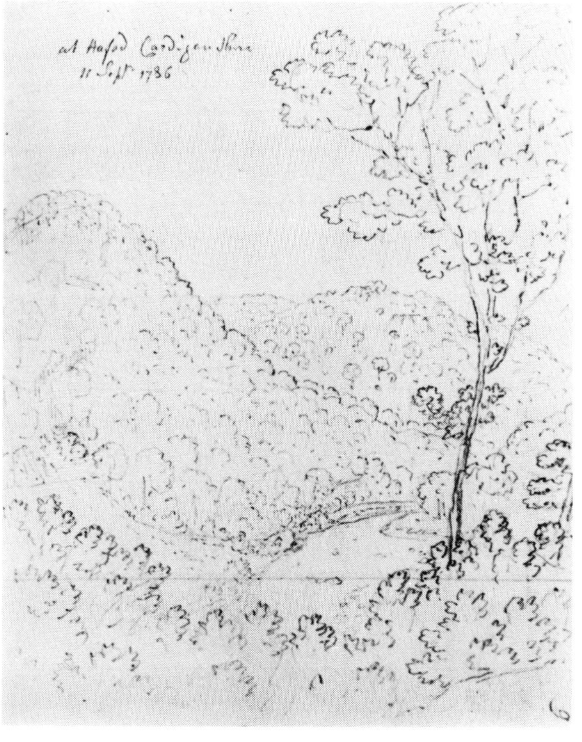

52 Jones, Thomas, Pencerrig, *Hafod Sketchbook,* 1786 folio 9 Private collection, Friends of Hafod Archive.

After an indifferent career in London he settled at Pencerrig and remained there from 1789.**(1)** His most significant work in Wales are his oils sketches dated mostly 1772 and 1776.**(2)** Such paintings were probably for his private use.**(3)**

He published by subscription, a set of engravings of Welsh Landscapes in c1775.**(4)** The majority of the subscribers were Welsh**(5)** and therefore his work probably represents an important native publication comparative with Paul Sandby's *Views in Wales.***(6)**

He kept close links with G. Marchi and other London-based artists even after his removal to Wales.**(7)**

Baker used some of Jones's views for illustrations to his work.**(8)**

1. *Memoirs* provides the main biographical details.
2. *Vide Thomas Jones* (1742-1803) GLC 1970 (exhibition catalogue) items 4, 5, 11, 12, 13, 14. Another useful source is Gere, J.A., 'Thomas Jones: an Eighteenth Century conundrum', *Apollo,* June 1970, Volume XCI, pp.469-470. This article specifically discusses the oil sketches.
   Gowing, Lawrence, *The Originality of Thomas Jones* (1986), contains a number of good colour illustrations of his work. Oliver, R.C.B., *The family history of Thomas Jones* (1970), has some illustrations.
   There is also a curious article by Neville Morris in *Y Casglwr* 39, Nadolig, 1989, 'Yr Arlunydd Mawr a anghofiwyd', pp.18-19.
3. They remained in his estate and a number are still owned by the family; *vide* Gowing, *ibid.*
4. *NLW*, BV202, *Six Views in South Wales drawn after nature by Thomas Jones F.S.A.G.B.*, approximately 22.7 x 29.9 cm, with list of subscribers and historical notes. Jones was elected F.S.A. in 1772.

Morgan, P., 'Thomas Jones of Pencerrig', *Transactions of the Honourable Society of Cymmrodorion*, 1984, pp.51-76, illustrates two plates from the set, *Caermarthen* [*sic*] & *Brecknock Castle*.
5. 65 Welsh subscribers and 27 English recorded in the list.
6. Sandby, Paul, *Views in South Wales* (1775) (BV3 4to).
7. *Vide* Marchi, G., *infra*.
8. Baker, James, *A Picturesque Guide to the Local Beauties of Wales* (London, 1791-94) (*vide* Lewis, M. Gwyneth, 'James Baker's picturesque guide through Wales', *National Library of Wales Journal*, Vol. XII, No. 4, Winter 1962). Lewis provides a list of all the artists used by Baker and Thomas Jones appears four times, one example is *NLW*, PZ 3535, A13 - A1, *Aber-Edow Rocks*. He also used original works by Ibbetson and Moses Griffith (*supra*).

JONES, Thomas (1820 - 1876)
'Taliesin o Eifion' Llangollen
Sign painter
[Portrait painter]

He is best remembered as a poet, and was a plumber and decorator. He painted a motto on the president's chair at the Llangollen Eisteddfod, 1858.**(1)**

Taliesin o Eifion was an important cultural figure in the region. One biographer relates that he followed his father's careeer & became mainly a sign painter. He was often seen in Llangollen: a tin of paint in one hand & brushes in the other. It appears he produced many shop signs in & around Denbighshire. Some which included his own poetry.**(2)**

The following account was recorded by Daniel Williams:

> Peintiwr a Phlymydd oedd galwedigaeth ddeublyg John Jones, tad Taliesin, a chan fod ysfa arlunio yn Thomas, a'i anfoddogrwydd i adael cartref, setlodd i lawr yng ngalwedigaeth ei dad, ond yn bennaf fel peintiwr. Mynych y gwelid ef ar 'strydoedd Llangollen, ei dun paent yn y naill law a brws neu ddau yn y llall, a'i hynodrwydd fel bardd bellach yn peri bod ei gyfeillion i ddieithriaid, yn pwyntio ato fel Taliesin o Eifion. Aeth y sôn amdano fel peintiwr artistig hwnt i ffiniau'r dref; ac am arwydd-fyrddau ychydig a oedd fedrusach. Beth a feddylier o"signboard" o'r teip cartrefol hwn a welid un cyfnod uwchben drws siop grydd yn y dref. Taliesin a'i lluniodd ac a'i peintiodd:
>
> Ha ! y troed noeth, tyred yn nes;—hwde
> Esgidiau rhad cynnes!
> Rhag oer hin, eira a gwres
> Nychlyd cei dirion achles.**(3)**

1. *Lord, 1992*, p.28, notes that Jones was a poet and also a sign painter.
2. Williams, Daniel, *Beirdd y Gofeb*, Pwyllgor Cyffredinol y Gofeb: [Llangollen?], 1951, pp.64-77. This also includes a portrait of the artist. I am very grateful to Huw Ceiriog Jones who lent me his own copy of this rare work.
3. *ibid* p.67.

JONES, Thomas (fl 1858)
Photographer Haverfordwest
Bridge Street

Slater's, 1858.

JONES, Thomas & William (fl 1837)
Slate-carvers Tregarth

Carved a slate fireplace with the signs of the Zodiac.**(1)**

1. Caffell, G., *Llechi Cerfiedig Dyffryn-Ogwen* (1983), p.17. *Lord, Barn*, p.33, illustrates the *Zodiac* fireplace.

JONES, Watkin Beynon (- 1839)
Painter Cardigan

SD/1839/113.

JONES, Watkin D.
(fl 1846 - fl 1855)
Sculptor Merthyr

Son of a monumental mason and brother of William and John Jones. Possibly trained at Merthyr and went to London to study c1846.**(1)**

1. *NLW* Ffrancis Payne Papers 847, p.8.

JONES, William (1775 - 1837)
Portrait painter Garthmyl
Montgomeryshire

Described as a land agent on his self portrait 1820.**(1)** Possibly a captain in the Montgomeryshire Militia, the portrait shows a uniform hanging in the background.**(2)**

1. *NLW*, PG 4585, oil on canvas, 47 x 39.5 cm. Noted as the youngest son of Thomas Jones (Lower Garthmyl). Donated to *NLW* 1993 from Humphreys-Owen family of Garthmyl.
2. *Montgomery Collections. Coll* Vol 16 p.119 notes officers in the Royal Montgomeryshire Militia**(2)** a 'Capt. Jones.' was promoted in 1812. This may possibly be the officer.

See Colour Illustration I.

JONES, William (c1786 - 1834)
Land surveyor Llanidloes

Gravestone 'William Jones, late of this town land surveyor who died March 23rd 1834 / Aged [4]8 years'.**(1)** He worked on a Montgomeryshire Enclosure Award map.**(2)**

1. Llanidloes churchyard, NLW Photofile, PG 1191.
2. *NLW*, Dept of Maps & Pictures, Llanidloes Parish Enclosure Award. *Eden* II p.431 possibly refers to this man living 'near Montgomery'.

JONES, William (1795)
Mason Llanfihangel Abergwesyn

BR/1795/42.

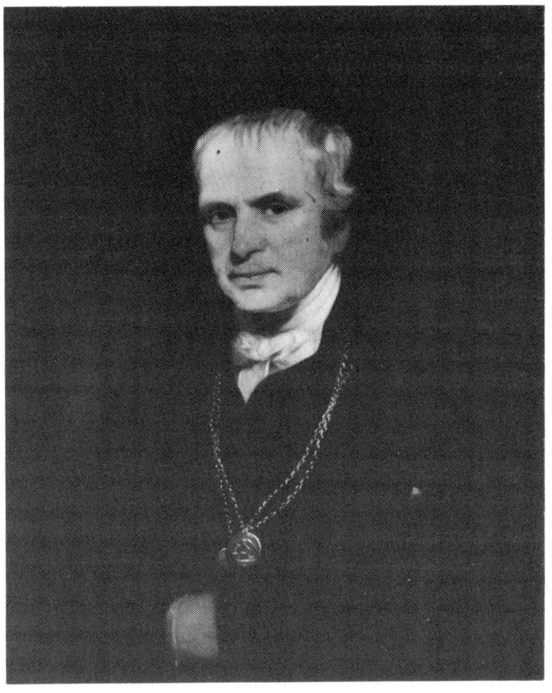

53 Jones, William, *Dafydd Ddu Eryri*, oil on canvas, 1821, PA8239.

JONES, William (fl 1835 - fl 1847)
Surveyor — Brecon, Belle Vue Place

Possibly the same man as *infra*.**(1)** It is evident that Jones also built houses using architects designs.**(2)**

1. *Davies Atlas. Eden*, II, p.150.
2. NLW St Davids, Bounty Plans 99, 1856 *Llanfrychan Rectory*, Breconshire. St Davids Bounty Plan 12, 1851. He built Boughrood rectory from plan by C. H. Howell of 31 Lincoln's Inn Fields, London (probably Charles Henry Howell 1823-1905) *Girouard* p.468.

JONES, William (fl 1835 - fl 1846)
Surveyor — Glyncastle, Neath

Davies Atlas. Eden, II, p.150.**(1)**

1. NLW PG4640 plan of Glyncastle House, Resolven dated 1840.

JONES, William (fl 1835 - fl 1843)
Surveyor — High Street, Brecon

Davies Atlas.**(1)**

1. Possibly the same surveyor as *supra*.

JONES, William (fl 1835 - fl 1843)
Surveyor — Mount Pleasant, Brecon

Davies Atlas. Not in *Eden*.

JONES, William (fl 1835 - fl 1847)
Surveyor — Newport

Davies Atlas. Eden, II, p.150.

JONES, William (fl 1836)
Slate carver — Waunfawr

Carved a large slate at Waunfawr, depicting St Ann's church.(1)

1. Caffell, G., *Llechi Cerfiedig Dyffryn Ogwen* (1983), p.13.

JONES, William 'Jones of Chester' (1787 - 1873)
Portrait painter — Beaumaris

He was born in Treffynnon and entered the *RA* schools in 1808.**(1)** He moved later to Chester but appears to have spent some years at his home.**(2)** One extant painting probably painted at Beaumaris is *Dafydd Ddu Eryri*.**(3)**

1. *Hutchison*, p.164, student 941, 'aged 19, a painter'. *Cadrawd*, p.73, gives details of Jones's life. *PL*.
2. At the *RA* he exhibited from a London address in 1819. In 1822 (44) *Painting a portrait* from a Beaumaris address, then in 1829 Chester (288) *The Bishop of London*. *Slater's*, 1828, p.1149, gives Jones at Chester. *See also* 'Artists Working in Chester'. From 1832 he again exhibited from London.
   Pigot's, 1828-9, p.1149, gives William Jones, 'Portrait painter, Church Lane, Beaumaris'.
3. *NLW*, PA8239, 75 x 62.5 cm, bears date 1821.
   Another example from this period is probably *John Williams Treffor* (1760-1826) in private collection, oil painting (*NLW*, Ports A, has copy).

JONES, William Edward (1825 - 1877)
Landscape painter — Rhewl Mostyn, Flintshire
Historical & portrait painter — Merthyr Tydfil

Born at Newmarket, Flintshire, he was trained at Liverpool and London.**(1)** It is reported that in 1856 he removed to Merthyr in the company of J.D. Williams, jeweller of London. Williams was a native of Merthyr.**(2)** He painted local portraits, such as Dr William Thomas and Holley records a number of other examples.**(3)**

His historical picture of *The Last Welsh Bard* was first exhibited at the Eisteddfod at Llangollen, 1859.**(4)**

> 'Mr Francis of Manchester, who acted as judge, awarded the prize to Mr William Jones...for his painting of "The Bard" which is undoubtedly a clever work and full of national character... The attitude of the venerable bard, standing undismayed on his dizzy height, is boldly conceived.'**(5)**

A verbose commemorative poem was written to Jones.**(6)**

1. Holley, T.F., 'William Edward Jones, painter of portraits', *Merthyr Historian*, Vol. 6, 1992, Merthyr: Merthyr Historical Society, pp.97-107. *Cadrawd* provides considerable information on this artist and notes that several good artists came from Merthyr.
2. *Cadrawd*, p.74.
3. *Ibid.*, p.99.

4. See *Lord, 1992* for details of this artist and the Eisteddfod exhibitions in general, especially pp.26-27.
5. Ibid., p.26.
6. Holley, *op.cit.*, pp.103-107:

   'Alas: The eye is closed the hand is still
   That could on canvas nature paint with skill.'

   Graves, B.I., notes pictures by W.E. Jones exhibited from a London address between 1853 and then intermittently until 1867.

JONES, William Ellis 'Cawrdaf' (1795 - 1848?)

Engraver — Dolgellau
Painter of religious works
Portrait and landscape painter

He was born at Abersoch and in 1808 was apprenticed to Richard Jones a printer at Dolgellau.**(1)** He removed to London, became a companion to a gentleman on a Grand Tour, and after some time working as a draughtsman in the West Country he returned to Wales. Evans states that 'he followed the same profession as far as he could find employment'.**(2)**

Extant works by Cawrdaf are rare.**(3)**

1. Richard Jones (1787-1855). For some description of his life and work, *vide* Jones, Ifano, *A History of Printing and Printers in Wales to 1810* (1925), p.158; *Libri Walliae*, p.281; *D.N.B*; *Gweithoedd Cawrdaf* (1851), pp.xii-xxii.
2. *Cadrawd*, p.75.
3. *Vide NLW*, photographs of two portraits in a private collection; both are stunningly simple, and probably painted in Wales. Also in *NLW* are two watercolours which were almost certainly painted on his continental tour. PB7193, *Joseph being sold by his Brothers*, 56.5 x 45.5, is a free copy of Friedrich Overbeck's fresco executed for the Casa Bartholdy in Rome, c1810. PB7194, *Jehosophat Riding*, 65.5 x 45.5 cm, may be a companion piece.

JONES, William L. (fl c1838 - fl 1847)

Sculptor — Merthyr

Son of a monumental mason, originally from Anglesea, who settled at Merthyr. He had two brothers, William also became a sculptor and John, the youngest, remained in Merthyr as a stone mason.

It is recorded that his first piece was *St Paul*.**(1)**

He moved to London in 1838.**(2)**

1. *NLW*, Ffransis Payne Papers 847, p.7: 'a bas-relief' carved from stone found at Penydarren Brook.
2. *Ibid.*, p.7.

JONES, William Lorando (fl 1840 - fl 1850)

Sculptor — Merthyr

He moved from Merthyr to London to work in the studio of Joseph Edwards.**(1)** Jones produced an important statue called *Taliesin Pen Beirdd*, which was exhibited at the Eisteddfod Y Fenni in 1845.**(2)**

1. *Gunnis*, p.221, also notes his bust of *Thomas Bevan*, 1845.
2. *Lord, 1992*, p.18. This was published in *Illustrated London News*, 25 October 1845. *PL* kindly gave me the original reference to this artist.

JOSEPH, John (fl 1847)

Builder — Cardigan

Designed & built rectory at Manordeifi, 1847.**(1)**

1. *NLW*, St Davids, Bounty Plan 137, 1847, well executed & detailed plans.

JOURNET, Monsieur F. (fl 1811/15)

Drawing master — Bangor

He published a trade card, dated in manuscript 'February 6 1811' [1815] which states:

> 'Mons F. Journet (Native of France)
> Professor of the French Language, Drawing and Fencing, Bangor'**(1)**

1. *UCW* Bangor, MS 3592 f34.

JULLIEN, Mr (fl 1843)

Photographer (daguerreotype artist) — Swansea, Neath

He advertised as 'of the Academy Royal of Paris', he visited Swansea in July 1843 and 1846. Jullien charged 'One Guinea and a half and two Guineas for Miniature and Water colour Portraits by the same unerring process, at moderate terms. Specimens may be seen at Miss Jenkins' Library, and at Mr John Morgan Jones's, Wind Street'.**(1)**

1. *Cambrian*, 3 July 1846, p.2.
   Ibid., 10 July 1846, p.[2].
   Ibid., 17 July 1846, p.[3].
   Ibid., 24 July 1846, p.[2].
   Ibid., 31 July 1846, p.3.
   Ibid., 7 August 1846, p.2.

K

KEITH, A. (fl 1855 - fl 1862)

Portrait painter — Tenby

Recorded as resident for the season at Haywood Cottage, Tenby.**(1)** He was based in London and exhibited there: 1846, 1847, 1850, 1853, 1861 and 1862.**(2)** It appears that he only visited Tenby once, and his portrait of Hon. W.H. Yelverton, signed and dated 1862, may have been executed in his London studio.**(3)**

1. *Tenby Observer*, 31 August 1855, p.3.
2. Exhibited at *RA*, *RSBA* and *BI*.
3. *Steegman*, Vol. II, p.80, records a portrait by Keith, dated 1862, at Whitland Abbey.

KENNEDY, Henry Edward (fl 1839 - fl 1897)
Architect — Bangor
Surveyor — Menai View**(1)**

He was a surveyor of tithe districts and worked from both London and Bangor.**(2)** A print after Kennedy is extant.**(3)** His plans show a surveyors attention to detail.**(4)** By 1883 he was still working at a solo practice.**(5)**

1. *Slater's*, 1844, p.9; 1849, p.11, 'High Street'. *Eden*, II, p.154, notes that he was in business with Johnson, *supra*.
2. *Davies Atlas* notes that Kennedy's address is 100 Chancery Lane, London, and also Bangor.
3. *NLW*, C3/1 - C16, *Church of Clynnog-Fawr*.
4. *NLW* Bangor Bounty Plans 32, *Llandyfrydog Rectory* plans signed & dated 1850. Also Bangor Bounty Plan 17, *Llandwrog Rectory* 1849 & Bounty Plan 48 Llanfairfechan Rectory 1852. St Asaph, Bounty Plan 103, 1846. Llys Faen Rectory.
5. *Girourad* p.522.

KNIVETON, William (fl 1800 - fl 1817)
Landscape painter — Caernarfon
[Drawing master]

He was born in Dublin and worked there before moving to Caernarfon.**(1)** By 1813 he was working in Caernarfon, but may have also visited other parts of Britain.**(2)**

Probably his most important work was the set of prints, eventually published postumously in May 1817, *Four Views in Northern Ireland*;**(3)** the set was published by subscription and advertised in the local press,

> 'William Kniveton of Carnarvon, Landscape Painter [etc.] Having by a very long continuance of pain and illness unfortunately lost his eyesight...The following subscribers inhabitants of the town and neighbourhood of Carnarvon, who have long known and respected the Author.'**(4)**

In 1816 Kniveton and his daughter organised a raffle which was a success;**(5)** after his death she was supported by local gentry.

Kniveton painted landscapes whilst at Caernarfon but may have worked mainly as a drawing master.**(6)**

1. Various examples of his work are mentioned by Strickland, *Irish Artists*, Volume 1, p.598. These included aquatints after him and works he exhibited in 1802 and 1804.
2. Strickland, *ibid.*, states that Kniveton 'resided for many years down to 1820 at 44 Leeson Street [Dublin]'. However, in 1813 whilst at Caernarfon, he received a letter from a former landlord at Shrewsbury demanding repayment of debt (Caernarfon Record Office, Poole MSS 5957).
3. There is a large correspondence on this venture, now at Caernarfon Record Office (Poole MSS).
4. *North Wales Gazette*, 19 September 1816, p.[3]. 31 subscribers were received.
5. Poole MSS 5956, dated 30 November 1816, an appeal for a raffle of a hearth rug made by Ellen Kniveton; 38 tickets were sold.
6. Poole MSS 5967, posthumous sale of Kniveton on 7 June 1817, held at Thomas Owen, Saddler's, Caernarfon, sold *Several Original Drawings of Views in North Wales*.

KRIENS, Mr E. (fl 1848)
Drawing master — Caernarfon
Bangor

Kriens worked as a French, German and drawing master.**(1)** He was also employed at Friar's School, Bangor.

1. *Caernarvon and Denbighshire Herald*, 14 October 1848, p.1.

L

LAMB, George (- 1842)
Mason — Fishguard
[Goveve]
Plas yr ŵyn

SD/1842/317 (I): Inventory includes 'household furniture & landed property'.

LANGDON, John Harries [Harris] (fl 1825 - 1853)
Architect — Newport
Stow Hill**(1)**

Langdon moved to Newport c1840? after a career in London. He designed the *Newport National School*, 1840, *Newport Alms Houses* at Stow Hill, c1840?, *Newport Town Hall*, 1842.**(2)** He is recorded as the architect of *The Friars*, c1845. By 1846-7 he was working in a Grecian style and produced a design for *Crane Street Baptist Chapel*, Pontypool.**(3)** He designed the rectory at Llangston, Monmouthshire, 1844.**(4)**

1. *Colvin*, pp.596-7. *Hunt*, 1844, p.115. *Slater's*, 1850, p.18.
2. *TL* kindly provided a short biography of this artist.
3. *TL* notes that a lithograph of *The Friars* is in *NPT*.
4. *NLW* Llandaff Bounty Plans 32, 1844 & Bounty Plans 15, *Caerwent rectory*, 1845.

LANGLOIS, Camille (fl 1838 - fl 1849)
Portrait and miniature artist — Swansea
Photographer — 5 York Place

Langlois was a resident of Swansea**(1)** and may be Langlois (Junior) who exhibited in the RA 1835-47.**(2)** In 1842 he published the following:

> 'Mr Langlois Artist
> Begs leave... of filling up a place in this Town for producting LIKENESSES on the new scientific principle called DAGUERREOTYPE but the execution of such a plan requiring the large outlay of four or five hundred pounds, upon an uncertainty, Mr C. cannot venture to go to that expense before he had obtained 150 signatures at a Guinea each (for a bust framed). To this end a book... is kept at Miss Jenkins' Library where specimens may be seen.
> Photographic Daguerreotype Portraits
> N.B.
> Subscribers will pay ten per cent less than non-Subscribers.'**(3)**

Unfortunately the venture seems to have failed, no further reference to the project can be found.

1. He is recorded in the following trade directories: *Hunt*, 1848, p.153, given as 'Langloss'. *Hunt*, 1849, p.153, not in *Hunt*, 1850.
2. Recorded as Camille Langlois, the son of Langlois (Senior), exhibiting at the *RA* 1839-47.
3. *Cambrian*, 7 May 1842, p.3.

LARGE, John (fl 1839 - fl 1840)
Surveyor Pembroke

He designed & built the vicarage at Castell Martin.**(1)**

1. St Davids, Bounty Plans 21, 1840. The plans are extremely vague concerning final details of the facade & interior. St Davids, Bounty Plans 158, 1839. Not in *Eden*.

LAWRENCE, Charles (fl 1848)
Surveyor Monmouth

Designed & built Llanfihangel Tor y Mynyth vicarage, 1848.**(1)**

1. NLW Bounty Plans 47, 1848, good, neat plans. Not in *Eden*.

LEDGEWOOD, Mr (fl 1835)
Artist Swansea

Visited Swansea in 1835, he had neither arms nor legs but, 'In the acquirements of Art and Education he will display various specimens of his ingenuity.'**(1)**

1. *Cambrian*, 19 September 1835, p.3.

LEWIS, Mr (fl 1834)
Teacher of calligraphy Carmarthen

London teacher, he visited Carmarthen and 'opened an Academy in Carmarthen for one month only'. Taught short-hand and penmanship, illustrating his advertisement with a profile. Also had an 'Exhibition of Penmanship at the Glass Warehouse'.**(1)**

1. *Carmarthen Journal*, 24 January 1834, p.2. This advertisement suggests that calligraphy was considered to include graphic art.

LEWIS, Edward (- 1834)
Mason Llandrindod

BR/1834/41.

LEWIS, Henry (fl 1832)
Builder Haverfordwest

Designed & built a rectory at Haverfordwest in 1832.**(1)**

1. *NLW* St David's Bounty Plans 57, 1832, very neat & clear drawings. Not in *Eden*.

LEWIS, John (fl c1735 - fl 1740)
Landscape draughtsman [Denbighshire?]
Engraver

He drew and engraved a series of North Wales views. These views were the largest early prints of Wales and each plate was patronized by local dignitaries. It is likely that Lewis lived or at least was associated with Denbighshire and returned to London to print and market his work.**(1)**

1. Ralph Hyde, Guildhall Library, London, is publishing an iconography, which will include this artist: *Prospects and Panoramas of British Towns 1575-1900*, forthcoming.
   Many sources mention a John Lewis (fl 1767 - fl 1776). For instance, Strickland, W.G., *Dictionary of Irish Artists* (Dublin, 1903), Vol. II, pp.20-24, gives him as a scenery painter. Grant, Colonel, *Old English Landscape Painters*

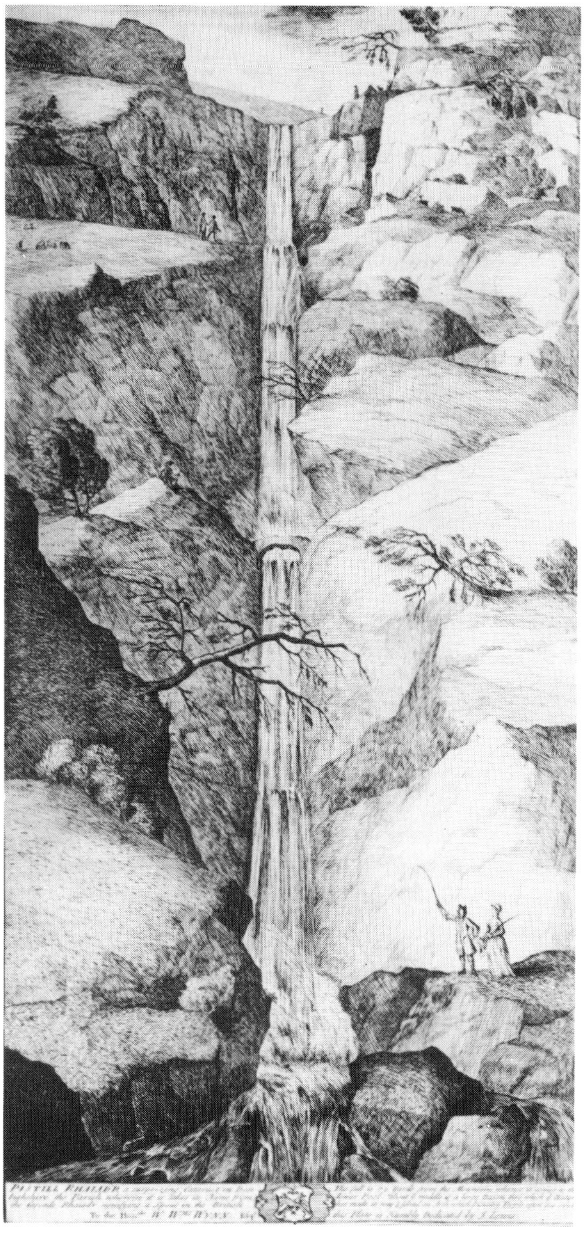

54 Lewis, John, *Pistyll Rhaiadr*, engraving, c1735-40, PZ5, PFC2M

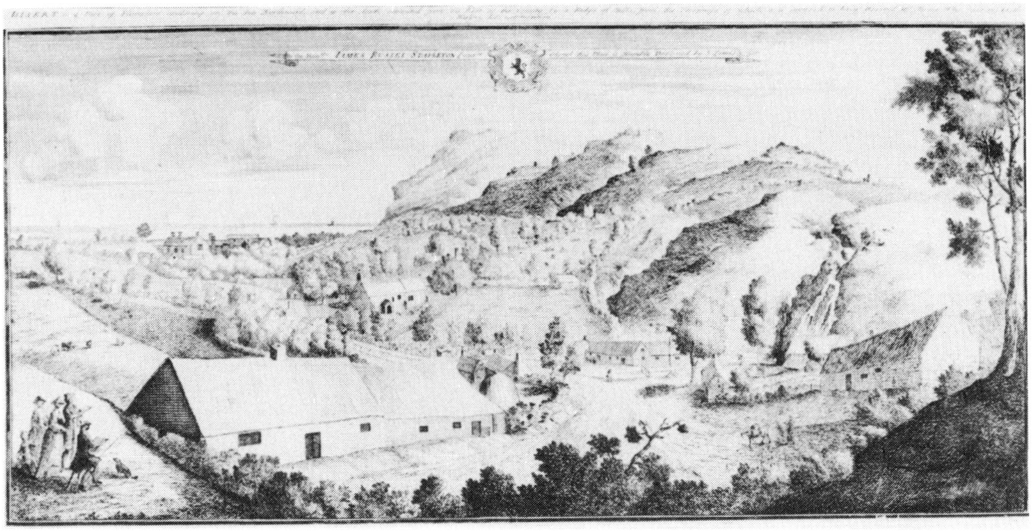

55 Lewis, John, *Disert* [sic], c1735-40, engraving, PB3044, PFC2M

(London, 1957-71), Vol. I, p.40, cites the same information. *Graves, S.A.*, gives Lewis as portrait and landscape artist. *Waterhouse* notes him as a scene and portrait painter. Edwards, Edward, *Anecdotes of Painters* (London, 1808), p.31, mentions that he resided 'chiefly in the country'.

2. *NLW*, has a good selection of his views: PB 3044; *Disert* [*sic*], Flintshire; T. Hon. J. Russel Stapleton; *St Asaph*, 'To Hon. Robert Davies Llannerch', P 404; *Pistill Rhaiadr*, a surprizing cataract..., 'To Hon. W. Wms Wynn', PZ 5; *Denbigh*, 'To Hon. Sir Robert Salusbury Cotton of Lleweir [*sic*]', PB 3048; *Ruthin*: 'To Hon. Willm Middleton', PB 3409; P 523, *Bangor*, 'To Hon. Ino [John] Wynn of the Abbey'.

LEWIS, John (- 1834)
Painter & glazier — Cardigan

SD/1834/37.

LEWIS, John (fl 1835 - fl 1843)
Surveyor — Dryslwyn Ucha, Llangathen, Carmarthenshire

Davies Atlas, *Eden* II p.164.

LEWIS, Joseph (fl 1835 - 1836)
Painter and glazier — Carmarthen, Woods Row, King Street

He was evidently a well-known artisan at Carmarthen and the *Tabernacle Church Book* records perhaps his introduction to the chapel.**(1)** He died early in 1836.**(2)**

1. *NLW*, MSS, Minor Deposit 746B (1835), p.19:

   'Mr Lewis Painter, King Street'
   Rhagfyr 7 'Daeth Mr Lewis y Painter i ymofyn ei lle. Dysgwylir i eraill dod Nos Fawrth bythefnos i heno. 30 Rhagf 1 adferia [*sic*] Mr Lewis Painter King Street.'

2. *SD*/1836/32.

LEWIS, Morgan (- 1823)
Mason — Llywel (Pentrebach)

SD/1823/264.

LEWIS, Thomas (fl 1760 - fl 1791)
Surveyor — Aberystwyth

Lewis became a burgess of Aberystwyth and worked in Pembrokeshire and a large number of areas in Cardiganshire.**(1)**

1. *NLW*, has Estate maps of these areas. *Eden* II p.165.

LINWOOD, Hannah (fl 1776 - fl 1820)
Painter of architecture — Emral Hall, Flintshire

Executed a volume of watercolours of her house in a bright, clear, delicate style. Probably taught by a drawing master.**(1)**

1. *NLW*, Drawing Volume 82.

LLANOVER, 'Gwenynen Gwent' Lady (Augusta Hall) (1802 - 1896)
Costume artist — Llanover
Silhouettist and landscape artist — Monmouthshire

Lady Llanover was deeply interested in Welsh culture, her craft reflects this emphasis. She designed a volume of Welsh costume with illustrations of traditional dress in South Wales. *Dull-wisgoedd Cymru*;**(1)** may have influenced other artists such as A.F. Rolfe and H. Jones**(2)** to produce similar genre images.

Her landscape drawings are highly Picturesque, similar to the work of Rev. William Green.**(3)** Llanover displays a multitude of influences and may not have had a consistent style.**(4)**

She painted a small self portrait in national dress in 1837.**(5)**

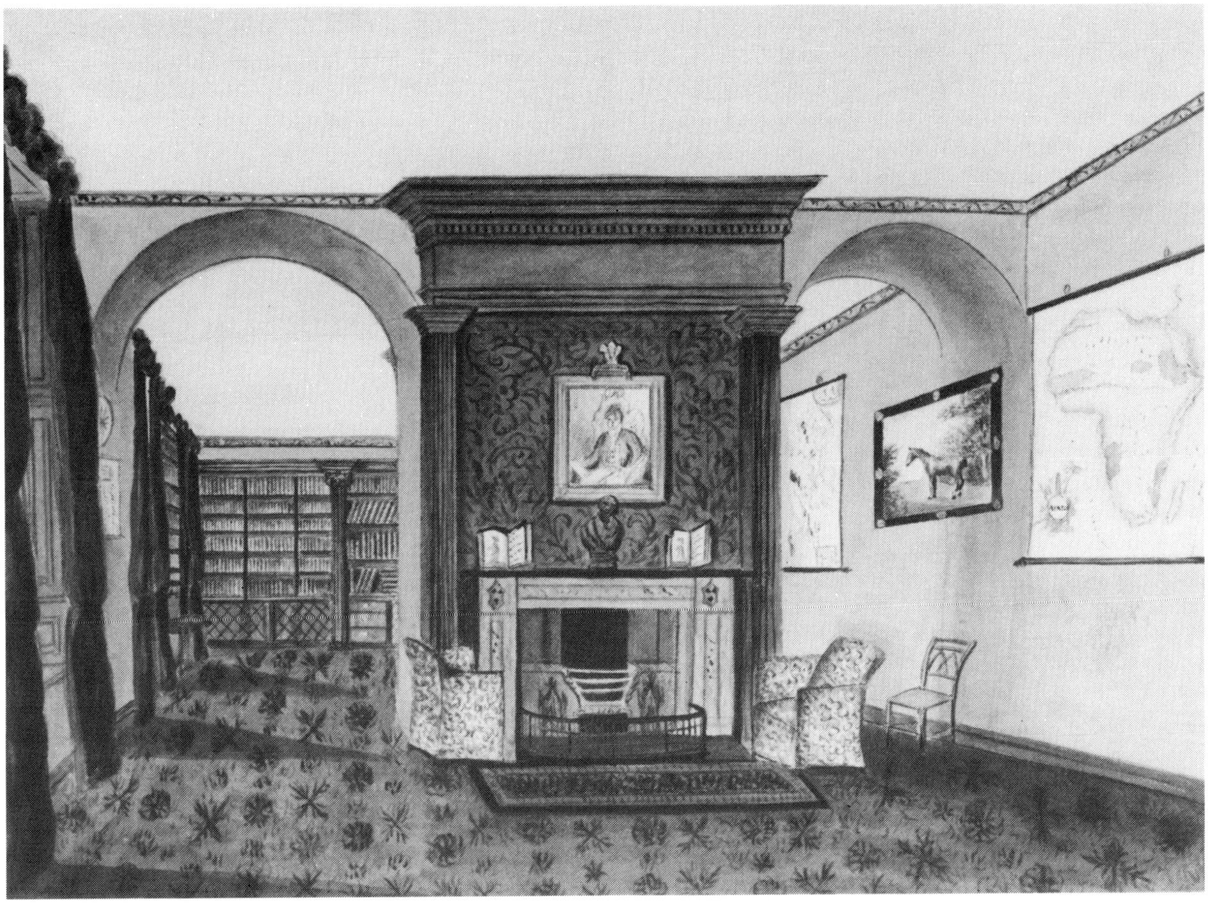

56 Linwood, Hannah, *The Library, Emral Hall sketchbook,* 1820, Drawing Volume 82, p.8, PA2755.

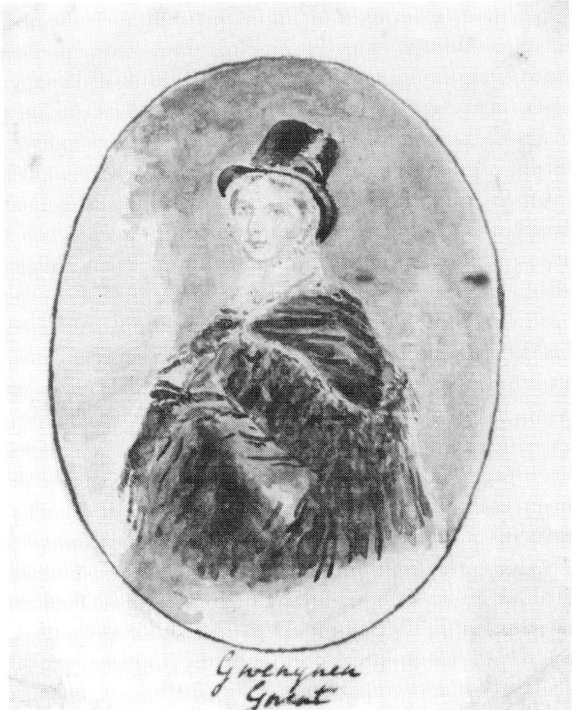

57 Llanover, Lady (Augusta Hall), *Self Portrait,* watercolour, 1837, PA3982.

1. The original watercolours are at *NLW* Drawing Volume 299 (4to), 17 watercolours. The most recent treatment of her life and work is Morgan, Prys, *Gwenwynen Gwent* (Casnewydd, 1988), a lecture which gives several references to other writings.
2. *Vide infra* and *supra.*
3. A series of her landscape prints are included in Williams, J., *The Literary Remains of the Rev. Thomas Price 'Carnhuanawc' vicar of Cwmdu, Breconshire,* 2 volumes (1845). I refer specifically to Green's Lake District etchings.
4. For instance, *NLW,* PB6178, *The Bard,* pastel 32.5 x 24.8 cm, undated, is in the style of James Barry or John Martin. Also in Williams, J., *op.cit.,* Volume 1, p.[233], is a full-length silhouette of 'Carnhuanawc', in a contemporary and accomplished hand by Llanover. Another portrait of Carnhuanawc, Thomas Price of Crickhowel (1778-1848), head and shoulders, signed & dated 1837 is *NLW,* Ad MSS 781A, p.31.
5. *NLW,* Ports A, PA 3982, oval, watercolour, 7.2 cm. In 1861 Charles Mornewick painted her picture, see *Western Mail,* 5 January 1989.

LLEWELLIN, (fl 1823)
Historical painter [South Wales]

Llewellin evidently had connections with Breconshire. One print after him, *The Welsh Army,* shows a simple engraver's style, suitable for publication.**(1)**

It may be that this is W.B. Llewellyn who was a South Wales gentleman/amateur and exhibited at the *RA* in 1812, 1814.**(2)**

1. One print (in XDA 1252 W29) in Rev. William Warrington, *The History of Wales* (Brecon, 1823) (2 vols), Vol. I. This has two plates: *Conwy Castle* by H. Griffiths & J. Shury and *The Welsh Army* (Roundel), 11.8 x 16.5 cm, 'Llewellin Del Johnson sc [sculpsit] Bristol'; a castle, something like Hay in the distance. A 'Llywellyn' exhibited at the *FS* 1780 *The bard from Gray's ode: a sketch.***(1)**
2. He was given as an honorary exhibitor at the *RA*: 1812 (734) *Views of South Wales*; 1814 (473) *Scene on the banks of the Wye*. *NLW*, W. Llewellyn, *Christ* (2768). There is a small file in the Witt Library which is given to S. Llewellin. No further details of this artist are available.

LLEWELLYN, Morgan (- 1847)
Architect/builder — Neath

LL/1847/49. Not in *Girouard*.

LLEWELLYN, W.B. (fl 1812 - fl 1814
Landscape and religious painter — South Wales

He was described as an honorary exhibitor at the *RA* in 1812 and 1814. Both exhibited pictures were of South Wales which suggests that he probably was resident there.**(1)** The *NLW* has a religious piece by Llewellyn which suggests that he was familiar with contemporary religious painting.**(2)**

1. *Graves, R.A.*:
   1812 (734) *Views in South Wales.*
   1814 (473) *Scenes on the banks of the Wye.*
   These may have been watercolours.
2. *NLW*, PZ 4027, *Christ crowned with thorns*, oil on canvas, 75 x 62.2 cm, signed 'W. Llewelyn'.

LLEWELYN, John Dillwyn (1810 - 1882)
Photographer — Penlle'r-gaer Swansea

Llewelyn was the first photographer in Wales, alongside Rev. Calvert R. Jones. He produced a number of very important photographs from 1839 onwards, and he continued photography throughout his life.

During the 1850s Llewelyn 'created some of his finest images'.**(1)** His most powerful and innovative images were the seascapes executed c1853,**(2)** and also the landscapes, for instance *Penrice Castle Gates*, 1852.**(3)**

His obituary appeared in *The Cambrian*. The author noted that 'Mr J.D. Llewelyn's chief contribution to modern science was in connection with photography. He had been experimenting for some years on the subject of taking sun pictures.'**(4)** The obituary also notes that 'he

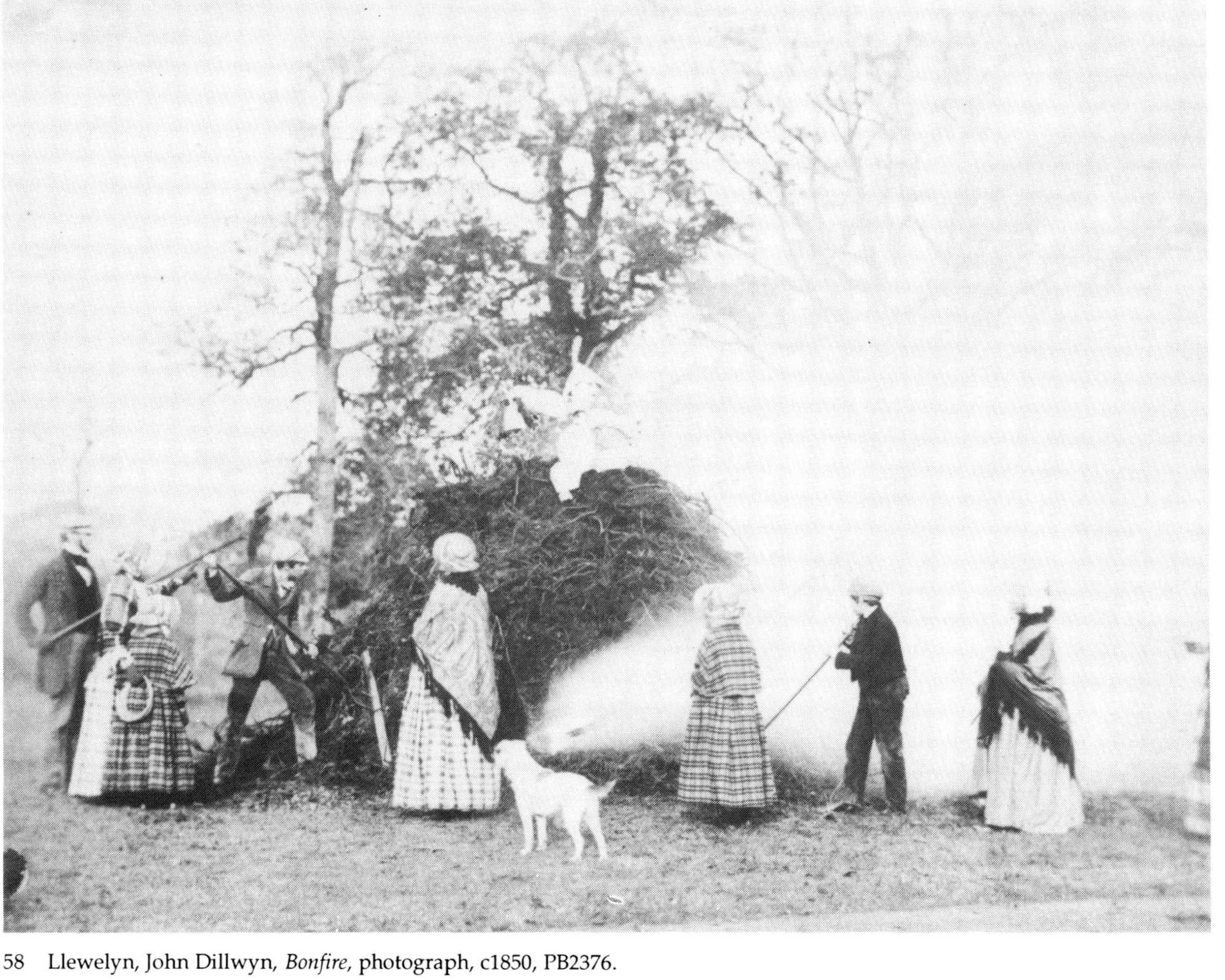

58 Llewelyn, John Dillwyn, *Bonfire*, photograph, c1850, PB2376.

brought his love of nature to bear in a somewhat singular way, getting the china painters to decorate the fictile ware with pictures of the flowers and grasses, the birds, insects and fishes which he collected and admired'.**(5)**

Llewelyn's work is considered amongst the finest of the period and one commentator has suggested that it has 'a grace and beauty virtually unmatched in the entire course of British, and any other, photography.'**(6)**

1. Painting, David, 'J.D. Llewelyn and his family circle', *History of Photography*, Autumn 1991, p.184. Painting provides a good account of Llewelyn's photography. See also Jones, Iwan Meical, *Scientific Visions* (1990).
2. *Ibid.*, facing p.129, illustrates *Thereza and Emma in Caswell Bay*, from a collodion negative, *NLW*.
3. Painting, David, *Swansea's Place in the History of Photography* (Swansea, 1982), p.4, illustrates *Penrice Castle Gates*.
4. Cox, Julian, 'From *The Cambrian* (Swansea)', *History of Photography*, Autumn 1991, p.173. *The Cambrian*, 7 November, 1877, p.8.
5. *Ibid.*, p.173.
6. Jeffrey, Ian, *The Real Thing: An Anthology of British Photography, 1840-1950* (London, 1975), p.117.

LLEWELYN, Mary Dillwyn? (fl 1824 - fl 1844)
Photographer — Penrice, Swansea

The sister of John Dillwyn Llewelyn, *supra*.

'She took many of the smaller photographs which required a shorter exposure and her work is usually more spontaneous, informal and approachable than that of her brother John. She deserves to be recognized as an important photographer in her own right.'**(1)**

She shared her father's and brother's interest in science and photography.**(2)**

1. Jones, Iwan Meical, *Scientific Visions* (1990), p.156. Booth, Mark Haworth (ed.), *The Golden Age of British Photography 1839-1900* (New York, 1984).
2. *Ibid.*, pp.122-123, notes that Lewis Weston Dillwyn, his son John and Mary Dillwyn attended lectures at the *RISW* in 1824. This practice continued until 1844.

LLEWELYN, Thereza Dillwyn (1834 - 1926)
Photographer — Penlle'r-gaer, Swansea

Thereza was the eldest daughter of John Dillwyn Llewelyn. She worked with her father on his scientific experiments, which included photography. In 1858 she married Nevil Story-Maskelyne, and both became 'equally involved in early photography'.**(1)**

One of her most important photographs is the portrait of her father c1856.**(2)**

1. Painting, D., 'J.D. Llewelyn and his family circle', *History of Photography*, Vol. 15, No. 3, p.184. Jones, Iwan Meical, *Scientific Visions*, p.159, notes the following: J.D. Llewelyn wrote to Henry Talbot on 17 October 1852, 'Thereza and I have made several sketches besides the photographic ones.'
2. Illustrated in Painting, D., *Swansea's Place in the History of Photography*, p.14. Kraus, Hans P., *Sun Pictures*, Catalogue 2 (New York, [c1985]), p.65, illustrates *Three Cliffs Bay*, 1854.

LLOYD, Charles (1733)
Potter — Hawarden

Hawarden Probate Records, 1733/1082.

LLOYD, Daniel (- 1804)
Mason — Prendergast, Pembrokeshire

SD/1804/240.

LLOYD, David (- 1853)
Mason — Swansea, Back Street

SD/1853/356.

LLOYD, David (- 1854)
Stonecutter/mason — Nevern (Nantycelyn)

SD/1854/16.

LLOYD, Edward (fl 1835 - fl 1843)
Surveyor — Penywenallt, Llandygwydd, Cardiganshire

Davies Atlas, Not in *Eden*.

LLOYD, John (- 1857)
Painter/glazier — Hay

BR/1857/32.

LLOYD, John (fl 1836 - fl 1848)
Architect — Mold

Lloyd was mainly an architect of churches. These have been described as 'mostly cheap churches of poor design'.**(1)** Several were rebuilt within 30 years of completion.**(2)** His designs were simple but the drawings could be very fine.**(3)**

1. *Colvin* p.621 main source of information. (Not in *Girouard, Eden*).
2. His first church, *Christ Church*, Pontblyddyn, Flintshire, built in 1836 was rebuilt in 1865. *Holy Trinity*, Gwernaffield, Flintshire, built 1838, rebuilt 1870.
3. For instance *Bounty Plans* Bangor 15, 1841 *Hen-Eglwys Rectory* (good, clear plan); Bangor 19, 1845 *Llanbeblig Vicarage* (plain & simple); Bangor, 22 1835 *Llanbeulan Rectory* (excellent drawing).

LLOYD, John (c1793 - 1867)
Architect — Caernarfon, Twt Hill

Lloyd was a versatile local architect who spent his whole career in the Caernarfon area. His first building was *St Mary's Church*, Caernarfon, 1828, shortly afterwards in 1829 he designed the *Wesleyan Chapel* & the *Gas Works* in his native town.**(2)**

In the 1840s he designed several bridges. He died at Twthill on 24 October 1867.

1. *Colvin* p.621 main source of information. *Slater's* 1844, p.16.
2. *Transactions of the Caernarvon Historical Society*, Vol. 32, 1971, p.32ff, mentions also the *Market*, 1832.

LLOYD, John (fl 1850 - fl 1865)
Portrait painter, Copyist — Rhaggatt, Merionethshire

Steegman records that he was

> 'An accomplished amateur artist; in addition to portraits of his family, he painted many copies of pictures in the National Gallery'.**(1)** Three portraits are recorded at Rhaggatt and two at Rhiwlas near Bala.**(2)**

1. *Steegman*, Volume 1, p.241.
2. *Steegman*, *ibid.*, p.241; Rhaggatt, *Edward Lloyd*, c1850; *Richard Lloyd Price*, c1850; *Vibart children*, c1860. At Rhiwlas (p.243), *Edward Lloyd*, c1850; *Richard Lloyd Price*, c1850 (another version of the portrait at Rhaggatt).

LLOYD, John William (1781 - 1870)
Landscape Artist — Danyrallt, Llangadog

Moved to Wales from Kent in middle age, but painted scenes in Wales whilst on holiday at Dale Castle. Produced watercolour dated 1802 of Pembrokeshire.**(1)** He had a good, topographical style.**(2)**

1. *TL*, informs me that there are a series of watercolours c30x45cm in a Welsh private collection.
2. *NLW* has an extant sketchbook (Drawing Volume 47), c1800-1802 views of Pembrokeshire. Various prints by its artist were sold by Jones & Llewelyn, Llandeilo, 18 September 1991 being contents of Dolau Bran, Cynghordy, Llandovery, lot 162, a *Country Lass* c1800 watercolour c40x33cm; lot 168 watercolour described as signed J. W. Lloyd *Female & Child* c25x28cm.

LLOYD, Owen (fl 1832 - fl 1843)
Surveyor — Cardigan

Davies Atlas, *Eden* II p.166.
NLW, Estate Maps of Cardiganshire and Carmarthenshire.

LLOYD, Robert Henry (fl 1849)
Portrait artist — Llandudno

Lloyd worked as an artist and teacher of languages.**(1)**

1. *Slater's*, 1849, p.4.

LLOYD, Thomas (- 1807)
Mason — Hay

BR/1807/23.

LLOYD, Walter (fl 1835 - fl 1843)
Surveyor — Pentowyn, Mydrim

Davies Atlas, *Eden* II p.166.

LLOYD, William (fl 1828 - fl 1843)
Surveyor — Wrexham, Chester Street

Davies Atlas. *Eden*, II, p.166.

LLWYD, Angharad (1780 - 1866)
Landscape painter — Ty'n y Rhyl, Rhyl

Daughter of John Lloyd, Rector of Caerwys (1733-1793), companion of Thomas Pennant.**(1)** She was a collector of genealogical and antiquarian history.

She collected an album of sketches by various hands, including her own and Augusta Hall's.**(2)** One of the most interesting is a portrait of Carnhuanawc.**(3)**

1. *DWB*.
2. *NLW*, Ad MS 781A.
3. Thomas Price (1787-1848), the inscription reads: 'Carnhuanawc AH fecit, Llanover, 1837'.

LOCKWOOD, Alfred (fl 1850)
Architect — Wrexham, King Street

Slater's, 1850, p.81.
Also at Chester, 2 Egerton Street.

LONGBOTTOM, Robert J. (fl 1830 - fl 1848)
Animal and landscape artist — Carmarthen

He appears to have moved from London to Carmarthen in c1835. At the *RA* he exhibited from a Carmarthen address in 1835 and 1837.**(1)** By 1848 he had returned to London.

1. He exhibited 1830-34 from London. In 1835 he exhibited from 'R.T.L. Carmarthen' *Morning* (669); 1837 *Belle Vue House, Carmarthen Scene in Wales* (62).

LOTHAM, John (fl 1800 - fl 1820)
China painter — Nantgarw

He worked with William Billingsley, *supra*, painting

flowers and birds. He returned to his native Shropshire.**(1)**

1. *Cadrawd,* p.83.

LOTT, James (- 1835)
Mason Narberth

SD/1835/275.

LOUGHOR, William (fl 1895)
Decorative house painter Neath
James Street

Hunt, 1849, p.90.

LOVEDAY, W.L. (fl 1829 - fl 1830)
Drawing master Union Street
Cardiff

He worked also as a French teacher.(1)

1. Bird, *Cardiff Guide,* 1829; *Pigot's,* 1830, p.82b, given as 'drawing master'.

LUGAR, Robert (c1773 - 1855)
Architect Carmarthen

He was born in Colchester, the son of a carpenter & from 1799 had an independent business in London. In 1796 he is recorded as 'Mr Lugar, Carmarthen', alongside John Nash & it appears he worked in Nash's studio for a short time, certainly his style reflected a Nash influence.**(1)**

1. *Colvin* p.625 main source for this reference. 1846, he designed *Wyelands* at Chepstow; 1825, *Cyfarthfa Castle,* Merthyr; 1825-33, *Glanusk Park,* Crickhowel; 1825, Greenmeadow, Tongwynlais; 1828-39, *Maeslwch Castle,* Radnorshire.

LYONS, Catherine (1794 - 1857)
Landscape artist South Wales

An amateur artist, the daughter of Vice Admiral Lord Lyons (1790-1858) She is believed to have spent a year in Wales & produced some views in South Wales, c1833.**(1)**

1. Information from Chris Wilson, Curator Radnorshire Museum, Llandrindod Wells. The museum has 120 watercolours of her journeys in the Alps c1835.

M

MADDOX, George Vaughan (1802 - 1864)
Architect Monmouth

Maddox was the only son of James Maddox *vide supra.* He was probably taught by his father and designed several buildings.

In 1826 his first known work was a *Theatre* at Crockertown, Cardiff, 1829-30 *The Hendre,* near Monmouth was built. By c1834 he designed *Pentwyn House,* Rockfield near Monmouth, 1840 houses & shops in Pontypool.**(1)**

1. *Colvin* p.635 main source of information. Another house was designed at Monmouth for Thomas Dyke, c1850 *NLW* PB 7779, PB 7780.

MADDOX, James (fl early 19th century)
Architect**(1)** Monmouth

He was the father of George Vaughan Maddox (1802-1864) *vide supra.* A collection of drawings, 'Practical plans etc for the new House of Correction proposed to be built in the town of USK',**(2)** show his considerable skill.

1. Not in *Girouard, Colvin.*
2. *NLW,* PB 1557-9, watercolours, various sizes.

MAINWARING, Daniel (- 1839)
Marble & stone mason Carmarthen

SD/1839/134.

MAJOR, Mr J. (fl 1843)
Waxwork artist Swansea

He exhibited his work at Swansea in 1843.**(1)**

1. *Swansea Journal,* 22 February 1843, p.48.
   Ibid., 15 March 1843, p.1.
   Ibid., 22 March 1843, p.3.
   He was unrecorded by *Pyke.*

MALIPHANT, David (fl 1792 - fl 1826)
Mason Kidwelly
Glazier & leather cutter**(1)**

Maliphant almost certainly, was related to George Maliphant (c1788-1865) who exhibited a *Cottage at Kidwelly* in 1826 at the society of British Artists.**(2)**

1. *SD*/1792/38.
2. *Colvin* p.636.

MANSION, L. (1785 - fl 1834)
Miniature painter Brecon

Born at Nancy. Exhibited at Paris Salon 1808-1822 and 1834.**(1)** In 1829 he exhibited at *RA* from Trebenshun House, Brecon, South Wales: (693) *'George Watford Esq'.*

It appears that he then moved to London.**(2)**

1. *Foskett* main source of information. One extant painting *'Unknown Lady'* is in the Wallace Collection, London.
2. In 1831 he exhibited at the *RA* from a London address.

MARCHI, Giuseppe (1738 - 1808)
Portrait and landscape painter Swansea
Mezzotinter Pencerrig

Marchi was born in Rome and brought back to England in 1752 by Sir Joshua Reynolds as 'his first pupil'.**(1)**

Later when Marchi's training was completed, Reynolds agreed to employ him as his assistant.**(2)**

By 1766 he was producing mezzotints and exhibiting in the *SA*.**(3)** In 1768 he visited the home of Thomas Jones, Pencerrig and painted various portraits of the family.**(4)** He and Jones then returned to London.

A few years later Marchi moved to South Wales, *Farington* reports that

> 'From the time of his first engagement till about the year 1770, he continued with Reynolds, who had for several years remunerated his services; but thinking that he might be able to obtain larger employment in another situation, Marchi began to practice in London on his own account; but being induced by some friendly offers of employment in South Wales, he shortly left the metropolis, and resided in or near Swansea in Glamorganshire. His encouragement in this place failing after remaining several years, it became necessary for him to remove. Accordingly Marchi removed to London... Sir Joshua having offered to receive him on a firm footing. Marchi willingly consented; and thus, after an interval of thirteen or fourteen years, he resumed a situation which he did not quit till the death of the great artist.'**(5)**

Several other sources provide evidence for the residence in Wales. Northcote writes that Marchi 'went to Swansea in Wales, where he practised as a portrait painter'.**(6)** The obituary on Marchi stated that 'he continued with Sir Joshua till the time of his death, except during an interval of a few years, which he passed at Swansea at Glamorgan'.**(7)**

It may be that the portrait of *Jane Deere* of Ystrad Owain near Cowbridge was painted in Wales.**(8)**

Commentators have assumed that Marchi was in Wales c1768-9.**(9)** This was based upon the evidence of extant works dated 1768, but actual documentary evidence links these portraits with the Jones/Marchi visit to Pencerrig. Clearly Marchi was working in Swansea at some other time. The most likely period was 1770-c1772.

Marchi's early Welsh connections were William Parry, who also trained with Reynolds**(10)** and Thomas Jones who even in 1768 wrote that he 'set off with my old friend Guiseppe Marchi'.**(11)** Although there is no documentary evidence to suggest a Swansea connection, he may have seen the potential for a resident artist in the region.

It is possible that Marchi wished to pioneer a practice in Wales to open out a market which previously tended to focus on London, Bath and Dublin. Only in 1772 did he not exhibit at the Society of Artists and this may represent the actual time while he was resident.

On the evidence of the 1768 works and comments on Marchi's painting ability by contemporaries he was a fine but not an exceptional painter.**(12)** His attempt to establish a portrait practice in Wales was one of the most important steps towards an independent portrait art in Wales.

It is possible that he returned in 1797; *Farington* mentions that Marchi 'is now painting ornaments in Wales'.**(13)**

Later his connections with Wales remained strong; it was to Marchi that Thomas Jones's daughters wrote concerning their father's death,**(14)** because in 1802 Marchi was 'going soon to Radnorshire to see Jones at his particular desire'.**(15)**

When he died, his sale contained some lots which suggested a special interest in Wales. He owned a copy of Sandby's *Views in Wales* (probably 1775-6) and several lots contained landscapes by Marchi of Wales.**(16)** It seems unlikely that he painted these at Pencerrig because Jones specifically stated that 'During Marchi's stay, he painted Portraits of many of the Family, and some few friends, while I exercised my pencil in my own Department'.**(17)**

Marchi exhibited a keen interest in Wales and despite no pictorial evidence, a Swansea residence seems quite possible.

1. Leslie, C.R., *Life and Times of Sir Joshua Reynolds* (1865), p.86. Penny, Nicholas, *Reynolds*, exhibition catalogue, 1986, p.57, has a short note on Marchi.
2. *Ibid.*, p.249, note: 'I find in one of Reynolds MS notebooks November 22, 1764. Agreed with Giuseppe Marchi that he should live in my house and paint for me one half-year from this day.'
3. He exhibited mezzotint portraits every year from 1766-1775, except 1772, from various addresses in London. Leslie, *op.cit.*, p.86: 'he was a very good engraver'.
4. Oliver, R.C.B., *Thomas Jones the Artist* (1970), illustrates portraits by Marchi: *Mr Thomas Jones* (1711-82) *Pencerrig* (frontispiece); facing p.20: *Major John Jones* (1739-87); facing p.38: *Mrs Sarah Humphreys* (1745-89). *Joyner, 1990*, Plate 5, illustrates *Thomas Jones Pencerrig*.
5. Farington, Joseph, *Memoirs of Sir Joshua Reynolds* (London, 1819), p.32.
6. Northcote, James, *Reynolds*, Vol.1, p.57.
7. *Gentleman's Magazine*, 1808, Vol. 1, April p.372. The article is unsigned but the present writer believes it was written by Baker, friend of Marchi and Farington, *vide Farington*, 6 April 1808 (Volume 9, p.3255).
8. Steegman, John, *Portraits from Welsh Houses*, catalogue (Cardiff, 1948). Item 63 records this picture from Ash Hall, signed by Giuseppe Marchi.
9. *Waterhouse*, p.231: 'attempting to start a portrait practice in Wales 1768/9'.
10. See entry under William Parry.
11. *Memoirs*, 14 September 1768.
12. Northcote, *Reynolds*, Vol. 11, p.488, records that in 1786 Marchi copied a Claude which was sold to the dealer Desanfans. *Farington* gives many references to Marchi's restoring ability, especially the work of Sir Joshua: *Farington*, 3 July 1796 (Volume 2, p.593); 3 October 1796 (Volume 3, p.739). *See also Waterhouse, Reynolds*, p.41.
13. *Farington*, 29 November (Volume 3, p.929).
14. *Farington*, 21 May 1803 (Volume 3, p.929). *Steegman*, Vol. 2, p.101 and 122, records *Rice Jones of Pencerrig*, 1785, and *Lady Mackworth*, c1780, which suggested Welsh patronage.
15. *Ibid.*, 10 June 1802 (Volume V, p.1786).
16. A catalogue of original finished paintings sold by Squibb, 30 June 1808: (The National Art Library, VAM, II RCDD 21) Lot 76 'One vol, containing etchings by Canaletti [*sic*]. *Views of Venice*; Etchings

by Marco Ricci and *Views in Wales* by Paul Sandby'. 'PICTURES': Lot 1, *Sketches, Views in Wales, Figures* [etc]. Lot 2, *Sketches* ditto (9 items). Lot 3, *Landscapes, Views in Wales*, a pair. Lot 6, *Six Views in Wales*.

17. *Memoirs, op. cit.*, 14 September 1768.

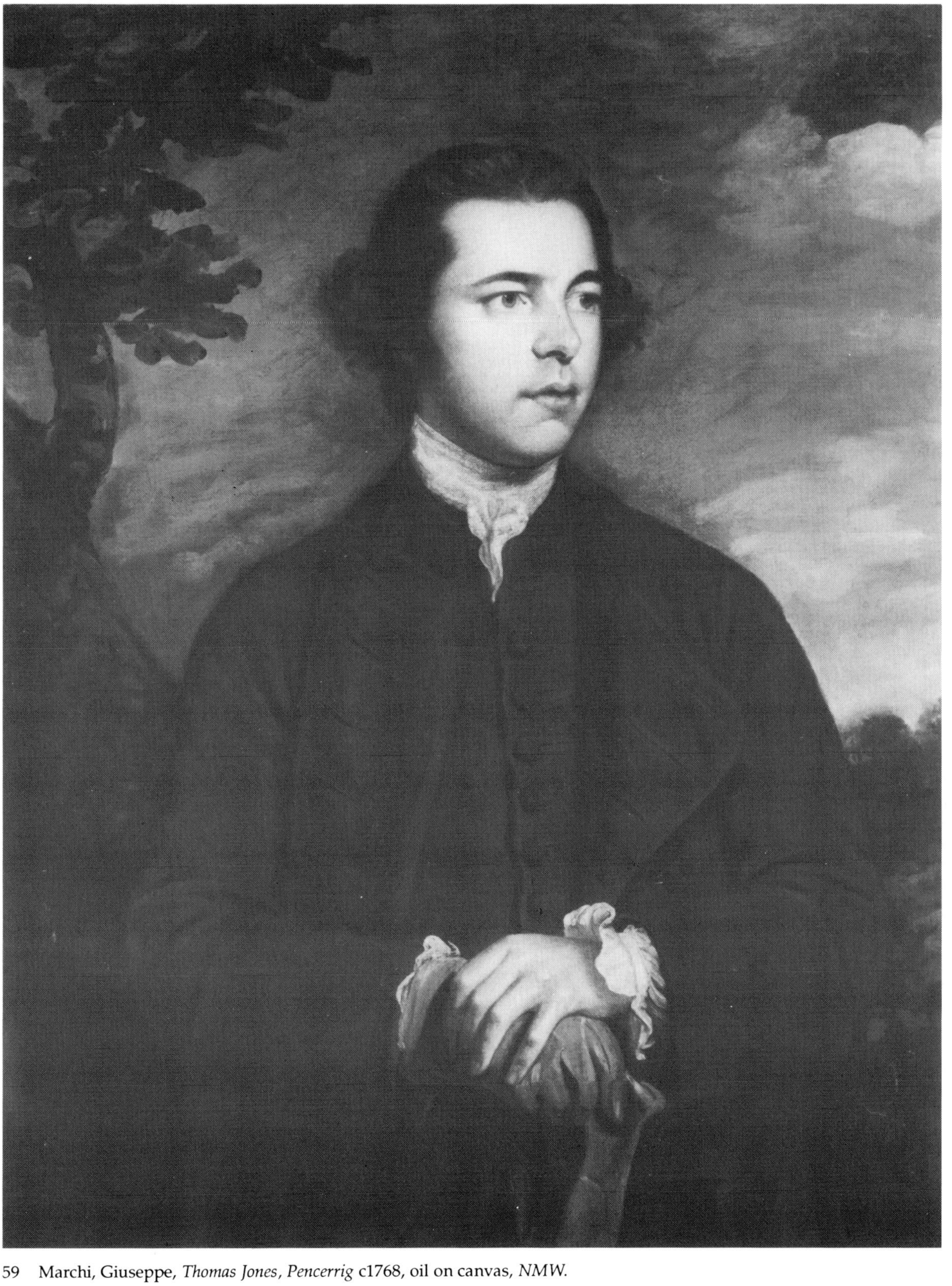

59 Marchi, Giuseppe, *Thomas Jones, Pencerrig* c1768, oil on canvas, *NMW*.

MARKS, Barrett Samuel(1) (1827 - 1916)
Portrait painter — Cardiff, St Mary Street

Born in Cardiff and 'there he received his first lessons in painting'.**(2)** He began a portrait practice, in the late 1840s. He moved to London c1867 where he was apparently successful.**(3)** He continued to be patronised by the Welsh in South Wales.**(4)**

1. *Mardy Rees* gives 'Bernard Samuel Marks', and *Wood* gives 'Barnett Samuel Marks'.
2. *Mardy Rees, op. cit.*, p.104, main source of information.
3. *Slater's*, 1850, p.22, gives Marks as St Mary Street. In 1855 *Wakeford*, p.23, gives Marks at the same address.
4. *NLW* has signed & dated portrait of *David Duncan* 1899, 126x100cm, oil on canvas (Deposit 1994).

MARTIN, Edward (fl 1807)
Surveyor**(1)** — Morriston

1. *NLW*, Estate map, 1807, *St Issell's*. *Eden*, II, p.175. Worked with David Davies of Crickhowel, *supra*.

MARTIN, J[ohn] (fl 1830)
Drawing master — Carmarthen
Painting master — The Parade
Portrait painter

Attempted to establish a portrait academy in 1830 by subscription:**(1)**

> 'J. Martin Drawing master...still continues to give illustrations in Drawing and Painting at reduced terms... He also has to inform them that he intends opening a society for Portraits in Oil at two guineas each, in which the purchaser will have the accommodation of paying for them by weekly payments of one shilling...warrant a current likeness... The rules of the society may be seen at Mr Davies's Six Bells, Peters Street where the Society will be held on every Thursday between the hours of seven and nine in the evening; where also a specimen is left for inspection.'

1. Information Sally Moss, *Transactions of the Carmarthenshire Antiquarian Society & Field Club*, Vol. XXII (1930), p.6. *Witt* gives John Martin (1789-1854) and J. Martin (1782-1838). Possibly this is the latter.

MATHEWS, Richard (- 1821)
Mason — Llangyndeyrn, Carmarthenshire

SD/1821/139.

MATHIAS, John Turner (fl 1858 - fl 1880)
Photographer — Pendwr Cardigan**(1)**

1. *Slater's*, 1858, other references in *NLW*, Dept Pictures & Maps, *Ffotograffwyr Cymru*, 1850-1920.

MATHIAS, Joseph (fl 1822 - fl 1830)
'Architect & builder' — Quay Street, Haverfordwest

Pigot's, 1822; *ibid.*, 1830, p.836. Not in *Girouard*.

MATTHEWS, John (fl 1835 - fl 1843)
Surveyor — Llanidloes, Aberystwyth

He worked at Llanidloes, then Aberystwyth where he became burgess.**(1)**

1. *Eden*, II, p.176, notes that he lived at Clydfanc, Llanidloes in 1823, then Aberystwyth from 1828. *Davies Atlas.*

MAUND, John (fl 1820 - 21)
Architect — Brecon

Noted as 'architect' in plan of *Brecon House* St Davids.**(1)**

1. *TL*, (Powys R.O.: Abercamlais B/D/ACA/2/432) countersigned by Maund & account for building given by William Owen, Haverfordwest.

MCLOUGHLIN, Mr (fl 1850)
Miniature artist — Swansea

He was 'the Teacher of Teachers of Writing' and painted 'Likenesses on ivory and in water-colours'.**(1)** McLoughlin worked in partnership with his daughter and he delivered a public lecture of the *RISW*, 'On the Proportions and Beauties of the Art of Writing'.**(2)**

1. *Cambrian*, 2 August 1850, p.2.
2. *Ibid.*, delivered on 5 August 1850.

MCLOUGHLIN, Miss (fl 1850)
Drawing mistress — Swansea

Worked with her father she taught 'every style of DRAWING and WRITING'.**(1)**

1. *Cambrian*, 2 August 1850, p.2. *vide supra* for Mr McLoughlin.

MERRYWEATHER, G. (fl 1834)
Miniaturist — Cardigan

Pembrokeshire Herald, 23 April 1834, connected with Hubard, *supra*.

METCALFE, William (fl 1835 - fl 1843)
Surveyor — Monmouth

Worked for some time in Monmouthshire, then moved to Gloucester after 1835.**(1)**

1. *Eden*, II, p.179. *NLW*, Estate maps of Monmouthshire (Estate Map Volume 26, 1835) and Herefordshire *Davies Atlas.*

MICKLEBURGH, Charles (fl 1832 - fl 1843)
Surveyor**(1)** — Montgomery

Possibly moved to Welshpool by 1858.**(2)**

1. *Davies Atlas. NLW*, Estate maps in Montgomeryshire and Cardiganshire.
2. (*NLW*, Estate map dated 1858).

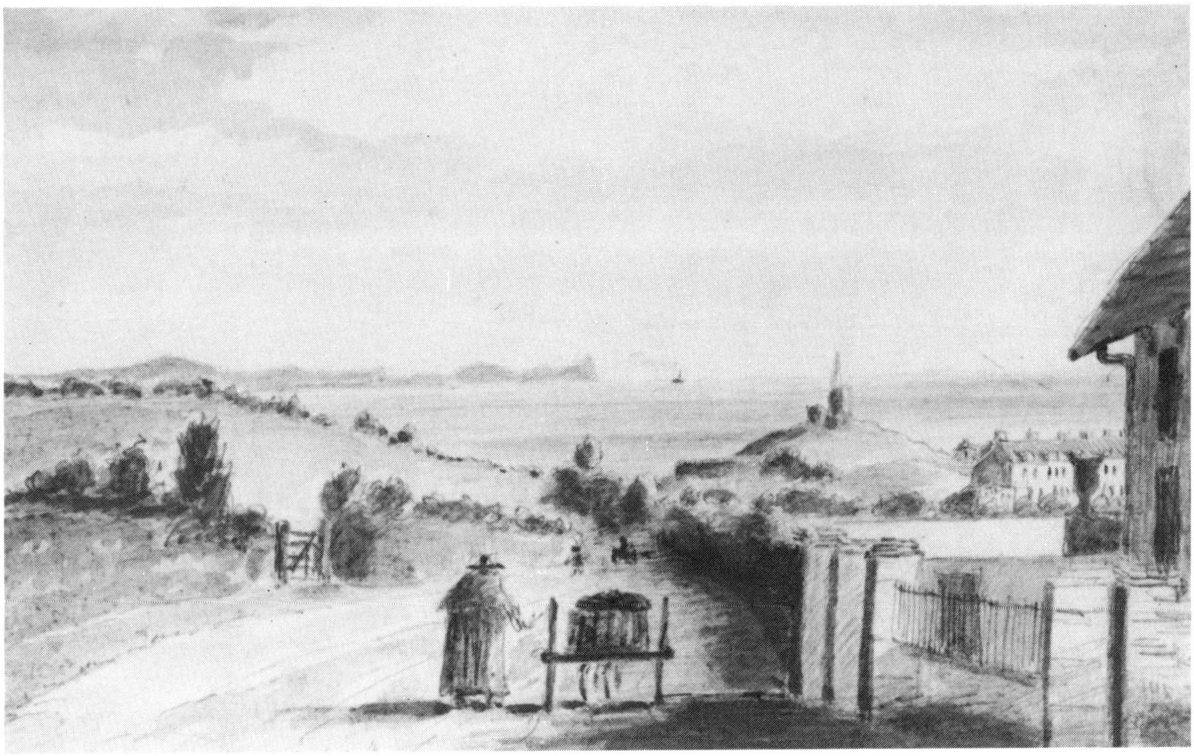

60 Morgan, Charles, *Tenby*, watercolour, 1851, *WPA*, Private Collection.

MILNE, James (- 1830)
Painter Steynton

SD/1830/343.

MORGAN, Ann (- 1804)
Japanner Usk (Monmouthshire)

Morgan probably worked at one of the Japanning works in South Wales.**(1)**

1. *LL*/1804/121.

MORGAN, Charles(1) (1796 - 1857)
Landscape artist Cae Forgan Llanrhidian Glamorganshire

Charles Morgan was trained as a solicitor & worked in that profession at Chancery Lane until moving to Wales c1833.

He was a collector of British Art & bought a number of important pictures from the studio sales of Philip Reinangle (c1760-1834) & Benjamin West (1738-1820).**(2)** The Fielding family were his lifelong friends.**(3)** In Wales he painted watercolours of local landscapes.**(4)**

1. Dr Prys Morgan kindly informed the author of the artist & provided details of his life.
2. Erffa, Helmut von & Staley, Allen *The Paintings of Benjamin West* (London University, 1986) gives 7 pictures owned by Morgan.
3. He was at school with one of the Fielding sons & often visited Mr Fielding senior when in London (after 1833).
4. These tend to be in a simple, topographical style.

MORGAN, David (- 1848)
Tiler/plaster Llandefaelog

BR/1848/34.

MORGAN, David (c1774 - fl 1851)
Architect [& builder]**(1)** Carmarthen Lammas Street**(2)**

Morgan was a prolific local architect who appears to have began working in Carmarthen c1790.**(3)**

He designed 'many houses' in the town, probably including *Picton Terrace*, 1834, *Trelech ar Betws* church 1843, *Carmarthen Gaol* [enlargement] 1843 & he repaired *Llandeilo Town Hall*, 1848.**(4)**
He is buried at Carmarthen cemetry.

1. *Colvin* p.663. Not in *Girouard*.
2. *Pigot's*, 1822, p.738.
   Robson's, 1840, p.6.
3. *NLW* Slebech MSS 3964 p.24.
4. *TL* notes the following references for this architect *Carmarthen Journal* 21 March 1834, 3 March, 19 May, 1843. Quoted in *Colvin* p.663.

MORGAN, David (- 1794)
Mason
Llan-ddewi
Breconshire

BR/1794/29.

MORGAN, Evan (- 1845)
Mason
Bronllys

BR/1845/3.

MORGAN, Jacop David (- 1818)
Mason
Llandeilo Fawr
(Pant y gelly)
Carmarthenshire

SD/1818/90.

MORGAN, John (fl 1836)
Surveyor
Swansea

Designed & built rectory at Llanmadog**(1)**

1. *NLW* St Davids, Bounty Plans 124, 1824. *Eden* II p.183 notes a John Morgan fl 1830 from ?Burrows Gardens, Swansea.

MORGAN, Richard (fl 1834 - fl 1843)
Surveyor
Talybont
Cardiganshire

Davies Atlas, Eden II p.183. *NLW*, Estate maps of Cardiganshire and Mongomeryshire (1836-1840).

MORGAN, Thomas (fl 1844 - fl 1855)
Sculptor
Cardiff
17 Trinity Street

Pigot's, 1844, p.19.
Wakeford, 1855.

MORGAN, William (fl 1850s)
Interior decorator
[Stained glass artist]
Haverfordwest

'House decorator, ornamental painter'.**(1)** Exhibited work of Mr W. Huston (*supra*) in 1851.**(2)**

1. *Pembrokeshire Herald*, 26 April 1850, p.1; 10 May 1850, p.1; 31 May 1850, p.1; 14 July 1850, p.1; 26 July 1850, p.3; 17 Jan. 1851, p.3.
2. *Ibid*.

MORGAN, William (- 1817)
Mason
Cathedin
(Bwlch)
Breconshire

BR/1817/9.

MORGAN, William (- 1783)
Mason
Llanywern
Breconshire

BR/1783/55.

MORGAN, William (fl 1823 - fl 1836)
Surveyor
Aberffrwd
Cardiganshire

He executed a map of *'Ty Bach'* in Llanrhystud.**(1)** It includes a portrait sketch of a clergyman and figures on a cartouche.

He also drew surveys in Carmarthen**(2)** and various parts of Cardiganshire.**(3)** Morgan was deputy steward of the manor of Perfedd.**(4)**

1. *NLW*, MSS Maps, Amphlett Lewis & Evans Deposit Collection (1968), Rack 14, signed and dated 1827.
2. *Conwil Gaio*, 1836, and Talley, 1836 (*NLW*, MSS Map, Volume 11).
3. Cardiganshire properties represented in *NLW* are Lordship of *Nant yr Arian* 1834; *Elerch*, 1823, 1824, 1828; *Nanteos* 1834.
4. *Eden*, II p.183.

MORGAN, William (fl 1835 - fl 1843)
Surveyor
Tanylan
Llansawel

Davies Atlas, Eden, II p.183.

MORGAN, William Llewelyn (- 1856)
Painter
Ystradgynlais

SD/1856/376.

MORRICE, Thomas [William] (c1777 - fl 1796)
Surveyor
Llanishen

He was born c1777.**(1)** Executed simple topographical sketches on some of his maps. For instance, *Llanbrodach* survey, 1795, is illustrated with a waterwheel.**(2)**

1. *Eden*, Supplement, p.450. *NLW*, Estate maps *Gelligaer* (Glamorganshire), 1796 and others. Possibly the same surveyor who recorded William Morrice, *Caerleon*, Monmouthshire, 1765 and *Mamhilad*, Monmouthshire, 1780.
2. Thomas H., *A Catalogue of Glamorgan Estate Maps*, Cardiff: GAP, 1992, pp.78-79. *Plan of Gwaelod Brithdir Farm, Glamorgan* signed, dated 1796. *NLW*, Cwrt Mawr Collection. Includes waterwheel, signed & dated houses and birds-eye view, 44.6 x 68.5 cm.

MORRIS, David (- 1850)
Mason
Swansea
Pottery Lane

SD/1850/323.

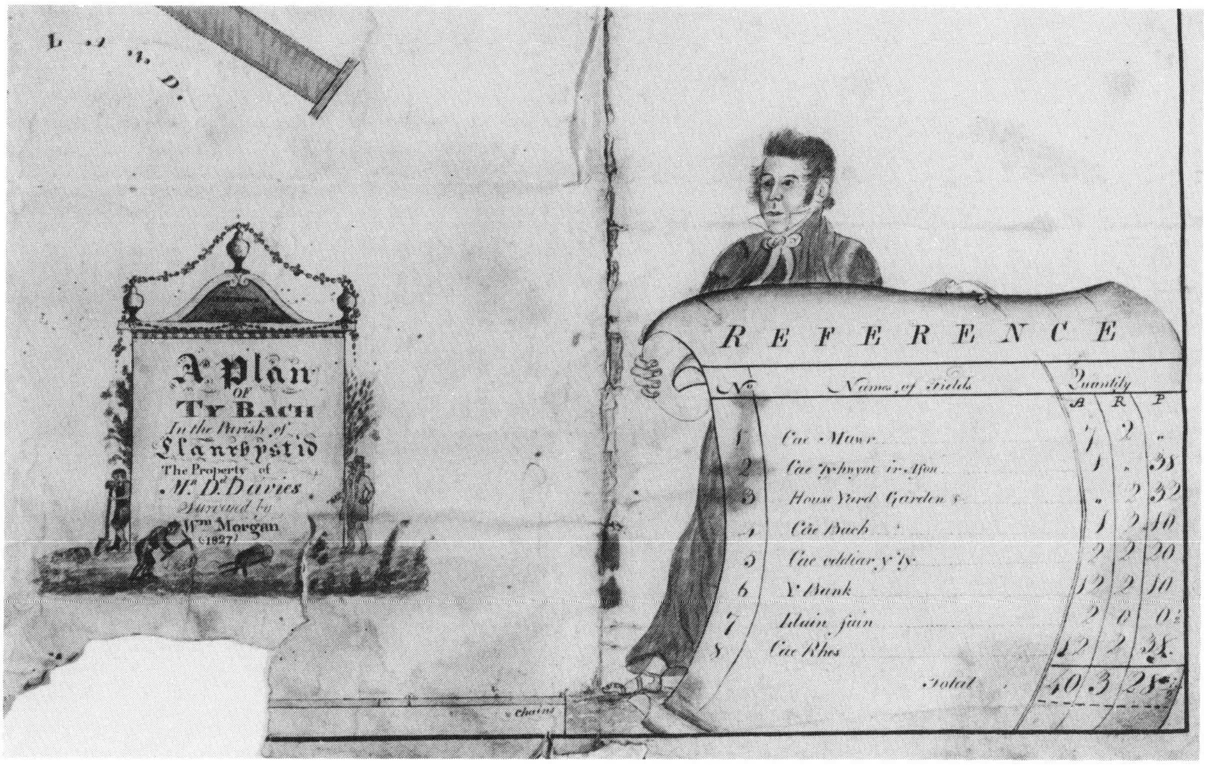

61 Morgan, William, *A Plan of Tŷ bach, Llanrhystid* [*sic*], pen & ink wash, 1827, Amphlett Lewis & Evans Deposit.

MORRIS, David (fl 1847 - fl 1879)
Lithographer
Newport
Llanarth Street

Published *Selections from a Sketchbook*, 1847, being 24 lithographs of landscapes.**(1)**

1. *NLW, BV* 321, approximately 27 x 37 cm.
   PL, portrait of *Rev Thomas Morris*, (*WFM*) after Mullock. Not given in Wilson, John, *Art & Society in Newport vide* Mullock *infra*

MORRIS, Edward (The Elder) (- 1836)
Mason
Llanddewi
Ystradenni
(The Hollies)

BR/1836/40.

MORRIS, Henry (1799 - 1880)
China painter
Swansea

Possibly born in Wales.**(1)**

1. *Nance*, pp.299-300.

MORRIS, Henry (fl 1844)
Coach painter
Bangor
Dean Street

Slater's, 1844, p.10.

MORRIS, John (1825 - 1835)
Surveyor
Abergavenny

Eden, II, p.184.

MORRIS, Lewis (1701 - 1765)
'Llewelyn Ddu o Fôn'
Beaumaris
Surveyor
Portrait painter?

Born at Llanfihangel Tre'r Beirdd, Anglesey.**(1)** By the 1720s he was working as a land surveyor. He may have received training for this at Beaumaris Grammar School.**(2)**

His work *Plans of Harbours...in St Georges Channel*, 1748, gives a good idea of his surveying.**(3)** His plan of mining in Cardiganshire has become a classic of its type. He appears to have painted a self portrait in 1740. This was published in 1810.**(4)**

He is buried at Llanbadarn Church, Aberystwyth.

1. Main sources are: *DWB*; Owen, H., *The life and works of Lewis Morris* (Anglesey Antiquarian Society, 1951), contains a short life and extensive extracts from his letters and other sources; Davies, Philip Wyn, *Astudiaeth o ysgolheictod hynafiaethol Lewis Morris (1701-1765)*, M.A. dissertation, Cardiff, 1982. *Eden*, II, p.184. Bick, David & Davies, Philip Wyn, *Lewis Morris* (Aberystwyth, 1994) for a portrait.
2. *Op.cit.*, p.xviii.
3. Morris, Lewis, *Plans in St George's Channel* (1748), (Beaumaris, 1987). This reprint includes a short discussion of the nature and facsimiles of the charts. This was reprinted by his son William Morris in 1801

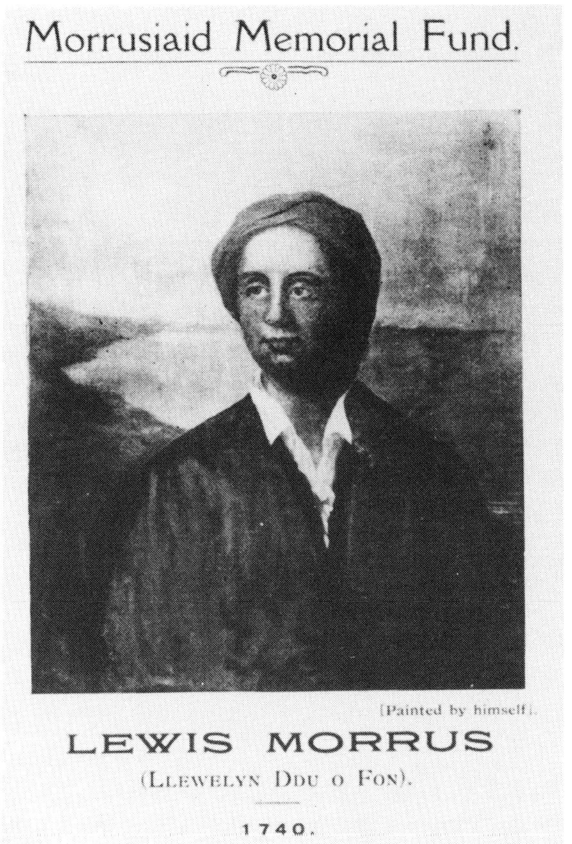

62 Morris, Lewis, *Self Portrait*, half-tone copy, c1900?, P8683. [Original, oil on canvas, 1740].

and published in Shrewsbury. *NLW*, Estate map, *Manor of Perfedd*, 1744 (Roller Maps, A118).
4. *Casglwr* (9), 1979, pp.8-9, 'Wynebau Lewis Morris', discusses this self portrait which is now at Sir Thomas Jones School, Amlwch.

MORRIS, Maria (1792 - fl 1841)
Painter on pottery — Swansea

She was born at Swansea and worked with her husband David Morris (c1796 - fl 1841) at the Cambrian pottery.**(1)**

'Painter on Pottery [Age] 49 Born in Glamorganshire'.

1. *Census Returns* [1841], HO/107/1426/455, Swansea district 12, p.37.

MORRIS, Thomas (fl 1821 - fl 1847)
Surveyor — Newport, Stow Hill**(1)**

Worked on estate, railway and tithe maps and also public works. He was trained by David Davies at Llangattock**(2)**

1. *Eden*, II, p.184, gives Stow Hill 1830-35. *Eden* also notes a T.T. Morris of 44 Commercial Street, Newport. *Davies Atlas*.
2. *vide infra & Eden Supplement* p.403

MORRIS, William (1705 - 63)
Botanical draughtsman — Holyhead

A botanist & antiquary, brother of Lewis Morris. One example of his art is a drawing of a fish taken from the Irish channel, dated 7 December 1759. NLW MS 21558E. With a letter addressed to Thomas Pennant.**(1)** William was multi-talented & his interest in botanical & naturalist illustration led to a working relationship with Pennant.**(2)**

1. Pen & ink wash with extensive inscriptions, showing upper & under side of the fish. c15x25cm.
2. Wiliam, Dafydd Wyn, *Cofiant Wiliam Morris (1705-63)* (Llangefni, 1995) pp.143-155 discusses this issue in some detail.

MORROD, Thomas (1755 - 1820)
Painter — Swansea

'of this town Painter who died Jan'y 20 1820'.**(1)**

1. West Glamorgan R.O., *St Mary's Burials*, p.296.

MOXHAM, Egbert (1822 - 1864)
Architect**(1)** — Neath, Queen Street

Recorded at Neath in 1849, 1850.**(2)**

1. *Girouard*, p.642. NLW Llandaff, Bounty Plans 65, 1854 *Llanmaes rectory*, well executed plans.
2. *Hunt*, 1849, p.83.
   Hunt, 1850, p.90.

MULLOCK, James Flewitt (1818 - 1892)
Portrait, animal, Landscape and Genre painter — Newport, Monmouthshire

Mullock was born in Newport.**(1)** His earliest extant picture is probably *Mr James Hodges and his two-year-old Hereford Heiffer*.**(2)**

In 1842 he published *View of the Docks, Newport*.**(3)**

He painted fine, animal and portrait pieces and later embellished his work with genre paintings such as *The Blind Beggar*.**(4)** The *Chartist riot* print remains his most popular image.**(5)**

Mullock suggested the first exhibition of art in Newport, 1841, only one year after the Monmouth exhibition.**(6)**

1. Wilson, John, *Art and Society in Newport: James Flewitt Mullock and the Victorian Achievement* (Newport, 1993). This is the first extensive piece on Mullock and it provides good illustrations, a biography and details of life in Newport up to 1892. The Mullocks were also important in the world of Rugby. For instance the 'Father of the Welsh Rugby Union', Richard Mullock (1851-1919) worked as an artist & rugby administrator (*info*) John Jenkins, Aberystwyth.
2. Sold at Sothebys, 31 October 1990, lot 381, oil on canvas, 44 x 58.5 cm (illustrated). Now at *NPT*. Wilson, *op.cit.*, p.54.
3. *Ibid.*, p.66.
4. *Ibid.*, p.63.
5. *Ibid.*, p.66: *The Attack of the Chartists on the Westgate Hotel, Newport, November 4, 1839.*

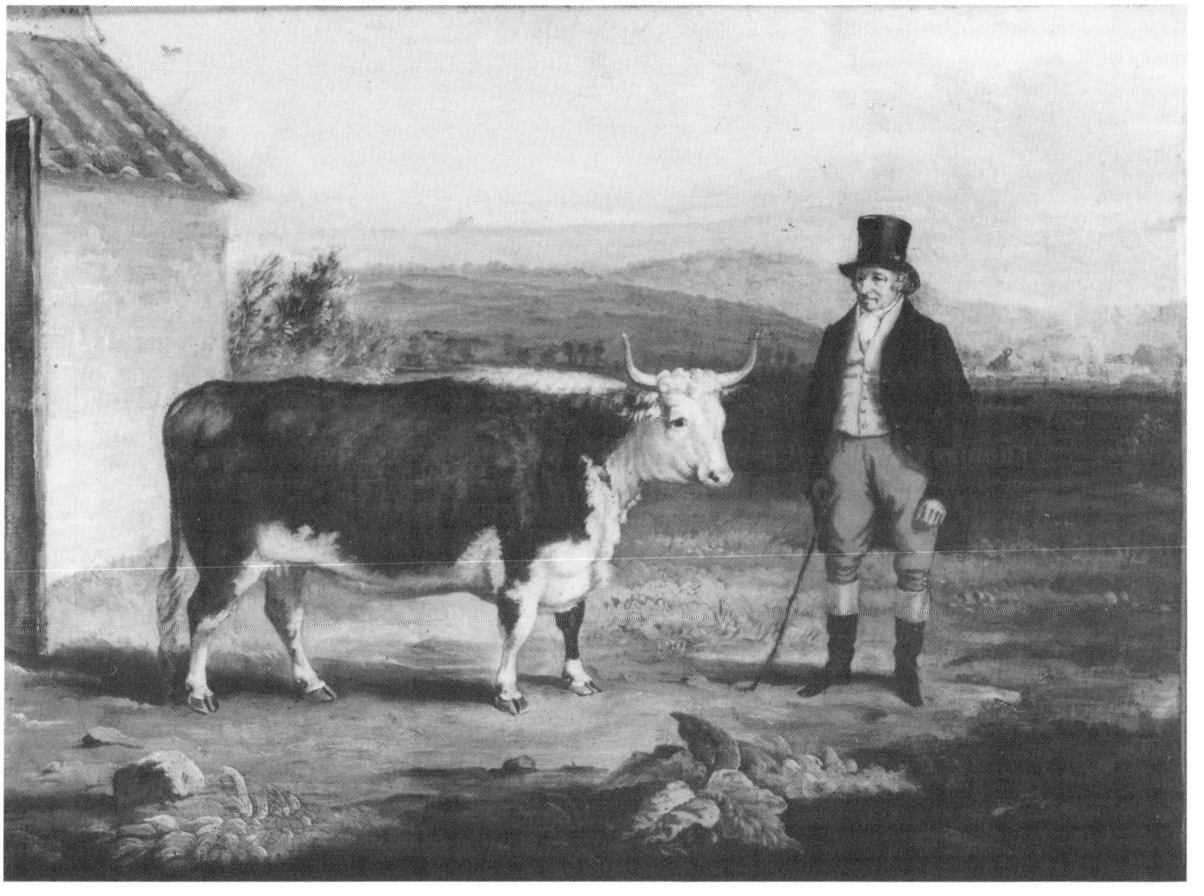

63 Mullock, James Flewitt, *Mr Hodges, Tredegar,* oil on canvas, c1843, *NPT.*

6. See *Joyner (1989)*, Volume 1, pp.163-172, for details of the Monmouth exhibition.

See front endpapers.

N

NASH, John (1752 - 1835)
Architect Carmarthen

His early career was in London but in 1783 he was bankrupt and moved to Carmarthen.**(1)** A number of important commissions in South Wales ensured that his 'Welsh exile had not been fruitless, for it was there that he emerged as the leading architect of the Picturesque. Nash's initiation...can probably be traced to his contact with Thomas Johnes.'**(2)**.

His known buildings in Wales include: (1785) work in *Carmarthen Church, Six Bells Inn;* (1788) *Castle House, Aberystwyth;* (1789-92) *Carmarthen Gaol.* In c1793 he employed A.C. Pugin as a draughtsman and they worked in *St David's Cathedral* (1791-2), *Tre-cefel Bridge,* Cardiganshire (1792-3), (1793) *Cardigan Gaol;* (1794-5) *Abergavenny Market.***(3)**.

Nash returned to London in 1796 and became an exceptionally popular architect.

1. Summerson, John, *John Nash: Architect to George IV* (1935), provides a good biographical account. Some details in *PP*, pp.10-11. The *NLW* mounted an important exhibition of this artist in 1995. The accompanying publication adds much to our understanding of Nash and Wales.
   See also: Davis, Terence, *The Architecture of John Nash,* London: Studio, 1960, and *John Nash The Prince Regent's Architect*, London: Country Life, 1966. pp.15-31 include numerous illustrations of his Welsh houses.
2. *Colvin*, pp.687-694. [quoting p.687].
3. *Colvin* provides a chronology of Nash's work & Suggett, Richard, *John Nash Architect Pensaer* (Aberystwyth, 1995), provides an invaluable architectural catalogue pp.107-128. Nash's Welsh buildings are dated 1785 onwards.

NEALE, Edward (fl 1835 - fl 1843)
Surveyor Laleston Cottage & Laleston Grange Laleston Bridgend

His early career was in London, Cheam & Ewell where he is recorded as an estate surveyor, he probably moved to Wales shortly after 1825.**(1)**

1. *Davies Atlas, Eden* II p.187.

NEDATH, Fredrick (fl 1858)
Photographer — Haverfordwest, Dew Street

Slater's, 1858.

NELSON, John Henry (fl 1840s)
Artist (unspecified) — Merthyr Tydfil

He was a member of the Cambrian Lodge of Freemasons, Merthyr in 1841. Originally from Ireland and described as an 'Artist' of Merthyr.**(1)**.

1. Fraser, J., *Illustrated History of Merthyr* (1914), p.310.

NEWNHAM, Thomas Garrett (fl 1841 - 1844)
Surveyor — Newtown

Described himself as civil engineer & surveyor & produced a detailed plan for the vicarage at Kerry, 1840.**(1)**. He worked at Llanbister, Radnorshire**(2)**

1. NLW, St Asaph, Bounty Plans 48, 1840.
2. NLW, St Davids, Bounty Plans 75, 1844.

Not in *Eden*.

NICOLETTI, Joseph (fl 1844)
Plaster figure maker — Cardiff, The Hayes

Pigot's, 1844, p.20.

NORRIS, Charles (1779 - 1858)
Antiquarian and topographical artist — Tenby
Etcher

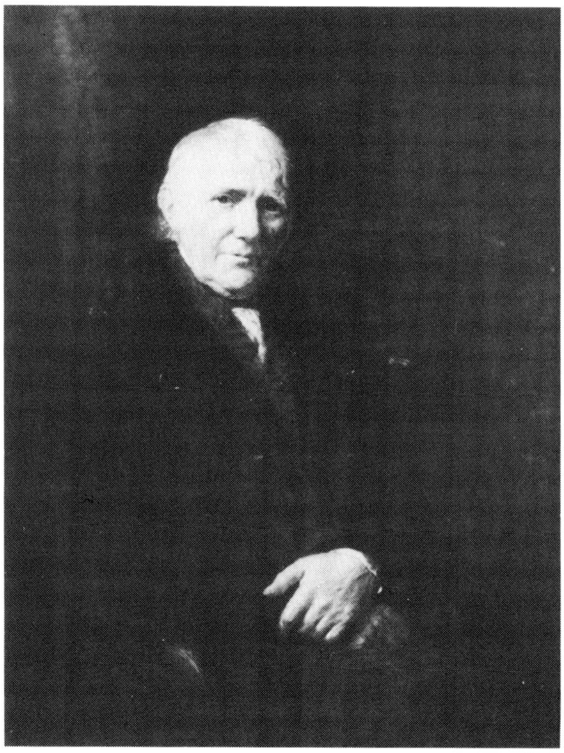

64 *Norris, Charles*, by John Linnell, oil on canvas, 1837, *WPA*.

Norris moved from Norwich to Tenby c1805. He was of independent means and was not patronised but appears to have drawn for interest alone.**(1)**

There is evidence to suggest that he travelled around part of South Wales.**(2)** He published a number of etchings, amongst the best were *Etchings of Tenby* 1812 which he says was 'intended to illustrate the most striking peculiarities in Early Flemish Architecture'.**(3)**

1. Leach, A.L., *Charles Norris 1779-1858* (1949), is a brief but useful guide to his art and life. Some etchings by Norris are illustrated. *See also NLW*, MS 19423C, Leach MSS, on Norris.
2. For instance, the *NLW*, Haverfordwest Museum and Cardiff Library have large collections of his watercolours.
3. Norris, Charles, *Etchings of Tenby*, 1812, title page. One example is *NLW*, PD 7069, A12/1 - A226, *Castle Gate* [Tenby], 1812.

NUNAN, James (fl 1835 - fl 1843)
Surveyor — Abergavenny

Davies Atlas, *Eden* II p.192.

NUNAN, M. (fl 1835 - fl 1843)
Surveyor — Abergavenny

Davies Atlas, Not in *Eden*.

O

OAKLEY, Elizabeth (1790 - 1859)
Landscape artist — Monmouth, Lydart House

An amateur watercolour artist who was reported 'untutored'. She was buried as Michel Troy, Monmouthshire.**(1)** Probably related to the Monmouth artist Mary Ellen Bagnall (1833-1904).**(2)**

1. *Vide Observer*, 9 March 1975, pp.1 and 3, see also *Western Daily Press*, 12 March 1975.
2. *Vide* [A. Helme], *Nooks and Corners of Old Monmouthshire* (Monmouth Museum, 1983). Most of her works are dated post-1850.

OLIVER, Thomas (fl 1762 - 1776)
Plasterer — Chirk

Worked at the New Drawing Room at Chirk. **(1)**

1. Beard, G., *Interior decoration in England*, (Edinburgh, 1981), p. 273. He also worked at Tabley House, Cheshire 1762-67 and was based at Warrington.

O'ROURKE, Michael Spain (fl 1850)
Architect**(1)** Cardiff**(2)**
Crockherb town

1. Not in *Girouard.*
2. *Slater's,* 1850, p.22.

OWEN, [Edmund] (fl 1704 - 1785)
Portrait painter [Penrhos]
Caernarfonshire

Owen painted a self portrait, and may have had a practice in North Wales.**(1)**

1. *NMW* files.

OWEN, Elias
Builder Eglwysfach

Built & designed the vicarage at Eglwysfach, 1828.**(1)**

1. *NLW* St Asaph, Bounty Plans 36, 1828.

OWEN, James (fl 1839)
Surveyor Haverfordwest

Designed a vicarage at Manordeifi, 1839.**(1)**

1. *NLW* St Davids, Bounty Plans 136, 1839, it was later re-commissioned to John Joseph 1847. Not in *Eden.*

OWEN, John (- 1842)
Mason Newport
St Mary Street

SD/1842/267.

OWEN, Nathaniel (- 1831)
Mason Cilgerran

SD/1831/48.

OWEN, Owen Davies (fl 1819 - fl 1838)
Land surveyor Rhuddlan
(Bryncwnin)
Flintshire

Also based in Shrewsbury.**(1)**

1. *SA* 1838/206. *Eden* II p.196.

OWEN, Richard (fl 1770 - fl 1814)
Surveyor [Llanynghenedl]
North Wales

He executed an elaborate frontispiece to a survey of Ynys y Maesgwyn Estate 1776. This includes Corinthian columns, sailing ships and classical imagery.**(1)** He is described as a'land surveyor' in his will.**(2)**

1. *NLW,* Peniarth Volume 2. *NLW,* Estate maps of Anglesey and Merionethshire and Caernarfonshire.
2. *B* 1814/53. *Eden* II p.196.

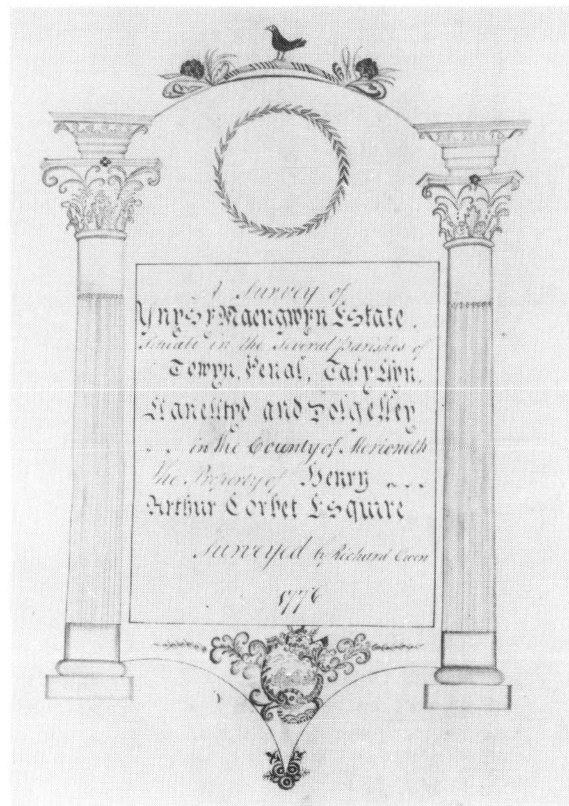

65 Owen, Richard, title page of *Survey of Ynys Maengwyn,* pen & ink with watercolour, 1776, Peniarth Volume 2.

OWEN, (Rev.) Robert (1803 - 1870)
'Eryron Gwyllt Walia' Caernarfon
House painter

He was apprenticed as a house painter and in c1818 to Robert Roberts. 'He continued to work as a house painter until he retired some five years before his death.'**(1)** He was a friend of Hugh Hughes (*supra*).**(2)** He spent several years in London and was a member of Jewin Crescent Chapel.

Owen may have been responsible for interior decoration [murals] at Glyn Llifon House.**(3)**

1. *DWB.*
2. *PL* kindly gave me this information.
3. *PL.*

OWEN, Thomas Davies (fl 1839 - fl 1845)
Land surveyor Aber-erch
Pwllheli

In his will he left £100.**(1)**

1. *B* 1845/51. *Eden,* II, p.196, notes that he undertook tithe map surveys. *Davies Atlas.*

OWEN, William (1791 - 1879)
'Architects & builders'**(1)** Haverfordwest
Short Row**(2)**
High Street

He was the son of William Owen (*ob*.1831) a cabinet maker & builder, Haverfordwest & he continued the family business with James his brother as a partner.

TL describes him as 'a remarkable man'.**(3)** He was the dominant figure in the business life of Pembrokeshire for over 30 years.

In 1832 he became County Surveyor & worked to improve Haverfordwest. His *Shire Hall* 1839 was a good design. Another of his important buildings was *Heol Awst Chapel*, Carmarthen, 1826-7.**(4)**

1. *Colvin* pp.718-19. Not in *Girouard*. *TL* very kindly provided me with a large amount of information on this architect.
   TL catalogues Owen's works as follows:
   1824 Haverfordwest, *New Market;* 1827 *Heol Awst Chapel;* 1826 *Mathri Rectory;* 1833-6 *Bridge;* 1839 *Shire Hall;* 1839 *Albany Chapel;* 1839 *Manordeifi Rectory;*1840-2 *Scolton Manor;* 1842-4 *Begelly Rectory;* 1847-9 Haverfordwest, *Corn Market.*
2. *Pigot's*, 1822, p.741.
   Pigot's, 1830, p.836, 'Owen & Son'.
   Pigot's, 1844, p.34, 'William Owen & Sons', High Street'.
3. *TL* MSS notes on the architect.
4. *TL* refers to *Carmarthen Journal* 6 April 1827 p.3 mentions the chapel as the biggest in Wales and states 'here is nothing gaudy - nothing superfluous but all is as it should be, solid & substantial, yet chaste & elegant'. He also designed buildings which were executed by a different craftsman, for instance St Davids, Bounty Plans 4, 1842 *Begelly rectory* has plans by Owen (& James Owen) but it was built by William Lewis of Haverfordwest. Also St Davids, Bounty Plan 138, 1826, *Mathry rectory* is a simple & convenient design.

P

PADLEY, John Weir (1813 - 91)
Marine and portrait artist Swansea
Burrows Place
25 Wind Street

Born of a Swansea family, his father was Silvanus Padley, Clerk of the Harbour Trust.**(1)** One source called him 'a talented amateur';**(2)** however it seems more likely that he was professional. He collaborated with A.F. Rolfe, painting shipping in a large *View of Swansea*, 1840.**(3)**

He exhibited in the *RSBA* in 1842 showing marine pieces:
(133) *Scene in Swansea Bay.*
(206) *A Ship under Close Reefed Topsails.*
(402) *Scene near the Nass Sand.***(4)**

His style is similar to John Attwood.**(5)**

1. *Cambrian Daily Leader*, 2 March 1912, p.3, gives a short biography with details on his style. *Cambrian*, 20 November 1891, p.5, has an obituary notice.
2. *Cambrian Daily Leader*, referring to Padley sketching members of the British Association on their visit to Swansea in 1848. This is illustrated in the article.
3. *Gamwell*, p.104.
4. His address was then 25 Wind Street, Swansea.
5. *Rogers*, p.57, illustrates a pen and ink drawing by Padley of *Swansea Harbour* dated 1839.

PADLEY, Paul (1778 - 1850)
Surveyor**(1)** Swansea
Landscape artist**(2)**
Pottery painter

Padley had a polymathic career and probably drew a number of landscapes in South Wales.**(3)** The most impressive was his *Swansea Panorama*.**(4)** He died in Leamington Spa & his obituary appeared in the *Cambrian*.**(5)**

1. *Eden*, II, p.197, estate maps and railway plans. May have moved to London by 1818. Morris, Bernard, 'Paul Padley's Swansea', *Gower*, XLI (1990) p.8 suggests he had moved by May 1803.
2. *Nance*, p.32, records a watercolour of Swansea.
3. Thomas, Hilary, *A Catalogue of Glamorgan Estate Maps*, (Cardiff, 1992), p.69, *Map of Gnoll Estate*, dated 1801, by Paul Padley who executed a decorative cartouche and sketch of Gnoll house.
4. Morris, Bernard, 'Paul Padley's Swansea: a view of the town in the 1790s', *Gower*, XLI (1990) pp.6-16.
5. *The Cambrian* 27 December 1850 p.3.

PALMER, William (fl 1845 - fl 1849)
Carver and gilder Swansea
Artists' colourman 41 Wind Street

Palmer moved from London and purchased the business of James Harris in 1845.**(1)** He was still recorded as an artists' colourman in 1849**(2)** and may have continued the Harris tradition of exhibiting and selling pictures.

1. *Cambrian*, 19 December 1845, p.2.
2. *Hunt*, 1849, pp.157 and 174.

PALRY, Henry (- 1840)
Land surveyor Chirk

SA 1840/19. Not in *Eden*.

PARDOE, Thomas (1770 - 1823)
China painter Swansea
Nantgarw

Born at Derby where he was an apprentice at the Derby Porcelain works 1785/1786. He moved to Swansea shortly before 1795**(1)** where he worked at the Cambrian and later Nantgarw Potteries.**(2)** About 1809 he removed to Bristol and returned to Swansea c1820 and died at Nantgarw.

1. *Nance*, Appendix VII on Thomas Pardoe, pp.480-487. *Cadrawd*, p.95, adds some information. *Bell* p.77. A plate by Pardoe, at *GVS*, illustrated p.112.
2. *NMW* has a number of studies for painted designs by Pardoe. These illustrate animals, birds and flowers, in a delicate hand.

PARDOE, William Henry (1803 - 1867)
China painter — Swansea

He was born in Swansea, and was the son of Thomas Pardoe, *supra*. He assisted his father at Nantgarw.

1. *Cadrawd*, p.95.

PARKER, Rev. John (1798 - 1860)
Landscape artist — Llanmerewig, Mont.
Architectural draughtsman & architect — Llanyblodwel, Salop.

Parker was born at Sweeney Hall, Oswestry, and educated at Eton and Oriel College, Oxford.**(1)** After a curacy near Oswestry he moved to Llanmerewig and then Llanyblodwel.**(2)** He designed and restored his two churches according to Neo-Gothic taste.**(3)**

Parker recorded in watercolour all the extant rood screens in Montgomeryshire and many other parts of Wales. His drawings of church interiors, especially details of Gothic ornament are amongst the most important sources of Welsh architectural history.**(4)**

He painted landscapes, mainly in watercolour, of North Wales and Mid Wales, and these are characterised by high-toned colouring.**(5)** They tend to concentrate on a Romantic view of Wales, wholly akin to his Gothic interests.

He produced a series of flowers native to Wales. These are large watercolours.**(6)** He is buried at Llanyblodwel churchyard

1. *DWB*. The *Arch.Cam.*, No. XVI, Oct. 1853, published his portrait by Halle and notes that he has 'visited, measured & delineated nearly all the antiquities of Wales, of an architectural character'. Not in *Girouard*.
2. Haslam, Richard, *The Buildings of Wales: Powys* (Harmondsworth & Cardiff, 1979), p.148, discusses Parker's additions. *Bell* pp.155-6, p.113 illustration of *St. David's Cathedral*.
3. Johnson, Rita, *John Parker*, BA dissertation, UCW Aberystwyth, 1994, discusses Parker's interest in the Gothic and architecture.
4. Jerman, H.N., *Reproductions of Water-colour Drawings by John Parker* (Aberystwyth, [1947]). Jerman notes that 'he made drawings of all the rood screens in Welsh churches; and of all the chief types of fonts. But through it all he remained the specialist: no other architecture but Gothic interested him.'
5. *NLW* has the main collection of Parker's works. Some are illustrated in Jerman, *ibid*. A list of the sketchbooks are included in Joyner, Paul, *Catalogue of Drawing Volumes in the Dept of Pictures and Maps*, [typescript] *NLW*, Aberystwyth, 1983, pp.59-63, give full references. *NLW* also has an extensive collection of loose watercolours by Parker.
6. *NLW*, for instance, *Wildflowers near Falls*, PZ 3774; *Daffodils*, PZ 3780; *Welsh Yellow Poppy*, PZ 4028. In addition he produced small watercolours. They are almost all painted showing the flowers in native habitat.

See Colour Illustration IX and Back Cover.

PARRY, Devereux (fl c1730)
Engraver? — Llanvetherine Church, Monmouth

An inscribed tombstone with shields in upper portions of the brass. Signed 'Devereux Parry sculpsit'. A good, slightly naive hand. The memorial was for Anne, wife of John Stephens of Usk.**(1)**

This may have been Parry of Hereford, identified as the father of Rev. William Parry (1686-?1756).**(2)**

1. *Lewis*, pp.98-99 (illustrations). The inscription was in Latin, with all names in Italic script.
2. *Ibid.*, p.23, quotes Bradney, Joseph, *History of Monmouthshire*, Part II: The Hundred of Abergavenny, p.272.

PARRY, Henry 'Senior' (fl mid-19th century)
Landscape artist — Monmouth

'Parry pere was a pupil of David Cox,**(1)** and one of his best! Many of his watercolours passing for those of his master. Parry Fils was a medical man - he painted in oils principally specially game and still life subjects. Both Parrys came into considerable [fame?] in their youth especially the father.'**(2)**

He exhibited at Monmouth in 1840.**(3)**

1. There appears to be at least one print after Parry, *NLW*, PE 634, B8/10 - B233, Swansea, Glam., 1836.
2. *Cadrawd*, Volume II, p.150, 'Reminiscences of the Parrys of Monmouth'. Parry is not mentioned in studies of Cox.
3. Monmouth Museum, *Monmouth Exhibition*, 1840, oil paintings: (125) *Game*, (129) *Castle in Ruins*, (134) *Snipes*, (137) *Cardiff*, (138) *Monnow Bridge*, (139) *Llanelly*; watercolours: (150) *Mill and Waterfall*, (159) *Barmouth*.

PARRY, Henry 'The Younger' (fl 1801 - fl 1841)
Animal and landscape painter — Monmouth

Various documents provide evidence for his residence in the town.**(1)** He exhibited a number of oil paintings and one watercolour in the 1840 Monmouth exhibition.**(2)** He may have worked with his father Henry Parry 'Senior'.

1. Gwent Record Office, Deeds W & T/624 628 dated 1833, 1841 bear the name 'H. Parry the Younger'. D25.0912, D412. 44/45 dated 1801, 1802 also relate to him.
2. Monmouth Museum, *Monmouth Exhibition*, 1840: (118-122) *Game*, (131) *Dog*, (135) *Snipes*, (136) *Ruins*, (140) Oil Sketch, (160) Watercolour *Cat and Dog Life*.

PARRY, Henry (- 1840)
Land surveyor — Chirk

SA 1840/19.

PARRY, J. (fl 1843)
Architect and land surveyor**(1)** — Pwllheli

Began a practice at Pwllheli. 'Land and Buildings

surveyed. Estimates and Plans made on reasonable terms, and with the greatest regard to economy and usefulness. Rents etc. collected.'**(2)**

1. Not in *Girouard, Eden.*
2. *Caernarvon and Denbighshire Herald,* 13 May 1843, p.3.

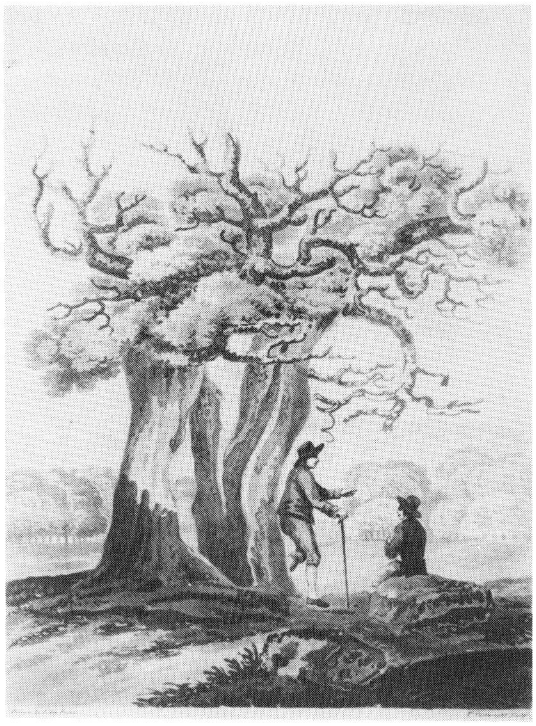

66 Parry, John, *Ceubren yr Ellyll,* lithograph, c1813, PB8227 Top B9/6.

PARRY, John (fl c1813)

Landscape artist — Wrexham, Brynyffynon

Parry drew a tree portrait c1813. This was published as a print. T. Cartwright probably embellished the original drawing with figures.**(1)**

1. Williams, Isaac, *List of Topographical Prints in Wales* (Cardiff: 1926). *NLW,* PB 8227, Top. B9/6 - B155, *Ceubren yr Ellyll, or the Spirits Blasted Tree,* c1813 (Eng. T. Cartwright, n.d.).

PARRY, William A.R.A (1742 - 91)

Portrait and historical artist — Wynnstay
Scenery painter — Denbighshire

The son of John Parry, the famous blind harper of Wynnstay.**(1)** William Parry was an artist of considerable ability. He trained at William Shipley's school c1760-61,**(2)** with Sir Joshua Reynolds**(3)** and from 1769 at the *RA*.**(4)**

In 1770, he worked at Wynnstay where he painted *Time Discovering Truth,* cleaned pictures and painted scenes for the theatre.**(5)** Whilst at Wynnstay he was probably employed as a Reynoldesque portrait painter. Examples of his work at this time are *Watkin E. Wynne, Miss Lloyd* and *Lady Williams Wynn*.**(6)** The two former paintings are clearly pastiches of Reynolds. In the same year, at the Society of Artists he exhibited from 'Wales', *Portraits of Two Gentlemen.*

The work which *Waterhouse* believed to have been Parry's best, *Sir Joseph Banks, Solander and Omai* has several direct quotations from Reynolds.**(7)** Another portrait, still owned by the Williams-Wynn family is *John Parry,* a tragic, psychological portrait similar to Reynolds' self portraits and *Dr Johnson composing the Dictionary*.**(8)**

Parry was patronised by Jesus College, Oxford, probably because of the college's Welsh connections.**(9)**

He probably travelled to Rome in September 1770 where he remained until at least 1776 or 1777.**(10)** In 1776 he was elected Associate of the Royal Academy.

Farington reported that Parry returned to Wales in 1778, remained a year, then returned to Rome.**(11)**

Parry may have continued his Welsh connections after the loss of patronage from the Williams-Wynn family because amongst the works in his posthumous sale was *The Celebration of St David*.**(12)** He also returned to Wales early in 1791 where he died**(13)** on 13 February.

1. Edwards, E., *Anecdotes of Painters* (London, 1808), p.163-165, has a good short biography of Parry. The *BM* copy of Edwards includes an etching by Parry of his father. This small print was used as an entrance ticket for his father's concerts. *DWB*. Parry played at London, Oxford, Cambridge and Dublin. *Lord, 1994* p.106 illustrates two portraits of this sitter including the picture recorded in *Joyner (1989)* I p.152 as at Llangedwyn Hall.
2. Allan, D., *William Shipley* (London, 1979), p.217, he won prizes for drawings in 1760 and 1761. These were *The Dancing Faun* (1760) and *Hercules and Atlas* (1761).
3. *Waterhouse* gives a summary biography and mentions his training under Reynolds. *By Gones* II, June 1890, p.382, reports that he was 'the favourite pupil of Sir Joshua'.

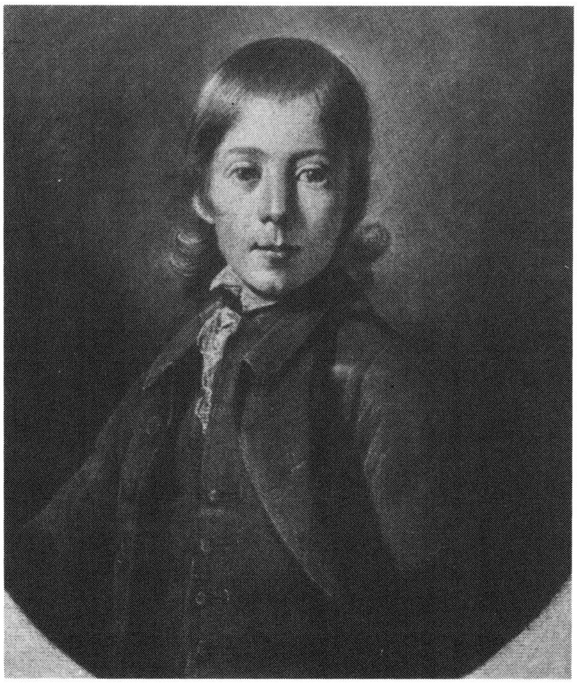

67 Parry, William, *R. Owen, Llwyn,* pastel on paper, c1770, PG2820.

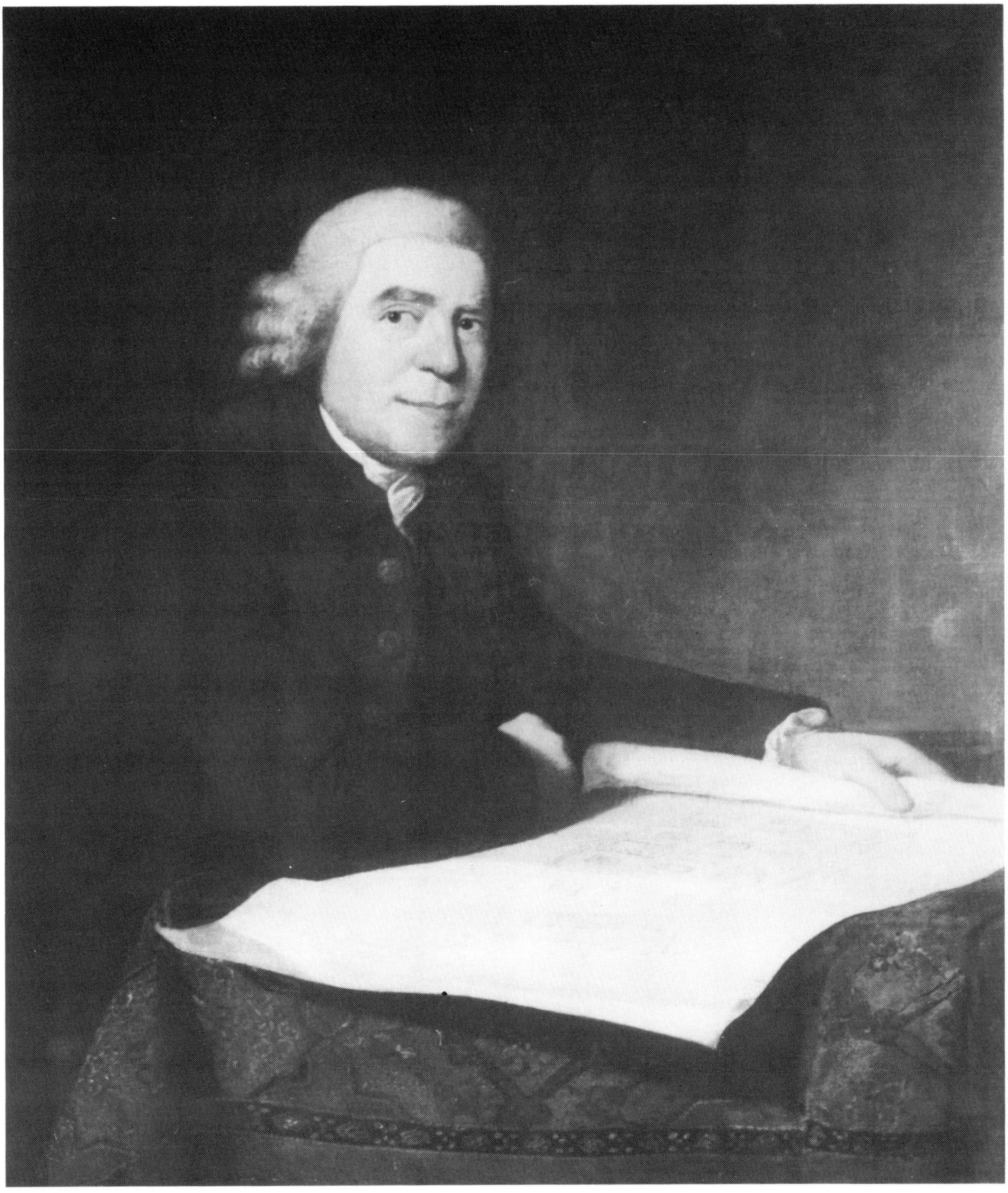

68 Parry, William, *Richard Jones*, 1770, oil on canvas, *WPA* (St David's School, Ashford).

4. *Hutchison*, p.133, Parry entered the schools on 14 February 1769 as a painter. He later exhibited at the *RA* from 1776-88 but never from Wales.
5. *NLW*, Wynnstay MSS, Box 115/2, p.29. No further reference to the painting appears in the Wynnstay papers.
6. *Lady Williams-Wynn* is mentioned in Wynnstay MSS, Miscellaneous, Volume 16, 1790 inventory, p.26.
7. This painting clearly illustrates how much Reynolds's pupils knew of his compositions and finish.
8. Another series of portraits was recorded by *Steegman*, Volume 1, at Nerquis Hall, Denbighshire: six pictures, all but two dated 1770.
9. Jesus College, Oxford, portrait of Eubule Thelwall (1562-1630), oil on canvas, 'copied by William Parry'.
10. Wynnstay MSS, volume 16, *op.cit.*, p.17; disbursements, p.12. He began exhibiting at the *RA* in 1776 giving a London address.
11. Farington, J., *Notebook* (Windsor Typescript), [p.75]. Published version not yet available.

12. Mentioned in *Morning Post*, 27 April 1791, no catalogue has survived but this advertisement gives an indication of his collection.
13. Bryan, M., *Dictionary of Painters and Engravers* Volume IV p.73. His wife Elizabeth died in childbirth in Wales, she was the daughter of Henry Keene (1726-1776). Presumably it occurred in North Wales but no details of her or her husband's death or burial has yet been discovered.

See Colour Illustration II.

PARRY, William (fl 1835 - fl 1843)
Surveyor — Morfodion, Llanidloes

Davies Atlas.

PARRY, William (fl 1835 - fl 1845)
House, coach and sign painter — Caernarfon

He had a partnership with Robert Samuel, which began c1835. Early advertisements emphasised 'prompt as well as careful execution'.**(1)** Later they were commended for their 'Style of House Painting'.**(2)**

After 1842 Parry continued the business alone. He offered a large range of services which included glazing, gilding, paper hanging and chinese japanning.

1. *Caernarvon and Denbighshire Herald*, 13 June 1835, p.3. *Ibid.*, 20 June 1835, p.2. *Ibid.*, 5 March 1836, p.2. *Ibid.*, 12 March 1836, p.2. *Ibid.*, 19 March 1842, p.2.
2. *Ibid.*, 19 July 1845, p.2.

PATENT DAGUERREOTYPE ESTABLISHMENT (fl 1843)
Photographic portraits — Swansea, At *RISW*

The *Cambrian* announced that

> 'it is only in Swansea that a *real Artist* has thought fit to manage this admirable result of chemistry and optics combined, the public may, therefore, expect more graceful, expressive and spirited Pictures from this establishment than even from those in London which are managed undoubtedly by skillful Photographists, but who understand only the *material* part of the execution without being able to govern the *spiritual* or *tasteful* part of the Picture.'**(1)**

Nothing more is known about this practice. In the mid-1840s Fox Talbot set up a 'Photographic Establishment' at Reading.**(2)** This venture at Swansea could have been instigated by Calvert Jones or Dillwyn Llewellyn, both of whom had connections with the *RISW*.

1. *Cambrian*, 8 July 1843, p.3.
2. Mentioned in Painting, D., *Swansea's Place in the History of Photography* (1982), p.8.

PATRICK, David (c1812 - fl 1851)
Portrait painter & House painter — 4 St Mary's Street, Carmarthen

Born in Carmarthen, where he is recorded living with his wife Elisa in 1851.**(1)** Carmarthen Museum has a portrait of John Williams 1850, & his wife with daughter.**(2)**

1. *Census Returns*, 1851, *DFHS*, Vol. II, folio 228, p.38. *WPA* 394/395 (1850).
2. Exhibited in *Trefi'r Gorllewin* 1995 No 4&5.

See Colour Illustrations V and VI.

PAYNE, Henry Thomas (-1832)
Landscape drawings — Breconshire

Some topographical, architectural and antique drawings.**(1)**

1. *NLW*, MS 4278C, *A Parochial Visitation...* Brecon, 1785 (information Dr S. Briggs, RCAMW). For example, p. 200 has a *Stone at Cwmdu*.

PAYNE, Thomas (fl 1835 - fl 1847)
Surveyor — Dolgellau

Davies Atlas., Eden II p.201.

PEMBERTON, James (fl 1821)
Architect — Hawarden

He designed and built Llanarmon [yn Iâl] vicarage.**(1)**

1. *NLW* St. Asaph, Bounty Plans 51, 1821, a particularly fine, ambitious plan with good facade detailing & well composed windows. Not in *Girouard*.

See Colour Illustration XIV.

PENNANT, Thomas (1726 - 1798)
Landscape draughtsman, Cartoonist — Downing, Flintshire

Executed several wash drawings in an antiquarian style. He usually employed artists to undertake art work**(1)** but was probably trained at some point. His early portrait c1738 shows Pennant with a sketchbook. This may represent his own copies from Old Master drawings.**(2)** He drew three cartoons *Modern Toilet*, 1781, *The Good Shepherd*, 1784, *Triumph of Turbulence*, 1785.**(3)**

1. *Vide* Griffith & Ingleby, *supra*. *DWB*. Dr R.P. Evans has recently completed a PhD dissertation on Pennant (1993).
2. *NLW*, PG 4534, Highmore, Joseph, *Thomas Pennant*, oil on canvas, c1738.
3. Illustrated in *Lord, WWP* pp.74-79.

See Colour Illustration XII.

PENSON, Richard Kirke (c1815 - 1886)
Landscape painter, Architect — [Carmarthenshire]

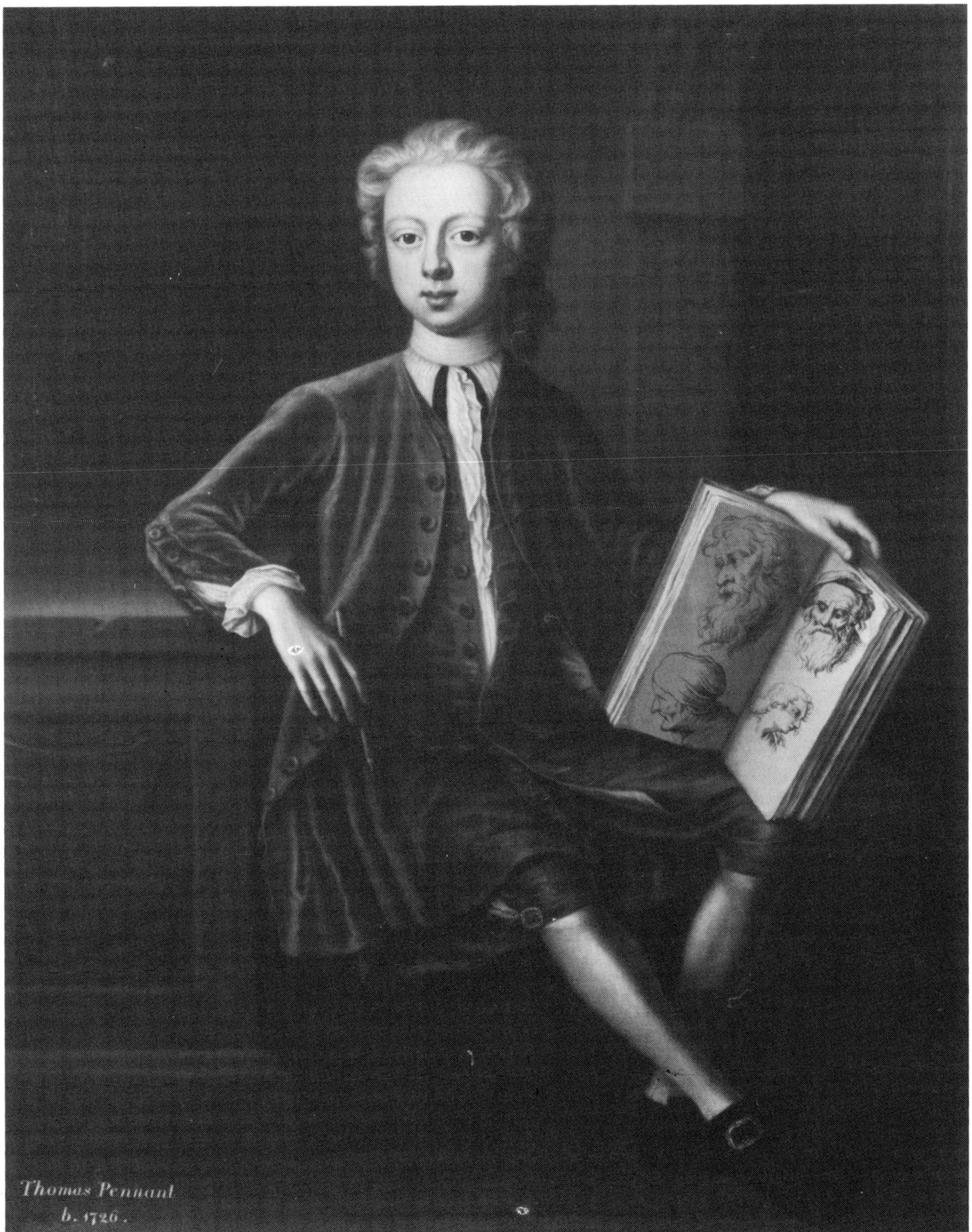

69 *Pennant, Thomas,* by Joseph Highmore, oil on canvas, c1738, PG4534.

He was the architect of Bronwydd, Llangunllo, did some work at St David's Cathedral and designed a lime kiln at Llandybie.**(1)**

By 1868 the *Carmarthen Journal* was defending Penson against London indifference.**(2)** He drew some fine Welsh landscapes.**(3)**

He was the pupil of Thomas Penson (*infra*).

1. *TL. Girouard,* p.749, provides further details of his training and profession. He notes that Penson was the county surveyor for Carmarthenshire and Cardiganshire c1857. *Eden,* Supplement, p.457, notes that R.K. Penson was 'a watercolour painter'.
2. I am grateful to my friend *TL* for this reference. *Carmarthen Journal,* 8 May 1868, note reproduced from the *Spectator*: 'Mr Penson is no new member of the

Institute but meets with little favour there.'
3. Prints after R.K. Penson include: *NLW*, P3401, A3/3 - A434, *Pass of Nantffrangon, Caernarvonshire*, c1850 (the other two prints do not appear to be in the *NLW* as loose items); *Chirk Castle; Pass at Llanberis, Caernarvonshire.*

PENSON, Thomas (1760 - 1824)
Architect — Wrexham
Flintshire county surveyor (1810-1814) — Charles Street, Beast Market
[Landscape painter]**(1)** — Caernarfon

'Founder of a dynasty of architects practising in Chester and North Wales'.**(2)** He lived in Wrexham and built various buildings in the town,**(3)** including his own house and the theatre. In 1784 he designed the County Gaol at Caernarfon. He died at Wrexham. There is an extant will in the hand of Thomas Penson.**(4)**

His two sons both followed his interests. Thomas Penson (c1790-1859) became a pupil of Thomas Harrison at Chester and established a practice in Oswestry and Shrewsbury. John William Todd Penson (c1790- fl 1850), was an artist and worked in Oswestry.**(5)**

1. *Pigot's*, 1822, p.731-732, given as 'Landscape Painter'.
2. *Colvin* pp. 748-9 notes a large number of projects completed in Wales. See also *PP*, p.226. *Girouard*, p.107-108. *Eden*, Supplement, p.457.
3. *Wrexham Market*, 1848, illustrated in *PP*, p.52. *Colvin* notes that he lived at Charles Street, Wrexham until c1818.
4. *SA* 1824/220. Penson is described as an architect, and the will is written in his own hand and signed by him.
5. *Slater's*, 1850, p.81, 'Penson, William, Oswestry'.

PENSON, Thomas M. (Junior) (1790 - 1859)
Painter — Wrexham
[Architect] — Oswestry, Chester

Penson was probably the son of Thomas Penson *supra*.**(1)** His early practice may have been in Wrexham, but by 1837 he had moved to Oswestry. From 1857 he was living in Chester.**(2)**

1. *Girouard*, p.708, mentions several drawings at the *RIBA*. *Eden*, Supplement, p.457, mentions this surveyor. *NLW* St Asaph, Bounty Plans, 62, Llandyssilio, 1850 'of Oswestry' 'architect'. He was working at Aberhafesp in 1828 & gave Oswestry as his residence. St Asaph, Bounty Plans, 2, 1828 & St Asaph, Bounty Plans, 59, 1847 address given as Oswestry, & Bounty Plan 137, 1843.
2. *Graves, R.A.*: He exhibited five pictures from 1836 to 1837, three from Oswestry (1837-39), all North Wales landscapes; in 1857 an architectural view, *Arle Court near Cheltenham*, for a member of the Bute family.

PETHERICK, John (1784 - 1861)
Landscape artist — Merthyr Tydfil

Petherick was born in Cambourne, Cornwall, the son of a mining engineer. His family moved to Merthyr, where the father and later his sons worked at Pen-y-darren.

In 1989 a series of watercolours by Petherick were discovered and sold at a London Gallery.**(1)** Views of Wales are dated from 1847 to 1855. They exhibit an interesting mixture of industrial scenes, landscapes and miniature studies of insects and natural life.

One example of his style is *Court Llangewydd*, 1854.**(2)**

1. Moore, D., *John Petherick* (London, [1989]), exhibition catalogue. Several of his oil paintings & watercolours were exhibited at the Merthyr Tydfil Exhibition, 1880.
2. *Ibid.*, item 46, watercolour, dated '22 July 1854'. Now *PG* 1292, 10 x 12 cm.

See Colour Illustration XI.

PHILIP, John (- 1771)
Mason — Crunwear (Caernarfonshire)

SD/1771/42.

PHILLIP, David (- 1766)
Mason — Kidwelly

SD/1766/39.

PHILLIP, William (- 1765)
Mason — Mathri, Pembrokeshire

SD/1765/174 (I).

PHILLIPS, John (c1820 - fl 1851)
Pottery painter — Llanelli
Printer — 18 Caedubach

Born in Llanrhidian, working at the ?South Wales pottery in 1851.**(1)**

1. Census, 1851, *DFHS*, Vol. I, folio 234, p.5. *Vide* Hughes, Gareth, & Pugh, Robert, *Llanelly Pottery* (Llanelli, 1990), p.84.

PHILLIPS, John (fl 1823)
Sculptor — Haverfordwest

Executed a monument of Richard, Lord Milford in 1823, at St Mary's Church, Haverfordwest.**(1)**

1. *WPA* file.

PHILLIPS, William (fl 1845)
Builder — Prendergast

Designed & built rectory at Rudbaxton, Pembrokeshire im 1845.**(1)**

1. *NLW* St Davids, Bounty Plans 162, 1845. Not in *Eden*.

PHILPOTT, H.P. [Goode] (fl 1835 - fl 1843)
Surveyor — Haverfordwest

Davies Atlas. Probably the same as *infra*.

PHILPOTT, Henry (fl 1835 - fl 1864)**(1)**
Surveyor Haverfordwest**(2)**

1. *NLW*, Estate map *Camrose*, 1864.
2. *Davies Atlas. NLW*, Estate map *Amroth*, 1847. *Eden* II p.204.

PIERCY, Robert (fl 1825 - fl 1847)**(1)**
Surveyor Chirk

A versatile surveyor, the father of Robert A. Piercy.**(2)**

1. *NLW*, MSS Estate map index.
2. *NLW*, Estate maps *Trefeglwys*, 1827, *Llanllugan*, 1823. *Davies Atlas., Eden* II p.204 notes R. A. Piercy as son of Robert, a civil engineer.

PILDITCH, John (fl 1844 - fl 1860s)
Architect Llandeilo
New Road**(1)**

He may have moved to London in the 1860s.**(2)**

1. *Pigot's*, 1844, p.44.
2. *Girouard*, 1993, p.718, notes a John Thomas Pilditch (fl 1868 - fl 1871) living in 98 Church Street, Chelsea.

POLLARD (fl 1814 - fl 1821)
China painter Swansea

Employed at the Cambrian Pottery 1814-1821.**(1)**

1. *Cadrawd*, Volume II, p.95.

PORTER, Isaac (fl 1835 - fl 1843)
Surveyor Oswestry
Brook Street

Davies Atlas., Eden II p.206.

POUGET, Major Robert (fl 1840 - fl 1841)
Landscape draughtsman Tenby

Moved to Tenby with the Royal Engineers**(1)**, working on fortifications for St Catherine's Rock. He produced a competent drawing of Tenby which was lithographed.**(2)**

1. National Army Museum, Chelsea, has no reference to Major Pouget. He does not appear in the *Army Lists* for this period.
2. *NLW, PA* 5345, B12/15 - B269, *Tenby Pier*, lithograph. The *Narberth Weekly News*, 14 October 1943, 'A Picture of Tenby', discusses Pouget and his picture.

POUNDLEY, J.W. (fl 1835 - fl 1865)**(1)**
Surveyor Newtown
Kerry**(2)**

1. *NLW*, Estate map *Llandysul*, 1865.
   Davies Atlas. Not in *Eden*.
2. *NLW* Estate Map Harrison Volume 1 signed J. W. Poundley, Kerry, Montgomeryshire.

POWELL (Powel) (fl 1767 - fl 1780)
Monumental mason Talgarth

Carved and painted tombstones in South Wales. Two good examples are at Llandefalle Church, Breconshire, both use 17th century motifs such as interrupted pediments.**(1)**

1. Information from Mr A. Parkinson, *RCAM*. The grave of Thomas Williams, 1767, is inscribed 'Powell Talgarth' and another stone, dated 1780, inscribed 'POWEL Talgarth'.

POWELL, Champney (1824 -)
[Landscape painter] Monmouth

He was the pupil of the elder Parry (*supra*), and is reported to have worked in watercolours and to have etched prints.**(1)**

1. *Cadrawd*, p.96.

POWELL, William (fl 1816 - 1834)
Architect Swansea
3 Nelson Place
Cae Bailey House

Powell worked as an architect in Swansea from about 1813.**(1)** He originally lived at Nelson Place and then moved up to Cae Baily in 1830. It was at this latter address that he is recorded in his will.**(2)** His first building was a 'commodious dwelling house in High Street'.**(3)** Later, he worked as a Surveyor for the Swansea Paving and Lighting Commissioners.

Rather surprisingly he was commissioned by Thomas Mansel Talbot to build a new wing at *Penrice Castle* & to repair Margam *Orangery*.

1. *Colvin*, p.777. *Swansea Guide*, 1813, Appendix. *Matthews Guide*, 1816, p.19.
2. *Swansea Directory*, 1830: 'Cae Baily Mount Pleasant'. *Pigot's*, 1830, p.862: 'Mount Pleasant'. *SD*/1834/355, described as architect. *Girouard*, p.734, records a William Powell (1839-1872) at 11 Crooked Lane, London. This is possibly a son or relation.
3. *Lloyd* architects p.64. He also illustrates *Slaughterhouse* c1825 plan at *RISW* & discusses his work. *Colvin* quotes *TL* who catalogues the works of Powell.

POWELL, William (fl 1805 - fl 1843)**(1)**
Surveyor Pantycorred
Breconshire

Davies Atlas. Eden, II, p.267.

1. *NLW*, Estate maps *Llanelieu*, 1818, *Llanddety*, 1805.

POWELL, William James (fl 1841 - 1844)
Surveyor Aberporth

Eden, II, p.207, notes that he executed tithe maps. Not in *Davies Atlas*. He may be the same person as William Powell, *supra*.

PRATT, John (fl 1835 - fl 1840)
'Architects & Builders' Crickhowell

Pigot's, 1835, p.755. He produced neat plans for a vicarage at Cwm du, Breconshire**(1)**

1. *NLW*, St Davids, Bounty Plans 40, 1840. Not in *Eden*.

PRATT, R. (fl 1850)
Miniaturist Haverfordwest
High Street

'Informs inhabitants...instructed in Science of Kalography... now prepared to take portraits in the above most beautiful style. No charge will be made for the portraits but for the morocco cases, in which they are enclosed.'**(1)**

1. *Pembrokeshire Herald*, 25 October 1850, p.3.
   Ibid., 1 November 1850, p.1.

PRICE, Anthony (- 1793)
Mason Llangatock

BR/1793/44.

PRICE, Francis (fl 1835 - fl 1843)
Surveyor Norton
Oystermouth

Davies Atlas., Eden II p.207.

PRICE, Henry (fl 1835 - fl 1843)
Surveyor Abergavenny

Davies Atlas. Eden, II, p.208.

PRICE, John (fl 1835 - fl 1843)
Surveyor Denbigh

Davies Atlas. Eden, II, p.208. *NLW*, Estate maps, *Llanfair Dyffryn Clwyd*, 1842. Possibly the same one as *infra*.

PRICE, John (fl 1835 - fl 1847)
Surveyor Ruthin

Davies Atlas., Eden p.208.

PRICE, Thomas (fl 1859)
Portrait painter Maenan
Caernarfonshire

Portrait of Rev. Thomas Davies, Rector of Llanddoget and Llanrwst.**(1)**

1. Private Collection, oil on canvas, 25.1 x 19.3 cm, 'Painted by [T.] Price [at] Park Maenon 1859'.

PRICE, Rev. Thomas (1787 - 1848)
'Carnhuanawc' Llanfihangel Cwm-Du
Landscape artist Crickhowell**(1)**

He was born in Pencaerelin in Llanfihangel Brynpabuan, Breconshire. He was ordained as deacon in 1811 and worked as curate and rural dean in Radnorshire and Breconshire. He knew Lady Llanover (*supra*) and this may account for his interest in landscape draughtsmanship. His landscapes are rare. He apparently offered two of his own views of Llanfihangel Helygen, 1811, for sale.**(2)** He produced decorative certificates for the Cymreigyddion y Fenni.**(3)**

1. *DWB* has an extensive article on Thomas Price.
2. No copies are extant.
3. *PL* kindly gave me this information.

PRICHARD, John (- 1851)
Painter**(1)** Llanbeblig
Caernarfonshire

1. *B* 1851/125. The will mentions Edward Prichard, No. 1 George Street, Chester, Painter - brother of J.P.

PRICHARD, John(1) (1817 - 1886)
Architect Llandaff**(2)**

He became the Llandaff Diocesan architect and restored Llandaff Cathedral 1843-67. He later entered partnership with J.P. Seddon (c1853) and worked on various churches in Wales.**(3)**

1. *Girouard*, p.239, gives Prichard (omitted from 1995 Edition) and notes he was born at Llangan, partner to John Pollard Seddon (1827-1906).
2. *Hunt*, 1849, p.17, gives 'John Pritchard, Architects & Surveyors'.
   Slater's, 1850, p.22: 'John Prichard, Architect and Sons'. His sons remain unrecorded.
3. *PP*, p.226, main source for entry. *NLW* Llandaff, Bounty Plans 111, 1847, *St Brides Major*, vicarage; Llandaff, Bounty Plans 102, 1857 *Peterstone Super-Ely* (with Seddon), also Bounty Plan 69, 1855 *Llansoy*, Bounty Plans 82, 1845 *Merthyr Tydfil Rectory*.

See Colour Illustration XIII.

PRICHARD, Owen (fl 1849)
Artists' colourman Port Dinorwig

Slater's, 1849, p.14.

PRICHARD, Thomas (- 1857)
Architect Llansawel

SD/1857/321.

PRIDE, Thomas
(fl 1814 - 16)
Surveyor Carmarthen

NLW, Estate maps *Ebbw Vale*, 1816, *Llanwinio*, 1814.
Eden II p.208.

PRIOR, James (1799 - fl 1841)
Artist — Swansea, Wind Street

Described in the Census of 1841 as an artist 'not born in Glamorgan'.**(1)**

1. Census returns, HO 107 1426, p.20, [36].

PRITCHARD, Edward
Mason — Clodock (Longtown)

BR/1834/12.

PRITCHARD, George (fl 1764)
Sign painter, Mural painter — All Saints Church, Llangar, Merionethshire

Painted texts, inscriptions in English and Welsh, possibly cherub heads.**(1)**

1. *RCAM (TP)*, c15 x 15 cm.

PRITCHARD, Thomas (1764)
[Sign painter] — Llanfair Church, Conwy

Probably an itinerant sign painter, he executed five large wall paintings.**(1)**

1. *RCAM* (*TP*). These paintings depict prayerbook texts and a skeleton symbolising Death.

PROSSER, John (fl 1827)
Stone Mason — Monmouth

He was the son of Benjamin Prosser who also may have been a stone mason. **(1)**

1. Gwent Record Office, W&T 1056 a release document dated 5 September 1827 describes John Prosser as the elder son of Benjamin Prosser.

PROTHEROE, Rees (- 1814)
Mason — Talgarth

BR/1814/91.

PROVIS, W.A. (fl 1820)
Landscape painter — Menai Straits

Produced several views of Menai Bridge. He was described as the resident engineer.**(1)**

1. *NLW*, PB 2507, E2 (E3), PFC 2/M, colour engraving. Also *NLW* P2816, A68, Top A1, dated July 1821. The bridge was opened in Jan. 1826. I wish to thank John Holmes for this information.

PUGH, Mr (fl 1809)
Miniature painter — Tenby

A London artist**(1)** who visited Tenby and exhibited his work at 'Mr Griffith's, Key Hill, Tenby'. His advertisement mentioned his 'faithful resemblance of the celebrated Gwillym Lloyd Wardle Esq MP'.**(2)**

1. This may have been Edward Pugh (1763-1813) or possibly T. Pugh (fl 1808-9). Neither possibility seems convincing.
2. *Cambrian*, 1 July 1809, p.3.

PUGH, Ed[ward] (fl 1739)
Engraver — Oswestry

Signed a brass at Llanfair Caereinion church, Mont. This brass was lost when the church was rebuilt in 1868.**(1)**

1. *Lewis*, p.23. Also gives *Transactions of the Monumental Brass Society* VIII, p.143, and *Montgomeryshire Collections* XVI (1883), p.355.

PUGH, Edward 'The Limner'(1) (1763 - 1813)
Miniature and landscape painter — Ruthin, Well Street

Pugh was born in Ruthin, but left for London in his youth. He exhibited a number of Welsh subjects at the *RA***(2)** and did not leave London until c1800. He spent some years in Chester until c1808, returned to London and by 1813 was back in his home town.

Theophilus Jones (*supra*) published an original drawing after Pugh as the frontispiece to his *History of the County of Brecknock*, Vol. I (1805).

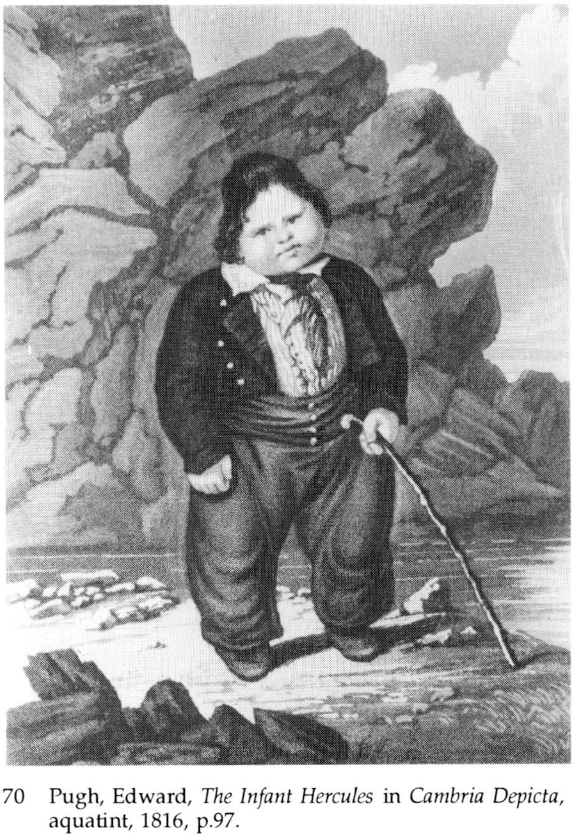

70 Pugh, Edward, *The Infant Hercules* in *Cambria Depicta*, aquatint, 1816, p.97.

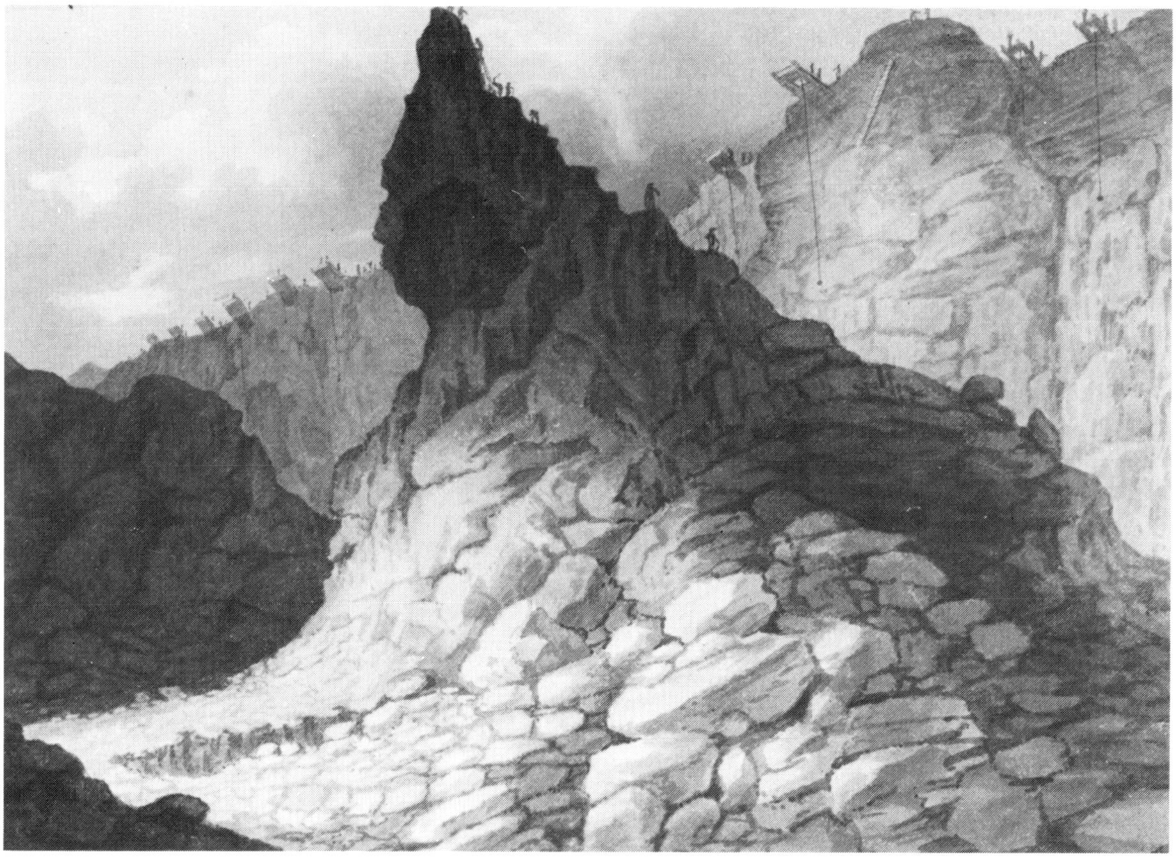

71 Pugh, Edward, *Paris Mines* in *Cambria Depicta, book of drawings,* pen & ink, Drawing Volume, 407, p.12, P.G672.

His best work was the *Cambria Depicta***(3)** which he wrote and illustrated. He wrote the foreword from Ruthin saying that he possessed 'a moderate talent as an artist'.**(4)**

Pugh drew a set of views of the Vale of Clwyd and also (at least) two large aquatints of Monmouthshire.**(5)**

An oil painting dated 1811 may have been executed in Wales.**(6)**

He died at Ruthin and was described as a 'Limner'.**(7)**

1. *Y Traethodydd* XII, 1910, p.43, described him as the 'Nature Artist'. *NLW,* MSS Dept, Bishops Transcripts Ruthin (2), 1751-1790, 'Edward son of David Pugh [Barber] and Dorothy his wife was Baptised...June 1763.'
2. He exhibited the following at the *RA* in 1799: (739) Portraits of *Mr Jackson of Holyhead,* and an *Officer;* (774) Portrait of *Mr Edwards the bard,* commonly called the Welsh *Shakespeare* [Twm o'r Nant].
   NMW has a miniature (A614) of *Lady Morris* [on ivory?] 9.5x7.6cm
3. Pugh, E., *Cambria Depicta,* illustrated with picturesque views (London, 1816). 'By a Native Artist', it contains a series of aquatints. Examples of these aquatints in *NLW* are:
   PA 4393, B1/3 - B4, *Bishop's Throne, Anglesey,* 1813
   PA 4393, A1/1 - A116, *Paris mines in the 1800,* 1814
   PA 4396, A1/1 - A114, *Paris mines in 1804,* 1813.
   NLW, Drawing Volume 405 (4to), *Cambria Depicta. Joyner, 1990,* Plate 7, illustrates *The perilous situation of Robert Roberts.*
4. *Ibid.,* p.vii.
5. *NLW* has examples of these aquatints. One particularly interesting print, date 1 June 1810, is *View of a Stone Bridge across the Valley and River at Risca in Monmouthshire.*
6. Grant, Colonel, *Old English Landscape Painters,* Volume 5 (1959), p.385, notes this picture.
7. *NLW,* Bishop's Transcripts, St Asaph diocese, Ruthin parish (3), 1791-1815, p.118, *verso* Ruthin Burials 1813, No. 9

PUGH, George (fl 1835 - fl 1850)

Surveyor — Machynlleth, Aberystwyth

He had a limited practice in North Cardiganshire & Merionethshire.**(1)**

1. *Davies Atlas. Eden,* II, p.209, gives 'Machynlleth'. *NLW,* Estate maps *Aberystwyth,* 1838, and *Llansaintffraid,* 1840, 1850. *NLW* MSS Gogerddan Collection has a survey at Aber Llolwyn house with a portrait of the dwelling c1840.

PUGHE, Lewis (1836)

Builder — Meifod, Montgomeryshire

Designed & built Rectory at Llanfihangel in 1836.**(1)**

1. *NLW* St Asaph, Bounty Plans 76, 1836, a simple design.

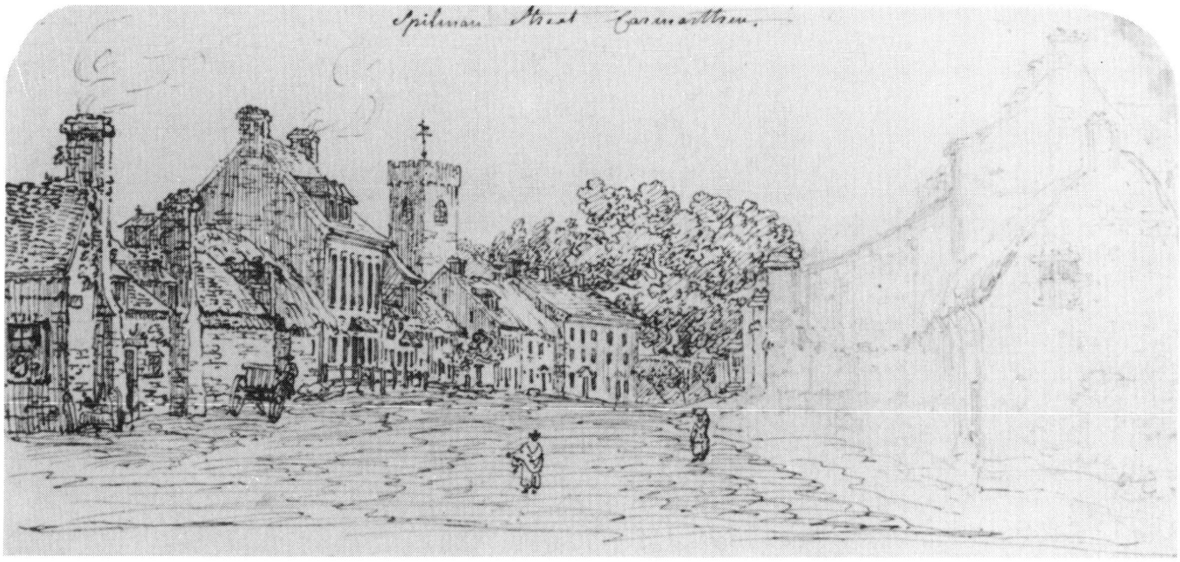

72 Pugin, Auguste, *Spilman Street, Carmarthen*, pen & ink, c1804, PE3753.

PUGHE, William Owen (1759 - 1835)
Landscape and portrait painter — Nantglyn, Denbigh

A famous scholar, poet & intellectual of great importance. Pughe was born at Ty'n y Bryn, Llanfihangel y Pennant Merionethshire, educated at Altrincham near Manchester & moved to London in 1776 where he remained until c1806.**(1)** He was an amateur artist, painting mainly in watercolours. He produced characterful portraits & tiny topographical landscapes. Stylistically his portraits are contemporary in feeling but his views appear to reflect the older, wash drawing technique of the late 18th century.**(2)**

Pughe had a wide circle of friends & aquaintances which included at least two other Welsh artists.**(3)** He also knew Sir Edwin Henry Landseer (1802-1873) & they shared antiquarian interests.**(4)**

His portrait of *Iolo Morganwg* is a unique record of another artist scholar of its period.**(5)**

1. *DNB*. pp.815-6. Mordaf Pierce, y Parch T., *Dr W. Owen Pughe* (Caernarfon, 1914) includes illustrations of Pughe's birthplace & home. G. Carr provides the authorative study on Pughe: Carr, Glenda, *William Owen Pughe* (Caerdydd, 1983). Includes portraits by T. George & Daniel Maclise (1806-1870) (*Daniel Maclise* NPG, (London, 1972) is a good study of his work). Carr also provides much information on Pughe's London connections (for instance *vide* pp.253-4). Another text by Carr concentrates on Pugh as a writer: *William Owen Pughe* (Caernarfon, 1993) (in the Llên y Llenor series *ed.* J. E. Caerwyn Williams).
2. *NLW*, has two sketchbooks by Pughe: Drawing Volume 57 (Previous called Mysevin MS 30), contains landscapes & portraits from his London period & later. They include some fine watercolours of Welsh landscapes dated between 1796-1832. Drawing Volume 58 is a larger format with many loose drawings, subjects include Nantglyn landscapes & portraits of his family dated between 1810-1832. This later sketchbook was probably executed entirely in the Nantglyn area. Also NLW MS 13,239c (Mysevin 19) has sketches of druids by Pughe.
3. *T. George* vide Carr 1983 *op.cit.*, p.253; Hugh Hughes *ibid* p.253.
4. *ibid* notes a visit to Landseer 29 October 1823 (in *NLW* MS 13248 p.333). It may be significant that Landseer began his Highland studies, after visiting that region for the first time in 1824. *vide* Ormond, Richard *Sir Edwin Landseer* London: Thames & Hudson, 1981, p.60ff.
5. *NLW* Drawing Volume 57, 'Iolo Morgannwg 1798' full length seated at a table writing, in a painted oval, 10.8 x 6.3cm. He is also known to have painted portraits of *Twm o'r Nant* & *Richard Owen* (information Dept. Pictures & Maps, *NLW*). It is interesting also to note that he inscribed his drawings with his own unusual vocabulary. This was also seen in his diaries. For instance he uses the terms 'ardebed' or countenance for a portrait & 'dyzelwad' for the actual image. *vide* Pughe, W. O., *Geiriadur* (London, 1793), & compare inscriptions on Drawing Volumes 57 & 58 & *Ivor*. Ivor was one of Pughe's sons, born 29 August 1826 & Carr p.206 notes Robert Davies 'Bardd Nantglyn writing '... Ivor dirion frawd arall ...'

See Colour Illustration X.

PUGIN, Augustus Charles (1769 - 1832)
Architectural draughtsman — Carmarthen
Scenery painter — Swansea
Landscape artist

Pugin is reported to have emigrated to Britain and arrived at Carmarthen.**(1)** He was employed by John Nash as an assistant and amongst Pugin's works are designs for the renovation of St David's Cathedral.**(2)**

He and Nash were also interested in the theatre, and Pugin worked for Mastermann at the Wind Street Theatre, Swansea, painting scenes.**(3)**

Nash and Pugin apparently left together for London and in 1792 Pugin entered the *RA* schools.**(4)**

An album of landscape and architectural views included a view of Carmarthen.**(5)**

1. *Mallalieu*. Not in *Girouard*; p.743 mentions A.C. Pugin in reference to his son Augustus Welby Pugin (1812-1852). *Colvin* pp.787-789.
2. The original drawings are held at Haverfordwest Record Office and illustrated in Evans, W. & Worsley, R., *St David's Cathedral*, 1981, pp.41-2. They are accurate and clear works.
3. Price, C., *English Theatre in Wales*, 1985, p.89; also mentioned by *Rogers*, p.162; Ferrey, B., *Recollections of A. Welby Pugin*, 1861, p.29, mentions Carmarthen Theatre.
4. *Hutchison*, p.153.
5. Christie's, 20 March 1984, lot 26, illustrated *View of Carmarthen*. This drawing was acquired by *NLW* (PE 3753), watercolour and pen and ink, 8.9 x 18.3 cm. Many of the drawings in the album (now broken up) were inscribed 'c1800', but the present writer believes that they were executed in the 1790s.

PURCHAS, Robert Nathaniel (fl 1835 - fl 1843)

Surveyor — Pilestone, Llandogo, Chepstow

Davies Atlas., *Eden* II p.209.

PURCHAS, Robert Whittlesey (fl 1823 - fl c1850)

Surveyor — Pilestone, Llandogo, Chepstow

Davies Atlas. *Eden*, II, p.209, mentions him as estate, tithe and road surveyor.

PYNE, Henry (fl 1801 - fl 1850)

Drawing master — Haverfordwest
Portrait painter — Goat Street, Hill Street

He was born at Haverfordwest where he seems to have lived all his life.**(1)** Pyne worked from his home in Haverfordwest and appears to have visited various gentry families,**(2)** but also organised his own school, and worked for private schools in mid Wales. He advertised as a drawing and dancing master, having been employed by 'the first schools of respectability, and Families of Distinction in Pembrokeshire, Carmarthenshire and Cardiganshire'.**(3)**

He was still working as a Drawing master in 1840 but by 1850 had become a portrait painter.**(4)**

1. Census, 1851, *DFHS*, Vol. IV, folio 22, p.11, gives Pyne as age 79, 38 Hill Street.
2. Haverfordwest R.O., D/TE/64, receipt for Pyne dated 18 June 1801 for 'Two pounds Ten Shilling from Mr Painter to a Bill drawn on the late Capt. Tasker of Upton for instruction in Drawing to the Miss Jones's'. Upton Castle Estate was in Pembrokeshire.
3. *Carmarthen Journal*, 23 January 1813, p.[3].
   Ibid., 30 January 1813, p.1.
   He charged 15s per quarter for his school with 10 shillings and 6 pence entrance fee.
4. *Robson's*, 1840, p.7, notes he had moved to Hill Street.
   Hunt, 1850, p.50, gives his profession as a portrait painter only.
   Pigot's, 1835, p.760.
   Pigot's, 1834, p.36, gives him as teacher of portrait painting.

Q

QUINTIN, Monsieur H.J. (fl 1838 - fl 1839)

Teacher of drawing — Monmouth, Newport

Mentioned in an advertisement as the son of Monsieur Quintin, French language teacher. He worked in Monmouth in 1838**(1)** and at Newport in 1839.**(2)**

1. *Monmouthshire Merlin*, 14 April 1838, p.2.
2. *Ibid.*, 2 February 1839, p.2.
   Ibid., 4 May 1839, p.2.

R

RAPHAEL, Mrs (fl 1849 - fl 1850)

Miniature painter — Swansea, 9 Camden Place

She advertised her second visit to the town:

'Miniature likenesses etc.

Mrs Raphael begs to inform the Inhabitants of Swansea and its Vicinity of her SECOND ANNUAL PROFESSIONAL VISIT, and is now prepared to take LIKENESSES in MINIATURE and WATER-COLOUR SKETCHES, for a short time.'**(1)**

1. *Cambrian*, 24 May 1850, p.2.
   Raphael had visited Swansea before 1850 and presumably returned because of sufficient patronage.

RATCLIFFE, Elizabeth (fl 1758 - ?c1823)(1)

Model maker — Erddig Hall
Landscape artist — Denbighshire

Ratcliffe was a maid at Erddig who showed considerable artistic skill as a copyist, modeller and artist. Thomas Pennant encouraged her and she may have produced some drawings for his grangerized volumes.**(2)**

She may have been commissioned to produce the model of the *Chinese Pagoda* (1767) and *Ruins of Palmyra* (1773).**(3)** Both are elaborate works probably based on earlier prints.**(4)**

One original landscape, *Conway Castle*, has a freshness and simplicity reminiscent of other native primitive artists.**(5)**

1. *SA* 1823/195 notes her as a widow, living in Wrexham.
2. *Waterson*, p.36, notes that Pennant lent Ratcliffe a print to copy. *Waterson* also mentions a letter from Anne Yorke to Philip Yorke, dated 10 May 1768, 'Mr Pennant has beg'd of Mamma to let Betty Ratcliffe copy for him, from a print, the youngest of Lord Hardwickes Daughters.'

3. *Ibid.*, both are illustrated.
4. The *Pagoda* may be after a design in Chambers, W., *Gardens and Buildings at Kew* (1763). The *Palmyra* may be a composition after prints in Woods, Robert, *The Ruins of Palmyra* (1753), plates VII and XXI.
5. *Waterson, op.cit.*, p.47 (illustrated).

REDMOND, Thomas (1745? - 1785)
Miniature artist
Brecon

He may have been born at Brecon, was the son of a clergyman.**(1)** He was apprenticed as a house painter at Bristol and then moved to London to study at St Martin's Lane Academy in 1762.

By 1767 he was again resident in [Brecon] and exhibited at the *SA*, *A Lady*.**(2)** He continued to exhibit at the *SA* in 1769 (from Bath) until 1771.**(3)**

1. *DWB*, pp.822-823. *Foskett*, p.463, notes that no incumbent of this name is recorded.
2. *Graves, S.A.*, p.210, notes a miniature.
3. *Ibid.*, records that he exhibited at the Free Society from 1762 to 1766.

REES, Daniel (- 1845)
Land surveyor
Tregaron

SD/1845/35. Not in *Eden*.

REES, David (fl 1835 - fl 1843)
Surveyor
Neath

Davies Atlas., Eden II p.213.

REES, David (- 1842)
Mason
Tregaron

SD/1842/111.

REES, Edward (- 1856)
Painter
Swansea
23 Orchard Street

SD/1856/154. Also described as a 'glazier'.

REES, Edward (fl 1835)
Surveyor
Marshfield
Nr Newport
Monmouthshire

Redesigned the vicarage at Coed Kernew, Monmouthshire.**(1)**

1. *NLW* Bounty Plans 18, 1835 in a neat, simple style. Not in *Eden*.

REES, John (fl 1765)
Mason
Carmarthen

BD/1765/23 (I).

REES, John (fl 1835 - fl 1843)
Surveyor
Cilgellisaf
Pencarreg
Carmarthenshire

Davies Atlas., Eden p.213.

REES, John William (fl 1835 - fl 1843)
Surveyor
Pencarreg Fawr
Llanilar
Cardiganshire

Davies Atlas. Not in *Eden*.

REES, Richard (fl 1849)
Builder
Alltgoed
Radnorshire

Designed & built rectory at Llanfinach, 1849.**(1)**

1. *NLW* St Davids, Bounty Plans 100, 1849. Neat surveyor-like plans. Not in *Eden*.

REKER, William (1813 - fl 1841)
Artist
Swansea
14 York Place

An unspecified professional not born in Glamorganshire.**(1)**

1. Census Return, 1841 HO 107, 1462, p.35, [p.21].

RELLY, Richard (- 1785)
Mason**(1)**
Haverfordwest

His will gave a particularly long and detailed inventory which included '1 Old Bible & other little Books, 1 looking glass'.

1. *SD*/1785/58 (I).

RENIE, John (fl 1830)
House painter
Monmouth
Monnow Street

Painter & 'ornamental' glazier/painter.**(1)**

1. *Pigot's*, 1830, p.520. He probably worked as an interior designer.

RICHARD, David (- 1842)
Mason
Brecon
Watton

BR/1842/6.

RICHARD, Thomas (- 1790)
Mason
Llandyfaelog
Carmarthenshire

SD/1790/71 (I).

RICHARD, Thomas (- 1807)
Mason
St Dogmaels
Pembrokeshire

SD/1807/274.

RICHARDS, David (- 1856)
Tiler/plasterer
Brecon

BR/1856/7.

RICHARDS, John (- 1842)
Mason
Laugharne
Butts
Carmarthenshire

SD/1842/293.

RICHARDS, John (- 1845)
Mason
St Issells
St Brides Hill
Carmarthenshire

SD/1845/183.

RICHARDS, John Inigo R.A. (1731 - 1810)
Scene painter
Wynnstay
Denbighshire

Worked at Wynnstay in September 1771**(1)** and painted a number of important scenes for the Theatre. He appears to have been the chief painter and was employed for '24 days' for that purpose.**(2)** He probably brought two scenes from London**(3)** but the best were executed *in situ*.

1. Wynnstay MSS Box 115/4, p.32.
2. Wynnstay MSS Box 115/21/1, describes the following scenes:
   p.[1] 'Detached Pieces'
   'D Distance behind cut wood 3 pieces'
   i 'Garden Back to Arched Flat'
   P 'Back of a Hiding Cave'
   d 'A Bark used in the Merch[an]t of Venice'
   p.[3] Wings No 1, 2, 3, 4 pairs of Palace Wings
   Two pairs of Wood Wings
   1 pair of Street Wings
   p.[4] rolling Scenes
   2 Salmon
   4 Cascade
   6 Street
   11 Best Chamber
   14 Landskip
   15 Palace.
3. Wynnstay Box 115/3, p.33.

RICHARDS, Richard (fl 1831 - 1856)
Architect**(1)**
Swansea**(2)**

He designed & built the rectory at Bishopston in 1831**(3)**

1. Not in *Girouard*.
2. *SD*/1856/311.
3. *NLW* St Davids, Bounty Plans 9, 1831, he describes himself as a builder & presents a neat, clear plan. St Davids, Bounty Plans 63, 1832 shows his designs for repair of Ilston rectory. Also St Davids, Bounty Plans 153, 1831, *Penmaen*.

RICHARDS, Thomas (fl c1837 - fl 1850)
Interior decorator
Carver & gilder
Swansea
2 High Street

Moved from London in 1845 where he had 'extensive practice in 8 years in Regent Street'. He regilded interiors and cleaned pictures.**(1)** He seems to have moved by 1850.**(2)**

1. *Cambrian*, 11 January 1845, p.2; *Hunt*, 1849, p.157, says address was 127 High Street, Swansea; also he is a carver, gilder and picture-frame maker.
2. Not in *Hunt*, 1850. Mentioned in *Dale-Jones* p.74.

RICHARDS, William (fl 1840 - fl 1854)
'Architect'
Swansea
Orchard Street

Richards was born in Swansea and is recorded at three different addresses between 1840 and 1851.**(1)** In 1854 he designed & built the vicarage at Llandeilo Talybont.**(2)**

1. *Robson's*, 1840, Glamorganshire, p.40.
   Hunt, 1849, p.152, gives his address as Worcester Place, Swansea. *Girouard* p.768 records a W. Fynone Richards at Swansea in 1868, possibly the same architect.
   Hunt, 1850, p.153, gives his address as Grove Place.
   PRO Census Returns, HO/107/1426/455, Swansea, District 8, p.44. Also recorded by *Scammell & Co* H52 p.190 at this address.
2. *NLW* St Davids, Bounty Plans 82, 1854 very detailed plans.

RICHERDS, John (- 1813)
Mason
Swansea
(Brynmelyn)

SD/1813/232.

RIGAUD, Stephen Francis Dutilh (1777 - 1861)
Drawing master
Religious artist
Portrait Painter
Milford Haven

Rigaud trained at the *RA* schools, entering the same day as Pugin.**(1)** He was successful in London**(2)** but moved to West Wales c1818,**(3)** perhaps when his wife wished to return to her native Pembrokeshire,**(4)** and open a school for young ladies.**(5)**

Rigaud worked with his wife as a French, Italian and Drawing master and was advertised as such in the local newspaper. He executed a number of portraits and topographical landscapes in Pembrokeshire.**(6)** By 1834 he had moved to 'Head Lodge near Pembroke'.**(7)**

In 1835 he gave a series of lectures on Perspective to the Pembroke Dock Mechanics Institution**(8)**

1. *Hutchison*, p.153. Pressly, W., 'Memoir of John Francis Rigaud', *Walpole*, L. 1984, p.1ff, provides a good account of S.F.D. Rigaud up to 1810.

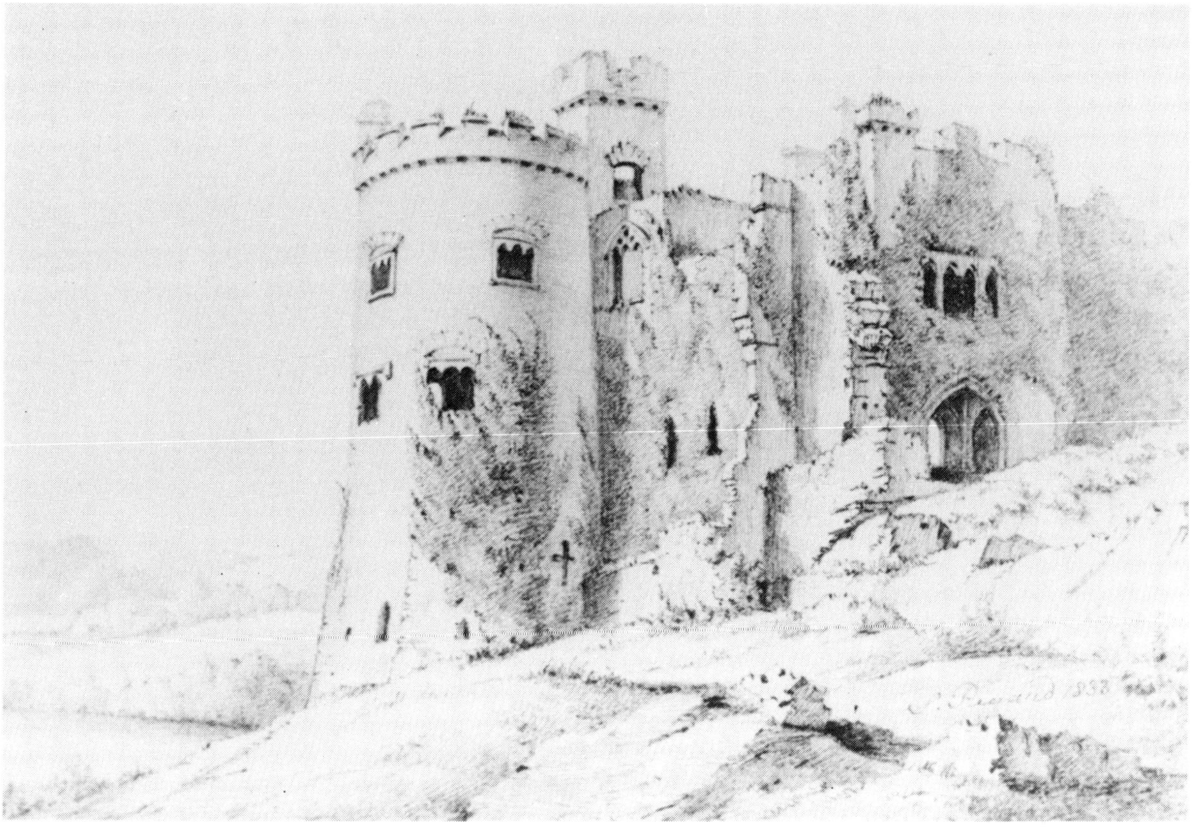

73 Rigaud, Stephen, *Carew Castle*, pencil, 1833, Private Collection.

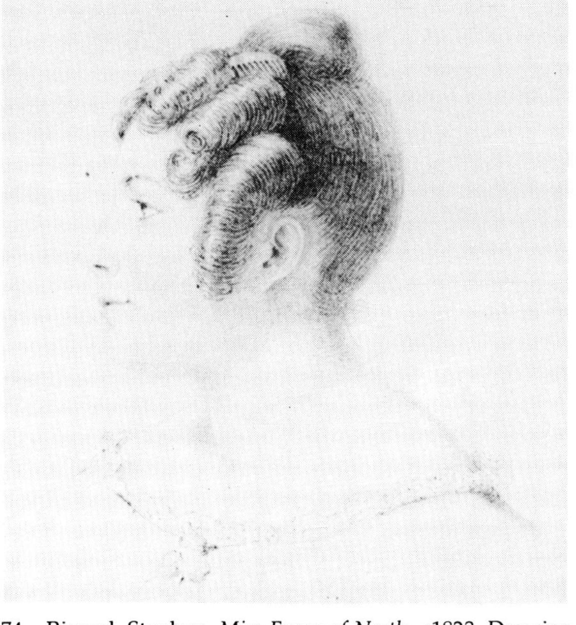

74 Rigaud, Stephen, *Miss Evans of Neath*, c1823, Drawing Volume 115, p.2, PB7026.

2. *Vide* Roget, J., *History of the Old Watercolour Society*, Vol. 1, 1818, p.276.
3. He exhibited *Madonna and Child* (152), 1.0" x 0.11", at the *BI* in 1818 from 'Jordenston near Milford'.
4. *Cambrian*, 15 January 1808, reports the marriage at Dale, Pembrokeshire of 'Stephen Rigaud Esq, son of the Royal Academician, to Miss Davies of Broom-Hill'.
5. *Carmarthen Journal*, 5 January 1821, p.3. *Ibid.*, 12 January 1821, p.2.
6. *NLW*, Drawing Volume 115 contains landscapes by Rigaud dated 1821 and some head and shoulder portraits of Pembrokeshire families.
7. *Ibid.*, inscribed on front endpaper 'S. Rigaud Head Lodge, near Pembroke, S. Wales 1814'.
8. *Carmarthen Journal*, 27 November 1835. *TL* provided much material on this artist.

ROACH, Thomas (- 1757)
Mason
St Ishmaels
Pembrokeshire

SD/1757/142.

ROBERTS, David (fl 1842)
Surveyor
Beaumaris

He designed & built at least one rectory.**(1)**

1. *NLW*, Bangor, Bounty Plans 25, 1842, signed & dated. Not in *Eden*.

ROBERTS, John (fl 1835)
'Engraver'
Aberystwyth
Bridge Street

Pigot's, 1835, p.734.

ROBERTS, John (fl 1820)
Portrait artist**(1)** Llanystumdwy
House painter,**(2)** ship painter

He painted a portrait of *Robert Owen* of Llanystumdwy, shoemaker which is very naive in style.

1. *WFM*, 65-253, oil painting, approx. 30 x 35 cm.
2. *(PL)*, kindly provided this information but no details are available at present.

ROBERTS, John (fl 1835 - fl 1843)
Surveyor Bryntirion
Llangar
Corwen

Roberts had a variety of skills.**(1)**

1. *Davies Atlas.*
Eden, II, p.216, also gives him as an insurance agent.
NLW, Estate maps, gives maps in Flintshire, 1756.

ROBERTS, Jonathan (fl 1850)
Portrait painter Bangor
High Street

Slater's, 1850, p.13.

ROBERTS, M. (fl 1840)
Surveyor Corwen

Eden, II, p.216. Not in *Davies Atlas.*

ROBERTS, Richard (fl 1835 - fl 1850)
Surveyor Caernarfon
Architect Castle Square

Davies Atlas. Eden, II, p.216.
Slater's, 1850, p.20.
Possibly same person designed vicarage at Nantglyn, Denbighshire in 1818. *NLW* St Asaph, Bounty Plans 117, 1818.

ROBERTS, Robert (fl c1818)
Painter Caernarfon

He was the employer of Robert Owen (*supra*) and had a painting and decorating business in Caernarvon.**(1)**

1. *PL*. For further details, *vide* Parry, G., *Cofiant a Chasgliad o Weithiau Barddonol y Parch. Robert Owen* (Manchester, 1880).

ROBERTS, Robert (fl 1828 - fl 1850
Architect Caernarfon
Surveyor Castle Square
Friar's Place
Bangor

A polymathic professional**(1)**

1. *Slater's*, 1844, p.9., p.16.
Slater's, 1849, p.11.
Slater's, 1850, p.11.
Pigot's, 1844, p.16, gives 'Castle Square'.
Not in *Girouard., Eden* II p.216.

ROBERTS, Thomas (fl c1850)
Sign, coach & ornamental painter Llangollen
36 Church Street

Roberts worked as a craftsman and purveyor of artists' materials in Llangollen. It is likely that visiting artists would have patronized his shop in Church Street. His trade card notes 'paints prepared for use, brushes, glue, varnishes'.**(1)**

1. *NLW*, Misc. Prints (A), illustration, engraved by F. Lewis, Salop.

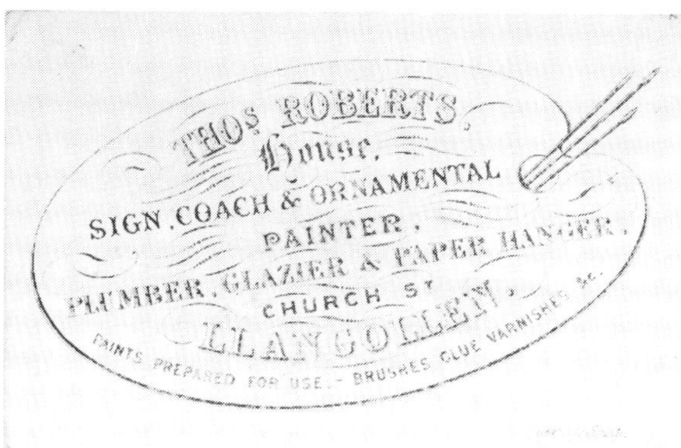

75 Roberts, Thomas, trade bill, 1840s. (Misc Prints, A).

ROBERTS, William (fl 1849)
Landscape painter Rhyl

May have been an amateur artist. Cox corresponded with him in 1849 and asked him to draw the landscape and to examine the condition of the sign board, executed by Cox in 1847.**(1)**

1. Solly, Neal, *Memoirs of the life of David Cox*, 1873, p.169. Letter sent by Cox to Roberts at Rhyl.

ROCHE, Sampson Towgood (1759 - 1847)
Miniature painter Swansea
Burrows

Roche was originally from Dublin but worked in Bath from 1792**(1)** until at least 1819.**(2)** He probably therefore visited Swansea from Bath during the summer holidays. His arrival was noted in the *Cambrian*: 'Swansea - this season's arrivals are... Mr & Mrs Roche.'**(3)**

He took rooms in the Burrows area of Swansea which was frequented by wealthy visitors.**(4)**

1. *Foskett* provides a basic biography. *Cambrian*, 6 August 1808, p.3, gives 'Roch'.
2. *Gye*, p.11, includes 'Roch, miniature painter, 12 Pierrepont Street'.
3. *Cambrian*, 6 August 1808, p.3.
4. *Ibid.*, 6 August 1808, p.3, staying 'at Mr Howell's'.
Ibid., 13 August 1808, p.3.

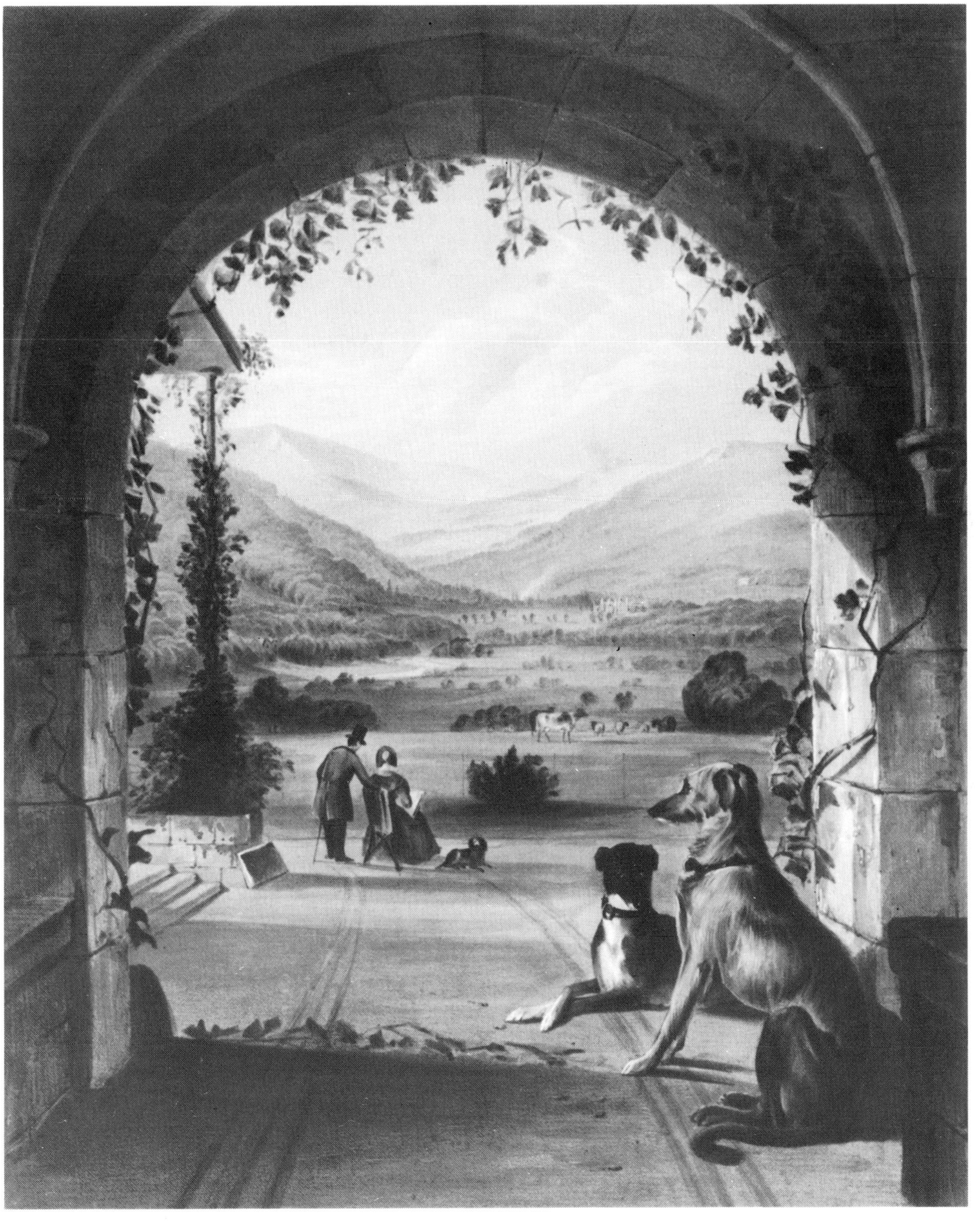

76 Rolfe, Alexander F., *Views at Crickhowell*, coloured lithograph, 1845, PB6379, BV2401.

ROGERS, Edward (fl 1835 - fl 1843)
Surveyor
Bryneithin
Flintshire

Davies Atlas, Not in *Eden*.

ROLFE, Alexander F. (fl 1839 - fl 1873)
Landscape, portrait and Animal painter
Swansea
Crickhowell

Rolfe originally worked in London**(1)**, but moved to Swansea c1840. Shortly after his arrival he painted a large and impressive townscape of Swansea, collaborating with John Padley, who painted the shipping, and offered the picture for raffle.**(2)**

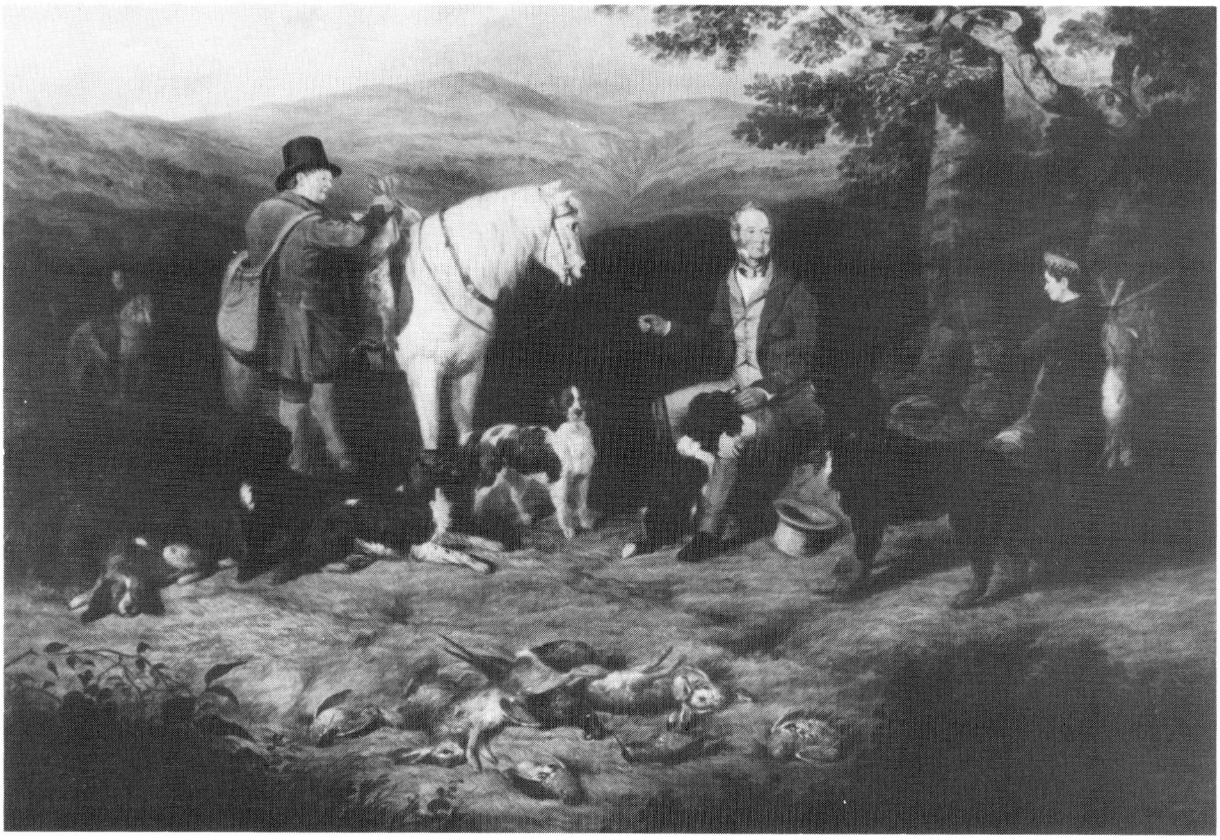

77 Rolfe, Alexander F., *Sir Joseph Bailey*, oil on canvas, c1849, *WPA*, Private Collection.

He often worked with other artists**(3)** and the fact that a suitable artist was available shows the level of competence attained in Swansea.

In 1842 he resumed exhibiting at Suffolk Street**(4)** and sent a version of his Swansea painting, *A view of Swansea*. By 1845 he had moved to Crickhowell where he remained until c1852. One of his extant portraits, *William Davis*, is a full-length, in a wooded landscape, dated 1847.**(5)** Whilst in the area he produced a number of paintings**(6)** and two sets of important lithographs, *Views in the Vale of Crickhowell*, 1844, and *Sketches in Breconshire*, 1845.**(7)** The former contained more accomplished designs.

Rolfe also executed a fine genre portrait print of *Sally Jones* whilst at Crickhowell.**(8)**

Rolfe received encouragement from Sir Joseph Bailey and his last picture in Wales was of Sir Joseph, now at Ilston Court, Chepstow.**(9)**

He retained connections with London whilst in Wales and produced works which suggest a knowledge of good art of the period.**(10)**

1. He exhibited at Suffolk Street, *RSBA*, from a London address from 1839.
2. The history is recorded by *Gamwell*, pp.104-5. It was raffled for £40 to Mr Tripp, a solicitor, then bought by F.E. Williams and presented to Swansea Council where it now hangs in the Mayor's Parlour. Given by *Gamwell* as 'approximately 3 ft 6 inches by 25 ft 6 inches'.
3. *Vide*, for instance, Christie's, 25 July 1974, lot 128, landscape dated 1873 by John F. Tennant & Rolfe, 59.7 x 64.8 cm, oils. Derrick Webley recorded that Rolfe copied two pictures by Penry Williams in 1846, 1852 both recorded at Penpont House, Breconshire.
4. 1842 (72); he also exhibited (618) *Sorento, Bay of Naples*; 1843 (147) *Dead Hare and Wild Duck*; (281) *A Group of River Fish*; (695) *View from Newtown Hill, Looking over Swansea Bay* (a watercolour).
5. Christie's, London, 11 April 1980, lot 51, oil on canvas, 101.6 x 126.4 cm, recorded as the property of late Mrs Reginald Fellowes. The painting is signed and dated 1847.
6. *RSBA* (Suffolk Street) exhibited from Crickhowell, 1845 (815) *View in the Neighbourhood of Crickhowel*, watercolour; 1846 (177) *Tre-Tawr, Breconshire*; from Herbert Hail, *Crickhowell*; 1847 (218) *An Old Mill on the River Usk, Brec*; 1848 (159) *View of Glanusk* [*sic*] *Park & House near Crickhowel the seat of J. Bailey Esq M.P.*; 1852 (346) *Scene near Llanberis-Snowdon in Distance*.
7. *Sketches in Breconshire*, published in Abergavenny, contained five lithographs with good landscapes. *Views in Vale of Crickhowel* (portfolio), 1844, had four lithographs in a similar style.
   One example of this is *NLW*, P1948, B2/1 - B25, *Porth-Mawr Gateway Crickhowel*, 1844.
8. *NLW*, PE 5409, *Sally Jones Blwch Hill, near Crickhowel Aged 105, April 10th 1846*; signed and dated A.F. Rolfe 1846, 34.6 x 25.1 cm.
9. *Steegman*, Volume II, p.135. He was patronised by Bailey in 1847 and produced a full length portrait of him with his hounds, oil on canvas 100x126cm (*WPA*: AB02336). In 1849 *Sir Joseph Bailey & Rev. Rees Jones*, oil on canvas, 128.1x179.8cm (*WPA*: AB02340). He also painted two exquisite views of Glan Usk

Park, oil on canvas, 69x110cm, with gypsy encampment, [1846] & another 59.5x90cm, indistinctly dated [1871]. His latest landscape was sold at Christies 3 June 1994 Lot 211. Oil painting of *Glynpedr*, signed & dated 1863 PG5237 29.5x44.8cm.
10. The *BM* has a mezzotint by Rolfe (1870-8-13-123), 5 x 7 cm, of a landscape, possibly White Castle. One innovative process which Rolfe used is identified as the 'Anastatic' print. There are two examples extant, dated 1849, *St Brides Super Ely Church* (south front and the re-opened church), c7 x 11 cm, PE 955 (Top. B8/9-B200).

ROMNEY, G.(1) (fl 1819)

Portrait and miniature painter — Carmarthen, Aberystwyth

Romney claimed to work in London and visited Carmarthen in the spring of 1819,**(2)**. He was in Aberystwyth in August of that year.**(3)**

1. This may have been John Romney (1786-1865).
2. *Carmarthen Journal*, March 26, 1819, p.[3]. *Ibid.*, April 16, 1819, p.[3]. He announced that crayon portraits cost two guineas, miniatures on ivory one guinea and 'shade profiles' two shillings.
3. *NLW*, MS 2844E, sales book of Samuel Williams, Aberystwyth, 30 August 1819, 'Mr Romney. Artist 150 Pointed cards 7s'. I am grateful to my colleague Eiluned Rees for bringing this material to my attention. The MSS is discussed in *Ceredigion*, Volume X, No 3, 1986, pp.255-267.

ROOS, William 'Gwilym Rosa'(1) (1808 - 78)

Portrait, animal, historical and miniature painter
Mezzotinter — Newtown, Caernarfon, Amlwch, Towyn

Roos was born at Bodgadfa,**(2)** near Amlwch and appears to have lived there for an extended period. He also lived at Towyn where his children were educated.**(3)** He painted a large number of portraits, including ministers, self portraits and some family groups. He moved to Caernarfon c1834 and advertised his services painting miniatures for one guinea, 'half size portraits in oils' at two guineas and 'Three Quarter lengths' at four guineas.**(4)**

By 1847 he was probably back in Anglesey and there painted a fine and important family group. This group of four portraits, two small images of sons, and larger canvases of the parents, exemplifies the best of Roos's work.**(5)**

His early work suggests that Roos was self-taught**(6)** and the mature style shows a possible interest in Rembrandt.**(7)**

He was a successful and popular artist in Wales,**(8)** winning prizes at Eisteddfodau**(9)**, his portrait of *John Elias* became the official image of that preacher and was hung in countless chapels.**(10)**

Roos wrote a *précis* of art history, in which he shows some understanding of the development of painting. He also mentions a love of Murillo, an artist who was seldom represented in Welsh collections.**(11)** Towards the end of his life he wrote:

> 'I have taken to Animal and Landscape painting for the last few years, this is the thing in art Photography can't do - I have painted a few hunters and hounds for the sporting gentry of this Country [or County] and have given great satisfaction.'**(12)**

This statement by Roos chronicles a change of taste in Wales in the 1860s-70s, towards the cheaper and more reliable photograph.

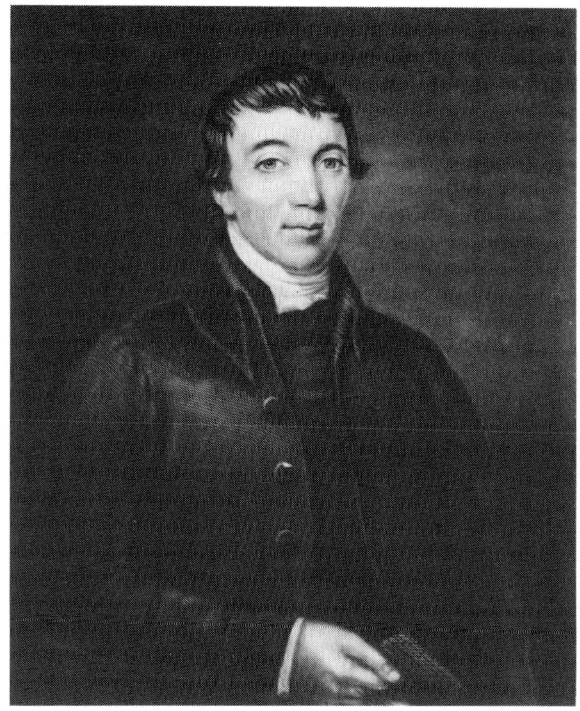

78 Roos, William, *John Elias*, mezzotint, c1840, P7701.

1. His name is sometimes given as Roose, and his pseudonym which appears often on his canvases is sometimes given as 'Gwilim', for instance *NLW, PA* 8159.
2. Jones, Bedwyr Lewis, *Gwŷr Môn*, pp.108-110.
3. *PL* notes that Roos's children attended Ysgol Edwin Jones, Towyn.
4. *Caernarvon and Denbighshire Herald*, 23 August 1834, p.2, mentions that he continues work at Caernarvon and exhibits pictures at the Herald Office. *Vide* note 9.
5. *NLW*, PE 5380-3, oil on canvas, *William Thomas* and *John Thomas*, 20.8 x 18 cm; *Hugh Thomas* and *Thomas* and *Margaret Thomas*, 75 x 62.2 cm. All signed on verso 'Wm Roos Pinxit 1847'. The family lived at Hendregadog, Anglesey.
6. *Vide NLW, Rev. John Williams, PA* 8159, signed and dated 'Gwilym Fecit 1827', oil on canvas, 76.2 x 59.7 cm.
7. Especially clear in his *William Morris, Cilgerran* (identified by *Lord, 1993*, p.44), *NLW*, PE 1684, 32 x 27.5 cm, [1850s] oil on slate. This portrait was traditionally always known as a self portrait by Roos. *Joyner, 1990*, Plate 6. *Vide* **illustration, 79.**
8. Many famous Welshmen sat for him, including Christmas Evans, Thomas Charles, John Jones

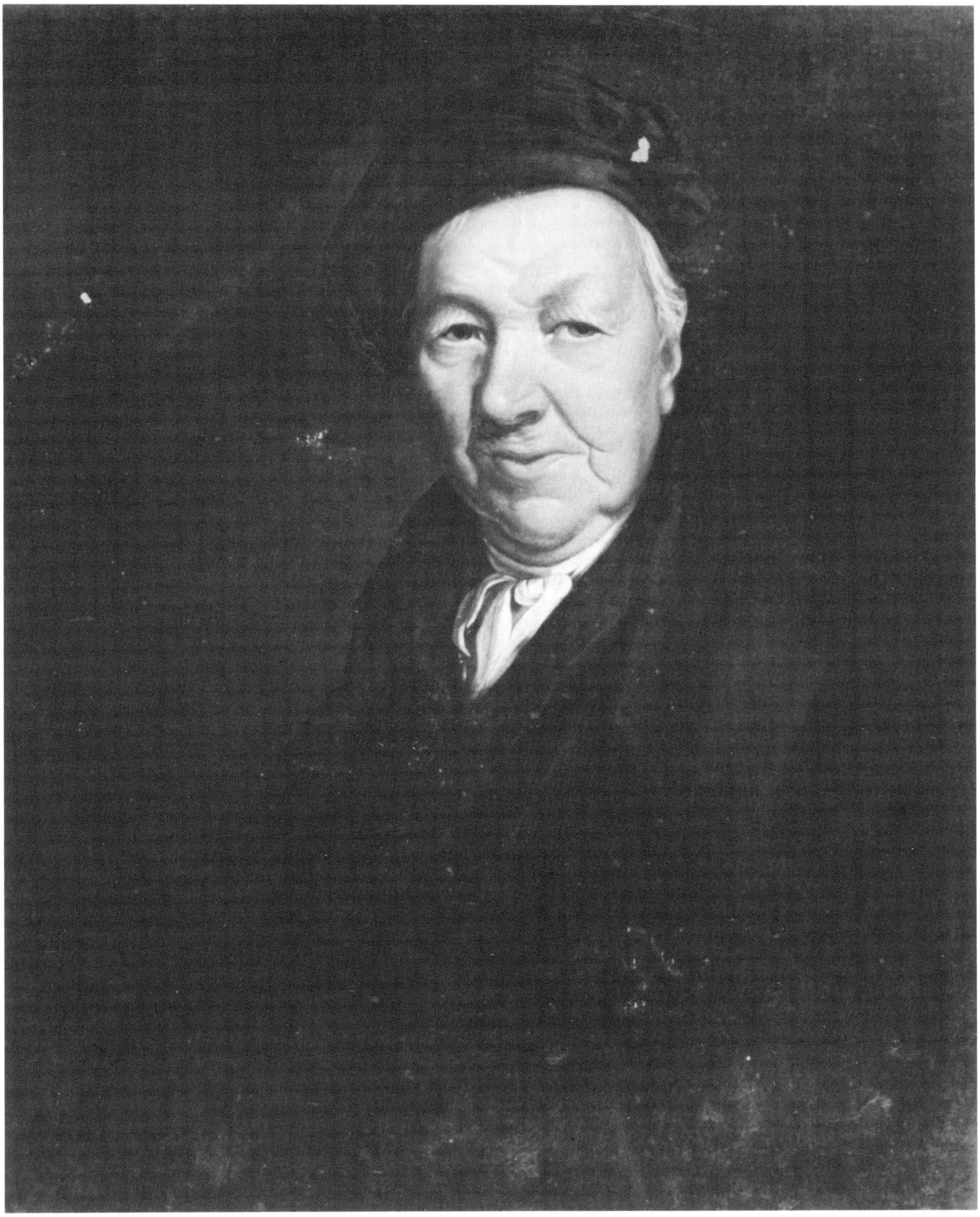

79 Roos, William, [*William Morris Cilgerran*], oil on slate, 1849, PE1684.

'Talhaiarn', Robert Williams 'Robert ap Gwilym Ddu'.

9. Carmarthen Eisteddfod 1867, *Marwolaeth Llywelyn* [Death of Llywelyn], 1st prize; Llangollen Eisteddfod 1858, 2nd prize for *Death of Owen Glyndwr (Hanes Cyflawn Eisteddfod Llangollen*, 1858, p.11). These are the only examples of his historical compositions and they may reflect his ambition to transcend face painting.

10. *John Elias*, mezzotint 'engraved by W. Ross [*sic*] from an original painting', 23.2 x 19 cm. *Vide* **illustration 78.**
He mentions another painting, *NLW* MS 7165D (Nefydd MSS 155), letter dated 13 September 1870 to Rev. William Roberts (f.l.): 'I beg to inform you that I have an Oil Portrait of the late Christmas Evans a first rate likeness. I painted and engraved his portrait at Caernarvon in 1835... I lived next door to

him.' *Revd Christmas Evans* 'painted and engraved by W. Ross', mezzotint, 16.5 x 12.5 cm (image size). He also engraved an ambitious print of *John Jones Talhaiarn* which is a fine example of his mature style (*NLW*, PA 3264, 47.5 x 37.5 cm).

11. *UCNW Bangor*, MS 5709, dated 26 January 1845, Newtown, letter to Hugh Hughes (Derfel). He may have been familiar with Pliny's account of Apelles as his comments are close to those found in *Natural History*, Book XXXIV. *Vide Joyner (1989)*, chapter one.
12. *NLW*, Add. MS 584B (Celynog MS 58), letter to Nicholas Bennett, Caersws, from Cardigan dated 16 May 1873. He also mentions, 'I shall return northward, they [Southerners] are void of taste for art and too fond of their only God, the golden calf.' Iona Antiquities, P.O. Box 205, London, in Catalogue 1993, item 2554, notes a painting of a dog, signed and dated 'Gwilym Rosa 1859', oil on canvas, 35 x 46 cm. The dog was the property of '[O.F. Meyrick] of Bodorgan, Wales'. Illustrated in the catalogue. Christie's, South Kensington, 22 February. 1984, lot 185, sold a signed and dated *Hunting Companion*, 1857. Miles K. Wynn Cato, stock list No.3 Winter 1994 item 5, oil on panel by Roos, signed & dated 1841, 'from birds killed by M. Webster Esq'. c53x41cm.

ROSSITER, John (1820)

Mason — Carew

SD/1820/18.

ROTHWELL, Thomas (1740 - 1807)

Engraver, topographical artist, enamel painter — Swansea

He worked first in Staffordshire potteries, then moved to Birmingham, and by 1790 he was resident in Swansea. *Nance* described him as the 'principal artist employed at the [Cambrian] Pottery up to the date of the arrival of Thomas Pardoe'.**(1)**

Rothwell was considered a highly skilled and creative engraver for china.**(2)** He also published the first known set of engravings at Swansea. These he engraved, printed and published between 1791-2 and printed on paper and plaster of Paris**(3)** are probably the best work published in Wales at that period. Rothwell clearly borrowed from the English masters,**(4)** and displayed a fine sense of design within a limited genre. The prints are clear, crisp and delightfully well observed. A certain flatness of image is compensated by the detailed treatment of landscape and architecture.**(5)**

He moved to London c1794 where he engraved reproductive prints**(6)** and later returned to Birmingham where he died.

1. *Nance*, Appendix VI, 'Thomas Rothwell', p.477.
2. The following are the chief sources of information on Rothwell:

a) Turner, W., *The Ceramics of Swansea and Nantgarw*, pp.199-202.

b) *Nance, op. cit.* Appendix VI.

c) Stretton, N., 'Thomas Rothwell, Engraver and Copper-Plate Printer 1740-1807', *Transactions of the English Ceramic Circle*, 1966, pp.249-53.

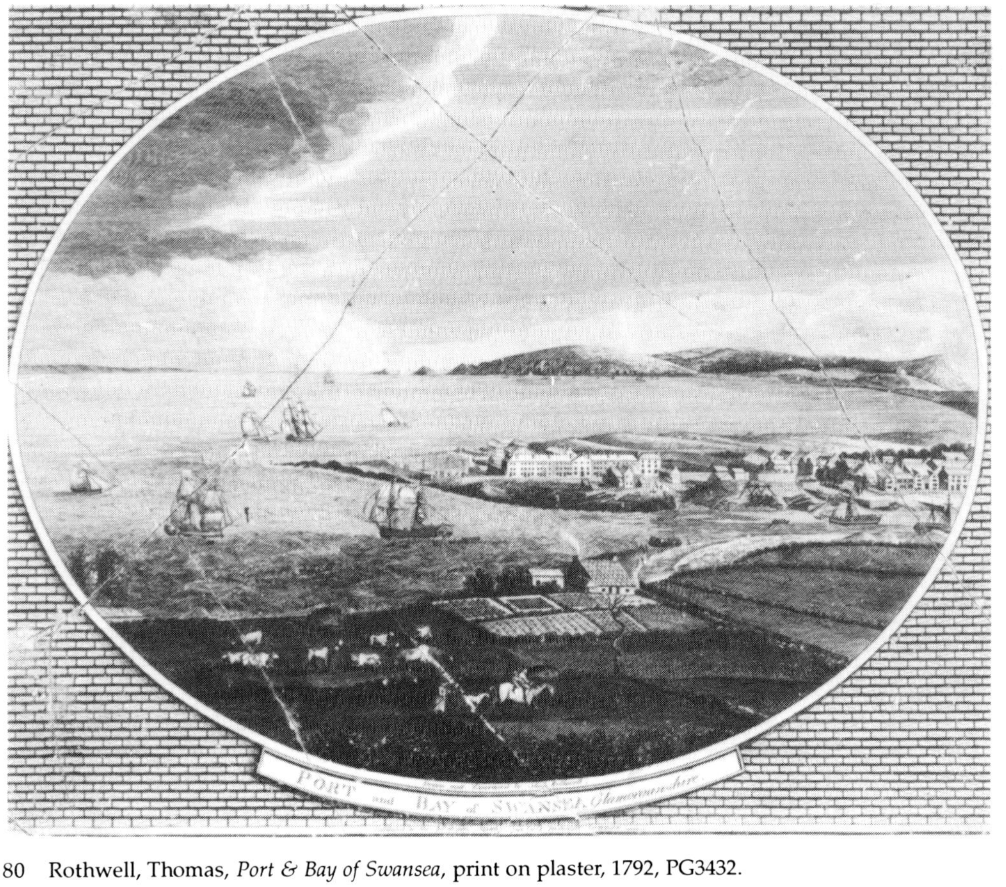

80 Rothwell, Thomas, *Port & Bay of Swansea*, print on plaster, 1792, PG3432.

d) Stretton, N., 'Thomas Rothwell Engraver', *The Antique Collector*, October 1971, pp.201-204.
e) Jenkins, E., 'Early Artists' in *Gower* XVI, pp.66-68, discusses Rothwell. Boorman, David, *The Brighton of Wales* (1986), illustrates three prints by Rothwell.

3. Known prints are as follows:
   1791, [19] January, *Briton Ferry*.
   1791, 29 [January?], *Copper Works at Forest*.
   1791, 12 September, *The Bathing House* [Swansea].
   1792, 25 March, *Port and Bay of Swansea*.
   1792, 26 March, *Sketty Hall*.
   1792, 25 July, *Clasmont*, *NLW*, P623, B8/3 - B63. [Paper version]
   1792, *North East View of Swansea*.
   ?1792, *Penrice Castle*.
   ?1792, *Heathfield House*.

   Sizes vary, but they are generally 14.5 x 17.7 cm. All have an oval surround with brick facing background. Examples on paper and plaster of Paris in collection *RISW*. *NLW* purchased two examples on plaster of Paris at the Sir Leslie Joseph sale (Sothebys) 14 May 1992 lot 1043. PG 3432 *Port & Bay of Swansea*, PG 3433 *Clasmont*. Both were exhibited at the Swansea Pottery Bi-centenary Exhibition 1768-1968, Nos 561, 562.
4. This is especially evident with *Heathfield House, Glamorganshire* where the figures are reminiscent of George Stubbs's *Reapers*, exhibited at *RA* 1786, then at the Liverpool Exhibition for Promoting Painting and Design 1787. Stubbs published prints of *Reapers* and *Haymakers* in 1791 which may have influenced Rothwell's use of this rural device. (See Judy Egerton, *Stubbs*, Tate Gallery Exhibition (1984), items 187, 188).
5. The delineation of architecture and landscape suggests an acquaintance with early 18th century landscape prints, both Dutch and English. It is possible that some of his figure groups were derived from pattern books or earlier works. Rothwell certainly used the work of *The Ladies Amusement*, c1760, by Robert Sayer, a London printer (Plate 50).
6. Rothwell engraved 24 portraits for the *Biographical Magazine*, dated from 1 August 1794. In 1795 he engraved from views after J.M.W. Turner, (*Wilton*, Andrew, *The Life & work of J. M. W. Turner* (London, 1979) 107, 110, 113, 114). He was employed as a jobbing engraver for various genteel publications.

ROWLAND, John (- 1776)
Mason
Llanrheithan
Pembrokeshire

SD/1776/129 (I).

ROWLAND, John (1819 - 90)
'Cambrian Lluniedydd'(1)
Aberystwyth
North Wales
Portrait and genre painter
Lithographer
Landscape artist

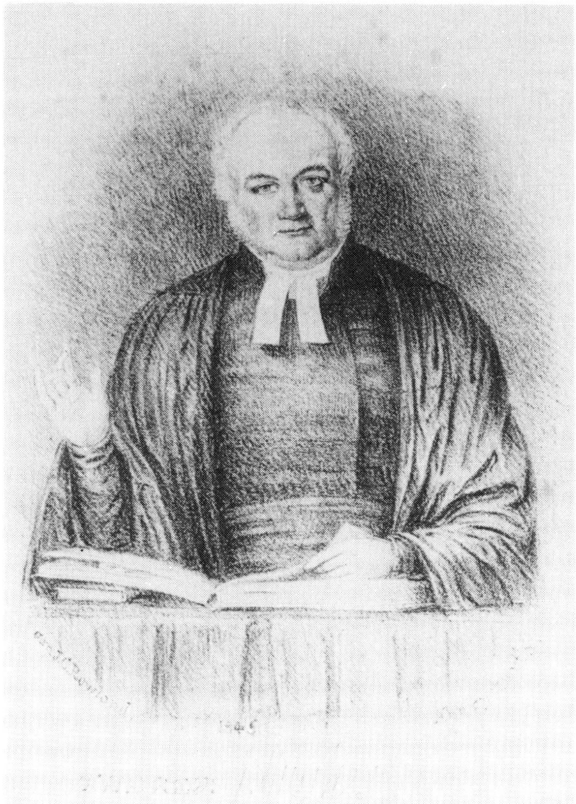

81 Rowland, John Cambrian, *Rev. John Hughes*, lithograph, 1845, P8492.

Born at Lledrod, Cardiganshire, 7 December 1819, he is reported to have studied in London.**(2)**

His earliest known work is a simple outline drawing dated 1839.**(3)** He published a portrait in 1845 which is considerably more accomplished and probably akin to engraved portraits of the period.**(4)**
A number of costume prints were published by Rowland in 1848. These were extremely popular and have become standard images of 19th century Welsh life. Whilst the compositions are competent, the anatomy is usually inaccurate.**(5)** *The Welsh Wedding* is a good example of his detailed subject pictures.

Later portraits generally have the same failings, good natural colour with little skill in the drawing and anatomy.**(6)** One biographer stated that 'he settled in North Wales, travelling, painting and drawing portrait commissions, also doing animal paintings and landscapes, and was also appointed Art Instructor of Caernarvon Church Training College'.**(7)**

He was one of the earliest artists to collaborate with a photographer.**(8)**

He also produced a series of landscape drawings of the area around Pont-rhyd-y-groes.**(9)**

1. Census Return 1841 (Transcript in Cardiganshire R.O. by E.A. Benjamin, p.71) states that a John Rowlands, 'Age 20, born in Cardiganshire, Artist' lived at Trefechan with his father Thomas Rowlands and Margaret Rowlands, possibly his sister. This is probably the same artist.
2. Note by Mrs Alan Gough, Nanhoron, Pwllheli, dated 20 April 1939, in files of the Dept of Pictures and Maps,

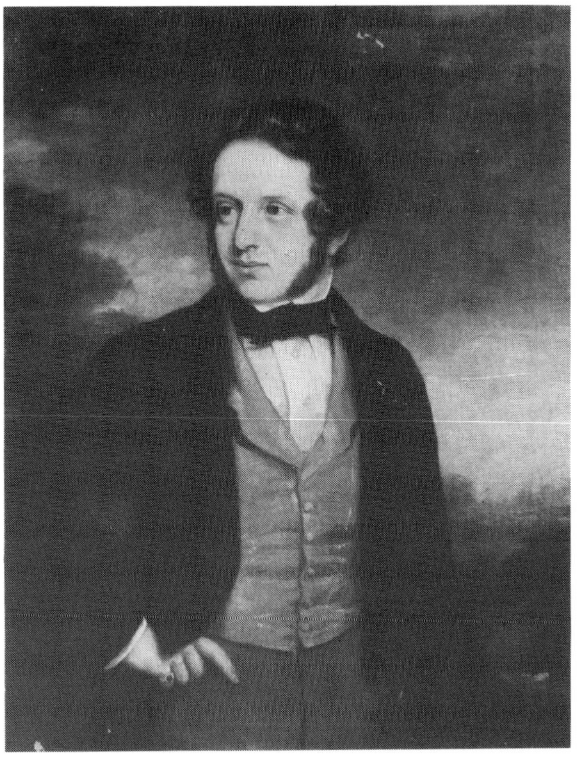

82 Rowland, John Cambrian, *John Salusbury Thelwall*, oil on canvas, 1849, *WPA* (Private Collection).

NLW. She claims that Rowland was at the *RA* schools and South Kensington but no supportive evidence can be found. His lack of anatomical draughtsmanship suggests the reverse because his work is reminiscent of many untrained artists.

3. Illustrated *Cymru*, Vol. 15 (1898), p.113, pencil drawing of *John Williams* (Sion 'Sgubor'), approximately 10 x 7 cm.
4. *NLW*, P8492, lithograph, *Rev. J. Hughes*, 'Gan J.C. Rowland', 1845, Aberystwyth, 21.3 x 16.3 cm. The face, neck and background probably derive from contemporary engravings. *NLW*, PB 7030 (Ports A), watercolour, *Sylvan Evans*, dated 1843, 18.7 x 15.3, is a good example of this style.
5. Published in Chester, 1848, lithographed by J. McCahey, all approximately 25.5 x 31cm. Prints known are *Welsh Costumes, Welsh Wedding, Running Away with the Bridge, Jenny Jones, Edward Morgan*.
6. Additional portraits are known from *Steegman*, Vol. 2, p.186, *J.B. Lloyd Philipps*, 1840; Hickman, G., letter in *Country Life*, 2 October 1958, p.706, describing four portraits of the Parry family signed and dated 1851; *NLW*, PB 1906, *George William Bulkely Hughes*, 75 x 63 cm. Also *WPA*, AB00580, *John Salisbury, Thelwall*, dated 1849.
7. Mrs A. Gough, *vide* note 2. His 1848 prints and portraits suggest a North Wales residence.
8. *NLW*, PA 1831 [*Welsh Black*], 'Presented to the Honourable T.J. Wynn of Glynllifin [*sic*] Park in his coming of Age the 31st December 1861 by his wellwisher Wm Griffith Tyranwr Clynnog'. Drawn in stone by J.C. Rowland from a photograph by H.J. Hughes and lithographed by H. Humphreys, Caernarvon, lithograph 28.2 x 39.8 cm.
9. *NMW* has this series of landscapes dated 1844.

ROWLAND, William (- 1823)
Mason — Haverfordwest

SD/1823/61.
Possibly father of Thomas Rowlands.
TL notes a William Rowlands (- 1850).

ROWLANDS, James (fl 1850)
Architect**(1)** — Haverfordwest**(2)**, St Martin's

1. Not in *Girouard*.
2. *Hunt*, 1850, p.42.

ROWLANDS, Thomas (1802/3 - 1883)
Architect**(1)** — Haverfordwest, Glenover

His father, William Rowland[s] (- 1850) was a mason & builder of Haverfordwest. Rowlands may have been trained in London & began his career well, alongside his father. He remodelled Picton Castle 1826-8 & this building remains his best project.**(2)** He was active until 1848.**(3)**

1. *Pigot's*, 1830, p.836, 'Mariners Square'; *ibid.*, 1844, p.34, Coat Street.
   Hunt, 1850, p.42.
   Not in *Girouard*. *Colvin* p.837.
2. *TL* MSS notes His extant plans are neatly drawn, *vide NLW* St Davids, Bounty Plans 70, signed by Rowlands.
3. *TL* MSS notes on Rowlands. *Colvin* p.837 quotes *TL* who catalogues Rowlands work to include: *St Michael's church*, Pembroke 1829-33; *Market Hall*, Narberth 1832-6 & houses; *Castle House*, Picton Terrace, Carmarthen, 1836; *Letterston church*, 1844.

S

SALMON, William Reynold Deer (1815 - 1858)
Landscape artist — Penlline Court, Glamorganshire

He was an amateur artist. One painting, *Penlline Court Cows*, was described as follows: 'The whole picture has the handling of a masterhand.'**(1)**

He may have also been a collector of art. *Cadrawd* mentions that Salmon was 'passionately fond of art'.**(2)**

1. *Cadrawd*, pp.105-106. *Cadrawd* tends to eulogise Glamorganshire artists and no doubt this is the reason for such a glowing criticism. *Cadrawd* mentions several pictures by Salmon.
2. *Ibid*.

SALTER, A.W. (fl 1830)
Portrait artist — Merthyr Tydfil

He painted a full-length of *William Williams Scethrog*.**(1)** *TL* gives a reference to *Carmarthen Journal*, 16 May 1834, portrait, presented to the Breconshire Architectural Society by Salter.

1. (*PL*).

SAMUEL, Robert (fl 1835 - fl 1844)
House and coach painter — Caernarfon, Market Street

Worked with William Parry (*supra*) from about 1835-1842 and then is recorded as a single craftsman.**(1)**

1. *Slater's*, 1844, p.18: 'Horse and coach painter', Market Street.

SANDBY, Paul R.A. (1731 - 1809)
Scenery painter — Wynnstay
Drawing master — Denbighshire

Sandby was employed by Sir Watkin Williams-Wynn to paint at Wynnstay in the summer of 1771 and 1772.**(1)** He may also have taught Sir Watkin drawing on the estate.**(2)** At the Wynnstay Theatre he painted *Llangollen Bridge, A Garden* and *A Castle*.**(3)** John Inigo Richards and Michael Angelo Rooker also painted scenes but evidence suggests that only Richards and Sandby worked *in situ*.**(4)** Sir Watkin also employed Sandby to travel to part of North Wales and presumably some of the Sandby pictures in the Wynnstay Collection came from that time.**(5)**

1. Hughes, P., 'Paul Sandby and Sir Watkin Williams Wynn', *Burlington Magazine* CXIV, 1972, pp.459-466, discusses his patronage and transcribes the relevant Wynnstay MSS and other sources.
2. Wynnstay Box 115/21/30, bill dated 21 June 1771 for 38 lessons and other services.
3. Wynnstay Box 115/28/3, contents of the Theatre, p.[4].
4. *Vide supra* Richards, J.I.; Rooker painted *A Square* Wynnstay MSS Box 115/28/p.[4]. He also engraved the Play Tickets for the Wynnstay Theatre (Box 115/5/p.5) in 1774.
5. These are included in the bill (Box 115/21/43) dated 22 July 1772, *Vale [sic] Crucis Abbey, Bala Lake*.

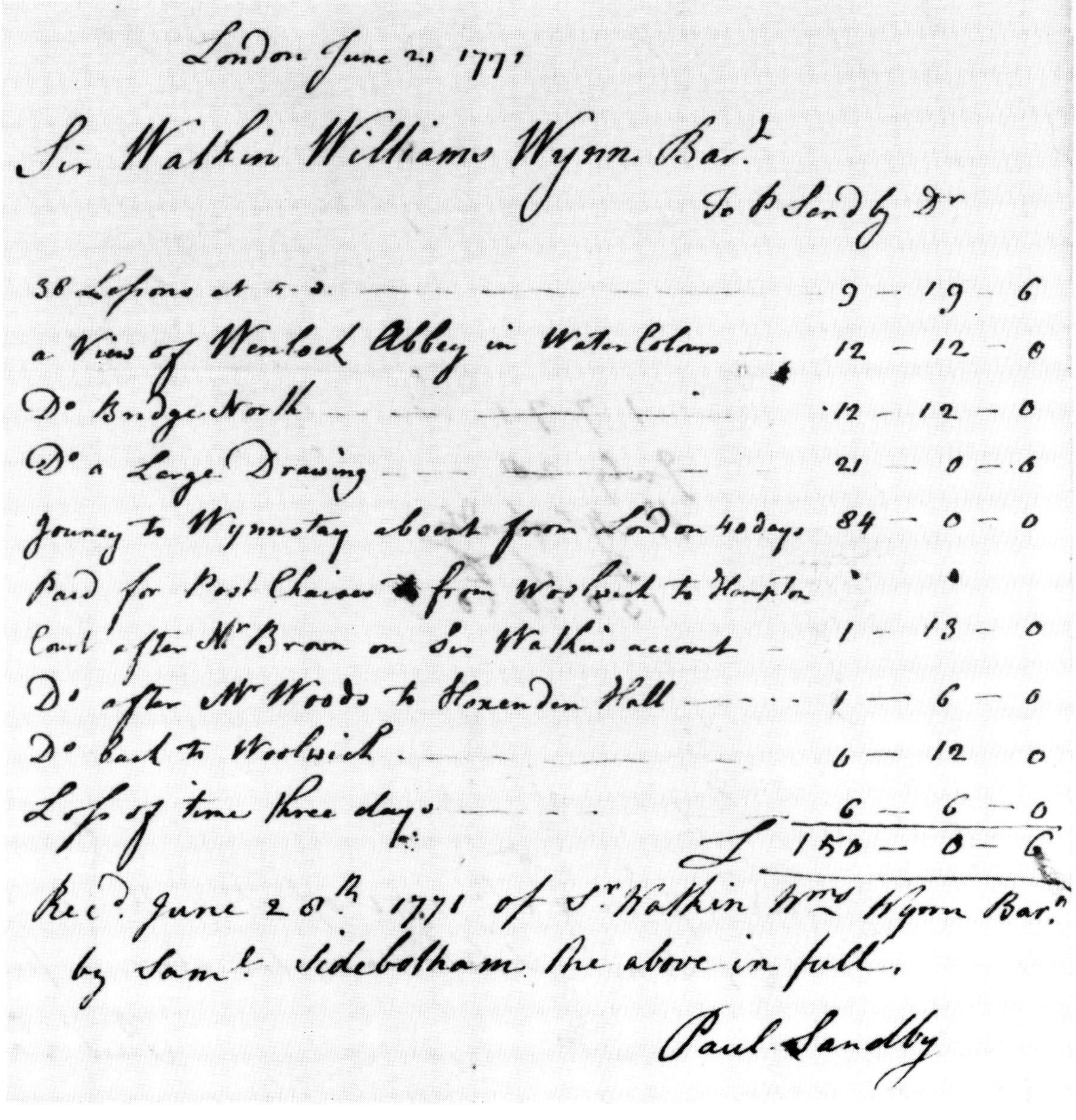
London June 21 1771

Sir Watkin Williams Wynn Bart

To P Sandby Dr

38 Lessons at 5-3.	9 - 19 - 6
a View of Wenlock Abbey in Water Colours	12 - 12 - 0
Do Bridge North	12 - 12 - 0
Do a Large Drawing	21 - 0 - 0
Journey to Wynnstay absent from London 40 days	84 - 0 - 0
Paid for Post Chaises from Woolwich to Hampton Court after Mr Brown on Sir Watkin's account	1 - 13 - 0
Do after Mr Woods to Hoxenden Hall	1 - 6 - 0
Do back to Woolwich	0 - 12 - 0
Loss of time three days	6 - 6 - 0
	£ 150 - 0 - 6

Recd June 28th 1771 of Sr Watkin Wms Wynn Bart by Saml Sidebotham the above in full.

Paul Sandby

83 Sandby, Paul, *Bill to Sir Watkin Williams-Wynn*, Wynnstay MSS, 115/21/30, dated 21 June 1771.

SANDERS, Charles (late 18th century)
Drawing master Llandovery
Scenery painter Carmarthen
Cardigan

Sanders, described as an artist from Bath **(1)** advertised that

> 'he will give lessons in drawing...offers instructions to gentlemen on the German Flute. Views, landscapes etc. taken or copied by Mr Santer [*sic*] at very reasonable terms.'**(2)**

1. *Gye*, 1819, p.11, 'Sanders, landscape painter and drawing master, 3 Westgate buildings'.
2. Quoted by Price, C., *English Theatre in Wales*, p.119.

SANT, George (fl 1856 - fl 1867)
Landscape painter Swansea
Myny-do-Gloys [*sic*] [Mynydd y Glais]

Exhibited from Swansea in 1859.**(1)**

1. *Graves, B.I.*, seems to have exhibited from a London address for the majority of his life but from Swansea for one year: 1859 (110) *Study in Clyne Wood, South Wales*, 20 gs.

SAUNDERS, Robert Cook (fl 1849)
Architect Neath
South Terrace
London Road

Hunt, 1849, p.83.

SAUNDERS, Thomas (fl 1835 - fl 1843)
Surveyor Undergrove
Lampeter

Davies Atlas, Eden III p.224.

SAXBY, Richard (fl 1858)
Photographer Tredegar
Church Street

Slater's, 1858.

SAXBY, Robert Scraze (fl 1850)
Portraits and miniature painter**(1)** Swansea
1 York Street

1. *Hunt*, 1850, p.132.
   Hunt, 1847, '500 portraits in week'.

SAYCE, Morris (fl 1808 - fl 1847)
Surveyor Welshpool
7a Church Street**(1)**

Worked in Monmouthshire, Montgomeryshire, Breconshire, Radnorshire, Cardiganshire & Carmarthenshire. He was in partnership with William Sayce (fl 1835-46) & who appears to have been based in Kington, & Hereford.**(2)**

1. Now home of the Powys Archaeological Trust.
2. I would like to thank my colleague Frazer Henderson for bringing this surveyor to notice. *Eden* III p.224. *NLW* has signed & dated plan *Bank Farm*, Churchstoke (M177 Powis Castle) which has a landscape cartouche.

SAYCE, Thomas (The Elder) (1) (- 1847)
Mason Ewyas Harold
Breconshire**(2)**

1. *BR*/1847/29. *BR*/1847/28 also notes Thomas Sayce, Mason, at the same address. This is an additional will of the same mason.
2. The address of this mason is problematic, it probably was a transcription error & he possibly lived in Breconshire.

SEABORN, John (- 1813)
Mason St Margaret's Island
Pembrokeshire

BR/1813/66.

SEDDON, John Pollard (1827 - 1906)
Architect Llandaff

Worked with John Prichard**(1)** from 1853-1869.**(1)** He later became Llandaff Diocesan architect.**(2)**

1. *NLW* Llandaff, Bounty Plans 54, 1855, *Girouard* pp.818-819. Llangattock Vibon Avel, Bounty Plans 66, 1857 Llanmartin, Monmouthshire. Darby, Michael, *John Pollard Seddon* (London, 1983) gives a good account of his practice. Seddon in 1864 designed a hotel now the Old College of University College, Aberystwyth.
2. *Girouard* p.818, notes 1886.

SEVILLE, [W.](1) (fl c1818 - fl 1845)
Miniature and silhouette artist Caernarfon
Teacher of landscape, flower painting,
Etching and wax flower designs

Seville was based at Manchester and visited Caernarfon in the latter part of 1838. *McKechnie* records that he charged one shilling for a 'Black shade' and 3 shillings and 6 pence for 'a Dog' in 1824. By 1838 his prices were similar or less.

> 'At Miss Williams's. Old Post Office, Caernarvon. Miniatures on ivory and coloured likenesses from 5s to 1.10.0. Full length likenesses, standing or walking. Family groups, Sporting Subjects, Dogs, Horses, [etc] taken from life...produced with common scissors, without drawing or machine of any description, a CORRECT LIKENESS...expression and peculiarity of character are pourtrayed [*sic*], in a style that has not been accomplished by any other artist.**(2)**

1. Possibly 'The Elder', *McKechnie*, pp.269-271, describes him solely as an artist not a teacher.
2. *Caernarvon and Denbighshire Herald*, 27 October 1838, p.2.
   Ibid., 3 November 1838, p.2.
   Ibid., 10 November 1838, p.1.
   Ibid., 17 November 1838, p.1.

Ibid., 24 November 1838, p.1.
Ibid., 8 December 1838, p.1.

SHARP, Mr [C.] (fl 1847 - fl 1850)
Silhouette artist — Caernarfon
Photographer — Rhyl

Sharp claimed to be based in London.**(1)** He travelled extensively in the 1840s, visiting Rhyl in 1847, 1848 and 1849.**(2)**

At Caernarfon he exhibited at Mr Sneades, Confectioner and produced photographs.

> 'with all the Natural Colours of Life; warranted permanent and second to no other taken in this or any other country...Portraits taken for lockets, Brooches, and Rings, Miniatures, Family Paintings and Engravings, accurately copied and Studies executed for artists.'**(3)**

He probably hand coloured photographs in oil to provide a permanence because the fixing of hue in photographs was not invented until the late 19th century.**(4)**

1. It is likely that this was correct, *vide* Pritchard, Michael, *A Directory of London Photographers 1841-1908* (Bushey, 1986), p.84. gives a C. Sharp living at 5 Duke Street & Tooley Street 1848.
2. *Caernarvon and Denbighshire Herald*, 22 December 1849, p.1, Sharp records that he had received testimonials from Rhyl residents and from a visit to Cambridge in April 1849.
3. *Caernarvon and Denbighshire Herald*, 22 December 1849, p.1; 29 December 1849, p.1; 12 January 1850, p.1; 16 March 1850, p.8; 23 March 1850, p.1.
4. Gernsheim, H. & A., *History of Photography* (1955), p.521ff, discusses this issue of permanence.

SHAW, Claudius (fl 1820 - fl 1843)
Surveyor — Bangor

He was a former officer in the Royal Artillery & surprisingly worked in Wales & Edinburgh.

Davies Atlas, Eden III p.227.

SHAW, William R.B. (fl 1849)
Landscape and portrait painter — Tredegar
Bridge Street

Hunt, 1849, p.158.

SHEY, Mr 'The Profilist' (fl 1824)
Silhouette artist — Cardigan

Working at Cardigan in 1824 and although he claimed to be well travelled he is unrecorded elsewhere.**(1)**

1. *NLW*, Cardigan file K5, hand-bill issued 28 August 1824 by Shey.

SHONE, Charles (fl 1808 - 1809)
Land surveyor**(1)** — St Asaph

He produced two designs for a bridge & embankment at Conwy. The earlier plan is embellished with topographical views of the castle & other features around Conwy.**(2)**

1. Not in *Eden*.
2. *NLW* PB 7434 watercolour *Design for a bridge...* 1808, 32.4x163cm. Signed as 'C&R Shone'. Also PB 4048 *A Plan of the Town & river of Conway*, watercolour, 1809, 45.9x74.8cm.

See back endpapers.

SHONE, Richard (fl 1805 - 1853)**(1)**
[Mason] — Rhuddlan
Land surveyor — Rhyl: 3 Mona Terrace
St Asaph

He worked with his brother? Charles on at least one, unrealised project at Conwy.**(2)** He worked also in Flintshire, on Tithe maps & was the clerk of the local savings bank 1843.**(3)**

1. *SA* 1853/211.
2. *Vide* Charles Shone. Presumably Richard was to provide the craftsman's skill for this project & Charles, the professional aspect.
3. *Eden* III, p.229.

SIMONNET, Julius Augustus
(fl 1849 - fl 1852)
Teacher of drawing — Newport
1 Clifton Place, Stow Hill

He also taught languages and was probably an immigrant.**(1)**

1. *Hunt*, 1849, p.131. *Scammell & Co.* 1852 p.152.

SISSON, John (fl 1835 - fl 1843)
Surveyor — Plas Coch
St Asaph
Flintshire

Davies Atlas. Not in *Eden*.

SLATER, A.W. (fl 1830)
Portrait artist — Merthyr Tydfil

(*PL.*)

SLATER & LEWIS (fl 1770 - fl 1784)
Surveyors — Denbighshire

Their survey of property owned by Watkin Williams in 1770-71 shows an interest in topographical draughtsmanship.**(1)** They also executed a later survey in 1784.**(2)**

1. Not in *Eden*. *NLW*, Peniarth Deposit Volume 4.
2. *NLW*, Estate Map Volume, 84.

SMITH, Henry (fl 1826)
Surveyor
Newport
Maindee

NLW, Estate map, *Christchurch*, 1826.**(1)**

1. *Eden*. III, p.232 refers to him as 'copyist only'.

SMITH, Miles (1811 - fl 1849)
Landscape painter
Swansea
16 Somerset Place

Smith was born in Glamorganshire**(1)** and may have established himself as an artist in Swansea. In c1843, he moved to London where he exhibited in the *BI*.**(2)**

An important sale of paintings, owned by Miles Smith took place in Swansea in September 1843 and included were works by or attributed to George Chambers, John Constable, Thomas Barker, J.M.W. Turner, R.P. Bonington 'also a number of sketches and Pictures of the neighbourhood of Swansea'.**(3)** Such pictures would probably be consistent with a landscapist's taste but not his finances.

1. Census Returns 1841 (HO 107 1426, p.10, [p.9]): 'Miles Smith Age 30 Artist'.
2. *Graves, B I*, 1848 (Covent Garden) (108) *Chiswick on the Thames*; 1849 (Regent Street) (172) *Llanrhidran* [*sic*] *Sands*; (279) *Caswall Bay* [*sic*]. The last two landscapes are of views near Swansea.
3. *Cambrian*, 9 September 1843, p.2. The sale of 'all the valuables of Miles Smith of Southall [?*sic*] Place, Picton Place, Swansea' on 25, 26, 27 September. Consisting of 150 oil paintings, magic lantern, camera and an excellent library. If this was the collection of a young man one would presume he had some inheritance. No catalogue of the auction is extant, therefore the attributions cannot be analysed.

SMITH, Thomas Haddon (fl 1849)
Drawing teacher
Caernarfon
High Street

He may have moved to Caernarfon in 1849 and advertised his services:

> 'announce to the Families of Caernarvon and its Vicinity, that his course of instructions in Water Colour, Crayon, Pencil (including Galpin's Broad Style) and Monotone Drawing, will commence on Wednesday next... Families attended at their residences.'**(1)**

He seems to have sought patronage mainly from ladies and families with children.

1. *Caernarvon and Denbighshire Herald*, 20 January 1849, p.4. The artist probably meant Gilpin not Galpin: Rev. William Gilpin (1724-1804) specialised in general picturesque effects.

SMYTH, Henry (fl 1850)
Landscape painter
Kidwelly

Hunt, 1850, p.55.

SPENCE, Mr W. Steers (fl 1824 - fl 1826)
Silhouette artist
Brecon, Bridgend
Cardigan, Carmarthen, Chepstow
Haverfordwest, Cowbridge,
Llandeilo, Llandovery,
Merthyr, Monmouth, Newport,
Newcastle Emlyn, Swansea

He worked in numerous towns in Mid and South Wales during the summers of 1824 and 1826. Afterwards he moved to Shrewsbury, therefore his Welsh visit was probably part of a larger itinerary.**(1)**

Spence considered his art a 'Singular Ingeniuty - A most striking likeness produced in a few seconds by scissors'.**(2)** He reported that on his visit to Swansea he took '1400 likenesses' in twelve days and 1100 at Carmarthen in eight days.**(3)**

1. *McKechnie*, p.273, mentions his visit to Shrewsbury but not to Wales.
2. *Cambrian*, 14 August 1824, p.3.
   Ibid., 15 July 1826, p.3.
3. *Ibid.*, 14 August 1824, p.3. He also advertised in the *Carmarthen Journal*, 2 July 1824, p.3.
   Ibid., 6 August 1824, p.3.

SPOONER, J.S. (fl 1854 - fl 1874)
Landscape painter
Llanrwst
Beaver Grove

Exhibited at *BI* and *RA*.**(1)**

1. I wish to thank John Holmes for discovering this artist. *BI*, p.507, 1859 (473), *Nant Llam Transcwl*. Also at *RA* from Llanrwst 1854, 1874 (moved to 'Tarry Vron, [Tan y Fron?] Llanrwst'). *Pavière*, p.122.

SPOONER, James & Sons (fl 1835 - fl 1843)
Surveyor
Morfa Lodge
Caernarfon

Davies Atlas. Eden III, p.235.

SPRATT, Henry (fl 1823 - fl 1835)
Drawing master**(1)**
Caerleon
Newport

Possibly moved to Newport in 1820s from Chelsea.**(2)**

1. *Pigot's*, 1835, p.258, 'Henry Spratt Drawing [Master?], Caerleon'.
2. Gwent Record Office, D1670 98/99 deed, dated 1823.

STEPHEN, Edward (- 1839)
Mason
Llangadog
Carmarthenshire

SD/1839/264.

STEPHENS, John (- 1848)
Mason
Mochdre
Montgomeryshire?

BR/1848/60.

STEVENS, James (fl 1852 -)
Portrait & landscape painter
'Tan Lan'
Park Street
Holyhead

NLW, Ffoto Album 6, 'established 1852'.

STONE, Richard (fl 1835 - fl 1843)
Surveyor
St Asaph

Davies Atlas, Not in *Eden*.

STOOKE, James (c1800 - fl 1850)
Silhouette artist
Llantrisant
Cardiff

He was a Bristol artist who visited South Wales in 1831 and 1847.**(1)** Three examples of his work in Wales are extant, they are considerably more elaborate than other recorded works.**(2)**

1. Reported by *McKechnie*, p.568.
2. *WFM* (59/-426/1): 'Ann Jacob taken by James Stooke of Clifton at Llantrissent in June 1831', (59/-426/2): 'Edward H. Jacob taken by James Stook [*sic*] of Clifton at Elm Cottage Canton on the 20th of March 1847'. (59-426/3): 'Meredith James Jacob taken by James Stooke of Clifton At Llantrissent in the year 1831 - July'. All approximately 6.1 x 4.8, painted on glass with traces of gilding, framed in black [ebony].

STORY-MASKELYNE, Nevil (1823 - 1911)
Photographer
Penlle'r-gaer
Swansea

Maskelyne was a scientist who was also interested in photography. The husband of Thereza Llewelyn, *supra*, he worked with his wife on photographic experiments.**(1)** J.D. Llewelyn mentioned in a letter, 21 December 1855, that 'my friend Mr Maskelyne sent me from Oxford a sample of Glycerine, with a recommendation that I should try it as a substitute for honey in the preservation of excited collodion plates.'**(2)**

1. Painting, David, *Swansea's Place in the History of Photography*, p.15. Kraus, Hans, P., *Sun Pictures*, Catalogue 2 New York, [c1985], discusses this photographer of the Llewelyn circle.
2. Cox, Julian, 'Photography in South Wales 1840-60', *History of Photography*, Autumn 1991, p.166.

STOTHARD, Robert Thomas (fl 1821 - fl 1865)
Miniature painter
Caernarfon

A London artist who claimed to be the son of Thomas Stothard.**(1)** In 1834 he visited Caernarfon for six weeks and invited the 'Nobility, Gentry and Inhabitants of North Wales to see his exhibition of miniatures at William Owen's, Castle Square Caernarvon'.**(2)**

He painted miniatures for lockets at five guineas, or ten guineas, the 'second size' and 'Sketches of Heads of children at full length' at two guineas each.

1. *Caernarvon and Denbighshire Herald*, 23 August 1834, p.2; for Stothard *vide infra*. *Foskett*, Volume 1, p.533, states, 'possibly the son of Thomas Stothard'.
2. *Caernarvon and Denbighshire Herald, op.cit*.

STOTHARD, Thomas (1755 - 1834)
Landscape artist
Drawing master
Hafod
Cwm Ystwyth
Cardiganshire

He taught Mariamne Johnes at Hafod, first visiting in 1803 for that purpose. 'In 1810 he painted grisaille scenes from Monstrelet for Johnes' library.'**(1)** Johnes wrote from Hafod in 1805 mentioning Stothard.**(2)**

1. Parris, L., *Landscape in Britain c1750-1850* (1973), p.70. Parris illustrates two landscapes of Hafod by Stothard, presumably c1810. Croft, Murray E., *Decorative Painting in Britain 1537-1837*, Volume II (1970), p.283, mentions that the frieze was in a London collection in 1858. Moore-Colyer, *A land of Pure Delight* (Llandysul, 1992) p.262 provides MSS evidence for this commission. T. Johnes wrote on 11 Nov. 1810 (BL Add. MS 36502, f.322) 'Mr Stothard is now here busily employed to finish his work to return to Town, which I suppose he will do in the course of next week'. Coxhead, A.C., *Thomas Stothard RA* (an illustrated monograph) (London, 1906), p.12, mentions this commission 'Decorate one room (at Hafod), the library, with scenes chosen from the medieval classics. Eight painted panels...in imitation of reliefs'. He notes that Stothard painted 'Two views of Hafod and a portrait of Colonel Johnes.' (p.203).
2. Moore-Colyer, Richard, *A land of Pure Delight* (Llandysul, 1992) p.199. 'Mariamne is making great improvement in her drawing under an old acquaintance of yours [George Cumberland] Stodhard [sic] he is very deft and, as the Scots say colded'.

STOWER, Mr (fl 1846)
Portrait and
Miniature painter
Haverfordwest

Visiting Haverfordwest and advertising for patrons.**(1)**

1. *Pembrokeshire Herald*, 6 November 1846. (*TL*). Not in *Foskett, Witt*.

STRAWSON, George Smith (fl 1831 - fl 1850)
Architect
Surveyor
Cardiff
Smith Street

Hunt, 1850, p.17.
Slater's, 1850, p.22.
Davies Atlas. *NLW*, Estate Map, *Cardiff*, 1837, 1846.
Eden, II, p.239.

STURKEY, Thomas Owen (fl 1835 - fl 1843)
Surveyor
Newtown

Davies Atlas, Not in *Eden*.

T

TAMLYN, John (fl 1810 - fl 1845)
Surveyor [near] Haverfordwest

He worked as a versatile surveyor for tithe maps, roads and taxes in the Pembrokeshire area.**(1)**

1. *Davies Atlas. Eden* III, p.244. There is another J. Tamlyn, *NLW*, Estate Map Volume, *Picton Castle*, 1773 - noted by R. Davies as possibly the style of Tamlyn.

TAYLOR, George (fl 1842 - fl 1847)
Surveyor Brecon

Taylor appears to have worked mainly in Breconshire & Montgomeryshire.**(1)** Like Tamlyn his career was varied, he did some work for railway & tithe surveyors, in addition to estate maps.**(2)**

1. *Eden* III, p.245.
2. *NLW*, Estate Map, *Llanfihangel Fechan*.

TAYLOR, Isaac (fl 1835 - fl 1843)
Surveyor Manor House
Bagillt
Holywell

Davies Atlas. Eden, III, p.245.
NLW, Estate Map catalogue, notes that he worked on Ystumllyn Estate.

TAYLOR, M. (fl 1798 - fl 1809)
Miniature painter Swansea
Burrows

Taylor lived at Bath**(1)** and visited the West Country and Wales.**(2)** At Swansea he took 'Striking likenesses' adding that he would travel to a day's journey in the surrounding regions to take group family portraits.**(3)**

At his Swansea studio he operated a 'Machine' which produced cheap portraits, presumably for a wider market.**(4)**

After Swansea he had 'several engagements in different parts of the country'.

1. *Gye*, 1819, does not mention Taylor. *Foskett* and *McKechnie* provide a short biography.
2. *Long* records that Taylor was at Exeter in January 1798 and Plymouth in February 1798, *Exeter Flying Post*, 11 January 1798, 18 January, 8 February, 15 February, 22 February.
3. *Cambrian*, 22 July 1809, p.3.
4. *Ibid.*, he charged two to five guineas for miniatures but only 10s 6d for a 'likeness taken by a Machine in Colours'. This was probably similar to the Patent Delineator used by Brooke (*vide supra*).

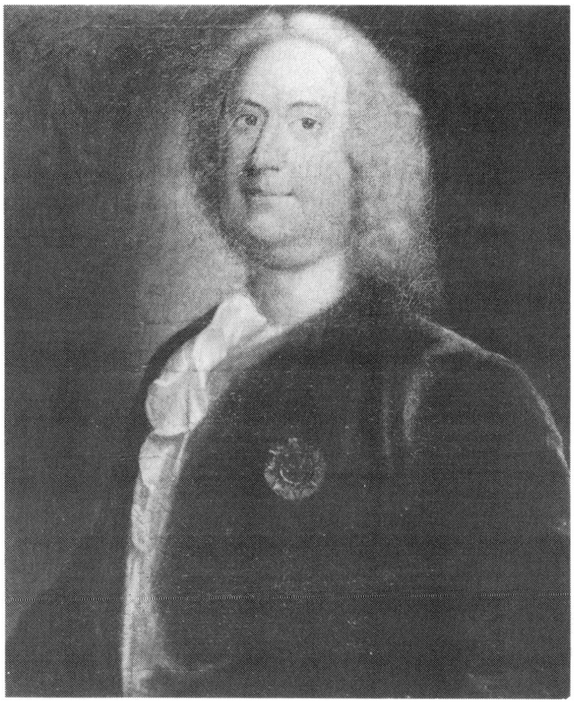

84 Taylor, Robert, *Richard Gwynne*, oil on canvas, 1740, *NMW*.

TAYLOR, Robert (fl 1737 - fl 1755)
Portrait painter Taliaris, Carmarthenshire

Taylor trained under Jonathan Richardson and followed his master's style closely.**(1)** He was given a major commission by an exclusive Welsh gentlemen's club, the Society of Sea Sergeants.

> 'When Mr Gwynne was President, Taylor the painter was employed to draw all their Portraits - which were executed in 1740.'**(2)**

The society had Jacobite tendencies which may be the reason for Taylor's being chosen for this task.**(3)** The series was fairly uniform in size and format, being half length portraits with the badge of the Society displayed on their jackets.**(4)** This was precisely the type of portrait Taylor was painting in London at the time.**(5)**

Taylor may also have been patronized by individual members of the Sea Sergeants in c1747, and possibly by other gentry families in South Wales.**(6)**.

1. *Waterhouse* described him as 'quite competent'.
2. Carmarthen R.O., Gulston MSS, 3, p.66. Twenty-nine portraits are described with a final note on p.70, 'Robert Taylor, the painter, who executed all the foregoing pictures, in a loose dress, a post [*sic*] Crayon in his hand, Wig [etc]. This is the best portrait in the room'. Another list in Gulston MSS (Derwydd 1a, p.33) gives the same sitters but less information. Jones, F., 'Portraits and Pictures in Old Carmarthenshire Houses', *Carmarthen Historian*, Volume 5, 1968, pp.43-66, gives some useful details of these MSS.
3. *Vide* 'The Sea Sergeants', *Cambrian Quarterly Magazine*, 1831, Volume 3, pp.55-57. *Waterhouse*, 'He escaped mention by Vertue because of Jacobite sympathies.'
4. The portraits were of 'Country Gentlemen' mainly of Wales. All approximately 75 x 62 cm, oil on canvas. Most of the portraits are now lost but the *NMW* has

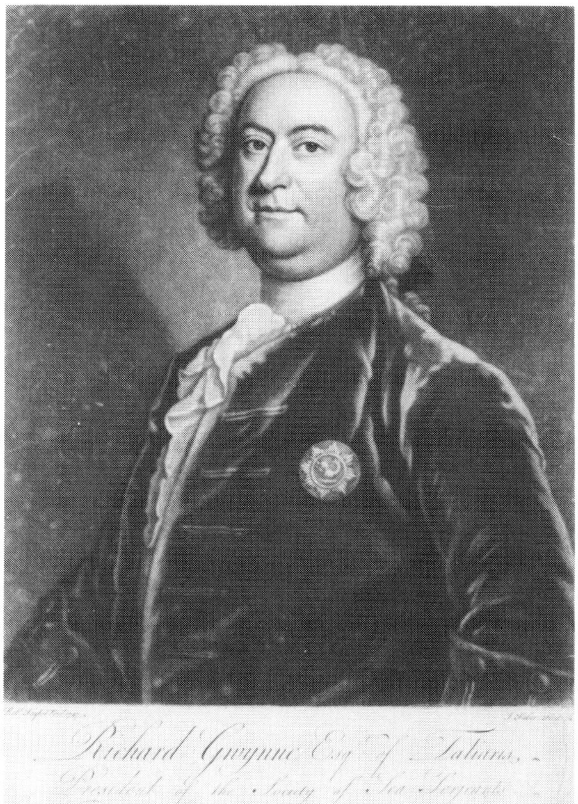

85 Taylor, Robert, *Richard Gwynne*, mezzotint, 1747, P8677.

two (on loan to the *WFM*): *Richard Jones Gwynne of Taliaris*, exhibited *AIW*, item 112; *John Williams, Congasser*. Some of these portraits were published in mezzotint, for instance *NLW*, P8677, *Richard Gwynne*, 'Pubt Taylor Pinxt 1747', mezzotint by J. Faber, 32.2 x 22.5 cm.

5. *Lord Digby*, 1743, signed and dated 'R. Taylor Pinxit 1743', oil on canvas, approx. 79 x 63.5 cm, Sotheby's, 17 July 1923, lot 62.
6. Three portraits are held in private collections: *Steegman*, Volume II, p.65, *Richard Gwynne*, c75 x 62 cm (Gulston list 1); *ibid.*, p.16; *Richard Gwynne*, c127 x 102 cm; *ibid.*, p.77, *Richard Gwynne*, signed and dated Robert Taylor 1747. All presumably duplicates.

TAYLOR, Captain [William] (fl 1839)

Landscape artist — Newport, Gwent

Taylor appears to have been resident of Newport in November 1839 & drew a view of the Westgate Hotel shortly after the riot.**(1)**

He may have had some interest in architecture**(2)** & produced a fine landscape drawing of the Monnow Bridge & Llanthony Abbey.**(3)**

This artist is somewhat of a mystery. If he was Captain William Ryvef Taylor of the Royal Artillery, he was a cadet at Woolwich in September 1839, 2nd Lt 1842, 1st 1843 & 2nd Captain 1849, retiring in 1850. If this is so, the date of prints after his drawings may need revising.**(4)**

1. *NLW* PG5542 *A View of the Westgate Hotel* lithograph 31x46.2cm Printed for W.T. by Lavars & Ackland, Bristol, 1839.
2. Newport Museum has a ground plan of the Westgate by Taylor, 30.2x46.5cm. 'Printed at the Lithographic Establishment, Quarter Master General's Office Home Guards, November 1839'. Taylor is described as 'Lieutenant' of the Royal Artillery so he presumably was promoted after the riot.
3. *NLW* P2452 (Top A10/1) *Entrance to Monmouth*. lithograph, 7x10cm, P2596 [Top A10] *Llanthoney* [*sic*] *Abbey* 6.9x9.5cm.
4. Information from the National Army Museum.

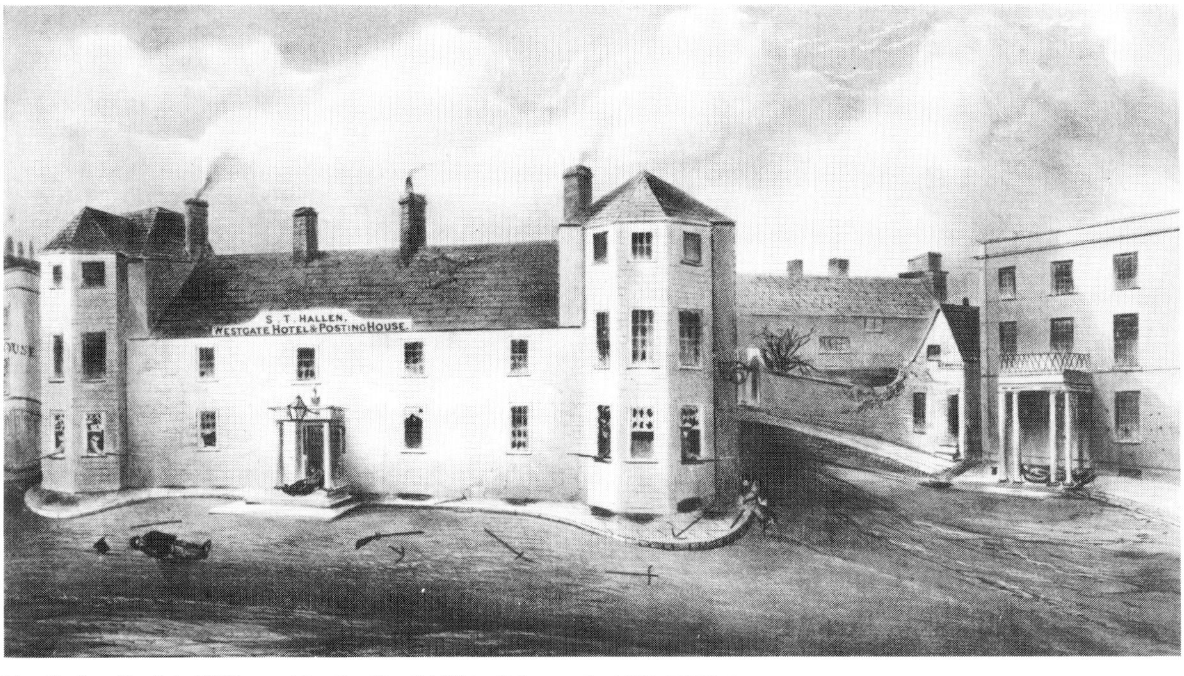

86 Taylor, Captain William, *After the Chartist Riots*, lithograph, 1839, PG5542.

TENANT, John (- 1818)
Mason Lamphey

SD/1818/67.

THOMAS, Alfred (fl 1835 - fl 1846)
Surveyor Haverfordwest
Carmarthen
Wellfield Villa

Davies Atlas. Eden, III, p.247, notes that he lived at St Peter's Street in 1835, Lammas Street in 1840.
NLW, Estate Map, *St Clears*, 1819, 1827 (gives him at Haverfordwest).

THOMAS, Betty (fl 1800)
China painter Nantgarw

Servant to William Billingsley. 'She was a native of Nantgarw.'**(1)**

1. *Cadrawd*, p.112.

THOMAS, Daniel (fl 1850)
Surveyor Cardiff

Worked on improvements to the rectory at St Nicholas.**(1)**

1. *NLW* Llandaff, Bounty Plan 116, rectory built in 1829 by William Griffiths. Not in *Eden*.

THOMAS, David (- 1816)
Mason Cellan
Cardiganshire

SD/1816/28 (I).**(1)**

1. Inventory includes 'household furniture' at '10.6.'

THOMAS, David (fl 1838 - 1856)**(1)**
Architect Mynyddislwyn**(2)**
Abercarn
Monmouthshire
Cardiff

1. *LL*/1856/61.
2. *Eden*, III, p.247, records Thomas at Penllwyn, Mynyddislwyn, 1838-42.

THOMAS, E[dward] (fl 1766 - fl 1797)
Land surveyor Cardiff
Margam**(1)**

A surveyor who embellished his works with landscape motifs.**(2)** He was Town Clerk of Cardiff 1766-1786.**(3)**

1. Probably the same hand as Edward Thomas, Margam, in *NLW*, Tredegar Deposit Collection, Volume 2, which has a magnificent coloured title page with a cornucopia, griffin and [portrait] head, all executed in watercolours. The *Town of Brecon* is particularly fine, with characteristic depictions of sheep and figures. *Eden Supplement* p.478, notes an E. Thomas 1772-97.
2. *NLW*, Estate Map Volume 28, *Estates in Glamorgan, Monmouth, Hereford*, 'Survey'd & Mapped by E. Thomas'. Title page includes pastoral scenes. This includes a sketch of Llandaff Cathedral.
3. *Eden* III, p.247.

THOMAS, Evan (- 1795)
Stonecutter Llanafan Fawr
Breconshire

BR/1795/25.

THOMAS, Evan (fl 1833)
Surveyor Cowbridge

Drew a simple plan for Llanharry rectory, 1833.**(1)**

1. *NLW* Llandaff Bounty Plan 60, 1833. Not in *Eden*.

THOMAS, George (-1837)
Mason Nash
Nash Back
Glamorganshire

SD/1837/226.

THOMAS, Griffith (- 1835)
Tiler, plasterer Brecon
Llanvase

BR/1835/5.

THOMAS, Inigo (fl 1821)
[Sign painter] [Newport]
Monmouthshire

He painted a panoramic view of *The Humfrey Coal Train*.**(1)** This is extensively inscribed and includes a detailed view of the coal trucks with the Severn estuary in the background.

1. *Lord, 1993*, pp.12-13, oil on panel, 86 x 376 cm, Cardiff: Industrial and Maritime Museum.

THOMAS, John Evan (Junior) (fl 1810 - 73)
Plaster modeller and sculptor Brecon

Working in Brecon on various commissions. 'The specimens Mr Thomas, jun. has already produced exhibits a grandeur of composition, a grace in grouping, and a flow in his draperies, equal to any that has been seen in the Principality.'**(1)**

He won a prize from Abergavenny Cymreigyddion in 1848 for the *Death of Tewdric, King of Gwent, in the moment of victory over the Saxons at Mathern, on the Wye*.**(2)**

He trained in the studio of Francis Chantrey and was recorded to have returned to Brecon in 1857.**(3)**

1. *DWB*, p.955, notes that he was assisted by his brother William Meredith Thomas (1819-1877). *Cambrian Quarterly Magazine*, 1833 (Vol. V), pp.147-8.
2. *Art Union*, 1848, p.354. *Lord, 1992*, p.20, illustrates this

sculpture, and also gives the wood engraving from the *Illustrated London News*, 1849.
3. *Gunnis*, p.390.

THOMAS, John (fl 1844)
Stone mason & sculptor — Haverfordwest, Picton Place

Pigot's, 1844, p.36, gives him as 'statuary'.

THOMAS, John (fl 1849)
Stone mason & sculptor — Brecon, Castle Street

Hunt, 1849, p.93.

THOMAS, John (- 1846)
Mason — ?Llangastyn, Breconshire

BR/1846/41.

THOMAS, Rees (- 1799)
Mason — Llansadwrn, Carmarthenshire

SD/1799/174.

THOMAS, Robert (fl 1851 ?)
Artists' colourman — Caernarfon

Advertised a range of paints including many artists' colours.**(1)**

1. *UCW Bangor*, MS 3592, No 51, printed catalogue of colours which included Dry Lake, Dutch Okre, Green Verditer, Prussian Blue and Spanish Brown.

THOMAS, Robert George (1820 - 1885)
Architect — Newport, 48 Commercial Street**(1)**

Began his practice in 1848, possibly at Newport, continuing there in 1861, moved to Australia in 1866.**(2)**

1. *Slater's*, 1860, p.23.
2. *Girouard*, (1975) p.909.

THOMAS, Samuel (- 1828)
Mason — Swansea

SD/1828/315.

THOMAS, Thomas (- 1850)
Mason — Llanbedr Felffre (Seven Acres), Pembrokeshire

SD/1850/297 (I): Inventory did not specify any craftsman's tools.

THOMAS, Thomas (1795 - fl 1841)
China painter — Swansea

Nance suggests that he was a native artist who painted 'second grade' Swansea china.**(1)** He is mentioned in the Census of 1841.**(2)**

1. *Nance*, p.329.
2. Census Return 1841, HO 107 1426, p.27, he is described as a 'China painter Aged 46 Born in Glamorganshire'.

THOMAS, Walter Richard (fl 1853)
Builder — Swansea

Designed & built the rectory at Penmain.**(1)**

1. *NLW*, St Davids, Bounty Plan 154, 1853. Not in *Eden*.

THOMAS, William (fl 1770 - fl 1772)
Surveyor — [Cardiganshire]

NLW has surveys executed from 1770-1772. Not in *Eden*.

THOMAS, William (- 1840)
Painter — Swansea, Wind Street

SD/1840/230: painter & glazier.

THOMAS, William (fl 1753 - 1810)
Architect — near Pembroke

Born in Pembrokeshire,**(1)** and moved to London to work. Hilling records that Thomas 'lived near Pembroke' and designed Stackpole Court in 1753.**(2)** In 1795 he exhibited a design for Upton Court, Pembrokeshire at the *RA*.**(3)**

1. *Colvin* p.973 does not mention that Thomas lived in Pembrokeshire.
2. *PP*.
3. He was then working in London.

THOMAS, William (Junior) (fl 1828 - fl 1835)
Architect & surveyor — Pwllheli, Penlan

Son of William Griffith Thomas (*infra*)?**(1)** He designed & built *Rhiw Rectory* in 1831**(2)**

1. *Pigot's*, 1828-29, p.1171
   Pigot's, 1835, p.719.
   Not in *Girouard*, *Eden*.
2. *NLW* Bangor Bounty Plan 80 signed & dated 1831, a simple plan.

THOMAS, William Griffith (fl 1844 - 1855)
Architect — Caernarfon
Surveyor — Pwllheli**(1)**

Described as an architect in his will and place of residence given as Pwllheli.**(2)**

1. *Slater's*, 1844, p.16: 'Shirehall Street'.
   Ibid., 1828, p.1171: 'Architect [?Pen-lôn]'.

Pigot's, 1828-9, p.1171, at [Pen-lôn].
Ibid., 1835, p.690, at Shirehall [Street].
Robson's, 1840, Vol. II, p.13, at Tithe Barn Street, Caernarfon.
Slater's, 1850, p.20, Bridge Street, Caernarfon.
2. *B* 1855/124. *Girouard*, p. 910, records a William Thomas (1799/1800-60), no residence mentioned but possibly the same architect. Not in *Eden, Colvin*.

THOMAS, William Meredith (1819 - 1877)
Sculptor — Brecon

Brother of J.E. Thomas (*supra*).**(1)** Went to London c1840.**(2)**

It is reported that he completed some of his brother's works. He specialised in 'allegories and medallions executed in marble'.**(3)**

1. *DWB*.
2. *Cadrawd*, [p.117].
3. *DWB*, p.955. *Lord, 1992*, pp.20-22, discusses this artist.

TODD, James (fl 1835 - fl 1843)
Surveyor — Abergavenny

Davies Atlas. Eden, III, p.250.

TRAHERNE, Charlotte Louisa (fl c1800 - fl 1869)
Landscape painter — Coedriglan
[Portrait painter] — Glamorganshire

There are several volumes of her sketches at the *NLW*.**(1)** Mrs Traherne was an amateur artist whose work was occasionally copied by A.F. Rolfe (*supra*), probably in his Crickhowell period.**(2)** She painted a portrait of Iolo Morganwg. She also produced lithographs of Glamorganshire for 'private circulation'.**(3)**

1. *NLW*, Drawing Volumes 24, 81, 118.
2. *NLW*, PD 3798, Top. C8/1 - C19, *West front of Llantrithyd place house*; *PA* 1690, Top. C8/1 - C20, *Drawing room, Llantrithyd House, Glamorganshire*.
3. *Cadrawd*, p.118. *NMW* has the portrait of Iolo Morganwg (A627) watercolour 8.2x7cm. This is a very fine example.

TROSSARELLI, Gaspari/Giovani (fl 1792)
Miniature painter — Hafod
Drawing master — Cwm Ystwyth

He was employed by Thomas Johnes to train Mariamne *supra* to draw & paint. Presumably he only spent a few months at Hafod.**(1)**

1. The Trossarelli brothers arrived in Britain from Italy in 1791. It is not clear whether Gaspari or Giovani was employed at Hafod, but either would have been capable of training young Mariamne. They were also dancing, music & Italian professors. *Vide* entry on Mariamne Johnes & Moore-Colyer, Richard, *A Land of Pure Delight* (Llandysul, 1992), p.93.

TROUGHTON, John Ellis (c1820 - c1872)
Painter — Hawarden (Flints)
Aberhafesp (Mont.)

He was an amateur painter who produced very accomplished 'embellishments' at his parish church.**(1)** Troughton was trained as a clergyman at Cambridge and was rector at Hawarden in 1860, then Aberhafesp.**(2)**

1. Hubbard, Edward, *The Buildings of Wales: Clwyd* (Harmondsworth, 1986), pp.64, 417, notes: 'Enrichments' at Pentrobin.
2. Venn, J.A., *Alumni Cantabrigienses* (Cambridge, 1954), Vol. VI, p.236. *Crockfords*, 1860, p.615, gives Troughton at Hawarden.

TUCKER, John (- 1851)
Mason — Ilston
(Parkmill)
Glamorganshire

SD/1851/132.

TUCKER, William (- 1814)
Mason — Knelston
Glamorganshire

SD/1814/69.

TUDOR, Miss (fl 1774)
Needleworker — Monmouth

Probably a relation of Thomas and John Tudor and may have kept a school in Monmouth.**(1)** Exhibited at the Society of Artists in 1774, (358): *A piece of flowers*; in needlework'.**(2)**

1. *Vide* Thomas Tudor: Monmouth Artist chapter in *Joyner (1989)*.
2. *Graves, S.A.*: Tudor given as 'A Honorary Exhibitor'.

TUDOR, John Owen (fl 1799 - fl 1824)
Landscape artist — Monmouth

The elder brother of Thomas Tudor. He worked on drawings for Cox's *History of Monmouthshire*,**(1)** in collaboration with Thomas and Owen Tudor. These, and two small sepia studies are the only evidence of his work in Monmouth.**(2)**

From 1809 he exhibited works at the *RA*, many of them Welsh scenes**(3)** and in 1816 he entered the *RA* schools.**(4)** From 1816 to 1824 he exhibited at the *BI*. First of all from the residence of his relative, J.S. Tudor and then presumably his own studio.**(5)** He did not return to Monmouth and gradually painted more historical works than Welsh landscapes.**(6)**

1. Coxe, William, *History of Monmouthshire*, Volume 1, facing p.203, four engravings by 'W.B.' after J. Tudor [Monmouth Country houses]. *The environs of Monmouth* was published in Coxe, one example of this print is *NLW*, PB 2392, B10/13 - B233.
2. Newport Art Gallery 78-178-1&3, *Raglan Castle*, *Monmouth Castle*, both approximately 14.5 x 20.5 cm. The latter is signed 'John Tudor'.

3. For instance in 1809 he exhibited four landscapes: *Tintern Abbey, Abergavenny, Monmouth* and *Scene on the Trothy brook, in a park of the Duke of Beaufort's, Monmouthshire.* His address 1809 given at J. Tudor, Lamb's Conduit St. 1810 his address was 15 Featherstone Buildings & he mainly exhibited North Wales Scenes.
4. *Hutchison*, p.169, entered on 9 August 1816 as a painter.
5. *Graves, B.I.*, 'J.S. Tudor, 15 Featherstone Buildings:
   1816 (183) *Conway Castle*, 2.1 x 1.6, 4 Haymarket.
   1818 (273) *Langollen Aqueduct*, 2.10 x 3.3.
   1819 (172) *On the River Wye near Ross*, 1.8 x 2.1.
   (255) *From Horace Lib. 2 Car.* 3 (Latin quotation), 3.9 x 3.1.
   8 Judd's Place East:
   1821 (143) *Conway Castle*, 2.10 x 3.3.
   1824 (76) *Abraham entertaineth Three Angels*, 4.0 x 5.0, My Lord, if now I have found favour in thy sight, etc. - *Genesis*, xviii.
   (275) *Eton College*, 3.2 x 3.10.'
6. By 1822 he was exhibiting subjects after Burns at the *RA, The Solitary*, 'How Blest the Solitary's lot / Within his humble cell...'

TUDOR, Owen (fl c1790 - fl 1810)

Landscape draughtsman — Monmouth

Owen Tudor was the father of Thomas and John Tudor. He had an important printing and bookselling business at Monmouth. He published several tours on the Wye and also tourist guides to Monmouth itself.

He collaborated with his sons, producing a bird's eye map of Monmouth in 1801.**(1)**

1. *Vide* Tudor *infra* and *supra*. *Vide Libri Walliae* for details of Tudor's published texts.

TUDOR, Thomas (1785 - 1855)

Landscape and portrait painter — Monmouth
Architect, surveyor — Wyesham

Tudor was born and worked most of his life in or near Monmouth. His brother John was also a painter and his father Owen Tudor kept a bookshop in the town.**(1)**

His first works were for the *History of Monmouthshire*, they were simple topographical drawings of little distinction.**(2)**

The early dated original drawings by Tudor are similar to the work of J.M. Ince or Samuel Prout.**(3)** Possibly this was because he learnt through prints and engravings.

By 1809 he was exhibiting at the *RA* and he entered the schools in 1817.**(4)** He exhibited always from Monmouth and the following are all his known exhibition pictures:

1809	(329)	*View on the river Wye between Ross and Monmouth near Coldwell.*
	(370)	*South-east view of Lanthony Abbey,* [*sic*] *now destroyed.*
	(392)	*South-west view of Lanthony* [*sic*] *Abbey, now destroyed.*
1810	(368)	*Snowdon, from the upper Lake of Llynniau Natle.* [*sic*]
	(373)	*View on the River Wye at Hadnock, near Monmouth.*
1811	(279)	*Rocks above new Weir on the River Wye.*
	(395)	*View of the Valle Crucis Abbey, Denbighshire.*
1812	(743)	*Monmouth.*
	(749)	*View of the Monmouthshire Hills from Staunton, Gloucestershire.*
1813	(651)	*Raglan Castle, Monmouthshire.*
1814	(21)	*Portrait of a gentleman.*
	(292)	*Portraits of a lady and child.*
1816	(75)	*Portrait of Mrs O Tudor.*
1817	(459)	*The Rev. Dr. Bell.*
1818	(406)	*Mrs Haffenden.*
	(517)	*Miss Walker.*
1819	(444)	*View of Raglan Castle, Monmouthshire.***(5)**

From 1822 he was employed as a land agent for Major Clifford, Monmouthshire. He also worked at Kentchurch Court and other sites as an architect.**(6)**

His *Diary* is one of the most important documents of the taste of a Welsh artist.**(7)** He was a collector of art and had a fine sublime work by J.M.W. Turner.**(8)**

There is a large body of work by Tudor extant, the best is close in style to Thomas Girtin and J.M.W. Turner.**(9)**

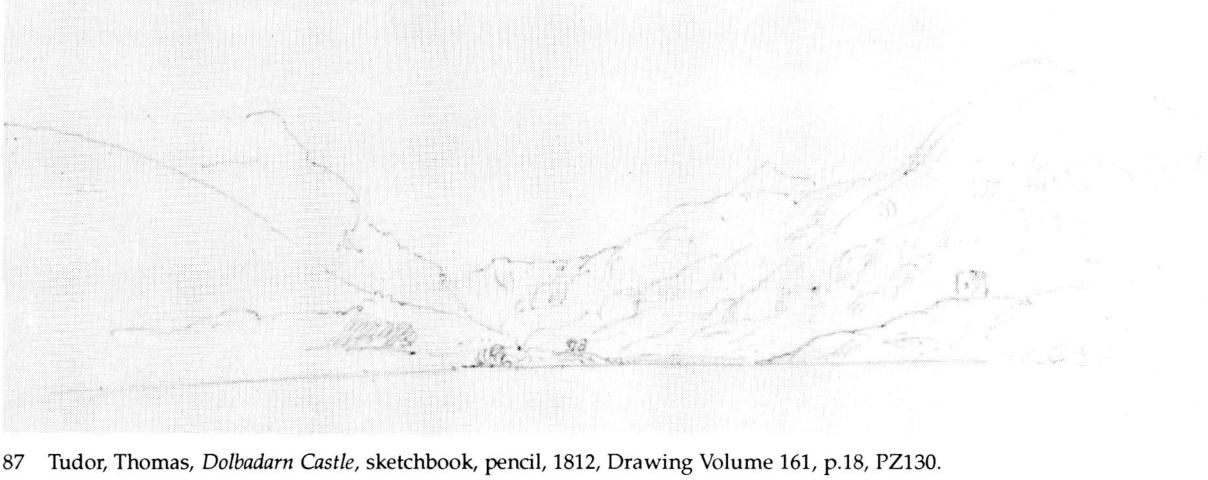

87 Tudor, Thomas, *Dolbadarn Castle*, sketchbook, pencil, 1812, Drawing Volume 161, p.18, PZ130.

1. *Vide* 'Thomas Tudor, Monmouth Artist', *Joyner, 1989*, pp.82ff. Not in *Girouard*.
2. Coxe, W., *History of Monmouthshire*, 2 volumes (1801); Volume 1, facing p.26, engraved by W.B. *Caerwent*; *NLW*, PB 8702, B10/1 - B27, *Eastern entrance of Caerwent*; facing p.89, *Caerleon*; *NLW*, P 4629, B10/1 - B26. In Volume 2 there are wood engravings by Lee, *Trelech Church*.
3. *NLW*, Drawing Volume 160 (8vo), sketchbook. Mainly outline drawings.
4. *Hutchison*, p.170, 26 March 1817, aged 29: 'Painter'.
5. *Graves, R.A.*
6. *Eden*, Supplement, p.480, gives Tudor working in Monmouthshire in 1802. *Joyner, 1989*, pp.82ff, discusses Tudor as an artist and surveyor. *NLW*, Estate Map *Llangasty Talyllyn*, signed T. Tudor, c1800 (RM:A152).
7. Collection of Major Clifford, MS *Diary*.
8. *Joyner, 1989*, Vol. I, pp.133-135; the collection is also discussed in *Joyner 1990*, p.90. The most important picture in the collection was J.M.W. Turner, *The Fifth Plague of Egypt*, 1800, 124 x 183 cm, oil on canvas, Indianapolis Museum of Art, USA. Butlin, M., & Joll, E., *The Paintings of J.M.W. Turner* (2 vols), (New Haven and London, 1984), discusses this picture in some detail.
9. *NLW* has a number of Sketchbooks, drawings and watercolours. Monmouth Museum has a fine collection; Newport has one large watercolour of *Llanthony Abbey* and three other lesser works. The *BM* has a single drawing 1978-10-7-9, *Bridge over Waterfall*. There is a collection of sky studies at the *VAM*. The best private collection is owned by Mr K. Kissack of Monmouth who pioneered work on Tudor. *Joyner, 1990*, Plate 3, illustrates a watercolour, *Monmouth*, c1830 from another Monmouthshire collection.

TURNER, Joseph (c1729 - 1807)
Architect — Hawarden

In 1760s and early 1770s he lived in Hawarden. He executed a number of designs, mainly remodelling and alterations to existing fabric.**(1)**

At the end of the century he became 'the leading architect practising in Cheshire and Flintshire and appears to have been a competent designer in an orthodox late Georgian style'.**(2)**

1. 1766-73, *Chirk Castle*, Staircase; 1767-72 *Garthewin*, remodelling; 1772-4, *Erddig*, alterations, 1773, Mold, *West Tower* rebuilt. From 1775 he tended to design new buildings, for instance, *Ruthin Gaol*, 1775; *Dyffryn Aled*; 1785, *Flint Gaol*.
2. *Colvin*, p.998 *vide* Artists working in Chester.

TURNER, Robert (fl 1841)
Surveyor — Denbigh

SA 1841/32. Noted as executor of the will of Thomas Cuming *supra*.

V

VAUGHAN, David (fl 1814 - fl 1815)
Builder — Meifod

Designed & built new Rectory at Pennant, Montgomeryshire in 1814.**(1)**

1. *NLW* St Asaph, Bounty Plans 128, 1812. Very rudimentary, Georgian building with a plain symmetrical facade. Describes himself as a builder & *NLW* St Asaph, Bounty Plans 80, 1815, Llangadfan Rectory, is similarly conventional.

VAUGHAN, David (fl 1842 - fl 1857)
Architect — Bonvilston near Cardiff

He designed the Town Hall**(1)** and Police Station at Bridgend**(2)** and a church in Merthyr Tydfil.**(3)** Designed vicarage at Bedwas**(4)**

1. *PP*, p.47 (illustrated).
2. *Ibid.*, p.48 (illustrated).
3. *Ibid.*, p.84 (illustrated). *PP*, p.227 also mentions Vaughan but *Colvin* omits him. Not in *Girouard*.
4. *NLW* Llandaff Bounty Plans 7, 1857 & *NLW* Llandaff Bounty Plans 114, 1846. NLW Llandaff, Bounty Plans 97, 1845 Pendoylan & Bounty Plans 65 Llansannor 1851, & Plan 73 Llantrilled 1845.

VAUGHAN, John (1745 - 1824)
'Sion Grythor/Sion Fychan'
London
Portrait painter — [Ruthin]

Born in Conwy, the son of Richard Vaughan, glover.**(1)** It appears that John and his elder brother William Vaughan (1743-1827) moved to London before 1802. Portrait attributed to him of *Bardd Alaw*.**(2)** A painting of *Twm o'r Nant* by this artist was presented by Goodman Roberts of Ruthin in 1814. This may suggest that the artist had been resident or at least visited Ruthin around this date.**(3)**

1. *DWB*, p.1005. *Arch.Cam.*, Vol. 20 (1920), pp.277-279, article by D. Lleufer Thomas provides biographical information not included in *DWB*. See also Ffransis Payne Papers 837, John Vaughan. His portrait of *Owen Myfyr* was exhibited at the *RA* in 1823.
2. *PL* kindly provided this information. *NMW* has a portrait of *Iolo Morganwg* (A702) watercolour, 7.9x6.7cm.
3. *Arch.Cam. op. cit.*, p.278.

VILLIERS & ANDREWS (fl 1858 - 1884)(1)
Photographers — Newport
59 High Street

1. The company moved many times in this period, information appears in the local Trade Directories.

W

WADE, H[enry] (fl 1848)

Surveyor — Pwllheli
Draughtsman — Brynberllan

Worked on one tithe map.**(1)** He recorded that he had just commenced business in 1848.**(2)**

1. *Davies Atlas*. He may have moved to Pwllheli after surveying this map. *Eden* III p.258.
2. *Caernarvon & Denbighshire Herald*, 14 October 1848, p.4.

WALKER, Samuel (fl 1808 - fl c1820)

Porcelain painter & worker — Nantgarw

Moved from Worcester to Nantgarw with William Billingsley in November 1813.**(1)**

1. John, W.D., *William Billingsley* (Newport, 1968), pp.32-60, describes Walker's and Billingsley's joint careers at Worcester, Nantgarw, Swansea and Coalport.

WALLACE, Alfred R. (1823 - 1913)

Architect — Neath
London Road

Born at Usk, Monmouthshire, he appears to have worked from Neath.**(1)**

1. *Davies Atlas. Eden*, III, p.260, notes surveys in Wales, the UK, Brazil and the Far East. Brother of William Wallace.
   Hunt, 1849, p.83; *ibid.*, 1849, p.83. (It also includes a John Wallace.)

WALLACE, William G. (c1809 - 1846)

Surveyor — Neath

The brother of A.R. Wallace.**(1)**

1. *Eden*, III, p.260, notes a William G. Wallace of Neath who was an estate and land surveyor.

WALLIS, Charles (fl 1800 - fl 1840)

Architect and builder — Swansea

He worked both in South Wales and Bristol.**(1)** In 1802-4 he remodelled Penpont House, near Brecon & worked at Dunraven Castle. In 1805 his plan for the *House of Correction*, Cowbridge was accepted. After various projects in South Wales he moved to Dorset in mid 1820s.**(2)**

1. *Swansea Guide*, 1813, Appendix [no pagination].
   Colvin p.1019. John Francis (Auctioneers, Carmarthen 1977), sold a *Plan for the Hotel Charles Bristol 1815.*
2. *Lloyd* pp.62-63 notes buildings in Swansea & The Countess of Huntingdon's Chapel, Penclawdd.

WALTERS, James (fl 1822)

Surveyor — Newport, Monmouthshire

Built the rectory at Michaelston-y-Vedw, Monmouthshire.**(1)**

1. *NLW* Llandaff, Bounty Plans 86, 1822. Not in *Eden*.

WALTERS, John (fl 1791 - fl 1830)

Portrait and sign painter — Denbigh

He painted portraits of Erddig employees in 1791-3, and again in 1830.**(1)** The paintings which are still hung at Erddig, show a range of influences suggesting that he developed considerably from a local genre to a more mainstream treatment of portraiture.

He was employed by Philip Yorke who was a liberal minded patron.**(2)** Yorke had been painted by Thomas Gainsborough and perhaps the fluid, free treatment of paint in the 1830 work was the result of Walters seeing the portrait at Erddig.**(3)**

1. *Waterson* illustrated as follows: *Jack Hemshaw* Gamekeeper, 1791, p.141; *Edward Prince* Carpenter frontispiece; *Thomas Jones* Butcher, 1796, p.79; *Jack Nicholas* Porter, 1790s, p.100; *Jane Ebrell* Spider Brusher, 1793, frontispiece (cover); *William Williams* Blacksmith, 1793, p.123; *Edward Barnes*, 1830, p.143; *Thomas Rogers*, 1830, p.57. *Thomas Pritchard*, 1830 (not in *Waterson*).
2. Yorke had considerable humour and compassion. Each portrait is inscribed with a poem by his hand. He recorded in his diary 1793: 'September 28 Saturday / Walters painted two portraits Paid 4.40 / Place in coach to [?] 2.20', Hawarden R.O., D/E/802.
3. Gainsborough Thomas, *Philip Yorke*, c1779, 124 x 99 cm; *Waterhouse, Ellis, Gainsborough* (1958), p.97, No. 746.

WALTERS, William (fl 1849)

Engraver — Penydarren
Merthyr Tydfil**(1)**

Possibly associated with the iron works.

1. *Hunt*, 1849, p.73.

WANKLYN, Philip Endell (fl 1835 - fl 1843)

Surveyor — Monmouth

He worked as an estate & tithe surveyor in Monmouthshire & Gloucestershire.**(1)**

1. *Davies Atlas*, location unknown *Eden* III p.260..

WARLOW, Thomas (- 1766)

Mason

SD/1766/57.

WATERS, Thomas (1814 - 1889)

Landscape painter**(1)** — Caerphilly

He was a cabinet maker, born at Navarius House, Caerphilly.**(2)** He was possibly trained as a cabinet maker in London and had moved back to Caerphilly by 1837. About this time he commenced 'the study of painting'. He was self-taught and continued painting throughout his life.

He executed scenes of Glamorganshire and Monmouthshire. One example after Waters is *Caerphilly Castle*.**(3)** A signed & dated picture *A Waterfall*, 1863 is in a private collection.**(4)**

His known work is meticulous & finely painted. He tended to use a stippling technique, similar to oil paintings of John Glover.**(5)**

1. *Witt*, p.239 (possibly the same artist), Williams, Isaac, *List of Welsh Topographical Prints*, *NMW*, p.33
2. *Cadrawd*, p.125.
3. *NLW*, PB 311, Top. C8/C10.
4. *Waterfall at Cwm Draw, Treherbert Rhonda* [*sic*] *Valley Glamorganshire* ink on paper 20x24cm.
5. Phillips, Cardiff 21 September 1994 lot 60, a pair of oil paintings *Pwllypant & Porset* 25.3x35.7cm. [*near Caerphilly*] c1850s. Both are signed. *NLW* PG 5538, PG 5539.

See Colour Illustration VII.

WATKEYS, William (1800 - 73)

Portrait and miniature painter — Swansea
Landscape painter — 29 Wind Street
2 Adelaide Place

He was born in Swansea, moved to London**(1)** for training and then returned c1832.**(2)** He continued to work in Swansea until at least 1850.**(3)**

A self portrait, c1830, and *Ann of Swansea*, c1833, are both competent examples of a well trained hand.**(4)** There are no doubt many works by Watkeys as yet unattributed. Watkeys drew several landscape views in and around Swansea. These are in the style of compositional sketches rather than finished drawings.**(5)**

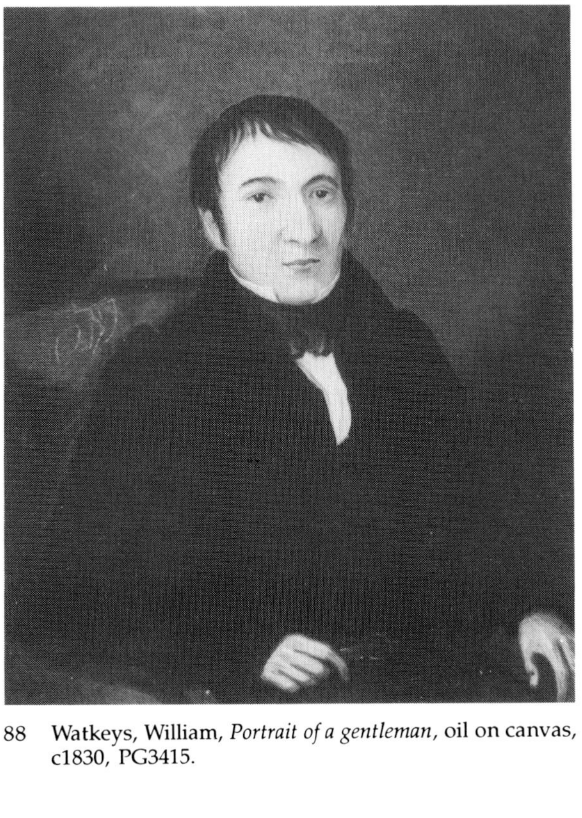

88 Watkeys, William, *Portrait of a gentleman*, oil on canvas, c1830, PG3415.

1. *Hutchison*, p.174, enrolled as a painter, 13 March 1821. He exhibited at the *RA* (two landscapes) from a London address in 1822 and 1823.
2. *Cambrian*, 20 July 1833, p.2: 'Removal, Mr W. Watkeys Portrait Painter...from Wind Street to Mrs Jenkins 2 Adelaide Place'. Also at the *RISW* there are portraits of *Dr William Hewson* and *Mrs Hewson* signed and dated 'W. Watkeys Pinx 1832'.
3. He appears in the following *Hunt*, 1848; 1849; 1850, p.132.
4. Both at the *GVS*.
5. *TL* informs me of *Oystermouth Castle*, lithograph, drawn by Watkeys & lithographed at Swansea by [J.] Grove c1830, watermarked 1830, c28x32cm (Private Collection).

WELCH, John (1810 - c1857)

Architect — Holywell
St Asaph
Conwy

Born in Overton, he worked in the Isle of Man c1830-1837, then returned to Wales c1838. All of his recorded Welsh buildings were in the North.**(1)** He provided exquisite plans for a Rectory at Llanbedrog, Caernarfon in 1838.**(2)** About 1843 he moved to Preston, Lancashire.

1. Not in *Girouard*. *Colvin*, p.1037, provides a fine biography & list of his buildings. He was the brother of Edward Welch (1806-1868) who designed & built a number of Welsh buildings, but did not live in Wales.
2. *NLW*. Bangor, Bounty Plans 21 signed & dated 1838. Also Bounty Plans 56, 1839 [Welch then at Conwy]. Possibly the same man as mentioned in *Eden* III p.265 working in 1805 in Shropshire.

WELSH PRIMITIVE (fl 1830 - fl c1853)

Landscape artist — ?Aberystwyth

Probably a local artist who had considerable talent. His work is carefully designed in great detail, using an oil painting technique for watercolour. The forms have a solid rounded appearance in the best tradition of folk art.**(1)**

The majority of the pictures are of the Aberystwyth area with a few views from North Wales. The Carmarthen Museum has about twenty pictures by this artist. These are from the same source as the collection at the *NLW*.**(2)**

1. *NLW* has a volume of drawings (56 4to), 29 x 36.5 cm, mainly of views in and around Aberystwyth, one watercolour is dated 'Dec 3 1846'. There is also a portfolio of drawings, PB 8185ff, of North Wales subjects, all approximately 29 x 36 cm. Joyner, Paul, *A Welsh Primitive* (exhibition catalogue), 1993. *Lord, Barn*, illustrates some of the watercolours. *Lord, 1994* provides several colour illustrations.
2. *Ibid.*, Joyner discusses the provenance of these pictures. They were collected by the Rev. George Eyre Evans (1857-1939). The identity of the artist is still unknown, despite great interest shown in the exhibition both at Carmarthen, Aberystwyth and Scolton Manor. Phil Garrett is submitting an M.Phil. on this subject 1996 at U.W. Aberystwyth

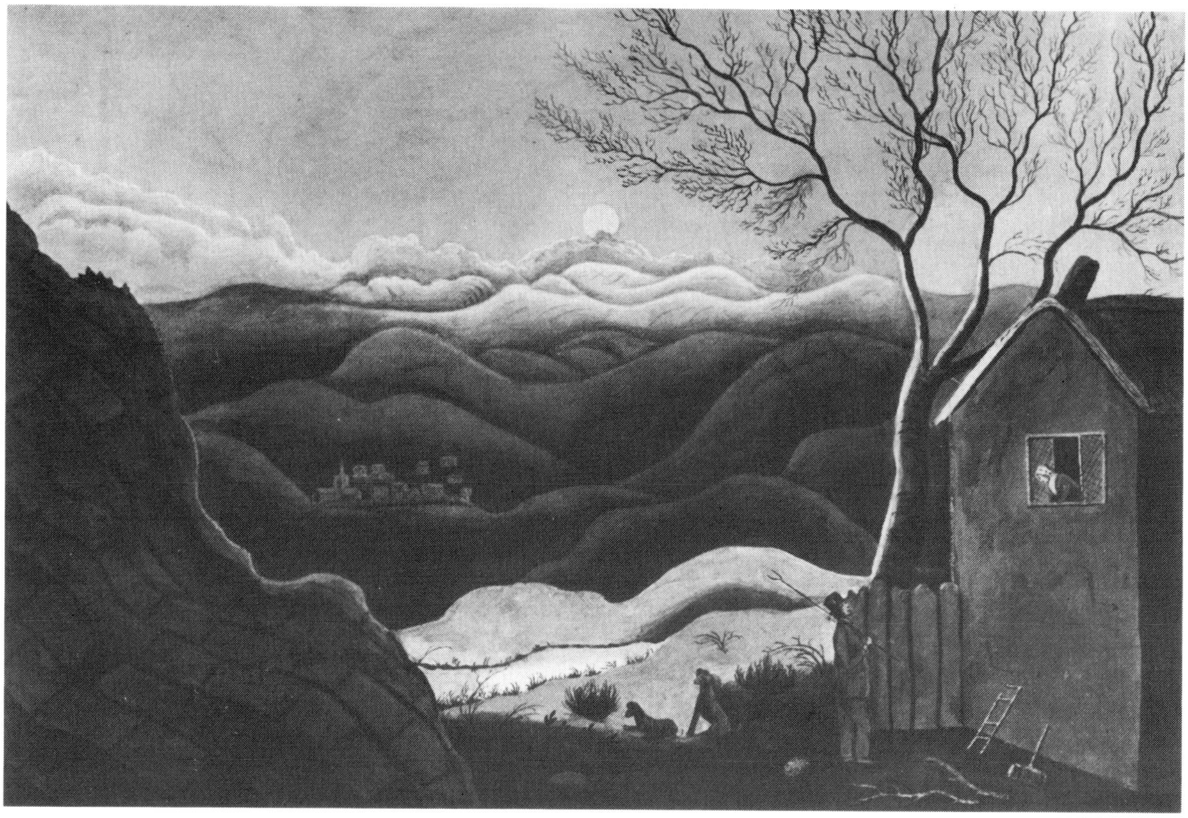

89 Welsh Primitive, *The Moon rising over Plynlimmon,* [*sic*] watercolour, 1846, PZ7329.

WHEELER, Joseph (?1775 - 1856)
Architect — Cardiff
Surveyor — Trinity Street, Aberystwyth

Wheeler was burgess in 1817. There are no known attributable works to this architect. He moved to Gloucester, probably late in life & died at his daughter's home.**(2)**

1. *Colvin,* p.1040 *Pigot's,* 1822, p.736, gives Wheeler as builder and architect at Trinity Street.
   Not in *Girouard, Eden.*
2. *TL* notes he was buried at St Mary le Crypt, aged c56.

WHITE, William 'of Swansea' (fl 1824 - fl 1839)
Portrait painter — Swansea

He was born in Swansea,**(1)** associated with J.D. Francis**(2)** and moved to London to work.**(3)** By the 1830s he was probably back in Swansea.**(4)** He may have had a practice at Swansea but did not advertise in the *Cambrian.*

1. *Mallalieu* describes White's style as 'a mixture of those of W. Henry Hunt & G. Richmond'.
2. *GVS* have two pictures from the Francis Collection by White, *Self Portrait* (DF 2454) and *Portrait of a fellow student at the RA* (DF 2032). *Walpole,* XXXVIII, has no reference to White as a student.
3. Watkins, W., *Life and Career of George Chambers,* (1841), p.87, mentions White as a friend of James Harris.
4. *BM,* 1971-10-11-7, drawing, inscribed 'W. White 1836 Swansea' 'Mrs White by her son'.

WHITLEY, Robert (- 1827)
[Mason] — Hawarden

Hawarden, 1827/1887 (I).

WHITTINGTON, William (1769 - 1849)
Surveyor**(1)** — Neath
Architect

Whittington worked as a contractor**(2)** & architect.**(3)** He was County Surveyor of Bridges from 1828. He died at Neath following an accident.

1. *Colvin* p.1046, information from *TL.*
2. For instance he built Glanusk Park to the design of Robert Lugar *vide supra.*
3. He designed Lampeter church, 1836-8; St John's, Clydach, near Neath 1847.

WHITTLE, E. (fl 1833)
Silhouette painter — Whitland, Tenby

Two portraits of ladies taken at Whitland or perhaps Tenby.**(1)**

1. *WPA,* signed and dated 'E. Whittle 1833, portrait painter, cut with scissors, Whitland'.

WILKINSON, George (fl 1777 - fl 1795)
Antiquarian draughtsman — Wynnstay
Scenery painter — Denbighshire

He was based at Chester**(1)** and worked on several occasions for the Wynnstay Theatre.**(2)** In the 1770s he also worked for Thomas Pennant and executed several Chester views included in the *Tour in Wales.***(3)** All display an excellent architectural hand and Pennant himself commented that

> 'The accurate representation of them [views of a Roman Eastern Gate at Chester] by Mr Wilkinson of this city, will give a stronger idea of them than words can convey.'**(4)**

1. *Vide* Appendix, 'Artists working in Chester'.
2. Rosenfield and Croft, Murray, 'A check list of Scene Painters working in Great Britain', *Theatre Notebook*, Volume 20, 1965, No. 1, pp.42-43, provides further evidence of his Wynnstay career and work elsewhere.
3. *NLW*, Pennant, Thomas, *Tour in Wales* (London, 1770, 1778), Volume 1, London, facing p.122, 3 pen and ink drawings, 2 approximately 20.4 x 24.5 and the other 31.5 x 26 cm. *Tour in Wales* 1778, Volume II, has a MSS list in the hand of David Pennant which states that three drawings of a hypocaust were drawn by Mr Wilkinson.
4. *Ibid.*, 1784, p.115; p.116 has a sketch of an altar by Wilkinson and the following page has a similar work.

WILLETS, Thomas (-1802)
Surveyor — Brecon

BR/1802/9. Not in *Eden*.

WILLIAMS, D. (fl 1818)
?Artists' colourman — Pwllheli

He was a general grocer and also kept a large variety of paints.**(1)**

1. *UCW Bangor*, MS 3592, no 53.

WILLIAM, David (- 1831)
Mason — Llangyfelach
Berllandywyll
near Clydau

SD/1831/181.

WILLIAMS, D.J. (fl c1850)
Sign painter — Menai Bridge
Anglesey

Painted a large panel inscribed 'I govern all I pray for all I fight for all I pay for all.'**(1)**

1. *MWAB*, Inn sign of the Four Alls, Pant Caerhun, c 120 x 70 cm, oil on board. *Lord, 1993*, p.15 (colour illustration) & *Joyner (1989)* (colour illustration).

WILLIAMS, David (fl 1841 - 1859)
Architect**(1)** — Pentref Poeth
Carmarthenshire

He is recorded as an architect and carpenter. He designed a new chapel at Carmarthen in 1841.**(2)** His death was recorded in 1851.

1. Not in *Girouard*. *TL* drew my attention to this 'architect'.
2. *NLW*, MSS, Minor Deposit 746B, *Tabernacle Church Book*, 1835-. This includes a reference to two artisans, Mr Lewis, painter, King Street, p.19, and Mr David Williams, p.38, '28 Gorff. 1841, Ail adeiladu y Tabernacle - Spring 1842', David Williams 'fo ido [*sic*] ef dynu y plan or ty newydd', and p.57 which records David Williams's bill (Dec.15 1841): Mr David Williams Carpenter 'brought in a Bill for doing the plans of the new chapel - amount £5. £4 - given'.

WILLIAMS, David (- 1857)
Land surveyor — Swansea
Chapel Street

SD/1857/179. Also described as a mineral surveyor. Not in *Eden*.

WILLIAMS, David (- 1844)
Mason — Cardigan
Pendre Street

SD/1844/183.

WILLIAMS, David (- 1853)
Potter — Llanelli
Pottery Row
Swansea

SD/1853/118.

WILLIAMS, David Robert (- 1849)
Architect & surveyor — Brynmawr
Bailey Street

Hunt, 1849, p.98. Not in *Eden*.

WILLIAMS, Edward (1747 - 1826)
'Iolo Morganwg' — Flimston
Architect — Glamorganshire
Monumental mason
Sign painter

Iolo Morganwg was born at Pennon, Llancarfan. He became apprenticed to his father as a monumental mason at Flimston and remained there most of his life.**(1)**

He is famous for his poetry and literary pursuits but was also a fine craftsman. In 1781 John Walters addressed Iolo 'Sculptor, linguist, poet, antiquary - which is your favourite title?'.**(2)**

He trained in Glamorganshire and England. When he returned to Wales in 1779 he advertised that he made 'all sorts of chimney-pieces, Monuments, Tombs, Head-

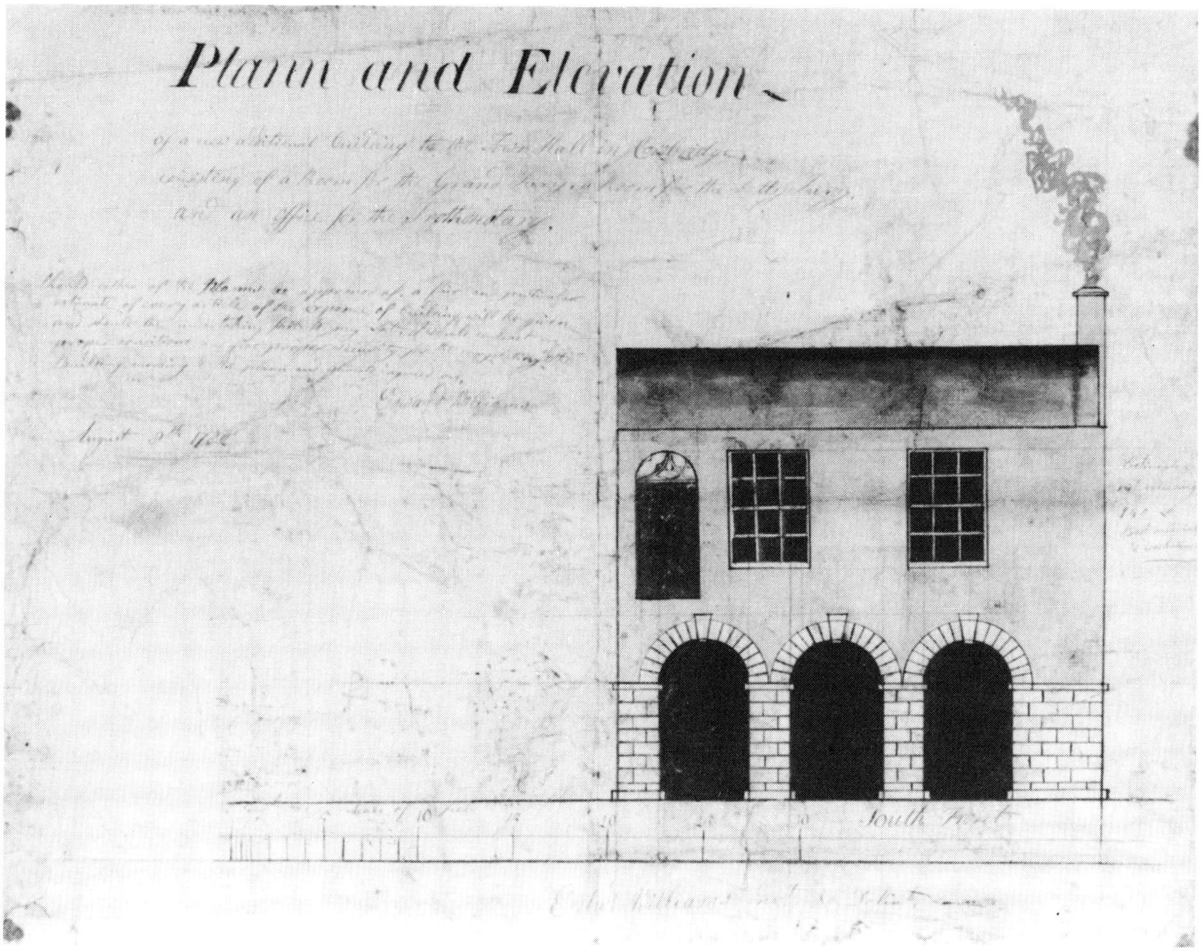

90 Williams, Edward, 'Iolo Morganwg', *Town Hall, Cowbridge,* pen & ink, 1782, MS 21416E (126), p.31.

stones, and every other Article in the MARBLE and FREESTONE MASONARY in the newest and neatest manner'.**(3)**

Extant drawings of his monuments are in a range of styles.**(4)** Evidence does suggest that he preferred Gothic ornament but he was capable of designing a modern Classical building.**(5)**

He also painted letters on gravestones, shopboards, coffin breast-plates, waggons and carts.**(6)** Iolo offered a comprehensive service to his community in a style probably far superior to the average craftsman.

1. *DWB* and Williams, G.J., *Iolo Morganwg,* (1956).
2. Williams, *ibid.*, Volume 1, p.349.
3. *NLW*, MS 2142OE (130), hand-bill published by Iolo. He also stated that he had worked 'for many years...under the best Masters'.
4. *NLW*, MS 2147E (127), contains a good collection of drawings of monuments by Iolo. A stone by Iolo is at St Mary's Church, Glamorganshire, *Robert Rees*, 1780 (cited - Williams, *op.cit.*, p.348.)
5. *NLW*, MS 2147E (126), pp.1ff, drawings for a Town Hall at Cowbridge, 1782, is Classical but has Gothic details. *See also* p.60, *Gothic Summer house*, drawing; *NLW*, MS 13120B, pp.257-8, notes on 'Gothic Cornices'.
6. Williams, *op.cit.*, p.358.

WILLIAMS, Edward (fl 1844)
Surveyor — Mold

Designed & built vicarage at Mold, 1844.**(1)**

1. *NLW* St Asaph, Bounty Plans 113, 1844. Not in *Eden.*

WILLIAMS, Rev. Evan (1816 - 1878)
'Ifan y Limner' — North Wales
Portrait and landscape painter — Caernarfon

Williams was born at Lledrod, Cardiganshire. He worked for some time as a missionary in London, then moved to Shrewsbury in 1848 and finally to Caernarfon in 1851.**(1)** He was ordained in 1859 but appears to have kept an interest in art.**(2)**

His portraits, despite awkward proportions are fine character studies.**(3)** From 1848-1849 he published the first attempt in Welsh to discuss the history and philosophy of painting.**(4)**
His landscapes of Snowdon are considered his finest work.**(5)**

In 1857 he published a review of the Manchester Exhibition. It is interesting that he saw the main importance of that event as a force for cultivating morality, especially in the young. He also focused largely on the works of Richard Wilson, who he thought was the most poetical of British landscape painters.**(6)**

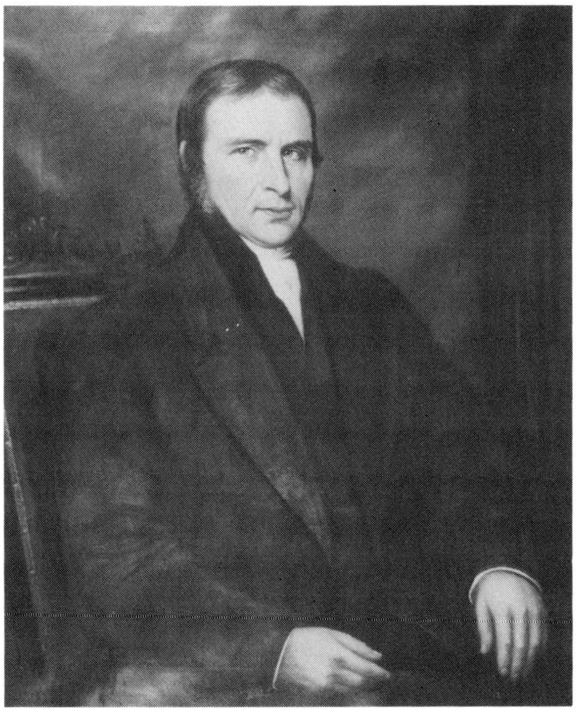

91 Williams, Evan, *John Jones*, oil on canvas, c1840, PZ3611.

1. *DWB* main source for biographical information.
2. *NLW*, MS 14026B, letter 30 to Mr Jones, Aberystwyth, dated 27 August 1865, signed 'Artist'.
3. *MWAB* has three portraits by Williams: *Eben Fardd*, signed and dated 'E Williams pinx 1851'; *Dafydd Jones* and *Edward Morgan*.
4. Articles appeared in *Y Traethodydd*, 'Y Gelfyddyd o Arlunio' [The Art of Painting], October 1848, pp.423-434; January 1849, pp.44-52; April 1849, pp.166-177; July 1849, pp.357-369; October 1849, pp.521-527.
5. *DWB*.
6. *Traethodydd* 'Arddangosiad Trysorau Celfyddyd [Exhibition of Art Treasures] July 1857, pp.329-341. Published catalogue: *Art Treasures of the United Kingdom*, Manchester: Bradbury & Evans, 1857 indicates a number of Wilson paintings.

WILLIAMS, Frances [Mrs] (fl 1850 - 1857)
Landscape artist — Glangwna, Caernarfon

Produced a panorama of Snowdon c1850.**(1)** She was married to Rev. James Williams (1790-1872).**(2)** The family were wealthy & Frances was able to devote considerable time to charity. She worked with the early lifeboat society & painted a view of *George IV at Holyhead*, which she lithographed & sold in aid of the Anglesey Association for the Preservation of Life from Shipwreck.**(3)**

Frances was probably taught to draw but rarely used her talent.

1. *NLW* Drawing Volume 65 watercolours, *Panorama of Eryri Mountains* c1850, 22.5x139.5cm, extensively inscribed. This was probably the original drawing for the several editions of *A Panoramic Sketch & Short description of Eryri Hills* (Caernarfon, c1851). The print is initialled N.M.G.
2. *DWB* p.1044. He was Rector of Llanfair-yng-Nghornwy & they lived at Glangwna.
3. Hughes, Rev. R. *Enwogion Môn* (Dolgellau, 1913), p.205 notes that Frances was 'yn arlunydd o fedr' & mentions the George IV picture. This is expanded in *The Transactions of the Anglesey Antiquarian Society*, 1957 pp.20-25. The landing occurred in August 1857.

WILLIAMS, H. (fl 1835 - fl 1843)
Surveyor — Swansea, Goat Street

Davies Atlas. Eden, III, p.270.

WILLIAMS, Henry (fl 1835 - fl 1843)
Surveyor — Newport

Davies Atlas. Eden, III, p.270.

WILLIAMS, Henry (- 1854)
Mason — Pembroke, Denbigh Dock

SD/1854/6.

WILLIAMS, Henry (- 1815)
Mason — Gwenddwr, Breconshire

Probably his son took over the mason's business at the same address.**(1)**

1. *BR*/1815/32. *Vide* Henry Williams *infra*.

WILLIAMS, Henry [Junior] (- 1844)
Mason — Gwenddwr, Breconshire

Possibly the son of Henry Williams *supra*.**(1)**

1. *BR*/1844/26.

WILLIAMS, Hugh Grecian (1773 - 1829)
Landscape painter — Hafod, Cwm Ystwyth

Recorded as staying at Hafod for some time in 1805 by Thomas Johnes.**(1)**

1. *NLS*, Liston MS 5609, letter by Thomas Johnes dated 1805.

WILLIAMS, J. (fl 1822)
Slate carver — Dyffryn Ogwen

Signed and dated a slate, 1833.**(1)**

1. Caffell, G., *Llechi Cerfiedig Dyffryn Ogwen* (1983), p.15.

WILLIAMS, J.T. (fl 1835 - fl 1843)
Surveyor
Pontypridd**(1)**
Glog
Pontypool**(2)**

1. *Davies Atlas. Eden*, III, p.270.
2. *NLW*, Bounty Plans 44, 1854 designed vicarage at Llanfaches, Monmouthshire.

WILLIAMS, James (fl 1842 - fl 1859)
Patchwork artist
Wrexham
College Street

A tailor**(1)** who assembled a patchwork quilt from 1842-52. It illustrates biblical and genre subjects in a bold naive style.**(2)**

1. *Slater's*, 1858-9, gives him as 'tailor'.
2. *WFM*, quilt, 305 x 274 cm. Illustrated in Ayres, J., *English Naive Painting*, p.154.

WILLIAMS, James (- 1859)
Mason
Johnston
?Vope Hill

SD/1859/226. Also described as a bachelor.

WILLIAMS, John (fl 1822)
Portrait painter
Merthyr Tydfil

Deaf and dumb brother of Penry Williams, he worked as a glazier.

> 'who also suffered from very weak eyes, was fond of making pencil sketches of his friends. I remember seeing some sketches of my parents and of myself - done when I was about three years old - and they showed a decidedly artistic feeling. But he lived and died in Merthyr.'**(1)**, **(2)**.

1. *Wales*, Volume 12, 1895, p.136. Also reported in Holley, T.F., 'Joseph Edwards & Merthyr Tydfil', *Merthyr Historian* (Vol. 4), 1989, p.88.
2. *CM* has a pen and ink portrait of *Thos Evans*, signed 'J. Williams 1822', 11.6. x 8.9 cm.

WILLIAMS, John (fl 1842)
Surveyor
Solva
Pembrokeshire

Designed & built vicarage at Whitechurch, Pembrokeshire.**(1)**

1. *NLW* St Davids, Bounty Plans 188, 1842. Not in *Eden*.

WILLIAMS, John (fl 1849 - 1850)
Portrait painter
Abergele
Market Street

Slater's, 1849, p.6.
Slater's, 1850, p.6.

WILLIAMS, John (- 1855)
Mason
Moylgrove
(Glandŵr-fach)
Pembrokeshire

SD/1855/379.

WILLIAMS, John (fl 1835 - fl 1847)
Surveyor
Swansea

Davies Atlas; Eden, III, p.270.

WILLIAMS, John (fl 1772 - fl 1811)
Surveyor
Newland near Margam

Surveyor to South Wales Association for the Improvement of Roads.**(1)** Worked in Glamorganshire.**(2)** W. Weston Young took over Williams's surveying and patronage in 1811.**(3)**

1. *Eden*, III, p.270.
2. *NLW*, Estate maps, *Bonvilston*, 1772, and *Neath Lower*, 1786, 1792 (just two examples of six surveys). Phillips, D. Rhys, *History of the Vale of Neath* (1925), 'John William, of Margam', p.324. Thomas, H., *A Catalogue of Glamorgan Estate Maps* (Cardiff, 1992), contains many references to this surveyor.
3. *Nance*, p.490, 'a leading Glamorgan surveyor died and Young at once took advantage of the opening thus made for him.'

WILLIAMS, John (c1772 - fl c1796)
Portrait painter
Llanddarog
Wernogydd

Drew a portrait of William Williams, Pantycelyn (1717-91) many years after his death. The sketch was executed in a MSS volume, originally the property of Rev. Robert Jones and recorded as at Swansea Library in 1934.**(1)**

This sketch was the original for the two portraits done of Pantycelyn, the small vignette published in Mackenzie's work and the larger version for display.**(2)**

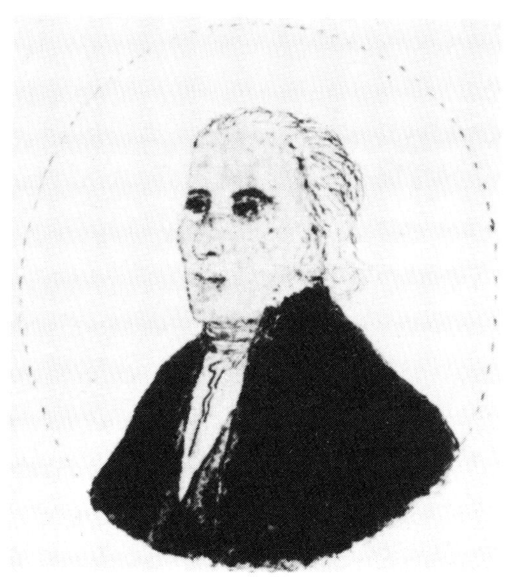

92 Williams, John, *William Williams Pantycelyn*, watercolour c1796?, PB8426 (Central Library, Cardiff has the original watercolour).

1. *W.W. Price*, Vol. XXX, p.76, copy of local newspaper (*Cambrian?*), dated 2/4/1934 (Swansea MS I/518). Photograph in Ports A, *PA* 8426. James, E. Wyn, 'Lluniau o Williams Pantycelyn', *Barn*, Awst/Medi, Rhifau 343-344, 1991, pp.62-63, illustrates this portrait.
2. Jones, J.R. Kilsby, *Holl Weithiau Prydyddawl a Rhyddieithol* (London, [1868]). Illustrated in Hughes, Glyn Tegai, *Williams Pantycelyn* (Cardiff, 1983), frontispiece.

WILLIAMS, Mathew (1732 - 1819)

Land surveyor — Llangadog, Llandeilo Fawr

He was born probably in the Llangadog area, where he is reported living in 1774.**(1)** He moved to Rhos-maen (Llandeilo) by 1788. He was a prolific surveyor in Carmarthenshire and surveys range from 1780 to 1805.**(2)** He produced several almanacks in Welsh, published from Carmarthen.**(3)**

He died and was buried at Llandeilo. He evidently had a good collection of books and texts in his home. Williams was unique as a land surveyor and scholar working and living in Wales.**(4)**

1. *DWB* has a detailed entry on this man. *Eden*, III, p.270.
2. *NLW*, MSS Maps, note surveys in the Llandeilo area, including Talley, Conwil Caio, Llangadog and Llanwrda. Many of these come from the Llwyn y Brain Collection.
3. *DWB*. These were dated from 1775 to 1815.
4. *SD*/1820/90 (I): the inventory is detailed including: 'Book case & books 12.00 - he had a considerable collection - 'Old watch 1.10.6 / Surveying Instruments 3.3.0.' His estate was calculated at £40.0.0, nearly a quarter of this being books and book cases.

WILLIAMS, Penry 'Cymro Bach'(1) (1802 - 1885)

Merthyr Tydfil

Portrait painter
Landscape painter

He was the son of a house painter and worked in his home town**(2)** before moving to London and training at the *RA*.**(3)**

Amongst the pictures produced in Wales are a series of South Wales waterfalls**(4)** and a townscape, *Merthyr Riots*,**(5)** both probably painted in c1816. In 1819 he worked at Aberpergwm for one month.**(6)** Williams moved to Rome in 1826 and remained there except for occasional visits to Britain.**(7)**

Just before he left for Rome he produced a fine series of watercolours, all similar to the Cyfarthfa watercolours.**(8)** There are several excellent examples of his small portraits of the Cyfarthfa foreman *William Williams*.**(9)**

1. *NLW*, MS 16704D, letter from Rome dated 1849, signed 'Cymro Bach'.
2. This is the traditional belief, mentioned by *Mallalieu* and *Mardy Rees*. A recent, extensive study of Williams also supports this belief. Mr Derrick Webley's monograph on Williams has recently been published by *NLW*. He notes that Penry's father William Williams also worked at one time as a stone-cutter.
3. *Hutchison*, p.175, 4 April 1822, 'painter'.

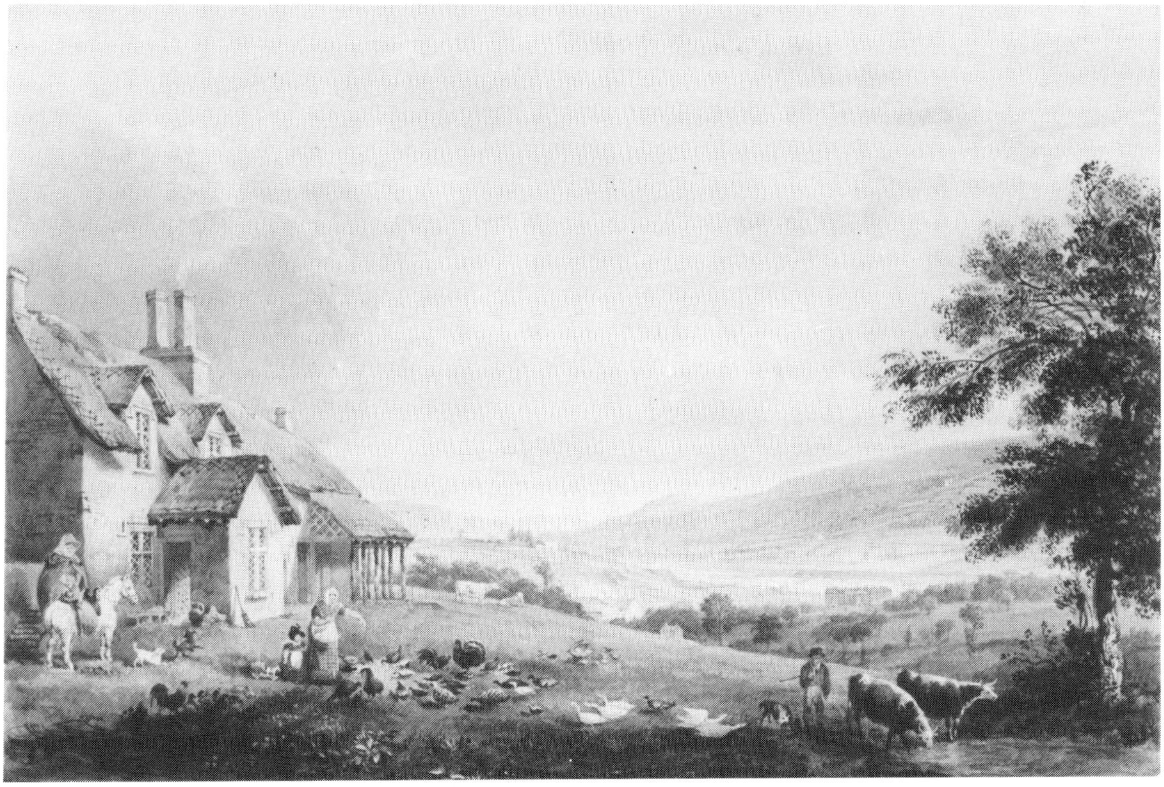

93 Williams, Penry, *Gwaelod-y-Garth*, watercolour, 1822, Drawing Volume 432, p.1, PG5346.

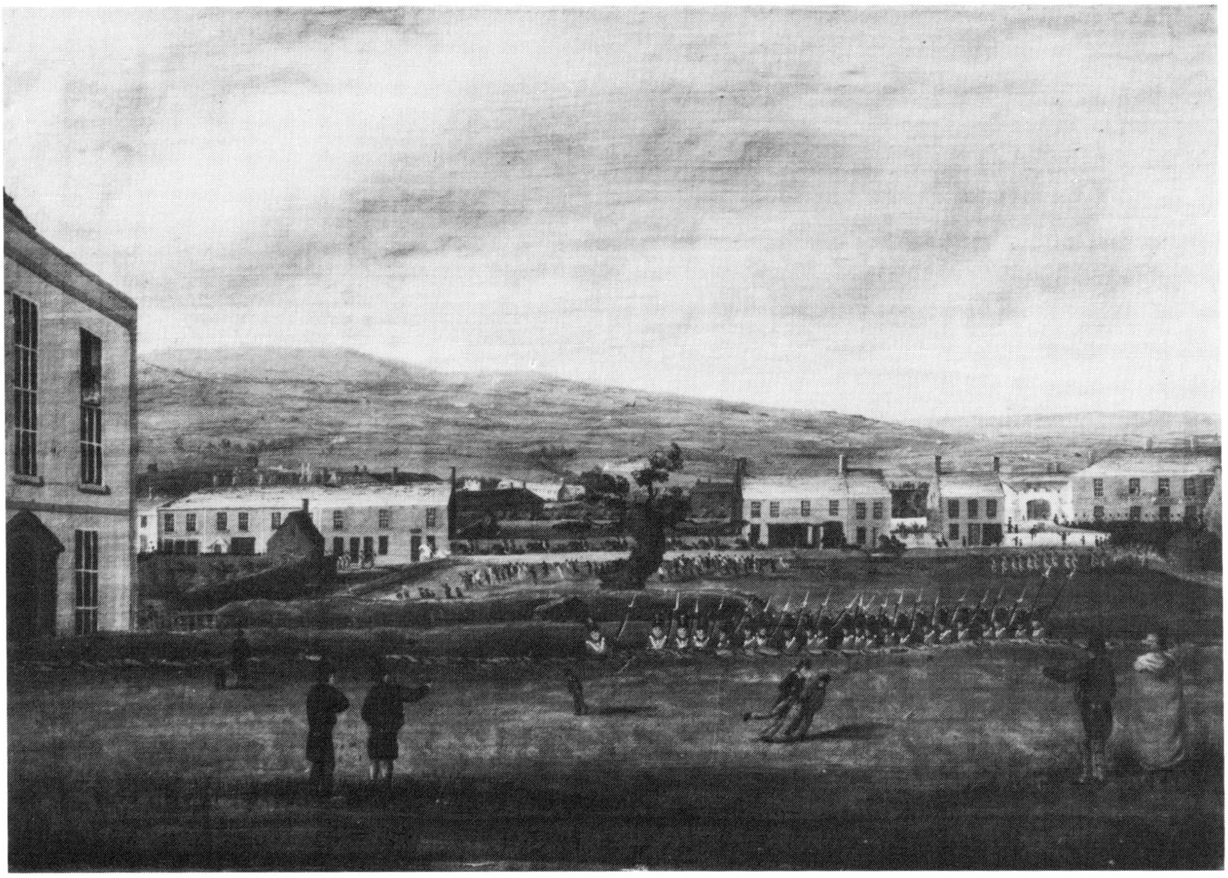

94a Williams, Penry, *Merthyr Riots*, oil on canvas, 1816, Cyfarthfa Castle Museum, Merthyr.

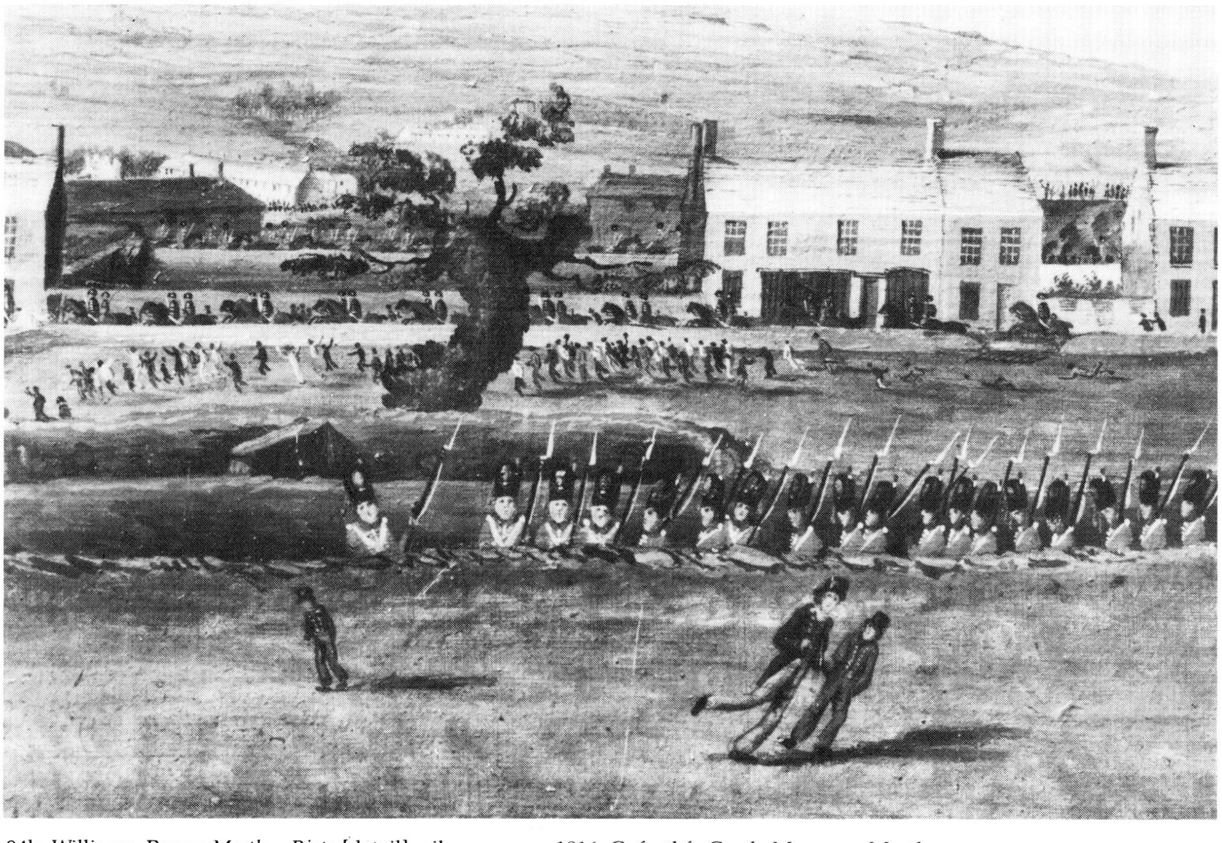

94b Williams, Penry, *Merthyr Riots* [detail], oil on canvas, 1816, Cyfarthfa Castle Museum, Merthyr.

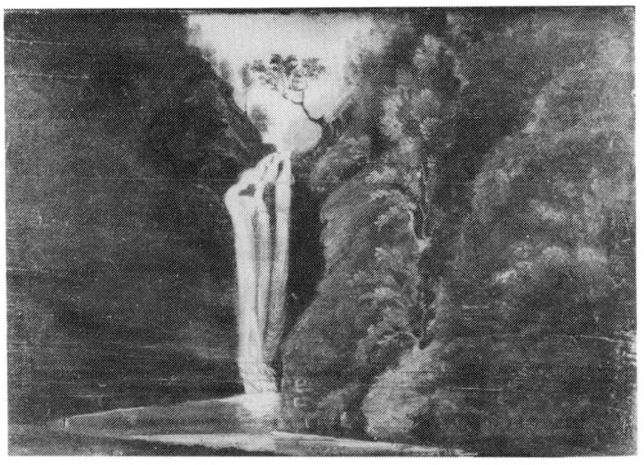

95 Williams, Penry, *Waterfall, [Ysgwyd Einion Fall]*, oil on board, c1819, Cyfarthfa Castle Museum, Merthyr.

4. *CM*, Merthyr Tydfil, all oil on board, c32 x 24 cm. (OP65) *Ysgwd Fall (or Scwd) Einion Gam on the Perddyn; [Waterfall]; Upper Clyngwyn Fall; [CilHepste?]*. A monumental series of pictures. This group was mentioned by Tomos, D., *Michael Faraday in Wales* [1972], p.147, letter by Faraday to J. Guest, 20 July 1819, referring to a series of eight or ten oil paintings of waterfalls which 'though rough convey an excellent idea of the places they represent'. *NMW* have several oil paintings in the style on display since re-opening their gallery in the early 1990s.
5. *CM*, *Merthyr Riots 1816*, oil on board, 41.2 x 54.1 cm, signed and dated 'Penry Williams 1816'. Another version in the Museum has cruder figures and brighter colours.
6. *Vide* Paul Mellon Centre for British Art, New Haven, USA, watercolour *William Williams*, and information given by D.Webley - note on *verso*, private collection.
7. He visited North Wales in 1856/7, 1867, 1868.
8. Drawing Volume 432 (PG 5346), bought at Honiton, Devon, July 1994. The only extant complete album by Williams from this period, 1822-24.
9. The *Williams* portraits are now at *CM*, watercolour, 18.5x15cm, c1825; another important portrait is *William Weston Young*, silhouette in black ink, 15.2x18cm, c1825, *NMW*.

See Colour Illustration VIII.

WILLIAMS, Richard (fl 1821 - fl 1825)
Painter Aberystwyth

Probably a house painter but may also have executed watercolours.**(1)**

1. *NLW*, MS 2844E (Sales Book of Samuel Williams, Aberystwyth) refers to 'Richard Williams Painter Aberystwyth' purchasing on 9 June 1821 a pocket book, 23 February 1824 '2 Quires Foolscap' and 17 October 1825 '1 White Block'.

WILLIAMS, Richard (- 1844)
Mason Pontarddulais
Llandeilo Tal-y-Bont

SD/1844/135 (I): Inventory only records animals owned by deceased.

WILLIAMS, Robert (fl 1799 - fl 1804)
Surveyor Llandegai, near Bangor

Eden, III, p.270.

WILLIAMS, Robert (fl 1804 - fl 1843)
Surveyor Llansantffraid
Merionethshire?

Davies Atlas. Eden, III, p.271.
NLW, Estate Maps *Llandegai*, dated 1804, and *Llangwstennin*, 1835.

WILLIAMS, Taliesin (1787 - 1847)
'Taliesin ab Iolo' South Wales
Landscape painter

He was the son of Edward Williams (Iolo Morganwg) and worked as a school teacher at Gileston, Glamorganshire until 1813. From 1813-1816 he was headmaster at Neath and then moved to Merthyr in 1816 to open a new school. **(1)**

There is no evidence to suggest where he painted, or why. He was a poor craftsman. His surviving works show an interest in Classical landscape. **(2).**

1. *DWB*, main source for biography.
2. *NLW* has five examples of his work: PE 4520 [*South Wales Landscape*], oil on board, 40.5 x 59.5 cm; PE 4521; PE 4522 [*South Wales Landscapes*] (?A Pair), 27 x 38 cm (each), oil on board; PE 4523 *Mumbles Lighthouse*, oil on board, 27 x 44 cm. All are possibly dated c1800-c1840, none are signed or inscribed.

WILLIAMS, Thomas (fl 1802**(1)** - 1805)**(2)**
Land surveyor Henllan
Denbighshire

1. *Eden*, III, p.271.
2. *SA* 1805/45.

WILLIAMS, Thomas (1787 - 1847)
Builder/Surveyor Llanfrechfa
Monmouthshire

Designed & built a rectory at Panteague in 1852.**(1)**

1. *NLW*, Llandaff, Bounty Plans 95. Not in *Eden*.

WILLIAMS, Thomas Jones (fl 1844 - 1850)
Portrait painter**(1)** Caernarfon
Bank Quay

He may have been the portrait and landscape painter who exhibited from a London address at the *RA* 1841 and 1850; *BI* 1835, 1837 and 1842; Suffolk Street 1831, 1835.

1. 1849, p.20.
   Slater's, 1850, p.20.
   PL informs me that there are MSS relating to this artist, dated 1844, in the Gwynedd Archive.

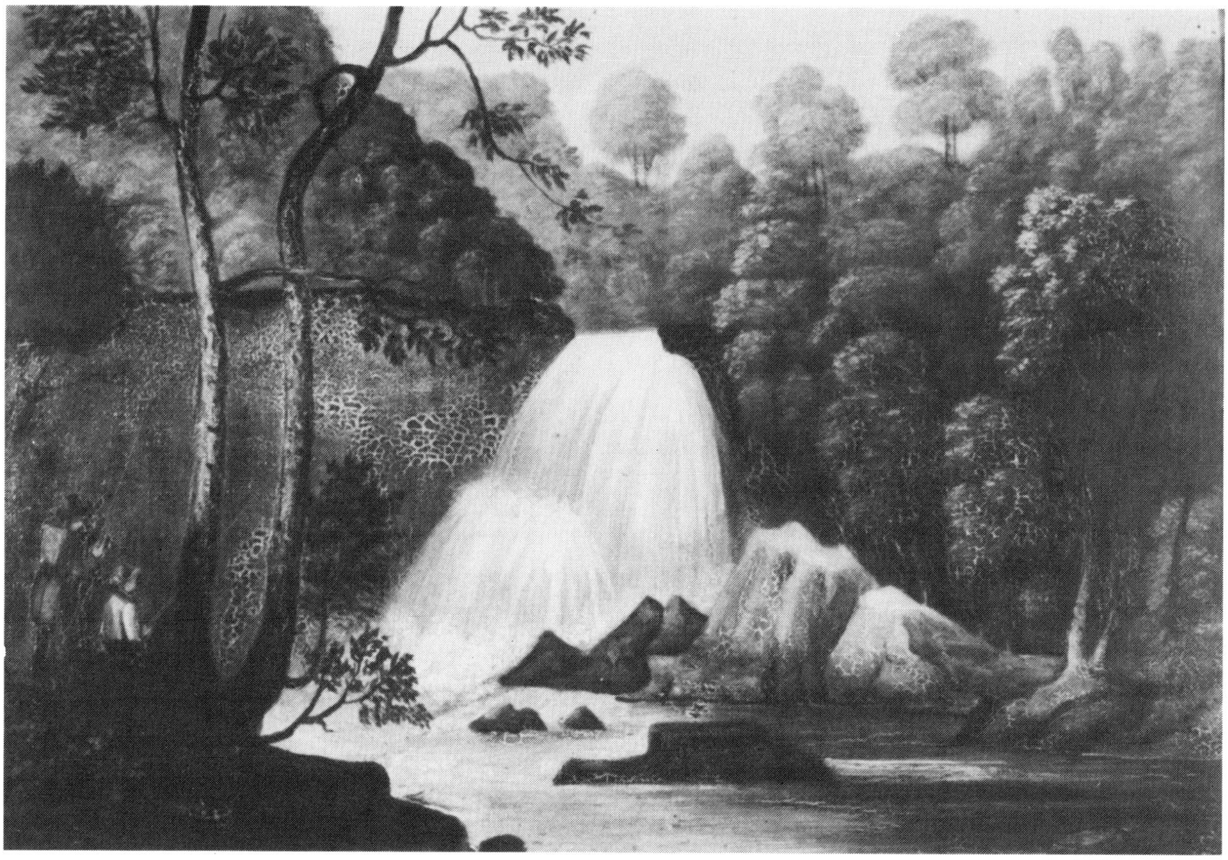

96 Williams, Taliesin, *Landscape, South Wales,* oil on board, c1830, PE4522.

WILLIAMS, W.P. (fl 1841)
[Artists'] colourman
Caernarfon
Bridge Street

Advertised that

> 'he has always on Sale on extensive Stock of white, black, green and other Paints together with all kinds of Oils and varnishes.
>
> Gentlemen who have been accustomed to procure these articles from England would, upon trial, find that they would be served upon equally liberal terms...'**(1)**

1. *Caernarvon and Denbighshire Herald,* 29 May 1841, p.2. *Ibid.,* 5 June 1841, p.1.

WILLIAMS, Watkin (fl 1756)
Engraver
Downing
Flintshire

Mentioned in a biography of Thomas Pennant as 'a person who resided at Downing, in the capacity of a humble companion to his father'.**(1)**

1. Pamphlet, undated, probably an extract from a contemporary periodical and written shortly after the death of Pennant (*NLW,* XCT 399, J33, pp.626-653. I am grateful to E. Rees for bringing this work to my attention). The engraving, was mentioned on p.633, published in 1756 in the *Philosophical Transactions,* Volume X, p.11 of 'Several coralloid bodies collected at Dale in Shropshire'.

WILLIAMS, William 'Llandygai' (1739 - 1817)
Surveyor
Llandygai
Caernarfonshire

Appears to have surveyed places in North Wales from 1774-1817. He was an important antiquarian and showed an interest in topography. In 1802 he published *Observations on the Snowdon Mountains.*

His connections with William Morris and the Gwyneddigion in addition to his work at the Cae-braich-y-cafn Quarry suggest his interest in delineation and surveying.**(1)**

1. *DWB,* pp.1079-1080. *Eden,* III, p.271, suggests this person is recorded as a surveyor.

WILLIAMS, William (fl 1802 - fl 1807)
Marble mason
St Florence
near Tenby

Williams excecuted mouments at Upton chapel **(1)** and Nash church **(2)**.

1. Haverfordwest Record Office. D/TE/73 Receipt dated 30 October 1802 to Williams £60 erecting monument to John Tasker at Upton.
2. Haverfordwest Record Office. D/TE/102 Receipt dated 4 July 1807 to Williams for engraving 93 letters @ 2d on a tombstone of Mary Rees at Nash church.

WILLIAMS, William (The Elder) (-1826)
Mason
Llan-faes
Breconshire

Probably the father of William Williams *infra*.

BR/1826/31.

WILLIAMS, William (-1842)
Mason
Llan-faes
Breconshire

BR/1842/42.

WILLIAMS, William (fl 1835 - fl 1843)
Surveyor
Mold
High Street

Davies Atlas. Eden, III, p.271.

WILLIAMS, William (fl 1835 - fl 1845)
Surveyor
Swansea
Waterloo Street, Gower Street

Davies Atlas. Eden, III, p.271.
NLW, Estate Map, *Ystradgynlais Lower*, 1845, noted 'Land & Mineral Surveyor, Swansea'.

WILLIAMS, William (fl 1830 - 1844)
Painter
?Artists colourman
Aberystwyth
Great Darkgate Street**(1)**

He was described as a painter and glazier.**(2)** Also appeared to have been colourman possibly for artists**(3)**

1. *Pigot's*, 1835, describes him as painter, plumber and glazier.
2. *SD*/1844/145: My colleague William Troughton has supplied me with the following information: *NLW* MSS, David Samuel Papers, 'Mr Williams was a painter and glazier, the chief of this craft in all the town. Mr Williams was the son of Betty Williams, proprietress of The Eagle [The Unicorn], the Methodist Vestry.'
3. *NLW* MSS Gogerddan Collection Box 17 'Miss Lovedon's receipts'. Headed note-paper dated 27 July 1830, gives Williams also as a 'furniture painter & artist's colourman'. I wish to thank my colleague John Holmes for this reference.

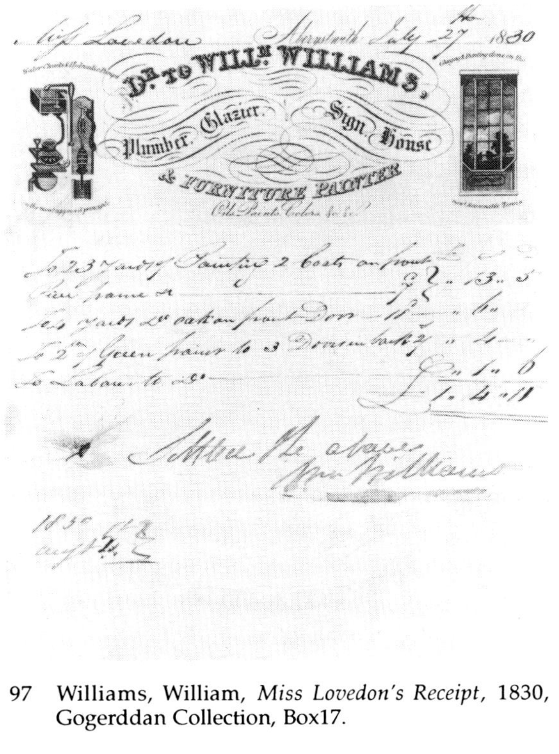

97 Williams, William, *Miss Lovedon's Receipt*, 1830, Gogerddan Collection, Box17.

WILLIAMS, William (fl 1858)
Photographer
Abergavenny
Brecon Road

Slater's, 1858.

WILLIAMS, William M. 'Ap Caledfryn' (1837 - 1915)
Portrait and landscape painter
Caernarfon

Williams was born in Caernarfon and a tradition states that his first drawing lesson at the age of six was given by Hugh Hughes.**(1)**

The earliest known example of his work was a portrait taken from a Daguerreotype.**(2)** His best work was accomplished in the latter part of the century.**(3)**

1. *DWB* main source of biographical details.
2. *NLW*, PZ 3637, *Portrait of the late Ieuan Gwynedd*, from a Daguerreotype taken in 1851, oil on canvas, 43.1 x 75.5 cm (very bad condition), signed and dated 'W.M. Williams - 5-60'.
3. Williams will be included in a proposed dictionary of the modern period.

WILSON, Alexander (fl 1850)
Artist
Cardiff
St Mary Street

Slater's, 1850, p.22.

WILSON, Richard R.A. (1713 - 82)
Portrait and landscape painter
Colomendy
Penegoes

Wilson was born at Penegoes,**(1)** 'under his father he received an excellent classical education, in the course of which he showed numberless instances of his prevailing love of the arts'.**(2)** Another early source notes that 'the walls of his father's house... were covered with rude attempts in outline: a burnt stick was his pencil'.**(3)**

In 1729 he was sent to London to study under Thomas Wright.

Wilson retained strong links with Wales through the patronage of Sir Watkin Williams-Wynn**(4)** and his own love of the Welsh landscape.

There were a few works which may have been executed before he left for London.**(5)**

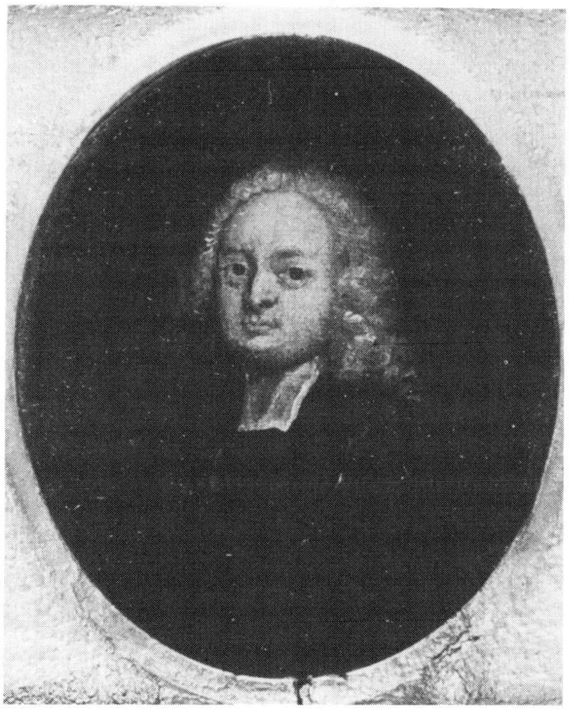

98 Wilson, Richard, *Rev. John Wilson*, oil on board, c1728, PE3545.

He returned to Wales in 1781 and lived at Colomendy; he was most probably too ill to work and died shortly afterwards. Several pictures by Wilson remained in the house after his death.**(6)**

1. Constable, W., *Richard Wilson* (1953), gives a good biography; Solkin, D., *Richard Wilson* (1983), confirms Constable's evidence. Morgan, Prys, 'Richard Wilson', *Barn*, Awst/Medi 1991, Rhifau 343-344, pp.27-35, discusses him in a Welsh context. *Bell* pp.125-134 also examines him within the 'Welsh' context.
2. Hodges, William, 'Richard Wilson' (obituary) *European Magazine*, June 1790, Volume XVII, pp.403-405, quoting p.403.
3. Anon., 'Biography of Richard Wilson', *Cambrian Quarterly Magazine*, 1831, Vol. 3, pp.161-170, quoting p.161. This source was not mentioned by Constable or Solkin but it provides some new anecdotal evidence, such as Wilson's early use of charcoal.
4. Solkin, *op.cit.* discusses this patronage; *see also* Solkin, D., 'Battle of the Ciceros', *Art History*, Vol. 16, No. 4, December 1983, pp.406-422.
5. a) *NLW*, PE 3545, *Rev. John Wilson*, oil on canvas, oval 11.4 x 9.5 cm, before 1728. A simple, generalised portrait almost certainly before his training.
   b) 'We Three Loggerheads', Inn sign mentioned in *Cambria Depicta*, p.11: 'Descending the hill I came to Loggerheads, a public house on the road. Here is a sign on the door, painted by the incomparable artist, the late Mr Wilson R.A.' The author examined this painting in 1991. It remains at the public house and is hung on the stairs. There is no reason to attribute this to Wilson on style or subject matter. Also, it appears later than 1782 and could even be a 19th century copy of the board seen by Pugh (oil on board, c200 x 200 cm).
   c) *Roland Jones*, oil on canvas, c75 x 80 cm. *At Chirk Castle*, Constable, *op.cit.*, plate 11b, dated by him 1757. Hussey, C., 'Chirk Castle', *County Life*, 5 October 1951, p.1067, states that this was 'painted by him in his native country'.
6. *Vide Constable* pp.129-131.

WINTTRAUD, Mr de (fl 1815)

Landscape painter — Swansea

Painter of the Golinos Oak, a print sold at Jenkin's office of the *Cambrian*.**(1)**

1. *Cambrian*, 22 July 1815, p.3.

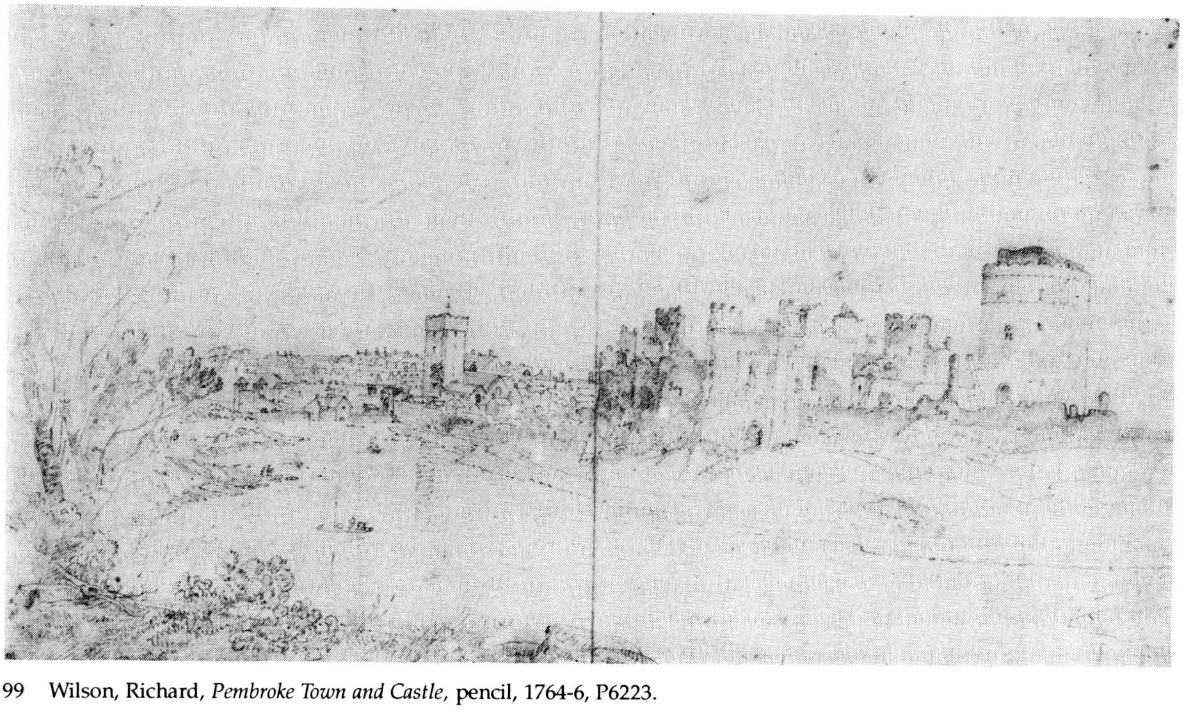

99 Wilson, Richard, *Pembroke Town and Castle*, pencil, 1764-6, P6223.

WOOD, Henry (fl 1801 - fl 1807)
Architect — Merthyr Mawr
[Mason]**(1)** — Glamorganshire

He designed and built Merthyr Mawr House, 1806-8. He is recorded in the files of the Great Sessions.**(1)**

1. *Colvin*, pp.1071-1072. He appears to have moved from London to Bristol where he worked as a mason/ architect. Presumably he moved to Merthyr Mawr by 1806.
2. *NLW*, MSS Dept, Great Sessions 4/632/5, records 12 & 13. These include his accounts and charges. I am grateful to Mr Glyn Parry for this information.

WOOD, John (1818 - 1847)
Surveyor — Caernarfon

Produced fine town plans of Aberystwyth, Bangor, Cardigan and Brecon.**(1)** He was resident in Caernarfon in 1834 & tended to move every few years.**(2)**

1. *NLW*, Estate Map index indicates that he may have also produced town plans of Merthyr Tydfil, Pwllheli and Caernarfon.
2. *Eden* III p.275 notes his career at London, Edinburgh, Northallerton, Croft, Caernarfon. He died near Edinburgh.

WOOD, Richard (- 1803)
Exhibitor of wax works — Haverfordwest

He was resident at Haverfordwest and appears to have moved from Bristol.**(1)**

1. *SD*/1803/62. A unique example of this type in Wales.

WRIGHT, Thomas(1) (fl 1815 - fl 1816)
Miniature painter — Carmarthen
Tenby
Haverfordwest

He claimed to be a London artist and offered 'This fair condition that no Lady or Gentleman, who favours him with a sitting, will be expected to take the Picture unless it is an approved likeness'.**(2)** Worked at Tenby and elsewhere for short time.**(3)** He exhibited his miniatures in his rooms at Lewis's, a Carmarthen grocer, hand painted on ivory and card.

1. This was possibly Thomas Wright (1792-1849) recorded by *Foskett*, Volume 1, p.588, an exhibitor at the *RA* in 1815, who in 1822 emigrated to St Petersburg.
2. *Carmarthen Journal*, 23 February 1816, p.[3]. *Ibid.*, 1 March 1816, p.[3].
3. *Carmarthen Journal*, 25 August 1815; *Carmarthen Journal*, 27 October 1815 at Haverfordwest.

WYNN, Sir Thomas 1st Lord Newborough (1736 - 1807)
Architect — Glynllifon
Caernarfonshire

Wynn was the son of Sir John Wynn Bart of Glynllifon. He was an eccentric & amateur architect, who built several classical monuments at Glynllifon, presumably using local craftsmen he designed & built *Fort Belan* & *Fort Williamsburg*, defences against French invasion.**(1)**

1. *Colvin*, p.1133-4.

WYNNE, Robert 'Ashbourne' (fl mid - 19th century)
Portrait painter — Garthewin Hall
Landscape painter — Llanfair Talhaearn

He painted a portrait of Colonel Robert William Wynne (1761-1844) at Garthewin.**(1)** Also his landscape of the house was executed in a similar, naive, carefully observed style.**(2)**

1. *NLW*, PB 5158, c1830, oil on canvas, 30.9 x 25.3 cm.
2. Private collection, 1837, oil on canvas, 23.8x28.9cm. Information from *WPA*. On the *verso* an inscription reads 'Robt Wynn, Ashbourne, Derbyshire'. Perhaps the artist visited his relations over the summer of 1837.

Y

YOUNG, James (fl 1830)
Oil & colour dealer — Newport, Monmouthshire
Cinder Wharf

Pigot's, 1830, p.524.

YOUNG, William Weston (1766 - 1847)
Engraver, landscape and china painter — Neath
Surveyor — Swansea

Born in Bristol and moved to Neath late 1791 or early 1798. By 1800 he was working from Aberdulais Mill. In 1803 he moved to Swansea to paint at the pottery.**(1)** His work on ceramics was particularly fine.**(2)**

He published a beautifully illustrated guide book in 1835 and he wrote, 'The drawing, etching, coloring [*sic*] and writing, being by his own hand, it is therefore truly a Welch or rather Glamorganshire work, perhaps the first of its kind.'**(3)**

Young was a competent estate surveyor. One extant map in his hand is of *Merthyr Mawr Place*, 1813. It includes a good elevation of the house and symbolic figures of Wisdom and Justice.**(4)** It appears that he worked as a surveyor between 1811 and 1814.

1. *Nance*, Appendix VIII, gives an excellent biography with extracts from the Young Diaries now housed at the Glamorgan Archives Service, Cardiff (D/D X, ch 1-30). *WW Price*, Vol. XXX, p.251, gives additional information on Young and his local connections. *Eden*, III, p.281, notes him also as a colliery surveyor. *Bell* pp.80-81 'One of the most interesting personalities who were connected with the pottery in its early days'.
2. The best collections of his china paintings are at the *GVS*, *NMW* and *RISW*. *NLW* has a sketchbook of drawings and watercolours, Drawing Volume 15.

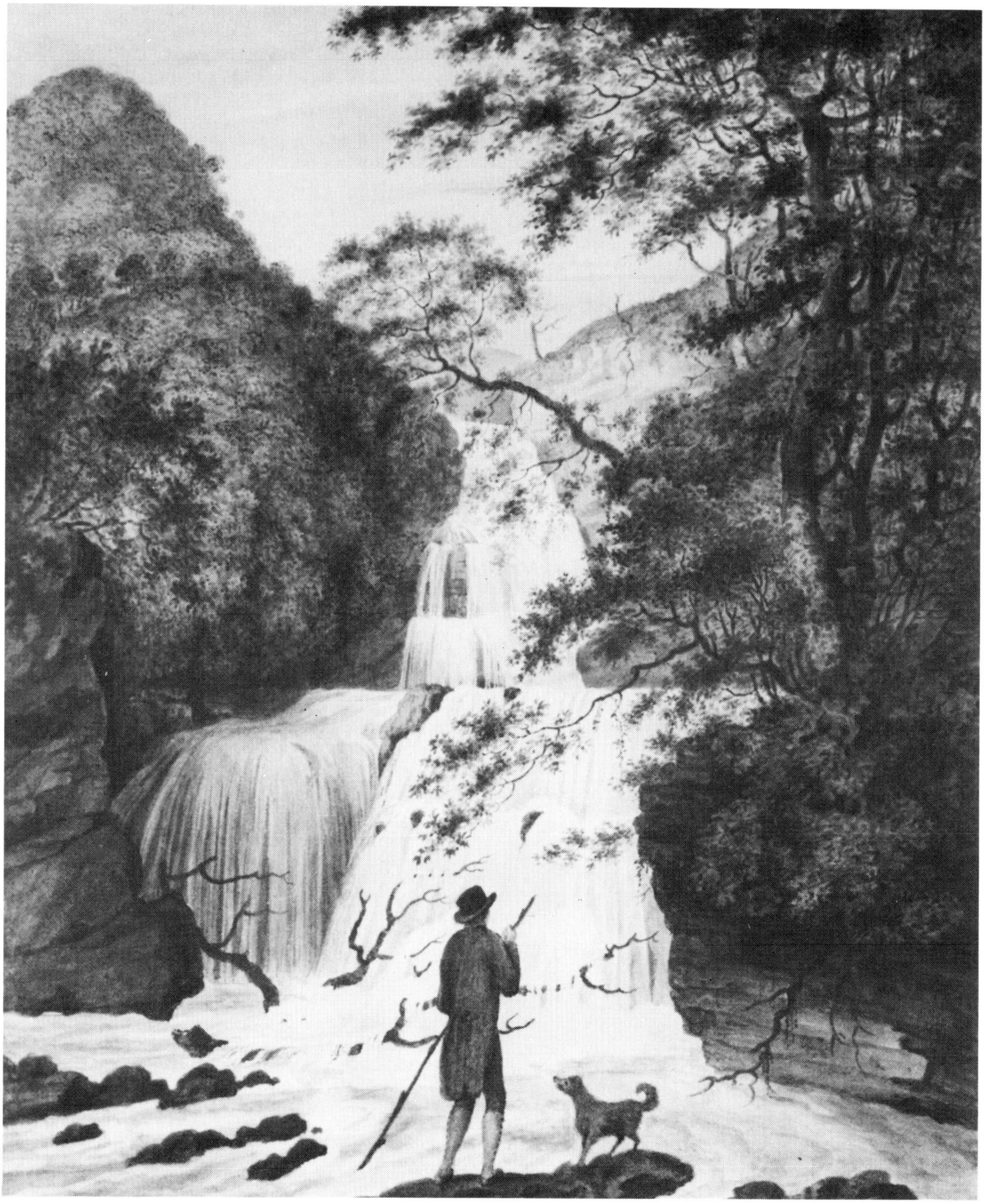

100 Young, William Weston, *Neath Waterfall*, watercolour, c1791, Drawing Volume 15, p.4 PD5765.

NMW has a portrait of Young on plaster, 15x12.5cm (A751) & another by Penry Williams c1825.

3. Young, William, *Guide to the Scenery of Glyn Neath* (London, 1835), Preface p.iv.
4. The original map is in a private collection. It is described and illustrated by Thomas, H., *A Catalogue of Glamorgan Estate Maps* (Cardiff, 1992), pp.91-92.

APPENDIX

A list of Artists working in Chester c1740-1850

Scope
The list includes artists who were resident in Chester. Sign-painters, banner painters, etchers and the more usual fine art professionals are mentioned.

Sources
The list is intended to be as comprehensive as possible. I have consulted all available sources including collections of Chester and Cheshire Record Office. Other main sources of the list were newspapers and trade directories. Occasionally I refer to *Braughton*: Mr Peter Braughton of Grosvenor Museum, Chester, who kindly lent his manuscript list of artists working in or near Chester. All the sources checked for the list of Welsh artists were also consulted for Chester artists.

As with the main list full bibliographic details will be given in the bibliography.

The *NLW* has a large collection of *Welsh* wills proved at Chester.**(1)** All have been checked. A selection of the wills at Chester from 1741-1837 have also been checked.**(2)**

Comment
A number of towns along the Welsh border had artists who worked in Wales. The architect Joseph Bromfield (c1743-1824) of Shrewsbury is a case in point. He designed several important houses in North Wales but had his residence outside Wales.**(3)** Shrewsbury**(4)** had fewer artists but had a similar commercial role in Mid-Wales as Chester in the North. Hereford, Worcester and even Bristol and Bath served the South Wales communities in the absence of local talent.

It is very likely that a number of new connections between Wales and Chester will appear as this list is used in conjunction with other material. For instance, Alfred Sumner (fl 1852) who was only known to us as a Chester drawing master is now recorded as a fine landscape painter who visited Anglesey c1852.

One point which has emerged from this listing is that from the early 1820s onwards the outlying villages and towns employed craftsmen rather than services being more centralised at Chester.**(5)**

Notes

1. I am very grateful to my colleague, Mr Tudor Barnes, for showing me his list of *Chester Wills* and for directing me to the recent editions of the *Chester*.
2. Some of the later volumes have indexed occupations and all references to architects, artists, masons, surveyors and craftsmen of that kind have been included here.
3. Caernarfonshire: *Nanhoron* 1797; Merionethshire: *Caerynwch* 1801; *Rûg*, 1802-3; *Glansevern*, 1803-7; *Nannau*, 1806; Montgomeryshire: *Churchstoke Church*, 1814-15. He owned a home at Llandrillo. *Colvin* pp.162-3.
4. The Bowen family, especially John Bowen, were particularly important. *A Panoramic View of Shrewsbury* was sold at Sotheby's 19 November 1986, lots 85 and 86 (c1740), illustrated. This shows a similarity with the work of John Attwood. William Bateman (*vide* list) worked both at Shrewsbury and Chester.
5. Compare the very few references to artists and masons working in Chester: *ibid.*, Volumes 107, 113, 120 (covering the period from 1821-1837). For instance a 'Fisher' of Bristol designed the Shire Hall, Monmouth 1724 *Colvin* p.363; John Collingwood (c1760-1831) of Worcester, designed a *House of Correction*, Swansea in 1826-8 *Colvin* p.267. Edward Haycock (1790-1870) Shrewsbury designed numerous public buildings & churches in Wales, *Colvin* pp.479-480. Anthony Keck (1726-1797) of King's Stanley, Gloucestershire built several important houses in South Wales, *Margam Orangery*, 1787-90 *Colvin* pp.569-570.

B

BAILEY, Thomas (fl 1808 - fl 1852)**(1)**
Landscape and portrait painter — Seller Street
Miniature painter

Bailey drew several views of North Wales.**(2)**

1. *Chester Directory*, 1840, p.48.
   Bagshaw, 1850, p.109.
   Williams, J., *Commercial Directory*, 1846, p.2.
   Illustration in *CAJ*, 1928, facing p.115 (William Tasker by TB).
2. *NLW*, PZ 3206, B1/1 - B56. *The Menai Bridge* is a good example of his work.

BAKER, J. (fl 1785)
Miniature painter — Apartments in Chester

Adam's Weekly Courant, 17 May 1785.

No will in *Chester*.

BASSANO, Francis (- d.1747)
Heraldic painter

Chester (1892), p.14.

BATEMAN, George [Junior] (ob 1821)

Braughton, otherwise unrecorded.

No will in *Chester*.

BATEMAN, William (1806-33)
Engraver

Bateman specialised in views of Chester and occasionally painted watercolours. He executed a fine print of Llangollen.**(1)**

No will in *Chester*.

1. *NLW*, Ffoto Album 725, 'Llangollen Bridge & Castell Dinas Bran', wood-engraving, c8 x 11 cm.

BATENHAM, George ([Senior]) (fl 1815 - 1833)
Etcher

Panoramic Delineations of the Four Principal Streets of the City of Chester, 1815 (Chester City Library).
The Stranger's Companion to Chester, 1821 (Chester City Library).

BELL, Mr
(fl 1795 - fl 1797)
Architect — Eastgate Street

The Chester Guide, 1795, p.74.
Ibid., 1797, p.75.

No will in *Chester*, not in *Colvin*.

BLOWER, William (fl 1789 - fl 1797)
Painter — Nicholas Street

Chester Cowdray, 1789, p.47.
Chester Guide, 1793, p.25 (Cuppin's Lane).
Ibid., 1795, p.75.
Ibid., 1797, p.75.

He may have been related to William Blower of Chester, a coachman who died in 1795, *Chester* (1902), p.17.

BOOTH, Miss (fl 1809)
Drawing and needlework teacher at Mrs John Wynn's

Chester Courant, 16 May 1809, p.[3].

No will in *Chester*.

BOWCOCK, William (fl 1766 - fl 1795)
Painter

Chester Record Office, examination dated 1766 (Q/E/15/51).
Chester Guide, 1795, p.[75].

No will in *Chester*.

BOWCOCKS, Miss (fl 1789 - fl 1797)
Drawing teacher — Abbey Street

Chester Cowdray, 1789, 'drawing school', p.47.
Chester Guide, 1795, p.75.
Ibid.

No will in *Chester*.

BOWMAN, Mrs (fl 1830)
Teacher of Oriental painting
Colourman
Fabric painter

Chester Chronicle, 30 July 1830, p.2, painted bell pulls and chair covers.

No will in *Chester*.

BROWN, Samuel (fl 1846 - fl 1850)
Heraldic painter

Williams, J., *Commercial Directory*, 1846, p.2.
Bagshaw, 1850, p.109.

BROWN, William and Thomas
(fl 1793 - fl 1795)
Painters — Further Northgate Street

Probably brothers/partners in business.**(1)**

1. *Chester Guide*, 1793, p.25.
Ibid., 1795, p.76.

No will in *Chester*.

BURT, Albin Robert (1783 - 1842)
Miniature painter — Northgate Street**(1)**

His mother was Welsh & Burt is recorded as having been in Wales, however although he evidently had connections with North Wales he lived in Chester, possibly London and died in Reading. He painted at least five Welsh portraits.**(2)** Burt also published an article on 'Dic Aberdaron' in the *Gentleman's Magazine*.**(3)**

1. *Witt; Mallalieu, Redgrave* p.65. *CAJ*, 1918 (Vol. 22), p.167.
2. *NLW*, D9922, *Lewis Hughes* (1750-1822), Cotterye, St Asaph, s. & d. 1820, watercolour, 31 x 22.1 cm. *R.R. Jones 'Dic Aberdaron'* (1780-1843), print after A.R. Burt published in Chester. Also: *John Jones 'Ioan Tegid'*,

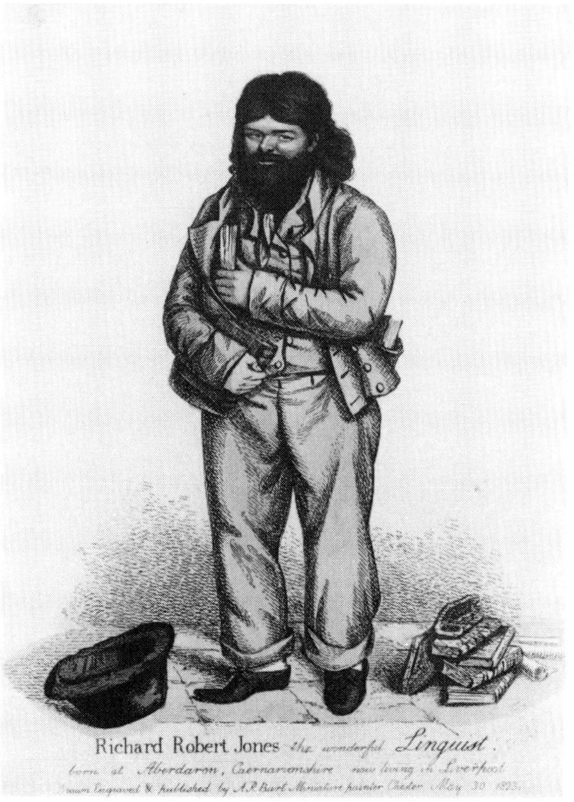

101 Burt, Albin Robert, *Dic Aberdaron*, engraving, 1812, PZ8297.

Thomas Jones engraved after the portrait by Hugh Hughes.
3. Jan. 1824, pp.65-66. I wish to thank Peter Lord for this information.

BUTLER, Mr and Mrs (fl 1831)
Drawing teachers

Chester Chronicle, 8 April 1831, p.2.

C

CALVELY, J. (fl 1784)
Land surveyor

Pennant, Thomas, *Tour of Wales* (London, 1784), p.iv, drawing of *Plastey Flints.*

CLARKE, W. (fl 1780)
Hair artist (portraits)

Adam's Weekly Courant, 19 September, 1780.

CLOWES, Daniel (1774 - 1829)
Animal painter

Edington, G., *The Clowes Family of Chester Sporting Artists* (1985).

No will in *Chester*. He sometimes used the North Wales landscape as a backdrop for his paintings**(1)**

1. Sotheby's Colonnade Sale 31 May 1995 lot 106, oil on canvas, 50.5x63.5cm shows a saddled bay outside a cottage & the Welsh hills.

CLOWES, Frederick (1801 - fl 1840)
House and sign painter

Edington, G., *The Clowes Family of Chester Sporting Artists* (1985), p.17.

CLOWES, Henry (1799 - 1871)
Landscape painter Watergate
House and sign painter

Chester Directory, 1840, p.48, 'H. and F. Clowes (Animal) Newgate Street', *CAJ*, 1918 (Vol. 22), p.167.
Edington, G., *David and Henry Clowes of Chester*, 1985.
Williams, T., *Commercial Directory*, 1846, p.2.

COLE, William (1800 - 1892)
Architect

Cole came from a family of builders from Chester. At fourteen he began a pupilage with Thomas Harrison *vide supra* & in 1829 he succeeded Harrison as County Surveyor. In 1840 he moved to Birkenhead.**(1)**

1. *Colvin* p.265-266.

COOKING, Mr (fl 1808 - fl 1820)
Miniature painter Northgate Street

Chester Courant, 28 June 1808, p.[3]. Charging two to three guineas per portrait.

No will in *Chester*.

COX, Mr (fl 1830 - fl 1831)
Miniature painter

Working at Chester for six months.

Chester Chronicle, 19 February 1830, p.2.
Ibid., 27 May 1831, p.2.

CRANE, Thomas (d.1749)
Pot [China] painter

Crane was originally from Liverpool, probably the father of Crane (1808-59), *Chester* (1892), p.45.

CRANE, Thomas (1808 - 59)
Portrait painter
Miniature and genre

Born in Chester, he moved to Liverpool, then London and returned to Chester. *Wood* states that he painted 'portraits of well known characters of North Wales'.

CRANE, W[alter] (fl 1830? - 1843)
Landscape painter
Portrait painter

Crane drew several views of Anglesey some of which were published by his uncle W. Crane.**(1)** He worked with his brother Thomas (*supra*) producing lithographs and portraits.

1. *NLW*, P 2838, B 1/2 - B33: *Beaumaris Castle.*

CUITT, George (The Younger) (1779-1854)
Engraver and landscape artist
Drawing teacher

He published various sets of antiquarian prints of Chester.

D

DAVIDSON, Ellis A. (fl 1851)
Drawing teacher

Worked at the Chester School of Art, *CAJ* 1918 (Volume 22), p.167.

DAVIES, John (fl 1835 - fl 1843)
Surveyor

Davies Atlas.

DELACOUR (fl 1777)
Heraldic painter

Mentioned in *CAJ* 1918 (Volume 22), p.167.

No will in *Chester*.

DOWNMAN, John R.A. (1750 - 1824)
Portrait artist — Eccleston, near Chester

He settled in Chester c1819.**(1)**

No will in *Chester*.

1. *Vide supra*.

E

ESTABLISHMENT OF ARTISTS (fl 1830)
Portrait practice

Portraits were taken using a delineator. This was an itinerant company of artists which had been at Liverpool for the previous two years.**(1)**

1. *Chester Chronicle*, 7 May 1830, p.2, advertised this service.

F

FERNAL (fl 1782)
Seal engraver
Miniature artist

This may have been John Fernell (fl 1724-1834) who worked mainly in Liverpool.**(1)**

No will in *Chester*.
1. *Adam's Weekly Courant*, 4 June 1782. (*Foskett*).

FINNEY, Samuel (1718/21-1798/1807)
Unspecified

Braughton, otherwise unrecorded.

G

GRIMALDI, Mr (fl 1773 - fl 1774)
Miniature artist

Adam's Weekly Courant, 6 September 1774.

He was also working in Shrewsbury: *Shrewsbury Chronicle*, 23 September 1773, p.[3] and 20 October 1773, p.[3].

H

HALTON, John Price (fl 1817 - fl 1821)
Draughtsman

He drew Chester scenes and illustrated Hanshall's *History of the County Palatine of Chester* (1817).

No will in *Chester*.

HAMLET, William (The Elder) (fl 1785 - 1816)
Portrait and miniature artist

Aris, B.G., 26 September 1785.

No will in *Chester*.

HARLING, William Owen (fl 1847 - fl 1878)
Portrait artist
Subject painter

CAJ, 1948 (Volume 22), p.167.

HARRISON, Catherine (1788 - fl 1825)
Drawing teacher

The Cheshire Sheaf 7428, August 1938, p.74.

This may have been Catharine Harrison who died in Stockport in 1837.**(1)**

1. *Chester* (1980), p.161.

HARRISON, John (fl 1801 - fl 1810)
Architect

Harrison was the nephew and assistant of Thomas Harrison *vide supra* and probably began an independant practice c1806, when he designed Sherdley Hall, near St Helens, Lancashire. By 1807 he designed *The Jewish Synagogue, Seel Street, Liverpool.***(1)**

1. *Colvin* p.465.

HARRISON, Thomas (1744 - 1829)
Architect

Harrison, the most important Chester architect in this period**(1)**, designed the *Moel Fammau Monument*, near Mold, in 1812 and the *Triumphal Arch* at Holyhead, 1822.**(2)** He also designed the *Denbigh Infirmary* 1810-13, *The Anglesey Column*, Llanfairpwll, 1816 and possibly *Glan-yr-afon*, near Mold, c1810.

1. *Colvin* pp.466-470, describes his career in detail
2. Exhibition catalogues *The Modest Genius* (Chester Museum, 1977) and *PP* included work by Harrison.

HAUCK, [Philip Elias] (fl 1783)
Portrait artist

Adam's Weekly Courant, 22 July 1783.

Possibly Philip Elias Hauck, exhibitor and member of the Society of Artists 1761-1765.

HAULTIER, George (fl 1782 - 1802)
Drawing teacher — Northgate Street
Artist (unspecified)

Chester Guide, 1782, p. (unknown).
Ibid., 1789, p.53 (Paradise Row).
Ibid., 1795, p.82 (Paradise Row).
Ibid., 1797, p.83 (Paradise Row).

It seems he retired by c1800 and was recorded as 'A gentleman' in 1802.**(1)**.

1. *Chester* (1911), p.168.

HODKINSON, Edward (fl 1851)
Surveyor

He worked on the Rectory at Llanfechan, Montgomeryshire in 1851.**(1)**

1. *NLW* St Asaph, Bounty Plans 72, 1851.

HUGGINS, William (1820 - 84)
Animal painter — The Groves

CAJ 1918 (Volume 22), p.168.

J

JONES, John (- d.1838)
Whitewasher and colourman

Chester Welsh Wills, 1838/18.

JONES, Thomas (fl c1837 - fl 1845)
Architect

He designed at least two buildings in North Wales.**(1)**

1. *Vide* main entry. *NLW*, PZ 3546/1, B7/4 - B119, *North View*, and *View of Talacre* in P 6781, B7/3 - B107 are good examples of his work. He also produced plans with a watercolour for the Rectory at Llanfachreth, Anglesey in 1837 & Llansantffraid Glynceiriog, St Asaph Bounty Plans 96, 1841.

JONES, William (fl 1810 - fl 1853)
Portrait painter — King Street

Williams, J., *Commercial Directory*, 1846, p.2.
Bagshaw, 1850, p.109.
CAJ, 1918 (Volume 22), p.170 (Queen Street)
See also *supra*.

L

LEADBEATER, John (fl 1777 - fl 1782)
Coach heraldic, Banner and sign painter — Foregate Street

Chester Chronicle, 18 April 1777, p.[1], also advertised picture restoration and cleaning.
Ibid., 25 April 1777, p.[3].
Chester Guide, 1781, p. (unknown).
Ibid., 1782, p.97.

No will in *Chester*.

LEADBEATER, Peter (fl 1781 - fl 1782)
Painter — Foregate Street

Chester Guide, 1781, p.98.
Ibid., 1782, p.97.

No will in *Chester*.

LOCKWOOD, Alfred (fl 1850)
Architect — 2 Egerton Street

Slater's, 1850, p.81. Also at Wrexham. Not in *Colvin*, *Girouard*.

M

METZ, Caroline? (fl 1773 - 1794)
Portrait Artist
Engraver

A German engraver who may have been the wife or a relative of Johann Martin Metz, *infra*. A G. Metz is recorded as painting one of the portraits at Plas Gwyn in 1777.**(1)**

Several prints are probably by the same artist.**(2)**

1. *Steegman*, Volume 1, p.20, signed and dated '[G.?] [C.?] Metz Fecit 1777'.
2. *NLW*, PZ 815, B 1/3 - B3. Baron Hill, in the Isle of Anglesey...1779; P 2818 B 1/2 - B15, View in the *Isle of Anglesey*, 1774.

METZ, ? Johann Martin (1717 - c1790)
Portrait and miniature artist — Watergate Street

Chester Chronicle, 11 April 1777, p.[3].
He was based in London and recorded as an immigrant to England in c1772.

No will in *Chester*.

1. *Waterhouse*.

MEYER, Mr [Jeremiah] (fl 1772)
Portrait and miniature artist — Northgate Street

Adam's Weekly Courant, 2 June 1772.

Possibly Jeremiah Meyer (1735-89) recorded in *Steegman*, Volume 1, pp.77, 217 (c1768 and 1765, Bronygader and Brogyntyn, North Wales).

No will in *Chester*.

MEYRICK, Robert (fl 1797)
Painter — Queen Street

Chester Guide, 1797, p.89.

No will in *Chester*.

MORLAND, George (1763 - 1804)
Miniature painter

Manchester Mercury, 27 March 1773 (*Foskett*): 'returned from Chester'.
Manchester Journal, 27 March 1773 (*Foskett*): 'miniature painter from Chester'.

No will in *Chester*.

MURRAY, Mrs (fl 1781 - fl 1782)
Engraver — Werburgh's Lane

Chester Guide, 1781, p.101.
Ibid., 1782, p.100.

No will in *Chester*.

MURRAY AND STUART (fl 1789 - fl 1797)
Engravers — Werburgh's Lane

Chester Guide, 1789, p.58.
Ibid., 1793, p.31.
Ibid., 1795, p.88.
Ibid., 1797, p.89.

No will in *Chester*.

P

PENSON, Thomas M. (Junior) (1836 - 1857)
Landscape painter
[Architect]

Vide supra

PERCY, Mr (fl 1783)
Modeller in wax

Adam's Weekly Courant, 6 May 1783.

PICKERING, George (1794 - 1857)
Landscape artist — Upper Northgate Street

He drew views of North Wales.**(1)**

Chester Directory, 1840, p.43 (Flookersbrook).
Bagshaw, 1850, p.109.

1. *NLW*, P 2832, B 1/1 - B 90: *The Menai Bridge, Bangor* (North Wales), c1850. Another example is PD1627 Top B6/5 Valle Crucis Abbey, c.1840.

PRICE, John (fl 1835 - fl 1843)
Surveyor — Chester

Davies Atlas, Eden II p.208, also notes him working at Denbigh & Ruthin.

PRICHARD, Edward (fl 1851)
Painter — No 1 George Street

Brother of John Prichard, Llanbeblig (-1851).

R

ROMNEY, George (1794 - 1857)
Historical engraver — Outlaw Place

Williams, J., *Commercial Directory*, 1846, p.2.
Bagshaw, 1850, p.109.

Owned premises at Outlaw Place from at least 1849 (Chester Record Office documents A/B/6/868-869).

S

STERNE, Mr (fl 1772)
Portrait artist and wax modeller

Adam's Weekly Courant, 31 March 1772.

No will in *Chester*.

STUART, J. (fl c1780)
Engraver of book plates

Two signed examples of his book plates, both for Welsh patrons, are recorded.**(1)**

1. *WBP*, pp.30 & 32, book plates for Richard Garnons, Colomendy and Marshall Griffith, Brynodol.

SUMNER, Alfred (fl 1852)
Drawing master — King's School
Landscape painter

He drew and lithographed views of North Wales.**(1)**

CAJ, 1918 (Volume 22), p.167.

1. *NLW, Beaumaris Castle* (pub. by T. Catherall, Bangor, Chester, August 1852), P2844 (Top B1/3-B13).

T

TASKER, George (fl 1808 - fl 1852)
Landscape and sporting artist — Queen Street
Animal painter

Chester Directory, 1840, p.48.
CAJ, 1928 (Volume 28), pp.124-126.
Exhibition catalogue Grosvenor Museum, Chester 1983-4. *Louis Rayner and William Tasker.*

TAYLOR, Richard (1758 - 1827)
Painter — Eastgate Street

Chester Guide, 1781, p.109.

No will in *Chester*.

TILSTON, Thomas (fl 1729 - fl 1772)
Smith

Beard (1981): worked at Hawarden Castle 1749-57 and 20 St James's Square.**(1)**

No will in *Chester*.

1. This was the house built for Sir Watkin Williams-Wynn in 1771-4 by Robert Adam *vide* Pritchard, T. W. *The Wynns of Wynnstay* (Caerwys, 1982). *Colvin* p.57.

TROUGHTON, J. (fl 1781 - fl 1782)
Engraver — Crane Street

Chester Guide, 1781, p.110.
Ibid., 1782, p.107.

No will in *Chester*.

TURNER, John (fl 1793)
Painter — Cuppin's Lane

Chester Guide, 1793, p.[33].

No will in *Chester*.

TURNER, J[oseph] (c1729 - 1807)
Architect — Paradise Row

Chester Guide, 1781, p.110
Ibid., 1782, p.107.
Ibid., 1789, p.64.
Ibid., 1795, p.93.
Ibid., 1797, p.96.

Probably Joseph Turner described as an architect, will proved June 1817, *Chester* (1924-5), p.173. I can offer no explanation for the delay in proving this will *vide* main entry for discussion of his career in Wales.

W

WILKINSON, George (or William) (fl 1774 - 1799)
Heraldic and coach painter — Werburgh's Lane
Scene painter

He worked for the Wynnstay estate in October 1774 on the Theatre, and painted a number of scenes.**(1)** 'Wilkinson was a stroller at the time, coming annually to Wynnstay, to do what he was wont to do, for the rest of the year, on this circuit - paint scenes, and daub characters, as occasion required.'**(2)** He died in Chester.**(3)**

1. Wynnstay MS Box 115/28/3 lists various scenes painted by Mr Wilkinson. He also retouched some scenes by Paul Sandby. The MS also has a 'W Wilkinson' which may be simply 'Mr Wilkinson'.
2. Colman, G., *Random Records*, Volume 2, pp.48-9.
   Chester Guide, 1781, p.113 (Coach painter).
   Ibid., 1782, p.109 (Herald and coach painter).
   Ibid., 1795, p.95.
3. *Chester* (1902), p.168, described as George Wilkinson 'of the City of Chester, painter'.

BIBLIOGRAPHY

NOTE

All sources cited in the work are to be found in this bibliography. Many of the texts have been cited several times and in this case they are used in abbreviated form in the main text. The list of abbreviations will cite the works in full and when this occurs the same work will not appear in the main body of the bibliography.

ABBREVIATIONS

Arch.Cam. — *Archaeologia Cambrensis.*

AIW — *Art in Wales*, WAC, Cardiff, 1964.

Aris, B.G. — *Aris's Birmingham Gazette*, 1746- .

B — *NLW* MSS, Probate Record Project, Bangor Probate Records.

BBA — Baillie, Laureen, ed., *British Biographical Archive*, Sauc, London, 1984.

Bell — Bell, David, *The Artist in Wales*, London: George G. Harrap, 1957.

Bennett — Bennett, Mary, *Merseyside Painters, People and Places* (2 vols), Liverpool: Walker ArtGallery, 1978.

BI — British Institution, London.

BL — British Library.

BM — British Museum.

Bounty Plans — NLW Dept of MSS Church in Wales Records, QueenAnne's Bounty Plans.

BV — *Book of Views*, Dept of Pictures & Maps,*NLW*.

BR — *NLW* MSS, Probate Record Project, Breconshire Probate Records.

Cadrawd — Evans, T.C. ('Cadrawd'), *Biographies of Welsh Painters, Architects, Engravers...*, c1895, South Glamorgan Libraries, Cardiff Central Library, MS 4.305.

Cambria Depicta — Pugh, Edward, *Cambria Depicta: a Tour Through North Wales*, London: W. Charles, 1816.

CAJ — *Journal of the Architectural, Archaeological and Historic Society...Chester*, Chester, 1849 -.

Chester — *Wills at Chester*, published by Lancashire & Cheshire Record Society.

Chester Wills — *NLW*, Welsh Wills proved at Chester, Probate Project, Dept of MSS.

CM — Cyfarthfa Museum, Merthyr Tydfil.

Colvin — Colvin, Howard, *A Biographical Dictionary of British Architects 1600-1840*, New Haven & London: Yale University Press, 1995 (3rd Edtion). The 1978 was also used for some references.

Cox, 1990 — Cox, Julian, *From Swansea to the Menai Straits: Towards a History of Photography in Wales c1800-1860*, M.Phil. thesis, University of Wales, 1990.

Dale-Jones — Dale-Jones, Edna, 'Three generations: the Jeffreys of King Street, Carmarthen (1846-1936)' *The Carmarthenshire Antiquary*, 1993, vol. XXIX, pp.73-88.

Davies Atlas — Davies, Robert, *An Atlas of the Tithe Maps of Wales*, forthcoming pub. *NLW*, Aberystwyth, 1997. All surveyors mentioned by Davies were working on Tithe Surveys between c1839-1845.

DFHS — Dyfed Family History Society, Transcripts of the Census 1851, Vol. I.

DNB — *Dictionary of National Biography*, ed. Smith (*et al.*), London, 1885-1900.

DWB — *Dictionary of Welsh Biography*, London: Cymmrodorion, 1959.

Eden — Eden, Peter, *Directory of Land Surveyors and Local Cartographers of Great Britain and Ireland 1550-1850* (3 vols & supplement), Folkestone: Dawson, 1979 (1976 earlier edition).

Farington — Farington, Joseph, *Diary*, New Haven & London: Yale U.P., 1978-1985 (16 vols, further volumes pending).

Foskett — Foskett, Daphne, *A Dictionary of British Miniature Painters* (2 vols), London: Faber & Faber, 1972.

FS — Free Society of Artists, London.

Gamwell — Gamwell, S.C., *The Official Guide and Handbook to Swansea*, Swansea: 'Cambrian' office, 1880.

Girouard — Girouard, Mark, *Directory of British Architects 1834-1900*, London: *RIBA*, 1993.

Graves, B.I. — Graves, Algernon, *The British Institution 1806-1867*, Bath: Kingsmead Reprints, 1969 (orig. 1875).

Graves, F.S. — Graves, Algernon, *The Free Society of Artists*, Bath: Kingsmead Reprints, 1969 (1907).

Graves — Graves, Algernon, *The Royal Academy of Arts* (8 vols), London: Henry Graves, 1905-6.

GVS — Glynn Vivian Art Gallery, Swansea.

Gye — *Gye's Bath Directory*, Bath: H. Gye, 1819.

Howells, 1987 — Howells, R.G., *Under Sail*, Swansea: *GVS*, 1987.

Hutchison — Hutchison, Sidney, 'The Royal Academy Schools 1768-1830', *Walpole Society*, Volume XXXVIII, 1960-62, pp.123-191.

Joyner (1989) — Joyner, Paul, *A Place for a Poussin*, (2 vols) PhD, unpublished, Cambridge University, 1989.

Joyner (1990) — Joyner, Paul, *A Place for a Poussin*, Denbigh: Gee and Son Ltd, lecture repr. from *Transactions of the Honourable Society of Cymmrodorion*, 1990.

Kissack — Kissack, Keith, 'Thomas Tudor, a Monmouth artist', *Gwent Local History*, no. 53, 1982, pp. 33-37.

Lewis — Lewis, J.M., *Welsh Monumental Brasses*, *NMW*, 1974.

Libri Walliae — Rees, Eiluned, *Libri Walliae* (2 vols), Aberystwyth: *NLW*, 1987.

LL — *NLW* MSS Dept, Probate Record Project, Llandaff Probate Records.

Lloyd — Lloyd, Thomas 'The Architects of Regency Swansea', *Gower*, XLI (1990), pp.56-69.

London — *Survey of London*, London: *RCAM*, 1930ff.

Long — Long, Basil, *British Miniaturists*, London: Geoffrey Bles, 1929.

Lord, Barn — Lord, Peter, 'Ystyr y llun naif', *Barn*, Rhifau 348, 349, 1992, pp.26-41.

Lord, 1990 — Lord, Peter, *Hugh Hughes: 1790-1863, Arlunydd Gwlad / Artisan Painter* (exhibition catalogue), Aberystwyth: *NLW*, 1990.

Lord, 1992 — Lord, Peter, *Y Chwaer-Dduwies - Celf, Crefft a'r Eisteddfod*, Llandysul: Gomer, 1992.

Lord, 1993 — Lord, Peter, *Arlunwyr Gwlad / Artisan Painters* (exhibition catalogue), Aberystwyth: *NLW*, 1993.

Lord, 1994 — Lord, Peter, *Gwenllian: Essays on visual culture*, Llandysul: Gomer, 1994.

Lord, WWP — Lord, Peter, *Words with Pictures: 'Welsh images & images of Wales in the Popular Press 1640-1840'*, Aberystwyth: Planet, 1995.

Mallalieu — Mallalieu, H.L., *Dictionary of British Watercolour Artists up to 1920*, Woodbridge: Antique Collectors' Club, 1979.

Mardy Rees — Rees, T. Mardy, *Welsh Painters, Engravers, Sculptors 1527-1911*, Caernarvon: Welsh Publishing Co. Ltd, c1911.

McKechnie — McKechnie, Sue, *British Silhouette Artists and their Work 1760-1860*, London: Sotheby, 1978.

Memoirs — Jones, Thomas, 'Memoirs of Thomas Jones', *Walpole Society*, Volume XXXII, 1946-48.

Millar — Millar, Oliver, *The Victorian Pictures* (Pictures in the Gallery of Her Majesty the Queen), C.U.P., 1992 (2 vols).

MWAB — Museum of Welsh Antiquities, Bangor.

Nance — Nance, E. Morton, *The Pottery and Porcelain of Swansea & Nantgarw*, London: Batsford, 1992.

NLS — The National Library of Scotland.

NLW — The National Library of Wales, Aberystwyth, Ceredigion.

NMW — National Museum of Wales, Cardiff.

NPT — Newport Art Gallery & Museum, Newport.

P-PG — Accession numbers, Dept of Pictures & Maps, *NLW*.

Pavière — Pavière, Sydney H., *A Dictionary of Victorian Landscape Painters*, London: F. Lewis, 1968.

PL — Peter Lord, information given in discussions.

POL — *Post Office London Directory*.

PP — Hilling, John, *Plans & Prospects*, Cardiff: WAC, 1975.

PRO — Public Record Office, London.

Pyke — Pyke, E., *A Biographical Dictionary of Wax modellers*, Oxford: Clarendon Press, 1973.

RA — Royal Academy, London.

RCAM (SB) — Royal Commission for Ancient and Historical Monuments in Wales - Dr Stephen Briggs, information given in discussions.

RCAM (TP) — Royal Commission for Ancient and Historical Monuments in Wales - Tony Parkinson, information given in discussion and correspondence.

Redgrave — Redgrave, Samuel, *A Dictionary of Artists of the English School*, Bath: Kingsmead *Reprints. 1970 (1878).*

Rees MS — Copy of *Mardy Rees* in the Art Dept. *NMW* with copious, unique, MSS annotations.

RIBA — Royal Institute of British Architects, London.

RISW — Royal Institution of South Wales, Swansea.

Roberts, I & M — Roberts, Iolo & Menai, 'Which John Evans are we talking about?', *The Map Collector*, No.46, Spring 1989.

Rogers — Rogers, W.C., *A Pictorial History of Swansea*, Llandysul: Gomer Press, 1981.

RSBA — Royal Society of British Artists, London.

RSPW — Royal Society of Painters in Watercolour, London.

SA — Society of Artists, London.

SD — *NLW*, MSS Dept, Probate Project, St David's Diocese Records.

Steegman — Steegman, John, *A Survey of Portraits in Welsh Houses*, Cardiff: *NMW* (Volume 1, 1957, North Wales; Volume 2, 1962, South Wales).

TL — Thomas Lloyd, information given in discussions and correspondence.

VAM — Victoria & Albert Museum, London.

Vaughan — Vaughan, G.H., *List of Artists and Engravers in Book Plate Collection*, *NLW*, 1940 (unpublished).

WAC — Welsh Arts Council.

Walker — Bennett, *Walker Art Gallery* (2 vols), Liverpool: Merseyside County Council, 1978.

Walpole — *Annual Volumes of the Walpole Society*, *BM*, The Walpole Society.

Waterhouse — Waterhouse, Ellis, *The Dictionary of British 18th Century Painters*, [London]: Antique Collectors' Club Ltd, 1981.

Waterson — Waterson, Merlin, *The servants' hall: a domestic history of Erddig*, London: Routledge & Kegan Paul, 1980.

WBP — Vaughan, G.H., *The Welsh Book Plates*, London: A.L. Humphrey, 1920.

WFM — Welsh Folk Museum, St Fagan's, Cardiff.

Witt — Witt Library, *Checklist of British Artists in the Witt Library*, London: Courtauld Institute of Art, 1991.

Wood — Wood, Christopher, *Dictionary of Victorian Painters*, Woodbridge: Antique Collectors' Club, 1971.

WPA — *NLW*, Welsh Portrait Archive.

WW Price — Price, *Biographical Index*, c1924- .

MANUSCRIPTS

Some of the MSS used for this study include the following:

National Library of Wales:
Cwrt Mawr 130A
  Hughes, Hugh, *Diary 1819-1820.*

Ffransis Payne Papers 847.

Glynne MS 57
  GLYNNE, Sir Stephen R., *Tour of South Wales*, 1824.

Wynnstay MSS.

MS 1890
  Letters to Rev. J. Jenkins, early 19th century.

MS 2258C
  SYKES, Christopher, *Tour in Wales*, 1796.

MS 5370C
  Sir Richard Colt Hoare, *Sketchbook*, 1799.

MS 5500C
  Letters of Thomas Pennant and Richard Bull, 1773-1798.

MS 6358B
  Material relating to Hugh Hughes.

MS 13248B I & II
  PUGHE, William Owen, *Diary 1821-1831.*
  Mysevin MS 28 I & 28 II, *Dyddgoviant William Owen Pughe*, 1811-1835.

MS 15190C
SHEPHERD, William, *A Tour through Wales*, 1810.

MS 18252B
PARKER, John, *Journal*, 1831.

National Museum of Wales
Steegman, J. *Files for a Survey of Portraits*.

Thomas, T.H. [*List of Welsh Artists*].

NMW files
A-Z artists files have been kept by the Department of Art of the *NMW* since the early 1920s. These include MSS and published material.

Anglesey Record Office
WCC/33/14
Inventory of portraits at Carreg Lwyd, early 20th century.

Cardiff Reference Library
3-127, Volume 6
Journal of Sir Richard Colt Hoare, 1796.

Welsh Folk Museum, Cardiff
MS 2295/213
Cardiff exhibition, 1855.
MS 3336
Valuation of Brynkinallt, 1838.

Caernarfon Record Office
Poole MSS.

Carmarthen Record Office
Gulston MSS (Derwydd MSS)
Gulston, Joseph, *Notebooks 1779-1785*.

Dolgellau Record Office
2/DCE/3/1
Inventory of Hengwrt, 1859.

Gwent Record Office
D1670 98/99
Deed, dated 1823.

Hawarden Record Office
B/923
Inventory of Gwysaney, 1833.

Ruthin Record Office
BA/A/459
Minutes of Ruthin Council.

University of Wales Bangor
MS 5709
Roos, William, letter dated 26 January 1845, to Hugh Hughes (Derfel).

MS 3592.

Private Collections
Jones, Captain, *Diary*, 1790s (Mrs C. Humphreys).
Tudor, Thomas, *Diary*, 1847-1851 (Major Probert).

Greater London Record Office
1302/113
Catalogue of Interesting and highly valuable oil paintings, Brecon, 1850.

Hereford Record Office
KENTCHURCH MS 2028
Notes on costs of work at the Cup Inn Monmouth.

National Library of Scotland
Add MS 29/5/5
Letter by T. Pennant, dated 13 May 1772.

National Register of Archives, London
S 3636
James Northcote?, letter dated 25 April 1823.

Victoria & Albert Museum, The National Art Library
86GG-22-26
Crosse, Richard, *Accounts and ledgers*.

UNPUBLISHED MATERIAL
BRAUGHTON, Peter, *List of Chester Artists*, c1985.

DAVIES, Philip Wyn, *Astudiaeth o ysgolheictod hynafiaethol Lewis Morris (1701-1765)*, MA thesis (U.W. Cardiff), 1982.

EVANS, Ronald P., *Thomas Pennant's writings on North Wales*, MA thesis (U.W. Swansea), 1985.

FARINGTON, Joseph, *Notebook* (Windsor Typescript), published version not yet available, typescript kept at Print Room, *BM*.

HACKFORTH-JONES, Jocelyn, *Views in Wales c1760-c1830*, PhD thesis (University of Sydney), 1988.

HARVEY, John, *Art and Nonconformity in Wales*, MA thesis (U.W. Aberystwyth), 1984.

HARVEY, John, *Nicholas Evans, aspects of the visualisation of religious concepts in the non-conformist tradition*, PhD (U.W. Aberystwyth), 1990.

JOHNSON, Rita, *John Parker*, BA dissertation (U.W. Aberystwyth), 1994.

JONES, Daniel, *Welsh Furniture*, MA thesis (U.W. Aberystwyth), 1933.

JOYNER, Paul, *A catalogue of drawing volumes in the Dept of Pictures and Maps, National Library of Wales* (Typescript Aberystwyth), 1983.

JOYNER, Paul, *Edward Pugh and Ruthin* (Lecture to the Denbigh Historical Society, 1992).

JOYNER, Paul, *Rev. John Dyer* (Lecture to the Carmarthenshire Antiquarian Society, 1993).

JOYNER, Paul & HOLMES, John, *David Cox and Betws y Coed Prints* (Lecture for Betws y Coed Festival, 1993).

MCCARTHY, Francis, *The treatment of mountain scenery by some British writers and artists in the eighteenth century - with some special attention to North Wales*, PhD thesis (Cambridge), 1963 (2 vols).

MONMOUTH MUSEUM, *Handlist of Thomas Tudor exhibition* (Typescript Monmouth), 1979.

PARKINSON, Anthony J., *Wallpaintings in Wales: handlist* (typescript), 1980.

Rhestr o Ffugenwau, [A list of pseudonyms], typescript National Library of Wales, n.d.

SLOAN, Kim M., *The teaching of non-professional artists in 18th century England*, PhD thesis (London University), 1982.

SMILES, Samuel A., *Plymouth and Exeter as centres of Art 1820-1865*, PhD thesis (Cambridge University), 1982.

WAKELIN, A.P., *Tours in Wales* (Typescript at *NLW* Aberystwyth), 1981.

WALTERS, Gwyn, *The tourist and guide book literature of Wales 1770-1870*, MSc thesis (U.W. Aberystwyth), 1967.

CONTEMPORARY AND MODERN NEWSPAPERS AND PERIODICALS

Reference is given to the earliest published issue of the work and (-) denotes that it was still being distributed in 1850. All available issues of the Welsh publications were checked. For details of the periodicals, the best source is Walters, Huw, *A Bibliography of Welsh Periodicals 1735-1850*, Aberystwyth: *NLW*, 1993. For Welsh newspapers *vide* Jones, Beti, *Newsplan Cymru*, BL/NLW, 1994.

Adam's Weekly Courant.

Art Journal, London 1849-.

Art Union: *see Art Journal.*

Bath Chronicle.

Biographical Magazine.

British Quarterly Review, London, 1845.

Burlington Magazine.

By Gones.

Caernarvon and Denbighshire Herald, Caernarfon, 1831-.

Cambrian, Swansea, 1804-.

Cambrian Daily Leader.

Cambrian Quarterly Magazine.

The Cambro-Briton, ed. J. Limbird, Volume 1, London, 1820.

Carmarthen Journal, Carmarthen, 1810-.

Carmarthen Historian.

Carmarthenshire Antiquary.

Chester Chronicle, Chester, 1775-.

Chester Courant, Chester, 1825-.

Chester Cowrdray.

Civil Engineers and Architects' Journal.

Connoisseur.

Country Life.

Cymru.

European Magazine.

Exeter Flying Post.

Gentleman's Magazine.

Gower.

Gwladgarwr, Caerlleon, Llanidloes, 1833-.

Hereford Journal.

Leisure Hour.

Manchester Journal.

Manchester Mercury.

Merthyr Historian.

Monmouthshire Beacon, Monmouth, 1837-.

Monmouthshire Merlin, Newport, 1829-.

North Wales Chronicle, Caernarfon, 1827-.

North Wales Gazette.

Y Papur Newydd Cymraeg, Caernarfon, 1836-1837.

Pembrokeshire Herald.

Y Pwnch Cymraeg, Caergybi, 1858-.

Radnorshire Transactions.

Salopian Journal, Shrewsbury, 1794-.

Y Seren Ogleddol, ed. J.T. Jones, Caernarfon, 1835.

South Wales Daily News.

The South Walian.

Swansea Journal, Swansea, 1843-1845.

Y Traethodydd, 1895-.

Transactions of the Honourable Society of Cymmrodorion.

Wales.

Western Daily Press.

Western Mail.

Welshman.

TRADE DIRECTORIES

All available Welsh trade directories have been checked. References are given in the individual sections on the artists concerned. A full bibliographical description will be found in Norton, Jane, *Guide to the National and Provincial Directories of England and Wales*, Royal Historical Society, London, 1984.

The *NLW* has an excellent selection of *Welsh* trade directories and many libraries have some local information. The Swansea Library is one of the best examples, which has early Swansea directories and guide books.

The following trade directories appear often in the text: *Crockfords Clerical Directory, Hunt, Master's Directory, Matthew's Guide, Pigot's, Post Office London, Robson's, Swansea Directory, Swansea Guide, Wakeford, Whittaker, The Boarding School & London Master's Directory, Slater's.*

OTHER PRINTED MATERIAL

ALTICK, Richard, *The Shows of London*, Cambridge, Mass.: Harvard UP, 1978.

ALLAN, D., *William Shipley*, London: Scolar Press, 1979.

AP GWYN, Llewellyn, *Celfyddyd a Chrefft yn Nghymru* [Art and Craft in Wales], Liverpool: Hugh Evans, 1946.

AYRES, James, *English Naive Painting 1750-1900*, London: Thames and Hudson, 1980.

BAILLIE, Laureen ed., *British Biographical Archive*, London: Sauc, 1984.

BARNETT, C., *Gwent as seen by the Artist*, Newport: Art Gallery, c1970.

BARNETT, H.V., 'A treatise on wood engraving', *The Magazine of Art*, 1882, pp.240-242.

BEANLAND, W.A., *History of the RISW*, Swansea: *RISW*, 1935.

BEARD, Geoffrey, *Craftsmen and Interior Decoration in England 1660-1820*, Edinburgh: J Bartholomew, 1981.

BEARD, Geoffrey, *Decorative Plasterwork in Great Britain*, London: Phaidon, 1975.

'Beauties of Cambria' (review), *Gentleman's Magazine*, 1823, p.162.

BELL, David, *Welsh Landscape in British Art*, Arts Council of Great Britain, Cardiff: William Lewis Ltd, 1947.

BICK, David & DAVIES, Philip Wyn, *Lewis Morris and the Cardiganshire Mines*, Aberystwyth: NLW, 1994.

BICKNELL, Peter, *Beauty, Horror and Immensity*, Cambridge: CUP, 1981.

'Biography of Richard Wilson', *Cambrian Quarterly Magazine*, Vol. 3, 1831, pp.161-170.

BOORMAN, David, *The Brighton of Wales*, Swansea: Swansea Little Theatre Company Ltd, 1986.

BOUGHTON, P.J., *The Clowes Family of Chester Sporting Artists*, Chester: Grosvenor Museum, 1985.

BRADNEY, Joseph, *History of Monmouthshire*, Cardiff: South Wales Record Society (various dates, most recent 1993).

BREEZE, George, *Society of Artists in Ireland*, Dublin: National Gallery of Ireland, 1985.

BROWNE, Turner, & PARTNOW, Elaine, *Macmillan Biographical Encyclopedia of Photographic Artists & Innovators*, London & New York: Macmillan, 1983.

BRYAN, M., *Dictionary of Painters* (5 vols), London: George Bell & Son, 1909.

BUCKMAN, Rollin, *The Photographic Work of Calvert Richard Jones*, Science Museum, London (HMSO), 1990.

BURGESS, F., 'Painted tombs', *Commemorative Art*, Vol. XXXIII, 1966, pp.238-242.

BUTLIN, Martin & JOLL, Evelyn, *The Paintings of J.M.W. Turner* (2 vols), New Haven and London: Yale UP, 1984.

BYNG, John, *The Torrington Diaries*, ed. C.B. Andrews, Vol. 1, London and New York: Methuen (et al.), 1977.

CAFFELL, Gwenno, *Llechi Cerfiedig Dyffryn Ogwen*, Cardiff: *NMW*, 1983.

'Cambro-British picture gallery', *Cambrian Quarterly Magazine*, Vol. 2, 1830, p.112 and p.255.

CAREY, William, *On the Probable Extinction of British Historical Painting*, London: Howlett and Brimmer, 1825.

CARR, Glenda, *William Owen Pugh*, Cardiff: University of Wales Press, 1983.

CARR, Glenda, *William Owen Pugh*, Caernarfon: Gwasg Pantycelyn, 1993.

CARTER, Harold, *The Towns of Wales*, Cardiff: UWP, 1965.

CAW, J.L., *Scottish Painting Past and Present 1620-1908*, Edinburgh: T.C. & E.C. Jack, 1908.

CENSUS Reports 1841, London: W. Clowes & Son, 1843-4.

CHATER, A.O., 'Early Cardiganshire gravestones', *Archaeologia Cambrensis*, Volume CXXV, 1976, pp.140-161; Volume CXXVI, 1977, pp.116-138.

CLARK, Kenneth, *Moments of Vision*, London: John Murray, 1981.

CLARK, Kenneth, *The Gothic Revival*, [London]: John Murray, 1974.

CLARKE, Michael, 'A Bangor architect of the early Nineteenth Century', *Transactions of the Caernarvonshire Historical Society*, 1954, pp.49-50.

CLARKE, Michael, *The Tempting Prospect*, London: B.M.P., 1981.

CLAY, Rotha M., *Julius Caesar Ibbetson*, London: Country Life Ltd, 1948.

CLIFFORD, Derek & Timothy, *John Crome*, London: Faber & Faber, 1968.

COLYER, Richard, *Roads and Trackways of Wales*, Ashbourne: Moorland Publishing Co, 1984.

CONSTABLE, William G., *Richard Wilson*, London: Routledge & Kegan Paul, 1953.

COOKE, William B., *Picturesque Views of the Southern Coast*, 2 vols, London: John & Arthur Arch, 1826.

COOPER, Douglas, 'Iconography of Richard Wilson', *Burlington Magazine*, Volume 90, 1948, pp.109-118.

COOPER, Emmanuel, *Celfyddyd yr Aelwyd / Bringing it All Back Home* (exhibition catalogue), Aberystwyth Arts Centre, Welshpool: Powys Printers Ltd, 1992.

CORNFORTH, John, 'Kentchurch Court Herefordshire', *Country Life*, 5 December 1966, pp.1632-1635.

COXE, William, *A Historical Tour Through Monmouthshire*, 2 vols, London: Cadell & Davies, 1801.

COXHEAD, A.C., *Thomas Stothard R.A.* (an illustrated monograph), London: A.H. Bullen, 1906.

COX-JOHNSON, Ann, *Hand-list of Painters, Sculptors and Architects Associated with St Marylebone 1760-1960*, London: Borough of St Marylebone Public Libraries Committee, 1963.

CROFT, Murray E., *Decorative Painting in Britain 1537-1837* (2 vols), Feltham Country Life, 1970.

CROUAN, K., *John Linnell*, London: Martyn Gregory Gallery, 1982.

DARBY, Michael, *John Pollard Seddon*, London: V&A, 1983.

DAVIES, Cunllo, 'Art in Welsh homes', *Wales*, Volume 2, 1895, pp.223-4.

DAVIES, Gareth, 'Trevecka', *Brycheiniog*, Volume XV, 1971, pp.41-56.

DAVIES, T.A. & PRYSE, W.T.R., *John Roberts Clock Maker*, Cardiff: *WFM*, 1987.

DAVIES, Williams, 'Joseph Edwards, Sculptor', *Wales* II, 1895, pp.134-137.

DAVIS, Terence, *The Architecture of John Nash*, London: Studio, 1960.

DAVIS, Terence, *John Nash, The Prince Regent's Architect*, London: Country Life, 1966.

DESMOND, Ray, *Dictionary of British & Irish Botanists & Horticulturalists*, London: Natural History Museum & Taylor & Francis, 1994.

DEW & SON, *Auction at Madryn Castle*, 29-30 June 1910.

DIBDIN, E.R., 'Liverpool art and artists in the Eighteenth Century', *Walpole Society*, Volume VI, 1917-18, pp.12-93.

DREW, William, *Auction Catalogue*, 1-3 August 1859.

DUNTHORNE, Kirstine, 'Art in Wales' (review), *Welsh History Review*, Volume 2, number 3, 1983, pp.400-401.

DUNTHORNE, Kirstine, 'Art and Artists', *The City of Swansea: Challenges & Change*, Swansea: West Glamorgan County Council, 1991.

DYER, John, *Poems*, London: John Hughs [*sic*], 1761.

EASTLAKE, Charles, *Materials for a History of Oil Painting*, London: Longman [*et al.*], 1847.

EDINGTON, G., *The Clowes Family*, Chester: Grosvenor Museum, 1985.

EDMOND, Mary, 'Limners and picturemakers', *Walpole Society*, Volume XLVII, 1980, pp.60-242.

EDUCATION in Wales 1847-1947, London: HMSO, 1948.

EDWARDS, Edward, *Anecdotes of Painters...*, London: Luke Hansard & Sons, 1808.

EDWARDS, Edward, *Anecdotes of Painters...*, annotated and grangerized copy, BM Print Room.

EDWARDS, Hywel T., *Gŵyl Gwalia*, Llandysul: Gwasg Gomer, 1980.

EDWARDS, Ifor, *Davies Brothers Gatesmiths*, Cardiff: WAC, 1977.

EGERTON, Judy, *Stubbs*, Tate Gallery Exhibition, 1984.

ELLIS, E.T., 'Domestic and decorative art in Wales', *Cymmrodorion Transactions*, 1896-97, pp.14-33.

EVANS, L.W., *Education in Industrial Wales 1700-1900*, Cardiff: Avalon Books, 1971.

EVANS, John, *North Wales*, Llwynygroes: John Evans, 1795.

EVANS, Wyn & WORSLEY, R., *St David's Cathedral*, 1981.

FARINGTON, Joseph, *Memoirs of Sir Joshua Reynolds*, London: T. Cadell & W. Davies, 1819.

FAWCETT, Trevor, *The Rise of English Provincial Art*, Oxford: Clarendon Press, 1974.

FERREY, B., *Recollections of A. Welby Pugin*, London: no imprint, 1861.

FINBERG, Alexander J., *Complete inventory of the Drawings of the Turner Bequest* (2 vols), London: HMSO, 1909.

FINCHAM, Henry W., *The Artists and Engravers of British American Book Plates*, London: Kegan, Paul, 1897 (incl. a number of *Welsh* plates done in London).

FLAXMAN, John, *Outlines* (*The Odyssey of Homer*), London: Longman (*et al.*), 1805.

FORD, Brinsley, 'Welsh Maecenas', *Apollo*, Volume 99, 1974, pp.435-439.

FORSHALL, Frederic H., *Westminster School Past and present*, London: Wyman & sons, 1884.

FRASER, James, *Illustrated History of the Royal Cambrian Lodge, Merthyr*, Merthyr Tydfil: W H Southaw, 1914.

FREDERICKSEN, Burton, *The Index of Paintings Sold in the British Isles during the 19th Century*, Oxford: Clio Press, 1990- (The Provenance Index of the Getty Art History Information Program).

GERE, J.A., 'Thomas Jones: An Eighteenth Century conundrum', *Apollo*, Vol. XCI, June 1979.

GERNSHEIM, Helmut & Alison, *L.J.M. Daguerre - The History of the Diorama and the Daguerreotype*, London: Secker & Warburg, 1956.

GERNSHEIM, Helmut & Alison, *History of Photography*, Oxford: Oxford University Press, 1955.

GOWING, Lawrence, *The Originality of Thomas Jones*, London: Thomas Hudson, 1986.

GRANT, Colonel M.H., *Old English Landscape Painters* (3 vols), London: Col. Grant, 1926-47.

GRANT, Colonel M.H., *Old English Landscape Painters* (8 vols), Leigh on Sea: F. Lewis, 1957-1971.

GRAVES, Algernon, *The Society of Artists*, Bath: Kingsmead Reprints, 1969 (1907).

GRAVES, Algernon, *Summary of Waagen*, London: A. Graves, 1912.

GREGSON, Matthew, *Portfolio of Fragments*, Liverpool: G.F. Harris's widow (*et al.*), 1817.

GUNNIS, Rupert, *Dictionary of British Sculptors 1660-1851*, London: Abbey Library, 1968.

HANES Cyflawn Eisteddfod Llangollen, 1858 (no imprint or author), *NLW*.

HARRIS, John (*et al.*), *Buckingham Palace*, London: Nelson, 1968.

HARTHAN, John P. & WIGHT, M., 'Brute Fecit: a vernacular art of the Welsh Border', *Architectural Review*, Volume 102, October 1947, pp.135-216.

HARVEY, John, *The Art of Piety* (*The Visual culture of Welsh Nonconformity*), Cardiff: UWP, 1995.

HASKELL, Francis, *Rediscoveries in Art*, London: Phaidon, 1976.

HASLEM, John, *The Old Derby China Factory*, London: George Bell, 1876, pp.125-126.

[HELME, Andrew], *Nooks and Corners of Old Monmouthshire*, Monmouth Museum, 1983.

HILLIARD, Nicholas, *The Arte of Limning*, Ashington: Mid Northumberland Art Group [et at.], 1981.

HILLING, John B., *The Historic Architecture of Wales*, Cardiff: UWP, 1976.

HOLLEY, T.F., 'Joseph Edwards and Merthyr Tydfil', *Merthyr Historian*, Volume 3, 1989.

HOLLEY, T.F., 'William Edward Jones, painter of portraits', *Merthyr Historian*, Volume Six, 1992.

HODGES, William, 'Richard Wilson' (obituary), *European Magazine*, June 1790, Volume XVII, pp.403-405.

HOWELLS, Roderick, *The Rev. Calvert Richard Jones of Swansea* (exhibition catalogue), Swansea: Glynn Vivian, March 1973.

HUBBARD, Clifford, 'A book at Random', *Kennel Gazette*, November, 1991, pp.33-37.

HUBBARD, Edward, *The Buildings of Wales: Clwyd*, Harmondsworth: Penguin Books, & University of Wales Press, 1986.

HUGHES, Gareth, & PUGH, Robert, *Llanelly Pottery*, Llanelli: Llanelli Borough Council, 1990.

HUGHES, Glyn Tegai, *Williams Pantycelyn*, Cardiff: University of Wales Press, 1983.

HUGHES, Hugh, 'Ar ryddid, cymdeithas, a Llywodraeth' [on freedom, society and government], *Seren Gomer*, No. 193, Volume 14, 1831, pp.289-293.

HUGHES, Hugh, *Beauties of Cambria*, London: H. Hughes, 1823.

HUGHES, Hugh, *Brut y Cymru*, Caerfyrddin: J. Evans, c1824.

HUGHES, Hugh, *Y Drefn Ddwyfol* [The Divine Order], Caernarvon: H. Humphreys, 1849.

HUGHES, Hugh, *Dysgedydd sef Cyfarwyddyd i Ddysgu Darllen yr laith Gymraeg* [Directions for learning Welsh], Dinbych: T. Gee, [n.d.].

HUGHES, Hugh, *Hynafion Cymreig*, Caerfyrddin: T. Evans, 1823.

HUGHES, Peter, 'Paul Sandby and Sir Watkin Williams Wynn', *Burlington Magazine*, Volume 114, 1972, pp.459-466.

HUGHES, Robert, *Hunan-Gofiant ynghyda Phregethau a Barddoniaeth*, Pwllheli: William Hughes, 1893.

HUMFREY, Belinda, *John Dyer*, Cardiff: UWP, 1980.

HUSSEY, Christopher, 'Chirk Castle', *Country Life*, 5 October 1951, pp.1067-8.

HYDE, Ralph, *Gilded Scenes and Shining Prospects*, New Haven: Yale U.P., 1985.

HYDE, Ralph, 'Thomas Horner: pictorial land surveyor', *Imago Mundi*, Volume 29, 1977, pp.23-34.

INGLIS-JONES, Elizabeth, *Peacocks in Paradise*, London: Faber & Faber, 1950.

JACKSON, J., *Wood Engraving*, London: Harry & Bohn, 1861.

JAMES, E. Wyn, 'Lluniau o Williams Pantycelyn: gwaith ditectif', *Barn*, Awst, Medi 1991, Rhifau 343, 344, pp.59-68.

JARMAN, A.O.H. & HUGHES, G.R., *A Guide to Welsh Literature*, Swansea: Christopher Davies, 1976.

JEFFREY, Ian, *The Real Thing: An Anthology of British Photography, 1840-1950*, London: Arts Council of Great Britain, 1975.

JENKINS, D.C., *The Diary of Thomas Jenkins of Llandeilo 1826-1870*, Bala: Dragon Books, 1976.

JENKINS, Ellis, 'Early artists', *Gower* XVI, pp.66-68.

JENKINS Ellis, 'Thomas Horner', *Glamorgan Historian*, Volume 7, 1971, pp.37-50.

JENKINS, Geraint H., *The Foundations of Modern Wales 1642-1780* (History of Wales, Vol. IV), Oxford: Clarendon Press, UWP, 1987.

JENKINS, Robert T. & RAMMAGE, Helen M., *A History of the Honourable Society of Cymmrodorion*, London: Cymmrodorion, 1951.

JOHN, William D., *Nantgarw Porcelain*, Newport: R.H. Johns Ltd, 1948.

JOHN, William D., *William Billingsley*, Newport: The Ceramic Book Company, 1968.

JOHNES, Thomas, *A Catalogue of Pictures, Busts etc at Hafod*, Hafod: Hafod Press, 1807 (*NLW*).

JOHNSON, Samuel, *Account of the Life of Mr Richard Savage*, ed. C. Tracy, Oxford: Clarendon press, 1971.

JOHNSON, Samuel, *The Lives of the Most Eminent English Poets*, London: C. Bathurst, *et al*, 1781.

JONES, Anthony, *Welsh Chapels*, Cardiff: *NMW*, 1984.

JONES, Bedwyr Lewis, *Gwŷr Môn*, Bala: Cyngor Gwlad, 1979.

JONES, Francis, '[Gulston notebooks]', *Carmarthenshire Historian*, Volume 5, 1968, pp.43-66.

JONES, Francis, *Historic Carmarthenshire Homes*, Carmarthen: Carmarthenshire Antiquarian Society & Dyfed Cultural Services, 1987.

JONES, Ifano, *A History of Printing and Printers in Wales to 1810*, Cardiff: William Lewis, 1925.

JONES, Iwan Meical, 'Calvert Richard Jones, the earlier work', *History of Photography*, Autumn 1991, pp.174-179.

JONES, Iwan Meical, *Scientific Visions: The Photographic Art of William Henry Fox Talbot, John Dillwyn Llewelyn and Calvert Richard Jones*, Denbigh: Gee & Son Ltd, repr. from the *Transactions of the Honourable Society of Cymmrodorion*, 1990, pp.112-172.

JONES, J.R. Kilsby, *Holl Weithiau Prydyddawl a Rhyddieithiol*, London: William Mackenzie, [1868].

JONES, Maurice, 'Yr arlunfa Gymreig', *Cymru Fydd*, Volume IV, 1891, pp.19-27.

JONES, Thomas, *Six Views in South Wales* [no imprint], c1775.

JONES, William, *History of the Port of Swansea*, Carmarthen: W. Spurrell & Son, 1922.

JOYNER, Paul, *Arlunydd Cyntefig Cymreig* [A Welsh Primitive] (exhibition catalogue), Aberystwyth: *NLW*, 1993.

JOYNER, Paul, *Dolbadarn Castle* (exhibition catalogue), Aberystwyth: *NLW*, 1990.

JOYNER, Paul, 'Some Sandby drawings of Scotland', *NLW Journal*, Volume XXIII, No. 1, Summer, 1983, pp.1-16.

JOYNER, Paul, *Dolbadarn: Studies on a Theme*, Aberystwyth: *NLW*, 1990.

JOYNER, Paul, *S.H. Grimm: Views in Wales*, Aberystwyth: *NLW*, 1983.

JOYNER, Paul, (*et alia*) *Trefi'r Gorllewin • West Wales Towns*, (exhibition catalogue) Aberystwyth: *NLW*, 1995.

JUNG, Carl, *Man and his Symbols*, London: Picador, 1978.

KALLIR, Jane, *The Folk Art Tradition*, London: Allen Lane, 1982.

KEYSER, C.E., *A List of Buildings Having Mural Decorations*, London: South Kensington Museums, 1883.

KISSACK, Keith, *Monmouth: the Making of a County Town*, London (etc): Phillimore, 1975.

KITSON, Michael, 'Hogarth's apology for painters', *Walpole Society*, Volume XLI, 1966-68, pp.46-111.

KNIGHT, Roy, *History of the Swansea Art Society*, Swansea: Christopher Davies, 1987.

KRAUS, Hans P. (Junior), 'The Reverend Calvert R. Jones', *Sun Pictures*, Volume 5, 1990.

LANDSEER, Thomas, *Life and Letters of William Bewick*, London: E.P. Publishing Ltd, 1978.

LEACH, Arthur L., *Charles Norris 1779-1858*, Tenby: Tenby Observer & County Times, 1949.

LEATHART, William, *The Origin and Progress of the Gwyneddigion Society*, London, H. Hughes, 1831.

LESLIE, Charles R., *Life and Times of Sir Joshua Reynolds*, London: [no imprint], 1865.

LEWIS, John, *The Swansea Guide 1851*, Bath: Adlib Books, produced for the Library & Information Service of West Glamorgan County Council, 1989.

LEWIS, J.M., *Welsh Monumental Brasses - a Guide*, Cardiff: *NMW*, 1974.

LEWIS, Mostyn, *Stained Glass in North Wales*, Altringham: John Sherrat & Son Ltd, 1970.

LEWIS, Richard, 'Arlunydd Gwalia', *Y Casglwr*, 1988.

LEWIS, Wilmarth, *Correspondence of Horace Walpole*, New Haven: Yale U.P., 1971 (ff).

LLOYD, Thomas, *The Lost Houses of Wales*, London: SAVE Britain's Heritage, 1987.

LLOYD-JOHNES, Herbert, 'Thomas Tudor', *NLW Journal*, Volume XXI, No. 3, Summer 1980, pp.243-245.

LONG, Basil, 'Richard Crosse', *Walpole Society*, Volume XVII, 1928-29, pp.61-74.

LONGSTAFFE, J.P., 'John Dyer as a painter', *Montgomery Collections* XI, 1878, pp.396-402.

LORD, Peter, *Hugh Hughes - arlunydd gwlad 1790-1863*, Llandysul: Gwasg Gomer, 1995.

LORD, Peter, 'Iconograffeg poblogaidd y pregethwyr', *Barn*, Gorffennaf/Awst, Rhifau 330/331, pp.37-52.

LUGT, F., *Repertoire de Catalogues...*, La Haye: Martinus Nijhoff, 1938-1964 (3 vols).

MACDONALD, Stuart, *History and Philosophy of Art Education*, London: University of London Press, 1970.

MACMILLAN, Duncan, *Painting in Scotland: The Golden Age*, Oxford: Phaidon Press, 1986.

MANCHESTER ART GALLERY, *Art and Industrial Revolution*, Manchester: City Art Gallery, 1968.

MARILLIER, Henry C., *The Liverpool School of Painters*, London: Heinemann, 1911.

MATTHEWS, Thomas, *Biography of John Gibson*, London: Heinemann, 1911.

MCCORMACK, Helen, 'Duplicate Books by Hubard', *Antiquary*, February 1944.

MCCORMACK, Helen, *W.J. Hubard and the Hubard Gallery* (exhibition catalogue), Valentine Gallery, Richmond, Virginia, USA, 1948.

MEACHER, E.E., *Auction of Graiglwyd Penmaenmawr*, 14 July 1910.

MOIR, Esther, *The Discovery of Britain*, London: Routledge and Kegan Paul, 1964.

MONMOUTH, *Monmouth Exhibition*, [Monmouth]: T. Farror, 1840. Monmouth Museum.

MOORE, Donald, *Artists' Views of Glamorgan*, Cardiff: Glamorgan Archive Services, 1988.

MOORE, Donald, *John Petherick* (exhibition catalogue), London: S. Somerville & A. Reed, [1989].

MOORE, Donald, *Moses Griffith*, Cardiff: WAC, 1979.

MOORE, Donald, *Wales in the Eighteenth Century*, Swansea: Christopher Davies, 1976.

MOORE-COLYER, Richard, *A Land of Pure Delight* Llandysul: Gomer, 1992.

MORGAN, Prys, *Gwenwynen Gwent*, Casnewydd: Eisteddfod, 1988.

MORGAN, Prys, 'From long knives to Blue Books', in Davies, R.R., *Welsh Society and Nationhood*, Cardiff: UWP, 1984.

MORGAN, Prys, 'Thomas Jones of Pencerrig', *Transactions of the Honourable Society of Cymmrodorion*, 1984, pp.51-76.

MORGAN, Prys, 'Richard Wilson: cynffonwr adweithiol neu broffwyd rhanmantiaeth?', *Barn*, Awst, Medi 1991, Rhifau 343-344, pp.27-35.

MORGAN, William & JONES, John, *Tadau Methodistiaidd*, Swansea: Lewis Evans, 1897.

MORGAN-CLIFFORD, Colonel, *Reminiscences of his Life* [Monmouthshire]: Morgan-Clifford, 1893.

MORRIS, Bernard, 'Paul Padley's, Swansea: a view of the town in the 1790s', *Gower* XLI (1990) pp.6-16.

MORRIS, Edward, 'John Naylor and other collectors of modern paintings in 19th century Britain', *Walker Art Gallery* Annual Report, 1974-5, pp.72-9.

MORRIS, E.R., 'A Montgomeryshire artist - Hugh Jerman Llanidloes', *Montgomeryshire Collections*, Volume 72, 1984, pp.45-52.

MORRIS, William, *Plans of Harbours*, Shrewsbury: William Morris, 1801.

NEALE, J.P., *Views of the Seats of noblemen* (6 vols), London: Sherwood, Gilbert and Pipet, 1828.

NEWELL, Rev. R.H., *Letters on the Scenery of Wales*, London: Gordon, Baldwin & Craddock, 1821.

NICHOLSON, Benedict, *Joseph Wright of Derby* (2 vols), New Haven: YUP, 1968.

NORRIS, Charles, *Etchings of Tenby*, London: John Booth, 1812.

NORTHCOTE, James, *The Life of Sir Joshua Reynolds*, London: [no imprint], 1818.

OLIVER, R.C.B., *Thomas Jones the Artist*, Llandysul, R.C.B. Oliver, 1970.

OWEN, H., *The Life and Works of Lewis Morris*, Anglesey Antiquarian Society, 1951.

ORMOND, Richard, *Early Victorian Portraits* (2 vols), London: HMSO, 1973.

ORMOND, Richard & TURPIN, John, *Daniel Maclise 1806-1870*, London: Arts Council, 1972.

PAINTING, David, 'J.D. Llewelyn and his family circle', *History of Photography*, Autumn 1991.

PAINTING, David, *Swansea's Place in the History of Photography*, Swansea: *RISW*, 1982.

PALMER, Alfred N., *History of the Parish Church of Wrexham*, Wrexham: Woodall, Minshall & Thomas, 1888.

PARRIS, Leslie, *Landscape in Britain c1750-1850*, London: Tate Gallery Publications, 1973.

PASSAVANT, J.D., *Tour of a German artist in England*, Wakefield: E.P. Publishing, 1978 (1836).

PEATE, Iorwerth C., *The Welsh House*, Liverpool: The Brython Press, 1946.

PEATE, Iorwerth C., *Welsh Society and Eisteddfod Medals and Relics*, Cardiff: *NMW*, 1938.

PENNANT, Thomas, *The Literary Life*, London: B. & J. White, 1793.

PENNANT, Thomas, *Tour in Wales* (2 vols), London: B. White, 1784.

PENNY, Nicholas, *Reynolds*, London: *RA*, 1986.

PEVSNER, Nikolaus, *Berkshire*, Harmondsworth: Penguin, 1966.

PEVSNER, Nikolaus, *The Englishness of English Art*, Harmondsworth: Penguin Books, 1964.

PIERCE, Rev. T. Mordaf, *Dr W. Owen Pughe*, Caernarfon: Cymru, 1914.

PLINY, *The Natural History* (6 vols), London: George Bell & Sons, 1855-1857.

PRICE, Cecil, *The English Theatre in Wales*, Swansea: UC Swansea, 1984.

PRICHARD, T.J.Ll., *The New Aberystwyth Guide*, Aberystwyth: Lewis Jones, 1824.

PRITCHARD, Michael, *A Directory of London Photographers 1841-1908*, Bushey: ALLM Books, 1986.

PRITCHARD, T.W., *The Wynns of Wynnstay*, Caerwys: Old Court Press, 1982.

PRITCHARD, W., *Picturesque Scenery in North Wales*, Caernarvon: W. Pritchard, c1840.

PUGHE, William Owen, *Geiriadur Cynmraeg [sic] a Saesoneg [sic]*, London: E. & T. Williams, 1793.

PYE, John, *Patronage of British Art*, London: Longman *et alia*, 1845.

PYKE, E.J., *A Biographical Dictionary of Wax Modellers* (Supplement), Oxford: Clarendon Press, 1981.

RAWLINSON, W.G., *Engraved Work of Turner*, London: Macmillan & Co., 1908.

The RECORD Society, *An Index to the Wills and Administrations of Lancashire and Cheshire*, 1892-1980.

REES, D. Ben, *Wales: The Cultural Heritage*, Ormskirk: G.W. & A. Hesketh, 1981.

REES, D. Ben, *Hanes Plwyf Llanddewi Brefi*, Llanddewi Brefi: Pwyllgor Etifeddiaeth a Diwylliant, 1984, p.76.

REES, Mardy, *Notable Welshmen*, Caernarvon: Herald Office, 1908.

REES, Eiluned, 'Pre 1820 Welsh subscription lists', *Journal of the Welsh Bibliographical Society*, Volume XI, 1973-4, pp.85-119.

REES, Williams, *Cardiff - a history of the city*, Cardiff: The Corporation of the City of Cardiff, 1969.

REPORT of the Commissioners of Education, London: [HMSO], 1847.

RICHARDSON, Jonathan, *An Account of Some...Statues, Bas-reliefs, Drawings and Pictures in Italy*, London: J. Knapton, 1722.

RICHARDSON, Jonathan, *Two Discourses: An Essay...on Criticism; Science of a Connoisseur*, London: W. Churchill, 1719.

ROBERTS, Askew, *Wynnstay and the Wynns*, Oswestry: Woodall & Venables, 1876.

ROBERTS, Gomer M., 'Dirgelwch Oriel y Beirdd', *Y Casglwr*, No. 17, August 1982, p.11.

ROBERTS, G.M., 'Gleanings from the Trevecka letters', *Brycheiniog*, Volume III, 1957, pp.127-156.

ROGET, John T., *History of the Old Watercolour Society*, London: Longmans Green & Co., 1891 (2 vols.).

ROSENFIELD, Sybil, & CROFT, Murray, 'A check list of scene painters working in Great Britain', *Theatre Notebook*, Volume 20, 1965.

ROWAN, Eric, *Art in Wales 2000 BC - AD 1850: An Illustrated History*, Cardiff: WAC & UWP, 1978.

ROYAL Institution of South Wales, *Annual Reports, 1836-48*, Swansea.

SANDBY, Paul, *Views in South Wales*, London: [J. Boydell], 1775.

SANDBY, Paul, *XII Views in North Wales*, London: P. Sandby, 1776.

SCHARF, George, *Catalogue of the Art Treasures of the United Kingdom*, Manchester: Bradbury & Evans, 1857.

SMITH, Peter, *Houses of the Welsh Countryside*, London: HMSO, 1975.

SOLLY, Neil, *Memoirs of the Life of David Cox*, London: Rodart Reproductions Ltd, 1973 (orig. pub. 1873).

SOLKIN, David, 'Battle of the Ciceros', *Art History*, Volume 16, No. 4, December 1983, pp.406-422.

SOLKIN, David, *Richard Wilson*, London: Tate Gallery Publications, 1983.

SPINTHER, 'Hugh Hughes yr artist', *Y Traethodydd* (Cyfres newydd), Volume XII, 1924, pp.42-50.

STEEGMAN, John, *Portraits from Welsh Houses* (exhibition catalogue), Cardiff: *NMW*, 1948.

STEEGMAN, John, *The Rule of Taste*, London: Macmillan & Co, 1936.

STRETTON, N., 'Thomas Rothwell, engraver', *The Antique Collector*, October 1971, pp.201-204.

STRETTON, N., 'Thomas Rothwell, engraver and copper-plate printer 1740-1807', *Transactions of the English Ceramic Circle*, 1966.

STRICKLAND, W.G., *A Dictionary of Irish Artists* (2 vols), Dublin & London: Maunsel & Co, 1913.

SUGGETT, Richard, *John Nash Architect • Pensaer*, Aberystwyth: RCAHM & NLW, 1995.

SUMMERSON, John, *John Nash: Architect to George IV*, London: George Allen & Unwin, 1935.

SUPER, Robert H., *Walter Savage Landor*, London: John Calder, 1957.

TAYLOR, Basil, *Joshua Cristall*, London: VAM, 1972.

THOMAS, Hilary A., *The Diaries of John Bird 1790-1803*, Cardiff: South Wales Record Society and Glamorgan Archive Service, 1987.

THOMAS, Hilary A., *A Catalogue of Glamorgan Estate Maps*, Cardiff: GAP, 1992.

THOMAS, John, 'Josiah Wedgewood and some prominent Cymmrodorion', *Cymmrodorion Transactions*, 1965, pp.137-147.

THOMAS, T.H., 'Sydenham Edwards of Usk' *Cardiff Naturalists Society Transactions*, Volume 43, 1910.

THOMAS, T.H., 'A Welsh Bewick', *The Red Dragon*, Volume XI, 1887, pp.457-466.

THOMPSON, Michael W., *The Journey of Sir Richard Colt Hoare, 1793-1810*, Gloucester: Alan Sutton, 1983.

TOMOS, Dafydd, *Michael Faraday in Wales*, Denbigh: Gwasg Gee, 1972.

TOOLE-STOTT, Raymond, *Circus and Allied Arts: A World Bibliography 1500-1962* (3 vols), Derby: Harper & Sons Ltd, 1962.

TRACY, Clarence, *The Artificial Bastard*, Toronto: University of Toronto & Saskatchewan, 1953.

TURNER, William, *The Ceramics of Swansea and Nantgarw*, London, 1897.

TWISTON-DAVIES, LEONARD & LLOYD-JOHNES, H.J., *Welsh Furniture*, Cardiff: UWP, 1950.

TWISTON-DAVIES, Leonard & EVANS, A., *Welsh life in the 18th Century*, London: Country Life Ltd, 1939.

VAUGHAN, Herbert M., *A List of the Artists & Engravers of Book Plates Culled from the Catalogues of Various Collections in the NLW & in the Collection of Welsh Book Plates made by Sir Evan Jones, Baronet, of Pentower*, Heathfield, Sussex: G.H.V., 1940.

VAUGHAN, Herbert M., *The Welsh Book-Plates in the Collection of Sir Evan Davies Jones, Bart., M.P.*, London: A.L. Humphreys, 1920.

VENN, J.A., *Alumni Cantabrigiensis*, Cambridge: University Press, 1954.

VERTUE, George, 'Notebooks', *Walpole Society*, Volume XVIII, 1929 [*et al.*].

WAAGEN, Gustav, *Galleries and Cabinets of Art*, London: John Murray, 1857.

WAAGEN, Gustav, *Treasures of Art in Great Britain* (3 vols), London: John Murray, 1854.

WALKER'S GALLERY, *Watercolours and Drawings by Thomas Tudor*, London: Walker's June 1961 (exhibition catalogue).

WALPOLE, Horace, *Anecdotes of Painting in England* (4 vols), London: J. Dodsley, 1786.

WATKINS, John, Life and Career of George Chambers, London: J. Watkins, 1841.

WATERHOUSE, Ellis, *Thomas Gainsborough*, London: Spring Books, 1958.

WEAVER, Mike, 'Early Welsh Photography', *History of Photography*, Vol. 13, No. 3, 1991.

WEBLEY, Derrick Pritchard, *Cast to the winds: the life and work of Penry Williams, 1802-1885*, Aberystwyth: The National Library of Wales, 1997.

WEBSTER, Roger, 'For Wales see England', in *Anatomy of Wales*, ed. R. Brinley Jones, Peterston-super-Ely: Gwerin, 1972, pp.227-247.

WHITE, Gilbert, *The Natural History of Selbourne*, London: T. Bensley, 1789.

WILIAM, Dafydd Wyn, *Cofiant Wiliam Morris (1705-63)*, Llangefni: O. Jones, 1995.

WILKINS, Charles, 'Joseph Edwards the sculptor', *The Red Dragon*, Volume 1, 1882, p.100.

WILLIAMS, Albert H., *John Wesley in Wales*, Cardiff: UWP, 1971.

WILLIAMS, Evan, 'Y Gelfyddyd o Arlunio' *Traethodydd*, Volume IV, 1848, pp.423-434; V, 1849, pp.44-52, 166-177, 357-369, 521-527.

WILLIAMS, Evan, 'Arddangosiad trysorau celfyddyd' *Traethodydd*, 1857, pp.329-341.

WILLIAMS, Glanmor, *Swansea: An Illustrated History*, Swansea: Christopher Davies Ltd, 1990.

WILLIAMS, Griffith J., *Iolo Morganwg* (vol. 1), Cardiff: UWP, 1956.

WILLIAMS, Isaac, *A Catalogue of Welsh Topographical Prints*, Cardiff: *NMW*, 1926.

WILLIAMS, Isaac, *Early Welsh Line and Mezzotint engravers*, Cardiff: *NMW*, 1933.

WILLIAMS, Jane, *The Literary Remains of the Rev. Thomas Price 'Carnhuanawc', Vicar of Cwmdu, Breconshire* (2 vols), Llandovery: William Rees, 1854-55.

WILLIAMS, John, *Digest of Welsh Historical Statistics*, Cardiff: Welsh Office, 1985.

WILLIAMS, John D., 'Dau bortread Hugh Hughes' [Two portraits by Hugh Hughes], *Casglwr*, No. 19, March 1983, p.1.

WILLIAMS, Jac L., *The History of Education in Wales*, Swansea: Christopher Davies, 1978.

WILLIAMS, Peter B., *The Tourists' Guide...Caernarvon*, Caernarvon: J. Hulme, 1821.

WILLIAMS, Ralph M., *Poet, Painter and Parson: The Life of John Dyer*, New York: Bookman Ass., 1956.

WILLIAMS, Terry, 'Hugh Hughes arlunydd', *Y Faner*, 8 Gorffennaf [July], 1983, pp.10-11.

WILLIAMSON, George C., *John Downman*, London: Otto Limited, 1907.

WILSON, John, *Art and Society in Newport: James Flewitt Mullock and the Victorian Achievement*, Newport: Newport Museum and Art Gallery, 1993.

WILTON, Andrew, *The Life and Work of J.M.W. Turner*, London: Academy Editions, 1979.

WINSTANLEY, T., *A Catalogue of Pictures*, Liverpool: 26-27 August 1840.

WOOD, John, *Wynnstay Park*, auction,. [Wynnstay, 12 June 1947].

WOOD, Robert, *The Ruins of Palmyra*, [no imprint], 1753.

WORDSWORTH, Jonathan (*et al.*), *William Wordsworth and the Age of Romanticism*, New Brunswick & London: Rudgers U.P., 1987.

WRIGHT, Christopher, *Old Master Paintings in Great Britain*, London: Sotheby's, 1976.

YOUNG, William W., *Guide to the Scenery of Glyn Neath*, London: [WilliamYoung], 1835.

INDEX TO TYPES OF ARTIST
Compiled by B. Morton and does not include Chester artists.

Animal painters:
ADOLPHE, 'Monsieur' Edgar
BARKER, Benjamin (Senior)
CHAPMAN, W.J. [John Watkins]
DAVIS, Tyddesley R. T.
HORLOR, M.
HUBARD, William James (and Company)
LONGBOTTOM, Robert J.
MULLOCK, J. F.
PARRY, Henry 'The Younger'
ROLFE, Alexander F.
ROOS, William 'Gwilym Rosa'.

Architects: Builders who also designed buildings will be included here, as will some surveyors.
BAGGALEY, John
BAGGALEY, Richard
BATCHELOR [& PROSSER]
BEDFORD, Thomas
BERNARD, C. E.
BLACKWALL, John
BOWEN, Thomas
BOWEN, W.
BRIGSTOCKE, Job (Senior)
CALVERT, John
CARVER, William
CHITTENDEN, G.
CLINTON, George
COLE, John
COOPER, John
COULTHART, William Ritson
DAVIES, David
DAVIES, Edward
DAVIES, Rees
DAVIES, Thomas
EDMONDS, Paul
EDWARDS, Robert
EDWARDS, William
ELLIS, Robert Lloyd
EVANS, Daniel
EVANS, David
EVANS, John
EVINS [*sic*] [EVANS], Joseph Hancock
FAIRCLOUGH, Henry, J.
GABB, Robert
GABE, William
GRIFFITHS, Evan
GUMMOW, Benjamin
HABERSHON, Matthew
HALL, John
HAMMON, Henry J.
HOARE, Hugh
HUGHES, James
HUMPHREYS, John
JAMES, Benjamin
JAMES, Richard
JERNEGAN, William
JOHN, Joseph
JONES, Edward
JONES, John 'Talhaiarn'
JONES, Griffith
JONES, James
JONES, Richard
JONES, Robert
JONES, Thomas (Oswestry)
JONES, Thomas (Chester)
JOSEPH, John
KENNEDY, Henry;
LEWIS, Henry
LANGDON, John Harries [Harris]
LLEWELLYN, Morgan
LLOYD, John
LOCKWOOD, Alfred
LOVEDAY, W.L.
LUGAR, Robert
MADDOX, George
MADDOX, James
MATHIAS, Joseph
MAUND, John
MORGAN, David
MOXHAM, Egbert
NASH, John;
OWEN, Elias
OWEN, William
O'ROURKE, Michael Spain
PARKER, Rev. John
PARRY, J.
PEMBERTON, James
PENSON, Richard Kirke
PENSON, Thomas
PENSON, Thomas M. (Junior)
PHILLIPS, William
PILDITCH, John
POWELL, William
PRATT, John
PRICHARD, Thomas
PRITCHARD, John
PUGH, Lewis
RICHARDS, Richard
RICHARDS, William
ROBERTS, David
ROBERTS, Richard
ROBERTS, Robert (Bangor)
ROBERTS, Robert (Caernarfon)
ROWLANDS, James
ROWLANDS, Thomas
SEDDON, John
SAUNDERS, Robert Cook
STRAWSON, George Smith
THOMAS, David
THOMAS, Robert George
THOMAS, Walter Richard
THOMAS, William
THOMAS, William (Junior)
THOMAS, William Griffith
TUDOR, Thomas
TURNER, Joseph
VAUGHAN, David
VAUGHAN, David (Meifod)
WALLACE, Alfred R.
WALLIS, Charles
WELCH, John
WHEELER, Joseph
WHITTINGTON, William
WILLIAMS, David
WILLIAMS, David Robert
WILLIAMS, Edward 'Iolo Morganwg'
WILLIAMS, Thomas
WOOD, Henry
WYNN, Thomas

Artists' colourmen:
DAVIES, Ann
HARRIS, James (Senior)
PALMER, William
PRITCHARD, Owen
THOMAS, Robert
WILLIAMS, D.
WILLIAMS, W. P.

Calligraphers:
ADOLPHE, 'Monsieur' Edgar
LEWIS, Mr.

Carvers:
ATKINS, Alex
BROOM, John
HUGHES, G.
JEFFREYS, Thomas
JONES, Elizabeth
JONES, John Waring
JONES, Thomas & William (Tregarth)
JONES, William (Waunfawr)
PALMER, William
RICHARDS, Thomas
WILLIAMS, J.

China painters:
BAXTER, Thomas
BEDDOW, George
BEVINGTON, Hannah
BILLINGSLEY, L[e]vinia
BROMLEY, Adelaide
CLULOW, Mary
DINGLY, Stephen
EVANS, Evan
ESSERY, William
EVANS, David
HANCOCK, John
HARLEY, Miss
HARRIS, John 'Old Harris'
HEWITT, Miss
HOOD, [Mr]
HUGHES, Samuel
JOHNSON, John
LOTHAM, John
MORRIS, Henry
MORRIS, Maria

PARDOE, Thomas
PARDOE, William Henry
PHILLIPS, John
POLLARD
ROTHWELL, Thomas
THOMAS, Betty
THOMAS, Thomas
YOUNG, William Weston

Coach painters:
CRIDLE, James
DINGLY, Stephen
FRANCIS, John Deffett
JOHN, William
JONES, Hugh
MORRIS, Henry
PARRY, William
ROBERTS, Thomas
SAMUEL, Robert

Costume artists:
CADWALLADER, A.
GRIFFITHS, R.
JONES, Hugh
LLANOVER, Lady (Augusta Hall)
ROWLAND, John 'Cambrian Lluniedydd'

Drawing masters:
ATTWOOD, John
BAKER, W. H.
BARNETT, Mr
BAXTER, Thomas
BUTEL, Alexander
BUTEL, Edmund
BUTEL, Louis
BUTLER, William
CARLISLE, R.
CLARE, Mr
COMER, Mr
COULON, Monsieur Pierre
COX, David
D'ALLEGRE, Monsieur Louis
DELAMOTTE, George Orleans
DODD, J. J. 'Arlunydd Gwalia'
DUPONT, Monsieur A.
ELLIS, Thomas
EVANS, Mrs
GARNAUT, Mr
GRAY, E. A.
GREIVES, Jonathan
HARRIS, James (Senior)
HART, Mrs
IBBETSON, Julius Caesar
JACKSON, Miss H.
JEBB, William
JERMAN, Hugh;
OURNET, Monsieur F.
KNIVETON, William
KRIENS, Mr E.
LOVEDAY, W. L.
MARTIN, J.
MCLOUGHLIN, Miss
PYNE, Henry
QUINTIN, Monsieur H. J.
RIGAUD, Stephen Francis Dutilh
SANDBY, Paul
SANDERS, Charles
SIMONNET, Julius Augustus
SMITH, Thomas Haddon
SPRATT, Henry
STOTHARD, Thomas

Engravers:
BAUGH, Robert
BAXTER, Thomas
BONNETT, John
BRINDLEY, E.H.
BRINDLEY, James
CHAPMAN, W. J. [John Watkins]
CLARE, Mr
COPE, James
EDWARDS, William Camden
EVANS, E.
EVANS, John
GRIFFITH, Moses
HUGHES, Hugh 'Hughes the Limner'
JEAVONS, Mr;
JONES, Charles
JONES, John
JONES, Thomas
JONES, William Ellis 'Cawrdaf'
PARRY, Devereux
PUGH, Ed[ward]
ROBERTS, John
ROTHWELL, Thomas
WALTERS, William
WILLIAMS, Watkin
YOUNG, William Weston.

Flower painters & Botanical artists:
CONWAY, Charles (Pontnewydd)
EDWARDS, Sydenham
EVANS, David
LOTHAM, John
PARDOE, Thomas
PARKER, Rev. John
SEVILLE, [W.].

Gatesmiths:
DAVIES, John
DAVIES, Robert
DAVIES, Thomas

Genre painters:
ALLEN, Joseph
BARKER, Thomas (of Bath)
GRIFFITHS, R.
MULLOCK, J. F.
ROWLAND, John 'Cambrian Lluniedydd'

Heraldic artists:
BEDDOW, George
CARTWRIGHT, J.
CLARE, Mr
DAVIES, David

House painters:
BARNETT, Mr
BRIGSTOCKE, D.
DAVIES, Ann
ESSERY, Timothy Brumble
ESSERY, William
EVANS, Thomas
JONES, Roger
LOUGHOR, William
MORGAN, William
OWEN, (Rev.) Robert 'Eryron Gwyllt Walia'
PARRY, William
PATRICK, David
RENIE, John
RICHARDS, Thomas
ROBERTS, John
SAMUEL, Robert
WILLIAMS, Richard

Landscape artists:
ALLEN, Lady Catherine [Lady Mackintosh]
ANTHONY, Henry Mark
ATTWOOD, John
AUSTIN, Samuel;
BARKER, Thomas (of Bath)
BEFFIN, Miss Sarah
BIRCHALL, Henry B.
BOND, Richard Sebastian
BOURDON, Toussaint
BROWNING, Miss
BOYDELL, Mrs
BURCHALL, William
BURTON, C.
BUTLER, William
CARTER, J. M.
CLARKE, Thomas E.
COX, David
CRACKLOW, C. T.
DAVIS, Tyddesley R.T.
DODD, J. J. 'Arlunydd Gwalia'
DYER, John (Rev.)
ELLIS, Ellis Owen 'Ellis Bryn-Coch'
EVANS, John
FENTON, [John]
FIDLER, J. (Junior)
GRENVILLE, Lady Charlotte Neville
GRIFFITH, Moses
HARRIS, James (Senior)
HAWKINS, Mrs Louisa [or Mrs W.]
HORNOR, Thomas
HUGHES, Hugh 'Hughes the Limner'

HUGHES, Robert
HUGHES, Samuel
IBBETSON, Julius Caesar
INCE, Joseph Murray
INGLEBY, John
JAMES, Horatio
JEAVONS, Mr
JERMAN, Hugh
JOHNES, Mariamne
JONES, Rev. Calvert Richard
JONES, Rev. Henry Longueville
JONES, Hugh
JONES, Theophilus
JONES, Thomas
JONES, William Edward
JONES, William Ellis 'Cawrdaf'
KNIVETON, William
LEWIS, John
LLANOVER, Lady (Augusta Hall)
LLEWELLYN, W. B.
LLOYD, John William
LLWYD, Angharad
LONGBOTTOM, Robert J.
LYONS, C.
MARCHI, Giuseppe
MORGAN, Chareles
MULLOCK, J. F.
OAKLEY, Elizabeth
PADLEY, Paul
PARKER, Rev. John
PARRY, Henry 'The Younger' (Monmouth)
PARRY, Henry 'Senior' (Monmouth)
PARRY, John (Wrexham)
PAYNE, Henry Thomas
PENNANT, Thomas
PENSON, Richard Kirke
PENSON, Thomas
PETHERICK, John
POUGET, Major Robert
POWELL, Champney
PRICE, Rev. Thomas 'Carnhuanawc'
PROVIS, W. A.
PUGH, Edward 'The Limner'
PUGHE, William Owen
PUGIN, Auguste Charles
RATCLIFFE, Elizabeth
ROBERTS, William
ROLFE, Alexander F.
ROWLAND, John 'Cambrian'
SALMON, William Reynold Deer
SANT, George
SEVILLE, [W.]
SHAW, William R. B.
SMITH, Miles
SMYTH, Henry
SPOONER, J. S.
STEVENS, James
STOTHARD, Thomas
TAYLOR, William
TRAHERNE, Charlotte Louisa
TUDOR, John Owen
TUDOR, Owen
TUDOR, Thomas
WATERS, Thomas
WATKEYS, William
WELSH PRIMITIVE
WILLIAMS, Rev. Evan 'Ifan y Limner'
WILLIAMS, Frances
WILLIAMS, Hugh Grecian
WILLIAMS, Penry 'Cymro Bach'
WILLIAMS, Taliesin 'Taliesin ab Iolo'
WILLIAMS, William M. 'Ap Caledfryn'
WILSON, Richard
WINTTRAUD, Mr de
WYNNE, Robert
YOUNG, William Weston

Marine artists:
AUSTIN, Samuel
BARRY, Joseph T.
BIRCHALL, Henry B.
BURCHALL, William
BUTLER, William
CHAPMAN, James
HARRIS, James (Senior)
HARRIS, John
HARRISON, J. H.
JONES, Rev. Calvert Richard
PADLEY, John Weir

Masons:
ARTHUR, John
BOWEN, David
BRUTE, Aaron
BRUTE, James
BRUTE, Peter John
BRUTE, Thomas
DANIEL, John
DAVIES, Griffith
DAVIES, Henry
DAVIES, Rees
DAVIES, Richard
DAVIES, William
EDWARDS, John
EDWARDS, Joseph
EDWARDS, William
EVAN, John
EVANS, David
EVANS, Griffith
GEORGE, Richard
GEORGE, Thomas
GRIFFITH, David
GRIFFITH, David
GRIFFITHS, Thomas (Llanelli)
GRIFFITHS, Thomas (Swansea)
GRIFFITHS, William
GROVES, Henry
HERBERT, Lewis
HUGH, Peter
JAMES, John
JENKINS (Bridgend)
JENKINS, Edward (Pen-tre)
JENKINS, John (Rhydypandy)
JENKINS, John (Swansea)
JENKINS, John (Cydweli)
JOHN, David (Llanybydder)
JOHN, David (Cardigan)
JONES (Llangynider)
JONES, David (Llangyfelach)
JONES, Edward (Llandyfair)
JONES, Hugh (Denbigh)
JONES, John (Llandyfriog)
JONES, John (Brecon);
ONES, John Emrys (Merthyr)
JONES, Phillip (Llanddewi Brefi)
JONES, Rees (Llanymddyfri)
JONES, William (Llanfihangel Abergwesyn)
JONES, William L. (Merthyr)
LAMB, George
LEWIS, Edward
LEWIS, Morgan
LLOYD, Daniel
LLOYD, David (Nevern)
LLOYD, David (Swansea)
LLOYD, Thomas
LOTT, James
MALIPHANT, David
MAINWARING, Daniel
MATHEWS, Richard
MORGAN, David
MORGAN, Evan
MORGAN, Jacop David
MORGAN, William (Bwlch)
MORGAN, William (Llanywern)
MORRIS, David (Swansea)
MORRIS, Edward (The Elder)
OWEN, John
OWEN, Nathaniel
PHILIP, John
PHILLIP, David
PHILLIP, William
POWELL (Powel) (Talgarth)
PRICE, Anthony
PRITCHARD, Edward
PROSSER, John (Monmouth)
PROTHEROE, Rees
REES, David
REES, John
RELLY, Richard
RICHARD, David
RICHARD, Thomas
RICHARD, Thomas (Llandyfaelog), (St Dogmaels)
RICHARDS, John (Laugharne)
RICHARDS, John (St Issells)
RICHERDS, John
ROACH, Thomas
ROSSITER, John
ROWLAND, John
ROWLAND, William
SAYCE, Thomas (The Elder)

SEABORN, John
SHONE, Richard
STEPHEN, Edward
STEPHENS, John
TENANT, John
THOMAS, David
THOMAS, George
THOMAS, John (Llangaston)
THOMAS, John (Brecon)
THOMAS, John (Haverfordwest)
THOMAS, Rees
THOMAS, Samuel
THOMAS, Thomas
TUCKER, John
TUCKER, William
WARLOW, Thomas
WHITLEY, Robert
WILLIAM, David
WILLIAMS, David
WILLIAMS, Edward 'Iolo Morganwg'
WILLIAMS, Henry (Pembroke)
WILLIAMS, Henry (Gwenddwr)
WILLIAMS, Henry [Junior] (Gwenddwr)
WILLIAMS, James
WILLIAMS, John
WILLIAMS, Richard
WILLIAMS, William (Llan-faes)
WILLIAMS, William (The Elder) (Llan-faes)
WILLIAMS, William (St Florence).

Medalists:
ARONSON, J.

Miniature artists:
ADOLPHE, 'Monsieur' Edgar
BEFFIN, Miss Sarah
BROOKE, Mr
CARLISLE, Mr
D'ALLEGRE, Monsieur Louis
DOWNMAN, John
FORSTER, Thomas
GARVIN, Henry
GEORGE, Thomas
GRIFFITH, Moses
HARGREAVES, Mr
JACKSON, Miss H.
JOHN, Alfred
JOHNES, Mariamne
LANGLOIS, Camille
MANSION, L.
MCLOUGHLIN, Mr
MERRYWEATHER, G.
PRATT, R.
PUGH, Mr (Tenby)
PUGH, Edward 'The Limner' (Ruthin)
RAPHAEL, Mrs
REDMOND, Thomas
ROCHE, Sampson Towgood
ROMNEY, G.
ROOS, William 'Gwilym Rosa'
SAXBY, Robert Scraze
SEVILLE, [W.]
STOTHARD, Robert Thomas
STOWER, Mr
TAYLOR, M.
WATKEYS, William
WRIGHT, Thomas

Model makers:
DUBOURG, Mr
RATCLIFFE, Elizabeth

Potters:
BENTLEY, George
CLARK, John
DAVIES, Hambury
LLOYD, Charles
WILLIAMS, David

Photographers:
ARNOLD, James F.
BIDDLE, Robert
BURNETT, Charles C.
CLARK, William
COMLEY, James
CROWE, William
DELAMOTTE, Philip
DYE, Charles
EVANS, David
FENTON, Roger
GUTCH, John Wheeley Gough
HARRIS, William
JONES, Rev. Calvert Richard
JONES, Thomas
JULLIEN, Mr
LANGLOIS, Camille
LLEWELYN, John Dillwyn
LLEWELYN, Mary Dillwyn
LLEWELYN, Thereza Dillwyn
MATHIAS, John Turner
NEDATH, Fredrick
SAXBY, Richard
SHARP, Mr [C.]
STORY-MASKELYNE, Nevil
VILLIERS & ANDREWS
WILLIAMS, William

Portrait artists:
ADOLPHE, 'Monsieur' Edgar
ALLEN, Joseph
BARKER, Benjamin (Senior)
BARKER, Thomas Jones
BATTERSBY, Mrs
BAXTER, Thomas
BEFFIN, Miss Sarah
BRIGSTOCKE, Thomas
BROOK, Richard
BROOK, Richard (Junior)
BROOKE, Mr
CHAPMAN, James
DAVIES, Dr [Thomas Woodwall]
DELAMOTTE, George Orleans
DOWNMAN, John
DYER, Rev. John
EDWARDS, William Camden
ELLIS, Ellis Owen 'Ellis Bryn-Coch'
ESSERY, Timothy Brumble
EVANS, David
EVANS, Simeon
EVANS, William Downing
FORSTER, Thomas
FRANCIS, John Deffett
GARNAUT, Mr
GARVIN, Henry
GRIFFITH, Moses
GRIFFITH, William
HAVERFIELD, Henry
HAWKINS, Mrs Louisa [or Mrs W.]
HUGHES, Hugh 'Hughes the Limner'
HUGHES, Lewis
HUGHES, Robert
HUMPHREYS, Robert
HUSTON, William C.
IBBETSON, Julius Caesar
JACKSON, Miss H.
JOHN, Alfred
JOHN, Daniel Llewellin
JOHNES, Mariamne
JONATHAN, Robert
JONES, Elizabeth
JONES, Hugh
JONES, Jonoval
JONES, Thomas 'Taliesin o Eifion'
JONES, William
JONES, William 'Jones of Chester'
JONES, William Edward
JONES, William Ellis 'Cawrdaf'
KEITH, A.
LANGLOIS, Camille
LLOYD, John
LLOYD, Robert Henry
MARCHI, Giuseppe
MARKS, Barrett Samuel
MARTIN, J.
MORRIS, Lewis 'Llewelyn Ddu o Fôn'
MULLOCK, J. F.
OWEN, [Edmund]
PADLEY, John Weir
PARRY, William
PATRICK, David
PRICE, Thomas
PUGHE, William Owen
PYNE, Henry
RIGAUD, Stephen
ROBERTS, John
ROBERTS, Jonathan
ROLFE, Alexander F.
ROMNEY, G.
ROOS, William 'Gwilym Rosa'
ROWLAND, John 'Cambrian Lluniedydd'

SALTER, A. W.
SAXBY, Robert Scraze
SHAW, William R. B.
SLATER, A. W.
STEVENS, James
STOWER, Mr
TAYLOR, Robert
TRAHERNE, Charlotte Louisa
TUDOR, Thomas
VAUGHAN, John
'Sion Grythor/Sion Fychan'
WALTERS, John
WATKEYS, William
WHITE, William 'of Swansea'
WILLIAMS, Rev. Evan 'Ifan y Limner'
WILLIAMS, John (Merthyr Tydfil)
WILLIAMS, John (Abergele)
WILLIAMS, John (Llanddarog)
WILLIAMS, Penry
WILLIAMS, Thomas Jones
WILLIAMS, William M.
'Ap Caledfryn'
WILSON, Richard
WYNNE, R. W.

Sculptors:
DAVIES, William 'Mynorydd'
DAVIS, Edward
EDWARDS, Alexander Wilson
EDWARDS, Joseph
JONES, Watkin D.
JONES, William L. (Merthyr)
JONES, William Lorando
(Merthyr)
MORGAN, Thomas
PHILLIPS, John
THOMAS, John Evan (Junior)
THOMAS, John (Haverfordwest)
THOMAS, John (Brecon)
THOMAS, William Meredith
WILLIAMS, Edward
'Iolo Morganwg'

Sign painters:
CARTWRIGHT, J.
DAVIES, Ann
DAVIES, David (Denbighshire)
DAVIES, David (Merionethshire)
ESSERY, Timothy Brumble
EVANS, Thomas
GRIFFITHS, Mr
JONES, Roger
JONES,
JONES, Thomas
(Pennant Melangell);
JONES, Thomas 'Taliesin o Eifion'
PARRY, William
PRITCHARD, George
PRITCHARD, Thomas
ROBERTS, Thomas
THOMAS, Inigo
WALTERS, John

WILLIAMS, D. J.
WILLIAMS, Edward
'Iolo Morganwg'

Silhouette artists:
ADOLPHE, 'Monsieur' Edgar
C., S.
HUBARD, William James
(and Company)
LLANOVER, Lady (Augusta
Hall)
SEVILLE, [W.]
SHARP, Mr [C.]
SHEY, Mr 'The Profilist'
SPENCE, Mr W. Steers
STOOKE, James
WHITTLE, E.

Sporting artists:
BARKER, Benjamin (Senior)
BARKER, Thomas Jones
SEVILLE, [W.]

Surveyors:
BALL, Samuel
BAMFORD, Samuel
BARBER, Edmund Scott
BARRETT, Richard
BARROW, John
BARRY, Thomas D.
BARTLEY, Samuel (Swansea)
BARTLEY, Samuel
(Pibwr, Carmarthen,
Llandefaelog)
BATE, Thomas
BAUGH, Robert
BLATHWAYT, Edmond
BOWEN, John
BRODIE, Henry
BROOKE, James
BURTON, Richard
CARTER, Robert
CARVER, William
CHAPMAN, James
CHRISTMAS, P.
CLINTON, George
COLLIER, Stephen
COULING, William
COULTHART, William Ritson
CUMING, Robert
CUMMING, Thomas George
DANIELS, Joshua
DAVIES, David
(Llangattock, Crickhowell,
Abergavenny)
DAVIES, David
(Froodvale, Conwil Gaio)
DAVIES, David
(Tyn y Coed, Myddfai)
DAVIES, R
DAVIES, Thomas
DAVIES, Thomas (Aberaeron)
DAWSON, Richard Godwin

DICKINSON, Joseph
DYOS, Edward
EDMONDS, Paul
EDWARDS, John (Cefn Bryn)
EDWARDS, John
(Dolaugwyrddion)
EDWARDS, Robert
ELLIS, Richard
ELLIS, Robert Lloyd
EVANS, Hugh
EVANS, John (Rhuddlan)
EVANS, John (Carmarthen,
Cardigan)
EVINS [*sic*] [EVANS], Joseph
Hancock
EVINS, Roger H
FAIRCHILD, Adolphius
FOORD, William
FURNIVAL, Edward
GABB, Robert
GISBOURNE, Edward
Sacheverell
GOODE, George
GOODE, Harry Phelps
GOODE, William
GRIFFITH, Hugh
GRIFFITHS, Evan Jones
GRIFFITHS, Lewis
GRIFFITHS, Lewis Jones
GRIFFITHS, William
GWATKIN, Walter
GWYTHER, George.
HALL, John
HAMMON, Henry J.
HAND, Thomas
HAND, William
HARRIES, Alfred
HARVEY, John
HASLAM, John Ralph
HASSALL, Charles
HEYDON, Christopher
HOARE, Hugh
HOOSON, William
HORNOR, Thomas
HOWELL, John
HOWELL, William Jones
HUGHES, E. B.
HUGHES, James
HUGHES, Meredith
HUMPHREYS, John
HUMPHREYS, William;
JAMES, Charles
JANE, William
JENKINS, David
JENKINS, George
JENKINS, John
JOHN, Henry
JOHNSON, E. & T.
JOHNSON, Kennedy
JONES, Aneurin
JONES, Benjamin
JONES, Edward
JONES, George

JONES, Hugh Lloyd
JONES, John
JONES, John (Amlwch)
JONES, Joseph
JONES, Meredith
JONES, Richard
JONES, Thomas (Oswestry)
JONES, Thomas (Chester)
JONES, William (Brecon)
JONES, William (Neath)
JONES, William (Brecon)
JONES, William (Brecon)
JONES, William (Newport)
JONES, William (Llanidloes)
KENNEDY, Henry
LARGE, John
LAWRENCE, Charles
LEWIS, Henry
LEWIS, John
LEWIS, John (Dryslwyn Ucha, Llangathen)
LEWIS, Thomas
LLOYD, Edward
LLOYD, John
LLOYD, Owen
LLOYD, Walter
LLOYD, William
MARTIN, Edward
MATTHEWS, John
METCALFE, William
MICKLEBURGH, Charles
MORGAN, John
MORGAN, Richard
MORGAN, William (Aberffrwd)
MORGAN, William (Tanylan, Llansawel)
MORRICE, Thomas
MORRICE, Thomas [William]
MORRIS, John
MORRIS, Lewis 'Llewelyn Ddu o Fôn'
MORRIS, Thomas
NEALE, Edward
NEWNHAM, Thomas
NUNAN, James
NUNAN, M.
OWEN, James
OWEN, Owen Davies
OWEN, Richard (Llanynghenedl, Anglesey)
OWEN, Thomas Davies
PADLEY, Paul
PALRY, Henry
PARRY, Henry
PARRY, J.
PARRY, William
PAYNE, Thomas
PENSON, Richard Kirke
PENSON, Thomas
PENSON, Thomas M. (Junior)
PHILLIPS, William
PHILPOTT, H. P. [Goode]
PHILPOTT, Henry
PIERCY, Robert
PORTER, Isaac
POUNDLEY, J. W.
POWELL, William
POWELL, William James
PRICE, Francis
PRICE, Henry
PRICE, John (Denbigh)
PRICE, John (Ruthin)
PRIDE, Thomas
PRITCHARD, John
PUGH, George
PURCHAS, Robert Nathaniel
PURCHAS, Robert Whittlesey
REES, Daniel
REES, David
REES, Edward
REES, John
REES, John William
REES, Richard
ROBERTS, John
ROBERTS, M.
ROBERTS, Richard
ROBERTS, Robert (Bangor)
ROBERTS, Robert (Caernarfon)
ROGERS, Edward
SAUNDERS, Thomas
SAYCE, Morris
SHAW, Claudius
SHONE, Charles
SHONE, Richard
SISSON, John
SLATER & LEWIS
SMITH, Henry
SPOONER, James & Sons
STONE, Richard
STRAWSON, George Smith
STURKEY, Thomas Owen
TAMLYN, John
TAYLOR, George
TAYLOR, Isaac
THOMAS, Alfred
THOMAS, Daniel
THOMAS, E[dward]
THOMAS, Evan
THOMAS, Walter
THOMAS, William
THOMAS, William Griffith
TODD, James
TUDOR, Thomas
WADE, H[enry]
WALLACE, William G.
WALTERS, James
WANKLYN, Philip Endell
WHEELER, Joseph
WHITTINGTON, William (Neath)
WILLETS, Thomas
WILLIAMS, David
WILLIAMS, David Robert
WILLIAMS, Edward
WILLIAMS, H. (Swansea)
WILLIAMS, Henry (Newport)
WILLIAMS, J. T.
WILLIAMS, John (Solva)
WILLIAMS, John (Swansea)
WILLIAMS, John (Newland near Margam)
WILLIAMS, Mathew
WILLIAMS, Robert (Llandegai near Bangor)
WILLIAMS, Robert (Llansantffraid)
WILLIAMS, Thomas
WILLIAMS, William (Llandegai)
WILLIAMS, William (Mold)
WILLIAMS, William (Swansea)
WOOD, John
YOUNG, William Weston.

Waxwork artists:
HATHAWAY, W.
MAJOR, Mr J.
PERCY, Mr
STERNE, Mr

Women artists: including women photographers
ALLEN, Lady Catherine [Lady Mackintosh]
BATTERSBY, Mrs
BOYDELL, Mrs
BEFFIN, Miss Sarah
BILLINGSLEY, L[e]vinia
BROMLEY, Adelaide
BROWNING, Miss
CLULOW, Emma
DAVIES, Ann
EVANS, Mrs
GRENVILLE, Lady Charlotte Neville
HARLEY, Miss
HARRIS, Sarah
HART, Mrs
HAWKINS, Mrs Louisa [or Mrs W.]
HEWITT, Miss
JACKSON, Miss H.
JOHNES, Mariamne
JOHNS, Naomi
LLANOVER, Lady (Augusta Hall)
LLEWELYN, Mary Dillwyn
LLEWELYN, Thereza Dillwyn
LLWYD, Angharad
LYONS, Catherine
MCLOUGHLIN, Miss
MORRIS, Maria
OAKLEY, Elizabeth
RAPHAEL, Mrs
THOMAS, Betty
TRAHERNE, Charlotte Louisa
TUDOR, Miss
WILLIAMS, Frances

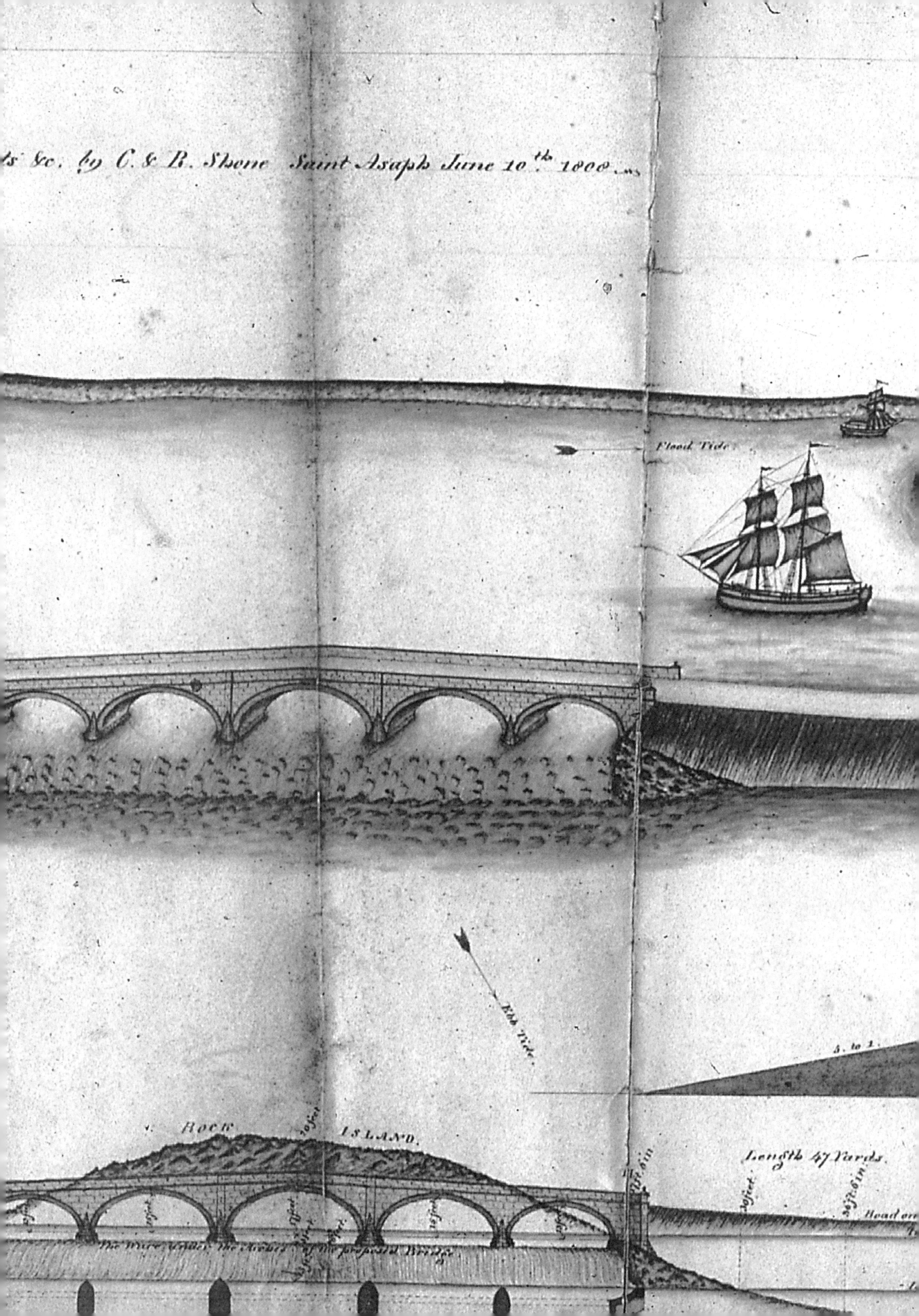
ts &c. by C. & R. Shone Saint Asaph June 10th 1808
Flood Tide
Ebb Tide
5. to 1.
ROCK
ISLAND
10 feet
Length 47 Yards
30 feet
The Weir under the Arches of the proposed Bridge